SPARDA BY THE BITTER SEA

Program in Judaic Studies
Brown University
BROWN JUDAIC STUDIES
Edited by
Jacob Neusner,
Wendell S. Dietrich, Ernest S. Frerichs,
Alan Zuckerman

Project Editors (Project)

David Blumenthal, Emory University (Approaches to Medieval Judaism)
Lenn Evan Goodman, University of Hawaii (Studies in Medieval Judaism)
William Scott Green, University of Rochester (Approaches to Ancient Judaism)
Marc L. Raphael, Ohio State University (Approaches to Judaism in Modern Times)
Jonathan Z. Smith, University of Chicago (Studia Philonica)

Number 52

SPARDA BY THE BITTER SEA
Imperial Interaction in Western Anatolia

by
Jack Martin Balcer

SPARDA BY THE BITTER SEA
Imperial Interaction in Western Anatolia

by
Jack Martin Balcer

Scholars Press
Chico, California

SPARDA BY THE BITTER SEA
Imperial Interaction in Western Anatolia
by
Jack Martin Balcer

© 1984
Brown University

Library of Congress Cataloging in Publication Data
Balcer, Jack Martin.
    Sparda by the bitter sea.

    (Brown Judaic studies ; no. 52)
    Bibliography: P.
    Includes index.
    1. Lydia (Kingdom)—History. 2. Ionia—History.
3. Iran—History—To 640. 4. Archaemenid dynasty, 559–
330 B.C. 5. Iran—Foreign relations—Lydia—(Kingdom).
6. Iran—Foreign relations—Ionia. 8. Ionia—Foreign relations—Iran. 9. Greece—Foreign relations—To 146 B.C.
I. Title. II. Series.
DS156.L9B35 1985   939'.22   83-20334

ISBN 13: 978-0-8913-0657-3

Printed in the United States of America

In memory of my parents

Alice Carolyn and John Peter

CONTENTS

ILLUSTRATIONS

Figures

Maps

Photographs

PREFACE

This monograph is a revisionist thesis of the processes of ancient imperialism and focuses upon the Persian satrapy of Sparda. This ensign satrapy of the Persian Empire lay in western Anatolia, west of the satrapies of Cilicia and Cappadocia, and south of the satrapy of Daskyleion. For more than a generation, my research has focused upon the littoral coast of Sparda, the area known as Ionia. Those studies were investigated primarily from the Greek view, and especially from the Athenian perspective. I now approach those same studies from the Lydian and the Persian point of view.

In order to understand better the western Anatolian littoral, I have come to belive it is necessary to view the ancient literary evidence in the context of its geographical setting. As a consequence of this belief, I have devoted the last two decades to archaeological, anthropological, and historical investigation of the regions under study.

With good fortune, I spent the last six months of 1976 in the remote rural village of Malyan in south-western Iran not far from Persepolis, Naqsh-i Rustam, and Pasargadae, and there the first outline for this study was written. The concept of studying the Athenian Empire from the Persian side developed further as I visited Susa and Bisitun. Earlier, in 1973, I had begun my investigation of western Anatolia and especially of Ionia and the Lydian capital city of Sardis, the necessary geographical autopsy by which I could better understand the ancient literary texts and the archaeological materials. Then, in 1978, I returned to Ionia and Sardis, and also visited the capital city of Daskyleion, with new questions and a more inquisitive eye. In the early summer of 1976, I investigated Cappadocia, and in late December of that year sailed the Nile in order to understand the nature of the satrapy of Egypt. Athens and Greece I have explored almost annually since 1965. Thus, in 1976 I began to study the interaction of the Persian and Athenian Empires in Ionia especially and throughout greater Sparda and Daskyleion in general.

Many years of archaeological field survey of the Ionian littoral and the Lydian regions of western Anatolia are still needed, however, not only to investigate the urban centers but also the rural villages and the agricultural demesnes. A complete archaeological study of this region within its historical context must be completed before we can continue our study of the landed gentry in western Anatolia as a key to the succession of imperialisms. We must also complete a similar study of Persian–controlled Thrace, the region of Skudra.

One need not repeat the age-long apologies for one's transliteration of ancient names. For the most part, I have transliterated them directly from the Greek with the exception of the very common English forms such as Aeschylus, Thucydides, and Attica. A few Spartan names I have transliterated from the Ionic to the Doric, notably Damaratos and Latychidas. Persian and Median names are also presented in their familiar Hellenized forms with the exception of persons who do not appear in the Greek texts even though their names could be Hellenized no less Anglicized. Some names such as Croesus, Cyrus, Darius, and Ecbatana I have also used in their familiar Anglicized forms. Most names will appear, however, as Themistokles, Perikles, Kimon, Byzantion, Samos, Lykia, and Karia. I trust the specialist and the non-specialist, the Classicist and the Orientalist, will accept my decisions.

Many friends have generously contributed their assistance in the development of this monograph. Special gratitude is extended to Professor Edith Porada, Columbia University; to the late Professor Richard T. Hallock, The Oriental Institute, Chicago; and to the late Professor George G. Cameron, The University of Michigan. Wise and constructive counsel, generously offered, has come from Professors Lyman L. Leathers and Donald W. Lateiner of The Ohio Wesleyan University; Terry E. Wick of the University of Wisconsin; John W. Eadie and Louis L. Orlin of The University of Michigan; John W. Snyder of Kent State University; and John C. Burnham, Susha Golomb, David Golomb, Brian Joseph, and William M. Sumner of The Ohio State University. From abroad, Professor Pierre Briant, Toulouse; George Huxley, Belfast; Mohammed Dandamayev, Leningrad; H. W. Parke, Epsom; Wolfgang Schuller, Konstanz; and A. Shapur Shahbazi, Göttingen; have also kindly assisted. Dana Dadson translated the studies written in Russian, Jonathan Gabel drew the maps, and Anne Allen and Yvonne Holsinger designed the figures. At The Ohio State University Library, Stephen Rogers, Robert Thorson, and Clara Goldslager assisted unstintingly; as did Inge Hynes of the Center for Hellenic Studies, and Francis Campbell of the American Numismatic Society. Students, Daniel Needham, Barbara Lake, and Louis Haas, also aided in the gathering of materials, and Jack Sokowski printed the photographs. To my typists, Judith Burke, Chris Burton, Helen Caldwell, Faye McCollister, and Georgia Meyer, I also offer my grateful thanks.

To the College of Humanities at The Ohio State University and its gracious Dean, G.

Micheal Riley, I am grateful for the subvention given for assistance in the preparation for this monograph. To the National Endowment for the Humanities and its generous subvention, I am also deeply grateful. To Scholars Press, to Mr. John Crowell and the other warm and kind persons on that Staff, I extend my thanks. To Professor Jacob Neusner, Editor of the Brown Judaic Series, for his acceptance of this "Herodotean" tome, I am honored to have worked with him. And to all of my students who endured these ideas in rough and polished form, thank you for being with me.

Jack Martin Balcer
German Village
4 July 1983

ABBREVIATIONS

AAH   Acta Antiqua Academiae Scientiarum Hungaricae

AC   L'antiquité classique

AMI   Archäologische Mitteilungen aus Iran

AJA   American Journal of Archaeology

AJAH   American Journal of Ancient History

AJP   American Journal of Philology

AJSL   American Journal of Semitic Languages and Literatures

ATL   Meritt, Benjamin D., Wade-Gery, H. T., McGregor, M. F. *The Athenian Tribute Lists*, v.1 Cambridge, Mass. 1939; v.2 Princeton 1949; v.3 Princeton 1950.

BA   Biblical Archaeologist

BASOR   Bulletin, American School of Oriental Research

BCH   Bulletin de correspondance héllenique

BSA   Annual, British School of Archaeology at Athens

BSOAS   Bulletin of the School of Oriental and African Studies

CAH   *Cambridge Ancient History*

CIG   *Corpus Inscriptionum Graecarum*. Berlin 1828-1859.

CRAI   Comptes Rendus de l'academie des Inscriptions et Belles-Lettres

CP   Classical Philology

CQ   Classical Quarterly

DGE   Schwyzer, Eduard. *Dialectorum Graecorum exempla epigraphica potiora.* Hildesheim 1960.

Diehl   Diehl, Ernest. *Anthologia Lyrica Graeca*. 3 vols. Leipzig 1949-1952.

FGrH   Jacoby, Felix. *Die Fragmente der griechischen Historiker*. Berlin 1923-1958.

FHG   Müller, G. and Müller, T. (eds.). *Fragmenta Historicum Graecorum*. Paris 1841-1872.

GDI   Collitz, H., Bechtel, F., and Hoffman, O. *Sammlung der griechischen Dialekt-Inschriften*. Göttingen 1884-1915.

GHI   Meiggs, Russell and Lewis, David. *A Selection of Greek Historical Inscriptions to the End of the Fifth Century B.C.* Oxford 1969.

GHI 1²   Tod, Marcus. *A Selection of Greek Historical Inscriptions to the End of the Fifth Century B.C.* v. 1 (2nd ed.) Oxford 1946; *A Selection of Greek Historical Inscriptions from 403 to 323 B.C.* v. 2 Oxford 1948.

GRBS   Greek, Roman and Byzantine Studies

HCT   Gomme, A. W. *A Historical Commentary on Thucydides*. v. 1 Oxford 1950.

HSCP   Harvard Studies in Classical Philology

HUCA   Hebrew Union College Annual

IG   Inscriptiones Graecae

JAOS   Journal of the American Oriental Society

JBL   Journal of Biblical Literature

JCS   Journal of Cuneiform Studies

JHS   Journal of Hellenic Studies

JNES   Journal of Near Eastern Studies

NC   Numismatic Chronicle

PFT   Hallock, Richard T. *Persepolis Fortification Tablets*. Chicago 1969.

PTT   Cameron, George G. *Persepolis Treasury Tablets*. Chicago 1948.

RA   Revue archéologique

RE   Pauly-Wissowa. *Real-Encyclopädie der classischen Altertumwissenschaft*.
          Stuttgart 1984-.

REG   Revue des études grecques

RSN   Revue Suisse de Numismatique

SEG   Supplementum Epigraphicum Graecum.

SIG   Dittenberger, Wilhelm (ed.). *Sylloge Inscriptionum Graecum*. 3rd ed. Leipzig
          1915.

Sources   Hill, G. F. *Sources for Greek History between the Persian and Peloponnesian
          Wars* (new edition by R. Meiggs and A. Andrewes). Oxford 1951.

SV   Bengston, Hermann. *Die Staatsverträge des Altertums: Die Verträge der
          griechisch-römischen Welt von 700 bis 338 v. Chr.* Munich 1962.

TAPA   Transactions of the American Philological Association

VDI   Vestnik Drevnej Istorii

ZDMG   Zeitschrift der deutschen morgenländischen Gesellschaft

"Persia, Media, and other lands, other tongues (where are) mountains and plains on this, the nearer shore of the Bitter Sea, and on that, the father shore of the Bitter Sea (as well as) on this, and on that, the nearer side of the region of thirst (the desert), and on that, the farther side of the region of thirst."

Darius Persepolis g.

"The pious minded Xerxes (greets) those upon the waters being the Ionian satrapy."

Aristophanes, *Acharnians* 100, 104.

"Remember that, throughout history, the rich littoral districts of Asia Minor have always fallen to continental Powers of Asia, unless there were a very strong maritime Power of Europe which desired them."

David G. Hogarth, *Ionia and the East*
Oxford 1909, 48.

"[Resolved by the Athenian Boule and Demos]: to summon all the Greeks whether they dwell in Europe or in Asia, both small poleis and large. . . [including] the Ionians and Dorians in Asia and the islands between Lesbos and Rhodes. . . ."

Plutarch, *Pericles* 17.

"The problem of the Greek cities of Asia Minor was the touchstone of Persian policy throughout Achaemenian history; these same cities led to the crusade of Alexander the Great."

Roman Ghirshman, *Iran*
Harmondsworth 1954, 130.

INTRODUCTION

Royal power rests upon the army, and the army upon money, and money

upon agriculture, and agriculture upon just administration, and just

administration upon the integrity of government officials, and the

integrity of government officials upon the reliability of the vizier, and

the pinnacle of all of these is the vigilance of the king in resisting his

own inclinations, and his capability so to guide them that he rules them

and they do not rule him.[1]

Mas^{c}ūdī, tenth-century Iranian scholar

Mas^{c}ūdī's words might also be applied to the imperial structure of the ancient Persian Empire. To their Persian kings, the Lydian and East Greek gentry of Sparda submitted military service and taxes, the wealth of their agricultural demesnes. It was upon those two requirements of vassalage that the Persian King of Kings structured his administration and ruling power. Decades earlier, similar gentry had submitted their services to the Lydian kings of Sardis, and decades later the Ionians and other East Greeks, Karians, and native Anatolians would submit services to a new type of imperial rule, the Athenian Empire. However, that empire was, paradoxically, not ruled by a monarch, a Lydian Croesus or Persian Darius, but by the democratic council (Boule) and assembly (Demos) of the Athenian city-state (or polis). For the Halikarnassian historian Herodotus, the relationship of town and cultivated lands marked civilized societies (4.127.2). For the Athenian historian Thucydides (1.2.2), the civilized state obtained security of commerce, free communications, a surplus of resources, and the systematic cultivation of land. The Ionian poleis, consequently, reached a high level of prosperity, accompanied by developments of every kind, and flourished with resources and power rarely achieved (Thuc. 1.2.6)[2] In response to similar conditions, the Greek historians and Mas^{c}ūdī focused upon the element fundamental to the growth of state, the agricultural desmene with services rendered by its lord to his suzerain.

The demesne's lord, a member of the gentry, possessed the fundamental responsibility for implementing three major imperial duties: the maintenance of civil order in his local region (a satrapal sub-division); the provision of revenues to the

1

superior officers of the satrapy and the empire; and the raising of troops to be supplied
to the higher satrapal authorities. Through this development of the rural demesne, its
land and its resources, the Persian king extended and maintained social, political, and
economic control. By these means, the king facilitated stable control within his empire
at the important basis of the social structure, the landed gentry (as demonstrated in
chapters 6 and 7).

As Roman Ghirshman correctly noted, the East Greek poleis scattered along the
western littoral of Sparda remained the "touchstone of Persian policy" throughout the
history of the Achaemenid Empire. Yet those same poleis were sought by the Athenians
(Plut. *Per.* 17). As David Hogarth noted years ago, the rich littoral districts of Sparda
had always fallen to the continental powers of Asia, of Lydia and Persia, unless they
were desired by a very strong European maritime power, namely Athens. As a reaction
to the attempts by the Persian Kings Darius and Xerxes to join the East Greek poleis and
the mainland Greeks, especially the Athenians, into a unified satrapy of Ionia (called
Yauna in Old Persian, Ar. *Ach.* 100, 104),[3] the Athenians resisted, counter-attacked, and
constructed their aggressive maritime empire. Thus, Sparda by "the farther shore of the
bitter sea" (Darius Persepolis g), the blue Aegean, remains crucial to any study of the
processes of ancient imperialism (cf. Strabo 15.3.23).

The major factor, which occurs as a constant throughout this monograph, is the
landed gentry. Whether the political structure was a small polis or an extensive empire,
the basic and vital military, economic, and political support for that structure came from
the landed nobleman, the country lord dwelling upon his demesne, and in some cases also
in his urban town house. The aristocratic/oligarchic family complex that developed as
the "household" (the oikos), therefore, remained synonymous with that demesne: in some
cases as a regular demesne, in others as a fortified or towered manor (the pyrgos), and in
most instances the non-urban districts as clusters of demesnes forming rural villages.

Too few scholars in the past have considered the fundamentally important point that
the Delian Confederacy, which became the Athenian Empire, would not have been
founded nor developed had not the Persian Empire penetrated forcibly into the Aegean
territories. To understand the Athenian Empire, in the past one used to study only the
obverse of the ancient coin—the Athenian obverse and its empire. Too often the reverse
was not analyzed—the Persian Empire. One must, therefore, study the "enemy" with

whom the Athenians struggled, and one must understand the nature of that Persian Empire and its control over Sparda. Unfortunately, most of the sources for that struggle between the two imperial systems are those from the ancient Greeks, the literary texts of Herodotus and Thucydides, and the fragmentary epigraphical sources. Yet when one does turn to the epigraphical, literary, and archaeological evidence for the structure and the development of the Persian Empire, including comparative studies from satrapy to satrapy, the picture is more fully developed. The final assessment of that study, not unsurprisingly, presents a picture very different from that which has heretofore appeared in the standard textbooks. In comparison to the Athenian Empire, the Persian Empire was for many of the East Greeks the more just, more stable, more satisfactory than that of Athenian imperial control.

The Persian Empire, rapidly assembled, ranged from eastern Parthia and Hyrkania across Media and Persia through Cappadocia to Lydia and the East Greek poleis. This empire consisted of a multi-ethnic, multi-linguistic, and multi-religious assemblage held together by the power of its king, the "Great King," and his aggressive noble army. The empire stretched from the tree-covered mountains of Parthia which ringed broad, well-watered valleys past the salt flats of the Kavir Desert, through Media and Parsa, and the mountain peaks of the formidable Zagros Range.[4] In northern Media, the upland valleys supported grazing areas for the famed Nesaian horses, sheep, goats, and cattle; to the south, the upland valleys of Parsa, watered by the qanat system of horizontal well irrigation,[5] supported the Persian nobles who had rallied with King Cyrus the Great to overthrow Median suzerainty. Ancient Parsa, however, was markedly more productive in agriculture and herding than today. Consequently, we must consider a decisively richer agricultural base for the Persian nobles and, thus, a powerful noble kinship system of landed gentry, which supported the two branches of the Achaemenid royal house.[6]

To the far west, the fine, well-watered plain of Sardis also supported a rich society, not only in gold and electrum but in agriculture.[7] In a contemporary setting, the lush, gently-rolling, low-lying hills are covered with wheat, olive trees, vines, and other agricultural staples. Along the northern edge of that plain, scores of Lydian grave tumuli dot the landscape some distance from Sardis. Within the plain, however, centuries of alluvial deposits from the Hermos River (modern Gediz) have filled in both the areas of the east-west river valley and the areas about the hills and hillocks on which Lydian remains are to be found. Today the hills are soft, some barren and brown, others covered with green scrub. Beyond the coastal regions of Ionia, north of Phokaia into Aiolis, the land begins to rise and rocky outcroppings increase as the present-day vegetation changes to wheat and olive trees, crops that require less water and irrigation than offered in the Hermos Valley. Beyond Aiolis looms the Ida Range, rocky arid areas with small verdant plains ringed by pine forests.

The western regions of Anatolia remained key to the future success and failure of the Achaemenid Empire, for here the Persians struggled at loggerheads with the East Greeks and the Athenian Empire.

Imperialism normally generates a distinct and widely encompassing political system of relatively highly centralized territories. At the center is the government with institutions to develop that imperialism. The empire created, usually based upon traditional institutions, embraces a wider and potentially universal political orientation beyond any of its dependent territories. This universal political orientation is often new and constructed specifically for the rising imperial structure.

Imperialism and its processes, consequently, assisted in generating a distinct series of interrelated cultures in western Anatolia. Each culture comprised its own unique combination of social organization, polity, economy, religion, language, art, and architecture; a complex of beliefs, customs, and behaviors. This study, therefore, focuses upon the succession of Lydian, Persian, and Athenian imperialisms within Persian Sparda and Daskyleion, and the role of the landed gentry within the context of those imperialisms. The gentry formed that institution fundamental to the political organization, social stratification, social interaction, and economic development of their cultures. The gentry were key because they controlled the government and social life, served in the military forces, promoted economic activity, controlled the temples and religious activities, and supported the other inhabitants of their urban centers. The purpose of this study is to determine the fundamental entities which composed ancient imperialism, and discover how those entities interacted with one another within the process of imperialism. The state and its culture, consequently, are investigated as societal organizations or organic phenomena that passed through stages of detectable societal transformation.

The direction of each imperial government rested upon the political and social elite, the leading landed gentry who held large demesnes and who utilized the other landed and non-landed peoples. That elite, the aristocracy (or in some cases the oligarchy), often responded to social and physical crises or challenges in order to preserve their status, wealth, and leadership. Yet, in Ionia between 550 and 450 B.C., their flourishing cultural systems were transformed into a cultural wasteland marked by a rapid decline in population due to the ravages of more than a generation of war. This study is the first to explore in detail the interactions of the Lydians, the East Greeks, and the Persians, and the first to study the Persian satrapies of Sparda and Daskyleion in relationship to the development of the Athenian Empire. It also offers a new approach to Athenian imperialism by analyzing not the development of Athens' foreign policy but rather the affect of that imperialism upon the several imperial regions. This study raises the fundamental question: Why did East Greeks, liberated from the Persian Empire by the confederated Greeks under Athenian leadership, rebel violently against the Athenians and rejoin the Persian Empire? Herein rests a new approach to classical Greek studies, which uses historical models and paradigms; the disciplines of anthropology, geography, and ecology; and the traditional studies of classical texts, epigraphy, numismatics, and archaeology. Consequently, it promotes the necessity for the application of new archaeological and anthropological methodologies for the future study of western Anatolia. In addition, this study offers a new approch to the history of the Persian Empire by analyzing several of the other Persian satrapies and their subdivisions (e.g., Judah, Egypt, and Babylonia) in relationship to the evidence from Sparda.

Empires arise as the deliberate, conscious, and organized revolutionary efforts of leadership, together with aristocratic support, for the purpose of constructing revitalized political forces in conjunction with military aggression (see chapter 1). By comparing the Lydian Mermnad and the Persian Achaemenid royal dynasties led by kings and nobles, leading aristocrats and landed gentry, with the Delian Confederacy led by Athenian generals in cooperation with allied representatives, the processes which generate empires are set forth within the context of the historical paradigm. In keeping with the current scholarly *communis opinio*, a critical re-evaluation of Herodotus' *History* is developed throughout this monograph. Similarly, a critical analysis of Thucydides' *History* offers a new thesis about the growth of the Delian Confederacy in Ionia and the transformation of that Confederacy into an empire. In essence, this study also compares King Darius' revolution and reorganization of the Persian Empire with the Athenian founding of the Delian Confederacy.

Many scholars who study Persia and Athens rely upon Photios' Byzantine epitome of the ancient Greek text of Ktesias, the *Persika*. Yet, persuaded by the studies of Joan Bigwood, cited herein, I only rarely and with caution refer to Ktesias. One might happily argue that the information contained in Ktesias *FGrH* 688 F 14.40, the notation of Megabyzos' revolution in Syria against the Great King at the mid-fifth century B.C., may be analyzed as a prime cause for the Peace of Kallias, a potentially valuable historical reference. But until our thorough historical analysis of Photios' epitome and other fragments of Ktesias' *Persika* is complete, we must remain suspect of Megabyzos in Syria.

Writing about imperial power, Thucydides was the first historian to submit his selected data to a logical analysis (1.1-19). For him, the successful imperial power was naval, ruled overseas territories, cleared the regions of pirates, and ensured the flow of trade (cf. Hdt. 3.122.2). As that empire created circumstances favorable for navigation, it secured greater wealth which generated a more settled way of life marked by the visible symbol of military security, urban walls. Because of its surplus of resources and technical advancements in military power (cf. Sophocles *Antigone* 365-7), the greater power subjugated small states, and as the weaker yielded it accepted subjugation. By vast naval strength and the fear it inspired, the ruler dominated its subjects (Thuc. 3.9-14) with the power not only of its own military forces but also of those subjects. Thus, for Thucydides, the landed imperial powers of Lydia and Persia could never have achieved the superior imperial domination developed by naval Athens. Yet empire and its wealth also fostered factionalism and revolution, namely, a disruption of the peace and security created by that superior naval power; it generated disunity; and it often led to total destruction.

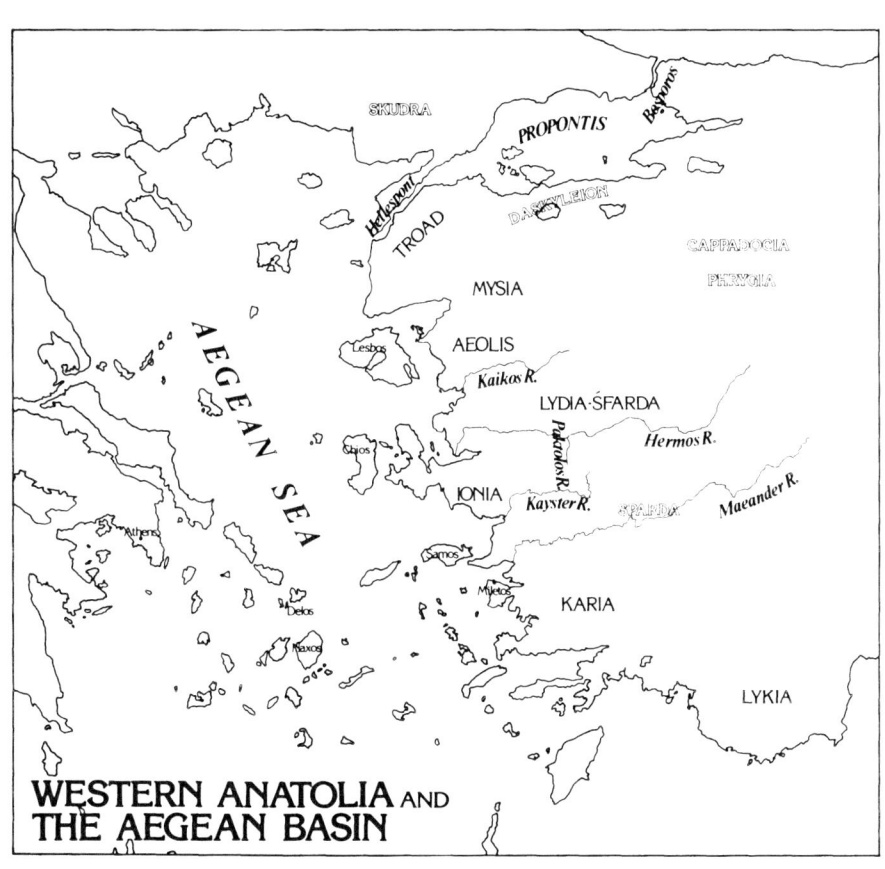

SKUDRA

PROPONTIS

Bosporos

TROAD

Hellespont

DASKYLEION

CAPPADOCIA

PHRYGIA

MYSIA

AEGEAN

Kaikos R.

AEOLIS

Lesbos

LYDIA·SFARDA

Hermos R.

Chios

Paktolos R.

SEA

IONIA

Kayster R.

SFARDA

Maeander R.

Athens

Samos

Delos

Mykos

KARIA

Naxos

LYKIA

WESTERN ANATOLIA AND
THE AEGEAN BASIN

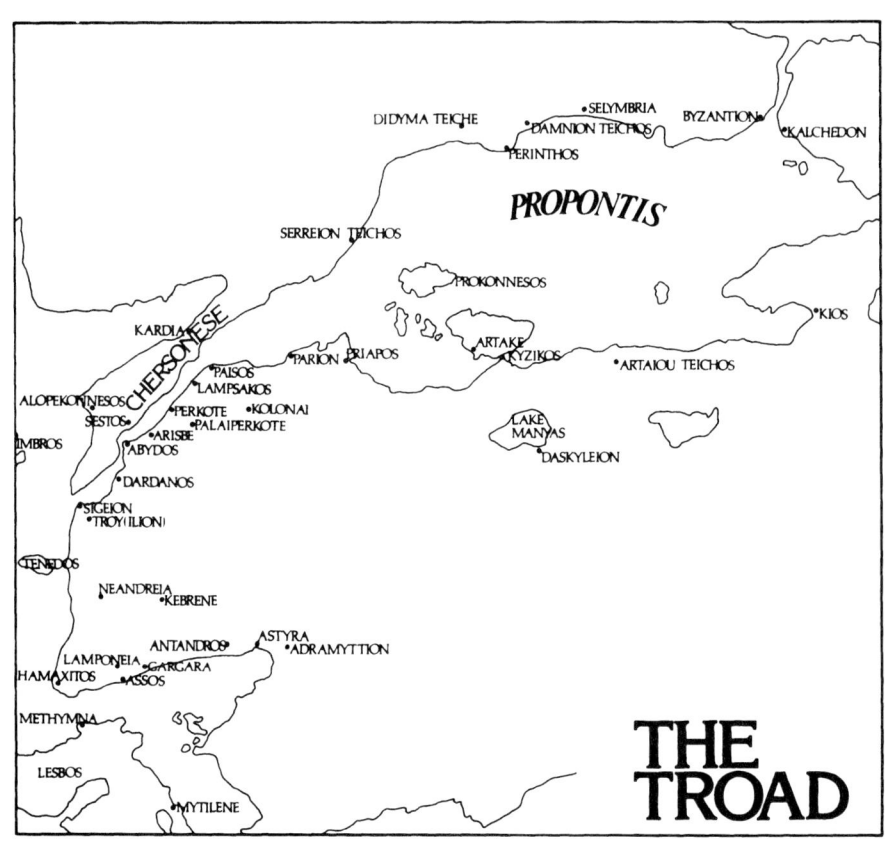

DIDYMA TEICHE
• SELYMBRIA
• DAMNION TEICHOS
BYZANTION
• KALCHEDON
PERINTHOS

PROPONTIS

SERREION TEICHOS

PROKONNESOS
• KIOS

KARDIA
ARTAKE
KYZIKOS
• ARTAIOU TEICHOS
PARION BRIAPOS
CHERSONESE
• PAISOS
• LAMPSAKOS
ALOPEKONNESOS
• PERKOTE
• KOLONAI
SESTOS
• PALAIPERKOTE
• ARISBE
LAKE
MANYAS
IMBROS
• ABYDOS
• DASKYLEION
• DARDANOS
• SIGEION
• TROY (ILION)
TENEDOS
NEANDREIA
• KEBRENE

ASTYRA
ANTANDROS
• ADRAMYTTION
LAMPONEIA
GARGARA
HAMAXITOS
ASSOS
METHYMNA

LESBOS
• MYTILENE

THE
TROAD

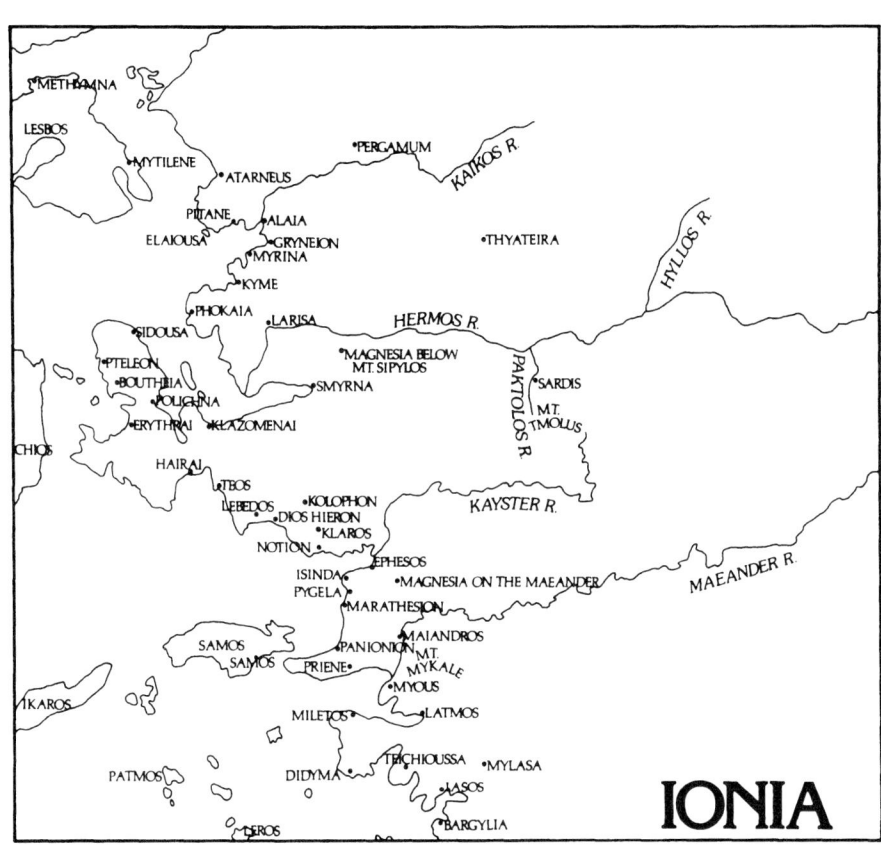

IONIA

PYGELA

MARATHESION

MAEANDER R.

MAEANDROS

PANIONION

TRIENE

MYOUS

LATMOS

MILETOS

DIDYM

TEICHIOUSSA

MYLASA

JASOS

OLEPISIMANDOS

LEROS

BARGYLIA

MADNASSA

KERAMOS

PEDASA

MYNDOS HALIKARNASSOS

KEDREAI

KALYDNIOI

TERMERA

KARYANDA

PELEA

KOS

AYLIATAI

KNIDOS

CHERRONESION

IALYSOS

XANTHOS

KAMEIROS

CHALKE

RHODES

LINDOS

KARIA

LESBOS

•MYTILENE

KAIKOS R.

ELAIOUSA

•MYRINA

•KYME

•PHOKAIA

HERMOS R.

•SIDOUSA

•MAGNESIA

•PTELEON

CHIOS

•BOUTHEIA

•SMYRNA

ERYTHRAI

•POLICHNA

•KLAZOMENAI

•HAIRAI

•TEOS

KAYSTER R

LEBEDOS

•KOLOPHON

DIOS HIERON•

•NOTION

•EPHESOS

CENTRAL
IONIA

SAMOS

•MAGNESIA

1

THE PROCESSES OF ANCIENT IMPERIALISM

In the great clashes of history, the triumph of the victor is never complete. Ironically, the victor never emerges unchanged but must forever bear traces of the defeated enemy. This commonplace is as familiar in the chronicles of the ancient Mediterranean as it is in the records of all regions.

What is unusual in classical or any other history is a clear understanding of exactly how and why this ineluctable legacy is transferred. In the succession of the Lydian, Persian, and Athenian imperialisms in the eastern Mediterranean, events that occurred do in fact fall into a pattern, an historical paradigm that reveals how and why this transference occurs. In addition to the continuity of an historical narrative, therefore, this history is valuable since it helps explain a phenomenon not fully understood.

Traditionally, classical history has been written from the point of view of the Athenians. Several historians, however, have tried to broaden their understanding of classical history by viewing it from the Persian perspective as well. The analysis which follows continues this tradition and adds to it the perspective of the Lydians. Two methods are used to restructure and extend our knowledge of the past: a narrative of events in western Anatolia during the period from c. 700 to 447 B.C., and a paradigm suggested by those events that is similar to those used in the analysis of cultures. The narrative begins with the development of Lydian imperialism and ends with Athenian imperial control of the western Anatolian littoral, the focus of this study. The scheme within which these events occurred is set forth in the pages of this chapter and is exemplified in the narrative of those which follow.

In the fifth century B.C. the vast Persian Empire clashed with the newly developed naval forces of the Delian Confederacy. The latter, which gradually transformed into the Athenian Empire, had come into being when the confederated Greeks under the leadership of the Athenians were attempting to stop the gradual expansion of Persia into the Aegean Basin and Europe by forcing the Persians out of Thrace and the western littoral zones of Anatolia. The confederation and Athenians mounted aggressions against Persia at a time when the Persian Empire had suffered a series of major military

13

setbacks in Greece, Thrace, and Anatolia at the hands of many of those same Greeks and when the problems of satrapal revolution against the Persian king had arisen once again in Judah, Babylonia, Syria, Egypt, and apparently in the east. The clash between the two imperial powers was inevitable, for the Confederacy had been established to attack the weakened Persian Empire. Yet the clash was not between two similar systems. The Delian Confederacy was new and aggressive, while the Persian Empire, already more than seventy-five years old, had shifted in 479 B.C. from an aggressive to a defensive force, at least in regard to the mainland Greeks and the Athenians.

This study concerns primarily the landed gentry in western Anatolia. Although it is not a complete history of the Persian Empire, the Delian Confederacy, or western Anatolia during the period c. 700-447 B.C., all three bear a relationship to the saga of the gentry since the gentry was fundamental of the political organization, social stratification, and economic development of the region throughout the succession of imperialisms. An historical analysis from the perspective of the landed gentry demands that one cast broadly throughout the Persian Empire, the earlier Lydian Empire, and the Delian Confederacy since the gentry was centered in the conflicts of the Persian Empire and the Delian Confederacy during the fifth century B.C. and provides a key to the succession of imperialisms. Thus, a fresh look is taken at western Anatolia through the eyes of its landed gentry within the context of imperialism by means of the comparative studies of anthropology, geography, and ecology. Finally, many facets of imperialism and its institutions are explored as they affected Greeks, Karians, Lydians, Persians, and Anatolians who made up the power elite, which was the landed gentry in western Anatolia. Along the shores of the salty Aegean bitter struggles between imperialisms made everday life for the Lydian and East Greek landed gentry full in strife (eris) and conflict (stasis). Since all history depends ultimately on social purpose, we can best understand the upheavals and alterations experienced by the noble gentry in western Anatolia by investigating that gentry.

My primary concern is not with substantive data: the customs, symbols, and relics of these people, but with the forms and functions of institutional relationship, which are the historical syntax of my literary and epigraphical sources and their vocabulary. By considering the noble, neither from the vantage point of the Athenian agora nor from the palace at Susa but from the acropolitan palace at Sardis, I attempt to reassess the complexity, the structure, the function, and the social evolution of the agricultural demesne. Although this inquiry has its roots in the Late Bronze Age, it focuses upon the demesne as it emerges in our literary, epigraphical, and archaeological sources c. 700 B.C. The study then traces those demesnes as they were conquered by Cyrus the Great c. 545 B.C., as they were subsequently placed under a confederate leadership in 477 B.C. that gradually became dominated by Athenian hegemony, and finally as they became central to the ensuing Athenian-Persian conflict in western Anatolia until 447 B.C. At that point, Athens finalized the structure of her empire, especially in the territory of Ionia formerly controlled by Lydia and Persia under similar imperial systems.

This account has one additional focus within the greater study of ancient imperialism: the demesne of the landed gentry in Lydia and Ionia, which became the Persian satrapy of Sparda. Since the historical matrix in which the noble demesne developed is exceedingly complex, I have attempted by means of historical and anthropological analysis as well as archaeological evidence and interpretation to uncover the nature of that demesne and its fundamental role in the seventh through the mid-fifth century B.C. The landed gentry and their demesnes are, together, the basic units of historical continuity throughout our very limited literary, epigraphical, and archaeo-logical sources; therefore, it is the investigation of the two which enables us to understand the complex problems of imperialism in western Anatolia. As the landed gentry supported the Lydian King Gyges and his Mermnad Dynasty, so too did that gentry serve the Achaemenid kings from Cyrus the Great to Artaxerxes I and beyond. Similarly, the landed gentry within the littoral East Greek poleis, when conquered respectively by the Lydians and then the Persians, served their foreign suzerains.

While no chart can begin to suggest historical complexity, figure 1 is offered as a means to understand the paradigm presented herein. Following the suggestions of Thomas S. Kuhn,[1] in constructing an historical paradigm one seeks to determine the fundamental components of imperialism and the interactions between those components and the processes of imperialism. To determine the complexities of imperialism, therefore, one must determine what questions may legitimately be raised about those components and what methodological techniques can be employed to understand them within the processes of imperialism. To analyze those processes by the establishment of a paradigm, in which the components often follow similar patterns, one must be alert to the anomalies thereby revealed. These anomalies, once isolated, must be accounted for. While at first seeming subversive of the basic tenets of the paradigm, in retrospect these anomalies often assist in perceiving the multifaceted variables of the components within the paradigm. In fact, the anomalies are themselves often different facets of a component; and, therefore, do not subvert the basic paradigm but illustrate its complexity and strengthen the fundamental principles of the historical model. Historical fact and analytical models are not categorically separable. An explanative paradigm, therefore, is not simply factual in its import but qualitatively transforms and quantitatively enriches the fundamental aspects of the factual account and the model of analysis. It has its limitations, however; it cannot nor does it need to answer all questions or confront all facts. Rather its purpose is problem solving. The existence of this paradigm, therefore, establishes the problems to be solved: Why did East Greeks, "liberated" from the Persian Empire by the confederated Greeks under Athenian leadershp, rebel violently against the Athenians and rejoin the Persian Empire?

The answer to the question of Ionian revolution against the Athenians can be determined by this paradigm. Some of the Ionians reacted violently to the processes of Athenian liberation of Ionia from Persia because of the strictures of Athenian subjugation. While the Lydian and Persian kings ruled the Ionian gentry as imperial lords over their subjects or vassals, the conditions of that subjugation and vassalage were defined from the outset within the regulations and treaties of vassalage. The Athenians, however, had offered the Ionian gentry an alliance structured upon articles of parity,

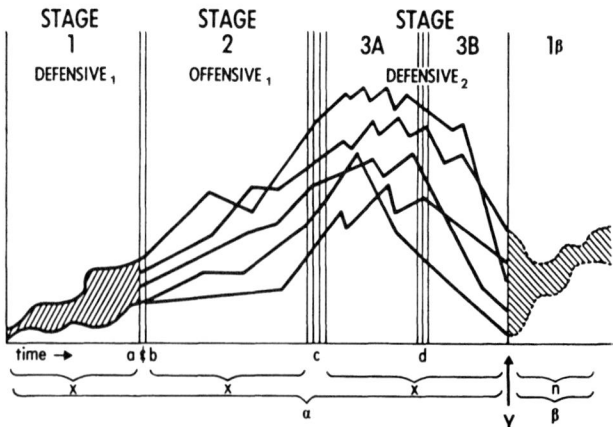

Figure 1: The Paradigm

of equal vote and of equal participation. Those principles were set out in the articles of the Delian Confederacy, founded in the spring of 477 B.C. But from the outset, the Athenians violated those articles, and within twelve years the processes of violation formalized into the processes of subjugation and vassalage. The landed gentry reacted against that subjugation. The gentry were, therefore, key to the rebellion since they controlled the government and social life of the East Greek poleis, served in the military forces, promoted economic activity in those poleis, controlled the temples and their religious activities, and supported the non-landed inhabitants of their urban centers.

For the landed gentry of the East Greek poleis, the strictures of foreign imperialism and its institutions came in three distinct phases: Lydian, Persian, and Athenian.[2] The first change of imperialism was a wrenching one. As Russell Meiggs properly noted: ". . . whereas Lydia by her long association with the coastal cities had become superficially at least Hellenized and could understand Greek political behaviour, the Persians were a completely alien power in language, religion, and politics."[3] Ironically, the Athenians liberated the East Greeks from Persian rule, only to subjugate them to their own imperial system from which many East Greeks revolted.[4] And finally, the Spartans seized some of the East Greek poleis from the Athenian Empire, subjugated them, and in a joint power play against the Athenians, gave the entire littoral region of the East Greeks back to Persian imperial control.

The Athenians, who were kinsmen and often military allies of several East Greeks, controlled the East Greeks with stringent imperial measures under the guise of liberation. At least the Lydians and Persians from the outset did not pretend that their motives and strictures were not imperial. In contrast, mainland Greeks, the quintessence of Hellenism, who understood East Greek political behavior, and whose language, religion, and politics bound them to the East Greeks as common Hellenes, ruthlessly subjugated their fellow easterners through modes not inflicted by the "foreign" Lydians or Persians.

In order to investigate the role of the landed gentry and understand the institutions of imperialism which directly affected it, we must turn first to the *nature of the state* and its basic form.[5] We shall consider the state as a societal organization or an organic phenomenon that passes through stages of detectable societal transformation. The nature of the state is applicable to the study of Lydia as the Empire of Sfarda, the East

Greek poleis, the Achaemenid Persian Empire as established by King Cyrus II (The Great) and significantly reorganized by King Darius I, and the Delian Confederacy, which the Athenians transformed into an empire. In each case, the state came into being at a specific moment within the historical constant of time (what we shall consider within the paradigm as the beginning of the historical period α). Let us consider four examples of the establishment of state as they occurred within western Anatolia, which we may place at the beginning of Stage #1. In the case of the East Greek poleis, states developed as colonies in various degrees of organization, which set out for new Anatolian territories. Lydian Śfarda, established by the Mermnad powers of King Gyges, emerged after a successful civil war against the former Lydian Tylonid dynasty. Achaemenid Persia, in overthrowing the older and ruling Median system, succeeded in revolution led by Cyrus the Great. In each of these three instances, the social system of the state underwent a dramatic shift as directed by the leadership of each respective society. In the circumstances of the Mermnad and Achaemenid dynasties that leadership acted in cooperation with the leading members of the two societies noted, and those members were of the landed gentry. The shift of the social system, at least in these two cases, generated a rapid and significant societal revitalization or alteration with positive rather than negative results. In the case of the Delian Confederacy, our fourth example, a dramatic change in leadership was also present yet was further complicated by a demonstrative process. The Confederacy experienced its dramatic restructure where it was and as it was, with its origins resting not in civil war or revolution but in counter-action to the Achaemenid Empire. The origin of the Confederacy, nevertheless, did incorporate a successful rejection of Spartan naval leadership, a rejection which parallels the Mermnad rejection of Tylonid leadership and Persian rejection of Median leadership. The Athenians, in organizing the Confederacy, assumed a leadership without the hallmarks of civil war or revolution; yet they manipulated the Confederacy so that it rapidly and significantly altered its own structure. This alteration basically arose from the complicated interrelationship which developed in the course of the fifth century B.C. with internal Athenian governmental procedures. All four states, however, emerged in Stage #1, the establishment of state, in what I have called a defensive primary (defensive$_1$) condition.

While in Stage #1, defensive$_1$, each state attempted to protect and to preserve the goals attained through restructure, revolution, civil war, or colonization (the four examples noted above), in essence to protect and to defend the newly altered state in order to protect its positive revitalization and to ensure that it would perform as specified. During Stage #1, political reorganization and the establishment of a military order or a sound protective system for the security of defense took place. A sound economic system was necessary to support the newly organized or reorganized societal organism. The economic base was land; thus, the wealthy land owners, the gentry of this study, who already participated in politics and the military, also provided the economic direction of the new state. Stage #1 was also a period of the establishment of new values, which were relevant to the new situation. These values were often transmitted through religion, positivistic propaganda, or heroic Sagen about the leaders of the revitalization phase.

The duration of defensive$_1$ (Stage #1) varied. In some cases societies never left this stage while in other cases societies progressed to Stage #2 rapidly. In every case in which a society shifted from Stage #1 to Stage #2, however, the transitional period can be located. During the period of defensive$_1$ mounting pressures from other societal systems conflicted with the state's military development; the growth of its economic systems; and its ethical, religious, and philosophical values. During the defensive$_1$ period, fear of foreign military intervention and fear of foreign domination of the institutions of art and architecture, literature, music, and the dissemination of information loomed large. The state, therefore, sought greater dependency upon outside powers allied for its support and sustenance in order to achieve success in becoming independent. While many states or societies never left this Stage, defensive$_1$, several of the East Greek poleis, Lydia, Persia, and the Delian Confederacy-cum-Athenian Empire did, in a relatively short and rapid period of change entered Stage #2, that of offensive primary (offensive$_1$). That change, however, was not marked by a specific historical event but by a series of closely related events within a brief transitional phase.

The period of transition from defensive$_1$ to offensive$_1$ occurred when a series of internal (a) and external stimuli (b) interacted. These stimuli, referred to in figure 1 as a and b, can be evaluated, but are often elusive in ancient studies because of the lack of literary and archaeological evidence. Nevertheless, they can be detected, at least in part. Stage #2 (offensive$_1$), therefore, may be disclosed by the appearance of an aggressive political system that exerted its influence, direction, or even power over groups of people, often those social or political systems which had aided, supported, or sustained the system in question during Stage #1. For example, the Persians had Babylonian support while winning dominance over their former lords, the Medes; but once Persia had become dominant after the fall of Lydia, Persia attacked Babylon, conquered it, and bound Babylonia into its imperial system by raising the Persian crown prince Cambyses as its king. Stage #2 aggression, therefore, was characterized by military activities and expansion or the lesser form of "police action" outside the realm of defensive$_1$ (Stage #1). This expansion and aggression was often linked to the offensive state's need for new or additional resources beyond its geographical limits. In seeking those new resources, the offensive state began to dominate the economic markets beyond its borders. Athens' development of the Delian Confederacy, for example, was primarily stimulated by the Athenian need for grain from the Black Sea regions. The conquests of Sestos and then Byzantion to control the Hellespont and the Bosporos and, thus, the opening of the Black Sea to Athenian and confederate ships were the primary motives of confederate military action against the Persian Empire. Thucydides' argument (1.96) that the Confederacy sought to ravage the king's domain and to gain booty for what the Persians had done to the Greeks outlined secondary motives, and Athens' argument that freedom was a prime motivation by this analysis becomes a tertiary motive and "legalistic" method by which to invade Asia and the king's domain.[6] Ravage and booty, nevertheless, were two additional facets of the primary economic dominative process.

Stage #2 was often accompanied by the cultural expansion of the offensive power over its spheres of domination. Changes in art and architecture, religion and philosophy, accompanied by propaganda that claimed the aggressive system and its component parts were good for all, were symptoms of this stage. We can, for example, detect a degree of Lydianization or Anatolianization of the East Greek poleis during the Mermnad control of Sfarda. The Athenianization of the Delian Confederacy is apparent to yet a greater degree. The Persianization of Sparda (the Persian satrapy of Sfarda and the East Greeks beyond Daskyleion), however, was all but absent. The archaeological and epigraphical materials do not provide for the historical demonstration of Persian control of western Anatolia or of Thracian Skudra. Persian arts, architecture, and religious practices for the late sixth century and the fifth century to 447 B.C. are almost absent in the western

Achaemenid satrapies. In fact, the Achaemenid propaganda set out by Cyrus the Great

at Babylon in 539 B.C. and then by Darius the Great in 519 B.C. implied that the Persian

system, unlike the preceding Chaldean or Assyrian systems, was good for all precisely

because it allowed local religious and cultural autonomy and did not impose Persian

Iranian and Zarathustrian policies upon its subjects. In Judah, this policy was most

obvious, as we may strongly conclude for Sparda, Thracian Skudra, and Daskyleion.

Ahura Mazda barely held a place in Sardis beside the great Lydian cults of Kuvava and

Artemis.[7] The Athenians, in contrast, eventually forced their confederate allies into an

empire under the guise of a religious amphictyony based in Athens and centered upon the

Parthenon and its chryselephantine statue of Athena Parthenos.

The aggressive system of the "imperial" state in Stage #2 was often facilitated by

smaller states that were willing, almost eager, to be dominated in order to obtain

positive political, social, economic, or even religious results, which the state in Stage #2

offensive$_1$ could offer the many smaller states still in stage #1 defensive$_1$. Examples are

the very small Ionian poleis of Dios Hieron, Isinda, Maiandros, and Notion. Within the

Delian Confederacy, approximately 68% of the allied poleis gained substantial direction

and stability as a result of being dominated by the Athenian Empire.[8] In Achaemenid

Persia, semi-autonomous regions such as Cilicia and the Phoenician mercantile city-

states also gained military security, a greater economic sphere of trade, and freedom

from brigandage set in motion by the extensive and wide-sweeping effects of King

Darius' key reorganization of the Persian Empire. In contrast, Egypt from the reign of

King Bardiya actively set in counter-motion actions whereby to sever Achaemenid

suzerainty, a motion which erupted several times during the sixth and fifth centuries

B.C. and which was essentially successful during the first half of the fourth century

B.C. In Egypt, consequently, the Athenians found a receptive faction which sought

Athenian military aid against the so-called "oppressive" forces of Achaemenid Persia. In

Judah, however, the problems were not external but internal, the basic problem being the

final definition of Judaism. Strikingly, we see no Persian influence or intrusion of

Zarathustrianism in the solving of this problem; whereas in the Athenian-dominated

poleis, cults to Athena the Protectrix arose[9] perhaps willingly among the subjected allies

and, apparently, in connection with Perikles' plans for the transformation of the Delian

Confederacy into an "imperial" amphictyony. Yet for the Jews, the great father Cyrus had been Yhwh's Anointed One, and King Artaxerxes' dispatch of the Jews Ezra and Nehemiah to establish order in Jerusalem according to Jewish law further confirmed Cyrus' and Darius' desires for the rebuilding of Yhwh's temple upon the foundations of the holy Solomonic temple.   In these aspects, Judah and Judaism rested within the Achaemenid fold.

In Lydia, Persia, and Athens, the three imperial states which developed into Stage #2 offensive$_1$ systems, the direction of each imperial govenment rested with the political and social elite. This elite held large landed estates or demesnes and within their states wielded control over the small and middle classed landed, the vast majority of each system, in addition to the non-landed, a minority who may not have exceeded 10% of the population.[10] In Persia, the elite consisted not only of the great landed nobles, but following King Darius' regicide and usurpation of the Achaemenid royal tiara, also of members of the royal family.

In western Anatolia the members of the non-landed classes constituted a notable exception because they dwelt in the aste, the urban nodes of the East Greek poleis. As a group they had become significantly diminished in number after the military struggles of 499-479 B.C. in the Aegean basin, yet they were instrumental in fostering factionalism (stasis) within the poleis during the mid-fifth century B.C., as will be explained below. Among the East Greek poleis throughout that region the landed gentry and its subserviant middle and small landed farmers, bound within a dendritic system of rural centers (komai), occasionally did function as a polis without an asty. Nevertheless, in several cases they became estranged from the urban dwellers of the asty, with the result that within stasis the asty functioned as a polis but without the dendritic chora or rural-village regions. Persian kings often gave these choric regions as gifts of land to Greek vassals such as Themistokles, Damaratos, and Gongylos, while the aste continued as independent poleis bound to the Athenian Empire.   Under these conditions of polis-division, the truncated aste, with their concentration of non-landed members, sought by absolute necessity the protection of the Athenian Empire and willingly submitted their political self-determination in order to gain economic and social stability. Because of greater needs such submission, therefore, became *douleia* or subjugation and the voluntary abandonment of the former political self-determination. In this transition, the original articles of parity which structured the Delian Confederacy had become articles of vassalage, not too dissimilar to the articles of vassalage imposed upon the East Greeks by the Lydians, the Persians, or in basic principle by the subsequent Spartans. The East Greek polis of Miletos is a prime case study of this transition from parity to vassalage.[11]

Each empire which developed from Stage #1 into Stage #2 by alteration and transformation maintained within each Stage the condition of a "steady state." This condition, as adopted from the anthropological model of Anthony F. C. Wallace,[12] allowed within the respective state or empire a tolerable degree of stress as generated by the settlement and growth of the community in question. As the state developed over time a gradual modification of those factors of social, political, and economic stress amidst the establishment and growth of the productive estate of oikos (demesne) systems was also tolerable. Moderate internal adjustment to problems of stress, therefore, both satisfied the state's needs and alleviated the transition of mini-crises or individual stress into maxi-crises or societal distortion. The mini-internal and external crises, essentially trivial, were all too often indicators of later major crises or the marks of crucial societal distortion. The mini-crises, therefore, were the signposts or "seeds" for later societal faltering and marked transformation, a transformation all too often simply termed "failure." The analysis that follows suggests a different interpretation.

While many states never transformed from Stage #1 to Stage #2, all states which entered Stage #2 must transform into Stage #3, defensive$_2$, which can be analyzed in two phases, A and B. It is, unfortunately, difficult to determine the precise or even relative moment of transformation from Stage #2 to #3 since the process of transformation is lengthy and is marked in Stage #3 as maxi-crises or societal distortion that evolved from mini-crises or individual stress characteristic of Stage #2. While individual stress in Stage #2 may have involved only a few members of the society under investigation, that stress was nonetheless significant since those few individuals were people who filled relatively important political, military, social, economic, or religious positions. The stress, which existed early in Stage #1 and increased throughout Stage #2, resulted from a breakdown in central leadership. That breakdown can be noted as a sporadic, periodic, or a continuous diminution in the efficiency of the central leadership of one or any combination of aspects of social government, which attempted to satisfy the needs of the community and in particular the important dominant elite. Stage #3 was reached once the stress experienced in Stages #1 and #2 increased to a point or, more exactly, to a series of points at which some alternative to that stress was sought.

Those seeking alternatives were the people within the society directly affected by that stress and the inefficient leadership. In seeking an alternative to stress, the substitute may have been less effective in relationship to those multiple and interrelated societal roles than the original mode of dealing with the mini-crises. In addition, there may have been increased stress as a result of the anxiety generated from fears that the new leadership would be less effective than the old in attempting to relieve the problems of increased individual stress. The anxiety generated a threat upon the intricate balance of societal factors, which formed the cultural "mazeway" or the accumulative societal complexity. For the Achaemenid kings, the factor of individual stress can be detected in the military activities of Cambyses against the Massagetai and the Scythians in the eastern zones of his empire and then, more acutely, in his Egyptian campaign and the imperial demands of the over taxed military forces to extend the imperial realm into Nubia. It may also be detected in the campaign of Xerxes against Athens and Sparta in 480 B.C. up to the pivotal crisis of societal distortion generated at the Battle of Salamis. For the Athenians and their empire, the major pivotal crisis occurred in Syracuse in 413 B.C. when the Peloponnesian and Syracusean forces defeated Athens' naval forces, a defeat that generated the oligarchic revolution, which overthrew the Athenian democracy, spawned revolutions in Ionia, and gave the Spartans the unchallenged ability to return Ionia and the western Anatolian littoral to the Persian Empire. In 412 B.C., Sparta had just entered Stage #2 (n), offensive$_1$. The factors of individual stress had been building against the Athenian democracy as it altered the Confederacy into an empire, and most noticeably increased its imperialism during the years of the Peloponnesian War preceding the reckless Athenian adventure against Syracuse.

The imbalance of acceptable individual stress, when increased to the degree of societal distortion, gave rise to a period of prolonged dissatisfaction and to the necessity of need-satisfaction the techniques generated by the leadership to relieve this dissatisfaction. The leadership's anxiety increased, however, since it feared that these need-satisfaction techniques might change societal patterns, which could be detrimental to that leadership. This process of increased stress is difficult to measure precisely, especially in antiquity, with our limited literary, epigraphical, and archaeological evidence. However, once it built to intolerable levels and societal distortion occurred, deterioration, disintegration, or marked degrees of decay or decline would follow unless a substantial act of societal revitalization occurred.[13]

A revitalization movement is a deliberate, organized effort by the members of a society to construct rapidly a more satisfying culture or state than existed during the period of societal distortion. From a cultural point of view, the revitalization movement generated a special kind of cultural change phenomenon as a deliberate intent by the society's members rather than the normal gradual alteration of that society amidst its coordinated activities. Thus, the Persian, Median, and Babylonian aristocratic conflict with King Cambyses and his overtaxation of the military forces by invading Nubia in 523-522 B.C. resulted in the successful revolution of Cambyses' brother, Bardiya. Many Persian, Median and Babylonian nobles rallied to Bardiya's cause, which offered an alleviation of that stress and its factors of military overtaxation. Darius, however, took advantage of this period of societal distortion, rallied other Persian nobles to his cause, overthrew Bardiya, ordered the king slain, suppressed the twenty-eight revolutions against his regicide and his usurpation of the Achaemenid throne, and after eighteen months of societal distortion initiated a penetrating revitalization movement. Within those eighteen months appeared all the factors, roles, and societal complexities of Stages #1, #2, and #3A and B, and the transformation into a new Stage #1 which we note as β or a new phase to be charted upon the constant base line of time.

A revitalization movement demanded superior and successful leadership to resolve the problems of stress and distortion that the previous leadership had failed to eliminate. But the leader could not function alone. He had to have a substantial base of support among the nobility or the landed gentry who, unlike the masses, had both the ability and the will to alter and transform the problems of stress and distortion. Revitalization indicated recovery, progressive positiveness, and the restructuring of elements and subsystems as conceived by the insight of the new leader. Charismatic leadership is typical. The new leader attracted followers who, in turn, generated oral Sagen to laud their leader, Sagen which became acceptable within the ancient historical traditions even if, in reality, unhistorical such as detected throughout Herodotus' History.[14] In addition, the leader and his followers established concrete positive activities which affected all aspects of the intricate and multi-faceted socio-political system, but most notably by the noble landed gentry. This is true for the Lydian nobles led by King Gyges during his revitalization movement, the Ariaramnes branch of the Achaemenid nobility led by Darius, and the Athenian Aristeides and the other Athenian officials in cooperation with the allied representatives establishing the Delian Confederacy in counterbalance to the Spartan directed Hellenic League.[15]

Each revitalization movement adapted a system to the new stresses. As a result, the system was culturally and socially transformed into a new steady Stage #1 (β) and/or Stage #2 (β). As Wallace noted: "Revitalization movements are defined as deliberate, conscious, organized efforts by members of a society to create a more satisfying culture."[16]

In order to understand more fully the development from Stage #3A into the markedly distorted Stage #3B and then to the processes of revitalization and alteration of the system to Stage #1 (β) and/or Stage #3 (β) ad infinitum (n), let us return to our analysis of the maxi-crises or major aspects of societal distortion within Stage #3A. It is necessary at this point upon the time line to investigate the condition and the problems of political centralization and its internal functioning in order to detect, if possible, the shift of the centripetal forces directed toward the common good to centrifugal forces of individualism in conflict with the collective body politic. During Stage #3A military failures began to outnumber successes, manpower weakened and/or declined, and fundamental resources became scarce. An unfavorable balance of trade may have developed, especially in the importation of basic food and grain products [although almost impossible to detect in antiquity, there is some evidence for this principle to be noted in Ionian Teos c. 470 B.C. (ML *GHI* 30)]. In addition, failures in the ethical, religious, and/or philosophical standards of the community in question may have arisen, which generated searches for the old values or the establishment of new standards.

There are several outstanding examples of attempts to recapture the past and its values in order to relieve the tensions of distortion. Kings Cyrus and Darius, for example, attempted to rebuild the temple at Jerusalem, and Cambyses tried to claim legitimate succession from the Saïte Pharaoh Apries (or Hophra) rather than Amasis whom he overthrew. As pharaoh, Cambyses alleged Amasis had usurped the Egyptian thrones of Upper and Lower Egypt (Hdt. 2.161-9). Similarly, the Athenian claims to ethnic and religious ties with the Ionians fostered Athenian metropolitan propaganda for the formation of the Delian Confederacy, for the transformation of that military alliance into a religious amphictyony centered at the Athenian acropolitan Parthenon, and for all subsequent imperial action against the allies and the Ionians specifically. And within his negotiations to regain Ionia in 411 B.C., King Darius II asserted prior occupation as the legitimate basis for his treaty with the Spartans which restored to the Anatolian satrapies of Sparda and Daskyleion the western littoral zones formerly held by Kings Cyrus, Cambyses, Bardiya, Darius I, and Xerxes (Thuc. 8.58).

In addition, we may detect pessimism and/or statements of negative propaganda characteristic of the transition from Stage #3B to the initial phases of Stage #1 (β). Examples of this can be noted in King Gyges' negative disposition toward the failures of the former ruling Tylonid dynasty in Lydia; in King Cyrus' negative approach to the "evil" rule of Nabonidus, the last of the Chaldean kings; and in Darius' negative statements about Bardiya, whom he called the "wicked magos." Similarly, Athenian propaganda against the Spartan prince Pausanias, general of the Hellenic League, was used to support and to justify Aristeides' direction of the splinter movement which created the Delian Confederacy. While Herodotus fell victim to the Persian oral traditions of Bardiya as the wicked magos, years earlier Aeschylus set that oral tradition aside and sought out the more reliable historical sources, which firmly noted that Bardiya was king after the death of Cambyses and that one of Darius' six co-conspirators, Artaphrenes, with dagger in hand slew King Bardiya in the palace at Susa. Even the attacks of Thucydides, the son of Melesias, upon Perikles' unethical and illegal use of confederate funds, and the transformation of the Confederacy into an Athenian Empire, generated counter-propaganda and attempts by Perikles and his claque to expunge the statements and the memory of Thucydides, the son of Melesias, from the ancient historical records.[17]

The major series of crises from c. 700 to 447 B.C., which formed the basic themes of Athenian and Achaemenid imperialism, occurred among the landed gentry. The pressures generated by crisis also affected the lower classes but without much overt reaction. The problems of poverty and the loss of resources were absorbed by the lower classes who composed the majority of any East Greek polis or of the western Anatolian communities. Even when the numbers of poor increased, the poor provided for more poor. The elite classes, however, the landed gentry or those whom we often label the aristocracy (or in many cases the oligarchy), did not sustain the mounting pressures of

competition for resources and land brought on by the crises. The ecological niches of the
poor could and did become narrower and narrower without counteraction, but the
ecological niches of the landed gentry, the ruling elite, could not become narrower.
Those niches had to remain broad and wealthy in order to sustain the socio-economic life
styles of the political elite. The rich, ruling elite could not absorb another member of
their class into a niche pressed to its maximum for support of those living in that niche.
Thus, a study of the landed gentry is not only imperative but will provide the key to
understanding the historical transformation of Ionia during more than two hundred and
fifty important years, from the rise of Gyges to the finalization of Athenian imperialism
in 447 B.C. All action originated within the ruling elite. Thus, when Robert L.
Heilbroner stated, "the revitalization of the polis is hardly likely to take place during a
period in which an orderly response to social and physical challenges will require an
increase of centralized power and the encouragement of national rather than communal
activities,"[18] he was incorrect. In Ionia, revitalization always occurred when the
centralized power increased neither as the result of communal attitudes nor the
encouragement of national attitudes, but rather as the response of the landed gentry to
the social and physical crises or challenges that threatened their status, wealth, and
leadership. National attitudes, of course, is a vague term to mask the propagandistic
claims or even Sagen which the elite generate to protect and to resolve their actions.
The lines of the "Empress of Inscriptions,"[19] Darius' great trilinqual monument at
Bisitun, clearly express those claims for the Persian elite and constitute the perfect
historical "mask."

We can detect societal crises in the decline of the arts, when the wealthy gentry
could no longer invest in the outward symbols of status but had to invest instead in the
processes of survival. This transition is all too clearly identifiable in Ionia between
c. 550 and c. 450 B.C. Ionia was transformed from a leading cultural and innovative
social system to a cultural wasteland.   The reasons for that decline were the
overtaxation of the landed gentry by the Persian overlords and then the rapid decline in
the numbers of the landed gentry because of the ravages of more than a generation of
Greco-Persian wars. Within the series of maxi-crises, however, the peak of artistic
expression altering into decline often fell after the peaks of economic, political, and
even philosophical-religious decline.

Stage #3, phase B, occurred when the cumulative major crises tipped the balance of the previous steady state and its ability to resolve the problems of stress and societal distortion, or when the negative peaks of the mini- or maxi-crises outweighed the positive achievements. These points we may note on figure 1 as c and d. At point d we can begin to describe the societal condition as that of decline or more properly transformation or alteration. In this phase, major changes occurred in most of the fundamental and even secondary institutions. This transformation either initiated civil war, new revitalization movements directed by new leaders supported by constructive factions, and thus a new Stage #1 (β), defensive$_1$ (β) state, or the state was absorbed by a dominant offensive system (Y) whereby the original state lost its self-identity and became part of the greater system (Y). In civil war, for example, Gyges revitalized the Lydian kingdom, and during revitalization following eighteen months of civil war Darius re-established a new phase of the offensive$_1$ system of the Achaemenid Empire. In contrast, the East Greek poleis were absorbed into the Lydian Empire of Croesus and the Achaemenid Empire of Darius; nevertheless, they retained significant aspects of their cultural identity in order to re-assert their political self-determination and individuality in 478 B.C. when they voluntarily (yet by unmitigated necessity) joined the Delian Confederacy. But by 449 B.C., the East Greek poleis had been absorbed into the Athenian Empire and had lost almost all of their earlier modes of self-identity. Only by means of revolution, as noted at Erythrai, Miletos, and Kolophon, could the landed gentry re-assert and attempt to revive or revitalize their self-identity. Yet they too failed. Thus, it was with relative ease that Sparta seized much of that littoral zone of western Anatolia and restored it without local Ionian opposition to the embracing fold of King Darius II's Achaemenid Empire. What opposition did arise in Ionia in 412/411 B.C. came not against Sparta or Persia, but against the Athenian Empire.

It is unfortunate that the processes of Stage #3A could only be perceived from the vantage point of Stage #3B. Because Stage #3B was a variable period, a phase of reshifting political power and economic bases of the elite, the maxi-crises became clearly identifiable and often subject to alteration by the power elite. Earlier, these crises were present but all too often unidentifiable and not subject to immediate rectification; or if these crises were identifiable, they were not rectified since they were integral parts of a positive alteration. Only in time would the negative aspects develop and outweigh the positive aspects. This condition is, unfortunately, the major problem for any society and for the people in that culture at that time. All too often during Stage #2 the creative minority, the elite or landed gentry, whose example was followed by the wider collective community, became a repressive dominant minority in Stage #3A, and grew even more repressive in Stage #3B. In this latter phase, the wider collective community no longer emulated the elite but became a sullen internal "proletariat" who did not hold power, but sought a new leadership out of the new elite or the revitalized elite who often later became the new ruling minority.

This analysis reveals two basic and extremely important factors in the study of the landed gentry in westen Anatolia. One, the clash between the Persian Empire and the Delian Confederacy came at a time when the two systems were at markedly different points on the time line of development. In 477 B.C., when the Athenians and the allies founded the Delian Confederacy, that system had just begun Stage #1. Within seven years, with the siege of the Persian fortress of Eion, it had transformed into Stage #2. In 470/69 B.C., with the fall of Eion, Stage #2 had a significant period of time yet to develop. By 477 B.C. Persia, however, transformed into Stage #3 and encountered the major problems of phase A of that Stage. The end of Stage #3B would not occur until Alexander III of Macedon burned the holy Achaemenid center of Persepolis in May of 330 B.C.[20] Two, in 477 B.C. Athens and the East Greek poleis, jointly forming the Delian Confederacy, were also at markedly different points on the continuum time line of development and transformation. The battles of Salamis and Plataia (480 and 479 B.C.) had rapidly transformed the polis of Athens from Stage #1 to Stage #2. In contrast, the East Greek poleis were in the critical throes of Stage #3, phase B. In order to revitalize their poleis, the East Greek gentry joined first the forces of the Hellenic League and then the Delian Confederacy. In 477 B.C. the Persian Empire offered little opposition to the transformation of the East Greek poleis, governed by their landed gentry, from Achaemenid suzerainty to Athenian hegemony of the Delian Confederacy. In 477 B.C. perhaps few Greeks envisioned the alteration of Athenian hegemony to Athenian tyranny and the transformation of the Delian Confederacy into an Athenian Empire. That Athenian Empire, however, would itself change. The opening year of the Peloponnesian War marked Athens' or her Empire's entrance into Stage #3A. Following the failure at Syracuse and the Spartan-Persian alliance for the restoration of the East Greeks to the

Achaemenid Empire, Athens and her Empire entered Stage #3, phase B. In the turbulent

days of 404 B.C. when the Spartan military forces occupied Athens and tore down Athens'

defensive walls, Athens altered into Stage #1 (β).

The principal lesson of this study, which most Classicists[21] and Orientalists have all

too often ignored, is that the history of ancient Greece and especially the East Greeks is

an integral part of the greater history of the Ancient Near East.[22] The paradigm

described above conceptualizes how cultures and politics met by the bitter sea. It allows

us to examine more precisely and concretely the complex interaction between the

Persian Empire and the Delian Confederacy which became Athens' Empire during the

fifth century B.C.

Note on the Paradigm

The paradigm described within this chapter, illustrated by figure 1, represents the

hypothetical movement of a single state through the full cycle of Stages 1 through 3.

The *horizontal axis* on figure 1 represents time. It is divided into historical units rather

than dated periods because of the unequal progression through the stages of

contemporaneous societies. The letter α is used to indicate one full cycle or unit (Stages

1 through 3B), and the letter β the following historical unit (also composed of Stages 1

through 3B), etc. The *vertical axis* indicates development (non-chronological) change in

the direction (upward on figure 1) of more structure, more discreteness, and increased

organization of the various societal institutions.

The *crosshatching* at the far right and left of figure 1 represents the combined

elements that gradually emerge to become distinct social structural elements in Stage 2,

e.g., political, economic and religious structure, social stratification, the dissemination

of the arts, and other notable societal factors, symbolized by the five rising and falling

(development change) *bands*. These *bands* progress into Stage 3 to points of crises

(downturn of bands) and eventual disassembly as shown by crosshatching in 1 β .

The *vertical lines* dividing the stages represent the transitions between the various

stages and substages. Lines a and b denote respectively the internal and external

stimulae which transform the state from Stage 1 to Stage 2. Lines c denote the multipli-

city of factors that lead the state from individual stress to societal distortion and usher

in the change from offensive$_1$ to defensive$_2$. Lines d, indicating an intermediate period, separate Stage 3 facet A from facet B, as the crises of societal distortion in facet A are essentially noted only during facet B. Line Y closes the cycle and indicates that a state in Stage 3 can be absorbed within another and lose much or all of its previous identity.

Time, in stages α and β, is further indicated as indeterminate periods labeled x, which continue indefinately as labeled by n.

LYDIA BEFORE THE PERSIANS

Cyrus the Great, the Persian leading his tribal armies, stormed out of the Iranian highlands in conquest of Lydia. In two decisive battles, traditionally dated to the autumn of 547 B.C. but perhaps as late as 545 B.C., he gained that kingdom and most of the Lydian subjects west of the Halys River.[1] Yet on the western coast along the Aegean Sea pockets of Ionian Greeks resisted the inevitable. The study will focus here, and reevaluate the trenchant Persian soverainty in Lydia and Greek Ionia and its ensuing conflict with the Athenian Empire during the fifth century B.C. For the Persians, Lydia and its subsidiary Ionian Greek territories functioned as a pivotal satrapy within Cyrus' newly-structured imperial realm; and it remained a key satrapy until the destructive military campaigns of Alexander III of Macedon in 334, more than two centuries later.

Lydia emerged as a nation c. 700-680 B.C. in response to the politico-economic pressures applied by the East Greek poleis along its western border and by Phrygia along its eastern border.[2] The increase in population in these three national zones produced competition for agrarian land and set into motion a Lydian politico-economic counter response.

The cultural origins of Lydia rest in the earlier centuries of the Neolithic and Bronze Age cultures in western Anatolia, more specifically the activities of the Bronze Age culture in the territory of Arzawa and its interaction with the highland Hittites.[3] The archaeological data are, unfortunately, sparse for the important transition from Bronze Age culture to the rise of the Iron Age Lydians, essentially because of a lack of archaeological exploration rather than a discrete lack of cultural evidence. The few known archaeological materials, nevertheless, indicate no major shift or hiatus in the cultural continuity in the Lydian territories during the four centuries between the end of the Bronze Age and the establishment of the Lydian Mermnad nation under King Gyges (c. 680 B.C.). We may suspect, however, a decline of population in western Anatolia due to the late Bronze Age internecine war and social upheaval[4] which parallel similar cultural phenomena on the mainland of Greece,[5] but add to such phenomena evidence showing movements of indigenous peoples and the intrusions of Europeans. The Early Iron Age kinship systems which structured the Lydian phenomenon, therefore, were essentially the descendants of the earlier cultural groups and the intrusive Europeans, who blended and became the Homeric Maionians.[6]

Out of the collapse of the Bronze Age Hittite Empire, a minor indigenous Anatolian clan seized sufficient power to form a weak Lydian kingdom, c. 1200 B.C. (?), which tradition labeled the Tylonid (or Heraklid) Dynasty.[7] This minor dynastic system remained politically amorphous until the beginning of the seventh century B.C. when the pressures from the East Greek poleis and Phrygia set in motion the struggles between the Lydian Tylonid and the rival Mermnad clans. Those struggles led to civil war and the success of the Mermnad King Gyges (c. 680-644 B.C.), who, seizing power, restructured the loosely organized Lydian clans into a centralized political empire with a military force, which attempted to push back the encroaching East Greeks and Phrygians. The civil wars and Gyges' victory resulted in the organization of a successful Lydian cultural and economic force, which succeeded for almost a century and a half until it fell to the more powerful onslaughts of the invading Persians.

Gyges' deliberate, conscious, and organized revolutionary efforts created the revitalized political force necessary to develop a militarily and economically aggressive nation. Supported by a substantial group of Lydian nobles, Gyges overthrew and killed King Kandaules of the ruling Tylonid clan and raised his Mermnad clan to power. The Mermnad reaction was stimulated by dissatisfaction with the Tylonidai's inability to prevent East Greek and Phrygian encroachment upon their agricultural estates.

For the rebels, the Tylonid system proved unsatisfactory. Our meagre ancient records, essentially Sagen sustained by Lydian oral tradition and organized by the Ionian logographers, indicate that before the revolution little more existed than a loosely structured suzerain Lydian society which vaguely traced its ancestry back to the heroic and Hittite era.[8] Even Herodotus' (1.7) and Plato's (Rep. 2.359D-360B) reports of the rebellious plot must be classed among these Lydian Sagen.[9] That Mermnad rebellion, however, produced a new discrete Lydian cultural system with specific new relationships: a strong royal house and an aggressive military policy against the East Greeks, Phrygians, and the indigenous population of the Troad; new, active diplomatic ties with Assyria, Babylonia, Cilicia, and Egypt; an aggressive mercantile system, which ultimately developed a bimetallic monetary system and coinage; and an increase in cultural monuments. Basic to the Mermnad revitalization movement was the extensive exploitation of the gold of Mt. Tmolos and the Paktolos River, which the dynasty developed and essentially retained as a royal industry.[10]

Although our ancient literary and archaeological sources dealing with this transition are few and the literature is heavily encrusted with Greco-Lydian Sagen, when analyzed by means of the paradigm described in chapter 1, the interrelated pattern of events becomes evident.[11] Following the turbulent period of internecine warfare, societal movements, intrusions of European tribes, and the collapse of Hittite control over western Anatolia in the twelfth century B.C., the early period of Tylonid Lydia witnessed a return to a relatively steady state of development. The Lydian clans settled the Sardian plain along the Hermos River and its connecting valleys, where water was readily available in densely populated hamlets and villages often not more than a kilometer and a half apart.[12] The Lydians resettled the plains, which were divided into areas owned and ruled by the aristocratic clans, a pattern which can be plotted by the clusters of early Lydian burial mounds and later Lydian inscriptions.[13] From Sardis and the royal mounds at Bin Tepe, approximately eleven kilometers to the north, the mounds are strung out following the main valley of the Hermos and its tributaries the Kogamos and Hyllos. Mounds in the southern regions of the inland Maeander and Kayster Valleys are connected to the Sardian plain by passes over the Tmolos range, as well as mounds in the northern regions past Thyateira and upon the plain of Daskyleion settled on the shores of Lake Manyas. The wealthy aristocratic clans probably owned much of the land informally organized as clusters or ribbons of villages upon the plains. The great burial mounds with stone markers, signs or pillars, and hundreds of chamber tombs mark these Tylonid settlements.[14] The nobles' burial sites reflect the oral traditions of Hittite and Bronze Age Sagen, of "Sesostris" at Kemal Pasha on the Karabel pass to the southern Kayster Valley (Hdt. 2.106.2)[15] and Niobe at Magnesia (Manisa) at the western end of the Hermos Valley below Mt. Sipylos (Il. 24.602-20). This Niobe is apparently the earlier Hittite Mother Goddess Hebat flanked by two lions, whom the Lydians venerated as Kuvava (Cybele).[16]

Sardis (95 m. above sea level) with its acropolis-refuge citadel, the Hyde (410 m. above sea level), developed as the Lydian metropolis, royal center, and unfortified urban area for the allied clans and their estates.[17] Here (Section HoB) the archaeological evidence reveals the continuity and cultural density from c. 1400 B.C. through the Lydian periods and into the Hellenistic era,[18] and it discloses Lydian contact with the Ionian Greeks and a limited importation of their Protogeometric and Geometric pottery. According to Greek legend (Hdt. 1.84.3), sometime in the eighth century B.C. the Tylonid King Meles fortified the Hyde acropolis, which was an ideal site, a spur extending northward from the Tmolos mountain flanks with the urban dwellings scattered down its slopes onto the plain about the Paktolos River and the fertile fields beyond. Here dwelt the Lydians (sometimes remembered as the Homeric Maionians, at other times as the tribe of Asias [Hdt. 4.45.3][19] of the Hittite region of Ashshuwa) and their ruling Tylonid clan and kings who had native and a half dozen Hellenized names essentially Sagen.[20] But legend did remember them in distinct contrast to the Greeks and to the Phrygians (Il. 2.864–6, 3.401, 18.291).

The noble clans and their families who settled about the burial grounds apparently owned sizable estates, which G. M. A. Hanfmann suggests included one or more villages.[21] The estates were suzerain holdings: the large and small agricultural villages, which partitioned the Lydian territory into fortified demesnes. The plains' villages developed as clusters of mud-brick and wattle-and-daub thatched buildings, and the mountain villages as clusters of flat stone houses. The Lydians congregated in tight units. Streets and alleys often did not provide access to their homes; rather, entrances were located on roofs covering those houses. These demesnes and villages strongly resemble the modern Turkish villages which today dot the Sardian plain: Celtiki and its 52 family units, which provide housing for approximately 600 people, is compactly clustered about three major intersecting streets much like Sardis' present village of Sart Mustafa.[22] The homes of these ancient and modern villages Hanfmann likened to Ovid's rustic description: "an oak and linden tree surrounded by a low wall . . . a marsh the hunt of divers and coots . . . one home . . . humble, indeed, thatched with straw and marsh reeds . . . the lowly door . . . the bench covered with a rough coverlet . . . the fire with the little copper kettle . . . the blackened beam . . . the bed of willow frame and grass; and the three legged table, the leg propped up by a sherd."[23]

Tylonid Lydia emerged from a variety of clans with distinct cultural identities and complex folkways, and with profound respect for the deep undercurrents and worship of the uncanny supernatural powers and gods. Holy precincts that probably controlled great agrarian estates arose first not as large temple complexes but as monastic clusters often near, but outside the villages. Together, the noble demesnes and the religious precincts formed the broad base of agricultural prosperity and exerted their economic influences upon the Tylonid royalty. The native Anatolian shrines at Klaros, Ephesos, and Didyma occupied and altered by the Ionians clearly indicate the sublime spiritual and emotional powers of similar Lydian centers, especially of the goddesses Kuvava and Artemis at Sardis.

While the demesnes, villages, and religious precincts remained small and agrarian, Sardis, the only Lydian "city," emerged as the Lydian Hauptstadt, the seat of the king and the shrines of Kuvava and Artemis below the Hyde-acropolis. A close association between the king and the vassalage nobility, a basic pattern of royal benefits and patronage and noble service within a broad interpretation of suzerainty,[24] fostered the rise and importance of the nobility, the famed Lydian horseman. This noble or qalmluś in Lydian,[25] equated as basileus by the Greeks, in a collective body was similar to Hesiod's Greek noble c. 700-680 B.C. (*Erga* 38), the great landowner who served in the king's cavalry (Mimnermos F 14 [Stob. *Fl.* 7.12]; Hdt. 1.27.3, 78-9) and ruled demesnes and suzerain clans such as at Adramyttion south of the Mt. Ida Range.[26] His wealth in agrarian products, wheat, barley, olive oil, vineyards, and wool from herding activities fostered the noble's growth; and his interests in Lydia's mineral wealth developed as placer mining activities. Internal Lydian commercial exchange and then, by c. 700 B.C., the first noteworthy external exchange with the Ionian Greeks to the west and the Phrygian kingdom to the east brought foreign products into Lydia. These exchanges marked the transition from internal to the first stages of external Lydian commerce, and increased the wealth of Sardis and the noble demesnes. Through King Mita's Phrygian kingdom, the products of Cilicia, Cyprus, and the wares of Assyria and early Media began to trickle into Lydia.[27] This new rise in trade and the accumulation of wealth in the royal hands apparently stimulated King Meles to fortify the Hyde and centralize Tylonid power there.[28] Along the eastern banks of the Paktolos flowing west of the Hyde (PN), the Lydian market area thrived. By the mid-seventh century B.C., urban sprawl filled in the Paktolos Valley from the Hyde (PC) and the red altar of Kuvava northward into the "gymnasium" sectors (HoB).[29] These residential quarters of densely constructed single-cell houses built of field-stone foundations, mud pisé walls, and colorful clay tiles standing compactly along the lanes and small open places are archaeologically less rustic than the reed and thatch houses claimed by Herodotus (5.101).[30]

From the Hyde and Sardis, the Tylonid kings ruled a loosely centralized kingdom through influential clans of landed gentry and horsemen, who were scattered along the valleys in their respective geographical areas. Daskyleion to the far north is a good case in point. Eight noble burial mounds mark the village(s) named after a Tylonid Sagen-hero,[31] which Lydian nobles ruled as a semi-autonomous and rival clan yet, no doubt, paid their annual tribe to Sardis (Dio Chrysostom *Orationes* 78.31).[32]

Greater Lydia and its extremely fertile agrarian plains rest as a natural geographical zone between the eastern highland plateau of Phrygia delineated by its western "burned zone" (Strabo 12.8.18) and the western Aegean harbor-dotted coast of Ionia. The major plain of the Hermos and its tributaries, the Hyllos and Kogamos, are linked to the southern Kayster River valley by passes at western Karabel (Hdt. 2.106.2); the Sardian pass across the Tmolos range, 2000 m. high (Hdt. 5.54, 100); and a pass from the upper Kogamos to the upper Maeander River valley, then link northward to Daskyleion. While the routes through the passes to Phrygia, southern Karia, Ionia, and northern Mysia cross barriers, the mountains were minor problems to the Lydians, and they easily crossed the western pass (Hipponax F 42, 50) to coastal Smyrna (Hdt. 2.106.2) or followed the Hermos route westward past Mt. Sipylos to the Greek settlements at Larisa, Phokaia, and Kyme. Phrygia to the east lay upon the great mass of the central plateau, 900 to 1600 m. above sea level. This volcanic landscape was a continuation of the central Asian highlands—vast, immobile, monotonous, and subdued, with long severe winters and short but hot summers, and with its fertile soil dependent upon uncertain rainfall. Ionia to the west with rugged mountains that sharply contrasted with its deep fertile valleys that gave way to the sea, and cape after cape with sheltered harbors and a tortuous physiognomy, offered Lydia easy routes to the sea: from south to north, the Maeander, Kayster, Hermos, and Kaikos flat-bottomed valleys from the Lydian heartland between the mountain ridges to the sea. The Gulf of Smyrna at the mouth of the Hermos and its Greek settlements provided Sardis, 100 km. inland, with its major western contacts and the subsequent effective Hellenization of Lydia. From Thyateira, the Lydians had easy access to the Pergamine plain of the Kaikos, the Makestros Valley northward to Daskyleion, and the trade routes into Mysia and the Troad on to the Hellespont. As a knot point for gradually developing overland trade and exchange, Sardis flourished among the seven valleys of the Paktolos and its fertile alluvial plain (Hdt. 1.80.1).[33]

Between the Lydians and Ionians, contact and exchange began c. 700 B.C. and directly affected both groups whose respective prosperities had produced a marked increase in populations, which, at that time, filled their available territories. The Aiolians from coastal Kyme north, who occupied the northern coastal agricultural belt to the Ida Range and were backed by rough-hill country, remained more secluded than the Ionians and barely developed commerce or contact with the native peoples and Lydian clans of the interior. Farther north, the Troad lay intrinsically isolated and sheltered by the massif of the Ida Range and the broken mountain country to its north, with its coast and Skamander Valley approachable best by sea. South of Lydia lay Karia and its pockets of native old Anatolian peoples speaking their non-Indo-European languages far into the fourth century B.C. and living as herdsmen in hilltop villages.

While the Ionian Greek poleis at the mouths of the Lydian river valleys flourished, the difficult long mountain ranges projecting westward into the Aegean hindered coastal traffic. The offshore islands, however, which continued the line of the mountain ridges, especially Samos, offered excellent opportunities to develop trade centers for the Lydian-Ionian contact with the Cycladic Islands and the emerging ports of Corinth and Aigina, among others.

In greater Lydia, the noble demesnes by c. 700 B.C. had reached a peak of production, prosperity, and population growth. The warm Aegean temperatures, the rainfall from October through early June, and the rivulets from the melting snows of the mountain ridges (Il. 20.382-5) brought to the gentrys' estates excellent climatic and geological conditions in the well watered fertile alluvial plains, criss-crossed with Lydian water-channels.[34] Pine, cedar, and oak trees crowned the higher slopes where vines flourished above the grain fields of wheat and barley dotted by vegetables of all kinds (Strabo 13.4.5-6). Here the Lydian wine god Bakillis (Bacchus later syncretized with the Greek Dionysos)[35] found a home. And in the cool mountain valleys fruits, apples, and nuts grew amidst the summer pastures for sheep (Plato Rep. 2.359 C-E). First in cottages and then in estate industries, the Lydians dyed their woolen yarn with special colors and wove them into textiles. On the plains, cattle and horses grazed. Unguents of herbs packed in the small lydion cups[36] and woolen tapestries[37] were the first Lydian products to pass beyond the Lydian borders to the Greeks. Later gold followed the same routes. Plato, the fifth century B.C. comic poet, noted the Lydian wealth of nobles who "recline on finery, on couches with ivory feet, with purple-dyed coverlets and red Sardis blankets" (Ath. *Deip.* 2.48b; cf. Herakleides of Kyme in Ath. *Deip.* 12.514e). With their wealth, the nobles fashioned great gardens as pleasure parks (Ath. *Deip.* 12.515d-f). But the Lydian landed gentry, unlike the Etruscans, were not interested in the acquisition of fine Greek pottery which they could easily have obtained.[38]

Homer's description of the Lydians from his native Smyrna, mid-eighth century B.C. (*Il.* 2.864-6), refers to well-peopled villages of renowned horsemen (*Il.* 4.141-5), of chariot-fighters and horse-breeders (*Il.* 10.431), the marks of the landed gentry. For the poet, the Lydians were similar to the Phrygians (*Il.* 2.862-3, 3.400-2, 10.431, 18.291-2): numerous, warlike, organized into clan systems headed by the noble chiefs, and concentrated in agrarian villages,[39] nobles whom the poetess Sappho observed as having chariots and armed footmen (F 38).

Famine, nevertheless, did stalk the Sardian plain (Plut. *de Tuenda Sanitate Praecepta* 20 [132F]). Both Herodotus (1.94.3) and Nicolas of Damascus (*FGrH* 90 F 45) noted a great famine that the latter placed in the reign of King Meles, c. 700 B.C. The famine was apparently the result of a brief and sporadic drought yet acute enough to cause the Lydian clans to sail from their port at Smyrna, westward to northern Italy, beyond the Greek settlements south of the mid-peninsula.[40]

During the early Tylonid era, the tolerable stress of clan settlement and growth had gradually modified Lydia into a nation of established and productive estate systems, with the nobles' needs adjusted and essentially satisfied. But this steady state gave way to individual stress and the continuous diminution of Tylonid efficiency to satisfy the needs of the rising-in-power nobles occurred. Economic stress arose in the agricultural areas as Phrygian and Ionian prosperities generated population growth. Caught between the eastward expanding East Greek settlements and the Lydian estates were the native clans that had given way to Greek encroachment, and now that encroachment extended into Lydian territories. The prosperous Lydian farms lay vulnerable to the East Greeks and the Phrygians, as periodic famine accentuated that stress. As the moderate degree of stress increased, the nobles sought an alternate solution to their agrarian problems, with some anxiety that any substitute might be less effective than Tylonid leadership. The stress began to threaten the intricate balance of factors, which undergirded Kandaules' kingdom. The prolonged stress then became a societal distortion with Kandaules' failure to ease the East Greek, Phrygian, and famine pressures; consequently, the decay of Lydian society would have set in had not revitalization occurred. The Lydian societal distortion during the last years of the Tylonid dynasty is underscored by the brief three year (?) reign of Kandaules who fell to the Lydian civil war spearheaded by Mermnad Gyges.[41]

Gyges' rebellion, supported and sustained by the Mermnad clan, its clients and apparently others, generated recovery. His leadership transformed Lydia from tribal to civic life.[42] Under Mermnad leadership, Lydia conquered the western lands of Phrygia, settled its old scores with the East Greeks, pushed back the Ephesians who had expelled the Lydians from Ephesos, and liberated the natives who had fallen into agricultural servitude under the Greeks.

As Gyges initiated activities, which affected the Lydian socio-political system, the noble gentry apparently generated oral Sagen about his conquest and about the earlier heritage of Lydia. From Gyges on, the Lydian sources became historically grounded and secure, which indicates that the Sagen were canonized at the time of the Mermnad rebellion when greater Lydia functioned as the Ortsage and Gyges as the Sagen-Pater Familias.[43]

The cultural transformation resulted in a new steady state, whereby Gyges and the Lydian nobility deliberately and consciously organized their efforts to create a more satisfying culture. Gyges' razzias upon the East Greeks and Phrygians for new lands and food gave material support to the agrarian estates and created a more powerful noble cavalry.

The impact of the new Lydian society did not reach fulfillment until the reign of the last Mermnad king, Croesus (561-547 B.C.); nevertheless, Gyges' revitalization activities were sufficient and successful enough to diminish the effects of the Kimmerian, Trerian, and Karian razzias, c. 660-620 B.C. Although the Kimmerians defeated Gyges' troops, killed the Mermnad king (644 B.C.),[44] and followed the broken Lydian army into Sardis, Gyges' son, King Ardys, was able to curtail the nomadic attacks, expel the Kimmerians, and settle many of the Trerians.[45] Ardys revived Sardis and the Lydian state and continued Gyges' policies.

The Mermnad revitalization movement, however, resulted not from Gyges' self-direction but from the Lydian nobles who supported and aided the rebellion against Kandaules. The nobles of perhaps both the Mermnad and Tylonid clans and the other Lydian clans that existed were agitated by the Ionian encroachments up the river valleys eastward into the Lydian heartland. Similar Phrygian encroachment westward down from the highlands of the east also challenged Tylonid rule and created a demand for a new aggressive and constructive socio-political system. The rebellious base, broad and under stress, suffered as Ionian and Phrygian conquests of agricultural lands seriously threatened the landed gentry. The stress led the nobles to seek a more satisfactory system than that which the weak and amorphous Tylonidai offered, and set in motion the successful and intricate Mermnad system. This was a pattern which Lydia would again experience under Persian rule during the last decades of the sixth century B.C.

Phrygia, ruled by King Mita, failed to respond to the stresses of the age. The Lydian campaigns upon its western slopes and the powerful and stayed empires of Urartu and Assyria to the east did not generate a successful revitalization response; and unlike Lydia, Phrygia fell to the nomadic Kimmerian razzias. With the Lydian blunting of the Kimmerian forces, western Phrygia fell prey to Lydian domination, a period which still rests in archaeological obscurity.[46] The fortified Phrygian villages of local estates and noble horsemen (Il. 2.862-3, 3.814-90, 3.400-1, 10.431, 16.719, 24.545) had progressed towards consolidation as a kingdom under Mita yet became subject first briefly to the Kimmerians, then to Lydian rule. At the Halys River, which divided western Paphlagonia from eastern Cappadocia (Hdt. 1.72.2), the Lydians now faced the well established Assyrian Empire, which had absorbed eastern Phrygia. Between c. 690 and c. 630/20 B.C., the Phrygian social system remained chaotic; but Lydian control brought a gradual revival to the noble demesnes and a revival of trade. Under Lydian rule, the capital city of Gordion revived. In c. 650 B.C. Gordion began to import eastern Greek wares across the Sardian plain, and between c. 600 and 550 B.C. it increased its imports of Ionian luxuries as the nobility again prospered. But the Phyrgian capital, Gordion, was destroyed by Cyrus the Persian during the violent end to the Mermnad rule in Sardis c. 545 B.C.[47] Herodotus knew little of the Anatolian plateau beyond Karia, Lykia, and Lydia up to Kelainai, and there is no Greek hint of Persian Gordion.

The Kimmerian death blows to King Mita and Phrygian centralization threatened Gyges and led him to seek King Ashurbanipal's (668-626 B.C.) Assyrian assistance. The

Lydian noble who entered Nineveh c. 657 B.C. (?) in a sensational diplomatic attempt to ally the Assyrians against the Kimmerians succeeded.[48] While this alteration of Lydian foreign policy brought Mermnad Lydia into the greater ancient Near Eastern world and fostered other foreign diplomatic alliances, the Assyrians mollified the Kimmerian striking force but also invaded Phrygia up to the Halys River border and in doing so established new military problems for the Lydians.

Within a few years, c. 655 B.C. Gyges turned against Ashurbanipal, assisted the rebellious Psammetichos in his bid for Egyptian pharaohship, and sent Ionian and Karian mercenaries to Egypt (Hdt. 2.152.4; Diod. Sic. 1.66.12). By aiding Psammetichos, Gyges sought to develop the common commercial interests of Lydia and Egypt, not that Lydia's overland routes to Assyria had been disrupted. But the Kimmerian aggression that resulted in the death of Gyges forced his son and successor, Ardys, to reestablish an alliance with Ashurbanipal to expel the fragmented but still destructive nomadic groups from Anatolia.[49] With Dygdamis and his Kimmerians in Cilicia, Ashurbanipal likewise acknowledged the merit of a new alliance (Hdt. 1.15; Strabo 1.3.21, 13.4.8, 14.1.40).

By the mid-seventh century the Kimmerian tide had been stemmed from Lydia as the hordes withdrew east beyond the Halys and struggled with Assyria; nevertheless, between c. 657 and 650 B.C. communication between Lydia and Cappadocia remained hazardous. By c. 600 B.C., however, Paphlagonia rested secure and accessible as Lydian territory.[50]

As Gyges' usurpation of the Lydian throne influenced notably the Greek structure of Lydian Sagen, so, too, did the death of Mita c. 676 B.C. (?)[51] become basic to Sagen which the Ionian logographers canonized as reflections upon emerging Anatolia.[52] Up to Mita's death, the Greeks neither traded with nor made major contact with Phrygia.[53]

The Kimmerians, however, while not destroying Lydia as they had Phrygia altered Lydian activities. Gyges had turned away the first Kimmerian attack upon Lydia in May 657 B.C.; following Gyges victory, however, the scattered marauding tribes wreaked further destruction upon the Lydians and coastal Greeks. Several years later (644 B.C.) the Kimmerians again attacked the Lydians, killed Gyges, and c. 638 B.C. raided and burned Sardis' lower town, setting the Sardians back for several generations. Kimmerian bands[54] wandering across the Hermos and Kayster Valleys and in the Kayster plain then fell upon Magnesia-on-the-Maeander and Ephesos, two strong native Anatolian centers

(Ephesos now with a notable Greek element). Rather than settling in the centers, the Kimmerians looted and burned them. Although Magnesia fell, Ephesos withstood the onslaught (Kallinos F 1, 3, 4). Unfortunately, sources fail to state what other devastations occurred or how long the Kimmerians continued their marauding.[55] In their wake, the Ephesians (or the Milesians?), took the opportunity to expand. They attacked Magnesia and occupied and restored the town.[56] Meanwhile the Kimmerians, led by their chief Dygdamis, turned back. After their chief's death, they dissipated while marauding in Cilicia, c. 630 B.C.(?). King Ardys (644-624 B.C.) and his son and successor, Sadyattes (624-612 B.C.), then faced the task of driving the marauding nomads east and recentralizing the Lydian kingdom.

Contemporary with the last thrusts of Kimmerian raids, c. 638 B.C., European tribes led by their chief Treres had crossed over into the Troad, sacked Sardis with the exception of the acropolis (Kallisthenes FGrH 124 F 29; Hdt. 1.15), raided as far south as Magnesia-on-the-Maeander (Strabo 14.1.40), also raided Ephesos perhaps at the end of the century, and destroyed the early temple of Artemis while sparing the city (Kallimachos Hymn to Artemis 3.251-258; Hesychios sv Lygdamis). The Ionian Greeks and Lydians, nevertheless, quickly mollified the Trerians and forced them to settle with some of the Kimmerians at Antandros south of Mt. Ida.[57] Lydia's expansion into the Troad and control of Adramyttion near Antandros and the regions north of the Kaikos Valley apparently resulted from this new threat, which the Mermnad kings faced.[58] Karian tribes from the south that had joined the Trerians at Sardis further complicated Lydia's problems.[59] Unhappy with the difficulties the settlement of these tribes produced, Sadyattes' successor, King Alyattes, later drove the Kimmerians out of Antandros (Hdt. 1.16.2).

As a consequence, the Lydian nobles and merchants, unable to maintain their land connections with the East and forced to repel the Trerian and Karian raids, turned to the Ionian Greeks for military cooperation and new trade connections, steps which accelerated the Hellenization of Mermnad Lydia during the reigns of Ardys, Sadyattes, and Alyattes (612-561 B.C.).

Gyges founded his complicated policy toward the Ionian Greeks upon several necessities: cooperation against the Kimmerians and greater use of Ionian mercantile activities. But Gyges also saw the need to attack several of those Ionian settlements.

Swooping in to plunder the Greek harvests, the Lydians from time to time raided Magnesia-below-Mt. Sipylos,[60] Kolophon, Miletos, and even the Ionian port town of Smyrna. The razzias for food and not land were similar to the Kimmerian and Assyrian raids, except for those near Ephesos. The Ionian poleis had arisen along Lydia's western coast in territories politically weak under Tylonid control. The poleis served as ports and sources of trade and supply, which the early Mermnad kings seemingly remained wary of seizing lest the foreign traders and others should shy away and trade dry up. In this fashion, the poleis offered Lydia a degree of military security while giving civil protection to traders: facilities of anchorage, debarkation and storage, and the benefits of Ionian judicial authorities and mercantile agreement.[61]

Magnesia turned for help against the Lydians first to Smyrna and then to Kolophon, two centers with extensive native Anatolian populations (Hdt. 1.14.4).[62] The subsequent Lydian raids upon Smyrna and Kolophon may have resulted from Magnesia's plea for assistance against Lydia. At Kolophon, the Lydians took the lower city while the Kolophonians successfully held their high acropolis as the noble cavalry of great repute repelled the Lydians (Strabo 14.1.28). Many Kolophonians, however, fled the strife for security at Polieion in southern Italy.[63] The remaining Kolophonians thereupon rapidly assimilated the Lydian customs and styles, as the irascible Kolophonian Xenophanes scoffed: "They learned useless luxuries from the Lydians, while still they were not subject to their hateful tyranny. They would proceed to their agora in purple cloaks, a full thousand of them as a rule, no less flaunting their comely locks and drenched in scented unguents."[64] Both the purple cloaks and unguents were Lydian marks. A symbiotic relationship, therefore, very rapidly developed between the Kolophonian and Lydian nobilities which bound the two systems of landed, horse raising gentry with extremely close economic and politically-minded ties.

Lydia's relationship with Miletos was also complex. While Gyges attacked and perhaps entered Miletos (Hdt. 1.14.1), he did not hold it and furthermore allowed the Milesians to settle Abydos in the Troad within Gyges' newly obtained territory of suzerainty (Strabo 13.1.22).[65]

In an effort to placate the mainland Greeks, Gyges used his newly obtained wealth, essentially Paktolian gold, to purchase major gifts for Apollo's temple at Delphi. These gifts further indicated Lydian Hellenization and the Lydian turn towards greater

Greece. Gyges' rich gifts, mostly silver but also six gold mixing bowls, which weighed thirty talents, certainly impressed the Corinthians who stored the Lydian offerings in their Delphian Treasury. Herodotus, however, was less impressed and considered both Gyges and Mita, who also gave gifts to Delphi, barbaroi, oriental, and foreign in speech (1.13-14).

Fundamental to Gyges' military, diplomatic, and commercial success was the royal control of gold. For Archilochos (F 15), Gyges was simply *polychrysos*, "rich in gold" (cf. Hdt. 1.14.1-2; Sappho F 219 [98], [a] 10-12, [b] 1-3), and Lydian gold-diplomacy made indelible marks upon the ancient world. Lavish gifts were given to Greek and Lydian sanctuaries, Ionian and Karian mercenaries were hired to supplement the Lydian military, and Ionian exiles were subsidized to return and foment revolution in their homelands (Alkaios F 42). Highly valuable, small in package, easily transportable, and extremely rare in the Mediterranean, Lydian gold persuasively influenced the essentially hostile and anti-Lydian Ionians to grant the Lydians trading agreements, and created a tolerable symbiosis based upon self-interest and mutual respect. At Ephesos, the noble oligarchic rulers intermarried with the Lydian royal house and reconfirmed the Lydian and native Anatolian interests and the chief sanctuary dedicated to the many-breasted Lydian Mother Goddess whom the Greeks addressed as Artemis.[66] Gold apparently also allied the landed Kolophonian nobles to the Lydians. Just as gold paid the king's bodyguard and sent mercenaries on foreign service, it also bought administrative service, luxury goods, and artistic commissions such as Gyges' great burial mound at Bin Tepe. His tomb, a strong ashlar wall heaped high with dirt, bore in the Lydian alphabet his name Gugu ("Grandfather"),[67] and marks Lydia's fertile country, rich in gold (Hdt. 5.49.4). The gold which underscored his mercurial and vacillatory diplomatic activities rebuilt a wealthy Sardis which impressed the seventh century Sardian poet Alkman sufficiently that he noted: "You are not simpleton nor clumsy fellow, nor a Thessalian nor an Erysichan shepherd, but you are a man of lofty Sardis" (F 16 [24B. 13 D]). While the Parian Archilochos could scoff: "I do not care for the wealth of Gyges rich in gold" (F 15), he could not avoid its power.[68]

The structure of socio-political Lydia, grounded upon the aristocratic agrarian nobles, their clans, and their retainers, reveals a system of suzerainty rooted in the Bronze Age Hittite societies, which emerged during Gyges' reign as a powerful institution basic to his revitalization movement. Within the early Hittite society during the Old Kingdom prior to King Telepinus (c. 1525-1500 B.C.), the village functioned as the basic unit. The village was a collection of houses much like the modern Anatolian village today, thirty-five centuries later. Only the Hittite capital Hattusha ranked as did Lydian Sardis as a major city. The nonurban majority dwelt in essentially self-contained and self-sufficient villages. The paternal heads of each household gathered as a council of elders, important figures forming a governing body. All effective power lay in the hands of a limited number of extended families or clans, which formed the agrarian aristocracy. The most important clan or "Great Family" provided the king and the highest officers of state. The aristocracy, consequently, held dual roles as warriors and administrators: the king's "fighting men and his servants."[69]

By oaths of loyalty, the Hittite kings bound their aristocracies and in return awarded grants of land for noble services. Newly conquered lands were first divided among the members of the royal clan and then among other aristocrats who served as military commanders and governors drawn from the aristocracies to include rulers of conquered states obliged to pay the kings homage, to fight in their wars, to pay yearly tribute, and to pledge loyal oaths. Interdynastic marriages often served as common political devices. As the Hittites expanded into the region of Arzawa (north-western Anatolia), they encountered ruling families and aristocratic organizations basically similar to those in Hatti. Especially in the Troad, the suzerains and their nobles sustained the basic Anatolian pattern of clan organizations.

While Lydian-Tylonid society endured large-scale movements of populations between 1200 and 700 B.C., the continuity of social institutions prevailed from the Hittite through the Mermnad eras. This continuity can be observed in the gradual transition of archaeological artifacts without evidence of a cultural break and in the similarity of Hittite and Lydian institutions. The continuity is also noted in the Anatolian language. Both the Phrygian and Lydian languages stem from the Indo-European Hittite-Luwian group, but Lydian retained closer ties with Hittite than did Phrygian.[70] This marked continuity between Hittite and Lydian societies is further underscored by the Lydian remembrance of Gyges' father, Myrsilus, whose name reflects the Hittite King Mursilis (Hdt. 1.7.2) and the Hittite meaning of "Grandfather" for Gyges. With the overthrow of the Tylonidai, Gyges' activities paralleled earlier Hittite noble threats to royal authority and challenges to the throne for command.

Basic to Hittite suzerainty, the oath of fidelity offered by the noble to the king obligated the noble to obey the stipulated commands. The primary purpose of this suzerain treaty was to establish a firm relationship of help and especially military support, whereby the king protected his nobles from the attacks or claims of others, essentially foreign states. The noble's obligation to trust the king rested in the benevolence of the suzerain.[71] During and apparently even before the brief reign of Kandaules (c. 683-680 B.C.),[72] that trust failed, which generated the aristocratic support of the rival Mermnad clan and its rise to power. Herodotus clearly noted (1.13.1) the rebels (stasiotai) in Gyges' faction and the other Lydians who plotted the overthrow of Kandaules.[73] Gyges' marriage to Toudo, Kandaules' widow and Mysian princess, not only legitimized Gyges' reign and adoption of the Tylonid harem but also bound the king closely to Toudo's Mysian clan (Nic. Dam. FGrH 90 F 47). Through the revitalization process, Gyges thwarted the Lydian centrifugal activities and imposed a strong centralizing centripetal royal power.

The Lydian suzerain ties did not develop, however, during the reigns of Gyges and Kandaules, but at earlier periods when the kinship ties had proved inadequate, particularly in their protective capacity, during the period of the weakened state (c. 1200-700 B.C.) and specifically during the age of the Greek colonization of Ionia, just as they had during the early Old Kingdom of Hatti.[74]

These elements of suzerainty appear in the Greco-Lydian Sagen in the terms of hegemonia for lordship (Hdt. 1.7; [Apollodorus] Bibliotheca 2.6.3),[75] genos and apogenos to denote clan and kinship (Hdt. 1.6.1, 7, 16; Nic. Dam. FGrH 90 F 63; Dionysius of Halikarnassos Ant. Rom. 1.27.1-2; [Apoll.] Biblio. 278), oikeia in reference to families (Polyainos 7.6.2-3), and hetairos to denote the association of the noble called basileus (Plut. de Herod. Malig. 18 [858E]; Tzetzes Chil. 5.456) as a companion or comrade-in-arms (Diog. Laert. 1.81; Plut. Quaest. Graec. 45 [302A]); or in the view of the third-fourth century A.D. Roman Arnobius (Adversus nationes 4.25) "to have served a mercenary servitude," an early medieval concept of miliary subordination.[76] Homer's Iliad (20.392-5) clearly refers to the Lydian "noble . . . as a leader of military men;" a type of noble whom Nicolas of Damascus (FGrH 90 F 16) identified with "manly courage and justice." Homer's noble "leadership" further reflects this concept of hegemonia or suzerainty and indicates a suzerain structure consisting of a network of ties of dependence extending from the top to the bottom of the social scale. Basic to this structure is the emphasis upon the noble as a horseman with an agrarian demesne and dependents (Mimnermos F 13; Nic. Dam. *FGrH* 90 F 62). The historical kernel fundamental within the Sagen which relates to Tylonid King Ardys (as noted by Nicolas of Damascus *FGrH* F 44.10) was the Lydian miliary force of cavalrymen, with their demesnes which Homer (*IL* 20.391) referred to as the ancestral estate, *temenos patrōion*.

With stability as the bulwark of Gyges' revitalization of Lydia and his royal power, the subordination of the nobles became necessary, as did the establishment of a complex socio-political hierarchy upon an agrarian economic base. Gyges essentially renovated the social relationship to establish his pinnacle of power. He extended his royal controls and bureaucracy outside of the standard suzerain relationships of the companion men, the king's cavalry, by hiring Ionian and Karian mercenaries loyal to the throne and its wealth. For a century, Gyges' Sardis prospered and formed Croesus' urban center where Lydians reached a superior state of social, political, and spiritual development, whereby Greeks, Babylonians, and Egyptians acknowledged the capital as one of the most powerful and richly endowed.[77]

Gyges' successor, Ardys (644–c. 624 B.C.), continued his father's policies: waged war against the fading Kimmerians (638 B.C.), seized briefly Priene, and raided Miletos for a period of eleven years.[78] In response, the Milesians and the other Ionians sought lands and raw materials elsewhere and began an active phase of Ionian colonization in Thrace, the Propontis, and ultimately along the Black Sea coasts. The Lydians had successfully blocked the East Greek encroachment upon their lands and were pushing the Greek borders back. With Ashurbanipal's renewed alliance of military assistance and the aid of the Cilician king, the new miliary coalition defeated the Kimmerian Dygdamis (c. 630 B.C.). For Sardis and Lydia, their Golden Age commenced.

Under Sadyattes (c. 624–612 B.C.), Ardys' son and dynastic successor, Lydian economic recovery blossomed following the Kimmerian depredations, although if we may trust the ancient sources, family intrigue and harem problems plagued the king.[79] To mark this revival, Sadyattes renewed the razzias for six years against Miletos during the second half of his reign.

Alyattes' succeeding reign (c. 612–561/60 B.C.) restored order to his father's ruling house, and for five additional years prolonged the war against Miletos. But a change in royal policy had shifted annual harvest-time razzias to an all out effort to gain Miletos as a Lydian port. The Milesians, then ruled by the tyrant Thrasyboulos, fought the Lydians with no Ionian aid save that from Chios. The particularism and parochialism endemic of the Ionian and other Greek poleis left Miletos alone to withstand Alyattes' advances and conclude a peace treaty with Lydia c. 605 B.C.[80] While our sources may retain more Sagen for this period than historical fact, Herodotus notes (1.19-22) that to replace the burned temple of Athena at Milesian Assesos the Lydian monarch built two temples as replacement for the Milesian loss. The thin line between Lydian and Greek religious practices often disappeared.

Undaunted by failure to seize Miletos, Alyattes turned upon Smyrna shortly after 605 B.C.; and raising a high siege mount against the city's northwestern walls, successfully besieged it by c. 600 B.C. Bronze arrowheads, spearheads, a cache of weapons, and an oriental style iron helmet excavated by archaeologists mark the downfall of that East Greek city.[81] But if the Lydians wanted the strategically positioned city as an Aegean port, they failed. Smyrna rapidly dwindled, perhaps due more to the silting in of its harbor than to Alyattes' destructions. And at Klazomenai, to the west of Smyrna, "evidently the Klazomenian hoplites proved superior to the Lydian horsemen,"[82] and Alyattes returned without victory (Hdt. 1.16.2).

Within the realm of foreign diplomacy, Alyattes' policies were extremely complex. Lydian treachery succeeded when Alyattes invited many of the leading Kolophonian landed gentry to Sardis for its festivals; but there Alyattes abused the principles of Guestfriendship, murdered the nobles, and deprived Kolophon of its powerful cavalry (Polyainos 7.2; Herakleides FHG 2.218 F 22). Failures at Miletos had turned Alyattes against the northern Ionian poleis, and success at Smyrna and Kolophon supported Lydian expansion into Cappadocia up to the banks of the Halys River. But to the east, new rulers had replaced the old as the Iranian Medes seized Nineveh in 612 B.C. and overran Urartu by c. 590 B.C. On the eastern banks of the Halys were King Cyaxares' Median troops and tribal cavalry. Battle ensued into military loggerhead until the total solar eclipse of 28 May 585 B.C. signaled to both warring nations the necessity of a truce (Hdt. 1.74.1).[83] The Lydian army stalemated the Medes and drew the international attention of the Babylonians and Cilicians, who sought to preserve the new military equilibrium throughout the Near East. Synnesis, the King of Cilicia, mediated for the Medes and Nabonidus, the Babylonian prince,[84] on behalf of Alyattes and secured the Halys as the international border between Media and Lydia. Babylon had begun relations with Lydia under Gyges and now tried to maintain a fragile alliance with the Medes. Cilicia actively sought to preserve her semi-autonomous status amidst it all. To seal the treaty, Alyattes offered his daughter, Aryenis, to Cyaxares' son, the Median crown prince Astyages (Hdt. 1.74.3-4; POxy. 2506 F 98; Cicero de Div. 1.49).

Alyattes' harem, as with similar Near Eastern collections of cloistered women, served not only to bind international alliances such as with Cyaxares and Melas, the tyrant of Ephesos (Aelian VH 3.26; Polyainos 6.50), but also served to bind the Lydian landed gentry to the throne. Sons were needed to help administer the empire, and Ionian, Karian, and Lydian women bore the necessary kinship blood-tied offspring to assist the king. Son of a Karian woman, the eldest prince and perhaps already heir apparent, Croesus (Hdt. 1.92.3) governed the turbulent and crucial village of Adramyttion. Alyattes' policy in the Troad increased royal power and brough about the suppression and expulsion of the hostile Kimmerians from Antandros, c. 570 B.C. In Alyattes' final years Croesus also served his royal father in renewed campaigns against Priene and Karia across the Maeander River (Hdt. 1.92.2-4).

For the Lydian nobles, Alyattes' fame and power surpassed Gyges'; and at Bin Tepe they supervised the building of his tomb, larger than Gyges' and rival only to Mita's at Gordion. Above the one hundred burial mounds at Bin Tepe, Alyattes' mound loomed among the great eastern cluster of three, of Gyges', Ardys' (?), and his own.[85]

The key to Mermnad success lay in the complicated interrelationship between the king and his nobles. Gyges had raised them as a collective nation into an international political power. Alyattes, however, sensed that this power was no longer adequate and, consequently, directed his nation toward new economic modes. The success of the noble demesnes relieved of Kimmerian devastations produced a greater need for international markets. With the preservation of Lydia's eastern border, the treaty with Cyaxeres of Media, and alliances of friendship with Nabonidus of Babylon and Synnesis of Cilicia, Alyattes reopened and renewed the safety of the overland trade routes into Mesopotamia. But western Sardis and the nobles of the Hermos Valley sought first Miletos then Smyrna and Klazomenai as outlets to Greece and Egypt. After the conquest of Smyrna, however, its harbor failed; and the direct land route between Sardis and Smyrna could no longer serve the economic functions of import and export either for the royal industries or the noble demesnes. Alyattes' successor, Croesus (561–c. 565 B.C.), would have to build a more aggressive, successful, and innovative policy; the conquest of Greek Ionia.

The fifth century B.C. tradition rather incorrectly labeled the Lydians effeminate, luxurious, and weak. The Lydian cavalry and infantry forces terrified the Greeks and fought the Medes from standstill to standstill. Alyattes transformed the Mermnad court into a brilliant cosmopolitan center marked by gold and luxuries as a reward for its support of his major change in policy to acquire East Greek land and ports. Near Eastern merchants and diplomatic envoys mingled with Greek poets, philosophers, and musicians, and Ionian architects and sculptors. The wealth accumulated at court and among the noble estates supported artists who created for their patrons the famed Lydian luxury envied and belittled later as effeminacy and weakness. The gold mining begun under Gyges remained largely under royal control, from placer to shaft mining; yet apparently some nobles also shared the riches of Mt. Tmolos.[86]

Croesus' reign over the Lydian clans and other indigenous peoples of his empire (Hdt. 1.53.2, 69.2) concentrated the institutional forces set into motion by Gyges' revitalization movement and Alyattes' development and expansion of those forces. Beneath the Herodotean dramatic novella (1.29-33) of Croesus' oriental luxury in contrast to Solon's elderly statesmanship, Croesus' innovative policies emerge clearly.[87] Harem factionalism continued to plague the royal house. After a bitter struggle with his half-brother Pantaleon (of an Ionian mother, Hdt. 1.92.3-4), Croesus, whom Alyattes had chosen heir apparent, emerged victorious. Kinship and clan politics compounded by the relationships of clientship underlay the royal selection of a successor, not racial factionalism against Croesus' Karian mother. This harem problem, present throughout the following Persian period, was endemic to many oriental empires. Swift in action and resolute of mind, Croesus immediately executed Pantaleon's chief supporter, seized his property, and successfully wielded power over the dissident Lydian nobles who had rallied to Pantaleon's cause. Croesus' support came from an Ionian faction led by the Prienian Pamphaes. Against the tyrant Pindaros of Ephesos, a grandson of the former King Alyattes, Croesus set his first attack. Pindaros, who had evidently supported Pantaleon, piqued Croesus' wrath and was forced into exile.[88] Nevertheless, in a magnificent gesture toward the Ephesians Croesus gave to the Artemision temple at Ephesos Pamphaes' wealth, an act which also gained the confirmation of Croesus' royal legitimany by the Ephesian priesthood (Nic. Dam. *FGrH* F 65; Aelian *VH* 4.27). In fulfillment of his vows to Artemis, Croesus offered golden bulls and carved column drums (Hdt. 1.92.1; Tod *GHI* 1^2.6), each carefully inscribed, "Croesus the king dedicated this."[89]

Croesus' diplomatic maneuvers toward the Greek sanctuaries were similar to the policies begun by Gyges. His gifts of gold of extraordinary artistic merit gained religious sanction for his imperial activities. Apollo Pythios at Delphi, Ismenian Apollo at Boiotian Thebes, Apollo Branchidai at Didyma in the polis of Miletos, and Apollo at Thornax in Spartan Lakonia could not fail to look upon Croesus favorably (Hdt. 1.92.1-2; 1.69.3-4; Marmor Parium 239A41). In antiquity Croesus' gold became proverbial no less a play on words: *Kroisos* (Croesus) and *chrysos* (gold)—(Favorinus *de Fortuna* 26-7; cf. Valerius Maximus 7.1.2).

Beneath this show of diplomacy, Croesus and his noble cavalry subjugated first the Ionian poleis, then the Aiolian poleis, and finally the Dorian poleis in Karia, and demanded annual tribute (Hdt. 1.26; Xen. *Cyr.* 6.2.10; Paus. 4.5.3). Croesus extended his protectorship over Ephesos, rebuilt Smyrna, and besieged Miletos, which bitterly resisted his domination. Upon the advice of the philosopher Thales, Miletos refused Croesus' initial overtures for alliance (Diog. Laert. 1.25); but as Smyrna could not serve Lydia's mercantile needs, Miletos did by forces. Additional campaigns into the Troad (Strabo 13.1.42) expanded Croesus' empire from the southern shores of Karia to the Hellespont and eastward to the Halys River when Sardis was at the height of her wealth (Hdt. 1.28; Schol. Plato *Rep.* 566C). Only the hardy mountain Lykians, the Cilicians subject to the Babylonian King Neriglissar 557/6 B.C.,[90] and the Median Phrygians east of the Halys, all of Anatolia, lay outside the Lydian realm; then an empire of tribes, clans, herders, farmers, landed gentry, and city folk, predominantly agricultural in character. Without a sufficient naval force, Croesus held no hope of subjugating the Ionian islands. Instead, he offered alliances of friendship (Hdt. 1.26-7). The Lydians would have been ineffective against the island navies even with their conquered Ionian fleets, just as the Ionians on land were ineffective against the Lydian cavalry.

The seizure of the Ionian poleis and their mercantile harbors radically altered Lydian policy. The Ionian poleis no longer functioned as a buffer zone between Lydia and the island and mainland Greeks, and Lydia now lay subject to their possible raids. At those harbors, the Lydian government had to offer the foreigners civil protection, the benefits of judical authority and mercantile agreement, and the facilities of those ports. Croesus' dramatic step brought Lydia directly into the world of Aegean and Mediterranean sea traffic and all the problems which that entailed.

At Sardis, Croesus ruled from his marble palace and an impregnable citadel within a city ringed by a massive mud-brick wall with battlements and beyond urban sprawl.[91] Hanfmann suggests a city population between 20,000 and 50,000 in addition to a Sardian rural population between 20,000 and 30,000; thus, 40,000 to 80,000 in total.[92] To secure his capital and empire, Croesus fostered international alliances which unfortunately failed him in his months of need c. 545 B.C. with the Saïte pharaoh of Egypt, Amasis; King Nabonidus of Babylonia; and the Spartans (Hdt. 1.77.1-2). Croesus' sister, Aryenis, as King Astyages of Media's queen continued to bind the Lydian-Median alliance and the Halys River border. Croesus also fostered diplomatic ties with the tyrants of Corinth, Athens, and the elder Miltiades in the Chersonese. What appears as an ambivalent attitude toward the Greeks, Lydian hostility to Ionians, and friendship to the mainland poleis, was in reality Croesus' clear perception of Greek parochialism and his success with gold-diplomacy.

Lydia's revived overland trade with Mesopotamia fostered in Sardis the development of the first gold and silver coinage (Hdt. 1.94; Pollux *Onomasticon* 9.83), a bimettalic monetary system patterned upon earlier Urartian and Assyrian noncoinage monetary systems and the preceding Lydian and Ionian experiments with electrum coinage.[93] Croesus introduced pieces of precious metal with his royal guarantee identifiable, the culmination of both the oriental use of metal for mercantile exchange and the long-used systems of control to encourage trade with the Ionian poleis and to pay Ionian and Karian mercenaries. Croesus' bimettalic currency solved the basic problem of market exchange of the two metals and their respective weights and values, and structured the organization of Lydian tax collection and Ionian tribute and the cumbersome payment of soldiers, mercenaries, and other state employees in bulky units of monetary exchange. The three basic uses of currency, a medium of exchange, a standard of value, and a means of payment were, however, not necessarily interconnected; perhaps each arose as an independent function, with silver and gold pieces used respectively for different purposes. The exchange of coinage, nevertheless, developed not from the random barter acts of individuals under Tylonid or early Mermnad rule but in connection with the organized external and internal markets of Croesus' age. Coinage, therefore, structured Lydian trade, encouraged noble participation in that trade, fostered the merchant dealers (Hdt. 1.94.1), and provided Croesus with monetary modes whereby he strengthened his royal power. The earlier barter and noncoinage monetary exchange of the agrarian estates and urban Sardis had structured an organized trade network interwoven within Alyattes' imperial structure, a network of merchants trekking overland to Babylonia and the Ionian poleis.[94] With access to Aegean ports and their maritime trade under Croesus, however, an innovative bimetallic coinage system raised Sardis to new levels as a major metropolis, an urban center of small shopkeepers who purchased a variety of goods. From Ionia, Aiolis, Attica, Corinth, Lakonia, Samos, Rhodes, and Egypt to Sardis came new products in exchange for Lydian perfumed unguents, seal stones, carpets, horses, ivories, and oriental wares carted overland by caravans from Phrygia, Media, Scythia, and Phoenicia. The royal device of Croesus, his coat-of-arms, marked many of the gold and silver pieces with the lion sacred to the goddess Kuvava.

Underlying Croesus' success was the relationship between the king and his landed nobility. With their support Croesus developed aggressive military policies toward the Ionians, Phrygians, and the indigenous populations of Karia and the Troad; active diplomatic ties with Babylonia, Cilicia, and Egypt; and aggressive mercantile system with its bimetallic coinage; and an increase in Sardian cultural monuments. The obligation of the throne to protect its nobles, to maintain or increase the steady state and to prevent individual stress, succeeded in molding a powerful royal house and the hegemony of the king. The several harem problems, which plagued the reigns of Sadyattes, Alyattes, and Croesus, signal the noble involvement and participation, limited though it may have been, in the selection of the heir apparent from the royal clan. Any individual stress or societal distortion had to be stemmed if the king was to succeed. Until Cyrus appeared at the Halys River c. 545 B.C., Croesus had succeeded magnificently. As basileus or qalmluś, Croesus ruled a large and progressive empire to which, at least in the Greek understanding, he also served as an hegemon and tyrannos. For the Greeks, namely Herodotus and Thucydides, an hegemon served as military "leader," "guide," or director,"[95] or as leader of a political faction.[96] Hegemony was the power of "rule,"[97]

yet with concern for one's subordinates. As Thucydides stated: "It is the duty of the

hegemons, while equitably considering their particular interests, to have special regard

for the common good, just as they are especially honored above all among other men"

(1.120.1).

Tyrannos, a word adopted by the Greeks and a pre-Indo-European word retained by

the "Pelasgian" substructure of indigenous Anatolian peoples, however, does not appear in

the few Lydian inscriptions which remain; and our understanding of the word and its

office is colored by the fifth century Greek writers, the same writers who labeled Lydian

life effeminate. Consequently, when Croesus conquered the Ionian poleis, the Greek

concept of tyrannos gained new meaning whereby the tyrannical life while being the most

enjoyable and desirable way of life was deplorable for the subjects.[98] For the Greeks,

the tyrannos' power arose in consequence of personal ambition, power, prestige, and the

manifestation of subjective will. For the Lydians, on the other hand, the concept of

tyrannos may have related to the word teri̅ meaning army to denote a ruler desirous of

being the master of armed forces and subject communities.[99] For Herodotus, basileus

was distinct from tyrannos: the former meant legitimate and hereditary rule, while the

latter indicated arbitrary, despotic, and evil government, a concept sustained by

Aristotle (Pol. 1295a and 1285a). For the Lydian nobles however, their king was neither

arbitrary, despotic, nor evil but chosen (even with difficulty) from the legitimate royal

house which had raised the Lydians to the fulfillment of Gyges' revitalization movement

and Alyattes' and Croesus' innovations. Without the support of the Lydian nobility, the

Mermnad kings could not have succeeded but would have been overthrown as the Tylonid

king had been. Great political power rested in the hands of each major Lydian landed

nobleman.

Under Croesus, Lydia reached a new, high level, centralized kingship structured upon

an hierarchical pyramid of interrelated kinship systems, which had transformed from

tribal units into a complex civic society centered upon the palace and its markets and

shrines in Sardis. The complexity of Croesus' regime underlay the development of

bimetallic currency, eastern overland trade, conquest of Ionian ports of trade, the

mercenary system, the bureaucratic system and its extension of the utilization of nobles

in the government, the royal and private gold industry, and the Sardian monuments.

These achievements were interrelated but not necessarily by cause and effect; nor were they absolutely contemporary with Croesus' initial innovative activities, which took place early in his reign. These innovative accomplishments, however, benefitted the nobles' estates by changing those demesnes from self-sufficient village clusters (as under the Tylonid rule) to complex economic areas dependent upon the political center. As a result, the military ties between the suzerain and his subordinate nobles increased. In this alteration, Croesus' Lydia emerged with marked distinction from the point of Gyges' revitalization movement. Croesus' system was also superior to that of the conquering Persian Cyrus but responsive to Darius' revitalization movement in 520-518 B.C. and able to integrate easily and extensively with Darius' system. The consequence of this easy integration was to secure a base for Achaemenid control in western Anatolia at the end of the sixth century B.C., a base which was violently disrupted by the Ionian rebellion of 499 B.C.

3

IONIA BEFORE THE PERSIANS

When Cyrus the Persian conquered Lydia, he incorporated that empire into his own, and Lydia known as Śfarda became his province or satrapy of Sparda. Śfarda flourished not only as the cosmopolitan Lydian culture brought to culmination under Croesus' reign but also as an Hellenized province, the product of its subsidiary East Greek populations. More than two centuries later, however, when Alexander III seized Sparda from the Persian Empire of King Darius III, Sparda was barely Persianized. In fact, the Hellenization had markedly increased and had spread extensively into Karia and Lykia. Between the East Greeks (especially the Ionians) and the Lydians a high degree of acculturation had occurred; while between the East Greeks and Lydians little acculturation with the Persians resulted. Beyond the fifth century B.C. literary evidence of Aeschylus, Herodotus, Thucydides, Xenophon and later Greek writers such as Ephoros and Arrian, the archaeological evidence alone would not bear witness to more than two centuries of rigorous Achaemenid rule in Ionia and Śfarda.

In this regard, to follow Robert Redfield, "acculturation comprehends those phenomena which result when groups of individuals having different cultures come into continuous first-hand contact, with subsequent changes in the original cultural patterns of either or both groups."[1] While the Hellenization of Lydia has long been noted, I suggest and demonstrate herein the Anatolization of the Ionian and Aiolian poleis. In doing so, I focus upon the Greek landed gentry and its demesne, the oikos, a phenomenon which had its origins in the Protogeometric era.

I

Social turmoil plagued Anatolia following the collapse of the Hittite Empire, yet it resulted in the centralization of peoples and especially the Hittite–Luwian speaking clans into the territory of Asia/Ashshuwa (the heartland of Lydia). The intrusions of European tribes also complicated the end of Mycenaean Greek contacts with Anatolia. While LH III C sherds have been uncovered at Miletos and at Sardis,[2] a distinct cultural hiatus appears between the Mycenaean contacts with Anatolia and the LH III B and C ceramics and the earliest appearances of Greek Protogeometric ceramics at coastal sites along the

59

Anatolian shores of the Aegean. The current thesis that Mycenaean LH III B and C contacts with Anatolia were essentially mercantile rather than colonial is credible,[3] especially when we note that the pattern of Greek Protogeometric and Geometric age settlements were distinct from the Mycenaean pattern of mercantile outposts.[4] The cultural hiatus was pronounced, and the lack of local Ionian Sagen referring to the thirteenth and twelfth centuries B.C. strongly reconfirms that hiatus.[5] Except for foundation Sagen, the Geometric Age bards from the Ionian region, Chios and Samos, had no Bronze Age Sagen to add to the Homeric Epics, while in contrast the bards of the essentially indigenous Anatolian regions of Lesbos, Lemnos, and Tenedos (settled by Greeks in the eighth century B.C.) had.

Our knowledge of the Greek Protogeometric settlements along the eastern Aegean coasts is unfortunately incomplete: excavated materials await publication in detail and further extensive excavation remains a prime desideratum.[6] Nevertheless, a pattern emerges. During the second century of Tylonid rule and the earliest phases of the Lydian steady state, mid-eleventh century B.C., small, scattered, and independent settlements of Greeks from the mainland dotted the Cycladic islands eastward to Miletos and Termera at the tip of the Halikarnassian peninsula. Both Anatolian settlements suggest strong local native populations marked by their local gray monochrome ceramics, but also tenuous oversea contacts with Athens and its rapidly diffused influence of Attic Protogeometric ceramics.[7] From this south-western coastal region, these new yet local Protogeometric styles spread to Dirmil, Iasos, Tsangli up the coast to Ionian Marathesion (at Kuṣadası), Teos, Smyrna, Boutheia, and into Aiolian Phokaia and Pitane.[8] The indigenous peoples at Emborio on Chios, Lesbos, as well as the remainder of Aiolis and the Troad, which were now relatively settled, continued as they had during the Bronze Age and without Greek contact.[9] The pivotal center was Smyrna, essential to Tylonid Sardis, where the native Smyrnaian population rapidly flourished and gradually developed that new socio-politico-economic institution, the city-state or polis.[10] While early Smyrna remained essentially neither East Greek nor Tylonid, the Smyrnaian polis was the result of the cultural assimilation of native Anatolians of a complex Greek cultural and political system.

The frontier between the newly settled East Greeks and the Lydians remained a broad zone marked with indigenous peoples who clung tenuously to their brief abilities for independence, such as at Smyrna. The East Greek settlements, however, in their initial stages absorbed many of the local inhabitants through intermarriage (Hdt.1.197), which structured a frontier of inclusion, and a markedly higher degree of inclusion than in Karia and Aiolis. The Greek settlement at Xanthos in the late eighth century B.C., by comparison, retained the highest degree of exclusion with the hardy and robust Lykians; a degree of exclusion which accompanied the Ionian settlements of Thrace and lack of interaction between the colonists and the indigenous Thracian tribes during the period of Ionian colonization and revitalization. The Lydians retained their distinct language, evolved and used their own script well into the fourth century B.C., and developed a fundamental cavalry-noble structure to their society; but they also became extensively Hellenized through the process of acculturation, so that the Lydians became similar to the Ionian Greeks, and conversely the Ionian Greeks were similar to the Lydians. The Ionians retained their Greek dialects (Hdt.1.142) and local Greek scripts, developed an aristocratic society often strongly based upon the nobles (or cavalry as at Kolophon), and gradually gained marks of Lydianization. The multifaceted similarities of the Lydian demesne and the East Greek pyrgos-demesne, therefore, fostered a high degree of social accommodation between the Ionians and the Lydians. At Miletos on the border of Ionia-Lydia and southern Karia, Ionian inclusion with the indigenous Karians also occurred.[11]

One of the more important processes of acculturation between the native Anatolians and the colonial East Greeks of Ionia occurred in the adoption by the Greeks of the local cult centers. At Didyma south of Miletos, at Ephesos, and perhaps at Klaros, for example, the open-air cult altars at which the local Anatolian tribes worshipped clearly preceded the more elaborate shrines built by the intruding Greeks. Through this adoption, the native Anatolian religious traditions, music and religious poetry, became deeply embedded in the developing East Greek cults.[12]

The process of East Greek and Lydian acculturation and the resultant high degree of social inclusion occurred gradually because the great lateral mountain ridges firmly divided the western Anatolian coast into small distinct geographical areas from north to south: Kyme, Phokaia, Smyrna, Klazomenai, Erythrai, Teos, Kolophon, Ephesos, Priene, and Miletos. During the tenth and ninth centuries B.C., consequently, the discrete mountain and distinct hill ridges isolated each area so that its own particular ethnic and dialectic forms developed. Ultimately these forms began to transform into a collective cultural koine as shorter and more direct sea travel developed, first centered at Samos and then Chios, but not flourishing until c. 700 B.C. While land travel over the mountain ridges of Mykale and Mimas-Korykos-Kaystrios may have been no more difficult than in Attica, or considerably easier than between many of the mainland Greek poleis,[13] the fundamental agricultural settlement of the East Greeks among the indigenous Anatolians and the process of acculturation fostered a high degree of regional parochialism until the eighth century B.C. This is demonstrated by the later evidence of strong dialect and script distinctions between the poleis,[14] as well as by the history of the conflict between these dissimilar groups for the same ecological niches.

The culturally egocentric Greeks, and in particular the Ionians, usually flaunted their superiority over the barbaroi, the exotic foreign peoples of strange speech. Yet, when the Kolophonian Xenophanes (F 171-172) stressed Ionian superiority over the Thracians and the Ethiopians he did not mention the Lydians. The Ionians and notably the Kolophonians admired the Lydians, and spoke of them not in their stereotypes for barbaroi as "savage, wild beasts or heathens," but in terms of envy: "rich in gold." The processes of acculturation and assimilation thereby eliminated exclusionist policies along Greek and Lydian ethnic lines; and the pockets of localized indigenous groups dotting the broad buffer zone of the frontier (except a majority of the Karians) were integrated, probably as lower class clients or subjection to serf status, and/or slavery, by a process of cultural interpenetration rather than habitational replacement.[15]

The process of acculturation developed gradually, as fundamentally noted by the role of mainland Greek ceramic influence upon western Anatolia from Attica to the Milesian-Termeran regions, which passed across the Cycladic island of Samos[16] and, consequently, affected essentially the Ionian region from Teos southward to Karian Termera. At the same time, Chios, the Smyrnaian Gulf and Lesbos to the north beyond the Erythraian peninsula (the Mimas-Korykos Range) gradually developed as fringe regions of Tylonid Lydia and its several indigenous populations. The Greek settlements in Ionia clung to the shores of the Aegean, rather similar to Plato's analogy of ants and frogs sitting along the edge of a great pond (Phaedo 109B); for clearly land was simply not available for expansion inland up the fertile river valleys and plains into Lydia.[17] The Greek settlements occurred apparently at a time of low population levels of indigenous peoples; they also occurred at a time when both groups were expanding in numbers of peoples and in their demands for more agricultural land. The East Greek settlements, therefore, were locked into their original territories with little room for expansion. The Ephesian expansion into the Maeander Valley (?) and brief occupation of Magnesia were notable anomalies. Ephesos and Kolophon were exceptions to the rule, with sufficient land to assume much of their population growths and rising standards of living, but the East Greeks in those two poleis had settled among concentrations of Anatolian inhabitants, a fact which subsequently produced high degrees of acculturation at those two non-trading port settlements (Hdt 1.197). Elsewhere, in Karia for example, the Greeks avoided obvious fertile and easily accessible areas. Mylasa, some twenty kilometers inland from the coast without intervening mountain barriers, lay well beyond the limit of Greek settlement, for here arose the Karian Hekatomnid dynasty (Hdt. 1.171).[18]

The extensive native Anatolian substructure in the East Greek coastal settlements focused upon the clan and its kinship system as evidenced by the predominance of multiple burial graves: cairns and circular and rectangular stone enclosures for inhumation, as at Termera, or clusters of cremation burials under tumuli, as at Kolophon. Outside of Halikarnassos, the native Lelegians, dwelling in the fortified hilltop villages, utilized rectangular tombs, chambers of corbelled masonry and entrance dromoi, covered by tumuli of rubble. These rather typical Anatolian family vaults began in the eleventh century and continued until the fifth century B.C.[19] At Ephesos and Klazomenai, cists and sarcophagi for the dead rested beneath small earth or stone tumuli, and at Smyrna the tumuli were ringed with fine stones walls to support the mounds, being similar in this respect to the hilltop tumulus near Ephesos at Belevi. At Aiolian Larisa closer to the Lydian tumuli and their influences, the mound walls were constructed with excellent revetted stones.[20] If we could chart the coastal burial mounds as Andrew and Nancy Ramage have charted the Lydian mounds,[21] we might have a better understanding of the settlement pattern of the coastal Greek and Anatolian landed gentry. In contrast, mainland Greeks abandoned extended family and kinship burials and adopted single burials, cremation and generally cist-tombs.[22]

What contacts existed between coastal Anatolia and mainland Greece were gradual, localized, and unspectacular through the Geometric era of the ninth and early eighth centuries B.C.[23] The evidence indicates connections with the Attic innovations of Protogeometric (c. 1050/1040 B.C.) and Geometric (c. 900 B.C.) ceramics. The mainland

Greeks who gradually infiltrated the native coastal settlements especially during the mid-eighth century B.C. originated from a wide variety of homes. Thessalians and Boiotians gradually settled Lesbos and its adjacent coasts of the southern Troad and Aiolis, Greeks from Attica and Euboia generally settled central Ionia, and Peloponnesians crossed the southern Cyclades to the Knidian and Halikarnassian regions.[24]   The Athenian origin for Ionia, touted by the fifth century B.C. writers, bears only traces of historical reality in addition to the hallmarks of the fifth century Athenian political propaganda.

II

The conclusion of this analysis contends that the Greek settlements along the Anatolian coast were ethnic complexities of indigenous native groups (the remnants of the Bronze Age societies and the Early Iron Age European intruders) and the infiltrating Greeks who gained agrarian demesnes scattered among the native demesnes and farms. Their coastal settlements remained just that, not because they desired extensive if not exclusive contact with the Greek mainland, but because Tylonid power prevented their expansion up the Maeander, Kayster, and Hermos valleys. The Greeks did not turn their backs to the Anatolian hinterland; they sought it, fought for it, but they were blocked and thwarted.

Two Anatolian poleis demonstrate this contention: Smyrna and Teos. Smyrna remained essentially Anatolian during the Protogeometric era, and developed the basic eastern polis. By c. 900 B.C., the settlement was dotted with oval houses, one story, often one room, with steeply pitched, thatched roofs competently built and carefully orientated. By the mid-ninth century B.C. the inhabitants had constructed a major stone wall, a fortification for that polis covering a low rise projecting into the gulf. A century later, a new wall fortification provided greater protection for the by then flimsy intramural houses. Smyrna was not only a coastal polis but also an agricultural center with its intramural houses marked by circular granaries, structures not dissimilar to the rural pyrgoi on the noble demesnes. The Smyrnaians had taken a vital step in the coordination of urban and rural life, an effective step in the development of the polis, and with a higher standard of mural architectural skill than found on the Greek mainland.[25] At Teos, in the low rolling countryside outside of the unwalled urban center and straddling the land between the two harbors, at least forty pyrgoi or agrarian demesnes dotted the landscape, pyrgoi of both Greeks and native landed gentry.[26] And at Miletos, the landed gentry also lived on landed estates or pyrgoi outside of the urban node (Hdt.1.17).

We may conclude that the agrarian demesnes of the Lydian nobles, the coastal native gentry and the newly settled East Greek aristocrats were similar in form and in function. The contrast occurred, however, between the urban center of Sardis structured about the palace and the newly emerging coastal poleis structured about the agorai, the altars or temples, and the stoas. Consequently, in regard to the fundamental agrarian institution in western Anatolia, the noble demesne or pyrgos, a high degree of acculturation occurred whereby East Greeks intermingling and interacting with Anatolian coastal natives generated substantial subsequent changes in the original cultural patterns of both groups. The East Greeks retained multiple burial graves, the indicators of their kinship units which extended broadly and deeply throughout the social scale. They also developed agrarian demesnes similar to the Anatolian demesnes, and, during the early stages of the East Greek poleis and demesnes, intermarried with the native inhabitants.[27] In turn, the coastal natives adopted more and more Greek material goods, joined the embryonic poleis and the rural agrarian structures, and sustained their local religious customs, which the East Greeks readily assimilated. By the reign of Croesus, the distinct identity of the buffer-zone natives in the Ionian region had been lost in the archaeological and literary evidence which remained.

Following the Norwegian anthropologist Frederik Barth, this argument stresses the ecological factors of Anatolia which determined the form and distribution of the Archaic Age cultures.[28] The East Greek and Lydian cultures acculturated because their ecological systems were similar, in sharp contrast to the highland Phrygians separated from Lydia by the "burned zone," the pastoral highland peoples of Karia and more notably of Lykia, and to a lesser degree the inhabitants of the Troad (western Mysia). Barth emphasized that the distributions of cultural types, ethnic groups, and natural areas rarely coincide; consequently, several ethnic groups (Ionic, Aiolic, Doric Greeks, Lydians, Karians, and pockets of residual Anatolians outside of the Lydian system) with markedly different cultures can co-reside in an area and develop symbiotic relations of variable intimacies. The distribution of these Anatolian and East Greek ethnic groups in the eighth century B.C. was not sustained by controlled objective and fixed natural areas but rather by the distribution of specific ecological niches; niches which each respective group exploited as its particular economic and political organization. If, however, the different ethnic groups exploited different ecological niches (such as the Lykians and Karians in contrast to the East Greeks) they could establish stable co-residences. But if they exploited the same niches (such as the East Greeks and the Lydians) then conflict and individual stress would arise and lead to societal distortion. The ensuing conflict, therefore, usually resulted in the militarily more powerful replacing the weaker, as the Lydians ultimately dominated the East Greeks. In Karia, where the different ethnic groups exploited the same ecological niches (at Melia, Miletos, Iasos, Halikarnassos, Termera, and Knidos), the weaker Karians utilized the marginal environments, and there the ethnic groups did co-reside in the one area. Cultural or ethnic groups of the same origin, analogous to biological organism, exist without rivalry within their ecological niche, yet cultural or ethnic groups of dissimilar origin cannot co-exist within one ecological niche without conflict.

The cultural distinctions between the East Greeks and the Lydians and their ensuing rivalries are apparent in the ancient sources, as also are the records of conflicts between the clusters of the East Greeks as they formed their early poleis, and the rivalries of the East Greeks with the other indigenous Anatolian peoples, such as the Karians. Wars waged by the East Greeks against Karian Melia and Anatolian Smyrna were similar to the wars waged by the Ephesians against the Anatolian inhabitants of Magnesia-on-the-Maeander, or by East Greeks against other East Greeks. Samians fought the Prieneians as Chiotes fought the Erythraians, in both cases for mainland agricultural territories. The hallmarks of ancient Greek societies, and in the case of this study of the early East Greek societies, were particularism and parochialism often manifest in rivalries and warfare among poleis. Consequently, greater political unity could not and did not arise from below or from the societal desires for unity. It was imposed from above by Croesus' conquest of the East Greeks and then Cyrus' conquest and Darius' reconquest of the combined empire of the Lydians and Anatolian East Greeks. The reciprocal processes of Lydian and East Greek acculturation, however, fundamentally determined the ease of Croesus', Cyrus' and then Darius' conquests.

While our literary evidence for the Lydian razzias upon the East Greek settlements suggest harvest time raids upon the agrarian fields and demesnes, we must also consider the plight of the Greek, Lydian, Karian, and other Anatolian pastoralists whose movements were generally determined by the seasonal availability of grass and the needs of their flocks.[29] The pastoralists along the lateral mountain ridges from Ionia inland to Lydia criss-crossed the broad frontier zones of cultural overlap and political instability, although not more than a few kilometers from their sedentary settlements, and increased the problems of individual stress.   This broad cultural frontier zone traversed by pastoralists and merchants from various communities generated an extended bilingual community of East Greeks and Lydians in which Ionic Greek gradually dominated as the lingua franca.   By degrees, the culturally dominant language, an Ionic Greek koine, replaced the numerous regional East Greek and Lydian dialects, but within a process which did not culminate until the end of the fourth century B.C.   By that time, Ionic Greek had also replaced the dialects of Karian and Lykian.   The development of Ionic Greek as the lingua franca, therefore, accentuated the Hellenic acculturation of the Lydians and the other indigenous Anatolian populations, yet the long retention of local Anatolian languages and their various regional dialects sustained the elements of stress between the East Greeks and the indigenous populations.

The process of Greek and Anatolian assimilation during the Protogeometric and Early Geometric eras, which fostered the acculturation, radically changed during the mid-eighth century B.C.   While the assimilation of Anatolians with East Greeks (specifically Ionians) declined, the process of acculturation, nevertheless, increased. Fundamental changes transpired throughout coastal Karia, Ionia, Aiolis, and their offshore islands.   For example, as a marked intensification of contact with the Greek mainland developed, Greek occupation of Kolophon and Ephesos occurred, advanced swiftly and produced prosperity.   Emborio on Chios similarly flourished, and Greek influence upon the Erythraian peninsula (the Mimas-Korykos Range) and the northern regions began earnestly.[30]   These events, coupled with the oral canonization of the Homeric epics, traditionally centered at Smyrna and Chios, also witnessed a vibrant archaizing movement marked by a revival of an outbreak of ancestral yearning, the conscious desire to establish links with the heroic noble ancestors to reinforce the hereditary principles of the now flourishing landed gentry upon their defined demesnes.

The decline in assimilation, essentially the fluid intermarriage of East Greeks and natives, had crystalized c. 800 B.C. with the conscious recognition of defined social units within the kinship system, and the closed parameters of the clan or phratra with its outward symbols—the horse and the cavalry.[31] In his *Politics* (1289b 39-40), Aristotle firmly noted the importance of the horse raising gentry at Magnesia-on-the-Maeander, and many other poleis in western Anatolia, in which the gentry during the archaic age formulated "cavalry politics." Membership in the tribe and its subdivisions, the phratrai, denoted citizenship, and membership within the phratra was now closed. Outside the phratra, any individual was excluded from the poleis' legal structure, a homeless "outlaw," while the landed "inlaws," the agrarian gentry, structured the administrative and military divisions of the state. Phratrai as clans centered upon households (oikoi), the extended families of the demesnes as at Smyrna, Teos, and Miletos. In Ionia (as in Lydia), they retained the political procedures of kinship, unlike Athens which replaced hereditary political office by first election and then sortition. Personal interests and familial ties remained substantially relevant and justified, with strong bonds of values and ideologies. In comparison, non-citizens, resident aliens (Anatolian and foreign) and freedmen, the landless, gathered within the mural urban nodes. Unions between paternal citizens and non-citizens may have occurred, but our sparse evidence barely hints at the possibility of their offspring becoming citizens and legitimate. The intermarriage of Ephesian aristocratic women and the Mermnad royal house, the exile of Mermnad families to Kolophon after the fall of Sardis to Cyrus,[32] and the structure of the Lydian international harem suggest some flexibility in the closed kinship-phratra system in Ionia. These, however, may have been royal perquisites and not normal flexibilities in the Ionian kinship system.[33] Strong native elements within the East Greek settlements, we must recall, occurred at Smyrna, Erythrai (Paus.7.3.7), Teos, Kolophon, Ephesos, Melia, Miletos, and Termera.

The basis of the East Greek kinship structure was the demesne (the oikos) and its land. Moses Finley, strongly influenced by the processes of anthropological analysis, has emphasized the decisive nature of the household's wealth, which served to seal and to preserve the social stratification of Homeric society.[34] In addition to convincing analyses of the eighth century B.C. gift-exchange economy, Guestfriendship, and the landed gentry's problems for the paying of these social obligations, funeral expenses, dowry guarantees, and the expenses of liturgies, Finley recognized the fundamental problem of the acquisition of the new land in settled regions. By c. 700 B.C., the demand for new lands, because of the increase in populations and the developing strictures of the inalienability of land, generated a conflict among the East Greeks and the Lydians, which not only caused the fall of the Tylonid royalty but apparently produced the first western Anatolian evidence of violent destruction since the LH III C period and particularly at Miletos.[35] It also caused Hesiod's father to move from Aiolian Kyme to Boiotian Askra.[36] Similarly, just north of Mt. Mykale and to the west of the Ionian Panionion center at the village of Melia, Ionians cohabiting with a considerable Karian element (as indicated by their burial customs) suffered a thorough destruction soon after 700 B.C. The stone circuit walls, roughly assembled, reveal a hasty attempt to defend the village's acropolis against East Greek attackers. The attack, and indicator of this general stress, came from the other Ionian peoples.[37] About the same time, the East Greeks successfully attacked and controlled Larisa and its position on the Hermos River just west of Mt. Sipylos where the river opened out into marshy estuaries; a position of influence for the eastern valley and Sardis as indicated by the beginnings of Greek influence upon the native pottery at Sardis.[38]

Future archaeological exploration will further enlighten our present limited scope of this rise of individual stress often erroneously attributed to the Kimmerians. For the landed East Greeks, the landed Lydians, and the landed indigenous peoples wedged in between the East Greeks and the Lydians, the problems of individual stress began to generate the conditions of societal distortion. Relief was primary for survival—relief which the Lydians sought with the new Mermnad leadership, relief which the East Greeks sought in the processes of colonization, but relief which did not appear for the indigenous peoples caught within the broad shatter belt frontier.

The primary demand for land was to increase pasturage and tillage: for horses and cattles, orchards, vineyards, and grainfields among the fertile plains, valleys, and soft mountains of western Anatolia. With the demesne or oikos as a unit of consumption structured for its noble and his people, additional new needs arose, which, if provided, would have allowed the demesne greater self-sufficiency: metals—iron, tin, and copper. But these were lacking in Ionia and in Lydia. Lydian domination of the hinterland and the dire need for land and metals complicated Ionian life at the moment when famine stalked western Anatolia. Consequently, the Ionians turned first to Thrace and then to the shores of the Propontis and the Black Sea. Colonization relieved the problems of individual stress and their subsequent societal distortions, and served the Ionians as a revitalization movement.

The center of the revitalization occurred in the traditional Ionic area, from the northern borders of Karia to the Hermos Valley (Strabo 13.1.2, 14.1.2), which during the Late Geometric period (c. 745-680 B.C.) shared a loose unity of ceramic styles and other common archaeological features such as bronze fibulae. From c. 900 to c. 750 B.C., while intermittent exchanges between the Ionian Greeks and Sardis had occurred, they increased c. 750 B.C. as the relative isolation of the East Greeks dissipated, when Corinthian pottery began to appear in Ionian setlements c. 700 B.C., and a cultural renascence quickened the Atticizing and oriental influences upon the East Greeks. But being neither travelers nor traders, the East Greeks on the Anatolian mainland were the receivers and not the initiators of the renascence blossoming offshore at Rhodes and Samos, the foci of the revived Levantine and mainland Greek trade. The Late Geometric art styles of the East Greeks, in comparison with mainland Greek standards, remained conservative, ill-disciplined, and somewhat unadventurous. The eastern Late Geometric contained a passive attitude with a lack of artistic initiative, which gradually moved the East Greeks from a parochial isolation into the mainstream of the cultural renascence but as the last Greek region to digest the quickening influence of oriental art. In contrast, Rhodes and Samos lay directly on the routes of Levantine ships sailing into the Aegean Basin with copious Near Eastern imports: Cyprian terracottas, Egyptian and Levantine ivories, Egyptian bronzes, and the Near Eastern bronzes of Urartu, Median Luristan, North Syria, Phrygia, and Cyprus. The orientalia imported to Samos by 700 B.C. were just beginning to enter the ports of the Greek poleis of Anatolia.[39]

At the same time, Karia in general began to produce a Hellenized Late Geometric pottery under Dodecanesian influence,[40] and in the Aiolian regions north of Ionia the first archaeological evidence of East Greek Late Geometric pottery began to appear, c. 730 B.C., at Larisa, Kyme, Myrina, Pitane, and Lesbos in general. After c. 700 B.C., the Aiolians at Larisa began to utilize the Subgeometric and then Orientalizing wares. In contrast to the ancient literary legends which date the Greek settlement of the Aiolian regions contemporary with the Ionian, the archaeological evidence indicates populations of native Anatolians producing the "somewhat featureless grey monochrome wares," the common Anatolian fabrics begun during the Middle Bronze Age and persisting as late as the sixth century B.C. As J.N. Coldstream noted: "At present [1977] we have no reliable evidence concerning the coming of the first Aiolians to Lesbos."[41] While Herodotus stated (1.150) that Kolophonians had wrested Smyrna from the Aiolian Greeks, the archaeological evidence does not indicate either Aiolian or Ionian occupation. At Smyrna the local grey monochrome ware predominated and co-existed with a local Late Geometric style, related to Chiote styles yet subject to mainland Greek influences.[42] This Late Geometric ware was gradually imported into Aiolis and Lesbos at a time when new settlements began along the western shores of the Troad, when Troy (VIII) was resettled after three and a half centuries of desolation. Late in the eighth century, East Greek settlements also arose at Hamaxitos and Kolonai, also in the Troad.[43] The archaeological evidence, therefore, suggests first that the geographical regions of Aiolis, Lesbos and the Troad retained their native Anatolian cultures while the Greeks settled the traditional geographical region of Ionia and the scattered coastal sites of geographical Karia; and second, that the Thessalian and Boiotian Greeks did not begin their migrations to north-western Anatolia until the eighth century B.C. Herodotus' early Aiolians appear then as geographic and Anatolian groups rather than as ethnic East Greeks; only in the eighth century B.C. can we identify the Aiolians in our literary sources as ethnic East Greeks. The Ionian aristocratic conquest of Anatolian Smyrna by the landed gentry from Kolophon, therefore, may have occurred c. 750 B.C. and produced that level of destruction and the subsequent magnificent stone walls which enclosed the squalor of the intramural houses. East Greek poleis normally remained unwalled while Anatolian Melia and Smyrna were unusual in that they were walled.[44] The walls were, perhaps, not East Greek fortifications and the result of the insecurity of the Greeks dwelling in foreign territories, but the insecurity of the Anatolian groups against the migrating Greeks. The ease with which the Mermnad Lydians expanded into the Kaikos Valley, into Mysia and the Troad, and controlled those regions from Adramyttion and Antandros to Abydos and Daskyleion, also indicates little East Greek resistance there, perhaps due to the only recent and yet sparse Aiolian East Greek settlement in those areas, and due to the Lydian acculturation of the native Anatolian inhabitants in that north-western territory.

Smyrna, hugging the raised promontory at the head of its gulf, contained a dense urban population by the late eighth century B.C., but with a marked contrast between the poorly structured houses (unlike the well built structures a century earlier) and the monumental, well-dressed masonry walls which encircled the urban node or asty of that polis. Sawn ashlar blocks almost a meter in length lie in regular courses, a wall repaired and thickened in the mid-eighth century with polygonal masonry and close-fitting dressed joints. By c. 700 B.C., the Milesians and the Antissaians of Lesbos adopted and improved this style, clearly an East Greek innovation during the period of individual stress and contemporary with the East Greek attack upon Melia. Smyrna, too, experienced destruction c. 700 B.C., but responded by replacing the hovels with a tightly knit rectilinear plan of intramural residential buildings, more solidly constructed, about open living spaces. The mural constructions c. 750 B.C. and the residential rebuilding c. 700 B.C. indicate substantial political change within Smyrnaian society. The massive and carefully constructed Smyrnaian walls were unlike the make-shift acropolitan wall of Melia thrown up to meet a specific danger. Their construction indicates a corporate enterprise, a high degree of political cohesion and pyramidal direction among the inhabitants, apparently the cooperative adventures of the rising landed aristocracy. The rebuilding of the intramural asty after c. 700 B.C. indicates, however, a reallocation of urban land by the aristocrats, to be used by the residents of the urban node, the early stages of the civic demos.[45] The inalienability of the aristocratic lands, rural and urban, ruled out a gradual cultural change in Smyrna whereby the demos gained status at the expense of the aristocracy, but a gain indicating the presence of a new and powerful political force which utilized the lands, and to some degree at aristocratic expense or compromise. This leadership was, apparently, one of the earliest phases of that political institution of the noble leader, the prytanis. The role of this aristocratic leader in Smyrna compares markedly with that of contemporary Gyges in Lydia. With the support of dissident landed nobles Gyges had replaced the ineffective Tylonid government during the period of individual stress and societal distortion when the East Greek poleis and settlements from Miletos northward rivalled the Lydian landed gentry for the occupation of agrarian lands. In Smyrna, if the Kolophonian nobility had occupied that polis c. 750 B.C., the challenge to Lydian, Anatolian, and East Greek pressures similarly caused stress and distortion for Smyrna at its pivotal geographical position between the coastal poleis of Kolophon, Teos, Klazomenai, and Phokaia, and the developing inland urban

center of Sardis. By c. 700 B.C., therefore, the necessity for the Smyrnaians to
centralize their socio-political organization more strongly than before may be indicated
by the new mural contructions and the suggested strong leadership of an aristocratic
prytanis.

In the eighth century B.C. Ionia lay essentially outside the mainstream of the
Geometric Age renascence which rapidly blossomed in the Cyclades and on the Greek
mainland. Yet in an Ionian context, traditionally at Smyrna and Chios, the master bards
called Homer orally canonized the heroic epics (the *Iliad* by c. 750 B.C. and the *Odyssey*
by c. 720 B.C.), the memory of Mycenaean exploits and achievements in essentially their
post-ninth century B.C. Ionic dialect. These epics rapidly spread throughout the Greek
mainland by the second half of that century. At Miletos, tradition also recalled that
shortly after Homer the bard Arktinos composed the *Aethiopis*, the sequel to the *Iliad*,
and a second work, the *Sack of Troy*; similarly Lesches on Lesbos composed the final
stages of the heroic epic, the *Little Iliad*.[46] While these master bards of the Mycenaean
Trojan Cycle were East Greeks of the eighth century B.C., the origins of these epics
remained in the Argolid of Late Helladic III mainland Greece and not in Geometric
Ionia. This Homeric archaizing movement arising among the East Greeks, nevertheless,
remained outside of the mainland Greek sphere of flourishing hero-cults often centered
on the Mycenaean tombs and the revival of "heroic" burials to emulate the previous
Mycenaean magnificence. Among the provincial art of these eighth century B.C. East
Greeks, the themes of the Homeric epics are notably absent.

The explanation for these apparently contradictory cultural phenomena is, however,
readily apparent. The Mycenaean mercantile settlements in western Anatolia had not
contributed to the Bronze Age Trojan Cycle, and the hiatus between LH III C and the
East Greek Protogeometric was distinct. The answer suggested by the seemingly
paradoxical information, the East Greek canonization of Homeric epic and the East
Greek provincialism outside of the Geometric Age Greek renascence, culminates,
nevertheless, in the reasons for the development of mural fortifications at Smyrna,
Melia, and Miletos, and the origins of the polis as a socio-politico-economic node first at
Smyrna and then at Miletos. Following the thesis presented in chapter 2, we may note
that during the eighth century B.C. the East Greeks, the Lydians, and the remaining
pockets of indigenous Anatolian peoples began their active competition for land. The

indicators of the competition were the increase of agricultural productivity and population as the result of increased productivity during phases of the steady state. In addition, the social and then political development of the phratra based upon the flourishing demesne or household (the oikos) and the phases of Greek settlement in the Aiolic and Troad regions came as the result of the search for unencumbered agrarian land. These phenomena, however, generated conditions and problems of individual stress during the last decades of Tylonid rule in Lydia, and resulted in major problems of societal distortion. The complexities of East Greek and indigenous Anatolian acculturation, the ensuing stress noted by destructions and walls at Smyrna, Melia, and Miletos and the accompanying conflicts of dissimilar groups for the same ecological niches, therefore, apparently produced the matrix for the heroic and militant epic; while, on the other hand, the absence of Mycenaean occupation did not foster heroic cults, "Homeric" art, or lavish heroic burials, as for example at the Athenian Kerameikos.

In response to this stress and distortion, the Lydians acted first, as groups of nobility supported Gyges' revolution, the overthrow of Kandaules, and the subsequent Lydian revitalization. The East Greeks responded later, for the basic element of East Greek revitalization rested with the development of the polis, which, when threatened by stress and ultimate distortion, had to develop a political cohesion, a pyramidal socio-political organization structured upon economic growth, as noted in Smyrna after c. 700 B.C. and similar early developments in Miletos, to allow leadership in the revitalization movement. The development of the polis from an embryonic stage to a vibrant political structure to foster revitalization rested first on the inherent health of each embryonic polis, Gyges' revitalization of Mermnad Lydia, and the subsequent razzias upon East Greek lands by the Lydians, Kimmerians, and Trerians. That the East Greek poleis sustained the stress from the mid-eighth century to the mid-seventh century B.C. indicates their fundamental health because of their acculturation with the Anatolians and the stimulation of trade from Rhodes and Samos, as well as the ultimate links with the renascent world of the Greek mainland and the Cycladic islands. Consequently, the polis was fundamental to Ionian development, but a polis now mature and dominated by the landed aristocracy, the agrarian gentry.

III

An economic dichotomy between the rural landed gentry within the polis and residing in the agrarian chora and the urban inhabitants of the asty, however, emerged. Few Geometric Age houses offer clues in regard to residential occupations, but spinning and weaving occurred (often the tasks of the household women), and there were concentrated quarters for potters and metal-smiths, specialist craftsmen who gradually increased their meager incomes by bartering their handiworks in the local markets rather than relying on limited agricultural incomes. Carl Roebuck has suggested that a large percentage of the polis' craftsmen, the potters and smiths, were native Anatolians of lower classes and East Greek counterparts not subject to the rigors of the aristocratic and patriarchal demesnes. Later, these elements turned to the mercantile exchange of products, ceramics, bronzes, and tapestries, which retained strong Anatolian influences. Guilds of workers in various crafts and traders in particular goods, the kapeloi or merchants of the urban nodes, emerged as distinct entities, like the rise of Lydian kapeloi in Sardis as they were part of similar economic systems.[47]

Other urban and village residences apparently comforted farmers and shepherds who walked to their ploughed fields and hillside pastures, who raised cereals, olives, grapes, and figs, and who herded sheep and goats, less often pigs, and rarely cows. And from the Levant to these farmyards, and rather recently, came domestic fowl (Theogonis F 864), Aristophanes' (Aves 483-5) "Persian birds." In the chora outside of the asty, with or without walls, the agrarian demesnes of the landed gentry, pyrgoi as at Teos, dotted the rich plains. The demesnes, however, developed at cross-roads and springs in clusters to form villages or komai, not as remote farmhouses and cottages. The asty as the prime urban node and the rural villages or komai as secondary rural nodules were agglomerated settlements similar to the Lydian pattern with few if any dispersed settlements or farmsteads.

By the time of King Gyges (c. 680-644 B.C.), all the East Greek poleis had long developed governmental rule by their hereditary noble clans. Political centralization of the Ionian clans for each respective polis meant that a president or prytanis was elected by the ruling powerful nobles to whom the prytanis was constitutionally responsible, but not to the population as a whole.[48]

Agriculture flourished among the Ionian poleis with fertile agrarian plains well watered and with a moderate climate, and with gentle wooded hill slopes and marshy estuaries to support herding. In contrast to mainland Greece, the Ionian plains were lusher and larger (Hdt. 1.142; Hippokrates *Aer.* 12) and their benefits resulted in a marked degree of agricultural specialization and population increase. But, by c. 700 B.C., the balance between food supply and population tipped, and the Ionian poleis were no longer able to feed their peoples adequately and consequently turned to colonization first of Thrace, then the Propontis, and ultimately the Black Sea, and to mercenary service notably in Lydia and Egypt in attempts to solve the problems of excess population.[49] The revitalization movement generated among the East Greek poleis, compounded by Lydian revitalization and expansion and the blunted and temporary razzias of the Kimmerians and Trerians, thrust the East Greeks into the greater eastern Mediterranean and Black Sea worlds. This, in turn, stimulated an extensive network of East Greek trade from the Black Sea to Iberia, a product of East Greek development and a characteristic of prosperity. The revitalization response answered, as Roebuck has carefully argued, the difficulties of the lack of land, food, and metals for an increasing population. It was, however, not the mark of political failure (as he considered) among the East Greeks but rather the political success of the rising leadership able to structure a revitalization movement.[50]

IV

The social morphology of the emerging East Greek polis, the asty and chora combined, focuses upon the social interactions of the East Greeks with East Greeks, and East Greeks with the native inhabitants, the political control by the landed aristocracy and its particular political subdivision of the military organization, the religious complexities of Greek syncretization with Anatolian cults, and the cultural distinctions between the asty and the chora in regard to life styles and the education of the young. We must also consider the existence of a variety of stages in a social bipolarization as a potential opposition between the asty and the chora. While the polis as a political conception, a combined asty-chora with its basic institutions, the aristocratic magistrates, councils, and emerging assemblies, centered in the urban and occasionally rural nodule with its public buildings; in Ionia the agrarian demesnes retained a particular political vigor in addition to their economic functions.[51] Beyond the political organization, existed the ethnos of the polis, the tribes, phratrai, and village-clusters, which structured a federal organization of aristocrats settled in the villages who controlled the political institutions of the polis but whose villages lacked the architectural characteristics of the asty (walls, monumental public buildings, and a density of residents). The existence of the asty and its institutions, nevertheless, influenced the institutions of those settled in the villages.

The polis, consequently, emerged as a broad cultural complexity, a synoecism of socio-political, military, and economic interrelationships with most of the segments of the polis detectable. With the political status and religion of the polis controlled by the aristocracy (East Greek and native), no sharp division of these institutions occurred between the asty and the chora as no sacred boundary to the asty existed. While some of the polis' sanctuaries rose in the asty others also existed in the villages. The tendency in ancient Greek political thought (and modern scholarship) to blur or eliminate the distinction between the urban dwellers and the rural dwellers (Plato *Leg.* 745b-c), for example in Kleisthenes' artificial system of urban-rural "tribes" and their subdivisions, has led to the erroneous assumption that the population of a given polis was homogeneous in income and consequently political inclination was evenly dispersed. The traditional interpretation of the polis is that which modern geographers label a "central place system": the central urban node or asty being the primate urban center for the rural, agricultural territory or chora, or in other more technical geographical terms the central urban node is the prime (or primate) settlement or aggregation of socio-political and economic functions, which serves as the focus (or as I have called it the node) of a hierarchical social system. This primate center, the central urban node or asty, may also serve a more complex regional system with several centers, essentially ports and villages (the komai), which function as nodules for several systems at various levels within the greater primate polis-structure; and this may still be labeled a "central place system" since the focus is the central urban node or asty.[52]

The Ionian poleis, however, were not "central place systems" as traditionally described but were what the modern geographer identifies as "dendritic systems" in which the pyrgoi-demesnes functioned as rural centers for their own estates and other smaller agricultural centers. These were apparently linked to rural villages as centers of exchange and under normal political conditions to the primate central urban node, the asty. The villages, perhaps, were much like the polis of Panopeos in central Greece which the ancient geographer Pausanias (10.4.1) degraded: "no government buildings, no gymnasium, no theater, no agora, no water conducted to a fountain, and where the people lived in hovels like mountain cabins on the edge of the ravine." But unlike Pausanias' rural polis, the Ionian poleis were composed of aste and pyrgoi-demenses, and the aristocrats of those demesnes as economic centers retained substantial political and military power.

As S. C. Humphreys correctly noted, the ancient Athenians had distinguished the urban type, the asteios, as witty, sophisticated, and cunning, while the rural type, the agroikos, was simply rustic. But that fails to distinguish the grouping of interests, of conscious solidarity corresponding to the division of economic manners and activities. Many of the urban craftsmen and traders, Humphreys notes, were resident non-citizens or semi-independent slaves who accentuated the struggle of the poorer citizens of the polis to de-emphasize the social distinctions which separated them from the ruling landed gentry, and the dichotomy between the asty and the chora.[53]

The well known pattern of East Greek colonization of first eastern Thrace, then the southern and eventually the northern shores of the Propontis, and finally ringing the Black Sea, emerged following the quest for grain and metals sorely needed in the East Greek poleis.[54] Colonization progressed fundamentally as the abilities of the organized aristocratic governments became sufficiently developed and politically structured to cope with the problems of their land shortages, over-population, Lydian revitalization, and the Kimmerian and Trerian razzias. While, unfortunately, our ancient literary sources conflict with the very limited archaeological data to prevent precision in charting this pattern of colonization, we may detect a general pattern in two phases. The first wave of colonization to eastern Thrace began essentially during the reign of Gyges as directly related to Lydia's aggressive policies against the East Greek settlements. Eastern Thrace offered the East Greeks a grim landscape of steep cliffs and marshy river deltas but also the fertile valleys beyond, which provided the needed grain for the East Greeks.

By the mid-seventh century B.C., the second wave had begun with settlements along the Hellespontine shores—first the southern shore and then the northern shore of the Propontis. Here, the colonial settlements were primarily at good harbors with good agricultural areas as the growth of Greek shipping into the Black Sea had begun and the growth of ports of trade structured the shift in colonial emphasis from agriculture to trade. Access to water traffic routes predominated the other demands for grain and metals, products which the Milesian, Phokaian, and Erythraian colonies provided. By c. 600 B.C., the shores of the Hellespontine and Propontic regions were filled; after mainland Megara's key settlement at Byzantion established that port of trade towards the end of the seventh century B.C., the Milesians essentially ringed the Black Sea with settlements at pre-existing native sites dominating good harbors, and controlled sailing routes and also the rich agricultural hinterlands (late seventh and early sixth centuries B.C.).

While Ephesos, Kolophon, Teos, and Smyrna remained agrarian and essentially without thriving Aegean ports and, apparently, without the acute necessities for colonization, Phokaia, Klazomenai, Erythrai, and especially Miletos exploited northern colonization. During the first wave of East Greek colonization, Ionian traders apparently had not ventured beyond Delos, Rhodes, and the Hellespont; during the second wave, and by the end of the seventh century B.C., they had expanded into not only the Black Sea but into Syria, Egypt, North Africa, Gaul, and Iberia. In Gaul, Iberia, and Egypt, trade preceded colonization.

Miletos, the most energetic East Greek polis in northern colonization and trade, just as actively entered the Near Eastern regions. Miletos' close interaction with Samos and the sea lands to Rhodes offered the Milesians advantages which they readily exploited. Miletos had become physically hemmed in by the Karians, the East Greeks of Myous and Priene, the sea, river, and mountains, and had turned outward, as had Phokaia also locked into a relatively small ecological niche. Milesian trade in the seventh century expanded to Al-Mina in Syria at the Orontes River delta and the new trading center founded c. 610 B.C. in Egypt's Delta at Naukratis.

Egypt, recently liberated from Assyria led by the new Saïte Pharaoh Psammetichos I (644-610 B.C.; founder of the XXVI Dynasty), opened Naukratis to Greek traders and his country to Ionian and Karian mercenaries. Naukratis, sixteen kilometers from the Egyptian capital Saïs, aided Psammetichos' restoration of native rule. This turned out to be a vibrant archaizing and revitalization movement in its own right, which encouraged East Greek trade essentially from the eastern Aegean islands (Rhodes, Samos, Chios, and

Lesbos) and also from the mainland poleis of Phokaia, Teos, Halikarnassos, Knidos, and from the active if not aggressive Miletos (Hdt. 2.178.3).[55]   Gyges, too, fostered Psammetichos' commercial offers, as Lydia's overland routes across Phrygia to Assyria had been disrupted.   For Phokaia, however, her major colonial and trading interests extended more to the western Mediterranean and to Massalia (c. 600 B.C.) in quest of the natural resources of the culturally undeveloped West.[56]

While the details of the East Greek colonization and trade have been outlined well, the impact of these phenomena as indicators of East Greek revitalization have not been considered heretofore.   The colonial and foreign supplies of grain, wheat and barley, Thracian wine and other agricultural products, Thracian horses (Mimnermos F 14; Anakreon F 88), the metals silver, gold, and copper, and slaves, stimulated the East Greek urban production of textiles and ceramics, as well as offered the rural demesnes sources of exchange for their olive oil.   The East Greek exportation of olive oil developed with the urban production of ceramics, and the greater aspects of the commercial exchange, determined the basic developments of the poleis' harbors as ports of trade. The colonization and trade relieved the pressures of stress, prevented major societal distortion, and therefore structured the processes of revitalization.   By the sixth century B.C., the prosperity of Ionian trade and colonization was necessary to support what Roebuck suggests was an East Greek population of over a quarter of a million free inhabitants.[57]

Each polis, however, responded in its particular way. We cannot determine precisely the degrees of stress for each polis nor measure exactly the degrees of revitalization, but a pattern can be sketched.   Kolophon, Ephesos, and Smyrna did not extend revitalization movements into colonization or trade; yet Kolophon and Ephesos structured a high degree of agrarian symbiosis with the Lydians, while Smyrna failed and became absorbed by the Lydians.   Lydian raids upon Kolophon, forcing elements out of that polis into flight to southern Italy, and the later brutal elimination of other Kolophonian nobles, left in that polis a strong pro-Lydian, horse-raising gentry which rapidly developed close economic and politically-minded ties with Lydia. It was, therefore, natural that following Cyrus' conquest and occupation of Sardis, the Mermnad royal families moved to Kolophon.[58]

The artistocratic structure of Kolophon and its high degree of acculturation with the Lydians appears similar to conditions in Ephesos.[59]   During the period of stress, the

Ephesians (or Milesians) had seized Magnesia-on-the-Maeander, but Lydia responded, gained Magnesia, and pressed upon Ephesos. The intermarriage of Ephesians and Lydians during the reigns of Gyges and Alyattes, and Croesus' special protection and benefaction to the Ephesian temple of Artemis, underscore the developed symbiotic relationship between Lydia and Ephesos and the high degree of acculturation between the two societies. King Ardys, Gyges' successor, had briefly seized Priene; subsequently that polis remained distinctly overshadowed by its powerful neighbors, Miletos and Samos. By c. 600 B.C., Alyattes had taken Smyrna after a long series of raids. Thereafter, Smyrna was distinctly linked with the Lydian village of Nymphaion just east of the Smyrnaian-Sardian low-rising pass with Smyrnaians settled in the rural villages of that district.[60] If the Lydians had wanted the strategically positioned urban harbor of Smyrna as an Aegean port (Hdt. 1.94), they failed. Smyrna rapidly dwindled, due more, perhaps, to the silting up of its harbor than to the destructions.

The poleis of Klazomenai, Erythrai, and Teos successfully thwarted Lydian control until Croesus' conquests. Klazomenai's brief experience in the unsuccessful colonization of Thracian Abdera (Solinus 10.10) and Teos' non-participation in northern colonization and trade, and apparently limited involvement at Egyptian Naukratis, were minor experiences in seventh century B.C. international activities. Klazomenai, consequently, controlled the northern fertile plains east of the Erythraian Mimas Range up to Lydian controlled Smyrna, while Teos dominated the slightly drier and less productive southern plains hemmed in by the bleak hills of the Mimas-Korykos Range and the minor East Greek polis of Lebedos along the east coast. Both poleis, therefore, remained moderately small, similar to Priene, and essentially agricultural with limited coastal shipping. Lebedos, even smaller, sustained a small agricultural area and engaged in only minor shipping. It ranked with Myous in tertiary importance.

The assimilative or acculturative processes between the Lydian agrarian units and the Kolophonian, Ephesian, and Smyrnaian agrarian units had been simplified by the geographical position of the three East Greek poleis. Kolophon and Smyrna formed the broad western agricultural plain just beyond the low pass at Kemal Pasha (or Bel Kave), which linked Sardis to the sea by a well-developed road (Hipponax F 42, 50). That broad rich agricultural plain also linked Sardis to Ephesos and to the Lydian occupation of the upper Kayster Valley and the Lydian occupation of Magnesia in the upper Maeander

Valley. In each case, numerous native Anatolian populations structured the ethnic complexities of those poleis. Similarly, the Lydian conquests of Magnesia-on-the-Maeander and Larisa on the Hermos were facilitated by the essentially native Anatolian structure of those poleis.[61] Myous, at the head of the Milesian Gulf and at the mouth of the Maeander River, also easily succumbed to Lydian control, essentially because its agricultural hinterland remained small and the potential opportunites for its large and good harbor were curtailed by Miletos' superior harbor to the west at the mouth of the gulf. The East Greeks at Myous never gained more than local importance.

Erythrai's importance rested in its close geographical position to commercially active Chios and its relatively isolated position behind the Mimas Range secure from Lydian and East Greek raids.[62] The urban center and the scattered pockets of rural villages and their agricultural lands supported a modestly active involvement in northern colonization and trade, and joined Parian settlers at the potentially rich port of Thasos and Milesian settlers at the agricultural settlement of Parion just east of the inner mouth of the Hellespont on the southern Propontic shore. Erythrai's scattered subordinate villages (Boutheia, Ptelion, Sidousa, and Polichna), which ringed the northern Mimas ridge, supported their urban center within a "dendritic system," which would be distinctly apparent in the mid-fifth century B.C. Erythrai's seventh century B.C. growth, I suggest, was due more to its proximity to Chios and Erythraian utilization of Chiote mercantilism than to the gradual growth of its geographically isolated chora structure of villages within a dendritic system. Erythrai, nevertheless, occupied a relatively isolated and secure ecological niche, unlike the more harried niches of Klazomenai and Teos to its immediate east or the extremely vulnerable niches occupied by Kolophon, Ephesos, and Smyrna. Yet factionalism had arisen in Erythrai, as elsewhere, with the ruling aristocratic landed gentry (the Basilidai, cf. Ephesos) attacked and overthrown by other factions (Arist. Pol. 1305b 18-22).

The rough, non-agricultural zone surrounding Phokaia, which nestled within fertile but very limited coastal agrarian plains about an excellent harbor, provided the Phokaians with an ecological niche relatively secure from harassment. From the hinterland of the Hermos Valley, from Sardis through Neon Teichos to Larisa, the Lydian east-west route crossed the north-south land route from Smyrna to central Aiolis and beyond.[63] Phokaia, therefore, functioned well as a Lydian port of trade with Phokaian merchants returning with Greek and Italian goods and natural resources (especially metals) from Gaul and Iberia.[64] Smyrna would have served Sardis more efficiently than Phokaia as a port of trade but Smyrnaian resistance to Lydian controls, her vulnerability to Lydian military pressures, and the suggested loss of Smyrna's harbor after Alyattes' conquest eliminated her from Aegean trade. Smyrna remained through the sixth and fifth century a placid collection of rustic and rural villages bound together within a dendritic system inside both the Lydian and Persian imperial structures. Klazomenai, Teos, and Erythrai lay too remote to serve effectively as Lydian ports of trade; and Kolophon and Ephesos developed within proper harbors. Lebedos, Myous, and Priene remained exceedingly small, and with constant Lydian harassment, which can be documented certainly at Priene and apparently at Myous.

Like Phokaia, Kyme in southern Aiolis served Lydia efficiently as a port of trade as it also served Phrygia during the halcyon years of King Mita's reign.[65] While Hesiod's father fled Kyme in poverty (Hesiod *Erga* 633–640; Ephoros *FGrH* 70 F 100), Phrygian traders from Gordion and central Anatolia crossed down into the Hermos Valley and joined Lydians traveling on to Kyme. With the Kimmerian raids, however, the Phrygian trade of bronze cauldrons, belts, and other metal objects, wool, sheep, and slaves ceased, yet the Lydians continued to utilize Kyme (Nic. Dam. *FGrH* 90 F 44). But the Aiolian poleis with better soil than Ionia yet inferior weather developed in a markedly different way from the Ionian poleis. Kyme, the focus of southern Aiolis, was similar to Smyrna and Phokaia, while from Pitane (at the Kaikos delta) north to Lydian Adramyttion and Antandros the local Anatolian and Lydian clans held control; no Greeks forced their entrance. The indigenous peoples and Greeks of Lesbos (the poleis of Methymna and Mytilene) settled the narrow southern Troad coast as their peraiai or rural districts as well as northward as far as Troy. Beyond Troy, Milesian settlements (after the Kimmerian period) ringed the southern Hellespontine and Propontic coasts by Lydian diplomatic agreement. Abydos, perhaps, served Mermnad Lydia as a military outpost of mercenaries.[66] But these Aiolic cities, barely poleis, remained exceedingly humble when compared with the Ionian poleis and their ports.

V

Of all the East Greek ports, Miletos was of prime importance to Lydian development and, consequently, the major focus of Lydian military campaigns. At the southern shore and corner of the Maeander Gulf, Greeks had seized the Milesian promentory, its excellent harbor, and the surrounding plains in search of land to farm. While initially the Greek Milesians married Karian women (Hdt. 1.146) and Karians within the city remained and worshipped at their native shrines, others (possibly conquered later) were subjugated by force to serfdom, the class called Gergithes (Hdt. 5.122.2; Ath. *Deip.* 12. 524a *apud* Herakleid. Pont.). The agrarian lands, however, were not plentiful, often rising to bleak ridges not unlike those surrounding Phokaia; beyond them the Karian mountain ridges of Mt. Latmos blocked Miletos' eastern borders. The activities of Thales, the Milesian philosopher, indicate a scarcity of olive oil[67] a short time after Smyrna had begun to import oil. On the other hand, our ancient sources do not suggest that the East Greeks imported either oil or grain from the Lydians.[68]

Where agriculture flourished in Miletos, the landed gentry developed pyrgoi-demesnes; and by the eighth century B.C., the urbanization of the asty was perceptible. While the asty suffered attack c. 700 B.C. probably from local East Greeks or natives rather than Lydians, the Milesians were extending their power into the Aegean, taking over Ikaros, the island west of Samos, for mercantile access to the Cyclades and the islands south of Samos—Lepsia, Patmos, and Leros—as access routes to Rhodes. These rocky islands served Miletos as the first steps in trade during the early seventh century B.C. as preludes to the Propontic mercantile centers of the mid and late seventh and the Black Sea settlements of the sixth centuries B.C.[69]

While Gyges attacked and possibly entered Miletos (Hdt. 1.14.4), the Lydians could not hold that polis;[70] apparenly subsequent diplomatic relations with Gyges enabled the Milesians (possibly as Lydian mercenaries) to gain Abydos along the Hellespont (Strabo 13.1.22). Gyges' razzias upon the East Greek poleis were basically harvest time raids and not conquests for land; yet his attacks upon Miletos may have been for other reasons. Miletos' early involvement in Aegean trade may have stirred Gyges to consider exporting Lydian and eastern goods brought to Sardis by the caravans from the interior. Gyges' conquest of Magnesia-under-Mt. Sipylos (Nic. Dam. *FGrH* 90 F 62) was apparently to open the route to Phokaia and Kyme; his utilization of Smyrna across the Kemal Pasha

(Bel Kave) pass served central Lydia and Sardis. But Miletos' deep gulf harbors and commanding exit to coastal and Aegean shipping accentuated by Milesian control of Ikaros, Lepsia, Patmos, and Leros offered Miletos (and consequently Lydia) greater commercial advantages. Miletos' volume of export trade normally rested upon grain, olive oil, wine, fish, pottery, luxury goods, and slaves. While Miletos' strong archaic walls thwarted Gyges' attempts to gain that port of trade, the Maeander Valley and its access to the sea remained a major priority for the Lydians.

The Kimmerian raids upon Lydia not only temporarily halted Sardis' desires to gain the lower Maeander but also structured a protective policy for the utilization of the independent poleis and their ports of trade. Apparently the Kimmerians never reached the growing wealth behind the Milesian walls, and Miletos continued to flourish. King Ardys' brief capture of Priene, the small, but for Lydia, important terminus of the caravan routes down the northern coast of the Maeander Gulf, had been the object of Lydian commercial interest. Both Sadyattes and Alyattes continued the Lydian attacks upon Miletos, and Alyattes' goal was clearly to obtain Miletos as a Lydian port. As Alyattes stormed (and later destroyed) Smyrna, his interests in Miletos increased. These military activities are distinct indicators of the Lydian control and use of the Kayster and Maeander Valleys, of Magnesia-on-the-Maeander and possibly Myous, for the subsequent control of Ephesos, which Lydia held easily, and the dogged resistance of Miletos to shake off Lydian domination. Alyattes' failure to subjugate Priene (Hdt. 1.92.23-4) apparently quickened his interests in taking Miletos.

Alyattes' desired conquest of Myous (?), Ephesos, and Priene would not have provided Lydia with the excellent harbor facilities which Miletos offered; Alyattes' new policy to dominate the Ionian ports of trade therefore ended the earlier Lydian respect and symbiotic relationship with that buffer zone. If successful, the new policy would have brought Lydia directly into the greater mercantile world of the Aegean. Alyattes' failure to obtain Miletos rested not upon Lydian weakness but in Miletos' response to the Lydian pressure and the centralization of political power in the hands of the tyrant Thrasyboulos who replaced the less effective political power of the Neleids, the Milesian aristocrats formerly in power. The five year war between Lydia and Miletos ended c. 605 B.C. with a treaty, which essentially preserved the status quo: Alyattes failed to gain Miletos, and Miletos remained independent. Smyrna now felt the brunt of Alyattes' wrath. Not only had Alyattes failed to subjugate Miletos, his appeal to the Delphic oracle came to naught, and Thrasyboulos' close friend Periander, the tyrant of Corinth, revealed to Thrasyboulos the oracular statement.

Thrasyboulos had organized a successful military defense of Miletos by centralizing political authority, but factional strife began to plague Miletos, which was internally torn between Thrasyboulos' innovations and revitalization of Milesian resistance to the Lydian stress and the disgruntled aristocrats who would ultimately regain power.[71] The opposition increased Thrasyboulos' ruthless reactions and his adamant suppression of all opposition, especially since the Lydian attacks had temporarily been quelled. Two generations of Milesian civil strife consequently ensued during which Phokaia took advantage of the Milesian set-backs and pursued the process of western colonialization and trade. Phokaians explored the Adriatic, founded Massalia (c. 600 B.C.), colonized the coasts of southern Gaul and Iberia with small villages, exploited the Samian discovery of the mines at Tartessos, and allied themselves with the Iberian chief Arganthonios of that region (Hdt. 1.163; Stesichorus 4; Strabo 3.2.11).

Thrasyboulos' diplomatic alliance with Alyattes and his close friendship with Periander enhanced his civic stature, as did his close relationship with the Pharaoh Necho, son and successor of Psammetichos, who offered dedications at Miletos following Egypt's victories over the Babylonian Nebuchadrezzar (c. 608–605 B.C.).[72] Yet among the East Greek poleis none except Chios came to Miletos' aid during the struggle with Alyattes. Herodotus noted (1.18) that because the Milesians had earlier aided the Chians in their war with the Erythraians, the Chians aided the Milesians, perhaps because of the strictures of diplomatic relationships rather than Panionian sympathies between Chios and Miletos. The problems of stress and societal distortion in each polis accentuated the latent tendency to overt parochialism and particularism in spite of the vague tribal and religious ties, which loosely ran through most of the East Greek clans and cities and the political thoughts of several East Greek intellectuals. Lydia's successful foreign policies concerning the East Greeks were often facilitated by that centrifugal particularism.

Miletos, however, during the last decades of Neleid aristocratic rule and Thrasyboulos' tyranny, economically flourished by means of her overseas trade and produced a cultural and intellectual milieu, which surpassed the creative activities elsewhere in western Anatolia. Miletos' resistance to Alyattes' attacks (while Alyattes stormed Smyrna, unsuccessfully attacked Klazomenai, violated Kolophonian nobles and the principles of Guestfriendship, allied himself with Melas the tyrant of Ephesos, forcefully expanded into the Troad, expelled the Kimmerians from Antandros, and occupied western Cappadocia) raised the philosophical question whether it was possible for the East Greeks to resist the Lydians.

VI

The stress wielded by the Lydians upon the East Greeks fostered political revitalization changes, which strengthened the control of the landed gentry within their respective poleis. The new sources of grain and metals, the accompanying opportunities of the landless and poor to obtain colonial land, and the changing of their political status because of this land acquisition relieved the inner tensions of the polis. The pressures generated by non-expansion, overpopulation, and the need to seek economic colonial and mercantile expansion into the greater Mediterranean and Black Sea worlds forced the ruling aristocracies to adjust the growth of their poleis in order to survive. The stress also set in motion the rise of tyrants in Ephesos, Miletos, Phokaia, and Erythrai.[73] In each case, however, I suggest that the origin of tyranny appears distinctly different from the origin of tyranny on the Greek mainland.

In Ephesos, without a thriving port, trade, or colonization, the rule of the landed gentry (the Basilidai) gave way to a higher degree of political centralization and the tyranny of Pythagoras and his successor Melas to obtain a positive symbiotic relationship with Lydia.[74] The Ephesian Melas (II), son-in-law of Alyattes, who gained tyrannical power, traced his lineage to an earlier Melas (I), a son-in-law of Gyges. The strong Anatolian clan structure in Ephesos, the basic importance of the landed estates with their Anatolian and Greek nobles, and the high degree of acculturation between the two ethnic groups, had produced an important landed gentry which centered on the shrine and cult of the Anatolian goddess whom the Greeks called Artemis. Gyges' major revitalization movement assimilated Ephesian economic and social life. But his efforts were occasionally marred by Lydian military excursions (against Magnesia-on-the-Maeander and Ephesos itself), which bound Ephesos closely to the Lydian Empire essentially as a geographical extension of the Lydian, controlled Kayster Valley and as an ecological niche common to Lydians, Anatolians, and East Greeks. While neighboring

Kolophon developed without tyranny, a similar process of Lydianization occurred there, which bound these two non-mercantile and non-colonial poleis closely within the Lydian economic and political structure based upon the importance of the landed gentry. At Ephesos, the nobles continued to control the ancient priesthoods, especially that of Artemis, and at Kolophon, the nobles controlled the oracular center at Klaros, which also had arisen from an earlier Anatolian cult.[75] Melas' (II) tyranny, consequently, arose as a means of political centralization to accommodate Ephesian interaction with Lydia in order to eliminate the stress, which had developed between the two political states.

Tyranny at Erythrai, Phokaia, and Miletos, however, differed from that at Ephesos. In these cases, it arose in response to the development of colonialization, trade, and the growing importance of their urban centers; yet it varied in degrees of resistance to Lydian imperial power. Erythrai, geographically secure beyond the Mimas Range and interacting closely with Chios and Lesbos, developed tyranny during the seventh century B.C. to replace the rule of the landed nobles (also the Basilidai). That transition appears directly responsive to the economic changes in the urban center and perhaps similar to the traditional Greek mainland tyranny at Corinth.

At Phokaia, during the first half of the sixth century B.C. and that polis' rapid and extensive expansion throughout the western Mediterranean, tyranny arose also in response to the urban development through trade. Phokaia's prime position at the Hermos River delta served Lydia (especially after Smyrna's fall) as the major outlet to the complex trading system developed in the western Mediterranean among the Etruscans, Carthaginians, Greco-Celtics, and Greco-Iberians. In this respect, Phokaia served the Lydian mercantile needs whereas Erythrai did not. The subsequent urban economic changes in Phokaia, however, apparently set the stage for Phokaian tyranny as they had in Erythrai.

Tyranny at Miletos arose as a third East Greek form. While the urban economic changes flourished because of the extensive colonization and trade relations built in the Propontic and Black Sea regions with Saïte Egypt, the tyranny of Thrasyboulos arose as Miletos faced the major onslaught of King Alyattes' attacks to gain that major port for Lydia. The Milesians also moved to greater political centralization and direction under Thrasyboulos' tyranny. The displaced Neleid nobility who retained their landed power and religious controls, especially at the pre-Greek Anatolian oracular center of Didyma,[76] resisted that rule and factional strife arose.

Factions within these poleis supported the rise of tyrants, a support emphasized by stress and the desired effects of revitalization, but the basic power of tyrants was the result of personal ambitions and the manifestations of their desires for power, prestige, and philotimia (the want of honor). The details of the origins and developments of the East Greek tyrannies are lacking in the ancient sources, and we can eliminate the older concept that tyranny arose as a result of the conflict of the city with the rural nobles. In Ephesos, the political power of the urban nouveau riches was lacking; with the ultimate elimination of tyranny at Erythrai and Miletos, the opposition to tyranny—the landed aristocrats—regained the power which the tryants had monopolized. In the ancient literature the position of the tyrant connoted arbitrary, despotic, and evil government; his position rested not on legitimate means to the rise to power but upon the transfer of power as an effective force, usually a violent coup d'état. In this coup, the military power came from professional mercenaries, adventurers who offered their valuable services to the politically ambitious. And that ambition was hybristic.[77] This interpretation, while historically more accurate than earlier urban economic interpretation, stems from ancient appraisals of tyranny after its historical role had been performed, and may not denote precisely the actual historical rise and role of East Greek tyranny. Gyges' rule has also been considered tyrannical, yet the interpretation offered in chapter 2 emphasizes the discontent of factions of the landed nobility which caused them to support the coup. Consequently, we must consider similar factionalism basic to the rise of tyranny in the four noted East Greek poleis. The interpretation for the rise of Gyges as a Lydian tyrant suggests that the origin of the East Greek tyrannies was not the urban support of tyranny since the urban centers remained concentrations of landless and non-citizen workers. Rather, factions of the landed gentry supported the tyrant in order to revitalize their poleis. In the case of Phokaia, Erythrai, and Miletos, the landed gentry found the mercantile activities of the urban center beneficial, as relief for the overpopulation of agrarian lands, as ports of export for the products of their flourishing estates, and as centers for the importation of foreign and exotic goods, which their increased agricultural wealth could afford and which reinforced their social standing among their wealthy contemporaries.

Within these landed aristocracies and not in the lower economic classes of the urban centers arose the Milesian and Kolophonian intellectuals who pondered the problems of East Greek symbiosis with or resistance to Lydian domination of western Anatolia. The intellectual concepts of the order and symmetry of nature which produced the development of government and new forms of justice within the poleis also originated in the same struggles for survival during the Lydian phase of disruption. The Milesian intellectual Thales, the father of Greek scientific thought, consequently urged the East Greeks to structure a united state of Ionia at geographically secure and central Teos (Hdt. 1.170). Unfortunately, the East Greeks rejected his advice. Thales' suggestion was clearly in response to the stress applied upon the East Greeks by the Lydians. But narrow, parochial views intervened. Similarly, Thales' kinsman and pupil the Milesian Anaximander, in constructing his great map of the Greek world, the first of its kind, during the reign of Croesus, must be seen in light of the conflict between the East Greek poleis and the Lydian Empire.[78]

The East Greeks never considered the Lydians as complete barbaroi since they were similar in many ways: the Lydians invented coinage which the Greeks quickly adopted, and Croesus was more of a friend than an enemy, and a king who generously gave to the Greek temples and oracular centers. The Ionian Greeks began to recognize a proud and haughty ethnic unity of their own, the distinction that they were Ionians. Lydia was open to Greek merchants, artists, soldiers, and oracles, but the Ionians began to circulate ideas of the superiority of the Greeks and their dominance over the indigenous peoples. The East Greek lyric and elegiac poetry stressed a positive Greek man's role in the cosmos for his anthropocentric interests. These were the products of the East Greek cultural growth and scientific interests. Within this intellectual productivity we must also place the East Greek canonization of the Greco-Lydian Sagen as a conscious effort to understand the conflict and stress between the East Greeks and the Lydians. An analysis of those Sagen emphasizes, of course, not the urban populace but the aristocracy, the role of the agrarian demesne and the generation of the noble anti-Lydian military.

One aspect of the rise of Ionian self-consciousness became centered at the Panionion shrine of Poseidon Helikonios on the northern shore of Mt. Mykale. Unlike the early Anatolian bases on the religious centers of Klaros, Ephesos, and Didyma, this Panionion shrine remained free of native accretions. After the Kimmerian period, it rapidly gained an ethnic and religious character—for a loosely bound union of Ionian poleis, which remained strongly parochial and particularlistic until Cyrus' conquest. By that time, the Panionion amphictyony provided a modicum of religious and ethnic unity for the twelve major and traditional Ionian poleis (Phokaia, Klazomenai, Erythrai, Teos, Lebedos, Kolophon, Ephesos, Samos, Priene, Myous, and Miletos: Hdt, 1.142) in sharp contrast to the northern Aiolic dodecapolis (1.149-152) and the southern Dorian hexapolis (1.144).[79] The functions of the Panionion and the collective mercantile enterprise of the group of Ionian poleis, rather than one particular polis, were not sufficient to weld Ionia into one state. The Panionion remained weak and politically ineffective, little more than a religious rallying point.

Within this complicated process of Ionian growth and change during Alyattes' reign, Miletos played a pivotal role. Alyattes' policy had changed from the utilization of the East Greek poleis as ports of trade and a buffer zone separating Lydia from the Aegean island powers to the positive desire to control Miletos and its harbor. The growth of Lydian agriculture and the limited but significant Sardian industries forced Alyattes, through the pressures of the flourishing Lydian gentry, to alter Lydian foreign policy. Lydian power would not shift from Sardis to Miletos but Miletos would remain as a port of trade from the inland capital, and it would exist peripherally to Sardis since Lydian trade remained peripheral to the agriculture of the aristocratic demesnes. Sardis would continue as the central focus of Lydian political and military preoccupations and power. Miletos, therefore, would retain its distinctive tyranny different from Sardian monarchy.[80]

Croesus' policy to gain Miletos began with the offer of diplomatic alliance, an offer which Thales successfully urged his fellow Milesians to reject (Diog. Laert. 1.25). Croesus piqued, then attacked and succeeded in subjugating the factionally strife torn Miletos and forced a treaty of suzerainty for Milesian acceptance. While Miletos retained municipal self-determination, it paid Sardis tribute (Hdt. 1.27), and furnished Croesus' army with men upon demand (Diog. Laert. 1.25). The alliance was not unlike the earlier Hittite alliances for western Anatolian subjects. Croesus' good will towards his new subjected ally arrived as rich offerings to Apollo's oracular shrine at Didyma. While under Lydia's rule, Miletos did not suffer by her great loss of independence, but flourished within a period of intellectual advancement, which later Greeks noted as proverbial luxury (Aristotle F 553). Croesus' aggressions had inflicted little harm while the presence of powerful Lydian utilization of that port of trade increased Milesian maritime ventures.[81]

Croesus' successful innovative policy based upon the conquest of Miletos and all the other East Greek poleis (Ionic, Aiolic, and Karian) produced a distinct new phase of Lydian imperial growth. Croesus' Śfarda of Lydia and the coastal Greeks and Anatolians transformed into a pluralistic society structured upon the combination of ethnic segmentation and economic interdependence, as a society developing upon a high degree of acculturation. Śfarda functioned as a synchronic association of East Greeks, western Anatolians, Karians, and Lydians.[82]

The Lydian domination of the Aegean coast widened Lydia's net of relationships with the Aegean Greeks, to whom the drain of Lydian gold and silver coinage passed as Lydia increasingly utilized Greek mercenaries. If continued too long the drain would have been harmful to Croesus' control; yet Cyrus quickly brought a halt to that economic drain upon Śfarda. In this rests an historical paradox. Lydia sought Aegean mercantilism and responded with the institution of bimetallic currency, which the East Greeks readily adopted and began to mint similar currencies. Yet the currency drain upon Sardis would have created economic havoc when the production of the limited Lydian gold and silver declined. Cyrus, in comparison, did not have to rely upon Sardian gold as the captured treasuries of Ecbatana, Babylon, and Susa contained wealth surpassing Croesus' gold.

Among the East Greeks, Lydians, and other western Anatolians (north of Karia), a marked degree of acculturation had occurred before the chaotic days of Cyrus' invasion. The different cultures with developed continuous first-hand contact underwent subsequent changes in their original and respective cultural forms. The contacts, which fostered assimilation, involved the total population of each group, whether through contact of friendship or of enmity; and of groups of various population size yet apparently of similar degrees of culturally material and non-material complexity. While enmity between the East Greeks and Lydians, and East Greeks and other East Greeks occurred, the elements of cultural exchange were readily and voluntarily received. The early stages of East Greek settlement, which witnessed intermarriage, had fostered some of the exchange while the lack of social and political inequality occurred. Later economic pressures upon each distinctive group furthered the acculturative process, but also produced the social superiority of the East Greeks over the Anatolians while the Lydians exercised political dominance over the East Greeks and other western Anatolians. The East Greeks, therefore, provided economic profit during the period of Lydian political dominance. But the aspects of social acculturation centered upon mutual religious considerations produced a Lydian conformity to the values of the East Greeks, just as the East Greek canonization of the Lydian Sagen produced a positive degree of East Greek conformity to Lydian values.

The traits selected and accepted by the several receiving groups were essential to their mutual economic advantages because of a basic congruity of their existing culture-patterns centered upon the landed nobility. The mutual adoption of functionally related traits quickened the time span of the integration and its process of adjustment within the acculturative process. During Croesus' reign over Sfarda, the several Greek and Anatolian cultural traits had combined producing an essentially smooth functioning cultural whole or historic and synchronic mosaic. Yet, while the reworking of cultural patterns had adjusted toward a meaningful and harmonious whole, the retention of conflicting attitudes was often reconciled. This cultural entity of imperial Sfarda, Cyrus conquered in the winter of c. 545/4 B.C.

4

THE PERSIAN CONQUEST OF ŚFARDA

I

Cyrus' conquest of Lydia (c. 545-3 B.C.) came directly in response to Croesus' ambitious imperial policies. The earlier Lydian conquest of the Ionian poleis and the adjacent territories of Karia, Aiolis, and the Troad had created for Croesus the centralized and unified extended Empire of Śfarda (Hdt. 1.28), an imperial system, which, in turn, fostered expansionist policies towards the East beyond the Halys River. Consequently, when Cyrus defeated Croesus' son-in-law, the Median King Astyages in the summer of 554 B.C.,[1] and seized the Median Empire, which loosely extended to the eastern banks of the Halys, Croesus ambitiously set out to gain Cappadocia (Hdt. 1.46), the highland territory beyond the Halys. While diplomacy had made possible the inevitable claim for Croesus to aid his allied but defeated son-in-law, Croesus could little hope to restore the Median prince to power beyond Mesopotamia in the Iranian highlands. He would, however, use the earlier alliance as a pretext to gain Cappadocia (Hdt. 1.71-3). It was here that Croesus hoped to check Cyrus' growing power, and in wielding blows against the Persian Empire Croesus firmly expected to succeed, as he mistakenly believed the message from Delphi that he would destroy Cyrus' power.[2]

Cyrus, in turn, spent little time in settling and organizing first the newly conquered Median territories with his own southern territories of Anshan, which the Persians renamed Parsa, then the eastern Indo-Iranian provinces of Hyrkania and Parthia, and ultimately the northern remnants of the once powerful Assyrian Empire and its important province of Urartu (which the Persians called Armenia). Within five or six years after his victory over Astyages on the highland plains of Anshan, Cyrus led his tribal cavalry, infantry forces, and baggage trains of camels and donkeys into eastern Cappadocia. Near the village of Pteria, Cyrus halted Croesus' eastward drive and forced the Lydian king to retreat to Sardis.[3] There, Croesus hoped to reorganize his army, to gain foreign military aid from Sparta, Egypt, and Babylon, and, after a five months winter's rest and recovery, to face Cyrus' Persian forces once again in a spring campaign. But Cyrus foiled the Lydian and drove on unexpectedly toward Sardis (Hdt. 1.77-80).

In Cappadocia, the Lydian military had burned farms, taken villages, and enslaved the inhabitants (Hdt. 1.76).   What limited Median control had been imposed upon

Cappadocia had apparently disintegrated.   As Lydia's ruthless conquest of Cappadocia

continued, Cyrus, leading his advancing army, sought just retribution for Lydian

destruction of his western province.   Cyrus, in order to check and disrupt Lydia

internally, sent invitations to the Ionian poleis to revolt against Croesus and to become

vassal states of the Persian Empire.   The Ionians, however, did not accept Cyrus'

overtures and remained loyal to Croesus in spite of decades of East Greek and Lydian

hostilities and the recently imposed Lydian military sovereignty over them.   While the

Ionians remained military subjects to Lydian sovereignty, Cyrus' offer of vassalage

treaties contained lenient terms, but with the Ionian refusal Cyrus began to treat the

Ionians as part of the Sfardian Empire and as co-participants with Lydia in active

military opposition to his Empire.   Their aggressions upon Persian sovereignty in

Cappadocia were, for Cyrus, cause for his declaration of war against the Ionian poleis

with punishment to be wielded following his intended conquest of Sardis.

    At Pteria, it was apparent to both military leaders that Cyrus' forces outnumbered

Croesus' (Hdt. 1.77).   For Croesus, therefore, it was imperative to gain time and foreign

military assistance.   But during that winter, he sent away his subject military forces—the

East Greeks and Karians—and retained only his well trained Lydian cavalry forces, the

military strength of the Lydian nobility (Hdt. 1. 79).   Cyrus' military counsel, in contrast,

advised him well, first at Pteria to march full speed to Sardis, and then on the broad

autumnal plain stretching north beyond the city of Sardis, counsel again and especially

the advise of Harpagos considered successful military tactics to rout the Lydian cavalry

and then to kill the Lydian soldiers to a man (Hdt. 1.80).   Lydia's failure, the reduction of

its cavalry, was precisely the key to Cyrus' victory.   In contrast, Cyrus led his cavalry

and infantry into Sardis, routed the remnants of the Lydian forces, breeched the city's

newly constructed walls, set fire to the lower city, and stormed Croesus' acropolitan

palace (Hdt. 1.80).

    Croesus expected a long siege with time enough to obtain aid from his foreign allies,

but after fourteen days the Persian army gained access to the Hyde-acropolis and

captured Croesus (Hdt. 1.88).   Croesus' rule had ended and the Sfardian Empire had

fallen.   And if Herodotus' report reflects correctly the essence of Croesus' reaction, the

Lydian king recognized in his military failures a concept basic to Near Eastern kingship.

In failure, Croesus recognized the abandonment by the gods of his sovereignty over Śfarda and their appointment of Cyrus as the new and victorious king to whom Croesus was now subject (Hdt. 1.89).[4]

While the East Greeks had not revolted against Croesus nor covertly aided Cyrus, they apparently (according to Herodotus' silence) did not send military aid to relieve the Persian siege of Sardis and its acropolis. Herodotus mentions only the forthcoming Spartan aid, which was about to depart for Śfarda when news arrived of the fall of Croesus (Hdt. 1.83). While Cyrus' army outnumbered Croesus' forces, man for man, in body it appears to have been inferior in ability. For Herodotus, the Lydian cavalry was superior, more valiant and warlike than any other Asian nation (Hdt. 1.79), and the East Greeks may have gambled that the Lydians would defeat the Persians on the Sardian plain. Had they revolted to provide Persia with a major disruption of the Śfardian Empire, and had the Lydians won, their lot would have been extremely precarious and subject to Croesus' continued military wrath. East Greek particularism, however, may have played the major role in the Ionians' non-support of their sovereign. During the previous centuries, the East Greeks fought East Greeks and rarely aided each other, especially when threatened by Lydian military power. The vague religious structure to the Panionion shrine had not generated a concerted military effort and would not for some time. The particularism was further underscored by Ephoros' note that the Ephesian Eurybatos had received money from Croesus to muster an army for the war against the Persians, but turned traitor, abandoned Croesus, and handed the money over to Cyrus (Ephoros FGrH 70 F 28; Harpokration sv Eurybaton; Suda sv Eurybatos). Eurybatos' treason, however, may have occurred after the fall of Sardis and the capture of Croesus, but at least it indicates the complexities of Ionian loyalties, sympathies, lack of sympathies, and petty parochialism endemic to the Ionian poleis and their societies, observable throughout the seventh, sixth, and fifth centuries B.C.

With the fall of Sardis, the Ionians and Aiolians realized their predicament and the strength of Cyrus' forces on the Sardian plain, and quickly sent messengers to Cyrus offering to be his subjects but under their terms and not his, and specifically the terms which they had as subjects of Croesus. Cyrus, in response, noting their earlier refusal clearly pronounced that he would dictate the terms of vassalage, not the Ionians (Hdt. 1.141). Now faced with the reality of Persian conquest, the Ionians began to resist the inevitable. Only Miletos submitted to Cyrus. The long history of Lydian attacks upon Miletos, first as harvest razzias, then Alyattes' firm desire to occupy the port polis and to utilize Miletos firmly within the economic structure of the Śfardian Empire, and finally Croesus' development of strong ties between Miletos and Sardis, evidently convinced the Milesians of the folly of resistance and, in light of rampant Ionian parochialism, of the inabilities of the Ionians to resist Cyrus' Persian armies any more than they had resisted Croesus' crack Lydian armies. Miletos wisely saved herself from Persian attack and disruption of her wide network of trade to the north and to Egypt. And because of Miletos' decision to submit, Cyrus did grant the Milesians a treaty under the terms formerly held under Croesus. With his alliance, therefore, the Persians divided the territories of Karia from those of Ionia and divided the East Greek and Karian resistance to them, in addition to gaining the immensely important ports of Miletos.

The nature of Cyrus' treaty with Miletos in contrast to the later Persian treaties with the Ionian poleis following their conquest remains problematical. Herodotus simply did not clarify the two, and any modern speculation or reconstruction remains tenuous. Yet three disparate sources shed some light upon the problem to enable a greater degree of reconstruction than not. Herodotus, in passing (1.22.4), noted that early in the sixth century the Milesian tyrant Thrasyboulos and the Lydian King Alyattes, following a stalmate in the Lydian war upon Miletos, ceased hostilities, whereupon the two leaders verbally agreed "to be friends one with another" and "to be military allies." The agreement also included Alyattes' promise to rebuild the destroyed temple of Athena at Milesian Assesos (of which he actually exceeded the agreement and built two). In essence, this treaty of mutual friendship and military support appears similar to that treaty which Croesus negotiated with Sparta (Hdt. 1.69.2) "wishing to be a friend and military ally without deceit or guile." The Lydian treaty with Sparta was clearly between equal military powers, in nature not a treaty of vassalage following defeat or subjugation but a treaty of parity of mutual friendship and military support. The fundamental aspects of this parity agreement can also be detected in earlier Hittite parity treaties with Assyria, Babylonia, and Egypt.

We may conclude, therefore, that the treaty between Alyattes and Thrasyboulos was not that of vassalage but of parity, whereby Miletos remained independent, sovereign, and in equality with Lydia. If war should arise with other powers, however, the ally would militarily aid the other under attack. The treaty of parity agreed upon apparently lasted only while both leaders remained alive and ended with the death of either one, to be renewed as desired by their successors. This, too, was an important aspect internal to Hittite treaties of parity. To this point, Diogenes Laertius (1.25) stated that the counsel of the Milesian Thales prevented the Milesians from consummating a military alliance with Croesus, "which provided the salvation of the polis when Cyrus obtained the victory." We may rightly assume, consequently, if Diogenes' statement is historical and it appears to be so, that the Milesians had not renewed the parity treaty with Croesus. Yet, following Croesus' conquest of Miletos, the Lydian subjugation of the Milesians prevented a resumption of parity as Croesus would have demanded the more favorable and restrictive clauses of a vassalage treaty. In this, Miletos became obligated to supply troops to protect Croesus if he were attacked. Yet when Cyrus attacked Sardis the Milesians rebelled against Croesus, refused to contribute a military contingent to aid Croesus, and instead supported the Persians, a decision which Cyrus gratefully rewarded.

What Cyrus renewed with Miletos, therefore, was a vassalage treaty yet one which placed the Milesians in a privileged status in marked contrast to the disprivileged status imposed by Harpagos upon the rebellious Ionians. But what denoted Milesian privilege remains questionable. As the major port for the Persian satrapy of Sparda, Miletos exercised that privilege, perhaps as either a reduction of tribute or clauses of less demanding military service. But rather than these, the privileged status may have been a clause which affirmed Milesian internal self-determination even while governed by a Persian established tyrant, Histiaios and then Aristagoras. The Milesian internal efforts to end the factionalism raging within the polis since the tyranny of Thrasyboulos may provide us with the key to the privileged status (Hdt. 5.29). Herodotus unfortunately wrote more about the internal affairs of Miletos than the other Ionian poleis, an imbalance which limits our understanding of similar or dissimilar events elsewhere of internal political self-determination. Nevertheless, the ability of the Milesians to bring in arbiters from independent Paros rather than from Persia indicates a high degree of internal self-determination, which simply does not appear among our sources for the rest of Ionia.

In this form, Cyrus' treaty raised Miletos to the status of a semi-autonomous province within the greater Persian imperial system, similar in nature to that which

Cyrus established with Cilicia, Cambyses would contract with the Phoenician harbor states, and Xerxes would unsuccessfully offer to Athens in 479 B.C. (Hdt. 8.140 α.1-2).

While the other Ionians fortified their cities with walls to stem the inevitable Persian sieges, at the Panionion shrine the ambassadors of the poleis finally met to consider the problems of their resistance. As subjects still loyal to the Lydian cause, the Ionians sent envoys to Sparta to seek the military aid, which the Spartans were prepared to send to Croesus (Hdt. 1.141). This crucial decision "Resolved by Common Agreement" (Hdt. 1.141) marks the first concerted military action by the collective Ionian and Aiolian (Hdt. 1.152) poleis, and their recent growth of identity and commonality as East Greeks (Hdt. 1.143-4). The Spartans, however, rejected the request yet dispatched one pentekonter with soldiers to observe first hand what Cyrus was doing in Ionia (Hdt. 1.152).

With Miletos in Persian hands, the Spartans sailed north to Phokaia, and from there the Spartan delegation led by Lakrines set out for Sardis. Once arrived, it delivered directly to Cyrus the Spartan proclamation not to harm a polis on Greek territory or else the Spartans would punish him (Hdt. 1.152). While this act seemed just and prudent to the Spartans and some relief to the Ionians, Cyrus considered it an act of war (Hdt. 1.153). The East Greeks and the Spartans, apparently, did not realize the gravity of the act nor the ultimate implications of Cyrus' declaration of war against the Spartans, which would not be resolved until 411 B.C.[5]

But for Cyrus, the entire matter of the rebellious East Greek poleis and the declared war with the Spartans were relatively unimportant, and he directly would not pursue either. The conquest of Babylon and the overthrow of Babylonian control of Mesopotamia and Syria-Palestine, then the conquest of Bactria and the eastern Scythians, and ultimately the conquest of Egypt, ranked as the top priorities of Cyrus' adventures. Thus, Cyrus set out for Ecbatana, the capital of Media (after about six months in Sardis), and left the Persian noble Tabalos in charge of that new imperial province and the suppression of the rebellious East Greeks. The war against Sparta would wait (Hdt. 1.153).

Tabalos and, we must assume, other Persian officers and soldiers held the Sardian acropolis and its ruined city below, and transformed the former Sfardian Empire into the Persian satrapy of Sparda. Sparda, therefore, became one of many satrapies in Cyrus' newly forming Empire. And although the empire remained loosely arranged because of the rapid conquest of Media, the union of Parsa and Media, the subsequent conquests of Hyrkania and Parthia, of Assyria and Armenia, and ultimately Cappadocia and Śfarda, Cyrus had had little time to organize a tightly knit imperial system. His subsequent campaigns against Babylonia and then Bactria and the eastern Scythians, therefore, only sustained his limited abilities to structure tightly that imperial system. The administration of the satrap Tabalos, consequently, continued the liberal policy of tolerance and conciliation, which Cyrus fostered among the other various ethnic groups within the rapidly emerging empire. Tabalos, therefore, directed a largely Lydian bureaucratic system from his acropolitan palace, in which the Lydian Paktyes directed the financial affairs of Sparda, affairs which Herodotus notes as "in charge of the gold of Croesus and the other Lydians" (1.153). As yet, Cyrus had not fixed tribute payments for the subject provinces but rather exacted gifts to be sent to him directly (Hdt. 3.89). In time, Cyrus and his satraps gradually established and initiated guide lines and rules by which "his enormously stretched civil service was to operate."[6]

The loose imperial structure, however, often faltered and in Sparda Paktyes rallied a Lydian revolt against Tabalos as soon as Cyrus set off toward Cappadocia and Ecbatana. From Sardis, Paktyes escaped into the East Greek coastal regions (from Priene to Kyme) and with gold pilfered from the Lydian treasuries hired mercenaries and bribed East Greeks to join his rebellion. Unfortunately, we do not know what success he had at Kolophon where the remnant of the Mermnad royal house had sought refuge. But elsewhere he did succeed and with a substantial army marched into the Sardian plain. The earlier Persian destructions to the city wall and the burned and pillaged houses may not have been restored sufficiently to offer resistance to the rebels, thus, Paktyes and his army besieged the Hyde–acropolis (Hdt. 1.154).

Herodotus' brief description of the rebellious activities and Cyrus' harsh reactions strongly suggest a substantial East Greek and Lydian uprising, which prompted Cyrus to contemplate the enslavement of the Lydians and the destruction of Sardis, which he had left essentially in Lydian hands. Patriotic Croesus escorted to court exile in the village of Barene (or Baryene near Ecbatana, Ktesias *FGrH* 688 F 9.4),[7] however, persuaded Cyrus not to destroy the "ancient city" but to disarm the Lydians, to turn the noble warriors into non-militant merchants, and to kill only the rebel Paktyes (Hdt. 1.155). As

with other conquered kings, princes, and chiefs, such as Cyrus' father-in-law the Mede
Astyages, Cyrus used Croesus to advise him in the administration of Sparda, the Croesus
who had earlier attempted suicide and whom Cyrus saved from the flames (Bacchylides
F 22; cf. Hdt. 1.87-91).[8] Wrathful Cyrus, however, rejected much of Croesus' advice, and
he commanded the Mede Mazares to return with Persian forces to Sardis, to quell the
rebellion, to enslave the revolutionaries "whoever they be," and to send Paktyes to him
alive (Hdt. 1.156). Satisfied that Mazares would succeed in suppressing the Lydian
rebellion and carrying the war to the walls of the rebellious East Greek poleis, Cyrus
marched on into Cappadocia and on to Media (Hdt. 1.157).

Paktyes and his rebels, upon learning of Mazares' march upon Sardis, fled down the
Hermos Valley to coastal Kyme and held up there. Mazares, therefore, had gained
control of Sardis and instituted Cyrus' commands to destroy the militant power of the
Lydian nobles. As Herodotus notes: "by his order they changed their whole manner of
life" (1.159). The crack of power of the Lydian cavalry, the landed nobility, which had
raised Gyges to power, had year after year raided the East Greek settlements, and had
finally taken Miletos and the other poleis during the reigns of Alyattes and Croesus, had
lost significantly its status in Lydian society. How Mazares accomplished this, Herodotus
unfortunately is not clear except to note Cyrus' decree whereby the nobles forced to
become merchants in order to soften them and to reduce their potential militancy and
rebellions. But in that, there is difficulty in comprehending a transformation from rich
landed gentry to merchants, unless Herodotus' statement beclouds a change, which
reduced the nobles from a high powered cavalry, armed with spears and swords, to a rural
landed gentry stripped of their horses and arms, reduced to only agricultural activities.
Neither Mazares nor Cyrus could afford to destroy the rural demesnes and reduce the
wealth of Lydia, which enriched the Persian royal coffers with gold and silver
indispensable to the financing of future campaigns against Babylon, Bactria, Sogdiana,
and Egypt.[9] With the fall of the Śfardian monarchy, private Lydian exploitation of the
gold mines provided new economic opportunities to the nobility, and by means of peasant
workers and craftsmen to gain wealth (Hdt. 7.28, Plut. *Mul. Virt.* 262d-e; cf. Hdt.
1.153). In a simplistic way, Herodotus notes the Persian dependence upon and utilization
of Lydian luxuries and comforts (1.71). Cyrus had, nevertheless, wanted the rebels
enslaved, and Mazares did wield that punishment by destroying the military power of the

other Lydian nobles.

Once the policy of destroying the nobles' military power was enacted and Sardis and Lydia were secure under Mazares' rule (Herodotus failed to mention what happened to Tabalos), Mazares sent imperial messengers to Kyme to demand the surrender of Paktyes in order to complete Cyrus' royal orders. The Kymaians, however, refused and, by arguing that Apollo's oracle at Didyma had advised them not to surrender the rebel,[10] sent Paktyes to Mytilene on Lesbos. But the Mytilenaians, in turn, desiring neither Apollo's wrath and devastation for giving Paktyes to the Persians nor Persia's siege for their keeping him, spirited the rebel leader off to Chios. In counter turn, the Chiotes sought a diplomatic agreement with Mazares: to surrender Paktyes in return for the rural areas (the peraia) of Atarneus across from Lesbos in northern Aiolis (Hdt. 1.160). With Paktyes secure, the Sfardian revolution ended, and Mazares apparently sent the unsuccessful rebel leader to Cyrus for the punishment in store. Only the rebellious East Greek poleis, which had refused Cyrus' offers of vassalage and which had supported Paktyes, remained to be punished.

In order to secure firmly the Persian connections between the allied vassal port of Miletos and the capital center of Sardis, Mazares campaigned vigorously in the Maeander Valley, first taking Priene and enslaving its inhabitants, then overrunning the remainder of the plain and, apparently, Myous, and pillaging the settlements therein and then moved farther inland and pillaged Magnesia (Hdt. 1.161). Mazares directed his attacks against the East Greeks who had participated in Paktyes' siege of Sardis as reprisals for their support of the recalcitrant Lydian rebels. In a frantic attempt for survival, Bias of Priene argued for refuge on Sardinia (Hdt. 1.170). Shortly thereafter, Mazares fell ill and died, and when news of this reached Cyrus, the king quickly appointed the loyal Mede Harpagos to succeed Mazares and raised him to the rank of general (Hdt. 1.162). Following his arrival in Sardis, Harpagos set out systematically to besiege the Ionian poleis. His first attack at Phokaia reveals several important factors: the Persians offered leniency, the oath of vassalage, the removal of one bastion of the city's wall, and the dedication of a house perhaps as the symbol of vassalage to the Persian king.

The Phokaians, however, rather than submit even on those terms prepared to abandon their city totally. Harpagos' offered of leniency, while in accord with Cyrus' general policies, may have arisen from the practical aspect of reducing the costs and

casualties to be sustained by the Persians during a long siege. But the Phokaian decision
to leave and sail for Chios in effect destroyed the importance of the port of Phokaia and
left essentially only Persian controlled Miletos as the major coastal port for the satrapy
of Sparda. The abandonment also destroyed the western mercantile zone, which the
Phokaians had developed, and, therefore, shifted the East Greek trade system more
strongly into the Milesian mercantile zone in the Black Sea. But why the Phokaians
fleeing from the Persians would have considered going to Chios, which had just
demonstrably aided the Persians, remains curious, unless we consider that the Phokaians
failed to see beyond their narrow parochial boundaries. The Chiotes, in turn, did not
reject the Phokaians on the basis of pro-Persian sympathies but rather with the argument
that if the Chiotes sold the Phokaians the Oinoussai islands (between Chios and the
Erythraian peninsula), the Phokaians would develop a commercial market to rival that of
Chios (Hdt. 1.165).

Following a dramatic yet drastic oath never to return to Phokaia, the Phokaians
prepared to sail for Corsica following a quick raid upon their former city to murder the
Persian guard, which Harpagos had left there. But as with so many resolute oaths, more
than half of the Phokaians broke theirs and returned from Corsica to their ancient city,
while a few settled on the Oinoussai islands (Hdt. 1.165).

With the northern area from Kyme to Smyrna and the southern region of the
Maeander Valley from Priene to Magnesia under Persian control, Harpagos and his forces
systematically besieged the central Ionian poleis. At Teos, as earlier at Phokaia, the
Persians raised their siege mounds only to find that the Teian inhabitants had sailed for
Abdera in Thrace (Hdt. 1.168), but gradually many Teians also returned to their
"fatherland" to live under Persian sovereignty.

The other Ionians, however, remained, faced the Persians in battle, yet failed and
were taken. With Harpagos' conquest of Ionia completed, the Ionians on the coastal
islands feared similar Persian attacks and quickly surrendered themselves to Persian
sovereignty (Hdt. 1.169). Unfortunately, Herodotus left the island-surrenders at that and
gave no explanation as to why the islanders would fear Harpagos' land forces. But
apparently, the Persians did have some naval forces, as Pausanias (7.5.4) recorded that
the Persians attacked Samos and in the conflict burned the Heraion complex, c. 540-39
B.C. Harpagos, consequently, now commanded Lydia, the Ionian poleis, the northern

Aiolian regions and the Ionian islands, and then turned to the subjugation of the southern Karians, Kaunians, and Lykians (1.171). And with Harpagos in the southern area, Cyrus appointed Oroites to the satrapal rule of Persian Sparda (Hdt. 3.121). This was, as Herodotus noted, the second time Ionia was subjected (1.169), but this phase of subjugation was markedly different from the first subjugation under Croesus (Hdt. 1.6).

The Persian conquest of the islands and especially of Samos, unfortunately, remains one of the major problems in modern scholarship and muddles what little we know of Cyrus' conquest of Sparda. Recently, however, B.M. Mitchell[11] cogently questioned the acceptance of Eusebius' chronology for the rise of Polykrates' tyranny on Samos (c. 532 B.C.) and his interaction with the Persians.[12] Consequently, by returning to the Herodotean text and Mitchell's suggestions for the course of events, it is possible to suggest a new understanding of those events. At the time Harpagos was systematically reducing the Ionian rebellions (in the late 540's), Polykrates and his two brothers seized control of the government and the island of Samos, and initiated a series of events which challenged Harpagos' military activities among the coastal cities (Hdt. 3.39). The civil war in Samos, first against the aristocratic rule of the landed nobility, the Geomoroi (Plut. *Moralia* 303C-304E; cf. Thuc. 1.115.2-5, 8.21), and then Polykrates' sole seizure of power, left Polykrates in tyrannical rule of the important mercantile island and in command of an extensive military force (Hdt. 5.94.1; Thuc. 1.13.6, 3.104.2; Polyainos 1.23.2). In a play to gain power while Harpagos' campaigns generated turmoil in Ionia, Polykrates seized control of many of the coastal islands from Lesbos southward to Rhodes[13] and attacked many of the East Greek mainland urban centers, Miletos in particular. From this, we may suspect that Polykrates attempted to gain control of the Maeander Valley and the Mykale range, which Samos had long sought as a peraia, a mainland territory, and to curtail the rival mercantile and naval powers of the Milesians. With Polykrates' control of Lesbos, the Samians may also have had control of the Chiote and central Ionian areas. But Harpagos succeeded in regaining those coastal urban centers and then led a naval campaign to subdue the islands and Samos.

Polykrates, therefore, was forced to submit and to accept Persian overlordship, which allowed him to remain in control of Samian affairs providing that he furnished tribute and armed forces and ships to the king when demanded. Polykrates' alliance with Egypt and the Pharaoh Amasis, while Amasis remained a neutral party, would not have

been at variance with Polykrates' vassalage to Cyrus, nor would Polykrates' activities in
the Aegean beyond the borders of Persia and Oroites' satrapy of Sparda.   Persian
overlordship in Sparda, consequently, created a unity and political calm, which for many
years neither the Lydians nor the East Greeks attempted to disrupt.

Throughout the Persian conquest of first Sardis and then the East Greek poleis, the
efforts of the Panionion council continued but to no avail.   Following Harpagos'
systematic conquest of the East Greek poleis, Bias of Priene counselled the East Greeks
to gather collectively and to sail to Sardinia where they would form one major polis and
rule the western regions.   But this the parochial East Greeks rejected just as they had
rejected Thales' earlier counsel to abandon their poleis and gather at Teos to secure unity
in centralization.[14]   The Ionians preferred the subjugation of their ancestral lands to
unity and a foreign home (Hdt. 1.170).   The return of Phokaians and Teians apparently
convinced the other Ionians of the greater problems they would face in contrast to
Persian subjection.

Herodotus' analysis of the two subjugations of Ionia is, unfortunately, vague and
unclear.   For the Father of History, Croesus' subjugation of the Aiolians, Ionians, and
Asiatic Dorians marked their transfer from "free" Greeks to tribute paying Greeks (Hdt.
1.6, 1.27, 1.91) and subjection (douleia, not to be understood as enslavement,
andropodismos, but the loss of political self-determination).   But even this concept must
be modified.   Croesus' articles of subjugation, which bound the Ionian poleis to his
imperial system, demanded from the subjected poleis tribute (Hdt. 1.6, 1.27) and military
forces (Hdt. 1.76).   These articles were also basic to the Mermnad control of the various
Lydian and Anatolian groups within the Lydian imperial system, and also reflect the
fundamental articles of earlier Bronze Age vassalage treaties dictated by the Hittites,
articles fundamental to several western Anatolian imperial alliances (as noted in
chapters 2 and 3).   But while Sardis governed foreign policy and diplomatic alliances, the
East Greek poleis maintained their local political organizations and their peculiar socio-
economic systems.

The liberty of a polis ranked first with the firm connotation of freedom from alien
domination or despotism.   In turn, the political liberty of a citizen within a given polis
ranked second; and the personal liberty, the independence of the individual ranked third,
as the freedom of expression.   For the ancient East Greeks and especially Herodotus, the

Ionian conflict with Persian was not a series of national wars, as the East Greeks had not developed a concept of nationalism, but rather was a conflict generating a fight for freedom from alien despotism at the same time for the external independence of a polis. As these two forms of liberty blended, Herodotus often implied both. Liberty and independence connoted the freedom of a polis for political self-determination and the freedom to live in accordance with its own laws.[15]

When before the battle of Pteria, Cyrus sought Ionian alliances and, consequently, the disruption of the Śfardian Empire, such alliances were counter to the Lydian rules of subjection of the Ionians and, clearly, an Ionian break with Sardis would have constituted rebellion. Yet what Cyrus appears to have offered were alliances of vassalage similar to if not exactly like those then operating between the Ionian poleis and Sardis. This type of alliance Miletos quickly accepted following the fall of Sardis, in which the Milesians swore their subjection to Persian sovereignty affirmed in a solemn treaty (horkion: Hdt. 1.141, 1.143) It was this type of vassalage treaty which the Ionian poleis, after initial resistance unlike that of Miletos, requested of Cyrus (to be "obedient subjects", katēkooi) but which Cyrus vehemently rejected (Hdt. 1.141).

Following Harpagos' conquest of the mainland East Greeks, a second type of vassalage treaty was imposed upon the rebellious poleis similar to the former Lydian treaty but clearly a firmer Persian treaty. Of this second phase of subjection and its vassalage articles, Herodotus is again vague. Ionian and Aiolian Greeks would serve in the Persian armies for the conquests of Karia, Kaunia, and Lykia (Hdt. 1.171), and the vassal poleis would offer tribute gifts. We must, however, note that while Croesus systematically taxed his subjects, Cyrus did not institute a similar program but rather accepted gifts on a less precise assessment system (Hdt. 3.89). Only the events at Phokaia hint at new regulations: the breach of part of the city's wall and the dedication of a house suggested vassalage symbols. And when the island Ionians surrendered we may assume that they accepted subject vassal status similar to the newly imposed Persian treaty arrangement. It remains unclear how that Persian system differed from the earlier Lydian system, but according to Herodotus it was markedly different. While we may only assume what new Persian restrictions were imposed upon the Ionians, we may consider that, as with Phokaia, Persian garrisons were established (Hdt. 1.165), the recently constructed defensive city walls were breached, and that greater local political restrictions were imposed.   In this, the first great change in western Anatolia was the establishment of peace, as the internecine wars among the East Greek poleis temporarily came to an end.

With Cyrus' and Cambyses' campaigns in the eastern regions of Bactria and Sogdiana (c. 535-525 B.C.), and then Cambyses' campaigns against Egypt (525-522 B.C.), the Persian kings and their still loosely constructed imperial system apparently allowed the Samian growth of power and control in the Cyclades, providing Polykrates remained a loyal vassal to the imperial crown and would supply ships and men for Cambyses' conquest of Egypt (Hdt. 3.44), in the same manner that the Aiolian and Ionian Greeks furnished Cambyses with troops (Hdt. 3.1) according to the stated vassal agreements. Polykrates' quick compliance to Cambyses' demands and his abrogation of the Samian alliance with Egypt (Hdt. 2.182, 3.39-44; Diod. Sic. 1.95.3) clearly note Samos' vassalage status within the Persian Empire, and Samos' subordination to the satrap Oroites governing from Sardis during the reign of the tyrant (Hdt. 3.120.1). Polykrates' main ambition was not to challenge Oroites, Cyrus, or Cambyses, but to control the Cyclades by means of the newly developed Samian triremes,[16] a plan which enraged the Spartans and Corinthians.[17]

In fulfilling his vassalage duties to Cambyses, Polykrates took that opportunity to remove from the city of Samos rebels to Samian and Persian control and sent them with other Samian troops to Egypt with the explicit directions that his sovereign lord Cambyses retain the rebels there, and thereby destroy the potential dangers to Samian and Persian rule. In this, Herodotus firmly notes the potential dangers of the Samian urban inhabitants and their rebellious attitudes towards Polykrates' tyrannical rule and the Persian overlordship (Hdt. 3.45).   But with the rebels' escape to Sparta, those malcontents were successfully instrumental in obtaining a military force of Spartans supported by Corinthians (Hdt. 3.48) to besiege the fortified city of Samos (Hdt. 3.54). Nevertheless, after forty days without success, the Spartans left Samos and abandoned the exiled rebels (Hdt. 3.56), and the Samian urban rebellion floundered. Samos, consequently, flourished under Polykrates' tyranny and within the Persian satrapy of Sparda.

For a generation, the Persian satrapy of Sparda remained relatively secured under Persian rule and administration and the East Greek poleis flourished, most notably Samos under the tyranny of Polykrates (Hdt. 3.60).   Only Phokaia subsisted markedly underdeveloped.   In Teos, while the urban center may not have advanced, the rural estates (the pyrgoi) continued unchanged.   Not until the events of the early years of King Darius I (July 522-519 B.C.) did civil wars and new Persian rules and regulations affect the East Greeks and the Lydians (see chapter 5).   In essence, Cyrus' Persian government installed at Sardis under the satrapal governance of Oroites, had replaced Croesus' Lydian government, and little else changed except at Phokaia.   We may conclude, therefore, that the East Greek, Lydian and Persian social systems structured upon agrarian communities locally governed by the landed gentry were to a large degree compatible.   But this view has long been rejected by Classicists.   For example, in his analysis of the Persian conquest of Šfarda, A. R. Burn stated: " . . . Herodotus (1.153) lays his finger upon an essential point: The economic basis of the 'temperamental incompatibility' between the Greek and Persian social systems.   That of the Persians was socially aristocratic, politically feudal, and economically based on a food-producing peasantry.   It was at a stage of development out of which the more progressive parts of the Greek world had been passing in recent centuries."[18]   Burn's analysis is, however, at variance with the evidence presented in chapters 2 and 3.

Under Oroites' satrapal rule for his imperial lords Cyrus and Cambyses, the Persian satrapy of Sparda contained two distinct types of social systems: the urban centers (the aste) and the rural agrarian regions (the chorai).   Of the the two, the urban centers controlled an extremely limited amount of land in comparison with the overwhelming majority of rural agrarian lands.   Sardis and the East Greek urban centers along the coast co-existed with, but in marked contrast to, the rural landed estates, the East Greek pyrgoi and the Lydian demesnes.   And in the East Greek urban centers, the landed gentry of the estates and pyrgoi dominated the civic activities of their poleis, as most notably at Teos, Kolophon, Ephesos, and Miletos.   The social system of Persian Sparda was distinctly dominated by aristocracies and their political vassal system,[19] based upon a predominantly food-producing economy.   This system was also common to the eastern regions of Parsa and Media with basic social systems of the aristocratic, agrarian demesnes and the landed nobility.   Both the ancient literary and archaeological evidence support this analysis.

II

Within Lydia, the Anatolian inhabitants structured five major tribes or phylai:
Mermnas, Tymolis, Masdnis, Alibalis, and Dionysias,[20] which, we may suspect from the
evidence of the above analyses of the Lydian and East Greek agrarian systems, were
similar in class structure rather than kinship structure to those of the East Greek
poleis. Common to most of the Ionian poleis were the Anatolian-Ionian tribes Boreis and
Oenopes, and the four tribes Geleontes, Hopletes, Aigikoreis, and Argadeis, which many
of the Ionian poleis shared with their titular metropolis Athens.[21] These were, however,
not socially restricted kinship structures but rather newly developed artificial systems,
which had modified the primitive kinship structure to accommodate Anatolian groups, as
notably at Miletos, Ephesos, Kolophon and Teos, in order to allow the growth of more
socially integrated communities. At those poleis, the organization of the phylai-tribes
included groups of early Greek metics and Anatolian peoples, an inclusion in response to
the pressures of urbanization as the East Greek poleis developed from predominantly
agrarian societies to societies with a growth of trade and limited urban production.
Central to Ionia, Miletos, Myous, Priene, Ephesos, Samos, Lebedos, and Teos, retaining
close tribal similarities, developed a greater conscious recognition of ethic affiliations,
which enabled them to function as a religious federation in the worship of Poseidon
Helikonios at the Panionion shrine on Mt. Mykale. In contrast, the poleis of Erythrai,
Chios, Smyrna, and Phokaia sustained strong Aiolian elements within their peculiar social
structures, which differentiated them markedly from the southern Ionian group. But
basic to the Ionian and Aiolian areas were the agrarian structure to the tribal units and
the standard interpretation that they were not kinship structures but rather social
structures, as Geleontes denoted the nobility, the Hopletes the warrior classes beyond
the nobility, the Aigikoreis the herding classes, and the Argadeis the non-noble farming
classes. Common to the three regional areas (Aiolis, Ionia, and Lydia) were class tribes,
which represented an aristocracy of landowners and lower classes of free farmers and a
few craftsmen.

In comparison with this class structure within Persian Sparda, Herodotus clearly
noted a parallel class-tribal system in Media and Parsa (1.125).[22] Herodotus stated that
under Cyrus the three major Persian tribes, the Pasargadai, Maraphii, and Maspii,
structured the noble cavalry, and to the Pasargadai belonged the clan and royal house of

the Achaemenidai to which Cyrus, Cambyses, Bardiya, Darius, and Xerxes belonged. Beneath those aristocratic class-tribes were those of the farmers, the Penthialaei, Derusiaei, and Germanii and those of the herders, the Dai, Mardi, Dropiki, Sagartii. In Media, Herodotus also presented a similar but not as well defined class-tribal structure of Bousai, Paretakenoi, Strouchates, Arizantoi, Boudioi, and the priestly Magoi (1.100), but he did note a breakdown of the army into distinct companies of cavalry, spearmen, and archers, which may parallel both the Persian and Ionian class and military organizations (Hdt. 1.103). While kinship and tribal structures to the Persian-Median and to the Lydian-East Greek systems are to be expected, and while such tribal systems are basic to ancient societies, the similarities of the breakdown of the class-tribal systems into cavalry holding nobility and the farming and herding classes, which serve in the other divisions of the military, are striking. To direct this analysis further, I suggest that the Persian nobility, which rode into Śfarda and conquered that satrapy, found a commonalty with the social structure of the landed agrarian nobility who formed the Lydian and East Greek cavalry units.

This concept of the construction and organization of Lydian, East Greek, and Persian-Median tribes, based upon Herodotus and Lydian inscriptions is, however, obviously not anthropological in definition. A proper anthropological definition of "tribe" and its cultural design, following Marshall Sahlins, stresses "a body of people of common derivation and custom, in possession and control of their own extensive territory." "Its economics, its politics, its religion are not conducted by different institutions specifically designed for the purpose but coincidentally by the same kinship and local groups: the lineage and clan segments of the tribe, the households and villages, which thus appear as versatile organizations in charge of the entire social life."[23] Our perception of Lydian, East Greek, and Persian-Median tribes, therefore, must surpass this conceptualization of primitive segmented societies and consider these ancient Greek and Near Eastern sources as indicators of advanced development of Lydian, East Greek, and Persian-Median societies beyond the cultural kinship design of tribe as outlined by Sahlins. The class structure of tribes, noted by Herodotus, indicates in contrast the establishment of societies with centralization and developing sovereign governing authorities, which altered the "primitive" tribal form into political class and occupational units, reorganized internally to serve the complicated military needs of the societies in question whereby primacy was placed upon the landed nobilities and their cavalry forces. Such transformations have long been noted for archaic Athens and early Rome and must also now be recognized as socio-political developments within the societies under scrutiny herein. The necessary reorganization of primitive cultural tribes into units artificially called tribes marks the advancement of political centralization and military stress. This transition, Sahlins states, occurs when cultural dominance is replaced by technical predominance whereby the cultural type develops power and resources within its ecological niche, and marks a predominant transition in advancing farming and herding societies.[24] Consequently, we must consider the East Greek and Persian-Median tribal divisions as societal class advancements similar to Solon's classification of archaic Athenian society, within political ranks which also mark their economic and military ranks, and to Rome's organization of the Comitia Centuriata, which reflects primarily a military and political reorganization of the greater community.

During the ninth and eighth centuries B.C., when the Persian and Median tribes were settling their respective highland territories, the nomadic extended-families, which formed clans of related families, began the process which, by the time of Cyrus' conquest of Media and Śfarda, produced the complex classification of tribes on higher forms of political and class organization. The Assyrians and Urartians, west and northwest of Media, the Babylonians to the west, and the Elamites of Susiana, west of Parsa, with established kingdoms and traditions of developed state and societal organization naturally influenced the development and reorganization of the Iranian tribes Media and Parsa.[25] In time, consequently, the early importance and structure of the primitive kinship tribe declined as Median and Persian kingship provided allegiances, which concentrated upon and solidified the landed nobility to provide the bureaucratic stratum of Cyrus' expanding dual-monarchy. Under Median rule during the years before Cyrus' revolt, the process of fusion and integration with the native settled peoples and the Iranians had occurred. Cyrus, therefore, inherited a developing "tribal" system of political and class stratification, as well as the Median concept of "king"[26] and developed political and social institutions which it implied. From scattered tribal chieftancies, the Medes had created the political systems, which the Persian inherited and rapidly developed. As the Medes centralized about their Hauptstadt of Ecbatana, "the Place of

Assembly" for the landed nobilities, so Cyrus and Cambyses utilized Ecbatana and the more recently conquered lowland centers of Susa and Babylon for their bureaucratic centers, to adopt and develop a political organization, which, to a certain extent, resembled that of earlier Assyria.[27]

The important step between the early "primitive tribe" and the developed class-tribal structured kingships of Astyages and Cyrus was the development of the advanced chieftancies and their chiefdoms, whereby the transforming tribal cultures anticipated in their complexities the later statehoods. Chieftancies established political superstructures upon wider and more elaborate bases of economic organization, ceremony, ideology and other cultural aspects.[28] Herodotus' view of early Media structured upon agrarian villages (komai: 1.96) with economies based upon herding (1.110-4), therefore, is strongly sustained by recent archaeological investigations of early Median and Persian sites which denote major centers of chieftancies. Similar to the sixth century B.C. Lydian and East Greek societies, Persian and Median societies were based upon the patriarchal family and clan and structured about the jurisdiction of the pater familias who served as the temporal and spiritual leader. In turn, the genos or greater association of numerous and different kinship groups formed communes, which gradually consolidated into larger political and economic units administered by provincial chiefs.[29] Basic to these structures were the noble families and the noble associations.[30]

To date, three Median centers have been explored and excavated in a region not more than 140 km. south and south-west of Ecbatana: Godin Tepe, Tepe Nush-i Jan, and Tepe Baba Jan. Unfortunately, the limited archaeological explorations at Ecbatana (modern Hamadan) have not revealed the Median palace, its habitation levels, or the subordinate village and agrarian units.

Throughout the area of Media, settlements developed with a notable increase in number during the Iron Age III Period, c. 750-550 B.C., in contrast to the lesser number of settlements during the Iron Age I (c. 1300/1200-c. 1000 B.C.) and Iron Age II (c. 1000-800 B.C.) periods.[31] In the northern Lake Urmia region, throughout the widespread plain of Ecbatana and among the Zagros valleys of Luristan, the traditional region of Media, recent archaeological investigation has revealed settlement centers, which represent the development of the loose confederation of Iranian tribes at the middle of the eighth century B.C.[32] While often the end of the Iron Age II phase and the beginning of Iron

Age III are marked by the destruction of sites, the pottery of phase III is a direct outgrowth of the earlier phase II.[33] Consequently, we may interpret the transitions of Iranian-Median settlements in phase III as the mark of population movements, the settlement of earlier nomadic or semi-sedentary groups, and the development of strong chiefdoms centered at the fortified phase III sites. This socio-political development of the earlier tribal groups may well be reflected by Herodotus (1.98) who noted a late seventh century B.C. Median centralization, the growth of noble power, the construction of fortified centers, and the construction of the royal center at Ecbatana.   The settlements of Iron Age III developed at sites with adequate water supplies, large expanses of arable land, and along the main migration routes of the nomads and the merchants from lowland Assyria, Babylonia, and Susiana. The Iron Age III sites developed as permanent settlements of large walled villages focused upon fortified manors of emerging strong chiefs.[34]

Within the Zagros range of Media[35] and in the Kangavar Valley, Godin Tepe emerged in the seventh century B.C. as the seat of an important petty Median chief or khan ruling over other minor sites in the valley.   Godin Tepe surrounded by a large towered fortification wall contained a single building complex of the chief's audience hall, kitchen and private apartments.   Beyond this fortified center, thirty-three smaller sites of agricultural units were scattered about the plain. These small agrarian units, subordinate to the fortified manor at Godin Tepe, ranged from small farmsteads to larger clusters of agricultural units with 79% of the sites smaller than two hectares and none exceeding five hectares.[36] The chief at Godin Tepe, therefore, ruled over a considerable settled agricultural population and this gradually emerging pattern of agrarian and noble settlements was not unlike the aristocratic settlements in western Anatolia. Related to these smaller and central Median agrarian settlements are the numerous Luristan bronzes of the Iron Age III period, of elaborate horse bits and trappings, which denote extensive horse raising communities and the development of the important aristocratic cavalries,[37] which supported the Median kings in their rise to power, and which supported Cyrus and his conquest of Media, Cappadocia, and Śfarda.

Tepe Nush-i Jan (c. 750-600 B.C.), also a small fortified hill with two buildings, a major fort, and a ceremonial fire temple complex with an encircling fortified wall, perhaps centralized a similar group of smaller agrarian units, but further publication of archaeological survey in that region will be necessary before we may postulate additional conclusions.[38] While we normally consider the early Median and Persian sites as chieftan centers for extensive nomadic populations without agrarian estates, the evidence of agricultural units about Godin Tepe indicates a systematic increase in non-nomadic settlements, which is also noted in the Marv Dasht region of Parsa (Anshan). The demographic analysis of this plain within the Kur River basin indicates a small sedentary population located in twenty-five settlements clustered around Persepolis. This marks an increase from the seventeen settlements in the preceding period, c. 1600-1000 B.C., but a sharp decline from the seventy-seven settlements during the Elamite-Kaftari period c. 2000-1800 B.C., or the one hundred and fifty settlements in the Bakun period, c. 4800-3900 B.C. In the Achaemenid period, a large percentage of the population, perhaps more than half, may have lived as tent dwelling nomads.[39]

Tepe Baba Jan, a third Median center, was similar in form to Nush-i Jan: a central mound with two fortified manors and a surrounding village.[40] Here, the small stone houses of earlier Level 3 were deliberately destroyed, and their foundations filled in with rubble to serve as a foundation for Level 2. In Level 2, one fortified manor consisted of a long room upon a court with other rooms attached. In the still later Level 1, the Iron Age III phase, the manor building became more massive and more sophisticated with building constructions, which further indicate the spread and political unification of the Medes.[41]

In the region of Anshan (Parsa) south of Media, the settlements of the Marv Dasht would, by the middle of the sixth century B.C., generate the development of Cyrus' Pasargadae ("the Encampment of the Persians") the settlements of the northern Achaemenid branch, the descendants of Teispes' first son Cyrus I (c. 640-600 B.C.), see fig. 2. To the south, Ariaramnes (c. 640-615 B.C.), the second son of Teispes, and his descendants generated the settlements of the regions of Parsa and Yautiya: Tel-i Zohak, Tarava, Parga, Tepe Yahya, and Mattezzish, which also flourished during the late sixth and fifth centuries B.C.[42]

In Media and Anshan (Parsa), the warrior class gradually settled and changed the land, as the vith (the clan) formed the village grouping and the surrounding agricultural territories under the jurisdiction of its chief or khan, the vithpaitish. His authority rested firmly upon the parcels of land and the number of individuals attached to the land. In time, the chief with tribal jurisdiction and prerogatives gained new aspects of social power derived from command of the aristocratic nobles and their lands. In this manner, Cyrus arose as a *vithpaitish* in Anshan, first under the domination of the Median overlords and then as conqueror of Media. His strength rested upon the aristocratic warriors who took their places in Cyrus' army, the bureaucracies of Pasargadae, Ecbatana, Babylon, and Susa, in his royal councils, and throughout the satrapal system. These nobles, consequently, insisted upon certain immunities in the new system, immunities in regard to their estates, their political and military positions, and their retainers.[43]

The early Median and Persian chiefdoms mark, as in the analysis of the anthropologist Morton Fried, the first transitional steps from a stratification to a state society and a development of state dependent upon the pressures, direct and indirect, from existing neighboring states. Within the stratified society, a shift of prime authority from earlier kinship to later territorial means occurred and set in motion the evolution of the complex forms of government associated with the state based upon the complex division of labor, which gave rise to the several arrangements of socio-economic classes. In this, the classes were structured by their access to strategic resources, which marked the privileged and unimpeded from the impaired. In the last step, the Median and Persian state emerged with highly developed regulative organizations, with authority and discipline essential to its large-scale achievements.[44]

The form and function of these Median sites and their chieftains are strikingly similar to Lydian sites and chieftains, in particular at Adramyttion and Daskyleion, and to the rural Ionian settlements of the oikoi in the dendritic choric organizations similar to the Erythraian centers at Ptelion, Boutheia, Sidousa, and Polichna, and to the more than forty pyrgoi scattered upon the plain of Teos. Consequently, when Cyrus conquered Sfarda and transformed that imperial system into his key western satrapy of Sparda, during those early decades of Persian rule under the satrap Oroites (the late 540's to 519 B.C.) the Persian control of the extensive choric regions utilized the Lydian and East Greek landed gentry and its noble-aristocratic socio-political organization in ways similar to the Persian control and utilization of the Persian and Median nobility at the center of that imperial structure. To govern the rural districts at the local level, early Persian imperial policy under Cyrus and Cambyses entailed the direct utilization by the satraps of the local landed gentries and aristocracies to deal with local problems, to raise

taxes and tribute, and to raise and structure the local military forces, essentially the

functions of noble vassal duties within the Persian sovereign system. Persian utilization

of local administration, therefore, fostered positive societal and governmental goals

from the rural dendritic systems to the centralized satrapal organization centered in

Croesus' palace on the Sardian acropolis.

III

Cyrus' conquest of Croesus' Sfardian Empire set in motion the process of political

inter-dependency between the ruling Persian nobility in Sardis and the landed gentry of

Lydia and the East Greek poleis, which fostered a wider development of ancient Near

Eastern trade and increase of urban crafts with the western satrapy. The highland routes

from Babylonia and Assyria through the Taurus passes into Cappadocia and Sparda, which

the Assyrians and Medes had fought for more than three and a half centuries to keep

open, became settled and secure as the Persian royal road from Susa to Sardis developed

with way stations for the imperial officers.[45]   With the Persian alliance with semi-

autonomous Cilicia, the key link between Mesopotamia and western Anatolia became

secure and free from foreign military dangers.[46]   In turn, the Persian conquest of Sfarda

halted the East Greek hostile attacks upon Persia's Phoenician ports. With Cambyses'

conquest of Egypt, the East Greek maritime trade with the Nile's ports increased, rather

than (as often argued) diminished. Under Pharaoh Amasis, whom Cambyses overthrew,

Greek commerce and mercenary services increased, at Naukratis in the Delta and at the

pharaonic center of Memphis. With Cambyses' conquest Greek mercantile activities at

Naukratis declined but, as M. M. Austin has wisely noted, Cambyses may have abolished

the earlier trade restrictions, which Amasis had imposed upon the Greeks (Hdt. 2.179),

and opened the country to more Greeks who flocked to Egypt in the wake of the Persian

army (Hdt. 3.139).[47]   Phoenician and Persian overland trade with Egypt also increased

through Syria and Palestine and linked with the long sought routes along the Red Sea to

southern Arabia.[48]   Cyrus' and Cambyses' ambitious attempts to gain and intertwine a

vast imperial structure were strongly governed by such economic considerations. As Max

Mallowan has noted, the cycle of Persian trade during the latter half of the sixth century

B.C. pierced the earlier political and geographical barriers.[49]   From the blue Aegean

ports to the muddy rivers of the Oxus and Jaxartes, from the green Nile banks of Nubia
to the brown shores of the Caspian Sea, the Persian imperial structure sustained the
acquisition of satrapal tributes which flowed into Babylon, Susa, and Cyrus' new imperial
center at Pasargadae, and also supported an increase in overland and maritime trade
based upon the development of agrarian units and craft centers. In this system, the
western Anatolian regions of Sparda functioned intricately and flourished, and often in
fierce competition with the Athenian merchants who also found the open Persian ports
lucrative centers.[50]

From the Assyrians, the Persians inherited basic concepts of an "imperial
community," and upon these developed their particular imperial system, which carried
the Persians beyond the compactness of their stratified Iranian communities into an
integral expanded territorial unity.[51] The Persians and Medes had impinged but lightly
upon the Assyrian Empire in the ninth century B.C., yet by the seventh century the
Medes had become a dominant factor in the Near East, and by the spring of 522 B.C. the
Persians ruled the Near East. While the urban centers from village to city rank provided
the bases to the material aspects of the Persian "community," bases which structured and
fostered the fundamental concepts of residence and economic exchange, the Persian
expansion to imperial territoriality drew upon the economic resources of the remote
areas in direct relationship to the central imperial zones. Beyond these material aspects,
concepts of sovereignty and rule existed but, in their own right, did not develop a strong
sense of community. Too often, the negative aspects of sovereignty developed as
overriding consequences of imperialism. Cooperation towards positive imperial goals
was, therefore, needed to systematize that stability needed to maintain the imperial
state and not to drain its productivity.

Unlike the earlier Near Eastern imperial structures since Sargon of Akkad's first
institutionalized empire in the late third millennium B.C., Cyrus ruled over a distinctly
new imperial organization. In the region of Anshan, the remnant of the highland
territories of the earlier Elamite civilization, the tribes of that region now called Parsa,
owed vassalage allegiance to their supreme tribal chief, victorious and elevated as king.
With the conquest of the vassal tribes of Media, Cyrus out of military necessity
amalgamated the two related yet distinct groups of vassal aristocratic kingdoms on the
basis of a dual-monarchy and then proceeded through conquest to add to that kingdom

the subordinate tribes, nations, and kingdoms of Anatolia, Syria, Palestine, Mesopotamia, and Bactria.

In a brilliant stroke of imperial propaganda structured by the Chaldean magi, the priests of Babylon disillusioned with the Chaldean King Nabonidus, Cyrus entered Babylon in 539 B.C. and offered his new subjects an imperial policy unlike the earlier Assyrian or Chaldean policies of terror, destruction of cities, the destruction of temples, the deportation of populations, and the transportation of the conquered peoples' gods to the imperial centers. In order to hold his vast and very disparate empire, newly won and not yet enmeshed into a vast network of imperial controls, Cyrus offered an imperial policy of peace, reconciliation, the return of deported populations to their homelands, and the return of the temple gods earlier seized and carted away by the Chaldean kings.[52] For this the writer of Second Isaiah (45:1; LXX) called Cyrus the Anointed of Yhwh, in Greek "the Christos."[53] Even Herodotus, so anti-Persian, praised the fatherliness of Cyrus and his good shepherd qualities (1.19, 1.86-91, 115-6, 123), themes and literary motifs echoed by Xenophon in his romantic *Cyropaedeia*.[54] Cyrus, the just and righteous savior, by good deeds and upright mind captured the hearts of the gods. Persians, Medes, Parthians, Bactrians, Sogdianians, Babylonians, Assyrians, Armenians, Phrygians, Lydians, Karians, Lykians, Cilicians, Phoenicians, Jews, and East Greeks, with their own peculiar political and social forms and institutions, were now joined together by the rule and edicts of the "King of the Universe, Great King, Mighty King, King of Babylon, King of Sumer and Akkad, King of the World Quarters,"[55] and the imperial edicts written in chancery Aramaic, the lingua franca of the earlier decades, which bound together the numerous and disparate linguistic subjects.[56] To this Empire, Cyrus' son and successor Cambyses added Egypt. Toward all the national and ethnic groups within the Persian Achaemenid Empire, the kings and governmental officials would be kind, gentle, and lenient but when piqued by rebellion or treason, destroyed cities, wrecked temples, deported people to the various satrapies of the empire, and impaled, beheaded, and crucified malcontents.

Cyrus' Empire (and that of Cambyses) fundamentally lay in the institutionalization of centralized leadership and the developing administrative functions of the satrapal bureaucratic positions held by Persian and Median aristocrats. The leadership and the bureaucracies together created and developed legislation, legal procedures, police, and militias as formal institutions purposely established and specialized for performing the

major political functions of the empire. In response to their rapid and extensive
conquests, Cyrus and Cambyses instituted the bureaucracies to rule the regional ethnic
populaces by right of their royal leadership. The ancient sources and in particular
Herodotus are unfortunately extremely sparse in regard to the specific structure of the
central imperial court and the various satrapal bureaucracies before the extensive
revitalization and institutionalization of the imperial system during the reign of King
Darius (see chapter 5).   The reconstruction of the early Persian imperial system,
however, can be generally perceived upon the bases of the anthropological studies of
Elman R. Service in regard to the origin and development of centralized states.[57] While
our knowledge of Oroites' satrapal rule over Sparda and his governmental relationship to
the imperial throne lack sufficient ancient evidence, we may assume, and with a high
degree of certainty, that the satrapal government in Sparda reflected the imperial
controls of other satraps within the Empire.

Persian political authority rested upon the hierarchical relationships which
maintained the social order within their respective communities while subject to the
imperial controls of power and authority directed by the satrap in obedience to the royal
demands. Through agreement and consensus to measures of compulsion by authority and
force the state sustained its centralized and permanent authority over the hierarchical
societies led by the ruling aristocratic classes. Yet, until Darius' extensive revitalization
of the imperial structure, Persian rule of Sparda remains obscure within an apparent
oversimplification of the formal governmental structure. Sparda, as with the other
satrapies, retained its earlier mélange of local Lydian and East Greek laws, customs,
traditions, religions, measures of weight and length, systems of currencies, local writing
systems and spoken languages, and remained a semi-independent socio-political unity
with local social institutions and an internal structure of its own.[58] As satrap, Oroites
demanded imperial allegiance and vassalage from the various subjected units, which
induced the imperial demands for tribute and, when required, armed forces for the king's
military campaigns. To obtain this imperial overlordship, an imperial *spasaka, or as the
Greeks referred to this officer a King's Eye (Hdt. 1.144.2), conducted a political and
administrative surveillance of the Spardian satrapy and communicated that information
directly to the king. His duties were distinctly separate from Oroites and his civil and
military administrative functions as the *spasaka supervised both the satrap and his

satrapy for the king. Within an empire of exteme ethnic, linguistic, and religious diversity, the Persian monarchs relied highly upon this network of espionage and communication.[59]

Fundamental to Oroites' satrapal system were not the Persian imperial officers and their duties, few as they may have been, but rather the socio-political organizations of the landed gentry who had gained power during the development of the Lydian Mermnad aristocratic system and the various East Greek aristocratic systems. As the Persian imperial structures utilized the Persian and Median landed gentry and their aristocratic hierarchies to govern those central satrapies and the imperial course, so, too, Oroites turned to the long established aristocratic structures throughout Sparda, allowed and encouraged them to continue their governance at the local level providing they did not interfere with satrapal rules and orders or the royal edicts.

Persian political utilization of the Lydian and East Greek nobles during the reigns of Cyrus and Cambyses, however, did not generate the complexities of acculturation. Most notably, without the ancient literary and epigraphical references to the Persians in Lydia and Ionia, archaeological evidence for the early Persian presence in western Anatolia is remarkably absent. With the contacts between Lydians and East Greeks within Sparda and the Persian officers and military personnel, elements of Persian culture were neither forced upon the Spardian inhabitants nor were they received voluntarily. The fundamental elements of the processes of acculturation remained absent. The process of accultural acceptance, which would have resulted in degrees of assimilation of the cultural aspects of the imperial rulers, affected neither the behavioral patterns nor the inner values of the Lydian and East Greek peoples. Similarly, accultural adaptation, which would have combined the original and foreign traits to produce essentially a smoothly functioning new cultural whole, with the reworking of the patterns of the two cultures into a harmonious meaningful society, also did not occur. Nor did Lydian or East Greek reaction arise as contra-acculturative movements due to the presence of Persians with their limited Iranian cultural traits at Sardis. The processes of acculturation failed to develop. Instead, the Persian officials in Sardis turned to the local aristocratic leaders in the urban centers and in the extensive rural estate regions and allowed them to govern as they had before the Persian occupation of Sparda. Consequently, a political symbiotic relationship developed without the cross-cultural processes of acceptance, adaptation, or reaction by the acculturated Helleno-Lydian society brought to the height of cultural assimilation during the reign of Croesus continued.

5

DARIUS' REORGANIZATION OF THE PERSIAN EMPIRE

King Darius' reconquest of Sparda in 519 B.C. dramatically set in motion new imperial institutions, which altered the lives of the East Greek and Lydian peoples. The imperial institutions established by the Mermnad kings and fundamentally sustained by Cyrus and Cambyses signficantly transformed into a distinctly new phase of imperial control. Darius I (522-486 B.C.) markedly revitalized the earlier controls to produce a strong imperial centralization. Darius' revitalized empire, built upon numerous vassalage forms among the subordinate satrapal and imperial officers from the satrap to the heralds and King's Ears, was more vibrant and intricate than that of Croesus or Cyrus. The fundamental issues, which affected the Spardians and specifically the landed gentry, focused strongly upon the legal strictures of taxation and military service, the pronounced elements of vassalage. By the end of the fifth century B.C., and the reign of King Darius II (423-404 B.C.), however, the satrapal activities moving toward greater independence from the Great King generated a radical failure of that centralization established by Darius I and this ultimately led to the demise of the Persian Empire at the hands of Alexander III, the Macedonian, in 330 B.C.

I

The Revolution

Darius' usurpation of the Persian royal throne temporarily shattered the loose political unity of the Achaemenid Empire. The series of events which led to his seizure, however, may never be clearly unraveled; consequently, numerous different interpretations have long been propounded. The major textual sources are two: Darius' own version of the events recorded on the face of Bisitun mountain and Herodotus' account, which essentially parallels but also elaborates upon the Bisitun version. As with the events related to the rise and expansion of Lydia and the Ionian poleis, scholars must use Herodotus' text with caution.

In evaluating the importance of that usurpation and revolution we must turn first to Herodotus and consider the historical reliability of his account, the degree to which it does reflect the Persian source, and then analyze Darius' Bisitun inscription. My

conclusions are that Herodotus gained his information through written and oral sources
(cf. 3.1), which, to a limited degree, reflect the official imperial version of that
revolution as inscribed at Bisitun. While Herodotus may have received accounts of the
revolution from the earlier and contemporary historians, including Hekataios of Miletos
(Hdt. 5.36.2)[1] and Xanthos of Sardis,[2] the paucity of fragments of their histories leads us
only to doubt that they provided Herodotus with information. Similarly, his
contemporaries Hellanikos of Lesbos[3] and Charon of Lampsakos[4] wrote essentially
histories of the Persian Wars and not extensively if at all of Persia or the Near East,[5]
and may not have considered the revolution. Dionysios of Miletos, a contemporary of
Herodotus and active c. 460-430 B.C., in comparison, did record some information about
the revolution but that, unfortunately, barely assists in a reevaluation of the usurpation.[6]

A major source for Herodotus was, apparently, the Persian noble Zopyros, the son of
Megabyzos, who fled Persia for Athens late in the 440's (Hdt. 3.160) and provided the
Halikarnassian historian with valuable information, the history of Persia and especially of
Darius' revolution.[7] Zopyros informed Herodotus admirably and ranks among the
greatest of the oral historians of antiquity.[8]

Zopyros rose to power in the inner circle of the Achaemenid court and within a
family which served foremost in the activities of Cyrus, Darius, Xerxes, and
Artaxerxes. As nephew of Xerxes, Zopyros was the son of Amytis and of Megabyzos, who
ranked as one of the six chief Persian generals whom Xerxes led against Greece (Hdt.
7.82-121; see fig. 15). From Zopyros, Herodotus gleaned information about the Persian
army (Book 7) and the affairs of Ecbatana and Susa. But, more important, Zopyros knew
the details of the Persian occupation of Babylon (Hdt. 1.192; 3.92, 153-60) and the details
of Darius' reorganization of the Empire and the official court version of Darius' rise to
power as outlined at Bisitun. Zopyros' grandfather and namesake, the satrap of Babylon,
served Darius well in aiding the structure and success of the usurpation (3.160).
Herodotus' essential ignorance of Darius' historical claim to the throne may, therefore,
be due to Zopyros' telling of the romantic story of the horse "trick" (3.84-8), which was,
it seems, a propagandistic veil for the usurpation.[9] Highly satisfied with this source,
Herodotus thought he spoke with authority about Achaemenid events (1.95), the satrapies
(Book 3), the army (Book 7), and the official Bisitun version of the regal usurpation (3.61-
88). With an accuracy of names and many details of Persian matters, Herodotus wrote of

the rise of the Achaemenid royal houses and their accession to the throne, and of the events of the inner court circles at Susa, Persepolis, and Ecbatana. Perhaps through Zopyros' oral transmission of Persian history, the Greek historian could demonstrate his excellent ability to transliterate Old Persian names, and Median and Persian terms into Greek.[10] But in spite of that accuracy, caution must prevail in uncovering Herodotus' use of Zopyros' information to assist the Halikarnassian's dramatic intent. Herodotus' account of Darius' rise to power simply does not correspond with the account in the Persian sources.

Others also served Herodotus in his quest for historical information. For example, the Persian Artabazos offered several personal and intimate stories (Hdt. 8.126, 9.41, 9.89). Other recollections could have come from the family of the exiled Spartan King Damaratos, living on landed estates in the Troad (Xen. *Anab.* 2.1-3, 7.8.17; *Hell.* 3.1.6), and possibly from Rhoesdakes who also deserted Persia and fled to the home of the Athenian Kimon (Plut. *Kim.* 10.9). But there is no evidence that they did.

The Harpagid family in Lykia, however, may have supplied Herodotus with valuable information not only of Cyrus whom the Mede Harpagos admirably served in his conquest of Media (Hdt. 1.108-9), and Sparda (1.80.108-29), but also of Darius' activities. This Median noble family held particularly strong control of its vassal estates, which remained as semi-autonomous family units within Sparda. Its funerary monument presented the faithful Median noble enthroned and surrounded by his attendants, a relief which marks the importance of the Median dynasty in Xanthos and its Irano-Lykian court ceremonies.[11]

Herodotus himself, as he traveled about in Egypt and in Babylonia during the mid-fifth century B.C., heard many stories which supported, corrected, or conflicted with his other sources; and these, too, altered and shaped his final literary view and his particular historical approach. If, however, he gathered oral stories in Babylon, a major center crucial to Darius' gaining the Achaemenid throne, the Halikarnassian does not reflect the strong Babylonian attitudes which held the Achaemenid royal house in contempt for its destruction of that city and its temple of Esagila in 482 B.C. We, therefore, must not rely heavily upon the idea that Herodotus gained in Babylonia important traditions about either Darius or his son Xerxes, the wielder of destruction upon Babylon.

As with all matters concerning the text of Herodotus' *History*, the ancient historian must constantly use caution in his analysis of the evidence presented. The long argued

realization that Herodotus' method was artistic, allows us to uncover in his *History* the

construction of a prose epic and drama in which irony, pathos, paradox, and tragedy

supported his imaginative exposition of the materials. Turning to invention and the

techniques of a poet, Herodotus used fictional devices to present the high truths of

drama which only fiction could convey.[12] Behind Herodotus' form and thought in which

he portrayed the failure of oriental despotism structured upon a pattern of an oriental

chronicle, the end Herodotean product was not a history of Persia. Herodotus' main

concern with the "accession" of Darius (3.39-87) was the dramatic representation of a

king who symbolized the high point of Persian power, a king not unlike the earlier

Assyrian Tiglath-Pileser III who gained power through revolution, and a usurpation which

first underscored a weakness within the imperial system and then resulted in a firm

reestablishment and reorganization of that imperial power. In this Darius played an

important dramatic role as the key of Herodotus' "accession logos" within a series of

logoi. While Herodotus offered an account of the accession, he wrote little about the

origins or the background events of Darius' rise to power. While this logos is very

detailed it is also dramatically stylized.[13]

Herodotus' literary method, to juxtapose failure with order or order with failure, is

pointedly demonstrated within his "sickness" motif for Cambyses' actions in Egypt (3.27-

38), a motif which contrasts with Darius' rule of order. Herodotus characterized

Cambyses' reign in Egypt as terror and impiety, but this view is inconsistent with the

Egyptian epigraphical records, which note Cambyses' restoration of order, the establish-

ment of strong pharaonic rule, the re-establishment of the ageless cults including the god

Apis, and the rebuilding of religious centers. Rather than impiety, Cambyses instituted a

regal policy of legitimate sovereignty as the rightful successor to the Saïte Pharaoh

Psammetichos in order to reclaim the throne from the usurper Amasis.[14]

Herodotus' organization of his prose epic of oriental despotism and Hellenic freedom

first considered the rise and extension of the Persian Empire from the time of Cyrus'

defeat of Croesus to the end of Darius' Scythian expedition[15] and the beginning of

Darius' Persian expeditions against Greece (Hdt. 5.27). The second half of the *History*,

which begins with the Naxian revolution (Hdt. 5.28), focused upon Greece and the final

stages of the conflict.[16] As Herodotus began with Croesus' subjection of the Greeks on the Anatolian seaboard, his tragic drama continued to focus upon Cyrus' and then Darius' imperial rises, and the subjugations of the Ionian Greeks. In linking the three imperial powers (Croesus, Cyrus, and Darius), Herodotus heightened his drama in preparation for the hybristic fall of King Xerxes and Persian failure.

Behind Herodotus' "accession logos," nevertheless, lay the stories and details obtained through oral traditions, which the Halikarnassian historian regarded as the principal means of gaining access to the past. This oral tradition, therefore, had already formed his judgment regarding the Persian king. Consequently, while Herodotus' *History* exhibited an essentially close connection between historical events and the oral traditions,[17] we must scrutinize the events of that tradition and carefully examine the sources which gave rise to those traditions. For Herodotus (and for Aeschylus) Darius embodied the "wise king," the Persian royal character at its highest, yet in a stylized if not generalized form.[18] For Herodotus, Darius developed from a clever usurper to a great and prospering ruler, but behind the usurpation rested a series of historical events, which Darius himself attempted to gloss over. The general traditions of the usurpation, which Herodotus gained from his border contacts with the Persian Empire, and which Zopyros transmitted in detail to the Halikarnassian, came directly from Darius' own presentation at Bisitun of the usurpation, from the copies carved into stone in the city of Babylon,[19] the copies written on parchment and papyrus distributed in Egypt,[20] and the numerous other copies now lost to the ravages of time.

While no one could reach the trilingual text at Bisitun to read Darius' official version of the usurpation, the copies which did circulate throughout the Empire brought to the people through their literati that official version. In the Babylonian palace of the Chaldean Nebuchadrezzar, which Darius took for his own, two fine diorite steles bore versions of the Bisitun Babylonian text,[21] and a copy of the relief.[22] These copies on public display in the extreme northern tip of the ancient capital bore important aspects of the official text, for they alone in contrast to the Elamite, Old Persian, and Aramaic texts note the numbers of soldiers killed and of prisoners taken, yet they are not close copies of the Babylonian text at Bisitun. Their contents are closer to the Elamite and Old Persian texts than to the Bisitun Babylonian.[23] For international purposes outside Babylonia, copies in Aramaic, the chancery script of the empire, followed closely and literally yet in free translation the Bisitun Babylonian text. In Egypt, as the Aramaic versions upon parchment and papyrus deteriorated and wore away, copies often illegible in themselves were produced for almost a century after the usurpation. In addition, Darius sent copies to the other centers of the empire including Sardis, even to some of the Ionian poleis,[24] and perhaps to Miletos and Halikarnassos.[25] These copies would have directly influenced both Dionysios of Miletos and Herodotus, and confirmed what Zopyros would later transmit to the Halikarnassian. But if Herodotus had knowledge of the Bisitun text, he rejected parts of it and wrote his account based upon what he thought were more persuasive arguments or evidence to fit his literary scheme.

Investigation of the official Bisitun texts, therefore, becomes necessary to understand first Herodotus' version and also to support the analysis and interpretation that the Bisitun texts reveal the propaganda and the extend of Darius' cover up of his usurpation of the throne following regicide. Event after event within Darius' offical version of the "accession" reveals not only his regal propaganda but a new outline behind the official version. These historical events, therefore, demonstrate not only the usurpation and regicide but also our consideration of corrections necessary to Herodotus' dramatic version.

In the preamble of the Bisitun text,[26] Darius touted his genealogy listing his father Hystaspes,[27] his grandfather Arsames, his great-grandfather Ariaramnes, his great-great-grandfather Teispes, and finally his great-great-great-grandfather Achaemenes, the founder of the royal house. Within this list, Darius by-passed Teispes' first son, Cambyses I, and his regal line which included Cyrus II (the Great and conqueror of Lydia), Cambyses II (the conqueror of Egypt), and the controversial brother of Cambyses II, the prince Bardiya. Darius, however, then stated that he was ninth in the line of succession of the Achaemenid kings whom the god Ahura Mazda established by divine sanction upon the throne. As ninth king, Darius purposely omitted Bardiya who did reign and did receive recognition by the inhabitants of Babylonia as king.[28] This omission was both deliberate and a firm disregard of any claim, legal or illegal, by Bardiya to the throne which he held for seven months (Hdt. 3.67.2). An equally glaring omission in the list of kings who reigned is Darius' father Hystaspes who was alive, militarily active, and who governed the Parthians.[29] But even more disturbing within this genealogy is the fact that Darius' grandfather Arsames, who Darius claimed was a king, was also alive.[30] Hystaspes apparently did not die until 514/3 B.C., and Arsames sometime between the accession of Darius to the throne and Hystaspes' death.[31] If the line of succession

passed, as Darius asserted, from the legitimate Cambyses to the royal line of Teispes'

second son Ariaramnes, King Arasames or Hystaspes and not Darius should have gained

the royal tiara.   In that Hystaspes did not challenge his son's activities but rather

supported them without his own claims to the Achaemenid throne further underscores

Darius' blatant usurpation of that throne from his rival, King Bardiya. Many years later,

Darius' son and successor Xerxes, in explaining the by-pass of Kings Arsames and

Hystaspes, claimed that while they were alive and possible candidates for the crown

Darius was clearly the best choice.[32] But the usurpation was again covered up by the

constant repetition, in order to drive home the propagandistic point, of Darius' accession

to the throne directly through divine sanction, of the fundamentally important ancient

Near Eastern claim to kingship. It was the same divine sanction, which Herodotus noted

Croesus recognized in Cyrus' victory at Sardis (1.89).   But Darius honed that point over

and over again, and rehearsed the argument of divine sanction by raising Ahura Mazda to

the theocratic position earlier held by Marduk-Bel. In this focus upon Ahura Mazda, to

whom Darius specifically referred as "the god of the Aryan,"[33] Darius also returned to

the propaganda touted by Cyrus upon his conquest of Babylon, his overthrow of the

Chaldean King Nabonidus, and the gaining of Marduk-Bel's sanction of his usurpation;

that is the concept that the accession covering the usurpation was necessary to combat

the Evil and the Lie. Thus Darius adopted the political and theocratic arguments and

propaganda from Cyrus and the concepts contained within the text of the Cyrus

Cylinder,[34] repeated by the Hebrew writer of Second Isaiah, and wove them into his

texts at Bisitun. In this, Darius raised the political and theocratic concepts of kingship

to a new theological level by focusing upon the divine sanction of Ahura Mazda in

opposition to the Evil and the Lie. The constant repetition of these themes by Darius

strongly suggests that it was absolutely necessary to impress and to assert time after

time that he was the legitimate king when in actuality he had usurped the throne by

murdering King Bardiya.[35]

In the first section of the Bisitun texts devoted to events among the Persians and

Medes,[36] Darius finally referred to the reigns of Cyrus and Cambyses, omitted in the

preamble, in order to discredit Bardiya and also to cast doubts upon the actions of

Cambyses.[37] Darius claimed that Cambyses had killed nis brother, a royal prince and son of Cyrus and Cambyses' own mother Kassandane, and that the murder and the absence of Bardiya remained unnoticed for several years by the royal family, by the members of the royal courts, and by the people.   The implication which Darius suggested is that Cambyses' murder of Bardiya created the Evil and the Lie, which arose among the Persians, Medes, Babylonians, Elamites, and the other but unnamed peoples,[38] which he, Darius, had to vanquish and did vanquish by assuming the royal tiara through the divine sanction of Ahura Mazda.[39]

Darius' account of Cambyses' subterfuge then claimed that while Cambyses was campaigning in Egypt, a priest, a magos, arose in the heartland of Parsa and Media and claimed to be Bardiya. Darius quickly glossed over this pretense apparently to ignore the question of how a priest named Gaumata could rise up among the Persian and Median nobles who had known Bardiya and yet could be tricked by an imposter. Not only did Darius try to convince his subjects that Gaumata was not the royal prince but Darius also glossed over the fact that the pretender led Parsa, Media, Elam, Babylonia and other regions in rebellion against the rightful King Cambyses. Darius then simply passed off the statement following Gaumata's accession to the imperial Achaemenid throne that "Cambyses died by his own hand."[40] Darius appears purposefully vague in regard to Cambyses' reaction to the accession of Gaumata to his throne and the revolution of Cambyses' homeland. On the other hand, Darius carefully suggested that many people indeed then did know that Gaumata was not Bardiya but feared for their lives and did not protest.[41]

That statement heightened Darius' next assertion that only he dared to oppose Gaumata and that with a "few men" killed the magos, but of course with the help and sanction of Ahura Mazda. In a magnanimous gesture which reflected Cyrus' imperial propaganda, Darius claimed that he restored the kingdom to the rightful regal family, "reestablished the kingdom upon its foundations," restored the holy sanctuaries which Gaumata the priest had destroyed, and restored the pastures and herds, the homes and the slaves to the people, things evilly done by Gaumata. At this point, with the slaying of Gaumata (29 September 522 B.C.), Darius claimed he became king.

But here again, numerous problems arise in trying to accept Darius' statements. Why did Darius cast Gaumata as an evil priest who destroyed sanctuaries and seized the pastures, herds, homes, and even slaves of the Persian and Median landed gentry? To this, Bickerman and Tadmor have argued, in fabricating Gaumata as a magos, Darius implied that only a wizard or an evil priest could pose as the perfect double of Cambyses' brother Bardiya, and was, therefore, both alien and a sorcerer. In contrast, Darius was "a Persian, an Aryan, of Aryan lineage," and a loyal servant of Right, Justice, and Truth (ṛta). His kingly, heroic, and religious deed necessitated the slaying of Gaumata (Bardiya) who became the perfect incarnation of the Evil, Deceit, and the denial of Divine Order (the drauga—which Darius stated four times within the Bisitun text). As the personification of Evil, Gaumata also embodied the total denial of holy power. Thus Darius supplicated Ahura Mazda thirty-four times (in all the god was referred to sixty-three times) to protect the empire from its enemies, invasion, famine, and deceit. Yet Darius' accusation that Gaumata destroyed the holy sanctuaries appears nonsensical, for Gaumata (false or not) as head of state and of the state religions would not have destroyed the altars and shrines where prayers for his well being were delivered.[42] The confusion of these events is further complicated by the account of the Bisitun text in which Darius noted the second Elamite and Babylonian revolutions against him because of his killing of Gaumata.[43] Again, we note the loyalty of the Elamites and the Babylonians to their sovereign whom Darius killed. In both provinces and in their capitals, Susa and Babylon, the new revolutions were extensive revivals of the older regal houses, which claimed legitimacy and divine sanction. In Babylon, the successful new king assumed the regal name of Nebuchadrezzar III, the son of King Nabonidus, whom Cyrus had over-thrown and taken into exile.[44] About Nebuchadrezzar III, the Bisitun text notes that at least forty-nine nobles rallied behind that rebellion.[45]

With Darius' killing of the Elamite Assina who had led the Elamite revolt,[46] following Darius' victory over that king on November 10, 522 B.C. (more than a month before Darius' victory in Babylonia, December 18, 522 B.C.), the Great King began to consider his victory in Elam pivotal to his reign. From the killing of Assina and the recovery of Susa and the Elamites, Darius marked his royal accession to the throne. What becomes glaringly obvious is that Darius did not mark his accession to Achaemenid power from the death of Cambyses or, more important, from his defeat and assassination of Gaumata, but rather from his victory in Susa, which he briefly noted in contrast to the more extensive references to the revolution in Babylon. The problem of why Darius chose the suppression of the Elamite rebellion as the mark of his reign is further complicated by Darius' insistence at five repetitive points within the Bisitun text that he had secured his rule "by the favor of Ahura Mazda *in one year*,"[47] when his final victory to gain the royal tiara occurred in Babylon on November 27, 521 B.C., more than a year later. If the problem of regal succession rested upon Gaumata's rebellion, or more fundamentally upon Cambyses' death, why did Darius postpone his accession until his victory over Assina a month and a half later? Yet, why did Darius deemphasize the importance of the Elamite rebellion? Or, in other terms, why was the Elamite rebellion crucial to Darius' imperial power? The suggested answer emerging is that Darius was feverishly trying to hide or to deemphasize many of the events of the crucial year of 522 B.C. in his propagandistic attempt to assert his legitimacy.

The matter becomes further complicated with Darius' victory over Nebuchadrezzar III and his killing of that king in Babylon. Immediately following Darius' suppression of the resurgent Chaldean royal house, rebellions in seventeen if not eighteen ethnic regions arose, not only to challenge Darius' usurpation of the throne but also, apparently, because of Darius' victories over the Elamites and Babylonians.[48] That the rebellions arose when Darius' power seemed secure suggests that they did not arise when Darius' power was being challenged by Assina and Nebuchadrezzar III but rather arose because of Darius' assumption of power in the key Near Eastern capital and holy city of Babylon on December 18, 522 B.C. Darius' own tribal Persians led the rebellion which quickly spread to Susa and the Elamites,[49] and a second rebellion erupted among the Medes where the resurgent royal family led a massive revolt in Ecbatana supported by the Median army and at least forty-seven nobles.[50] To the north of Media, the Armenians also rebelled not in support of an Armenian king but in loyal support of the Median royal resurgence.[51] Following a winter battle against the Medes, on January 13, 521 B.C., Darius' troops suppressed the Armenians, having earlier battled against them first on December 31, 522 B.C., then later on May 20, 521 B.C., again on May 29, 521 B.C., and a fourth time on June 21, 521 B.C. With a victory over the Medes at Raga (just south of modern Teheran) on May 5, 521 B.C., Darius' armies continued their operations against the Armenians and against the eastern Sagartians who had rallied around a second branch of the royal Median family also in rebellion against Darius.[52] This rebellion lasted throughout the summer of 521 B.C. until September 24, well after the Armenian and Median rebellions were suppressed, among which Darius mentions the Sagartian affair, and into the period of the third Babylonian rebellion.[53]

The massive rebellion against Darius also included revolutions by the Parthians and Hyrkanians (?).[54] In Parthia, Darius' father Hystaspes the local satrap led a successful campaign against the Parthian insurgents and following a victory on May 8, 521 B.C. (while other divisions of Darius' army fought against the Armenians, Medes, and Sagartians), Hystaspes finally defeated the Median king of Parthia on July 11, 521 B.C. Rebellion had also erupted among the eastern Margianians during that troublesome autumn of 522 B.C., but fortunately for Darius the Bactrians and their Persian satrap suppressed that rebellion on December 10, 522 B.C.[55]

Darius unfortunately but apparently purposely omitted the suppression of the rebellion in Parsa yet noted a second Persian uprising. From the Persian heartland of Anshan and the territories of Pasargadae[56] and the royal estates near the soon to be developed royal center at Persepolis,[57] the Persian army rebelled and supported a young man who claimed that he was Bardiya, the son of Cyrus, and the legitimate king. Following a victory over the rebellious Persians on May 24, 521 B.C., Darius finally defeated the new Bardiya on July 15, 521 B.C.[58] This Persian rebellion had been going on since the previous December if not November of 522 B.C., as the eastern satrapy of Arachosia had supported the new Bardiya.[59] Against the Arachosians, therefore, other divisions of Darius' army battled their rebellion first on December 29, 522 B.C., and finally won later that spring. Meanwhile against the Sattagydians, other loyalist forces battled those rebels and defeated them on February 21, 521 B.C., before the final fall of the Arachosians.[60]

As Babylon was key to the extensive rebellions which Darius elaborated upon, Babylonians continued for a third time to oppose Darius after the fall of Nebuchadrezzar III in December of 522 B.C., and supported a second claim to the resurgent Chaldean royal throne.[61] That king also chose the royal title, Nebuchadrezzar (IV) the son of Nabonidus. Darius noted that this rebellion erupted while he was in Parsa and Media, apparently in the early winter months of 521 B.C., as Darius had suppressed the second Babylonian rebellion on December 18, 522 B.C. and then moved into Parsa and Media to direct the numerous campaigns to suppress the other rebellions. But the new Babylonian rebellion occupied much of Darius' activities during the summer and early autumn of 521 B.C. as the rival to the Babylonian throne and his supporting nobles were not captured and impaled until November 27, 521 B.C.[62]   This ended the third Babylonian rebellion

against Darius since the rise of Gaumata.

Darius recapitulated an account of these events following the fall of the third

Babylonian rebellion but that recapitulation contains new problems, which raise further

doubts about the king's story. In this account, Darius drove home the point that he had

accomplished these events after he became king and "in one and the same year." But in

contrast to his earlier statements, Darius now counted the overthrow of Gaumata and

Assina among those events. While Darius had earlier claimed that he became king

following the fall of Gaumata, he did not begin to count his accession until November 10,

522 B.C. with the fall of Assina. Also in this recapitulation of the rebellions, Darius

acknowledged that the rebels were kings, and offered a bit more information about the

third Elamite rebellion. Here Darius noted that that rebellion was led by a Persian. This

information only suggested earlier now increases the complexities of the Persian and

Median rebellions after the second fall of Babylon.[63]

In Parsa (ancient Anshan), the Persian nobles had factionalised. Leaders of six noble

families[64] supported Darius' Achaemenid branch of the Pasargadai tribe, while other

noble families vehemently objected to the course of events and strongly opposed Darius.

Both Gaumata (Bardiya) and Vahyazdata who claimed to be Bardiya gained the support of

many Persian nobles at Pasargadae, and Vahyazdata also found support among the nobles

in Darius' home region of Yautiya, the chiefdom still ruled by his grandfather King

Arsames.[65]   Darius' claim to the royal throne had clearly divided Parsa. Some Persians,

including the noble family of Vaumisa who aided Darius' suppression of the Armenians[66]

but was not part of the seven noble families (including Darius' own family headed by

Hystaspes), rallied behind Darius, while others rebelled as the Persian Martiya raced off

to spur the second Elamite rebellion. The Medes were also divided, and while many

rallied around the revival of the Median royal family, other Medes such as Takhmaspada

who suppressed the Sagartian rebellion loyally supported Darius.[67]   Clearly, the

rebellions of the Persians and Medes threatened Darius' major base of support, and Darius

himself campaigned against Ecbatana;[68] but because of the absolute military necessity

to hold Ecbatana as the Iranian Hauptstadt he could not venture even to Raga.[69]   The

heartland rebellions of Persians and Medes were extremely acute and seriously

threatened Darius' claim to the throne. Consequently, Darius deliberately noted that certain Persian troops had not revolted against him. Following his victories over fifty-two rebellious Persian nobles, only then did the Persians become his subjects.[70]

Darius' account of the rebellions against him contains additional historical problems, which further undermine the acceptance of the text as Darius would want us to believe. After the second fall of Babylon, Darius listed the rebellions against him: Persians, Elamites, Medes, Assyrians, Egyptians, Parthians, Margianians, Sattagydians, and the eastern Scythians.[71] But within the account, the rebel Egyptians were omitted in addition to the numerous confusions noted. Assyria, for example, was mentioned only in passing as the location of a battle against the Armenians.[72] In the Old Persian text the Hyrkanians were included among the rebels, but in the Babylonian text Darius claimed that they were Margianians whom he did comment upon when he noted that the Persian satrap of the Bactrians, Dardashi, led his loyalists to victory.[73] To the problems and omissions of the account of the rebellions we may add the Lydians and the Ionians, and the rebellion of Oroites against Darius, as will be considered later.

The constant and immediate repetition by Darius that these events occurred "in one and the same year" is paralleled by a similar constant and immediate repetition that these events were accurately described and that people should believe them, and if they did not they are the Evil and the Lie thus Darius coupled them with the suppressed political rebellions in opposition to Ahura Mazda and his divine edicts and sanctions. This vehement insistence that he was the legitimate king, Darius further underscored by asserting that he was neither the Evil nor the Lie and that neither he nor his family had done any wrong. This entire section resounds with hypocrisy and strongly suggests what Albert T. Olmstead had earlier concluded, and more recently Muhammed A. Dandamayev, that Gaumata was Bardiya the legitimate king whom Darius killed and whose throne Darius usurped.[74] Because many Persians and Medes who had close contact with Bardiya and Darius did not accept Darius' propaganda about a false magos named Gaumata, we must consider that Darius' several stories perpetrated against Bardiya and the creation of a false magos were part and parcel of the suppression of historical facts by Darius and his supporters.

The resulting historical confusion within the Bisitun text and the stories about Gaumata obtained and written by Dionysios of Miletos and Herodotus, therefore, must be traced back to Darius.[75] Herodotus' explanation of the failures of Cambyses and the rise of the magos Bardiya, whom he correctly transliterated as Smerdis,[76] we now realize contains two elements: the basic outline of Darius' propaganda set forth at Bisitun and circulated throughout the empire, and Herodotus' expansion yet violation of that account into an elaborate dramatic logos whereby the hybris of Cambyses was followed by revolution led by the false magos who pretended to be the royal prince Bardiya. This, in turn, set the necessary Herodotean stage for Darius' usurpation of the throne in order to create a powerful and flourishing empire based upon despotic orientalism, which would soon meet its defeat at the hands of the freedom loving Greeks. Herodotus' account, however, markedly conflicts with Darius' own account. Darius claimed that Cambyses had killed Bardiya before he departed for Egypt (DB E and OP 10, B 10), yet Herodotus wrote that Cambyses sent Bardiya from Egypt back to Persia out of envy, and upon his return the prince was murdered (3.30). But where and how, Herodotus did not know exactly and reported two different stories: that Bardiya was assassinated while hunting at Susa or was drowned in the Persian Gulf (3.31.1). As an historical narrative, Herodotus' exposition of these events is historically valueless yet fundamentally essential and important to his dramatic literary development of this basic theme.[77] For the Athenian poet Aeschylus, a contemporary of Darius, the matter was less complex.[78] Bardiya, whom he transliterated as Mardos (or Mardis), the legitimate king and successor to Cambyses, was slain not in battle by Darius but in the royal palace (unnamed but perhaps Susa [Hdt. 3.31.1]) by Darius' half-brother prince Artaphrenes who faithfully supported Darius' usurpation (*Persians* 774-6). These details, Hellanikos of Lesbos also knew (*FGrH* 4 F 181 = *SchoL* Aesch. *Pers.* 778), although he called Artaphrenes, Daphernes (cf. Hdt. 3.78).

The outline of events which Olmstead and Dandamayev[79] present, but which other historians have often ignored,[80] remains valid. The Median conquest of Anshan (Parsa) in 629 B.C. had reduced the petty Persian chiefs Cyrus I (c. 640-600 B.C.) and Ariaramnes (c. 640-615 B.C.)—to common vassalage serving the ruling power in Ecbatana, just as they had served the Assyrian King Ashurbanipal. But while Cyrus' grandson, Cyrus II (the Great) rebelled against the Median overlordship of Astyages in the summer of 554 B.C., the second line under Ariaramnes remained a petty chiefdom, and Darius' grandfather Arsames (c. 615-c. 520/514 B.C.) continued as a local khan in the southern region of Yautiya.[81] Nevertheless, with Cyrus' rebellion against Astyages and his rise to imperial power, Arsames and his son Hystaspes supported the Persian king who, in turn, appointed Hystaspes to the governship of the eastern Parthians and Hyrkanians. With the death of Cyrus the Great at the hands of the eastern nomadic Massagetai, Scythian tribes across the Araxes River whom Hystaspes also battled (Hdt. 1.209.2), Arsames, Hystaspes, and Darius remained loyal to Cyrus' house and their new King Cambyses (August 530 B.C.).[82] Because of that loyalty, Cambyses appointed the young Darius as his personal and honorific spearbearer, and Darius accompanied his king to Egypt (Hdt. 3.139.2; Xen. *Cyr.* 5.2.46).

But, while Cambyses was completing the settlement of Egypt into his imperial system, on March 11, 522 B.C. (Hdt. 2.1-3.38) his brother Bardiya began his challenge for the Achaemenid throne and by July 1 had won over many of the Persians, Medes, Elamites, Babylonians, and several other ethnic groups. Cambyses then quickly departed from Egypt for Parsa and Media but in Palestine died. How he died also rests amidst confusion, and while Darius claimed that Cambyses had committed suicide we may suspect that it was Darius' hand rather than Cambyses' own which dealt the mortal blow.[83] From Palestine, Darius raced to Parsa (Hdt. 3.73) and there, with the support of six noble families and a sizeable Persian army, challenged his royal cousin whom Artaphrenes fatally stabbed. The six privileged Persian families would soon occupy prime places of administration and organization within Darius' Empire. This regicide, consequently, generated the Elamite and Babylonian rebellions, but with Darius' victory over Babylon and the revival of the Chaldean royal house almost the entire empire rebelled against the regicide and usurper and supported their national and legitimate royal resurgents (cf. Hdt. 3.127.1). But against all, by military strength, Darius won and with the support of the conspirators assumed the royal tiara and mounted the Achaemenid throne (Hdt. 3.61-116).

Darius' empire, however, was still not secure. The Egyptians, the Jews, and the peoples of Sparda, the Lydians and the Ionians, were still rebelling; amidst which a new rebellion among the Elamites broke out in the spring of 520 B.C. This was the fourth rebellion within less than two years among the Elamites opposed to Darius. Against the crucial region of Elam and its pivotal capital city of Susa, Darius sent the faithful Persian Gobryas, his father-in-law and one of the six conspirators, to crush that rebellion.[84] The security of Parsa, Media, Elam, Babylonia, and the eastern regions was a fundamental necessity before Darius would wield his imperial strength against the western rebels.

The rebellious events in Sparda and Egypt suggest that the satraps established there by Cyrus and Cambyses remained loyal to Cyrus' royal house and opposed Darius' usurpation. In Egypt, the Persian satrap Aryandes installed by Cambyses opposed Darius (Hdt. 4.165-7, 200, 203) and continued to lead the Egyptian rebellion against the new king until Darius himself invaded in November 519 B.C., killed Aryandes (Hdt. 4.166), replaced him with Pharandates, and for six months Darius himself demonstrated his imperial power there.[85] In demonstration of his rebellion, Aryandes had invaded Libya in a pattern similar to that of Oroites in Sardis who had invaded Cappadocia, Daskyleion, and Samos.[86]

In Judah, Jewish rebels taking advantage of the rampant chaotic conditions throughout the empire also rallied around a legitimate royal faction, similar to the legitimate factions which had arisen in Parsa, Media, Elam, Babylonia, Armenia, Sagartia, Margiana, Hyrkania (?), Parthia, and Arachosia. The Jewish group intrigued to raise to the throne in Jerusalem a descendant of King David, Zerubbabel (Ezra 1-6; Haggai 2:22-3; Zechariah 4:6-10; I Esdras 2:30, 5:4, 7; cf. II. Chron. 36:22-3). To quell this Davidic movement, Tattenai, a high Persian official and the local governor of Judah, ordered work stopped on the rebuilding of the Jerusalem temple.[87] But even though a Jewish embassy sent to Darius argued the right to rebuild the temple, and Darius' secretaries located in Ecbatana the original memorandum dictated by Cyrus to let the Jews rebuild, Darius still took severe measures against the Davidites. The king and not the Jewish community installed the high priest Joshua to govern the subordinate theocratic unit within the Syrian satrapy (Zech. 6:9-15).[88]

In Sparda, Oroites spurred that rebellion. With Bardiya's rise to power in the east while Cambyses was still in Egypt, the Persian satrap Oroites rebelled and attempted to increase his own power and to expand his newly obtained kingdom (Hdt. 3.120-6) in a pattern similar to that of Aryandes in Egypt and the nine other kings noted in the Bisitun texts.[89] Herodotus is unfortunately not precise in regard to the date of Oroites' rebellion and simply noted that it occurred "about the time of Cambyses' sickness" (3.120.1). The "sickness" motif, however, may be attributed to Bardiya's and then Darius' propaganda, the latter issued upon Darius' assumption of the throne and may mask a later date, which would coincide with the uprisings following the death of Bardiya and the second fall of Elam. We may consider, therefore, that in the chaotic thirteen and a half months between Darius' regicide of Bardiya and the final conquest of Babylon and the regicide of Nebuchadrezzar IV, Oroites seized power in Sardis and then struck out against the Persian satrap of northern Daskyleion, the noble Mitrobates and his son Kranaspes, and killed them both (3.126). It is also unfortunately unclear whether they were merely the brunt of Oroites' expansionist policies or were loyal to Darius' claim to the royal throne. At the same time, Oroites campaigned against the Cappadocians and claimed that region, too, for himself (Hdt. 3.127).

Oroites' revolutionary activities also extended to Samos and the tyrant Polykrates who had loyally served Cambyses. In a cruel act of duplicity, Oroites dispatched his Lydian aid, Myrsos the son of Gyges, to bring Polykrates to Magnesia-on-the-Maeander, and there killed and then crucified the Greek tyrant. In addition to the regions of Daskyleion and Cappadocia, Oroites sought control of the Samian regions of the Cyclades (Hdt. 3.122). Herodotus was again extremely vague about these events and failed to hint at the reaction of the other Ionian poleis. His dramatic account of Oroites' rebellion barely hints at the historical substructure, but fortunately the events recorded at Bisitun enable us to uncover the rebellious pattern in Sparda. Herodotus' sources were vague and contradictory and he, too, doubted their veracity about this rebellion, noted the contradiction among them (3.121.1), and warned his readers to "believe what they will" (3.122.1).[90]

Darius' omission within the Bisitun texts of Oroites' revolution and the loss of Daskyleion and Cappadocia, of the problems in Judah, and only the brief mention of the Egyptian revolution, apparently occurred because of his inability to subdue those four regions within the "year" framework of his accession to the throne (Hdt. 3.127.1). But once that throne was secure in Parsa, Media, Babylonia, Elam, and the eastern regions, his subjugation of Sparda, Judah, and Egypt outside of the "one year" framework became relatively unimportant in comparison with the crucial suppression of the fourth Elamite rebellion and Darius' personal campaign against the rebellious eastern Scythians.[91] Within the Bisitun text, Darius was concerned mainly with events east of the Euphrates.

While Darius was occupied with the eastern rebellions, Herodotus claimed that the king sent Oroites a firm command to submit. But rather than recognize Darius as his regal lord, Oroites slew the messenger (3.126). Darius then sent the Persian Bagaios, the son of Artontes, to Sardis and there generated among the Persian guards stationed in that capital city a revolution against Oroites (Hdt. 3.127). Upon hearing Bagaios' reading of the royal edict stamped with Darius' regal seal, "King Darius charges the Persians in Sardis to kill Oroites," the guards cut down the rebellious satrap (Hdt. 3.128.4). Following this success, Darius then sent the Persian general Otanes, one of the six conspirators, to subdue and regain Cappadocia, Daskyleion, Sardis and the Spardian regions including the Ionian poleis. To complete his campaigns, Otanes then led a naval expedition, and, after some bitter fighting in strife torn Samos, raised Syloson, Polykrates' brother, to tyrannical power and restored Samian vassalage to the Achaemenid throne (Hdt. 3.139-49; 6.13.2).[92]   At the same time, Otanes apparently regained Achaemenid lordship over Chios and possibly Lesbos (cf. Hdt. 4.4.138).

Following his usurpation of the Achaemenid throne, Darius quickly set about to reorganize the Empire. The immediate necessity to quell future rebellions, to demand and enforce the vassalage of his satraps, bureaucrats, and subjects to his imperial lordship, and to legitimize his kingship, generated a complex revitalization movement similar to that which I have considered in Lydia with Gyges' accession to the throne. Following the conquests of Sardis and Babylon, during the latter years of Cyrus' reign and through most of Cambyses' reign, until the uprising of Bardiya in March 522 B.C., the conditions of the steady state existed throughout the Achaemenid Empire. For the vast majority of the numerous ethnic populations, the retention of local administrators, social and cultural practices, and the restoration of religious liberties, satisfied sufficiently their local needs and desires whereby their various regions could function. The small degrees of chronic stress within the then loosely structured Achaemenid imperial system remained within tolerable limits. But with the rapid series of events ushered in by Bardiya's rebellion in March, Cambyses' death in July, Bardiya's death in September, and the advent of twenty-five rebellions following Darius' conquest of Babylon in November 522 B.C., disruption of that steady state rapidly projected the empire through the period of increased individual stress into a period of cultural distortion.

The rebellions had produced acute political, economic, social, and religious uncertainties throughout the various imperial regions with violent disruption to the institution of Achaemenid kingship. Moderate degrees of individual stress accelerated and social anxiety increased, as imperial controls disintegrated and temporarily failed to produce satisfactory changes within cultural patterns. From eastern Sattagydia and Arachosia to western Egypt, Sparda, and Samos, stress led to critical levels of cultural distortion whereby satisfactory techniques failed to alter or relieve cultural anxieties accentuated by the rapidly changing political and military events. The process of societal deterioration was checked, however, by Darius' final victories over Nebuchadrezzar IV, the last Elamite rebel Atamaita, Oroites, and Aryandes. Darius checked the twenty-eight attested factional disputes segmenting the state, from Bardiya's rebellion in March 522 B.C. to the suppression of Aryandes' rebellion in November 519 B.C., by instituting reform, reorganization, and new cultural patterns to restructure the secular and religious elements and their subsystems within the critically distorted imperial societies.

Intrinsic to Wallace's analysis of a revitalization movement, which produces a new steady state, are six major societal innovations, each of which is identifiable within Darius' reorganization of the Achaemenid empire. The first, a complex-societal reform-ulation, is a restructuring of the institutional elements and their subsystems, which had already attained common acceptance among the majority of the ethnic regions. Their new form, a reorganization of the earlier mode which had constituted an internally consistent structure, however, is both abrupt and dramatic. The reorganization, in this instance, occurs at the direction of the leader rather than grows out of group deliberation. New leadership and sudden change are the primary characteristics in this alteration of the familiar institutional forms and their functions. The second task is communication: the dissemination of the doctrines that the society will benefit by the acceptance of the new complex-societal reformulation. At this step, the new leader declares that the collective society has or will come under the care and protection of a supernatural being.

To inaugurate the reorganization, the leader undertakes the third task, organization, whereby he gathers about him a small group of people who are persuaded by the arguments and principles and accept him. Expediency and opportunity in addition to emotional appeal are often important factors, which the small group considers in its support of the revitalization movement and the new leadership. The fourth task, adapta-tion, accompanies these first three and emphasizes the complexities of the reformulation processes. As the new movement is revolutionary and generative in its organization, it is almost inevitable that it will encounter resistance. The resistance, therefore, as a positive and resourceful phenomenon challenges the reformulation movement to adopt various new strategies of adaptation: doctrinal modification, political and diplomatic maneuvers, or force. As Wallace noted, "these strategies are not mutually exclusive nor, once chosen, are they necessarily maintained through the life of the movement. In most instances the original doctrine is continuously modified . . ." by the leader.[93]

As the controlling administrators and other subordinates within the empire accept the complex-societal reformulation, the fifth task of cultural transformation occurs whereby a noticeable social revitalization reduces earlier and still present factors of increased individual stress and the resulting and accumulative cultural distortion. While some factors are eliminated others result in successful projects of further social, political or economic reform. Some of these projects, however, are momentary and circumstances often lead to their later failure or defeat. If the reforms are successful, the sixth task is accomplished, the routinization of various economic, social, and political institutions and customs which become normative. "Once cultural transformation has been accomplished and the new cultural system has proved itself viable, and once the movement organization has solved its problems of routinization, a new steady state may be said to exist. The culture of this state will probably be different in pattern, organization . . . , as well as in traits, from the earlier steady state; it will be different from that of the period of cultural distortion."[94]   Each step outlined above can be detected within Darius' revolution, his development of kingship, and the reorganization of the empire and specifically of Sparda.

To these basic principles of revitalization movements, I.C. Jarvie, considering similar stages of stress, distortion, leadership, and reorganization, added three additional stages, which also clarify our understanding of the complex events in Persia initiated in 522 B.C.[95]   Jarvie noted that once the collective experiences of stress and distortion generate a movement in which the leader and his followers interact, several different movements can arise contemporaneously and produce many other revolutions. To this we can relate the twenty-eight rebellions throughout the Persian empire. Jarvie's second point notes that within the revitalization movement each leader, successful or not, believes his cause to be true; a doctrine not created out of fancy or simple personal desire but to solve specific problems, in essence to resolve a complex problematic issue. Jarvie's third point indicates that once the circumstances generated the situation ripe for a revitalization movement, attempts to explain the new order in traditional terms produced anacronistic Sagen, for example the traditions gathered by Herodotus, which helped to develop the organization necessary for the new movement.

Like Augustus and his reforms in Rome, Darius set in motion at the beginning of his reign a reform program, which gradually developed, altered, and changed. In Egypt many legal aspects were not initiated until 503 B.C., in Babylonia fiscal reform occurred in 500/499 B.C., and in Sparda was eventually finalized in 493 B.C. with the registry of land, military forces, and taxation. By the time of the Persian expedition to Marathon (490 B.C.), Sparda lay tightly within Darius' imperial controls.

II

The King

Bardiya's claim to the Persian throne on the 11th of March, 522 B.C. violently upset the steady state previously developed by Cyrus and Cambyses.[96] Parsa, Media, Elam, Babylonia, and the other regions in rebellion against Cambyses rapidly set in motion the forces of individual stress and societal distortion. While the extreme western and eastern regions apparently remained loyal to Cambyses, the records indicate that as early as the 14th of April, the Babylonians hailed Bardiya as king.[97] The Babylonians from whom Cyrus had gained a triumphal entry in 539 B.C., and for whom Cambyses was crowned King of Babylon to celebrate the ageless Babylonian New Year's festival (akitu),[98] openly or coercively repudiated Cambyses and rallied around his princely brother.

Dandamayev has persuasively suggested that Bardiya's rebellion against Cambyses marked the bitter struggle between a strong centralized royal leadership and the Persian nobles' demands for participation in that leadership[99] (Plate 1). The failure of Cambyses' military expedition against Nubia (Hdt. 2.25) marked the turn of the nobles and the army against the king, and in a bold attempt to ingratiate himself with the disgruntled nobles, Bardiya declared a remission of taxes for three years (Hdt. 3.67.3). Individual stress among the nobles generated by Cambyses' actions quickly produced the societal

Plate 1. Persian nobleman from Parsa, east staircase, apadana, Persepolis (photograph by author)

distortion to which Bardiya reacted by seizing the Achaemenid throne. Basic Zarathustrian principles stressed that the state was a federation under the control of a council of leading representatives and not under the control of a single ruler, and these Cambyses apparently violated.[100] But Bardiya's rebellion also generated Darius' claim to the throne. Cyrus' imperial strength had rested upon his cooperation with the nobles and his utilization of them within his imperial structure, still developing and loosely organized. For Bardiya and later for Darius, Cambyses ruled as the cruel despot, a sick old man, an epileptic; events of a reign essentially incorrect[101] but persuasive in the propaganda disseminated by Bardiya and sustained by Darius. The problem rested not in Egypt in the early months of 522 B.C. but in Parsa. Bardiya's rebellion erupted as a fraternal quarrel resulting in political chaos of which his distant cousin Darius took advantage. Each prince had his loyal noble supporters and with the death of Cambyses Darius' position became stronger.[102] Darius immediately branded Bardiya an impostor, and with the successful aid of six Persian nobles killed the king and quickly reduced the extensive rebellions throughout the empire. As Dandamayev noted, from the beginning to the end the death of Bardiya was the work of the tribal nobles, and this Aeschylus knew stating that Darius' half-brother prince Artaphrenes slew Bardiya in the royal palace.

This Persian yet universal conflict between a strong monarchy and the aristocracy Herodotus wove into his interpretation of the events. The romantic speech by the conspirator Otanes emphasized the self-determination of the people while a second conspirator Megabyzos urged the continuation of aristocratic rule (Hdt. 3.71-84).[103] Darius' success, we may conclude, rested firmly upon the support of the conspirators, their emphasis upon aristocratic participation, and upon Darius' acute awareness of the conspirators' importance to his regicide, usurpation, and revitalization of the empire. This, Herodotus understood. Darius, consequently, felt compelled by the circumstances of his revolution to have inscribed later upon the face of his tomb at Naqsh-i Rustam (OP DNb) his personal justification, the motive for his rule, and the ideological bases for his kingship.[104] Ahura Mazda, Darius claimed, had established the Ordinance of Good Regulations, which became manifest in happiness, wisdom, and the king. The king, therefore, ruled fairly, justly, and without anger. Basic to that rule was the cooperation of the king with men who would act in accord with the divine rules, and the king as established by those rules. The king was friend to the right, and foe to the wrong, a help to friends, and protector of both the weak and the strong. The men the king sought were similar to himself: good battle fighters, fighters of rebellion, good horsemen, and good bowmen and spearmen on foot and on horse. Assistance would be rewarded and wrong doers would be punished.

The nobles who supported Bardiya's rebellion against Cambyses forced other nobles to rally around Darius, and the latter won. The individual stress, which arose among the leading tribal nobles, generated the societal distortion to which Darius responded. Basic to his revitalization movement, which produced the reorganization of the Persian Empire, were the conspirators who formed the "Gang of Seven" and the other nobles loyal to Darius' cause. At first those loyal to Darius, in addition to the six conspirators, such as Darius' father Hystaspes as satrap of Parthia,[105] were joined by the Persian nobles Hydarnes,[106] Vaumisa,[107] Dadarshi the satrap of Bactria,[108] Artavardiya,[109] Vivana the satrap in Arachosia,[110] and by the key foreign nobles Dadarshi of Armenia[111] and Takhmaspada of Media.[112] Following their victories with the death of the rebels and their nobles, other came into Darius' fold by persuasion and coercion. And with the death of Nebuchadrezzar IV in Babylon on November 27, 521 B.C., Darius responded positively to his nobles' support, their desires and demands, and, consequently, set in motion an extensive revitalization movement, the reorganization of the empire.

Darius immediately set about to restructure the institutional elements and their subsystems in the empire's heartland, Parsa, Media, Elam, and Babylonia, and among the several widely scattered imperial ethnic regions, from Arachosia to Sparda. New concepts of king and kingship ranked foremost in Darius' reformulation of the imperial structure. At Bisitun, consequently, artisans began to prepare a section of the mountain's southern face for the pictorial and epigraphic presentation of the new leadership. By April 519 B.C. work had begun at Bisitun and continued for about eighteen months.[113] Both the relief and the texts sustained recognizable earlier forms. The schema followed the traditional formulae of the Babylonian and Assyrian kings, into which Darius several times echoed a regal Armenian (Urartian) formula: "With god . . . have I these things in a year accomplished."[114] The relief, too, closely paralleled an earlier Akkadian era monument at Sar-i Pul, eighty km. west of Bisitun on the same caravan route from Ecbatana to Babylon. That monument carved in the twenty-second century B.C. to exalt the victory of King Anubanini of the Lullubi and his praise of the goddess Inanna, had also been based upon earlier and established traditions.[115] With his bow in his left hand and his left foot upon his enemy, amidst eight other enemies bound in fetters, Anubanini hailed Inanna who extended to him the ring of kingship. But at Bisitun, Darius, bearing his bow in triumph[116] over the imploring Bardiya beneath his left foot before eight additional enslaved rebels, altered the traditional form and raised his right hand not to an Assyro-Babylonian divinity but to a new Achaemenid symbol, the anthropomorphic winged ring, the encircled sacred *xvarnah*.[117] Based upon an earlier Assyro-Babylonian concept, the awe of the terrifying sheen or mask with which gods, kings, and even temples were clothed, this *xvarnah* also symbolized Darius' regal lineage, the collective kingship of the royal Achaemenid house, which extended to him the Great King's ring, the symbol of cosmic power and the source of kingship. A. Shapur Shahbazi has recently suggested that the winged figure is indeed a divine figure representing the heroic King Achaemenes through whom Darius claimed his royal *xvarnah*. But once Darius had established his own power, his need to rely upon a remote ancestor became unnecessary. On Darius' Naqsh-i Rustam tomb relief, the winged daemon is Darius himself, and on Xerxes' tomb relief nearby the *xvarnah* wears Darius' crenelated crown.[118] At Bisitun, behind Darius, in support of the new kingship and representative of the "Gang of Seven" and the broad base of noble Persian support of Darius' accession to the throne, stand Aspathines and the conspirator Gobryas. Gobryas played a special role in Darius' usurpation. As the king's closest friend he perhaps helped to mastermind the plot. While the elements of the relief and inscriptions sustained millennia old forms, Darius' schema for Bisitun was abrupt, dramatic, and perhaps the product of his mind alone.

To mark this change, Darius also commanded the construction of a new regal center. Pasargadae had served Cyrus, Cambyses, and Bardiya as a coronation center and royal residence,[119] yet Darius ordered elaborate architectural plans for a new palatial center, Persepolis. In Babylon, the ageless akitu festival would still be conducted in the Esagila ziggurat dedicated to Marduk-Bel,[120] but at Persepolis the Persian Now Ruz or New Year's festival would mark each vernal equinox, and the annually renewed vice-gerency of Ahura Mazda upon Darius and his successors.[121] Persepolis functioned as the crux between the divinely appointed king, that Aryan, that Achaemenid crowned by the

Righteousness and Truth, the legitimate kingship, and the people, the Medes and Persians and all the Asiatic peoples whom Darius ruled (cf. Arrian *An.* 2.7.6). For "Darius the Great King, King of Kings,[122] king of nations, son of Hystaspes, an Achaemenian . . . " (DPa), "Great Ahura Mazda, the greatest of gods—created Darius is King, he bestowed on him the kingdom, by the favor of Ahura Mazda Darius the King. Saith Darius the King: This country Parsa which Ahura Mazda bestowed upon me, good, possessed of good horses, possessed of good men—by the favor of Ahura Mazda and of me, Darius the King, does not feel fear of (any) other. Saith Darius the King: May Ahura Mazda bear me aid, with the gods of the royal house; and may Ahura Mazda protect this country from a (hostile) army, from famine, from the Lie! Upon this country may there not come an army, nor famine, nor the Lie; this I pray as a boon from Ahura Mazda together with the gods of the royal house. This boon may Ahura Mazda together with the gods of the royal house give to me!"(DPd).

At Persepolis, the iconography of the enthroned king prevailed, and upon the reliefs at Bisitun, Persepolis, and Naqsh-i Rustam, Darius himself represented the empire impressively slaying its enemies and receiving its tribute-bearers. The monarch cloaked in the vestments of sacred kingship sat upon the throne and platform under the sacral and royal *xvarnah* woven into a canopy of embroidered god and prophyry cloth supported by four gold posts (Ath. *Deip.* 12.514C). The same throne platform also formed the central relief of Darius' tomb at Naqsh-i Rustam, and upon each royal Achaemenid tomb thereafter, to the last, that of Artaxerxes III, 359-338/7 B.C.[123] In each, the king stands upon a small raised dais placed upon a large sacred platform which is carried, raised in the air, literally borne by the national representatives of the empire whom it nourished and protected. The platform is carried toward the *xvarnah*, the living king's regal ancestor, kingship flying within the royal ring of the world who extends to the worshipping king the sacral kingship. In turn, the living king, as at Bisitun, raises his right hand toward the *xvarnah* in a gesture of his cosmocratic power, that fundamental link between heaven and earth, and the nations which bear him. To the right, rests the king's sacred Zarathustrian fire altar, above which is the crescent moon embracing the sun.[124]

Darius' kingship was also heroic. While his new Achaemenid art motifs continued the Neo-Assyrian and Neo-Babylonian styles, Darius introduced the king as hero, identified by his attire.[125]   The royal force symbolized by the royal tiara and the royal beard

overcame the violent forces of nature, monsters, horned griffin-lions with scorpion tails,

bulls and lions, the bull who fought the oppressive lion,[126] symbols within a ceremonial

palace constructed upon a geometric axis for the specific determination of the Now Ruz

celebration, newly fundamental to the kingship sustained within.[127]

Sovereignty, rule, and kingship, in essence the royal tiara of the Achaemenid Empire

in toto and in each of its satrapies, and everything they contained, their peoples, palaces,

and treasuries, became embodied in Darius' new and dramatic concept of the sacral

heroic king.   For the people, Darius functioned as the key link between them and Ahura

Mazda and the other gods whom they served.   He was the force through whom Ahura

Mazda regulated the state.[128]   For the representatives of those people, those who bore

the enthroned king and who offered their annual gifts at the sacral vernal Now Ruz

festival, the king sat upon his "royal throne beneath the golden vault of heaven" (Plut.

Alex. 37.7).[129]   For Aeschylus and other Greeks who knew Darius and his royal son

Xerxes, the Persians, they claimed, regarded their kings as gods or like gods (Pers. 80,

150, 157, 634, 643, 711, 856).

Darius' new concept of Achaemenid kingship rested directly upon Persian Sagen, the

oral traditions which formed the bases of secular epics.   The Persian magoi who

transmitted the singing of theogonies (Hdt. 1.132) also recited the Sagen of Cyrus (Xen.

Cyr. 1.2.1), and developed the traditions of the western Iranian heroes, which ultimately

influenced the eastern Iranian traditions, which the poet Firdousi wove into his great

heroic epic, the Shah-Nameh.[130]   To parallel other Near Eastern traditions of great kings

and leaders rising from humble origins, Sargon I of Akkad,[131] Joseph[132] and Moses,[133]

for example, about Darius traditions also arose to indicate his humble rather than

princely origins.   Like Lydian and East Greek Sagen elaborating Gyges' origins as a

shepherd (Plato. Rep. 2.359d–e) or as the king's bodyguard (Hdt. 1.8), similar Iranian oral

traditions stressed Darius' humble origins as a horseman who won the kingship, the "horse

trick" (Hdt. 3.85-8), and the bodyguard motif (Hdt. 3.139.2; Xen. Cyr. 5.2.46).[134]

The oral traditions, which grew out of the Persian world of vassalage and

Heldensagen, intertwined with the early Zarathustrian Gāthās, Yashts and the other early

oral aspects of the Avesta.   Of these, the magoi chanted the theogonies and the heroic

Sagen, the exploits of the gods and great men for the edification of the noble youths

(Xen. *Cyr*. 1.2.1; Strabo 15.3.13). For the heroes of the royal house in the *Avesta*, chapters 9-11 of the *Yasnas*, the *xvarnah*, the fiery glory of kingship (*Yasht* 19), generating the Iranian national spirit and chronicles, molded the traditional role for the model king, the founders of dynasties, the reorganizers of dynasties, the creators of political and social institutions, and aristocratic education.[135] The social forces, which developed the Bronze Age oral traditions into the Homeric epics and the Ionian Sagen in the eighth and seventh centuries B.C., were, in essence, similar to those which developed the Zarathustrian principles basic to the Heldensagen of Cyrus and Darius.[136] As George G. Cameron noted: "The Achaemenids felt very keenly their debt to the past and built upon past experiences more explicitly than did the Assyrians. One finds repeatedly the attitude: 'Here is something new, something good for what was not good before, justice where there was injustice.' "[137]

Darius' development of the centralized kingship necessitated the cooperation and imperial utilization of not only the six conspirators but also the other nobles, Persian and Median, for whom the new Iranian concepts of kingship had specific meaning. The early Assyrian title "King of Kings"[138] adopted by Darius also drew extensively upon the Urartian and Median titles "King," "Great King," "King of Kings" and the accompanying concepts of power, leadership, the royal *xvarnah*, and the regions of the empire.[139] Thus, the opening lines of Darius' tomb inscription at Naqsh-i Rustam (DNa:1) emphasized both the Median regal inheritance and Darius' adoption of the Zarathustrian religious principles: "A great god is Ahura Mazda, who created this earth, who created yonder sky, who created man, who created happiness for man, who made Darius King, one king of many, one lord of many."[140] But more important is the emphasis at Naqsh-i Rustam, as throughout the Bisitun text, upon Darius' leadership of the nobility and the implicit realization that his usurpation and the subsequent revitalization of the Persian Empire necessitated the cooperation and participation of the nobility in the development of the imperial reorganization. It was, as Plutarch would note for Cyrus the Younger, a kingship as the hegemony of the Persians (*Per*. 24.7). Darius' kingship, his interaction with his leading nobles, and noble support of his revitalization parallel, but on a more extensive scale, the revitalization movement in Lydia led by Gyges more than a century and a half earlier. Darius' rule centered upon the complex interrelationships between a king and his nobles, lord and vassals, lordship and vassalage; an interrelationship in which the king functioned as the strong and successful innovator.

Throughout the Avestan texts, the descriptions of kingship strongly indicate that while the king's rule was legalistic it was not arbitrary. The king was clearly bound to the acknowledged obligations entered into with his vassals, obligations which modified his rule. In the *Mihr Yasht*, the king in command of many nations ruled in council with the first men of those nations,[141] a lord-vassalage condition, which prevailed in central Asia in the sixth century B.C.[142] Darius ruled with authority but was also bound to duties and his own lordship undertakings, for as his state of affairs reflected cosmic order, the eternal Zarathustrian law of righteousness (ṛta) obtained primacy.[143] Out of the early centuries of nomadic life and the fundamental structures of vassalage developed the principles of "primitive aristocratic vassalage" as suggested at Godin Tepe. These, in turn, produced in the late sixth century B.C. royal Achaemenid concepts, the principles of order and rightness that governed the natural world and directed society. The ruling imperial power of the king necessitated vassalage loyalty and obligation to him. As the agent of justice and righteousness on earth, the vice-gerent of Ahura Mazda, the king strove against the Evil and the Lie.[144] Between the king and his vassals lay the important covenant, contract, or pact, the agreement entered into by noble men with rich religious and moral overtones; loyalty to the ethical aspects of early Zarathustrianism. Thus, covenant as a philosophical and religious concept had become personified as the god Mithra,[145] to whom Cyrus may have been personally devoted.[146] Darius, however, shifted the Achaemenid regal emphasis from Mithra to Ahura Mazda, a basic principle within his revitalization movement, yet retained Mithra as one of the unnamed supporting gods, symbolized as the sun upon his tomb. Several decades later, Xerxes set about to purge the religion of the pre-Zarathustrian Indo-Iranian deities (X Ph), to emphasize Ahura Mazda and his righteous guardian Mithra.[147]

Iranian kingship, both Median and Persian, interwove inherited socio-political and sacral aspects, aspects of its Indo-European origin and the influences exercised upon it by Assyro-Babylonian culture. The election or selection of a king was restricted to candidates from a specific family, as was the case among Germanic tribes. In counterbalance, the group or assembly, which elected or selected the king, represented the larger body of people and served as the noble class fit for military service, the horsemen and infantry. The king's authority remained restricted and dependent upon the support first by his own family, second by his personal followers, and third by his military

retine.   The king's authority, therefore, interacted with the significant influence

exercised by the vassal lords. The king, consequently, functioned as primus inter pares,

the King of Kings, with the vassal lords themselves ruling as petty kings or nobles in

various parts of the empire. The council of the six conspirators may have advised Darius

but it is doubtful that it became a regular bureaucratic institution. His companions were

simply his friends, yet ranked above the many Achaemenid princes, and the other

Persian, Median, and non-Iranian nobles.   Their position at court remained more

important than their military or bureaucratic office.[148]

The king, as lord of vassals, was also different, in principle holy and inviolable,

protected by the unwritten religious law, which Bardiya and Darius transgressed. Darius'

regicide and usurpation, nevertheless, were sacrilegious acts liable to punishment. At

Bisitun, Naqsh-i Rustam, and Persepolis, consequently, Darius purposely omitted the acts

of regicide and usurpation, created the false and wicked magos Gaumata, and stressed his

rightful inheritance of the throne through the divine sanction of Ahura Mazda and

through the concerted efforts of the six conspirators whose importance he could not

omit. At Bisitun, Darius displayed his regal *xvarnah* arising from the eponymous heroic

King Achaemenes, and at Naqsh-i Rustam the *xvarnah* as himself in close relationship

with the Zarathustrian fire altar and his celestial brothers the sun and moon. Darius

ruled as the vice-gerent of Ahura Mazda, the elect of the gods and the noble vassals.

Darius' holy status carved into stone reflected the developing court ceremonials and

insignia of his royalty, which had their origins among the Assyrians and Babylonians, and

more directly among the Medes and court ceremony and insignia at Ecbatana. Under the

gold and porphyry canopy supported by four gold poles, the king sat upon a gold throne

(Plut. *Them.* 13.1) with his feet resting upon a gold stool (Dinon *FGrH* 690 F 26).[149] He

alone wore a porphyry edged white tunic (Ath. *Deip.* 12.38, 12.40, 13.10; Xen. *Cyr.*

8.3.13), a porphyry mantle, scarlet trousers, red stockings, and blue shoes.[150] About his

upright crenelated tiara, dark purple variegated with white (Curtius 3.3.17), a fillet

marked the king holding a gold scepter (Esther 5.2, 8.4; Xen. *Cyr.* 8.7.13).[151] In the

palace, he walked beneath a gold parasol (Plut. *Them.* 16.3) before his chamberlains

bearing the royal napkin and fly wisk (Diod. Sic. 11.69.1; Plut. *Reg. imp. Apophtheg.*

173E), and ushers and mace-bearers holding knobbed staffs and wearing gold torques

(Hdt. 3.84, 113; Xen. *Cyr*. 8.4.2). His ensign bore an imperial golden eagle with outspread wings mounted upon a long shaft (Xen. *Cyr*. 7.1.3; cf. Aesch. *Pers*. 205-9).[152] In the south palace of Persepolis, the king lived in godlike seclusion (Justin 1.1.9), the epitome of royal authority (Aesch. *Pers*. 691), leading a successful life among the Persians, like a god (*Pers*. 711). "The invincible Darius equal to god ruled the land" (*Pers*. 855-6).[153] He was the King of Asia who ruled over his subjects (Xen. *Cyr*. 8.1.6) to whom he awarded honor and benefactions, marks of their servitude and vassalage (Esther 4.3; Hdt. 3.138, 140, 5.11, 8.85, 9.107; Thuc. 1.138). He was also a god born in Susa for the Persians (Aesch. *Pers*. 643), god's counselor called by god for the Persians, to steer well the noble armies (*Pers*. 654-6). But his court was inaccessible to most of his subjects (Esther; Xen. *Cyr*. 7.5.41), with no one allowed before the presence of the king and everything arranged by means of messengers (Hdt. 1.99). Those who did come before him bowed low, the proskynesis or homage adopted from the Median and Assyrian courts, not prostration but a kiss by the hand reserved for gods and kings.[154]

The king divinely appointed and sacrosanct sacrificed for the well being of his people and performed the important priestly functions at the Zarathustrian fire altars (Xen. *Cyr*. 8.5.26).[155] At the Now Ruz festival in the context of mythic-ritual he slew mythical monsters thereby creating fertility for the world. His mace and dagger served as the tools of righteous power over evil.[156] At his coronation at Pasargadae at the hands of the Persian magoi (Plut. *Arta*. 3.1) the king gained his royal and priestly robes, and at the Now Ruz transferred to Persepolis annually reenacted his assumption to the throne as cosmic ruler dressed in the dual nature of his secular and sacred garb. At death, his personal regal fire was extinguished and his body prepared for the stone tomb at Naqsh-i Rustam to protect his royal body inviolate with *xvarnah*. Nearby, the Ka^cbah tower, constructed about 500 B.C., housed his royal and sacral robes and regal paraphernalia.[157]

God-like, the vice-gerent of Ahura Mazda and the other gods, Darius increased his imperial legitimacy through a cautious and successful cooperation with his nobles. Fundamental to this interrelationship was Darius' royal harem.[158] Often the center of intrigue, rebellion, and assassination, the harem served an important role in binding the throne close to the noble families, and tying Darius to the legitimate Persian royal line, which he had overthrown (figs. 6-13). Among the numerous marriages contracted with the first ladies of the Persian nobility, Darius' marriage with Atossa, which placed her as sovereign queen, was crucial. Atossa was Cyrus' daughter in whom the legitimate royal blood flowed, and was also queen of Cambyses and Bardiya. With her came the other noble women in Cambyses' and Bardiya's harem to link Darius by dynastic marriages and assert his legitimacy (Hdt. 3.88).[159] He also brought into his harem Artystone, a second daughter of Cyrus hitherto unmarried, who bore him a cherished daughter also named Artystone; and Parmys, Bardiya's daughter. To bind himself closely with his conspirators, Darius also married Otanes' daughters, Phaidyme (Hdt. 3.68.3) and Amastris (Hdt. 9.108-13), who had also been in the harem of Bardiya and who would ultimately enter the harem of King Xerxes; and the daughter of his faithful and chosen lancebearer, Gobryas (Hdt. 7.2.2). Among the other important women Darius gained was Nitetis, the daughter of the Egyptian Pharaoh Hophra (Gk. Apries) who bound Darius into the legitimate Saïte royal line, which Amasis had overthrown (Hdt. 3.1, 10).

Darius' harem, an important royal institution, functioned fourfold. It bound Darius into the royal line of Cyrus, Cambyses, and Bardiya, and enabled him to assert further his newly attained legitimacy won on the battlefields and demonstrated at Bisitun. It also bound Darius to his conspirators and his supporting nobles, and emphasized Darius' important and fundamentally necessary reliance upon them. The harem also produced children, men to go out into the provincial regions and assist the king's rule, and women to marry nobles and conquered princes. For Darius, Queen Atossa bore four sons and two daughters, Gobryas' daughter bore three sons, and princess Artystone bore two sons and a daughter.[160] Three of his royal daughters, Darius gave in marriage to his military commanders Daurises, Hymaies, and the conspirator Otanes (Hdt. 5.116). Cambyses' rejection of noble involvement in royal rule forcefully molded Darius' recognition of noble participation in the imperial administration. Finally, the harem bound Darius legitimately to the royal houses he overthrew and linked their conquered regions as vassal states to the king. It is extremely unfortunate that we do not know whether Lydian or Ionian noble women entered Darius' royal harem, yet we may suspect that they did enter the satrapal harem at Sardis (Plut. Them. 31.2).

Key within Darius' harem, as it traveled from Babylon, to Persepolis, Susa, and Ecbatana on its seasonal move (Xen. Cyr. 8.6.22), was Atossa. Herodotus (7.3) called her "all powerful" and Aeschylus hailed her as "O Lady, Queen, whom the Persians revere"

(Pers. 623). For Aeschylus, she was also "consort of the god of the Persians and mother of their god" (Pers. 156-7, implicit in lines 150 and 152) who bore to the purple the royal son and heir apparent, prince Xerxes. Like the romantic Queen Esther, Atossa held an important role as adviser and respected sage. In Persian imperial history, she was rivalled only by the wife of King Darius II, the Queen Parysatis who bore thirteen children, nine of whom died young, and of the four survivors two were boys (Xen. An. 1.1.1)[161] As consort Atossa ranked as the king's chief wife and mistress of the harem, and as queen mother after Darius' death her influence increased as she dominated her son Xerxes. In the history of western civilization, Atossa ranks with Queen Eleanor of Aquitaine.

Like Bathsheba, Atossa ruled the harem, and like Livia and Agrippina exerted tremendous force behind the throne. With Darius' death in November 486 B.C., harem plots thickened as Gobryas' daughter asserted the claims of her sons Ariamenes and Ariabignes (fig. 12). As satrap of crucial Bactria, Ariamenes set out to contest Xerxes' claim to the royal tiara, but the crown prince won over his half-brother with gifts and the promise that he would be second in the empire. Xerxes' ploy worked; Ariamenes placed the tiara upon Xerxes' head and remaining loyal became the Admiral-in-Chief of the Persian Imperial Fleet (Plut. Reg. imp. apoptheg. 173B; De Amor. frat. 448D). Atossa had worked through the Achaemenid nobles Artabanes, son of Hystaspes and brother of Darius, and Artaphrenes, Darius' half-brother and also Hystaspes' son, and ultimately satrap of Sparda (figs. 3, 22). The cooperation among the "Gang of Seven" and their descendants had begun to break down and generate vicious harem politics, which would plague the Achaemenid royal house until its demise.

The harem, therefore, was an institution fundamental to the integral parts of Darius' empire and his lordship over the Persian and imperial nobles. As on the Greek "Darius Vase" in the Naples Museum (c. 350 B.C.), Darius ranked below the gods but on a level with the important nobles of the empire. Below them were the ordinary people of the empire who delivered to the king their contributions and beseeched him for succor.[162] Noble women who entered the harem, and harem children who married nobles or served in the imperial government and army, reinforced that concordat which Darius established with the Persian nobles following his regicide and usurpation, and which was fundamental to the return to the condition of the steady state and his reorganization of the Persian Empire.

Achaemenid Genealogy for Western Anatolia
During the Late Sixth and the Fifth Centuries B.C.[*]

The genealogy of the royal Achaemenid family is both complicated and incomplete. Until all the Persepolis Fortification Tablets are published and analyzed it will be impossible to correlate the names in Herodotus' *History* with the few published names found in the PTT and the PFT. Thucydides and Xenophon assist in adding names for the late fifth and the early fourth centuries B.C. While Ktesias' historical and archaeological observations are essentially incorrect, it may be that his harem tittle–tattle has merit, and that his genealogical information may also have merit.[163] In the following charts (figs. 2-23) I have given the familiar Greek names of the Achaemenid khans, kings, queens, men, women, sons, and daughters. The stem khans are in medium type, the ruling kings in bold type, and the others in small type. In figs. 3-23, I have noted Kübler's entries with K numbers. This assists in identifying each person correctly, especially those who have the same name. Following R. Hallock, I have linked the Aramaic inscription "Seal of Farnaka, Son of Rshama" with Darius' grandfather Arsames and his uncle Pharnakes I (fig. 3) and the hereditary satraps of Daskyleion (fig. 23). Darius' royal line (figs. 2-5) should be read together, and similarly the complicated harem interconnection (figs. 6-13) should be read together. Rather than complicate the charts beyond legibility, I have tried to design readable genealogical relationships, and have often repeated key persons to facilitate that legibility. Many of the aids to Darius I and Xerxes I will be found in figs. 14-21, but certainly not all. Fig. 22 contains the satraps of Sparda to the end of the fifth century B.C., and fig. 23, the satraps of Daskyleion.

---

[*]Based upon the study of Paul Kübler, "Die persische Politik gegenüber dem Griechentum in der Pentekontaetia," an unpublished inaugural dissertation, Ruprecht-Karl-Universität, Heidelberg, 1950.

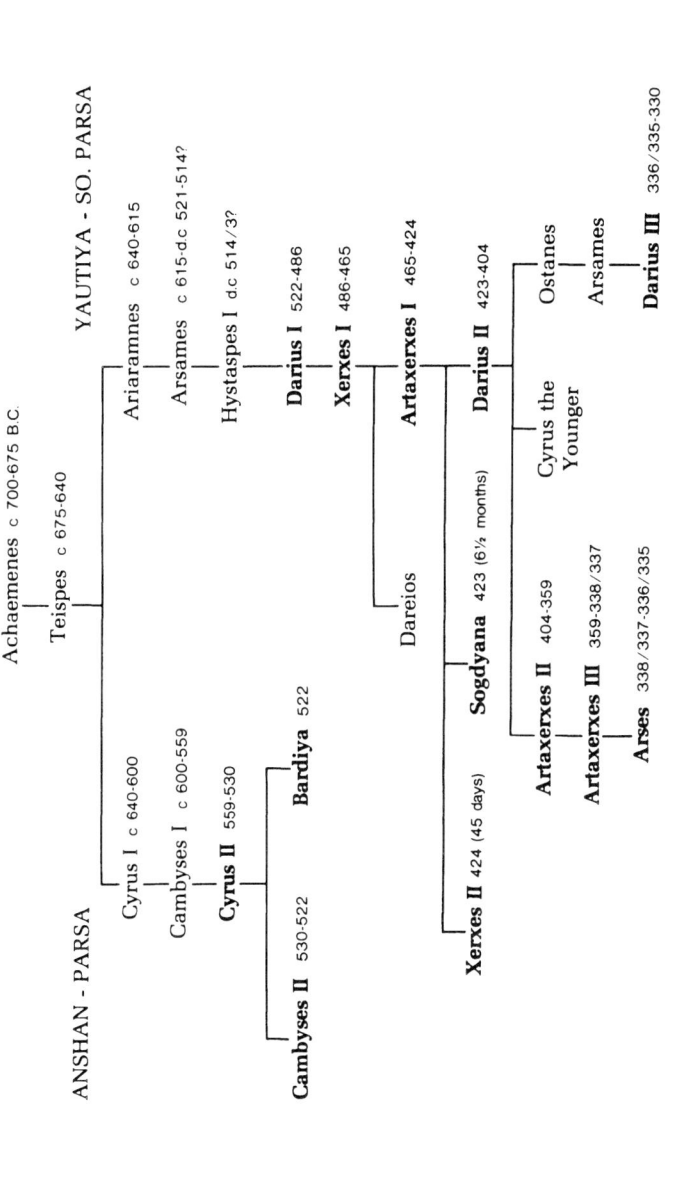

Figure 2. Achaemenid Royal Family

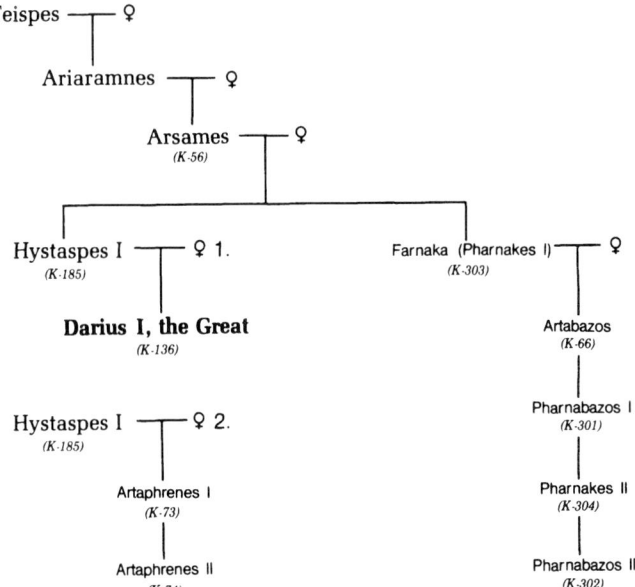

Figure 3

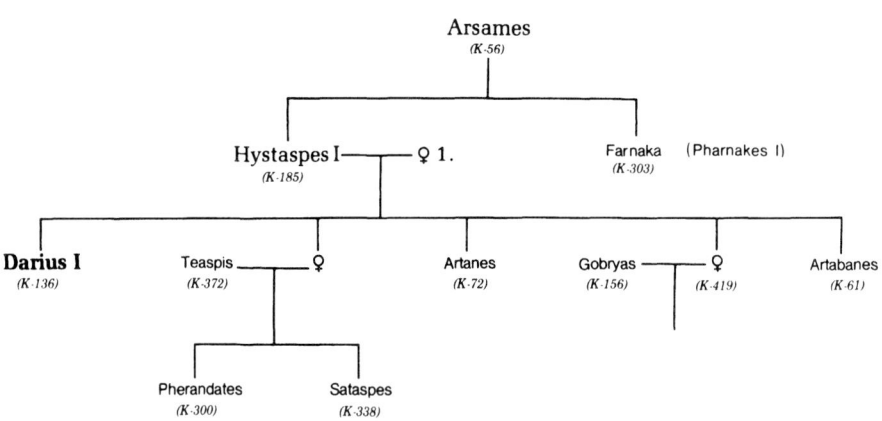

Figure 4

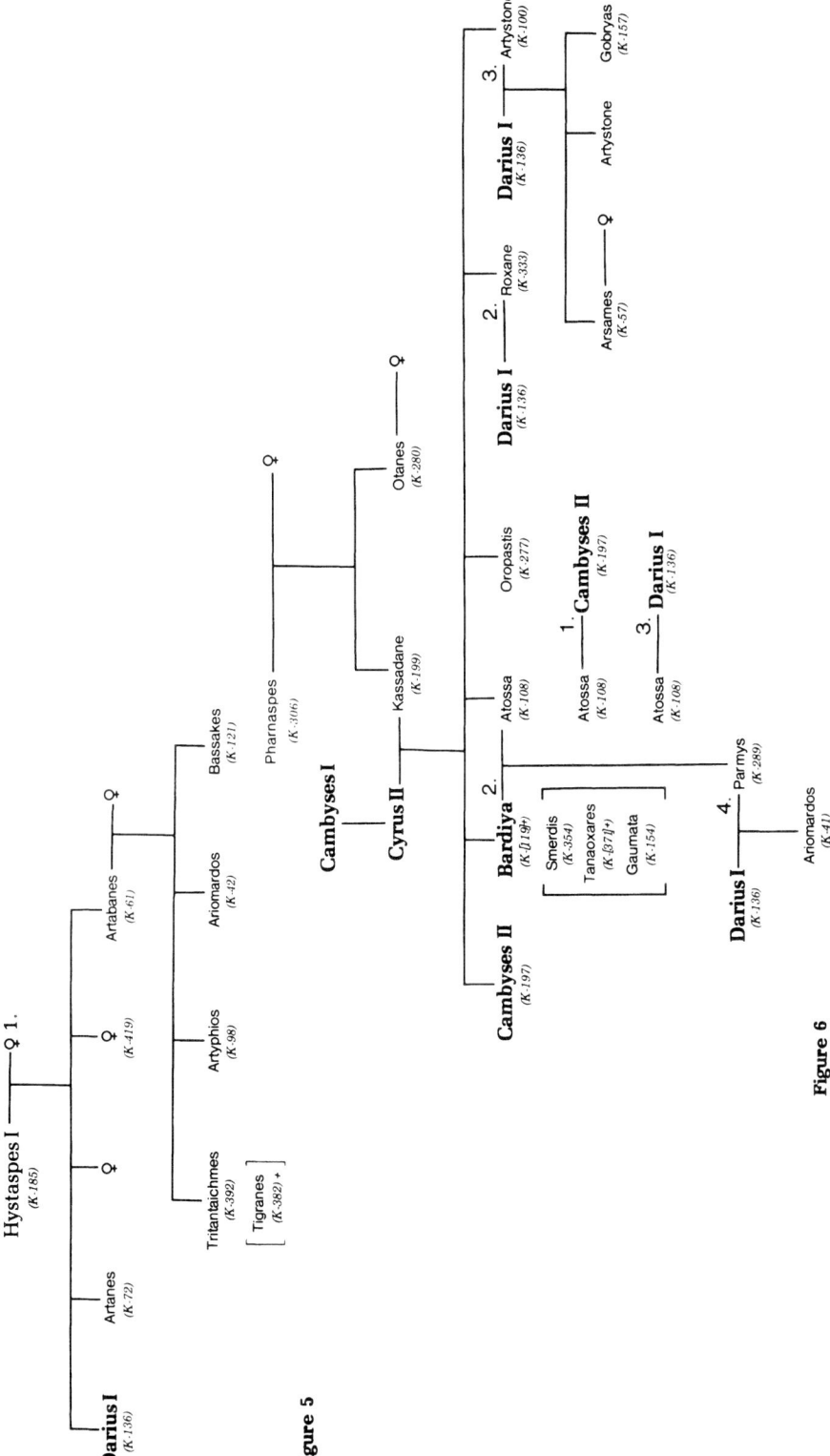

Figure 5

Figure 6

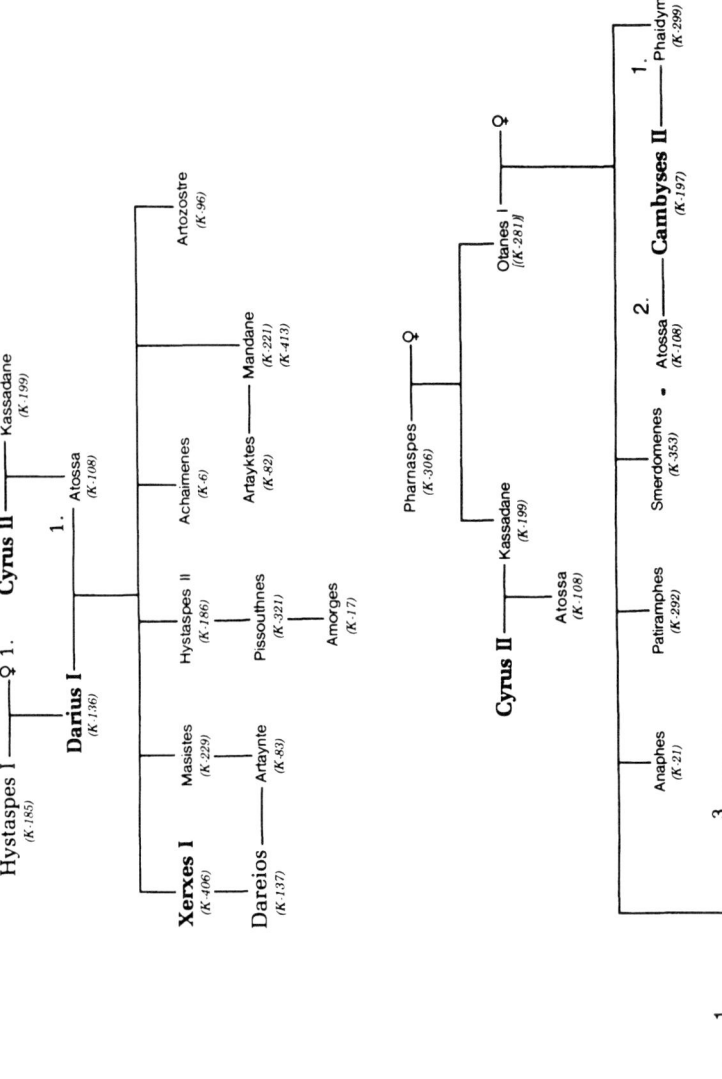

Figure 7

Figure 8

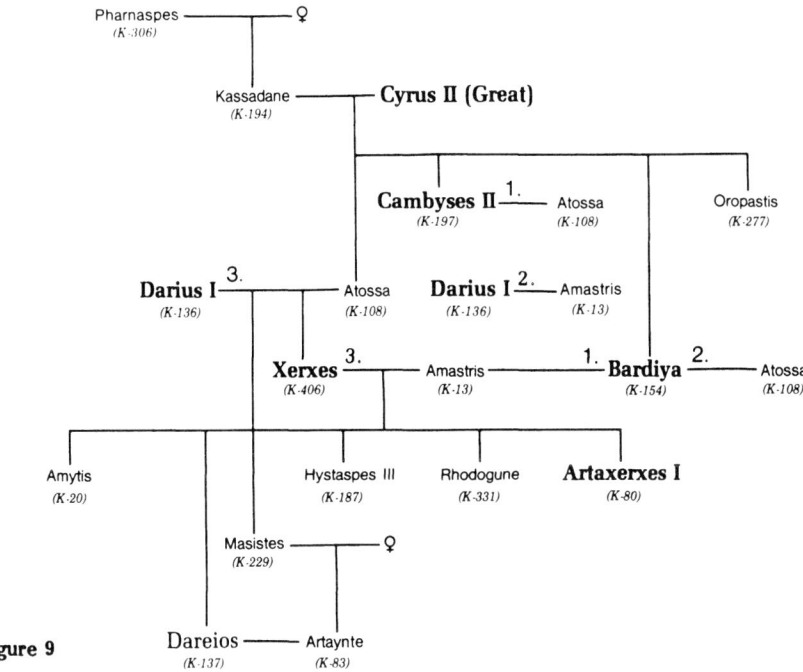

Figure 9

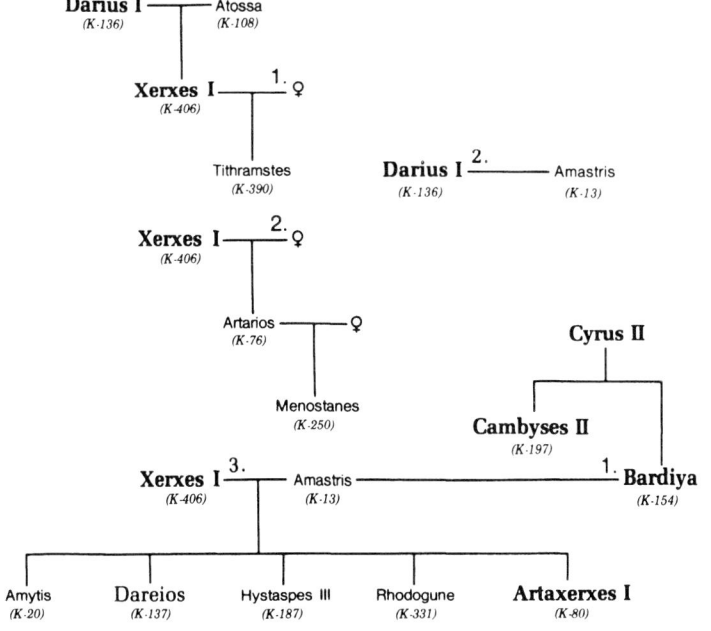

Figure 10

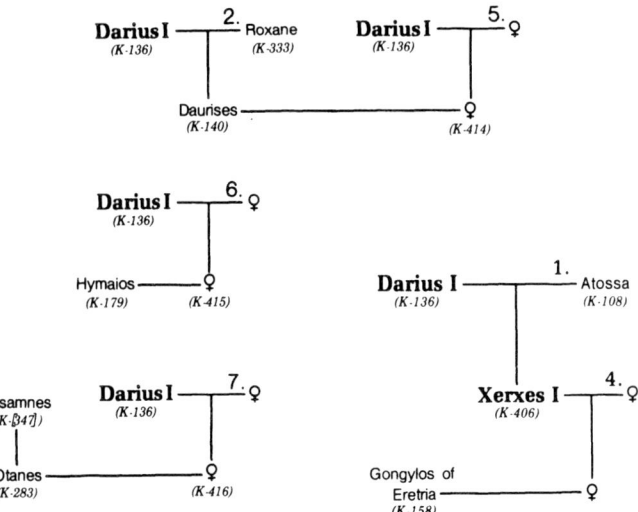

Figure 11

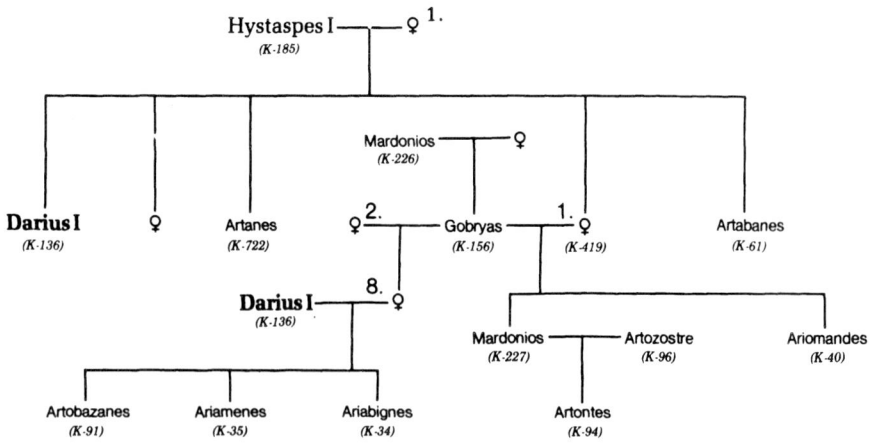

Figure 12

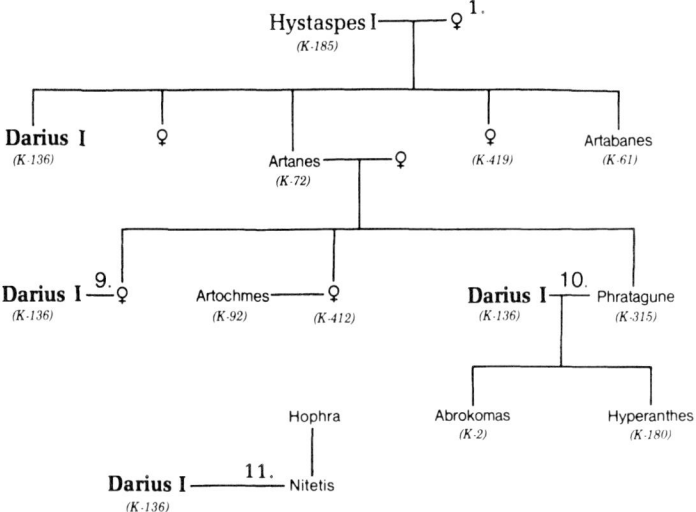

Figure 13

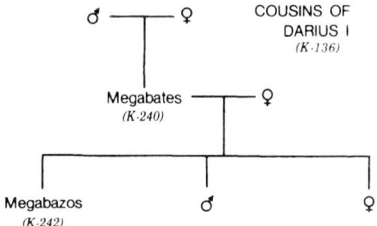

Figure 14

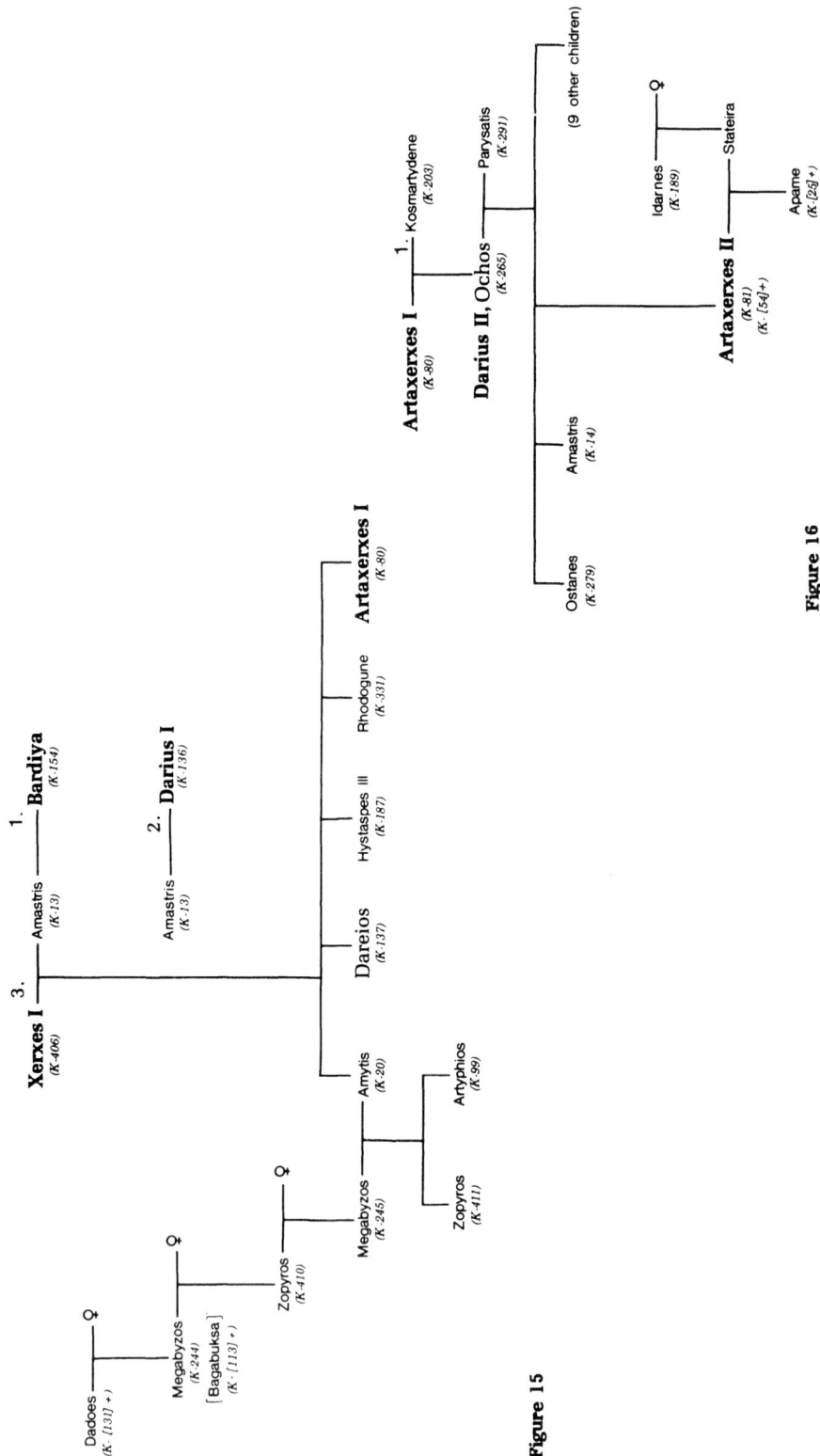

Figure 15

Figure 16

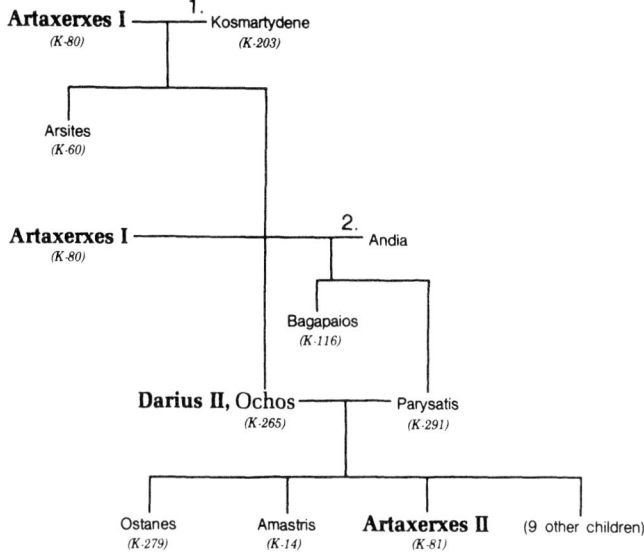

Figure 17

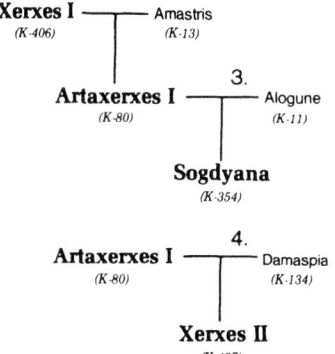

Figure 18

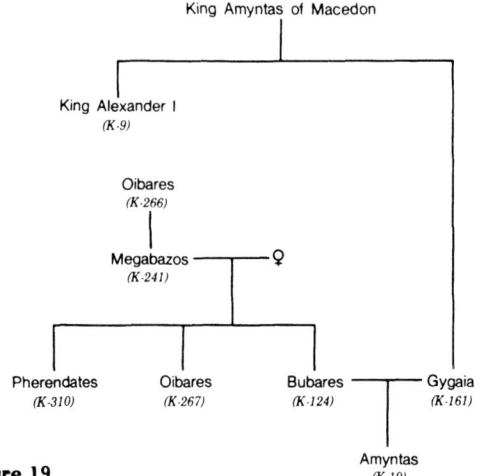

Figure 19

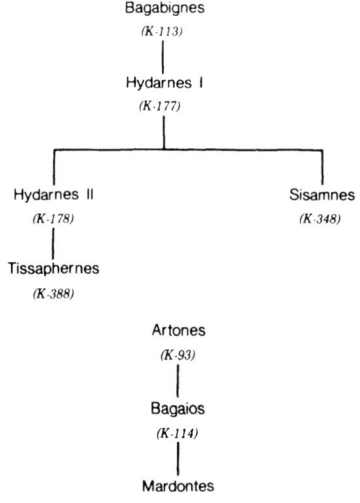

Figure 20

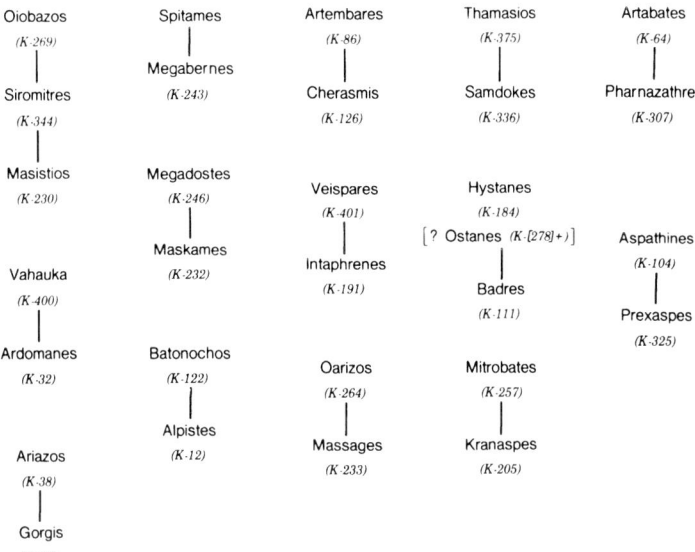

Figure 21

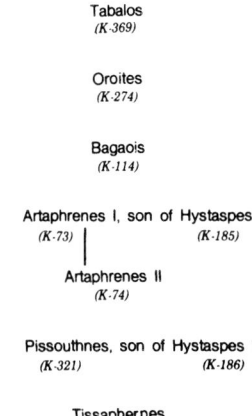

SPARDA - Satraps

Tabalos
(K-369)

Oroites
(K-274)

Bagaois
(K-114)

Artaphrenes I, son of Hystaspes I
(K-73)   (K-185)

Artaphrenes II
(K-74)

Pissouthnes, son of Hystaspes II
(K-321)   (K-186)

Tissaphernes
(K-388)

Figure 22

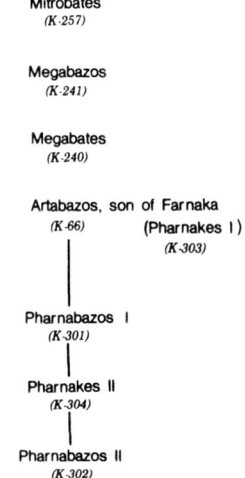

DASKYLEION - Satraps

Mitrobates
(K-257)

Megabazos
(K-241)

Megabates
(K-240)

Artabazos, son of Farnaka
(K-66)   (Pharnakes I)
              (K-303)

Pharnabazos I
(K-301)

Pharnakes II
(K-304)

Pharnabazos II
(K-302)

Figure 23

6

SPARDA AND THE EMPIRE

For the Greeks, Darius ruled all of Asia, and its peoples were his subjects (*katēkooi*: Hdt. 3.88.1)[1] whom he ruled for the gods who had appointed him to govern their earthly realm (Aesch. *Pers.* 762-5; Hdt. 7.53); as "shepherd of his flocks," he dictated their laws (Aesch. *Pers.* 763-4). For Darius, "the lance of the Persians had gone forth afar . . . , the Persian had smitten his foe. . . ." (DNa 4).

Several years after the restoration of rule in Sparda and Egypt, and the campaign against the European Scythians, which added to the empire European Thrace called by the Persians Skudra (c. 514-512 B.C.),[2] Darius ordered inscriptions to be carved upon his tomb at Naqsh-i Rustam (DNa) and to grace the imperial audience hall and palace at Susa (DSe) c. 493 B.C.[3] In both texts, Darius praised Ahura Mazda and his divine sanction of the king's vice-gerency over the god's empire: "A great god is Ahura Mazda, who created this earth, who created yonder sky, who created man, who created happiness of man, who made Darius king, one king of many, one lord of many" (DNa, DSe 1). Once again, Darius asserted his claim to royal legitimacy: "I am Darius the Great King, King of Kings, King of nations containing all kinds of men, King in this great earth far and wide, son of Hystaspes, an Achaemenian, a Persian, son of a Persian, an Aryan, having Aryan lineage" (2); a claim which the Greeks perceived as the divine rule of Asia.

Darius then enumerated the peoples beyond Parsa whom he ruled (3). Implicit in this statement, as in similar statements, was the recognition that the nobles of Parsa were not subjects but rather assistants to the king in fulfilling the commands of Ahura Mazda and the other gods. The Persians, consequently, did not pay tribute to the king, the tribute demanded through the royal edicts, the law (*data*) which bound the subjects firmly to the king. Darius apparently reacted to Bardiya's three year remission of taxes with a perpetual remission of taxes for all Persian nobles.[4] Among many subjected peoples, Darius enumerated the Cappadocians, the Lydians (or Spardians), the Ionians of western Anatolia, the Karians, the European Scythians "across the sea," the Skudrians, and the Thracian Greeks or "petasos-wearing Ionians"[5] who had colonized eastern Thrace from Ionia. At Naqsh-i Rustam, these subjects, Darius noted, bore the throne, which Ahura Mazda had given to him in order to quell rebellions (DNa 4-6), and at Susa, Darius

169

stressed that the rebels feared and respected his law (data: DSe 4): "Nations were in commotion; one man was smiting the other. The following I brought about by the favor of Ahura Mazda, that the one does not smite the other at all, each one is in his place. My law—of that they feel fear, so that the stronger does not smite nor destroy the weak."

For Herodotus, the ethnic groups in western Anatolia formed three distinct administrative units, which he labeled archai and satrapies (3.89.1).[6] In the first unit, Herodotus listed the Ionians, Magnesians of Asia, Aiolians, Karians, Lykians, Milyans, and Pamphylians who jointly offered a tribute of four hundred Babylonian talents of silver (3.90). In a second unit, the Lydians, together with the Mysians, Lasonians, Cabalians, and Hytennians gave five hundred talents. The third unit comprised the Asian Hellespontines, Phyrgians, Asian Thracians, Paphlagonians, Mariandynians, and Anatolian Syrians who contributed three hundred and sixty talents. Beyond these, Skudra remained separate (3.96.1).[7] These three Herodotean units, however, are in marked contrast to the attested administrative boundaries of the satrapy of Sparda centered at Sardis, which included Karia, Lykia, Ionia, Aiolis, and the western Troad, and the second satrapy of Daskyleion centered about its administrative center by the same name, which included the region between eastern Troad and the Halys River. A third satrapy, Cappadocia governed from Gordion, constituted much of the highland plateau. Of these, the military activities of the rebel satrap Oroites in 522-521 B.C. from Sardis against Daskyleion and Cappadocia confirm this distinct tripartite division, which the Persians maintained throughout the fifth century B.C. Cilicia completed the Anatolian region as a semi-autonomous kingdom and satrapy within the Persian Empire, a unit which Herodotus properly delineated (3.90.3). Many of the mountainous regions of Lykia, however, may also have remained semi-autonomous and tenuously held by the satrap in Sardis who attempted to govern the local Lykian dynasts and their urban councils.[8] The Mede Harpagos, who conquered Lykia, had faced fierce resistance (Hdt. 1.176) and the Persians may never have completely subdued Lykia (Isocrates Panegyr. 161), at least until the second half of the fifth century B.C. Although Lykians served in Xerxes' army in its campaign against Athens (Hdt. 7.92), there were apparently no Persian forces garrisoned in Lykia (Diod. Sic. 11.60). But this may be attributed to the fact that the Harpagid family, which held strong dynastic control in Xanthos and over Lykia, ruled its vassal estates as special demesnes, as semi-autonomous units, given to Harpagos by Cyrus.

Herodotus' lists, therefore, do not delineate the satrapal administrative units as he claimed but reflect, instead, three tributary regions as fiscal subdivisions of western Anatolia, called by the Halikarnassian nomoi (cf. Xen. Oec. 4.11), which crossed the three satrapies of Sparda, Daskyleion, and Cappadocia.[9] The center of the three fiscal nomoi was apparently Sardis, which served as the western capital for the empire and the western terminus of the Royal Road, which stretched from Susa, the eastern administrative capital of the empire, across Elam, Babylonia, Cilicia, Cappadocia, and Sparda. The suggestion by John L. Myres that the survey of the nomoi (Hdt. 3.89-94), like the catalogue of Xerxes' forces (7.61-99), must be derived from Persian documents accessible to Herodotus at Sardis has merit. As Myres noted, the tributary regions and the military contingents do not correlate in precise geographical terms. The authenticity of both lists, therefore, may be considered with an emphasis upon Sardis as the fiscal center for western Anatolia and the source of the tributary text, a list drafted early and before the accession of Skudra (Hdt. 3.96.1).[10] Dandamayev has suggested that Herodotus had obtained the list from Hekataios.[11] Tribute, fundamental to the inner structure and maintenance of the empire, went to the king and his imperial treasuries, and also to the local satrap toward the support of the local government and court, and the complex system of local garrisons and governors and the other imperial and satrapal officials. Only a small proportion of the direct taxes paid to the king, however, found its way back to the satrapal regions.

The importance of Sardis and the satrapy of Sparda is clearly noted in the trilingual inscriptions engraved upon the gold and silver plates placed in the foundation boxes at Persepolis (DPh), and similar plates placed in the palace at Ecbatana (DH): "Darius the Great King, King of Kings, King of countries, son of Hystaspes, an Achaemenian. Saith Darius the King: This is the kingdom which I hold, from the Scythians who are beyond Sogdiana thence into Ethiopia; from Hindush, thence into Sparda—which Ahura Mazda the greatest of the gods bestowed upon me (cf. I Esdras 3:2). Me may Ahura Mazda protect, and my royal house." These inscriptions date to the period after the European Scythian expedition, which gained Skudra and the conquest of Hindush (? perhaps c. 512 B.C.),[12] and also reflect Darius' inscription carved upon the south wall of the terrace at Persepolis (DPe). In this, Darius listed the ethnic groups, which bore him tribute, and noted, among many, "the Spardians, the Ionians who are of the mainland and (those) who are by the sea, and the peoples who are across the sea." In this inscription, also carved after the Indian campaign, Darius enumerated four groups: the Lydians, the inland East Greeks, the coastal and island East Greeks, and the Greeks and Thracians of Skudra. This list vaguely reflects Herodotus' list of tributary nomoi and may have been the origin of that Sardian source obtained by the Halikarnassian with its tripartite north to south division of western Anatolia.

Sardis remained pivotal in the scheme of Persian control of the Lydians, Lykians, Karians, Asian Dorians, Ionians, Aiolians, the remaining pockets of indigenous Anatolian natives, and Jews in exile (Obadaiah 20)[13] who collectively formed the peoples of the satrapies of Sparda and Daskyleion, as Sardis appears to have had a role in the direction of fiscal affairs in Daskyleion. From Croesus' palace on the slopes of the Sardian acropolis, the Persian satrap governed western Anatolia. At Sardis, his palace rose up a considerable part of the steep acropolitan slope beside the monumental staircase of green sandstone and white limestone, a complex of many pitched roof structures built upon stone foundations with mud-brick walls and terracotta friezes of winged horses and chariots,[14] in addition to a white marble hall built by the Persians (Eustath. *Comm.* 366.15-20). To this palace, Darius would entrust his half-brother Artaphrenes, the assassin of Bardiya and the son of Hystaspes, Darius' father the regal satrap of Parthia (Hdt. 5.25). Artaphrenes' royal presence in Sardis emphasized the role of that administrative center and the importance of the satrapal rule of Sparda.

Within the rebellions of 522-519 B.C., Darius recognized the centrifugal tendencies of the diverse nations of the empire toward autonomy. The reorganization of the empire and especially Sparda remained crucial, thus Darius utilized the Persian nobles who had supported his usurpation and members of his own family to occupy the key satrapal and administrative positions.[15] The king, however, remained the head of state, the commander-in-chief of the armed forces, and the last court of appeal in judicial cases. Sparda retained its several native languages (Lydian, the several Ionian, Aiolian, and Doric Greek dialects, Karian, and Lykian), its multiple ethnic individualities, its local social and political institutions, its particular economic structure based upon a long developed coinage system, and its numerous Greco-Lydian religious cults, yet gained the imperial political and military benefits of the Persian state. Artaphrenes' governance attempted to check rebellion and the inherent centrifugal forces, which would, unfortunately, shatter Sparda in 499 B.C.

Throughout the Bisitun, Persepolis, Naqsh-i Rustam, and Susa inscriptions, Darius stressed his Persian and Aryan origin. But to the various ethnic groups within the empire he took on native appearances. To the Egyptians he appeared as an Egyptian, to the Jews he was concerned with Judaism and the building of the Second Temple, and to Aeschylus, Herodotus, and Xenophon he often appeared as a Greek.[16] For Sparda, he must have appeared as a Lydian king and in the image of Croesus. In Egypt and Judah, as in Babylonia, Media, and Elam, he never denied that he was a Persian and, in the case of Egypt, had seized that country (DZe 3), but he did assert, as had Cambyses, that he was the innate pharaoh.[17] Darius, nevertheless, did assume in each ethnic region the guise and rituals of local kingship. We may suspect, therefore, that in Sardis the Lydians accepted the concept that Darius held the divine sanction of the goddess Kuvava. During Cyrus' reign, the Persians in Sardis had modified the great stone fire altar dedicated to Kuvava during the reign of Alyattes (c. 570-560 B.C.), and immured the lions poised at each corner, the symbols of Kuvava and the royal Mermnad house. The Persians, thus, transformed it sufficiently to be adopted as a Zarathustrian fire altar,[18] just as they adopted the oblong and stepped red stone fire altar nearby dedicated to Artemis.[19] The altars, however, remained essentially Lydian. The conclusion is, therefore, that Darius and his representatives, the satraps of Sardis, raised offerings at these altars not just as Persians but as Lydian rulers.

In 518 B.C., following the restoration of Egypt to the empire, Darius instituted his extensive reforms for the reorganization of the imperial system. In this, he clarified and defined the political structure of the satrapal organization, whereby he gave greater power to the Persian nobles who served as his vassal satraps than had been held under the reigns of Cyrus and Cambyses. The character of this administrative reform is apparent in the evidence for the administration of the satrapies of Babylonia and Egypt, which reflect a complex administrative organization similar to that of Sparda.[20] Under Cyrus, Babylonia, centered upon the administrative and holy city of Babylon, included the eastern Mesopotamian regions between Elam and Assyria and the western regions of the area Across the River, the subsidiary regions of Phoenicia, Lebanon, Syria, Cyprus, and Judah.[21] In Babylon, the faithful general Gobryas, whom Cyrus had established as satrap

535/4 to 525/4 B.C.[22] and who, as conspirator, aided Darius' usurpation of the throne, continued to govern. Darius' marriage to Gobryas' daughter confirmed the familial rule of the empire and its satrapies, the noble cooperation and joint rule of the empire, and the oaths of lordship and vassalage between the king and his satrap. Yet in 515 B.C. Darius divided the satrapy into two units and raised the region Across the River to the status of full satrapy governed by Persians from the satrapal palace at Tripolis. This satrapy Herodotus listed as the fifth nomos or tribute district offering three hundred and fifty talents annually (Hdt. 3.91.1).

The satrapy of Across the River, as with Sparda, contained various diverse ethnic and national groups, which the Persians not only tolerated but fostered to continue their particular religious and commercial activities. The Phoenician trading centers, Byblos, Sidon, Arados, and Tyre for example,[23] continued as semi-autonomous units within the satrapy in a political relationship to the empire similar to the Lykian dynasts of Sparda, and the autonomous satrapy of Cilicia. The Phoenician cities served the empire as did the Ionian poleis, especially Miletos, as the termini of caravan routes from Babylonia and the Iranian highlands, and generated the wealth of their respective satrapal treasuries as indicated by Herodotus' financial list. Thus at Sidon, Persian nobles built a royal pavilion within a "paradise" hunting park (Diod. Sic 16.41), in the style of Darius' new constructions at Persepolis and Susa,[24] and the earlier Achaemenid pavilions at Pasargadae, Naqsh-i Rustam, and Borazdjan on the Persian Gulf.[25] At Aleppo, the satrapal family erected a second pavilion and paradise park (Xen. An. 1.4.10). For Darius, the Phoenician fleets ranked most important within his imperial plans, as they enabled him to control Cyprus and the Ionian islands.

Darius referred to each of his satraps as a *bandaka*, in Old Persian his subject and servant, which also had the concept of "one in fetters." Some ancient Greek, therefore, translated this as *doulos* or "slave" but it is more accurately to be translated into English as vassal or servant.[26] The Lydians, similarly, adopting the Persian word, referred to subordinates as *bantakashash*.[27] The satrap governed the king's protectorship, a region or petty kingdom, called in Old Persian a *xšaçapavan*, which some Greeks transliterated as satrapeia or satrapy (Thuc. 1.129.1).[28] Herodotus, however, called the satraps hyparchoi, simply the administrators of provinces or hyparchies (3.70, 120, 4.166, 5.25, 73, 123, 6.1.42, 7.6), and Aeschylus similarly labeled the satrap an aparchos (*Pers.*

327).[29]   Below the satrap were numerous advisors, military commanders, and local officials. In some ancient Greek texts, especially Herodotus, these too were labeled hyparchoi, meaning colleagues or local administrators, and in other texts were given several similar generic titles such as *syndouloi* (LXX Ezra 5:3, 6, 6:6, 7:13), *synetairoi* (LXX-1 Esdras 6:27; cf. Dan. 3.7), *toparchai* (LXX I Esdras 3:14, 4:47, 4:48), and *hypatoi* (LXX I Esdras 3:14), in addition to the specific titles and functions of the finance ministers (*oikonomoi*—LXX I Esdras 4:47) and commanders (*strategoi*—LXX I Esdras 3:14, 4:47). And these were often the king's relatives and other Persian nobles (LXX I Esdras 3:7, 9, 14). The satrapal administration of Across the River included these subdivisions with their administrators, such as in the districts of Samaria, Idumaea, Moabitis, and Ammonitis.[30] Sparda, Daskyleion, and Skudra were similarly divided, as Herodotus noted the appointment during Darius' reign of the Greek Sandokes as the judicial administrator of Aiolian Kyme within Sparda (7.194.1), the Persian administrator of Sestos in Skudra (7.33), Maskames the commander of the Persian forces at Doriskos also in Skudra (7.105), Lykaretos the Greek administrator of the islands of Lemnos (5.27), and the other local administrators of Persian imperial rule throughout Skudra and the Hellespontine region (7.106), in Macedonia (5.20.4) and in Greece (7.6.1). The faithful Otanes, conspirator and noble Persian, whom Darius appointed as judicial administrator of the Troad, the island of Lesbos, Lemnos, and Imbros, and the European regions around the polis of Byzantion, also commanded Darius' armies stationed in the region of Daskyleion (Hdt. 5.25-8).

Darius' conquest of the empire rapidly transformed a relatively simple structure to one of complexity governed by an imperial bureaucracy bound to the king's centralization policies. To faciliate this new administration, by 500 B.C. Darius' orders to draft a map of the empire had been completed, and in particular the political subdivisions of the satrapies of Sparda and Daskyleion, a copy of which was deposited at Sardis. Of this, a second copy was cut in bronze (Hdt. 4.36) and obtained by the Milesian nobleman Hekataios (Hdt. 2.143) for his mythological and geographical treatise on the tribes subject to Darius, the *Periegesis* (Hdt. 5.49).[31] The map was apparently intended for the satraps and their subordinates the military commanders and the tax officials who, by edict, collected the tributes in precious metals to equal the value of silver talents and in kind, valuable objects, and animals.

In Sparda and in Daskyleion, the pivotal role of the new satraps directly bound those provinces to Darius' imperial reorganization. In Sardis, Darius replaced the Persian noble and rebel Oroites with a second Persian noble, Bagaios who governed temporarily until Darius himself visited Sardis and installed his half-brother Artaphrenes I, who was apparently succeeded by his own son Artaphrenes II. Sometime after the mid-century, Pissouthnes, a grandson of Darius I and the son of Hystaspes II (Thuc. 1.115.4) gained that position (fig. 22). During the turbulent years of King Darius II and the political disruptions in western Anatolia, Pissouthnes was replaced by Tissaphernes of another noble Persian family (fig. 20). In Daskyleion, Darius replaced the murdered nobleman Mitrobates with his loyal general Megabazos who temporarily held that position until the Great King appointed Megabates, a Persian cousin of Darius (Thuc. 1.129.1) who also faithfully served Darius' son King Xerxes (Aesch. *Pers.* 983). He, in turn, sometime in the second quarter of the century was succeeded first by the Persian noble Artabazos, the son of Pharnakes I, who also served kings Xerxes and Artaxerxes I (Hdt. 7.66; Thuc. 1.129.1; Diod. Sic. 12.3.4), and then in hereditary succession by Pharnabazos I, Pharnakes II who served Artaxerxes and his successor Darius II (Thuc. 2.67.1, 5.1, 8.108), and Pharnabazos II (fig. 23). In Cappadocia, Darius appointed the Persian noble Ariaramnes to the satrapal throne (Ktesias *FGrH* 688 F 13). Accession to either the imperial throne or its subordinate positions was not simply due to primogeniture but careful selection and the chances of assassination plots (cf. XPf 4).

Each satrap as "Protector of the Kingdom" ruled his satrapy as the successor to the former ruler or king of that region. He was, in fact, a minor monarch surrounded by a miniature court, reflective of Susa, through which he directed the civil administration, collected the satrapal levies, and commanded the satrapal armies (Xen. *Cyr.* 8.6.3-7). As royal commander within the empire, the satrap proudly wore the military fillet about his Persian hat.[32] In Media, Assyria, Babylonia, Egypt, and Sparda, the satraps ruled over powerful kingdoms conquered by the Achaemenids and bound to their empire as important vassal states. Beneath them, Persians and local officials governed the subdivisions of the satrapy, local offices which varied from satrapy to satrapy. But to check the satrapal control, which as it became an hereditary position threatened the centralized authority of the Great King, the king's representatives sent from his palace inspected the satrapy and caused many officials anxious hours. While the satraps wielded power over vast areas, the king's assent had to be obtained for all major decisions. When

Artaphrenes sought military conquest of the Cyclades, he could not act without Darius'
approval (Hdt. 5.31.4). The firm controls for imperial centralization which Darius
established nevertheless rapidly disintegrated during the fifth century essentially because
of growing satrapal independence and factionalism, so that by the early fourth century
the empire had weakened considerably. From the late sixth century to the mid-fourth
century B.C., Persia altered from a Völkerkosmos to an empire marked by increasing
deleterious political competition among the Persian nobles dwelling in the numerous
satrapies.

Darius' efforts at centralization built upon the previous Assyrian and Babylonian
adminstrations and the imperial Achaemenid foundations established by Cyrus.[33] Darius'
goals were to increase the receipt of information from within and without the empire,
and when necessary to direct military units to the areas vulnerable to rebellion or
attack. This necessitated the extensive and elaborate system of roads, road stations, and
the postal system, which spanned the empire. As major land routes linked Susa to
Babylon, Ecbatana, and Persepolis, so, too, the royal road linked Susa to Sardis. Between
Susa and Babylon, a caravan route across the Kerkha River, which took three days to
traverse, extended on to Sardis, marked by one hundred and eleven relay stations and
good hostelries (Hdt. 5.52).[34] A second caravan route from Babylon crossed the
Khurdistan mountains past Sar-i Pul and Bisitun to Ecbatana. A third route along the
eastern highland flanks of the Zagros Range linked Ecbatana with Pasargadae and
Persepolis, and a fourth passed over the Zagros range from Persepolis past Bishapur and
across the Karun River to Susa. From Susa to Sardis, the normal caravan took ninety
days to travel, completing about 24 km. or 150 stadia each day, an exhausting rate of
travel. Past the Cilician Gates (Hdt. 5.52), the Royal Road followed the earlier Lydian
and Assyrian route through Cappadocia and Sparda, about 817 km. From Sardis to
Ephesos, a subsidiary route passed directly south over the Tmolos Range to the Kayster
Valley, a route which took another three days to travel (Hdt. 5.54). Across the Royal
Road at a faster pace raced the king's couriers, undaunted by snow or rain, heat or
darkness (Hdt. 8.98; Xen. Cyr. 8.6.17).

Amidst the caravans of merchants and artisans, couriers and armies, travelers in the
service of the king also criss-crossed the empire and often on foot. At Persepolis, the
travel-ration texts (PFT 1285-1579, 2049-57) report the daily operations of men and boys

who journeyed to that palace westward from Bactria, Areia, Kerman, and Hindush, and eastward from Babylon, Egypt, and Sardis. For messengers, fast-messengers, caravan leaders, and elite guides, the daily rations of food recorded reveal the highly developed system of communication, transportation, and travel. At hostelries, each group received a day's rations, usually 1 or 1½ quarts of food per person, and at the next hostelry presented a sealed document issued either by Darius or one of his named officials for the receipt of the next day's rations. On one tablet, a royal scribe noted that two men had set out with twenty-eight camels (*PFT* 1418), and on a second that twenty men and thirty boys had departed with seven horses (*PFT* 1508). A third tablet noted an elite guard with a group of Spardians (*PFT* 1409) and a fourth a group of Skudrians (*PFT* 1363).[35] Into this collection of travel records, a single clay tablet inscribed in Greek bears witness to an Ionian, perhaps a Samian, who somewhere noted c. 500 B.C. in the month Tebet (Dec.-Jan.) the ration of two ten-liter measures of wine (*PFT* 1771).[36]

Prestigious imperial officers whom the Greeks called the King's Eyes (*spasaka) and Ears, who were not subservient to the satraps but to the king directly, also traveled the Royal Road to Sardis. The Eyes conducted political and adminsitrative surveillance of the satrapies, and communicated the information gathered to Darius. Their duties were distinctly separate from the satrap and his civil, military, and financial administrative functions, yet the Eyes supervised both the satraps and their satrapies for the king, essentially to prevent rebellion. Within an empire of extreme ethnic, linguistic, and religious diversity, the Achaemenid monarch relied highly upon this network of espionage and communication. Several years earlier, Cyrus had established this office, adopted from an earlier Median magistracy, an office which Darius expanded, and who may have appointed at least one Eye for each satrapy. The Eye was an itinerant officer who traveled with a small imperial guard and was concerned with the local problems of administration, taxation, judicial matters, the imperial armies, the cultivation of land, and the protection of the king's subjects. Perhaps it was an Eye who reported to Darius the illegal activities of Gadatas (ML *GHI* 12 [Tod *GHI* 1².10])[37] a local official at Magnesia-on-the-Maeander (Paus. 10.32.6). In response, Darius sent Gadatas an imperial letter, perhaps dated between 494 and 486 B.C.: "Thus saith Darius, King of Kings, son of Hystaspes, to his servant Gadatas. I hear that you are obedient to my commands but not accordingly to all. In so far as you cultivate my land by transplanting the gardens of

Beyond the Euphrates to the territories of Lower Asia, let me laud you with public notice
and because of these things, a great gratitude is laid up for you in the House of the
King. But in that you have obliterated the property of my gods, I shall not give you
territory in exchange for this misjudged anger. For you exacted tribute from the holy
gardeners of Apollo and ordered them to cultivate the profane land, being ignorant of the
intent of my ancestors to the gods who have spoken all truth to the Persians. . . ." In this
report, the Eye may have been assisted by the King's Ear, a type of state's attorney who
represented the government in legal cases.[38]   As with other high ranking imperial
officers, the Eyes were very close to the king and with sufficient social status to be
honored with marriage into the royal family.[39]   Both Aristophanes and his audiences
knew well the King's Eye whom the poet parodied in his comedy the *Acharnians* and who
spoke in perfect Old Persian (100, 104): "The pious minded Xerxes (greets) those upon
the waters being the Ionian satrapy."[40]

Beyond the borders of the empire, Darius also dispatched reconnaissance groups and
spies. Under the command of Skylax, a Karian from Karyanda, several ships set out to
explore the Indus River and southern Ethiopia (Hdt. 4.44; *FGrH* 709 F3),[41] and to Greece
and southern Italy three ships sailed from Sidon to chart and make records of the peoples
and resources there (Hdt. 3.136). As Persian spies infiltrated foreign areas (Xen. *Cyr.*
6.1.46, 2.2, 2.11, 3.2, 3.5, 3.6), Greek spies crossed into Sardis to take note of the armed
forces stationed there (Hdt. 7. 146-8).[42]   In addition to this information, at Sardis,
Artaphrenes' intelligence corps found also useful the Lydian archives, which contained
the correspondence with Assyria, Egypt, Babylon, Media, and most of the East Greek
poleis and their sanctuaries, in addition to the documents received and issued by
Oroites.[43]

Greeks from Athens and Sparta, fleeing political crises at home, also contributed
valuable information to the courts at Sardis and Susa. In return, Darius favored them
with estates, Persian noble wives and other royal gifts (Hdt. 8.5). For the Athenian
Metoichos, the son of Miltiades the victorious general at Marathon, Darius provided a
house, property, and a Persian wife who bore him sons whom the parents claimed as
Persians (Hdt. 6.41).[44]   Of Sparta, with which Persia was at a state of war, the exiled
King Damaratos supplied valuable information and would guide King Xerxes to
Thermopylae in 480 B.C.; but Damaratos angered Darius and his cousin Mithraustes by

riding through the streets of Sardis wearing a Persian tiara upright in the manner of the king (Plut. *Them.* 29.7). Damaratos, nevertheless, continued to live on his landed estates in the Troad (Xen. *An* 2.1-3, 7.8.17; *Hell.* 3.1.6).[45] Hippias, the former tyrant of Athens, also served Artaphrenes and Darius. For information of Attica, his service as vassal to the king, and as assistant to the commander at Marathon, the Mede Datis, Hippias also received estates in Sigeion in the Troad, honorific titles, and privileges in the court at Sardis (Thuc. 6.59.3; Hdt. 5.62-5, 73; *Ath PoL* 19).[46] These Greeks in exile served Darius with valuable evidence on peoples he would soon attempt to conquer, just as Phanes of Halikarnassos had served Cambyses with his valuable knowledge of Egypt (Hdt. 3.4). In addition, Histiaios, the Greek tyrant of Miletos whom Artaphrenes raised to power (Hdt. 5.25.1), when summoned by Darius traveled to Susa and served as the king's advisor for Milesian and Ionian affairs; the Egyptian priest Oujahorresne, who had earlier served the pharaohs Amasis and Psammetichos, and King Cambyses, went to Susa at the beginning of Darius' reign to serve faithfully as advisor for Egyptian affairs.[47]

A variety of East Greeks, Lydians, Cappadocians, Karians, and Skudrians also went to Susa (DSe) and Persepolis as artists, architects, and technicians.[48] Among these, the Persepolis fortification tablets record Lydian blacksmiths (*PFT* 873) and other Lydian workers receiving rations of flour in 500 B.C., and the Persepolis treasury tablets record wages of silver given to Karian goldsmiths (*PTT* 37). Other tablets note the presence of Ionian mothers (*PFT* 1224), Ionian grain handlers (*PFT* 1942, 1965), Ionian women irrigation (?) workers (*PFT* 1224), and a series of other Ionians (*PFT* 1798, 1800, 1808, 1810, 2072, *PTT* 21). At Susa, some of the Ionians and Karians had transported great cedar timbers from Babylon to Susa, while other Ionians and Lydians worked stone (DSf: 3g and j). At Persepolis, still other Ionians labored upon the columned halls (*PTT* 15).[49] Among the Elamite scribes who recorded the rations for many of these western Anatolians, in addition to the Samian who recorded the two measures of wine, a Phrygian from Cappadocia recorded other rations.[50]

Several East Greeks in contrast to these laborers held important positions within the Achaemenid empire. Darius employed the Phokaian artist Telephanes, who ranked with his contemporaries Myron and Polykleitos (Pliny *NH* 34.68), and the Samian engineer Mandrokles to build the bridge across the Bosporos for the expedition into Skudra and against the European Scythians (Hdt. 4.87-9).[51] Greek doctors also served the court of

Darius, as did Demokedes of Kroton in Magna Graecia (Hdt. 3.125.1, 129-37), the first in

a long sequence of Greek doctors to serve the Achaemenid royal family, the most notable

being the gossip monger Ktesias from Knidos. In all, the Greeks in Persian service

included tyrants who governed poleis, soldiers and mercenaries,[52] dragomen, political

agents, exiles, artists, engineers, philosphers, doctors, athletes, seamen and explorers,

priests and oracle-agents, women, Persian "mixlings," eunuchs, miscellaneous friends, and

others. Among these, many East Greeks and Lydians who labored at Pasargadae for

Cyrus and Cambyses and at Persepolis for Darius and Xerxes were humble artisans,

craftsmen, and quarrymen who held lowly positions and were badly paid. Many were

prisoners of war, deportees and even slaves, menials who had little opportunity to

influence the Achaemenid court. The East Greek and Lydian artisanship, however,

contributed substantially to the development of Achaemenid art and left its distinct

mark in technique, forms and motifs, style and structure by the experienced workmen

and their foremen.[53] Five of these lowly stone cutters, nevertheless, left graffiti upon

the walls of the quarries west of Persepolis: Pytharchos, a contractor from an Ionian

polis who marked his section for himself, Nikon from either Kea or Kos, Pab[. . .] whose

name compares to Pabis of Kolophon who had carved his name at Abu Simbel in Nubia a

century earlier, a pious Greek moved to inscribe "to the gods," and a nameless East

Greek, probably from Mysia or perhaps Pitane or Lampsakos, who drew a six-pointed star

on the rocks.[54] To these names, we must also add the Greek Eumenes, Polyanor, and

Polys who worked in the palaces nearby, and apparently were also East Greeks.[55]

Similar to these quarry workers and irrigation ditch diggers, deportees forcibly

removed from their homes and transported to distant satrapies also lived out their lives

uprooted. Centuries earlier, the Assyrians began the extensive practice of removing

rebellious subjects to foreign lands, among these King Shalmaneser who transported

Israelites from Samaria to the villages of Media (II Kings 17:6), and settled Samaria with

Elamites from Susiana. This method to reduce rebellion Darius adopted. In 494 B.C.,

many defeated Milesians were moved to Susa and Karians from Pedasa given their

Milesian farms (Hdt. 6.20). Similarly, from western Skudra, Paeonians were sent to

Cappadocia (Hdt. 5.12-17) by way of Sardis (Hdt. 5.23). Some of these, however, escaped

and returned to Paeonia (Hdt. 5.98). The rebellious Ionians, Darius threatened with

removal to Phoenicia and to repopulate their poleis with Phoenicians (Hdt. 6.3).[56]

Hyrkanians and Bactrians had already been settled in the Kaikos Valley.[57]

Toward all the national groups within the empire, Darius and his governmental officials would be kind, gentle, and lenient, but when piqued by rebellion or treason did destroy cities, temples, deport the rebels, and impale, behead, and crucify malcontents. Yet the policy of tolerance established by Cyrus and avidly maintained by Darius prevailed. In direct antithesis to the previous Assyrian and Neo-Babylonian policies to assimilate conquered territories rather than to rule them, Darius kept to a minimum the central and satrapal interference with the local traditions, customs, and religious practices. Without this policy, Cyrus would not have gained control of Babylonia as he had, nor would Darius have been successful in instituting his extensive reorganization of the empire. Darius was content to let the local regions alone, providing the inhabitants remained loyal subjects, kept peace, and paid their taxes.[58] The satrapy of Sparda, no exception to this practice, therefore, remained a complex of East Greek poleis with their respective governments and Lydian estates bound to Sardis and its particular socio-political organization. This policy of tolerance is most notable in Darius' support of the Lydian, East Greek, and native Anatolian religious practices.

The religious struggles which erupted in Parsa and Media in 522 and 521 B.C., initiated by Bardiya, remained there. Under Darius, a compromise was soon reached in the conflict between the old Iranian religious practices, which centered upon the early Zarathustrian deities, Sun, Moon, Earth, Fire, Water, Wind, and other elements (cf. Aesch. *Pers.* 49, 205-9, 497-9; *Mysi* F 144), and the Zarathustrian religious reforms instituted in the late sixth century B.C.[59] Even Xerxes' attack upon the pre-Zarathustrian deities of the early Indo-Iranian communities barely went beyond Parsa and Media; and his destruction of the ziggurat of Marduk-Bel, the Esagila temple in Babylon, was essentially a political repression of the rebellious Babylonians rather than a rabid religious reform.[60] From these activities, Sparda was exempt, as religious tolerance was a fundamental principle of Darius' administration. Without that tolerance it would have hardly been possible to hold the empire together, yet at the same time, the evocation of tolerance implied a relaxation in the imperial claims to absolute truth over the local cultures.[61] Thus, the seeds of centifugal forces and rebellion were sown among those of Darius' reforms. Although Darius derived his power from Ahura Mazda, no imperial cult developed for the empire and the distinction between the official court religion and the local religions accentuated the retention of local autonomies.

As Darius fervently defended the cult of Apollo at Magnesia-on-the-Maeander from the local official Gadatas who demanded tribute from the holy gardeners there and who ordered them to cultivate profane lands, Darius adamantly reminded Gadatas that he was ignorant of the intent of the king's ancestors toward the gods who had spoken all truth to the Persians. By his policy of religious toleration Darius found support among the local priesthoods, and essentially the same priesthoods which had collaborated with Cyrus: the priests of Babylon, Miletos, and Didyma, of Jews, Medes, Phoenicians, Cilicians, and, with little doubt, the people of Sardis. There the cults of Kuvava and Artemis remained inviolate and, as suggested, at their altars the Persians celebrated the old rituals. At Troy, Xerxes would sacrifice to Athena (Hdt. 7.43), and at Halos to Athamas (7.197), and late in the fifth century Tissaphernes, the satrap of Sparda, would sacrifice to Artemis at Ephesos (Thuc. 8.109); acts of maintaining Darius' religious program. Only in the reign of Artaxerxes II (404-359 B.C.), did the Persians require the worship of the statute of Anahita at Sardis (Berossus *Babyloniaca* 3.5.2),[62] and in 365 B.C. set up a statute of Zeus with the Old Persian title of "Legislator" (*Baradateō*).[63]

About the cult of Kuvava, the process of acculturation among the Phrygians, Lydians, and East Greeks had raised the earlier Anatolian Mother of the Gods to one of the extreme popularity, and several other goddesses among the East Greeks such as Hera and Artemis may have owed in part their origin in this cult, Artemis at Ephesos as a specific example.[64] At Sardis, both Kuvava and Artemis dominated religious life,[65] with a Lydian pantheon which also included a father god Tavśaś, Levś, Artemides of Koloë, of Ephesos, and of Smyrna (?), the native moon god Mên Axioteinos,[66] and the Babylonian Shamash, Marduk,[67] perhaps Ba^{c}al, and Kuoad, the primitive Asia Minor deity *Koas or *Korias. Among the East Greek poleis, the Greek Olympic pantheon dominated religious life, but there too, eastern gods such as the Cyprian god Adonis (Hesiod *Cat.* 21; Sappho F 25, 103, 136) had intruded early. But until the reign of Artaxerxes II, the activities of Zarathustrianism barely affected the lives of the people of Sparda. The Persians, on the other hand, paid great respect to the oracular shrines of Apollo at Didyma and Klaros, and at Apollo's holy sanctuary on Delos (Hdt. 6.97). These shrines of Apollo and others throughout the Greek world may have been conceived by the Persians as local units of a greater unified cult, just as they considered the Zarathustrian fire altars reflective of the single Ahura Mazda.[68] The Greeks, however, did not hold the same opinion of the unity of the Apolline cults.

The effectiveness of Darius' reforms rested squarely upon the king, his energetic personality which drove him during the first decade of imperial rule to crisscross the empire. Following Gobryas' reduction of the fourth Elamite rebellion in 520 B.C., Darius himself invaded eastern Scythia *(Saka Tigraxauda)* in the summer of 519 B.C., quelled the rebellion which had erupted there in the autumn of 522 B.C., killed the local khan who had opposed his invasion, and set up another khan who would remain loyal to him.[69] Since Cyrus had lost his life fighting the Massagetai in eastern Scythia and Cambyses had spent several years also attempting to quell eastern Scythia, as heroic king Darius was adamant in his efforts to control the Scythians. This special victory prompted Darius to order his artisans to cut into the Elamite text at Bisitun and carve Skunkha's portrait. The rebellious Scythian khan had been executed, and Skunkha was the prize of the conquest, hence he was carved larger than the nine rebels. Similarly, Darius was relentless in his invasion of Egypt in the autumn of 519 B.C., and spent six months in that satrapy to return to the imperial fold a region conquered by Cambyses. Once again, the necessity as heroic king to fulfill the military role established by his predecessors psychologically spurred Darius on from eastern Scythia to Egypt.

Several years later, c. 514-511 B.C. Darius traveled across the Royal Road through Cappadocia and Sparda and perhaps through Sardis in order to invade Europe, to gain the Thracian satrapy of Skudra, and to attack the European Scythians in order to obtain tribute of the famed Scythian gold (Hdt. 4.104).[70] While his expedition across the Danube into the Ukraine was less than successful, upon his return to Sardis (Hdt. 5.11-3), Darius commanded his faithful Persian noble, one of the conspirators, Megabazos to conquer the Hellespontine polis of Perinthos (a Samian colony) and to campaign across southern Thrace to reduce the inland tribes and the coastal Greek poleis. As Herodotus wrote (5.2), "As Perinthos was taken, Megabazos marched the army through Thrace and subjected to the king's will every polis and every ethnic group; for these commands came from Darius, to conquer Thrace." Megabazos campaigned westward to the Mt. Pangaion district of the Paeonian tribes along the border of the Strymon River and Macedonia beyond. The Paeonian resistance, however, could not block Megabazos who harshly deported the Paeonians to Cappadocia and then demanded that King Amyntas of

Macedonia subject himself to Darius and offer the symbols of vassalage—earth and water—which Amyntas did (Hdt. 5.17-8). But while the Persians now held Skudra securely, Macedonian subterfuge continued and Amyntas and his son Alexander continued to thwart the Persians (Hdt. 5.22). With Megabazos' return to Sardis to join Darius, the king appointed the conspirator Otanes to take military command of Skudra, to conquer Byzantion and Kalchedon on the Bosporos, Antandros and Lamponion in the Troad, and the islands of Lemnos and Imbros still populated by "Pelasgian" natives (Hdt. 5.26).[71]

From Sardis, Darius traveled back to Susa (Hdt. 5.11-2), and from there soon campaigned through Sattagydia to reaffirm his control there, and on into the Hindush region, c. 512 (?) B.C. From the Indians, Darius gained annually three hundred and sixty talents of gold dust, the equivalent of four thousand six hundred and eighty talents of silver (Hdt. 3.94-5), and added to Skudra and Macedonia, a third region, which he conquered in his drive to surpass the territories subjected by Cyrus and Cambyses, and to gain new tributes to fill the coffers at Persepolis and the other treasuries.[72]

At Boryza on the Black Sea, the Persians established an administrative center (Hekataios *Periegesis* F 177), [73] and perhaps here Darius ordered the construction of a building noted in the Old Persian cuneiform inscribed upon a clay plague: "[Darius the Great King, the King of Kings, the] King [of Countries, son of] Hystaspes, the Achaemenian [(is the one) who had this palace] built."[74] Over the Thracian tribes and the Ionian colonists who dwelt along the Aegean, the satrapal administration of Skudra governed the islands and inhabitants of Europe up to the borders of Thessaly (Hdt. 3.96). By 504 B.C., hundreds of Skudrian laborers filled the halls of Persepolis.[75]

Darius' residency at Sardis was crucial to his reorganization of Sparda and Daskyleion, and to the addition of Skudra to the empire. There he appointed his half-brother Artaphrenes satrap of Sparda, and Otanes commander of the Hellespontine regions (Hdt. 5.25-6). The king's presence in Croesus' palace reconfirmed Bagaios' control of Sparda after Oroites' abortive rebellion, and Otanes' early campaigns to regain Samos, Chios, and Lesbos. At Sardis, Bagaios apparently governed until Darius' royal visit and the appointment of Artaphrenes to the satrapal throne. Darius' energetic campaigns to eastern Scythia, Egypt, Skudra, and Hindush enhanced his regal stature as a divinely appointed and heroic king who fought the Evil and the Lie, and who succeeded except in western Scythia (Hdt. 2.110). His presence in Sardis, nevertheless, facilitated the reforms instituted throughout Sparda and underscored Artaphrenes' satrapal authority. Imperial edicts and letters issued by Darius from Sardis and later from Susa and other administrative centers bound the East Greeks and Lydians directly to the king. Messengers traveled constantly between Sardis and Susa over the Royal Road, as did special envoys who bore important letters from the king written in chancery Aramaic (Thuc. 4.50).[76]

In the administrative centers of Susa, Babylon, and Ecbatana, Darius maintained archives of his edicts and letters, with numbers of scribes to prepare new documents and to translate others. The Persian kings had inherited these institutions from the Assyro-Babylonian empires, and perfected the traditional bureaucracies (cf. Jeremiah 36:17-32; Esther 6.1, 10.2). For the central satrapies of Parsa, Media, Elam, and Babylonia, the scribes prepared clay tablets inscribed in Elamite and Babylonian, but for the western satrapies of Babylonia, Across the River, Egypt, Cappadocia, Daskyleion, and Sparda they wrote in Aramaic with ink upon leather scrolls (Ktesias *FGrH* 688 F 1; Ezra 5:17, 6:1-2, 7:11).[77] Old Persian was never used except for monumental inscriptions, and its cuneiform script had been invented for the Bisitun monument.[78] With Bagaios and Artaphrenes, Darius communicated in chancery Aramaic (DB OP 70; cf. Esther 1:22), which rapidly became the lingua franca of the empire,[79] yet in a variety of dialects without uniformity.[80] By this, nevertheless, Darius transcended the numerous language barriers in his empire, as in Sardis Artaphrenes maintained a group of scribes capable of translating the Aramaic texts into Lydian, Lykian, Karian, and the East Greek dialects. The efficiency of the archives, nevertheless, was often inadequate. Documents were often not duplicated, their labels less than informative (Ezra 5:17-6:2); and the presence of numerous royal scribal centers throughout the satrapies compounded those difficulties (Hdt. 3.128; Xen. *An.* 1.2.20). Edicts and letters mingled with historical annals (Plut. *Them.* 13.1; Ezra 4.15; Esther 2.23) and records of men who served their king and were to be rewarded (Hdt. 7.100, 8.85, 8.90).

In Babylon, during the reigns of Nabonidus and Cyrus, the recording of documents in Aramaic began to replace cuneiform, and at Persepolis the last known tablet inscribed in Elamite was dated 458 B.C., in the reign of King Artaxerxes I.[81] Of earlier Elamite tablets from Persepolis, forty-four bore short Aramaic glosses written in ink, and others recorded the delivery of hides of sheep, goats, cattle, and camels, "tablets on hides," and

Babylonian scribes writing upon those hides.[82]   Decades later, artisans in eastern

Arachosia systematically wrote "stock-taking notes" in Aramaic upon vessels sent to

Persepolis for use during the Now Ruz festivals.[83]   Darius' own language was a south

Persian dialect of Old Iranian from Yautiya and not the Old Persian dialect of the Bisitun

inscription. More than likely as a young military officer in Egypt he acquired a working

knowledge of Aramaic.   That lingua franca became the language of diplomacy par

excellence, of administration and law, and remained in use until the years of the bilingual

Seleucid chancery. For a large part of the Achaemenid empire, the official chancellery

Aramaic (which differed from the local Babylonian Aramaic dialect) served the king as

the mode of imperial communication with his vassals and his subjects, and his satraps

with their administrative officials. Most notable are the thirteen letters written upon

leather rolls c. 410 B.C. by scribes for the Egyptian satrap Arshames, the son of

Achaemenes, the brother of King Xerxes; letters in Aramaic but saturated with Old

Persian loan words.[84]

The Persepolis tablets, more than thirty thousand small clay records, are essentially

prosaic administrative accounts written in the hostelries west of Persepolis half-way to

Susa and in hostelries east of Persepolis near Lake Niriz. At Persepolis, the scribes

gathered them simply for accounting purposes, to note the transfer of food commodities,

which ranged from the transport of huge amounts of animals and produce down to the

payment of a man's ration for a single day, and even the grain fed to a chicken. Many

written during 500 and 499 B.C. indicate that the royal magazines throughout Parsa were

opulent. In Sardis, the Lydian scribes must have gathered similar records, as in Kyme

nearby Herakleides noted that the salaries of the Achaemenid officials were normally

paid in food rations (*FGrH* 689 F 2; cf. Thuc. 1.138.5, Plut. *Arta.* 4.1-3). Both the Samian

(?) Greek tablet and the Phrygian tablet, which recorded commodities for a man called

Mane, were similar records, which also traveled from hostelries to Persepolis, and

ultimately mingled with other tablets, which mentioned such persons as Yaunaparza, the

"Ionian panderer," and the scribe nicknamed "Mouse."[85]

The contents of Arshames' letters and documents and the Persepolis treasury and

fortification tablets reveal complex administrative activities of which the meagre

documents for Sparda suggest similar bureaucratic operations. Arshames' sixth letter, a

kind of passport, was issued upon the satrap's orders for Nehtihur, an Egyptian treasury official who traveled from Parsa to Egypt. The document instructs the officers stationed at the hostelries to supply the official, his companions and servants and their horses with food.[86] The ninth letter addressed to the same Egyptian official notes that the sculptor Hindanu, whom Arshames employed in Egypt, had also worked at Susa. The Elamite fortification tablets from Persepolis, and the single Greek tablet, note similar daily rations given to travelers setting out toward that center.[87] The Arshames' documents also deal with a second subject; the administration of estates in Egypt held by highly placed Persian officials and the difficulties of their administration, the mutual relations with the subordinate local officials, the problems of their subject peoples, and the collection and transport of the demesne revenues.

Although the Egyptian scribes wrote upon papyrus, abundant and cheap in their satrapy, it was not exported on a large scale beyond Egypt. Elsewhere, scribes wrote the important and official documents upon the more costly leather parchments, and placed those documents in leather pouches to be carried by the imperial messengers. The pouches bound with cord also bore clay bullae imprinted with cylinder seals which identified the sender (Nepos *Lys.* 4.2); of the Egyptian satrap the Aramaic inscription noted: "the seal of [Arshames] the son of the [Royal] House." At Persepolis, the scribes employed similar seals, and even an Athenian silver tetradrachm.[88] In the satrapal palace at Daskyleion, about three hundred clay bullae marked the archives of the satraps Megabates and Artabazos during the first decade of the reign of King Xerxes, 486–476 B.C. Ten bullae marked with stamp and cylinder seals bear Aramaic inscriptions; another a fragmentary Greek inscription, Mas. . . (or Sam. . .). Of these, thirty fragmentary bullae bear two lines of incomplete Old Persian cuneiform: "I am Xerxes, King." In identifying the royal correspondence between Xerxes and his satraps, and the palatial officials of Persepolis, Susa, and Daskyleion, the cylinder seals reflect the glyptic styles of seals employed at Persepolis: the heroic king fighting the horned and winged lion, and two man-bulls beneath the *xvarnah*.[89]

Under King Darius, the imperial chancelleries flourished. At Ecbatana, probably, the scribes prepared the texts for the Bisitun monument, first the official and prime text in Elamite, and then in Babylonian. It is not certain that the scribe who prepared the latter was a native speaker of Babylonian, yet he wrote in a colloquial rather than a literary Neo-Babylonian style, and had at least a limited knowledge of the formulae of

Neo-Babylonian royal inscriptions.[90] Then some learned scribe or committee of literati invented a new cuneiform syllabary for Old Persian by a careful and systematic development of the cuneiform wedge. Very few scribes, however, could read the new Old Persian.[91] The vocabulary of all three texts carved upon Bisitun is meagre and repetitious, and perhaps reflects that Darius spoke in a language in which he was not fluent. Yet the Old Persian text bears a poetic ring not unlike the early Zarathustrian *Gāthās*.

At the chancellery in Sardis, in 455 B.C., a satrapal decree issued in Aramaic was freely translated into Lydian, and both texts were inscribed upon a stone stele. The decree proclaimed: "On the fifth of Marheshwan, in the tenth year of King Artaxerxes, in the fortress Sardis. This is the stele and the tomb-cavern, the fire altar, and the vestibule which are above Sardis. This is the vestibule of the descendants of Mani, the son of Kumli, of the family of Siruk. Whoever seizes upon this stele or the tomb-cavern, or takes away the pillar at the front of this vestibule of the cavern, whoever destroys or injures anything; Artemis of Koloë and of the Ephesians will take away his estate, his house, his property, soil and water, and everything belonging to him shall be scattered both for him and his heirs." The Lydian Mani and his family had espoused Zarathustrianism, which practice had begun to spread through Anatolia, particularly Armenia and Cappadocia (Strabo 11.8.4, 14.16, 15.3.5). But the Achaemenid policy of religious toleration continued to respect Artemis of Koloë and of Ephesos.[92]

At the end of the fifth century B.C., the satrap of Sparda Artimas ordered the preparation of a rock cut tomb at Limyra in Lykia, with the Aramaic inscription: "Artimas the son of Arzifiya made this ossuary, anyone who . . . of him." The companion inscription in Greek declared: "Artimas, the son of Arziphios, of Limyra, and the great-grandfather of Artimas of Korydalla, first constructed this tomb for himself and his descendants." This tomb also conformed to Zarathustrian burial principles for a Persian whose personal cylinder seal (in a Greco-Persian style, a Persian horseman spearing a rampant monster), bore in Aramaic his name: "Artimas."[93] Generations later, in June/ July of 337 B.C., at Xanthos in Lykia a limestone stele at the Letoon was inscribed in chancery Aramaic, Greek, and Lykian. The official chancery Aramaic begins: "In the month of Siwan of year one of Artaxerxes (IV = Arses) King, in the citadel of Xanthos, Pixadoros the son of Katomno, the satrap in Karia and in Lykia decreed." The secondary

Greek text continued: "When Pixodaros, the son of Hekatomnos, became satrap of Lykia,

he appointed Hieron and Apollodotos archontes (governors) of Lykia and Artemelis

epimeletes (overseer) of Xanthos. The Xanthians and their perioikoi resolve to set up an

altar in honor of Basileus Kaunios and Arkesimas and they have chosen as priest Simias,

the son of Kondorasis. Let Pixodaros have the (final) authority." For the Xanthians who

lived in the urban center and the Lykian perioikoi who dwelt in the villages in the rural

plains of Xanthos, the satrap had to ratify the local decisions of his subordinate civil

officials. The tertiary Lykian text diverges only slightly from the Greek.[94]

In the late sixth century B.C., as Darius prepared to cross the Bosporos to conquer

Skudra and invade European Scythia, he ordered two white marble stelae to be erected on

the Asian side before the bridge designed by the engineer Mandrokles of Samos. Both

bore lists of the ethnic groups which marched in his army, one in Greek and the other in

Aramaic, which Herodotus called Assyrian (Hdt. 4.87). Both were later carted off to the

city of Byzantion.[95]

In nearby Daskyleion, a funerary stele bore the Aramaic inscription "These are the

reliefs of 'Elnap son of 'Shy. It was he who made them for his funerary monument. I

adjure thee by Bel and Nabu, whoever passes by this way let no one do harm (to my

tomb)."[96] 'Elnap was clearly not an East Greek, a Lydian, nor an Anatolian but a

Babylonian living in that satrapal center.

The letter which Darius sent to Gadatas, the governor of Magnesia-on-the-

Maeander, was apparently written in Aramaic, and upon its receipt in Sparda translated

into Ionic Greek. The Greek edition inscribed upon stone during the second century A.D.

contains traces of the earlier Ionic and several unusual syntactical problems, but

unfortunately the Aramaic original cannot be detected with any certainty. The opening

formulae do suggest chancery salutations. These, however, were often easily copied by

the Greeks, notably by the Spartan secretaries who forged the correspondence between

King Xerxes and Pausanias, the regent of Sparta (Thuc. 1.128-132).[97]

At Sardis, the scribes were important links in the complex administration and its

bureaucracy.   They were translators, copyists, writers, literary men, scholars, and

perhaps judicial experts, among whom the chief scribe kept and used the royal seal, the

sign of authority of the king and his satrap.[98] Within the archives at Persepolis, two

tablets record that in 496 B.C. a scribe at Sardis recorded and sealed a message from

Artaphrenes to Darius and, in the following year, four fast messengers carried a sealed document from the king back to the satrap.[99] In addition to the learned scribes, the bureaucracy included the ubiquitous dragomen, the bi- and trilingual interpreters (Hdt. 1.86, 3.140; Plut. *Them.* 28.1; Xen. *An.* 4.4.5, 4.5.34), such as the Karian Gaulites who served the satrap Tissaphernes and spoke Greek and Persian in addition to his native Karian (Thuc. 8.85.2). One of the more important duties the interpreters performed was to translate the imperial demands for vassalage, the royal exactions of earth and water (Plut. *Them.* 6.3)

The dragomen also accompanied the imperial heralds or sometimes acted in that capacity as well. To the king's subjects and to his enemies they announced the royal desires, commands, decrees, the demands for surrender and for earth and water. Often they returned bearing the latter (Hdt. 3.121, 6.48, 7.32, 131; Xen. *An.* 2.1.9; *Cyr.* 4.5.57, 5.4.24).

Royal edicts served not only to bind the satrapies to Darius' imperial reforms but also to reiterate the Persian policies of ethnic and religious toleration. For the Jews returning from Babylon to Judah in 538 B.C. the scribes in Cyrus' court at Ecbatana had prepared a written Aramaic memorandum, the record of the oral report or discussion among the king's advisors to allow the Jews to rebuild their temple to Yhwh (Ezra 6:3-5). But during the crisis in Jerusalem when the royalists supported Zerubbabel of the Davidic house, Tattenai the satrap of Across the River refused to allow work to proceed until he received Darius' confirmation of that edict. Tattenai's letter to Darius in 520 B.C., therefore, requested that the scribes search the royal archives in Babylon to locate the decree (Ezra 5:6-17). The search in Babylon was fruitless, but in Ecbatana the memorandum was located, and Darius acknowledged validity of Cyrus' ordinances, which had been brought into force by oral promulgation. Darius' scribes, consequently, prepared a new and more formal text, which they sent with a herald to Jerusalem to announce in that city: "Thus says Cyrus King of Persia." But as the new text apparently praised all powerful Ahura Mazda, the Jewish rendition of the edict into classical Hebrew, the official language of Jerusalem (Neh. 13:24), substituted the Jewish god Yhwh and continued: "All the kingdoms of this earth has Yhwh, the god of heaven, given me, and he commanded me to build him a house in Jerusalem, which is in Judah. Who is there among you of all his people? May his god be with him and let him go up to

Jerusalem, which is in Judah, and build the house of Yhwh, the god of Israel, which is god in Jerusalem. And all who remain, in any place where he sojourns, have to help him, the men of his place, with silver and gold, and with goods, and with riding-beasts, beside the freewill-offering from the house of god which is in Jerusalem" (Ezra 1:2-4).[100]

Through messengers and heralds, Bardiya had earlier announced his accession to the throne, even to Cambyses' soldiers in Egypt (Hdt. 3.62). To the Persian soldiers stationed in Sardis, Darius dispatched with Bagaios his edict: "King Darius charges the Persians in Sardis to kill Oroites" (Hdt. 3.128.4). And to the commander Megabazos in Thrace, Darius sent messengers with letters containing the order to remove the native Paeonians to Sparda (5.14). Many years later, in 416 B.C., King Darius II similarly dispatched a messenger to Arshames in Egypt with the edict: "[By order of Ahura Mazda and by order of the] King, [keep away from the] Jewish garrison."[101] Local officials, in turn, issued edicts for the administration of their constituencies (Ezra 10:7; Neh. 8:15).

Persian law emanating from the king permeated each satrapy and its ethnic groups to the lowest members of the imperial society. Essentially, each satrapy was a semi-autonomous and socio-political unit with its own internal administrative structure. This, consequently, produced extremely favorable conditions for the development of its social and economic institutions, and its political machine continued to employ native officials who developed fundamental knowledge of the local conditions and their functions. In Babylonia, for example, the Persians preserved the juridical legacy of the Assyro-Babylonian systems and maintained legal conservativism as Cyrus and Darius adopted the juridical phraseology, which stemmed from Hammurapi's Codex. The local royal officials were, therefore, charged with overseeing the application of the customary laws, as the king's laws, in the courts. This Achaemenid respect for local legal traditions and local autonomy produced a federative character to the empire, and gave to each satrapy its own code or *data*. In some satrapies the code was formal, in others less formal, a collection of laws and customs. The important factor was the subjects' attitude toward the law, and their concept of the law. In Babylonia, the king was the servant of the law, in Egypt he was the master of the law.[102] In Sparda, Darius' legal role had to reflect that of Croesus.

An adherent of the Zarathustrian admonitions to fight the Evil and the Lie, Darius revered as his highest judicial principles his prophet's teachings, the *Gāthās*. Centuries earlier, c. 1200 B.C.,[103] Zarathustra had pronounced: "Let those of good rule rule over us—not those of evil rule—with actions stemming from good understanding and with piety" (*Yasna* 48.5). "That good rule must be chosen which best brings good fortune to the man serving it with (strength). In alliance with truth, it shall encompass the best for us through its actions, O Mazda. This very rule shall I now bring to realization for us" (*Yasna* 51:1). "Yes, the person indeed who shall try to destroy us, O Mazda, is different from us: he is a son stemming from deceit's creator and thereby maleficent to those who exist. I therefore summon truth to me, to come to good reward" (*Yasna* 51:10).[104] These principles, Darius pronounced as this Ordinance of Good Regulations (*ṛta* = righteousness) which artisans carved upon the facade of his tomb at Naqsh-i Rustam (OP DNb).

In Mesopotamia by 519 B.C., the priests and scribes had prepared a code which applied to both Babylonia and Across the River, the remainder of the Assyrian and Chaldean empires, and to the Iranian areas. This Ordinance of Good Regulations was not new but a revision of the ancient Babylonian laws kept in the archives of the Esagila ziggurat, of Hammurapi's Codex housed in Susa, of Assyrian laws issued by Sargon II and Ashurbanipal, and numerous other judicial archives classified and categorized into a new casebook.[105] Several years later, in Egypt, a council of wise representatives of soldiers, priests, and scribes recorded the Egyptian laws as they existed down through the last year of Amasis, just before Cambyses' invasion. After Darius' return from Egypt to Susa in 518 B.C., he sent to the new satrap Pharnadates the edict to begin the codification, which the scribes completed by 503 B.C., and the finished work edited by Darius himself was distributed throughout the satrapy in 495 B.C. written upon papyrus rolls in Aramaic and native demotic.[106] And in Jerusalem, the Jewish priests had begun their edition of the Mosaic laws (P) to which Ezra in the middle of the century under King Artaxerxes I would add other rules to the basic and distinct Jewish code (Ezra 7:11; Neh. 8:1). The king's laws benefitted the upright and punished the guilty (Xen. *Oec.* 14.6) with sentences pronounced speedily, whether for death, for exile, for fine, or for imprisonment (Ezra 7:26). The most serious offenders, the king's officers impaled (Hdt. 3.125, 159, 4.43; Ezra 6:11).

For Sparda, in light of Darius' juridical activities in Mesopotamia, Egypt, and Judah, we may suspect similar orders for the reorganization of local law codes. For the Lydian region centered upon Sardis the law of Croesus and his Mermnad predecessors and the innovations of Cyrus and Cambyses may also have been categorized and codified during the last years of the sixth century B.C. under the satrapal direction of Artaphrenes. These would have stressed the Lydian nobility and the judicial regulations of the rural landed estates and the urban problems of the administrative center of Sardis. The East Greek poleis along the coastal zone similarly had their own local governments with ancient laws and customs, which the newly appointed Greek governors, or tyrants as the Greeks called them, would guide to adjust to the prevailing imperial laws of their overlord King Darius and his reorganization of Sparda.

Throughout the empire, the king's local counselors, his royal judges, wielded the local laws and jurisprudence of the prosperity of the king and his lands (cf. Hdt. 1.132); and these "sages" (Esther 1:14; Ezra 7:14-5; Dan. 6.8), both high Persian and Median dignitaries and local administrators, often retained their juridical functions through hereditary rights (Diod. Sic. 15.8, 10). In the case against Teribazos, a Persian military commander in Sparda (Nepos *Conon* 5.3) charged with negligence prejudicial to the interests of the empire, King Artaxerxes II chose three judges from several illustrious Persians to try him (Diod. Sic. 15.8-10). For the entire empire, Darius maintained the mosaic of national and governmental diversities sustained by a collection of regional codifications, much like the succeeding Seleucid empire. The Achaemenid empire obtained a unity by means of this diversity, and the tolerance of each ethnic group within its socio-ecological niche.

But in the urban centers of the East Greek Poleis important political roles began to emerge and develop in contrast to the Achaemenid court procedures at Susa and at Sardis. Within Darius' unifying forces, which structured the reorganization of Sparda, the expanding political institutions there tended to initiate revolutionary processes, which created new and conflicting orders as Darius' imperial procedures, contained intrinsic limitations. Achaemenid imperial expansion reversed the natural direction of the East Greek causal relations between socio-political development and culture in the Ionian poleis. Conflict would, therefore, eventually erupt between the East Greeks and their imperially imposed governors, the people (the landed gentry and the urban dwellers) and the local Greek tyrants, and then between the landed gentry and the urban dwellers as factionalism and new aspects of imperialism continued.

VASSALAGE AND THE LANDED GENTRY

The economic elements fundamental to the Achaemenid Empire were the institutions of rural agriculture: the peasants' small farms, the landed gentry's demesnes, and the small rural village clusters. Darius' extensive reorganization of state rested intrinsically upon those who supplied the imperial magazines and treasuries with tribute in kind and valuable metals and who served in the imperial armies (Hdt. 1.192, 6.42, 6.48).[1] In Egypt, where long established irrigation farming produced relatively stable, high yields, great estates (cf. Hdt. 2.109.1) lined the Nile's banks. In southern Babylonia in the district of Nippur, the great vassal estates, the hatru which supplied, in addition to taxes, vassal retainers in military service, the men of "bow-lands," "horse-lands," and "chariot-lands," passed on to the Murashu firm in Nippur their tribute for the Great King. In Cappadocia (cf. Hdt. 1.76.1) and Sparda, other landed estates, the oikoi or demesnes of the landed gentry, also provided taxes and military men to their satrapal centers, according to the fiscal nomoi outlined by Herodotus (3.90).

For the Greeks the taxes were "the revenues . . . collected by the king . . .,"[2] gathered by his tax collectors and noted by the tax recorders (Plut. *Kim.* 19.4);[3] tax and tribute payments based not merely on the amount of land held, but upon its potential for producing profits, the kinds of cultivation and average yields.[4] For the writer of the Aristotelian pamphlet the *Oeconomica* the sources for satrapal revenues varied [1345b-1346b (2.1.4)]: " . . .arising from agriculture, from the special products of the chora, from markets, from taxes, from cattle, and from other sources. The first and most important of them is revenue arising from agriculture, which some call tithe and some produce-tax. The second is that from special products; in one place gold, in another silver, in another copper, and so on. Third in importance is revenue from markets, and fourth that which arises from taxes on land and on sales. In fifth place we have revenue from cattle, called tithe or 'first-fruits'; and in the sixth, revenue from other sources, which we term head-tax, or tax on manufacturing." For Polyianos, the system was just and equitable (7.11.3), and for Plato it had been established by multiples of laws and regulations (*Leg.* 3.695d), which, in turn, produced the revenues carefully guarded in the treasuries (Strabo 15.3.21). For Herodotus, Darius acted as a kapelos, an "entrepreneur,"

which the nineteenth century translators deigned to read as "huckster." Darius' reforms
lasted neither modified nor changed by Alexander III (Arrian *An.* 3.16).[5]

I

From Egypt, Aramaic papyri and leather documents contain evidence for the
divisions of agricultural land and records of their taxes and military services rendered to
the king.[6] One papyrus, dated to the reign of Darius, 515 B.C., notes in detail tenant
farmers contracting for the share–cropping of parcels of land. In this instance, the
tenant was an Egyptian who signed a contract with a Jewish proprietor.[7] Several years
later, on the 22nd of October 495 B.C., a second document indicated that the Jewish
mercenaries at Elephantine at the first cataract had received allocations for agricultural
lots.[8] Both legal documents bear notations to the Achaemenid calendar, which had
spread throughout the empire during Darius' reorganization. Other papryri contain the
records of the distribution of rations and food stuffs to the Jewish mercenaries, records
similar to those of the Persepolis fortification tablets, which also note the records of
supplies sent to the royal magazines.[9] These legal documents from Elephantine, strongly
reflective of Neo–Assyrian legal traditions, had assimilated Egyptian, Babylonian, and
Persian elements, which structured the recent legal codification and reorganization of
Egypt, and their parallels throughout the empire.[10] The Jewish colonists whom the
Persian government employed as mercenaries at that strategic fort between Egypt and
Nubia had settled the island and river banks at Elephantine with their families and their
possessions, and participated in the buying, selling, and other legal transactions among
themselves and with the native Nubian and Egyptian populace. At that center, the local
scribes recorded the cultivated plots and the taxes incumbent upon the mercenaries, and
imperial heralds transmitted the governmental edicts, the military orders, and court
sentences.[11]

Among the more important land holders in Egypt was the Persian satrap Arshames,
whose products and revenues from his estates provided him with great agricultural
wealth. In turn, Arshames had to deal with the administration of Egypt and the problems
of the other estates, their landowners, tenant farmers, and revenues. Of these, the
satrap supervised the collection and transport of the revenues from administrative
estates, in addition to a variety of land tenure problems, which included the assignment

of a father's revenues to a son who had succeeded him to office, the transfer of a tract of land to the son of a deceased tenant, the care and protection of his own estates and the employment of a subordinate staff for his needs, and the supervision of military affairs. Among the letters from the satrap to his subordinates to carry out his orders to expedite those matters, the officers were referred to as servants or "slaves," terms which denoted their subordinate vassal status to their overlord. As Arshames was the "servant-slave" or vassal of his king, his subordinates were his "slaves" or vassals. In freely employing natives within the administration of the regional territories, the Persians bound their subordinates within vassalage relations and rewarded them with the necessary and important parcels of land. At least in Egypt, these subordinate positions passed on from father to son, who were responsible for delivering the revenues of estates to the higher officials.[12] In Egypt, therefore, the political hierarchy proceeded from the king who vested provincial authority in the satrap. At the local level, superintendents governed with their main functions being to collect rents from the various individual farms, to pass the rents on to the satrapal office, and to maintain order in time of unrest.[13]

From the records of the Murashu family of Babylonian business men centered at Nippur, hundreds of cuneiform tablets (the majority of the texts dated to 424-417 B.C.) reveal the complexities of business practices in relation to the local conditions of land tenure within the greater imperial problems of the royal treasuries and their connections with land holdings and administrative responsibilities.[14] Many of the tablets written in Babylonian cuneiform bear short Aramaic inscriptions written in ink or lightly scratched into clay while wet, and seal impressions with the names and titles of the various owners of those seals.[15] This archive gathered in a single room, with tablets which occasionally refer to other documents written on parchment, bears witness to the complicated hatru system of land tenure and military obligations and of the persons involved who had a variety of ethnic names. Jews,[16] West Semites, and Iranians prevailed among Egyptians, Arabs, Lykians, Lydians, and others, from India to Anatolia, from Egypt to the Caspian Sea.

These records identify the nature of the Babylonian landed demesne, the holdings of agricultural serviles or vassals who, as groups of patrilineal relatives, held those properties on the condition of the payment of annual taxes, in kind or in silver, and of military service. The payments of taxes were not in coinage but rather in ingots or pieces of silver as measures of weight, similar to the payments of silver noted among the Persepolis fortification and treasury tablets. The numerous individuals grouped into hatru associations held properties, which were specifically designated according to the type of military service they supported: "bow-lands," "horse-lands," and "chariot-lands," or the military divisions of archers, cavalrymen, and charioteers. For hatru groups, the lands held were inheritable and divisible among their occupants, but also inalienable. In supervision of each hatru, the overseer and his assistants were directly responsible for the allocation of the lands and for the collections of taxes due from them. The hatru as a collective estate of soldiers or functionaries was often also held by groups of foreign troops, garrisons of imperial soldiers gathered from India, Armenia, Bactria, Arabia, Phoenicia, and Sparda. While many of the hatru divisions were small, other estates, essentially large landed tracts, were the demesnes of nobles, courtiers, and other administrators of the satrapy and the empire. The Persian nobles, royal eunuchs, and other high ranking officials held their lands as privileged demesnes, as did Queen Parysatis, the wife of Darius II, who owned estates in Syria and in Media (Xen. *An.* 1.4.9; 2.4.27).[17] These, too, were taxed. The king also maintained considerable demesnes in Babylonia, which were managed directly in his interests but which were tax exempt.

As each vassal hatru organization was divided into landed units held as benefices of an entire family undivided and inalienable, each noble, officer, and landed family also held its estate in vassalage subordination to the king. In the reorganization of the military empire, Darius fostered in Babylonia a formal hierarchy of communal organizations, the garrisons and military colonies, and the hatru organizations, and rewarded their civil and military services with lands. This, unfortunately, did generate a certain degree of instability as the divided inheritance of lands produced a diminution of properties available to individual vassals and the struggles of new financial opportunities. Absentee ownership of estates also created problems within the requirements of local managements. This absentee ownership, complicated by the intrigues of court politics, often made the ownership of great demesnes precarious. These circumstances, therefore, favored the development of management services such as those of the Murashu firm to supervise the nobles' estates and hatru organizations specifically for the collection of taxes. While members of the Murashu family and agents within its firm also held "bow-lands" of their own, for the majority of the other estates, the family firm acted as an important intermediate agency, which undertook the management of the agricultural properties of others. The Murashu firm leased lands and water from their owners and paid rents and taxes to them or to their representatives. In turn, the banking firm sublet to tenants divisions of those lands, in addition to supplying livestock, equipment, and seed. The hundreds of cuneiform documents within the Murashu archive contain the leases of properties to the firm, the subleases of land to tenants, and the receipts of rents and taxes paid by the firm to the vassal landlords. In fulfilling its services the firm often had to convert farm produce in kind into silver by selling the large stores of crops obtained from the tenant farmers to the inhabitants of Nippur and southern Babylonia for the silver necessary to transmit to the landlords. The firm did this not only for hatru organizations and landed estates of the vassal nobility but also for crown lands. The firm's records, consequently, contain a list of landowners and tenant farmers and an evaluation of their properties for the purposes of imposing taxes and assigning of military responsibilities, both obligations as prescribed by the imperial government.

Within the district of ancient Nippur, crisscrossed by irrigation canals which carried water for the agricultural lands, hundreds of "bow-lands" (the unit being the *bit qashti*) dotted the plain, in addition to about nine "horse-lands" and two "chariot-lands." Of these, the "bow-land" division was the smallest, the "chariot-land" the largest, with the "horse-land" employing more workers than the "bow-land," and the "chariot-land" employing still more. In each, the nature of the plots varied, as the "horse-land" included orchards and fields of grain. Often members of a single extended family cultivated the "bow-land" while other "bow-lands" and "horse-lands" formed more than seventy hatru organizations cultivated by larger clans or groups of clans. Of these, for example, diasporic Jews formed four clans, which resided in thirty-seven settlements, among Tyrians and Philistines, and cultivated farms of small and middle sized tracts, herded, and fished, but together did not play important roles in the economic life of Nippur.[18]

The institution of a census, the registry of land for the assessment of tax and military obligations, occurred at Nippur and throughout Babylonia in 500/499 B.C. as part of Darius' sweeping imperial reorganization.[19] As with all aspects of that reform, the institutions and problems of land tenure in Babylonia, as in Egypt, underwent continuous transformation as inheritance problems occurred, political upheavals altered nobles' claims, and commercial activities changed. These complications compounded the Murashu firm's administrative activities as incomplete records of land transfer indicate the historical realities of those transformations of the agricultural management and economy throughout Babylonia. The Achaemenid system of land tenure remained strongly based upon grants of parcels of land given by the king to his vassal warriors on the condition of service to the crown. In turn, the archers, cavalrymen, and charioteers rendered taxes in kind and in silver, and military service. Smaller units of these lands were similarly granted on condition of service to satrapal officials, down to those of lowest servile and vassal rank. In regard to these vassals, the documents usually listed them as "slaves," but their status was clearly vassalage.[20]

In Judah, about the same time, Nehemiah recorded the problems of poor Jews who, forced to pay their royal taxes, mortgaged their fields, vineyards, and houses, and borrowed money against future harvests. Many also had to face giving away their sons and daughters as indentured servants and slaves to stave off the economic crises and famine (Neh. 5:1-12). Nehemiah did not specifically refer to military service within this passage, nevertheless, the reference to the king's taxes clearly relates the agricultural problems in Judah during the late fifth century to the agricultural taxation records of the Murashu firm and similar tax records among the Aramaic documents from Egypt. While each satrapy and its subdivisions retained its essential regional nature, its local administrations and officials, and its peculiar and particular ethnic and religious customs and activities, the imperial reforms instituted by Darius extended into each satrapy and subdivision in the form of the fundamental and universal requests of taxation in kind or in silver and of military service.

In a recent article, Pierre Briant persuasively argued that the Achaemenid Empire was essentially a military monarchy held together by warrior forces imposed upon the numerous diverse peoples, in a relationship between military constraint and rural dependency. The rural and agricultural villages tributary to the satrapal administrations supported military servicemen in addition to occupation troops in the form of garrisons and military colonies, which ensured the Achaemenid politico-military subjections and the fiscal gains of the imperial system. In turn, the garrisons provided security to the farmers working the fields and the pastoralists herding their flocks. Taxes, therefore, provided the maintenance of the garrisons and colonies, and supported the standing armies of the satrapies and the empire. As Polyainos noted (7.29.1), three institutions basic to all rural areas were the agricultural villages (the komai), their tribute or taxes (phoros), and the royal garrisons (phrouria). Peasants furnished the royal treasuries with agricultural products in kind and administrative units with corvée labor, while the military units defended the country against foreign attack, local brigands and rebels, and maintained the obeisance of the king's subjects. Briant, in identifying the Babylonian hatru as a fiscal and military unit, equated that organization to the rural fortresses and garrison posts in Sparda, the choria and the phrouria.[21] Among these, colonies of eastern Hyrkanians dotted the Sardian plain (Strabo 13.6.29),[22] and other Hyrkanians dwelt along the Kaikos valley.[23] Babylonian and Hyrkanian soldiers guarded the north-western region of Anatolia in Mysia (Xen. An. 7.8.15), and a guard post on top of Mt. Tmolos protected the Lydian plains (Strabo 13.4.5.). In Cappadocia, Briant noted seventy-five Achaemenid fortified posts which survived into the Hellenistic period.[24] In addition to military posts, throughout Anatolia numerous officials held palaces, large estates, and parks with hunting preserves, gardens, and meadow lands.[25] Briant, consequently, equated the Greek unit of land for agricultural production and military support, the kleros, with the agricultural units of the Babylonian hatru organization.[26]

We can, however, refine this comparison of the Spardian system of land holdings to the Babylonian system at Nippur and to the Egyptian system. While the specific conditions of land holding may have differed in form from place to place, the functions were clearly similar. The hatru as a collection of lands, essentially a large "enclosure," contained basic parcels of land, each designated as the "bow-land" or the bit qashti.[27] In Sparda, the kleros as the equivalent to the bit qashti formed the oikos, the demesne of the landed noble, which in many cases was also a pyrgos: the demesne with the noble's rural home and related agricultural buildings, the homes of associated free peasants, of tenant farmers, and of slaves.[28] In each case, Spardian, Babylonian, and Egyptian, the demesne (and in Sparda specifically the oikos or the pyrgos) contributed to the imperial fisc the assessed revenues and to the imperial armies the required military contingents. At Nippur, consequently, the Persian army incorporated the military contingents there, ethnic groups which included Phoenicians of Tyre, Lydians of Sardis, Armenians, and Arabs from Syria. In each region, the ownership of land marked the landed noble's membership into the community of armored warriors.

The Ionian oikos and pyrgos resembled the earlier Lydian estates (*Il.* 20.391) controlled by the family (oikeia: Polyainos 7.6.2-3) or the genos (Hdt. 1.6.1, 7, 16: Nic. Dam. *FGrH* 90 F 63) of Lydian nobles and leaders of military contingents (Nic. Dam. *FGrH* 90 F 16). Of these hereditary landed gentry, bound to the Persian vassalage system who led armed retainers and governed agrarian tenants, clients, and slaves, the Lydian Pythios of Kelainai in Cappadocia at the head of the Maeander River was probably exceptional. Herodotus reported that Pythios entertained King Xerxes and his entire army on their march to Athens, and provided the Persian king with money for the war effort. Some years earlier, Pythios had given Darius the gift of a gold plane-tree and vine, and was considered the richest man in the empire second only to the king (Hdt. 7.26-9).[29] Later in the century, in Mysia, the Persian noble Asidates governed vast estates and pastoral flocks, with a towered fortress which six hundred of Xenophon's veterans failed to take by storm (*An.* 7.8.17).

Exiled Greeks in vassalage to the Great King also held vast estates. Gongylos the Eretrian, who collaborated with the Persians when they attacked Eretria in 490 B.C. (Xen. *Hell.* 3.1.6), gained for his services territories in the poleis of Myrina, Gryneion, Gambreion and Palaigambreion scattered in the Troad, and confirmed his vassalage to King Xerxes by marriage to one of the king's daughters (Thuc. 1.128.5; Diod. Sic. 11.44.3; Nepos *Paus.* 2.2; Justin 2.15.14). Generations later, the estates still remained in the family, then headed by Gongylos' grandsons, the brothers Gongylos III and Gorgion. Gongylos III held Gambreion and Palaigambreion, while Gorgion held Myrina and Gryneion (Xen. *An.* 7.8.8).[30] Damaratos, the former Eurypontid "king" of Sparta who had defected to Darius' aid, also received from Xerxes as benefits for his loyalty estates throughout the Troad in Pergamon, Teuthrania, Halisarna, and in Gambreion as well. In 400 B.C., Damaratos' descendants Eurysthenes and his brother Prokles still held the estates; Eurysthenes in Pergamon and Prokles in the other poleis (Xen. *Hell.* 3.1.6.; *An.* 7.8.17; Paus. 3.7.7).[31] As with the Harpagid family in Lykia, the Greek vassals structured hereditary dynasties bound loyally to the Persian kings. These grants of vassal land ranked similar to Cyrus' grants of land to the deposed monarchs Croesus, the village of Barene near Ecbatana (Ktesias *FGrH* 688 F 9.4), and Nabonidus in eastern Karmania (Berossos *FGrH* 680 F 9; Abydenos *FGrH* 685 F 6); and to those which Xerxes gave to

Amyntas, the son of the Persian Bubares and Gygaia, the sister of King Alexander I of Macedon, in the Karian city of Alabanda (Hdt. 8.136), (fig. 19). In similar manner, the commander Harpagos, a superb tactician and conquerer of Lydia, Ionia, Karia and Lykia (Hdt. 1.80, 108-13), a Mede of royal blood related to Kings Astyages and Cyrus, obtained Lykia as his vassal demesne. A century and a half later, Pharnabazos, the satrap of Daskyleion, awarded the renegade Athenian nobleman Alkibiades with a fortress (castrum) at Gryneion north of Aiolian Kyme, from which the Athenian supposedly received annually a revenue of fifty talents (Nepos *Alc.* 9.3.).[32]

From Athens, the deposed tyrant Hippias, within the Persian Empire, also found refuge as a loyal vassal of Darius who hoped to be restored and rule Attica as a vassal state. Dwelling in the Troad, Hippias governed Sigeion at the southern mouth of the Hellespont, a polis long under the control of his aristocratic family, the Peisistratid house of Brauron in Attica (Hdt. 5.62-5; Thuc. 6.59; *Ath. Pol.* 19; Marmor Parium *FGrH* 239 F 45; Aristoph. *Lys.* 1153 and *Schol.*). His son-in-law Aiantides, tyrant of Lampsakos also in the Troad and at the northern mouth of the Hellespont, was another Greek vassal loyal to Darius (Hdt. 4.138; Thuc. 6.59.3), as was Aiantides' father the tyrant Hippoklos who served the Great King on his European Scythian expedition.[33] Elsewhere in the Troad, at Kolonai, east south-east of Lampsakos, Pausanias, the Agiad regent of Sparta, briefly held Persian vassal rank in the mid-470's B.C. (Thuc. 1.131.1; Nepos *Paus.* 3.3). During that time, the Spartans claimed that he had married one of King Xerxes' daughters (Thuc. 1.28.5; Diod. Sic. 11.44.3; Nepos *Paus.* 2.2; Justin 2.15.14), as reported by their forged correspondence between Pausanias and Xerxes, but more accurately he had married the daughter of the Achaemenid Persian Megabates, the satrap of Daskyleion (Hdt. 5.32; Aelian *VH* 9.41).[34] Several decades later Themistokles, the Athenian political leader and military general also in exile in Persia, received from King Artaxerxes I vassal estates in the Ionian poleis of Magnesia-on-the-Maeander and Myous, and in the Troad poleis of Palaiskepsis, Gambreion, Perkote, and Lampsakos.[35] At the latter, Aiantides and his family still held estates (Thuc. 6.59.3-4). For the Great King and in Old Persian terminology, each Greek functioned as a *martiya-*, a vassal no less as a *bandaka-*, or "slave-servant."[36] To these vassals or benefactors (the *orasaggai*; Hdt. 8.85), the king had given such landed estates.[37]

For Sparda, the institution of vassal demesnes and the processes of vassalage had origins in the Lydian period, phenomena also evident within the earlier Hittite system. As crown prince, Croesus governed Adramyttion and the plain of Thebe (Nic. Dam, *FGrH* 90 F 65). Later, to his friend the Greek Pytharchos of Kyzikos, Cyrus granted seven cities in the Troad as rewards for special services rendered to the crown. The cities (or demesnes within those cities) had earlier been controlled by the Lydians since the reign of Gyges (Strabo 12.4.6; 13.1.22). But Pytharchos, according to the Babylonian Agathokles, discontent with that gift alone raised an army and with force became tyrant of Kyzikos *(FGrH* 472 F 6). Unfortunately, we do not know whether Cyrus or Harpagos intervened or assisted, nor whether it remained purely a local affair.

The problems which have long plagued scholars, how Gongylos, Damaratos, and Themistokles could hold Gambreion, Aiantides and Themistokles hold Lampsakos, and Gorgion and Alkibiades hold Gryneion as Persian territories; and how Myous, Magnesia-on-the-Maeander, Lampsakos, and Gryneion in the fifth century B.C. could be controlled by both the Persian and the Athenian Empires; are solved when we realize that the several Persian vassals held not entire poleis but landed estates within those East Greek poleis. And as we shall consider in chapter 10, during the fifth century Persia apparently controlled the landed estates within the chora of the four controversial poleis while the asty in each was controlled by the Athenians.

II

In 493, the satrap Artaphrenes ordered the registry of land for taxation and military obligations, which entailed the careful administrative survey of land, as in Babylonia, Judah, and Egypt, and in Sparda (Hdt. 6.42). The official surveyors measured the regions of the Ionian poleis and the Lydian territories of Sparda into units of parasangs, the Persian units of land measurement each equal to about 5.6 km., and from these units of agricultural lands drew up the registry and its concomitant census records. This registry, Herodotus noted, listed taxes about the same as they had been earlier, and here he may be referring to the records of the fiscal nomoi, which he listed in book 3.89 and as established by Darius apparently in 520 B.C. Artaphrenes' registry, Herodotus also noted, remained fixed during the fifth century and was, we assume, adopted by the Athenians and Aristeides in their taxation registry of the Ionian poleis, which in rebellion against

Persia joined Athens' Delian Confederacy.[38] The great map of Sparda and the Persian Empire, a copy of which Hekataios in Miletos used, and which may have been the source of Herodotus' fiscal records for the Persian Empire (3.89-94), aided greatly in the original drafting and organization of this registry, checked by Artaphrenes and his satrapal officials, and counter-checked by the records and observations of the King's Eye in Sparda.[39] The ramifications of Darius' reorganization of his empire transmitted throughout Sparda entailed the essential factors of this registry for tax collection and conscription for military service, aspects of the reorganization which reached down to the fundamental elements of the great landed estates and the smaller farms of the landowning peasantry. For Darius, Great King and overlord, the taxes and military services marked each Spardian nobleman's vassalage to the state, of services for the royal and imperial protection and its benefices (see Plate 2). Upon the walls of the north and east staircases of the apadana hall at Persepolis, Darius' artisans carved each imperial ethnic group in military service bearing their encomium tributes; the same military groups Xerxes led against Athens (Hdt. 7.61-99).

Darius' registry of land, census, and tax allocations was not the first. When Croesus had subdued the East Greeks he, too, had demanded tribute from them (Hdt. 1.6, 27.1), and upon the basis of this registry and apparently a similar registry for Lydia, Croesus called up Lydian and East Greek military forces to fight Cyrus (Hdt. 1.77). And when Cyrus defeated Croesus and the Lydians, he made them subject to Persia as vassals and also imposed the imperial demands of tribute and military obligations (Hdt. 1.95.1). For the East Greeks before Croesus' conquests, their lands had been free from regular taxation and any tithe or other form of land tax, which they claimed were the marks of tyranny. In political terms, the Greeks noted a pronounced distinction between the liberty of the citizens of a polis and the lack of liberty, relative or total, under empires; a distinction marked by the loss of political self-determination and the payment of tribute to the subjugating power.[40] Herodotus, consequently, stressed throughout his history the political leitmotif of political freedom versus tyranny (cf. 1.62.1, 96.1), and labeled the Mermnad, Median, and Achaemenid kings tyrants and despots.[41]

With Cyrus' conquest of the East Greek poleis, the Ionians for a second time became "enslaved" (Hdt. 1.169.2), and in swearing oaths to the king as did the Milesians and offering the customary symbols of earth and water, they became the king's vassals. To

Plate 2. Representatives from Sparda presenting encomium gifts to the Great King, east staircase, apadana, Persepolis (photograph by author).

rule the East Greek poleis effectively, and especially after the rebellion of Oroites, Darius appointed in each case a local Greek nobleman to the office of governor, the regional hyparchos or "tyrant" as the Greeks referred to them.[42]   In each polis, therefore, the tyrant was responsible for the allotment of taxation and the mustering of troops for the king's army. Because of their own personal interests in political power and personal gain, the tyrants became devoted to the Achaemenid cause of the imperial reorganization and its laws, and with military constraint ensured the confidence and the fidelity of the citizens of the poleis.   While carrying out the imperial measures, the tyrants were sincerely concerned with the internal life and development of their poleis, and, as East Greeks, had the facilities to understand and to interpret the imperial measures compatible with the interests of their subjects. The local aristocratic councils and assemblies may not have been abandoned, but the tyrants did dominate the political direction of their poleis.   Local laws, tribunals, magistracies, priesthoods, and aristocratic control of private properties continued as they had under Croesus and earlier under absolute political freedom, but only as long as they were compatible with Artaphrenes' satrapal demands in the name of King Darius. When the security of his subjects seemed in jeopardy, as military commander for Darius, prince Artaphrenes did intervene.[43]

The most dramatic display of these tyrants and their military contingents occurred during Darius' expedition into Skudra and against the European Scythians when the king employed the major East Greek tyrants commanding important naval forces to assist in his crossing of the Danube River: Miltiades the Younger of the Chersonesos, Daphnis of Abydos, Hippoklos of Lampsakos, Herophantos of Parion, Metrodoros of Prokonnesos, Aristagoras of Kyzikos, and Ariston of Byzantion, all from the Hellespontine region; Aristagoras of Kyme in Aiolis; and from Ionia, Laodamas of Phokaia, Strattis of Chios, Aiakes the son of Syloson of Samos, and Histiaios of Miletos (Hdt. 4.137-8). After the expedition, Darius appointed Koes tyrant of Mytilene on Lesbos in reward for his helpful advice given in crossing the Danube (Hdt. 4.97.6, 5.11, 37.1).   Had Darius been overthrown or died in Scythia, the tyrants knew their authority would end (Hdt. 4.137), and the aristocrats would regain control.

In that realization of the loss of political position, which Herodotus attributed to the tyrant Histiaios of Miletos, we uncover the explicit difference between the Persian established tyrannies and the earlier tyrannies, for instance those of Thrasyboulos of Miletos and Polykrates of Samos. In these earlier cases, tyranny arose marking an internal condition of individual stress and societal distortion whereby the revolutionary elements of the evolution of political factionalism occurred. Because of the firmly held considerations of one or more aristocratic factions within the polis that the then present political and economic conditions were untenable, they supported a leader from their own group to seize power forcibly rather than to rise to a political position through election or sortition. There was, therefore, no sharp distinction between the tyrannos and the regularly chosen aisymnetes, the civic magistrate. As internal factionalism, in essence, created the conditions for the tyrannical revolution so, too, internal factionalism and not necessarily external factionalism could structure the political and military mechanisms for the removal of tyrants and the return to governments controlled by the landed aristocrats. While Herodotus wrote that Histiaios said "for each of the poleis would consider to become democratized rather than tyrannized," we must understand the Halikarnassian's use of *dēmokrateesthai* in relation to the later passage (6.43.3). In that passage Herodotus noted that in the spring of 492 B.C., following Artaphrenes' survey of Ionia for the land registry (6.42), Darius' son-in-law the commander Mardonios, son of Gobryas, "deposed all the Ionian tyrants and set up *dēmokratias* in the poleis." In this Herodotean leitmotif of freedom and popular government in contrast to tyranny and imposed despotism, we must understand "democracy" not as that form of government in Periklean Athens but rather as a government determined by the political forces formerly and still potentially in control of the Ionian poleis. Those governments after 492 B.C. were distinctly "constitutional governments" as demokratia can indicate, in which the rural aristocratic factions regained political control (Diod. Sic. 10.25.2).

The tyrannies established by Darius and Artaphrenes, and specifically those tyrants which Herodotus listed as being on the Danube (4.137-8), did not arise internally but were imposed externally upon the poleis. Darius' imperial conquest of Sparda through his agents Bagaois, Otanes, and Artaphrenes, a conquest reinforced by imperial reform and edict, and Darius' own presence in Sardis, produced unnatural alterations in the governments of the East Greek poleis. The Greek tyrannies imposed by the Persians upon their subject vassal poleis had not arisen by aristocratic factionalism even though many East Greek and native Anatolian families with pro-Persian sympathies accepted and supported the tyrants, at least temporarily. As tyranny in these cases had not occurred out of the regular internal conditions of stress, distortion, and internal factionalism, the regular mechanisms for the removal of those tyrants were also absent. The Persian king, his satraps, his commanders, and his armies enforced the tyrannies, and only rebellion against the king and his empire could remove them. This is precisely what occurred throughout Ionia in 499 B.C. and what prompted Darius to command Mardonios in 492 B.C. to remove the tyrants. To reinforce his "freedom" leitmotif, Herodotus stressed Miltiades' fictional debate with Histiaios on the Danube to foreshadow the eventual Athenian victories over the Persians.[44] Herodotus, therefore, noted that "Miltiades the Athenian, commander and tyrant of the Chersonesites of the Hellespont," argued that the Ionian tyrants should destroy the bridge across that river, abandon Darius to the European Scythians, and "set Ionia free" (4.137).[45] In the early fifth century B.C., Ionia remained firmly aristocratic.

In the Ionian poleis of Sparda, as throughout the ancient Greek world, the ownership of land, of agricultural demesnes, marked the political status of the aristocratic gentry. Only rarely and then under extreme conditions were citizenship and its political prerogatives ever extended to individual foreigners. Within the polis, therefore, citizens were classed in relationship to their agricultural productivity: first, the landed gentry who owned estates large enough to live off the labor of others, second, the farmers or peasants who worked their lands themselves, and third, those who did not own the means to farm but worked as tenant farmers or laborers for the landed nobles. Economic class rank and status consciousness were inextricably interwoven with political and religious factors within the polis.[46] In the aristocratic communities, full political participation within the government, therefore, was restricted to the aristocrats or landed gentry who held the great estates and to the relatively larger number of peasant farmers who worked their own but smaller farms. To Artaphrenes and the Great King, both the landed gentry and the peasants paid their taxes and fulfilled their obligations of military service, according to the land registry, which the satrap assembled. But unlike the gentry, the peasants had little economic protection in reserve to survive bad harvests and the depredations of war. The tenant farmers, in comparison, as laborers for the gentry were protected by their lords from the dispossession from the land and the harsh laws of debt, which affected the free and landed peasants, and generally not owning armor did not serve in the hoplite military. East Greek hoplites were armored foot soldiers of the gentry and peasant classes, often accompanied by their dogs. The hoplites did not serve as archers, cavalrymen, or charioteers, yet were accompanied by the gymnetai, the "naked men" of light-armed troops, who threw stones and occasionally javelins.[47] Against Athens in 480 B.C., King Xerxes called up the military units of Sparda, Lydian and Mysian hoplites and East Greek sailors who manned two hundred and ninety ships, all wearing Greek armor except the Mysians and Karians who carried some of their native equipment (Hdt. 7.74, 93-5).

The interrelationships of lordship and vassalage, of financial and military obligations, and of homage or proskynesis prevailed throughout the Persian Empire and in Sparda. The landed estate or demesne, the kleros or agricultural unit, which Xenophon noted as the oikos (Cyr. 8.4.28., 6.5) held by the landed gentry, bound the subservient nobles to the Great King within the institution of vassalage.[48] For Gadatas at Magnesia-on-the-Maeander, for example, who served Darius as *doulos*, or *bandaka*, in essence his "slave-servant" or vassal, the king had "laid up great honor in his house" (ML *GHI* 12:4, 15-7)[49] The relationship of Gadatas as nobleman with a demesne to Darius, for whom he served as an official of Magnesia, was clearly that of a vassal in the service of his protector and benefactor. In Egypt, Babylonia, and Judah, among the examples cited above, the particular form of vassalage duties to the king reflected the problems of their specific local regions, but the functions of vassalage transcended those particularisms, and were also apparent throughout Sparda. The agricultural lands, the chora, with the vassal estates, the oikoi, supported the landed gentry and peasantry who served their satrap and king by means of vassal services, *hypēkooi*, the rendering of taxes and military obligations. As each satrap throughout the empire was obligated to pay fixed sums to the central royal treasuries, each was also responsible for the collection of those sums, and the conscription of soldiers for military service. The Babylonians and Assyrians who marched with Xerxes towards Athens wore the armor characteristic of armed soldiers possessing land. Herodotus described them as wearing helmets of twisted bronze in an extremely unusual design, linen breastplates, and bearing shields and daggers of an Egyptian style, and wooden clubs studded with iron spikes (Hdt. 7.63). Some of these apparently had come from the "bow-lands," "horse-lands," and "chariot-lands" of Nippur, where the Akkadian texts note that the breastplates had been of iron rather than linen.[50]

The pyrgoi of Teos, similar to the pyrgoi of Smyrna, Erythrai, Miletos, and Karia and apparently elsewhere throughout Ionia and Sparda, reveal the fundamental elements of the landed estates of the Ionian aristocracies. In Teos, the great families, East Greeks, Lydians, and Anatolians, had divided extensive low rolling fertile fields rich in barley, cattle, and sheep. Each family as a genos, the kin tie unit of the extended clan, held its pyrgos as the economic structure of the oikos, and in many cases since the early days of Anatolian settlement and East Greek colonization. Some of the more than forty estates had passed out of the hands of the original families, but at least ten (and possibly others) remained into the Hellenistic era in the possession of the families descended from the early East Greek colonists. Ten other estates, by the Hellenistic era, had become vacant, perhaps with the extinction of the genos, or were then in dispute or held by minors.[51] The pyrgos as a large rural house with a tower appeared similar to the Hellenistic baris,[52] the rural estate (LXX Ps. 44 [45]:9; Dan. 8:2), and the modern Greek chorion or village. Walled villages in Ionia also occurred but significantly different from the pyrgoi and were referred to as teiche, often used as places of refuge and similar to the Greek pergama or citadels. Xenophon in citing the fortified houses of rich Persians in Mysia used pyrgos alternatively with tyrsis (An. 7.8.8), and other fortified estates in Thrace and Anatolia (4.4.2, 5.2.5, 7.2.21).[53] In each case, the pyrgos or teichos bore political and military significance.

The remains of ancient pyrgoi are common throughout the Aegean islands, Attica, and the Crimean Chersonese, and are the archaeological remnants of great tower-like structures, which were the central buildings of the flourishing agricultural estates. The towers, common in the archaeological remains from the late sixth to the early third centuries B.C., used for the storage of farm crops and tools, stood within or near the great farm courtyards and the manor houses; the centers of agriculture with wine presses, olive-presses, mills, and threshing-floors for grain.[54] These great country estates were often more than a single manor, usually compact units of farms arranged in a system which we may label a "village," the Greek kome. This settlement pattern of farms clustered about manorial estates with pyrgoi arose in the rural choric districts because of the dependence of the village upon central springs.[55] Isolated manors rarely occurred while clusters of homesteads and manors as rural villages (komai) commonly appeared. When fortified, the village as a teichos meant not simply "wall" but rather a walled village, or a walled or fortified great manor. In this, the Ionian teichos was similar to the early medieval Burg, being a walled place for refuge. Similar towers and fortified manors are common today throughout southern Europe, in Albania, and the Greek Peloponnesos, and in each case are associated with feuding clans.[56] The pyrgoi and teiche, consequently, functioned as centers of the kinship structured agricultural, aristocratic families and their subsidiary clients, tenants, and slaves.

Among many factors, the Ionian manors and villages were similar to the demes or rural townships in Attica: agricultural districts with one or more inhabited centers or villages from which each district locally administered its own secular and religious affairs and, where necessary, had its appropriate buildings and shrines.[57]

In the polis of Teos, some forty rural pyrgoi dotted the broad agricultural plains beyond the central urban node and its two harbors,[58] and the aristocratic families of those manors controlled Teos throughout the sixth and fifth centuries B.C., a group similar to the Board of Magistrates or aeinautai in Miletos (Plut. *Mor.* 2.298C) and in Chalkis during the third century B.C. (*IG* 12.909 and 939). The selected aristocratic magistrates, the timiouchoi, guided the polis and their abbreviated names may appear on the Teian silver staters minted in that city during the reign of Darius.[59] Neither the literary nor numismatic evidence suggests a change in government during the period c. 700 to 411 B.C. (Thuc. 8.16.3, 19, 20.2, 31.3).[60] In Miletos, the refuge center at Teichioussa was exactly what its name implies, a teichos or fortified manor, and a second Milesian refuge center on the island of Leros had early in the fifth century been under consideration by the Milesians for the contruction of a teichos, as a place of refuge from the Persians (Hdt. 5.125).[61] In Erythrai, the villages of Boutheia, Ptelion, Sidousa, and Polichna were, apparently, similar towered or fortified manors and centers of refuge. These manors fortified and unfortified collectively supported the rich agrarian families, which structured the politically powerful and militarily strong aristocratic and, in some cases, oligarchic factions in their respective poleis. In Teos, the magistrates were the timiouchoi, the "honored people or the worthy people;"[62] in Miletos, the Molpoi, the aristocratic priesthood and leading economic class;[63] and in Erythrai they were from the aristocratic families which the Athenians removed from power in the mid-fifth century B.C.[64]

The physical form of the fortified manor, for example of Teichioussa in the polis of Miletos, was that of a massive stone wall of irregular quarry-faced trapezoidal stones which completed the circuit of a low hill; a stone wall about 2.60 m. thick, with six quadrangular towers within the circuit, towers about 6 m. wide which project at present to a height of 4 m., a towered fortified manor above a sheltered harbor protected against the winds. For the central urban node of Miletos, Teichioussa served as an outpost east of the Milesian holy sanctuary and oracular temple to Apollo at Didyma, an outpost towards the polis of Iasos and the Karian poleis and tribes, a defence along the vulnerable south-eastern border of Miletos.[65] The fortified refuge at Leros, however, was apparently never constructed.[66] Other teiche may have been structures of little more than earth embankments and presently not identifiable, but may be noted in the small settlements of Damnion teichos,[67] Didyma teiche,[68] and Serreion teichos[69] on the northern coast of the Propontis, and in Pergamon teichos—"the acropolitan fort"—in the Mt. Pangaion district east of the Strymon River near a second and similar fort Phrages.[70] On the southern coast of the Propontis, the Milesians had settled the Koraxikon teichos and the Koraxike chora (Hekataios FGrH 1 F 210), and east of Kyzikos and the satrapal center of Daskyleion lay the Artaiou teichos on the Rhyndakos River.[71] The small Persian fort called Dareion in Mysia near the Propontis, apparently established during the months of Darius' Scythian campaign, also ranked among these small teiche,[72] and during the mid-fifth century B.C. each teichos may not have contained more than about 125 people.[73] Harpageion, similarly, between Lampsakos and Kyzikos also on the southern Propontic coast, may have been settled by Harpagos, a small outpost with no more than about fifty inhabitants.[74]

The construction of Teichioussa in Miletos is strikingly similar to the archaeological remains of a teichos in western Thrace, perhaps ancient Antisara,[75] located about 3 km. due west of the modern city of Kavalla on a small promontory on the western arm of the wide bay of Kavalla. Stanley Casson described this fortified demesne as an exceedingly small city, that which we have considered as a rural village or kome, for the purposes of trade with the barbarian tribes of the Thracian hinterland, and it would have been similar to other fortified manors on the Thracian mainland belonging to the island poleis of Thasos and Samothrace (Hdt. 7.108.2).[76] In a similar manner, the Persian fort at Doriskos, built on the vast plain of the Hebros River in eastern Thrace, was labeled by

Herodotus as the Royal Teichos—the Teichos Basileion (7.9), which the Persians

established when they had invaded Skudra (7.59.1) and their forces had occupied that

region up to the borders of Macedonia to the west.[77] And Doriskos was similar to the

Persian fort of Eion on the Strymon River, the western border of Skudra,[78] and to Neon

teichos, the "new" castle of the Athenian general Alkibiades constructed at Didyma

teiche on the northern coast of the Propontis, a refuge for that controversial Athenian

noble (Plut. *Alk.* 36; Nepos *Alc.* 9.3, 5).[79]   Other Persian garrisons also dotted the

Thracian landscape (Hdt. 7.106), little forts similar to those built by the Persians and the

Milesians in 500 B.C. for the exiled Naxian aristocrats (Hdt. 5.34.3).

III

The estates throughout the Persian empire and specifically within Sparda, while

essentially similar in agricultural and economic functions as related to the landed gentry,

differed in form and the nature of their relationship to the Great King. Some lands were

held without vassalage obligations, what medievalists term allodial lands (Hdt. 3.83.3;

Xen. *Hell.* 3.1.6; *An.* 1.4.9, 2.4.27).[80]   Other lands were held in vassalage obligations to

the king through the satrap and his provincial officers, and still others as benefits from

the king to his vassals, such as Gongylos, Damaratos, and Themistokles. In each case, the

evidence indicates hereditary possession of lands, and often hereditary office, and the

distinct references to vassalage benefits, the receipt of land (chora) and estates (oikoi)

were, in turn, for services rendered (*hypēkooi*), taxes and military duty (cf. Xen. *Cyr.*

3.1.10). Among the Lydians, the Old Persian word *bandaka-* was, therefore, adopted as

the Lydian *bantakashash* to refer to the vassal,[81] and among the East Greeks, and

especially for Herodotus, the term *doulos* (e.g. 5.49.2) usually indicated a subject or

vassal. But for the Greeks, while indicating subjection and vassalage, the term *doulos*

also carried the barbed connotation of servant and pejorative "slave" or menial.[82] This

condition of vassalage was markedly different from the western medieval relationship

between dominus and vassus, free and equal military men. In the Achaemenid empire,

the *doulos* remained inferior and subject, restricted by the laws of his superiors and the

imperial laws of the Great King. In essence, the Achaemenid system was similar to the

earlier Anatolian Hittite and Lydian structures of the landed gentry to their king, but in

the late sixth and fifth centuries B.C. were bound by the particular strictures of the

Persian religious oaths and offerings of "earth and water," an innovation established by Cyrus.

Throughout the empire, the king rewarded his officers and soldiers for their bravery and service with special titles, positions, and objects of their rank, gold laurel leaves, robes of honor, special daggers, bracelets, and similar objects (Hdt. 8.120).[83] Darius' bow and lance bearers, Aspathines and Gobryas, and the other conspirators received such rewards, as did members of the Achaemenid family, and each bore a special insignia or crest of their vassal families. The seigneurial lands, the vithpaitish, bit qashti, or oikos, lay fundamental to the imperial organization and basic to Darius' reforms. Of these, each satrapal and imperial chancery staff registered the levies exacted, and bravery was recorded and compensated.[84]   Upon this vassalage system rested the military organization and strength of the empire. At each Now Ruz festival at Persepolis, when the king reviewed his armies and received their tributes, new benefits of the vassalage system were distributed.[85] And when the king campaigned, the richer gentry and family nobles often quartered his armies (Hdt. 7.26-9; Xen. An. 1.2.7, 4.7). But as the king gave estates, such as Cyrus' gift of lands in Karmania to the deposed Chaldean king Nabonidus, Darius could take back some of that land for himself (Berossos FGrH 680 F 9; Abydenos FGrH 685 F 6).[86]

Affection and fidelity (Xen. An. 1.8.29) bound the Persian nobles and the other landed gentry to their king, with fidelity specifically expressed within an oath of allegiance and the fundamental Zarathustrian offerings of "earth and water." To the age old Near Eastern oaths,[87] the Achaemenids added the early Zarathustrian principle of "moral contract," rta, the cosmic and moral power materialized as light or fire (Yasna 31:7). It embodied the truth and order of things found in nature, liturgy, and vassalage oaths, a cosmic law controlling the behavior of men, in stark contrast to the Lie, Evil, fault, sin, and the non-observance of the law.[88] This principle of rta, Darius himself stressed in his Ordinance of Regulations and the other legal reforms throughout the empire. Extending their right hands, the Persians thus swore oaths to do justice (Xen. An. 2.3.28; 2.5.3, 2.5.7, 2.5.8, 2.5.39, 5.1.22; Ktesias FGrH 688 F 48, 50, 52), yet could also violate them (Plut. Arta. 18). Adhering to the legal force of the god Mithra, whose name denoted "contract," a force associated with the divination of time, vassals and vassal poleis offered the king the Zarathustrian symbols of "earth and water," the first two elements of creation, which arose after the formation of the celestial bodies and before the development of plants, animals, and ultimately man. As surrogates for the Great King, the satraps and their subordinate imperial officials contracted the oaths binding the vassals to their liege lord, the king, and to imperial centralization.[89]

From Sardis in 481 B.C., King Xerxes sent to all the Greek states imperial heralds to demand their allegiance and vassalage, and the symbolic offerings of "earth and water" (Diod. Sic. 11.2.4). Many decades earlier, Harpagos had demanded similar offerings (Hdt. 1.164), which apparently the Milesians had freely given to Cyrus following the overthrow of Croesus (Hdt. 1.143, 169). Such offerings apparently underlay the other treaties of allegiance, which Harpagos had obtained throughout Lydia, Ionia, Karia, and Lykia, and which bound each East Greek tyrant to Bagaios, Artaphrenes, and Darius following the failure of Oroites' rebellion against Darius' usurpation of the Achaemenid throne. Several years later, in 507 B.C., even the Athenians bound themselves as vassals to Darius.

Because of the Spartan intervention and military occupation of Athens, initially at the invitation of the Athenian noble Alkmeonid family, many Athenians including the Alkmeonid Kleisthenes quickly became disenchanted with Sparta's hostility and, therefore, sought an alliance with Artaphrenes and Darius for assistance against Sparta, Persia's old enemy (Hdt. 5.73). But to obtain that assistance, Artaphrenes insisted upon a formal alliance, Athenian recognition of Darius' suzerainty, and the symbols of earth and water. These, the Athenian embassy in Sardis eagerly offered, but upon their return to Athens, the Athenian assembly quickly disavowed the oath. Both the Athenians and the historian Herodotus forgot the oath of vassalage, and considered the Athenian repudiation valid. But neither Artaphrenes nor Darius accepted that Athenian view. For Darius, Athens was a rebellious vassal polis and would be properly beaten into submission and returned to the imperial fold. So too, did the former Athenian tyrant Hippias understand the grave political implications of the embassy's submission in Sardis, and when the Athenians repudiated the contract he immediately began to intrigue with Artaphrenes to restore him to power in Athens, and to add Attica to the imperial fold.[90] Aware of these complications, the Athenians again dispatched envoys to Sardis (perhaps 505 B.C.) to persuade Artaphrenes not to support Hippias (Hdt. 5.96), but to no avail. Athens had violated the important religious oath of vassalage, and the Persians had vowed to punish her. Kleisthenes, apparently deeply concerned with the reaction of the Athenians to his reforms, disowned the Persian alliance as it rendered danger to his political position and policies, and a temporary banishment from Athens. The Athenians, consequently, glossed over their failure at Sardis in 507 B.C., but emphasized their military attack upon Sardis in 498 B.C. (which Darius considered a flagrant violation of his sovereignty by a rebellious nation) for the positive yet propagandistic goals of freedom for the Ionians and offensive aggression to punish tyranny. Totally intrigued with the motif, Herodotus focused not upon the violated Athenian-Persian alliance, but upon the Athenian attack upon Sardis. In this, he simply failed to relay that Darius had declared war upon Athens in 507 B.C., a war which would not be resolved until the Peace of Kallias in 450 B.C.

Darius, in contrast to the Athenians, believed that he had gained Athens as a permanent vassal, which willingly submitted to the overlordship of Ahura Mazda and had taken its place within the Persian Empire in accordance with $r̥ta$. Against treaty-breakers, consequently, the king acted as the agent of Mithra, the war lord and controller of war and peace among men (*Avestan Hymn to Mithra* 1:2, 2:7-8, 5:18-9, 8:29, 9:35-9, 27:111, 29:115-7).[91] In moral and legal relationship to the early Zarathustrian principles of Mithra and the "contract," earth represented right-mindedness, humility, and propriety, and water wholeness and completeness. As with all ancient Near Eastern treaties, the deities of each side ratified the compact, and the kings, governors, or envoys involved ranked secondarily as human agents.

In the Avestan Hymn or *Yasht* to Mithra, dated to the second half of the fifth century B.C., Mithra as a divine being or genius, governed treaties, and especially international treaties. A cosmic power associated with light, Mithra preceded the rising sun and followed its setting, and symbolized vassalage, "fidelity," "peace," and the "contract." It was he who brought the rain, vegetation, and health, and those who lived according to their vows remained without illness. Similarly in early Zarathustrian thought, between the rain and vegetation, the king's moral behavior generated the welfare of his subjects, their health and the fertile conditions of agrarian societies. Mithra, consequently, bestowed blessings upon those countries faithful to the king's treaties. Violations produced drought and pestilence.[92] Among the Achaemenids, treaties were presumably concluded before the blazing fires of the Zarathustrian altars,

with Mithra's seat in that fire, and in Sardis the converted Lydian altars served
Artaphrenes and the other Persian officials in formalizing the vassalage contracts with
the landed gentry as vassals, with subordinate officers as imperial servants or vassals,
with the East Greek poleis, and the foreign poleis such as Athens. Each contract Mithra
supervised with his thousand perceptions, his thousand ears, ten thousand eyes, and ten
thousand spies, reflections of the Achaemenid imperial order, and he punished its
infringement and rewarded its observance.[93]   Carved upon the staircases of Darius'
apadana at Persepolis, Mithra in the form of a lion reared as the god of death to slay the
bull; there he was Mithra the Tauroctonus god. During the sixth and fifth centuries B.C.,
the Achaemenids with religious prohibition in representing their deities (Hdt. 1.131.1)
rendered them as animals to indicate symbolically their presence.[94]

The fundamental characteristics of both the personal oaths of vassalage and the
Persian treaties with the East Greek and other poleis were the provisions imposed under
oath and placed under the sanction of the divine witnesses invoked. Subsequent curses
within the oath underscored the dreadful fate of the transgressor. To the blessings, the
vassal answering accepted both the divine sanctions and the stipulations of the suzerain.
As a technique for imperial administration, the vassal treaty incorporated weaker states
into provinces and subjects as vassals bound by divine sanctions and the quid pro quo
pronouncements of the king.

IV

The fundamental element of rural agriculture throughout the Persian Empire, and
specifically in western Anatolia, interrelated closely with basic ethics of early
Zarathustrianism, in which attention to agriculture remained a cardinal virtue, and the
duty of the soldier and the landed gentry to protect agriculture (Xen. Oec. 4.15).
Throughout the Gāthās, Zarathustra stressed the maintenance of life through cattle-
raising and agriculture in order to sustain one's self and to procreate. The life of the
herdsman and agriculturalist was, consequently, in contrast to the village and city
dwellers, the tradesmen, potters, carpenters, and metal workers. The values of the
Iranian nobles, their love of virtue (Hdt. 1.138), their fidelity to their king (Xen. Cyr.
8.5.25-7), their respect for the law and customs (Hdt. 1.169, 7.136), their bravery (DNa
4), and their love of justice (Hdt. 5.16-25, 7.194; Diod. Sic. 15.10), found modes of

aristocratic expression in their agrarian lives (Hdt. 3.97; Xen. *Cyr.* 8.8.9; Plato *Leg.* 695a), which maintained the honorable precepts of Zarathustrianism.[95] For the Lydians and East Greeks these, too, were aristocratic virtues, and as the Aristotelian writer of the *Oeconomica* noted: "agriculture is the most honest of all occupations" [1343a (1.22)].

In Sparda, with "wide plains of fruitful acres" (Seneca *Phoenissae* 60-25), of rich ploughed fields (Lucan *Pharsalia* 3.209-10; Propertius 1.6.31-2; Virgil *Aeneid* 10.139-42), with mountains covered by vineyards (Ovid *Metamorphoses* 11.85-88; Pliny *NH* 5.110; Strabo 14.1.15), the Persian overlords found compatible agricultural vassals. As Xenophon, in his *Oeconomica* remarked: "to the local governors (*archontōn*) who are able to show that their country is densely populated and the land is in cultivation and well stocked with trees and with crops, the king assigns more territory and gives them presents, and rewards them with seats of honor" (4.8). For the Great King, Xenophon stated, husbandry and the art of war remained the noblest and most necessary of pursuits (*Oec.* 4.4). The wealth of this agriculture provided the troops and maintained the garrisons throughout the western satrapy (Xen. *Oec.* 4.5-6). For the Persians, Zarathustra had uttered: "Ahura Mazda who created cattle and Righteous Order, created waters and good plants, created light and earth and all good things (*Yasna* 37:1),"[96] and these principles they fostered among the receptive landed gentry in western Anatolia. For them, Mithra the life-giver and bestower of sons, brought life, fat herds, wide pastures, and as replenisher of waters and rain, fostered agriculture.[97]

With the development and expansion of the East Greek poleis, and the rise of population and prosperity throughout Sparda in the sixth century B.C., gradual inroads upon the heavy forestation throughout Anatolia had begun but was apparently kept in check. Yet, by the fourth century, the Mt. Ida range in the southern Troad was almost deforested (Theophrastos *HP* 4.5.4-5).[98] While it is extremely difficult to assess the problems in Sparda and its environs in regard to deforestation, logging for ship and house timbers, the burning of wood for charcoal, the general needs for wood, and the goat and pig herding in the forests evidently had begun to make acute marks upon the landscape. The Great King and his officials, however, carefully preserved forests, and developed throughout the rural districts and at Sardis carefully planted garden parks or paradises stocked with fine trees (Xen. *Oec.* 4.13-4).[99] At Sardis, Cyrus the Younger escorted guests through the paradise to admire the beauty of the trees, carefully spaced, planted in straight rows at regular angles, with a "multitude of sweet scents" (Xen. *Oec.* 4.20-1). And at Magnesia-on-the-Maeander, Darius I had praised the work of the local governor Gadatas in transplanting trees from Syria to Sparda (ML *GHI* 12). For Herodotus, one of the many reasons Xerxes hated the Athenians so vehemently was that they had burned the sacred groves and the temples in Sardis in 498 B.C. (7.8); and again late in that century the Spartan admiral Agesilaos destroyed the gardens and paradise of the satrap Tissaphernes "set out artfully and expensively with plants and all else that contributed to luxury and the quiet enjoyment of good things" (Diod. Sic. 14.80.2).

Pliny noted that the Persian kings had planted frankincense trees at Sardis (*NH* 12.57), apparently with special care and protection, and also the more mundane alfalfa (*NH* 18.16.144). As the paradises also contained wild and exotic animals, Pharnakes, the son of Pharnabazos and satrap of Daskyleion, introduced to his parks a fertile breed of wild mules from Syria (Arist. *HA* 580b1-9), and perhaps from similar paradises the Greeks obtained domestic chickens, Aristophanes' Persian birds (*Aves* 483-5). But the trees, evidently, held special importance; as gifts to Darius, the rich Lydian Pythios the son of Atys gave a plane-tree and a vine in gold (Hdt. 7.27); and along the Maeander River near the village of Kallatabos Xerxes, after admiring a plane-tree, adorned it with gold and established a guard before it (Hdt. 7.31). In their courts, the kings had artificial plane-trees of gold and jewels (Xen. *Hell.* 7.1.38), which symbolized the older cult of the local sacred trees associated with springs of water and the healing properties of their bark and fruit.[100]

V

Agriculture, a livelihood and the fundamental way of life,[101] collectively produced "the good things of Asia," the wealth which the acting-tyrant of Miletos Aristagoras reported to the Athenians in 499 B.C. (Hdt. 5.97). Beyond the several urban centers, which could truly be called aste, the overwhelmingly majority of land in Sparda belonged to the rural districts of the chora. By 500 B.C., Sardis, Miletos, Erythrai, Klazomenai, Kyme, and perhaps Ephesos alone ranked as major aste while the other urban centers such as Phokaia, Smyrna, Teos, Kolophon, Myous, and Magnesia-on-the-Maeander ranked well below and essentially as sacred centers of urban nodes not much larger than villages or komai.[102] The landed gentry and the rural peasants, consequently, not only held and cultivated the majority of Spardian land, but dominated and controlled the socio-political life. Among the East Greek poleis, as elsewhere in the Greek world, the ownership of land with no exceptions marked the political status of citizenship.

In contrast, many (but not all) who lived in the urban centers, were non-citizens, those engaged in trade, money lending, and a variety of small crafts and industries. Political power in each polis, therefore, rested squarely upon the landed and specifically upon the powerful aristocracies who retained religious domination within their societies. Most communities, whether aristocratic or oligarchic (terms essentially synonomous), restricted political rights and participation (steps beyond basic citizenship) to the landowners among their own groups.[103]

Throughout Sparda and the adjacent satrapy of Daskyleion the rural oikos of the landed gentry remained the fundamental economic institution and the dominant political center, and not the urban asty. By means of their extended clans and kinship systems (the gene), the landed gentry preserved the unity of their inheritable and inalienable landed estates and control of the local peasantries.[104] In Athens, during the fifth and fourth centuries B.C., many landowners possessed from three to six estates in different parts of Attica,[105] and although the evidence for a comparative study is absent this scattered pattern of landownership may also have occurred in Sparda, in both the Lydian and the East Greek regions. Here, clusters of estates, at springs and crossroads, formed the dendritic system of small rural villages, the komai similar to the many Greek villages of today scattered over a wide area with their present average population of less than eight hundred people.[106] According to our rough estimate, the population of the fifth century B.C. teiche averaged about one hundred and twenty-five people; an ancient village slightly larger would not be too dissimilar in population size from the modern figures. At the end of the fifth century B.C., Xenophon noted that a large village (kome) in western Armenia did contain a palace for the satrap (An. 4.4.2), and that village would not have been dissimilar from those under consideration for Sparda. Spardian villages, no doubt similar to Attic rural demes (in essence villages), would generally have possessed one or more inhabited centers or nodules, and each administered its own religious and secular affairs, and where necessary had appropriate buildings and shrines.[107] Thus, for the writer of the Aristotelian *Oeconomica*, the polis was an assemblage of houses, lands, and property, sufficient to enable the inhabitants to lead a civilized life [1343a (1.1.2)].[108]

In an important analysis of ancient Greek poleis, J.M. Wagstaff has recently offered an interesting series of observations toward an hypothesis not proved but for which, he noted, no contradictory evidence has been found. His study indicates that the basic type of settlement was the village, ranging in size from a few hundred to just over a thousand inhabitants, within an average territory of 24.4 sq. km., a structure similar to that of modern Greek villages. In conclusion, Wagstaff defined a village as a unit in which the inhabitants engaged in cultivating the soil, rearing livestock, or fishing, a unit which "can consist of several very small settlements dispersed within farmland but operating as a single social and economic unity, sharing common facilities comparable to our present-day school, church, and local administration. Such a community may consist of one or more built-up settlements."[109] And these observations are highly compatible with those stated above for the ancient East Greek and Lydian villages throughout the coastal and inland regions of Sparda and Daskyleion. Many villages would have been as [Dikaiarchos] described: "the streets are nothing but miserable old lanes, the houses mean, with a few better ones among them" (Paus. 1.43-7).[110]

Within the social hierarchy, the gentry ranked first, with the subordinate and dependent peasantry ranking second and above the non-citizen artisans and traders, the neglected and down-graded workers whose manual labors were not worthy of the nobles. Beneath all ranked the slaves.[111] The symbiotic relationship among the four classes, however, bound them closely through economic ties of necessity. Rents and other levies from the peasantry paid in kind to the gentry and the produce of the estates provided the means for the exchange of goods and coinage through the traders and merchants for objects and materials not produced by the essentially highly self-sufficient estates: ship timber, grain, metals, and slaves. At fairs and in the agorai of the komai and the aste, the products of the oikos, therefore, were exchanged for those products in demand yet not available. Among the East Greek poleis, at least, in the sixth century B.C. a dependence upon imported grain appeared as a factor, which led to the political activities of the aristocratic states to supplement their own production since private commerce was apparently inadequate to ensure proper provision. To this end, some aristocrats may have in whole or in part invested in joint enterprises, and perhaps in the support of some native and foreign merchants, to obtain the commodities necessary to sustain the high cultural level reached during the reign of Croesus and essentially maintained throughout that century under the early Persian kings. While these conditions often led to a higher degree of piracy than previously, because of the increased prosperity and shipping, the limited Persian naval control of the Anatolian and Thracian coasts and guard of the Bosporos and Hellespontine straits rapidly created a Pax Persica, which generated a sphere of trade from the Pangaion districts in western Skudra past the East Greek ports, Cyprus, the Phoenician city-states, to Palestine and to Egypt.[112]

In contrast to the relatively highly self-sufficient rural estate, the residents of the asty found it necessary to purchase most of their commodities from others, in exchange for the wealth of their specialized single or multiple craft production or activities. Each estate provided most of its food, clothing, housing, clay for roof tiles, mud for the crude building bricks, vineyards and olive groves with their own wine and olive presses, and animals. Trade, with the exception of certain crafts produced either in the villages or to a greater extent in the asty, functioned essentially to dispose of the surpluses from the aristocratic estates.[113] Trade, therefore, operated at two distinct levels: one, that required by the politically powerful aristocratic gentry who set in motion the processes by which to obtain materials and goods necessary for the operation of the landed estates; and two, that required by the former, the variety of products obtained by the urban merchants through numerous means and predominately through self-motivation and without specific state assistance.[114] Concerning the latter, the gentry played no direct role except to be receptive buyers of the foreign and often exotic goods to enhance their own status. The gentry, as kaloi k'agathoi ("the noble and the good") deployed every effort to preserve their society of physical and moral quality; and conservative in nature, to participate in state and military affairs and not in the mundane activities of the resident non-citizens of the asty.

The choric gentry retained political control of the East Greek poleis as a minority class or social group based upon hereditary inheritance of inalienable land and hereditary control of the priesthoods;[115] a social group gradually infiltrated by new landed wealth groups over the course of centuries, oligarchs who tended to assimilate into the aristocratic societies. Their common conservative natures generated a cohesiveness or solidarity yet counterbalanced by the political rivalries among them. The East Greek aristocracies (earlier allied with local Anatolian groups) during the sixth century B.C. gradually incorporated Lydian Mermnad aristocracies, most notably at Kolophon and Ephesos, and then Achaemenid, Median, and Cappadocian aristocrats who held great landed estates as vassal lands from the Great King. Mainland Greeks also gradually joined these prestigious groups. By the fifth century B.C., therefore, the ethnic complexity of the Spardian landed gentry structured a vast aristocratic network from the Median Harpagid nobles in Lykia to the mainland Greek nobles in northern Heraklea Pontika, an outpost of Daskyleion.[116] As political power related directly to the control of land, as on Samos where the ruling gentry were the Geomoroi ("those with a share of the land"), throughout Sparda the ruling nobility, aristocratic yet oligarchic, established policies from their landed estates.

In Stanley Burstein's study of Heraklea Pontika, that village is a good case in point. That center, founded c. 560 B.C. at the first good harbor on the northern Anatolian coast about a day's sail east from Byzantion, became part of the Lydian policy to utilize Greeks to settle outlying provinces of the Śfardian kingdom. (Hdt. 1.28). The ruling elite of Megarian and Boiotian settlers who dominated the native Mariandynoi possessed kleroi or divisions of land and continued to hold political control of that region as a Persian dependency, and under treaty contributed the necessary vassal obligations of tribute and military service (cf. Diod. Sic. 11.2.1). With annual eponymous magistrates called basileis, the Greek overlords controlled Heraklea by means of their landed status and their religious duties.[117]

Among the East Greek communities, the priestly order came from the aristocratic clans, occasionally chosen by lot from a group of qualified candidates, and often annually. Consequently, no independent priestly order arose as in Egypt or Judah to form ranked and unified organizations entered only after rigorous religious training, nor bound by strict normative codes of ascetic and ritual rules. The aristocratic clans, therefore, controlling the religious activities added further status to their political, military and economic domination of the western Anatolian societies.[118]

The transition from the chora and the estates of the ruling gentry to the walls of the asty was rather gradual and subtle, with no clear or profound division between the countryman and the cityman, as the chora began immediately outside of the urban walls in the extramural settlements of the proasteion (cf. Hdt. 1.78.1, 3.54.1, 4.78.3,

5.1.2).[119]   Here and within the walls, the gentry often did hold property and urban dwellings,[120] no less interests in the development in civic monuments, temples, and the aggrandizement of the agora. The relationship between the urban centers and the rural agricultural regions ranged from complete dependence to highly integrated and symbiotic functions. The contrast was not between the urban center and the rural estates as much as between the poor and the rich. For the urban centers, which ranged from small village or even teichos size to large city and metropolitan centers such as Miletos, growth was not measured in small craft industry and manufacturing but in less complex relationships of the exchange of commodities, the surplus products of the rural estates and the desires by the gentry for commodities of different soils and climates and the specialized products of the variety of urban centers. Aste were, therefore, centers of consumption rather than particular centers of production, and centers of exchange of rural surpluses, urban crafts, grain, metal, and slave imports.[121]

The aste, however, did support numbers of craftsmen, traders, foreign freemen, freedmen, and slaves; often not easily distinguishable from one another in appearance. In the minds of the gentry they held the despised positions, lodging-house keepers, tax-collectors, auctioneers, cook-house keepers, and employees of the small and unpretentious ergasteria or workshops. There they worked, compressed among the urban buildings, along the narrow streets, in small often shabbily built structures little more than shanties. To work for someone else was tantamount to being subject to him, as freeman did not live to benefit another (Arist. *Rhet.* [1367a32], 1.9) From such crafts, Plato proposed that citizens be banned (*Leg.* 846d-847b); activities which Xenophon also rejected as smacking of the workshop (*Oec.* 4.2).[122]

Those engaged in crafts and trade were outsiders with no access to the political power demonstrated by the aristocrats or oligarchs who held their political and religious functions within the asty's walls. Governed by the Persian appointed tyrants who themselves came from the aristocratic and landed classes, the East Greek governments similar to the Persian controlled Lydian government at Sardis functioned essentially for the well being of the imperial structure and the welfare of the landed gentry. Consequently, the construction of civic monuments and religious buildings within the urban centers arose from the revenues collected from the landed and for the benefit of the landed. The Ionian revolution in 499 B.C. and the subsequent events of Persian suppression and reprisals, however, quickly brought an end to that construction and the onset of a general economic depression throughout western Anatolia during the entire fifth century B.C.

8

THE "IONIAN" *REVOLUTIONS*

499 – 478 B.C.

I

The Milesian Affair

Since the days of King Cyrus, throughout the East Greek poleis and settlements in Ionia, Karia, Aiolis, and the Troad, factionalism and city-state parochialism continued to thwart thoughts of rebellion against the Persian king.[1] When rebellion did occur against King Darius, the East Greeks, consequently, failed as their hasty attempt to develop their religious federation at the Panionion shrine into a military alliance faltered because of those same ever present problems. In comparison, the Lydians remained faithful vassals of their foreign king and aided the Persian efforts to regain control of the important satrapies of Sparda and Daskyleion.

The Ionian Revolution against Persia, which exploded in 499 B.C., occurred basically from factional problems internal to Miletos. In 494 B.C., this revolution—essentially a Milesian affair with Ionian military participation—failed largely because of Persian military superiority and the failure of Ionian military cooperation. When revolution again erupted in 479 and 478 B.C.—this time essentially a Samian affair—the East Greeks succeeded. The intervening years—during which the Persians attacked and punished Athens several times for earlier having broken her vassalage obligations (in 507 B.C.) and then in aiding the Ionians in an attack upon Sardis in 499 B.C.—cost Persia dearly. The Samian affair succeeded not because of successful Ionian military activities but rather because of a series of Persian military strategic errors in Greece followed by King Xerxes' willingness to abandon the coastal areas of Sparda and Daskyleion strategically less important than Egypt, Babylonia, Bactria, and Sogdiana, which had to be controlled at all cost, and also because of a successful Athenian and allied military intervention in Ionian territories. To these three phases, Herodotus added his literary leitmotif, Greek liberty versus Persian subjugation, the conflict between oriental despotism and Greek freedom.

Basic to the imperial policies of Kings Croesus and Cyrus, and then Darius, the linchpin of foreign control of Ionia remained Miletos, a polis, which since the days of

Croesus, suffered from factional strife (Hdt. 5.28).[2] For the Lydian and Persian kings,

Miletos existed as the important port center to serve the naval and mercantile needs of

Sardis as it linked Sparda and Ionia by sea to the Persian ports of Cyprus, Cilicia, and

Phoenicia. And after 520 B.C., Miletos also maintained harbors for the Persian Imperial

Fleet for the control of the offshore islands of Samos, Chios, and Lesbos, and the control

of the coastal settlements of Skudra and the important straits of the Hellespont and the

Bosporos. For Darius, therefore, the political role of his appointed governor and tyrant,

the Milesian Histiaios, became more and more crucial as the reorganization of the

Persian Empire and the subsequent Pax Persica throughout Sparda, Daskyleion, and

Skudra increased the control and utilization of the four magnificent Milesian harbors.

At the Danube River, after Darius and his army had invaded European Scythia,

Histiaios had effectively and energetically commanded the other Greek tyrants and their

naval contingents assisting the Great King at that crossing (Hdt. 4.137-143). Upon his

safe return to Sardis, Darius consequently rewarded Histiaios by presenting him with the

vassalage gift of the polis of Edonian Myrkinos in western Skudra (Hdt. 5.11.1-2).[3] The

Persian general Megabazos, meanwhile, had left Darius' entourage at Perinthos, as

commanded by the Great King (Hdt. 5.1-2), expelled the Athenian tyrant Miltiades from

the Thracian Chersonese,[4] campaigned across southern Skudra to the troublesome regions

of the Paeonians (many of whom he deported to Phrygia: Hdt. 5.12.1-23.1), and met great

resistance from the other Thracian tribes of the Mt. Pangaion district (Hdt. 5.16). Mega-

bazos, nevertheless, did obtain from the Macedonian King Amyntas the desired offerings

of earth and water and the vassalage oaths sworn to Darius (Hdt. 5.17-18).[5] Darius' gift

of Myrkinos to Histiaios, therefore, came not only as a reward to a loyal and valuable

vassal, but as an important imperial step to control the volatile Pangaion district and to

sustain the Persian link with Macedonia.

But the undercurrents of unrest throughout the Greek regions of Sparda and Dasky-

leion, in spite of the far reaching aspects of Darius' imperial reforms, necessitated that

while the Great King held court in Susa he have Histiaios there to advise him directly and

thoroughly in regard to East Greek affairs. Darius, therefore, summoned Histiaios from

Myrkinos to Sardis and appointed him to the high office of King's Counselor (symboulos:

Hdt. 5.24).[6] This second important reward to a faithful and successful vassal no doubt

sent rumors throughout the imperial halls of Sardis, where Persians, Lydians, and other

East Greeks jockeyed for similar rewards and court positions. For Darius, Sardis and the Spardian satrapy were crucial, and following his command that Histiaios depart with him to Susa, the king appointed his half-brother Artaphrenes to the satrapal chair in Sardis. The loyal conspirator Otanes he appointed as general to succeed Megabazos, to conduct the imperial expeditions against rebellious Byzantion and Kalchedon, and to complete campaigns against Antandros and Lamponion in the southern Troad and the Pelasgian offshore islands of Lemnos and Imbros (Hdt. 5.25-6, 136.2). While Darius had campaigned across the Danube, Byzantion revolted, and upon his return to Sardis the Lemnians plundered his army (Hdt. 5.27). Otanes would handle those problems. At Miletos, meanwhile, Darius appointed Aristagoras, the cousin and son-in-law of Histiaios, as acting tyrant (epitropos) to govern for Histiaios while he was in Susa (Hdt. 5.30.1).

But for all of Miletos' prime position and importance in Sparda, and her favored alliance with Persia freely and beneficially offered by Cyrus, Miletos remained plagued with internal and external troubles. The Samians under Polykrates had attacked Miletos, and Samian naval mercantile activities and then the advent of Athenian mercantile expansion developed with its resultant harsh blows upon the Milesians. And about 510 B.C., with the fall of Sybaris in southern Italy, Miletos lost a crucial market in the west (Hdt. 5.44). Consequently, between c. 510 and 500 B.C., the Milesians' fortunes were curtailed.[7] As the new tyrant, Aristagoras avidly sought to revive his native polis, even though it ranked above the other mainland East Greek poleis, then at the height of its fortunes as "the ornament of Ionia" (Hdt. 5.28). More than two generations of factionalism since the death of Thrasyboulos c. 570 B.C. had compounded Miletos' problems.[8] With Persian consent and support, Aristagoras obtained Parian aristocrats from the Cyclades to arbitrate the Milesian strife (Hdt. 5.29.1). Throughout the fertile and rugged Milesian chora, the Parians inspected the landed estates (oikoi), some sadly wasted, unworked, untilled, unproductive, and only a few in the general desolation of the land remained well tilled under the guidance of their landed nobles called despotai by Herodotus, or simply lords of vassal demesnes: 5.29.2.[9] These despotai, the Parians reported to the Milesians gathered in the asty, would govern the internal affairs of the state. A narrow aristocracy (or oligarchy), which included the priestly clan of the Molpoi, gained control as a politically moderate faction, which held the offices of aisymnetes and prytanis, and maintained interests in the development of agriculture and commerce. It was the monied faction (the Ploutis) in contrast to the poor (the Chairomacha: Plut. QG 32.1), which apparently supported Aristagoras and sought bolder political and mercantile policies throughout the Aegean. Political strife (eris) lay fundamental to the political structure of the polis, intricately bound to aristocratic concepts of "freedom" (eleutheria) and "the equality of law" (isonomia), a world in which factionalism (stasis) flourished.[10] For the landed gentry who formalized the political structures of their poleis, the concept of "freedom" implied the legal privilege to engage in factionalism and strife.[11] Of this, Miletos in 500 B.C. was a prime example.

Wealthy nobles from the central Cycladic island of Naxos, the "Stout or the Fat," came to this new and energetic government in Miletos, which had brought a temporary end to the rigors of earlier factionalism, to seek aid. Factionalism had also torn asunder the Naxian polis, and the powerful factions, which formed the political community, had banished the "Fats" (Hdt. 5.30.1). Epigraphical evidence suggests that the "Fats" belonged to the kinship group then in power in Miletos, the Onites genos which included the Milesian Molpoi,[12] a confraternity of sacred priests, singers and dancers who governed Apollo's shrine at Didyma. Aristagoras as son of Molpagoras was also of the Molpoi families and brother to the two eponymous Molpoi priests, Daphnis who held that office in 498/7 B.C., and Leonax, eponymous priest in 492/1 B.C.[13] Herodotus supports this contention by stating that the Naxian "Fats" earlier had been "friends" (xeinoi) of Histiaios (5.30.2). The aid they sought was Milesian military assistance, a military fleet in the name of their blood kinship ties (cf. Hdt. 5.49.2), so that they could gain political control of Naxos and suppress the opposition (Hdt. 5.30.3).

Aristagoras responded favorably to these pleas of kinship ties and friendship. As Persian appointed tyrant of Miletos, he also governed the Milesian dependencies, the islands of Ikaros and Leros, and hoped that he would be given Naxos as well, and thus turned to his immediate superior lord, prince Artaphrenes, to obtain his imperial diplomatic sanction for the expedition and Persian military assistance (Hdt. 5.30.3-5). Aristagoras knew that the Naxian opponents had an army of eight thousand hoplites and a great number of ships (Hdt. 5.30.4). Artaphrenes as satrap of the coastal peoples of Sparda also had a great army and numerous ships, a powerful force for which the Naxian "Fats" promised from their own personal fortunes not only the expenses of the satrapal army and fleet but lavish gifts besides (Hdt. 5.30.5-6). The "Fats" tantalized Aristagoras and Artaphrenes not only with the addition of Naxos to the imperial system, but also the islands then subject to Naxos including Paros and Andros among several, and the hint of the entire central Cycladic region in addition to the large and wealthy island of Euboia (Hdt. 5.30.2-31.3). At Sardis, Aristagoras reported glowingly to his satrap the request, and the addition of a large island near Ionia to the Spardian government; a wealthy island with many slaves (Hdt. 5.31.1), for Naxos surpassed all the Cycladic islands in prosperity (Hdt. 5.28). In turn, Artaphrenes could report to the Great King the addition of the Cyclades to the empire, the acquisition of wealth over and above the costs of the expedition, and a government of the restored exiled "Fats" as loyal Persian vassals (Hdt. 5.31.1-2). But to take Naxos, Artaphrenes needed Darius' imperial approval, for even the satrapal prince could not act independently without incurring the king's wrath (Hdt. 5.32).

Aristagoras had suggested that a fleet of one hundred ships would accomplish the goals, but Artaphrenes, while considering his vassal's counsel good, reacted cautiously and apparently knowing that the Imperial Persian Fleet was considerably weaker than the Greek fleets, and especially the powerful and well-trained Naxian fleet, and thus proposed in his request to Darius a fleet, which Herodotus reports numbered two hundred ships (Hdt. 5.30.4).[14] And during those weeks in 500 B.C., as the imperial messengers raced back and forth across the Royal Road from Sardis to Susa, Aristagoras returned to Miletos to await news of Darius' consent (Hdt. 5.32).

With the king's directive to proceed, obviously after consultation with Histiaios his advisor in Greek affairs who apparently approved of his cousin's requests, in the spring of 499 B.C. Artaphrenes mustered at Miletos two hundred triremes manned with a great number of Persians and other imperial forces. To command this armada, Artaphrenes, perhaps upon the command of Darius, appointed the Achaemenid Megabates, cousin to himself and to the king (fig. 14), as general, and sent a large satrapal army to Miletos to join Megabates (Hdt. 5.32).

In the late spring of 499 B.C., Megabates' imperial armada sailed from the Milesian harbors, triremes teeming with Persian and other eastern imperial forces, Ionian soldiers, the Naxian "Fats," and Aristagoras who would be established as tyrant of Naxos. But Megabates was cautious, having listened carefully to the local Greek naval advice, and sailed not directly westward to Naxos but north to the harbor of Kaukasa in southwestern Chios in order to take advantage of the northern winds then blowing and turn and sail swiftly and unobserved across an open stretch of water southward to Naxos. Megabates' well developed plans, however, were quickly marred by two independent events. At Kaukasa, the Persian clashed violently with Aristagoras when his subordinate, the tyrant, attempted to give military orders without the consent of his superior (Hdt. 5.33.2-4), while news from Miletos reached Naxos of the sailing of the armada.[15] With sufficient forewarning, the Naxians prepared a teichos within their city for the Persian siege, stocked it well with grain and drink brought in from the chora, and set about to fortify their walls. Thus, when Megabates arrived, the Naxians were prepared and held their position successfully for four months. For this, Megabates was not prepared, and after four months, with his imperial funds exhausted, as well as the Milesian funds which Aristagoras contributed to the expedition, the Persians prepared teiche on Naxos for the "Fats," settled them there, and abandoned the royal plans to take Naxos and the Cyclades. Megabates reluctantly but by necessity ordered the fleet to return to Miletos (late summer-early autumn 499 B.C.: Hdt. 5:34).

Aristagoras was in trouble.[16] His quarrel with Megabates and then his failure at Naxos generated heated personal antagonisms between the Persian and the Milesian, and then Artaphrenes' personal anger resulting from the failures of his subordinate, the Greek tyrant of Miletos. Within the palatial halls at Sardis, the Achaemenid staff in reviewing the recent events concluded that Aristagoras was incapable of being the imperial governor of Sparda's key naval polis (Hdt. 5.35.1). He had discredited the satrap's advice to Darius, had overstepped his subordinate position to his commander Megabates, and had drained the satrapal treasury without obtaining the rich rewards of Naxos, Paros, Andros, and other Cycladic wealth. The Persians reached their decision quickly: Aristagoras would be replaced.

But it was not just Aristagoras who would lose but his familial faction in Miletos, which would also lose power, position, and wealth, and to that faction Aristagoras turned to seek its counsel. The decision reached collectively (individual stress transformed into societal distortion and the resultant revitalization) favored rebellion against the Persians, the development of the other latent rebellious desires throughout western Anatolia, and the seeking of foreign military assistance for success (Hdt. 5.35.2-36.1).[17] Only Hekataios the logographer dissented from the revolutionary council's decisions, and advising the Milesian nobles not to rebel against the powerful Darius he reminded them of his catalogue of the many ethnic groups throughout the Persian Empire indicative of the Great King's military strength. But the Milesian council remained persuaded of its decision. Thus Hekataios, realizing that the rebellion was imminent, joined his kinsmen in their decision and outlined plans necessary for success: to muster a great fleet of Eastern Greeks in order to defeat the Imperial Persian Fleet and to build that fleet with the wealth stored in the temple treasuries at Didyma, which would also prevent the Persians from seizing the treasuries for their own use (Hdt. 5.36.2-3). Much of his argument pleased the revolutionary council, and it moved to revolt and to gather a great fleet, but as many of the counselors were priestly Molpoi attached to Apollo's oracular sanctuary at Didyma they rejected outright the idea to use that temple's treasuries (Hdt. 5.36.4).

The personal issue of Aristagoras' loss of his governorship altered rapidly into the issue of Milesian political self-determination. In rebellion against Darius, the Milesian revolutionary council abrogated the vassalage treaty sworn to Cyrus and, thus, eliminated the payment of tribute and the duties of military service to the Great King. By this abrogation, the council also had to eliminate the office of the Persian governor or tyrant, and urged the exceedingly willing Aristagoras to renounce his office, the last vestige of Persian overlordship in Miletos. Aristagoras had no other choice, and by his formal but absolutely necessary abdication of tyranny raised the Milesian revolutionary council, his supporting faction, to power within the polis, with rights of equality in political decisions (isonomia: Hdt. 5.37.2).

The revolutionary council then resolved to send the Milesian fleet up the Maeander Gulf to the small polis of Myous where the fleet, which had just returned from Naxos, still lay in the harbor. This bold move was designed to tear away the East Greek contingents and their commanding tyrants from the Persians and the other easterners stationed at Myous. In its boldness, the council succeeded. The Milesian Molpos (?) Iatragoras sailed to Myous and with a military force captured the Karian tyrants Oliatos of Mylasa and Histiaios of Termera; Koes, the faithful and loyal vassal of Darius, the tyrant of Mytilene; Aristagoras the tyrant of Aiolian Kyme; and "many others" from under the noses of the Persian generals (Hdt. 5.37.1). With the news of Iatragoras' success, Aristagoras boldly announced his abdication and the rebellion, and set about to eliminate Darius' imperial control of the East Greeks first in Ionia and then through Aiolis and the

Troad and ultimately in Karia.

Amidst the confusion at Myous, many of the loyal tyrants fled to Artaphrenes' protection: but those captured, the Milesians handed over to their respective poleis for the local revolutionary governments to decide the tyrants' fates. Many governments, including that at Kyme, exiled their tyrants to Sardis, but the angry Mytilenaians stoned Koes (Hdt. 5.38.1). Persian taxes, military obligations, and tyrannies ceased, and the cry of Greek liberation and freedom after three subjugations reverberated along the shores of Sparda and Daskyleion. To head the revolutionary governments, each polis elected a general to command its military forces, and the Milesian revolutionary council elected its own Aristagoras. But beyond these measures, no formal federated military plans immediately developed. The Milesians, therefore, independently sent Aristagoras as their envoy (*apostolos*) aboard a single trireme to seek military assistance from the mainland Greeks (Hdt. 5.38.2).

As the Persians maintained that a state of war existed with Sparta since Cyrus' conquest of Sardis c. 545 B.C., and with Athens since c. 507 B.C., when she repudiated the vassalage treaty sworn at the Sardian altar, Aristagoras set sail for those two poleis. Sparta obviously had the better military force and was the Milesian council's first objective (Hdt. 5.38.2-54.2). With a bronze tablet inscribed with a map of the Greek and Persian worlds, all the seas and all the rivers, Aristagoras tried every means to persuade King Kleomenes to aid the "Ionians,"[18] but to no avail.[19] At Athens, Aristagoras argued more persuasively, noting among several things (if Herodotus' account is essentially accurate) the wealth and importance of the Milesian oikoi, his faction's wealthy rural demesnes, and adding passionate appeals to ties of blood kinship (Hdt. 5.97.2). After what must have been a lively and heated debate, the Athenian Assembly voted to send twenty ships (*neas* rather than triremes) as aid for the Ionian cause, and appointed the Athenian aristocrat Melanthios the son of Phalanthos to command that fleet.[20] Factionalism also abounded in Athens,[21] and while some groups rallied behind Aristagoras, the Peisistratid faction looked forward to the day when Darius would restore Hippias as vassal tyrant to Athens. But the majority of Athenians supported the Milesian cause and voted to send part of their fleet to Ionia.[22] Whether they understood the implications of their violation of the vassalage oath of 507 B.C., they fully did understand that Hippias was at Sardis urging Artaphrenes to take action and return him to Athens (Hdt. 5.96.2).

Ionian patriotism meant little if nothing to the Athenians, perhaps only a yen for booty became the persuading factor.[23]

Aristagoras, in some manner omitted by Herodotus, also contacted the aristocratic government of Eretria in central Euboia, and, appealing to an ancient alliance between the two poleis during the Lelantine War, gained the pledge that five Eretrian triremes would sail with Melanthios (Hdt. 5.99.1), and that a second fleet would sail immediately to attack the Persian Imperial Fleet off Pamphylia and at Cyprus (Lysanias *FGrH* 426 F 1). The earlier Persian desire to conquer Naxos and then Andros had alienated the Eretrians who dominated the islands of Andros, Tenos, and Keos (Strabo 10.1.10). This, rather than the appeal to ancient alliances in parochial Greek world, may have piqued the Eretrians to rally to arms.

With the pledges of military assistance, limited though they may have been, Aristagoras quickly departed to Miletos well before Melanthios could muster the fleet at Phaleron Bay (Hdt. 5.98.1). Meanwhile, the Milesian military council had been actively seeking East Greek support and upon Artistagoras' return to his city he found "all 'Ionia' in revolt against the king," or at least that is what Herodotus would have us believe (Hdt. 5.98.2).[24] In reality, the revolution had not spread much beyond the traditional regions of Ionia and Aiolis. The discontent with imposed tryants,[25] taxes, and military services, while not burdensome, had been bearable, yet bore the marks of vassalage in addition to the absence of a philosophical ideal (rather than political) of "freedom."[26] Aristagoras' personal and extremely precarious political position, however, had generated the spark of revolution, which found its first success in Iatragoras' raid at Myous. The Ionians, nevertheless, failed to perceive the implications of Hekataios' warnings and the realities of Darius' well developed political power and the strength of the Persian armies. The basic ties of Ionian nationalism or of a coordinated military federation were still markedly absent; further Aristagoras acted not as a popular Ionian national hero but rather as a scared politician who sought any means to survive.[27] Even during the lengthy winter months of 499/498, before the Athenians and Eretrians arrived in Ionia, the revolutionaries failed to prepare a systematic military offensive policy. At bottom, the "Ionian Revolution" was a general anti-Persian struggle and in part, at least, anti-tyrannical, but also uncoordinated (Thuc. 1.18.2, 89.2; *Ath. Pol.* 23.4).[28] The East Greeks failed to comprehend the effective reorganization of Darius' empire and the consolidation of the

Spardian satrapy under Artaphrenes intended to counteract the "Ionian" centrifugal forces of factionalism, parochialism, and particularism.

Artaphrenes' response to this rebellion was swift and decisive: to dispatch the imperial troops stationed at Sardis down the Maeander Valley and lay siege to Miletos (Plut. *de mal. Hdt.* 24, 861 B-C), the heart of the rebellion and its revolutionary council. If Miletos would fall immediately, the remaining disparate revolts would quickly fade. But unfortunately for Artaphrenes, Miletos stood firm for six years.[29]

The blow to Artaphrenes' military strategy came from abroad, from the rebellious Athenians and the hostile Eretrians. The Greek agents who had penetrated Phrygia to foment unrest essentially had accomplished little (Hdt. 5.98). In the late spring of 498 B.C., Melanthios commanded his combined Athenian-Eretrian fleet into the Milesian harbors safe from the Persian siege armies. There, in the city, Aristagoras laid before the Athenians, Eretrians, and other, unnamed military allies the Milesian revolutionary council's plan to attack Sardis, a plan which he apparently had designed (Hdt. 5.99.1). But faced with the problems of the Persian army stationed in the Milesian chora, Aristagoras was forced to remain in Miletos to direct the local counter-siege operations and to appoint his brother Charopinos and another noble of the Milesian asty, Hermophantos, to execute the Milesian plan (Hdt. 5.99.2). A raid upon Sardis might devastate the Sardian center and relieve Miletos of the Persian siege. The decision had been made not to use the Athenians and Eretrians against the Persians in the Milesian chora.

From Miletos, the revolutionary fleet (now perhaps including Milesian ships) sailed around the Mykale cape and set in at Koressos, a small port near Ephesos. The majority of Ephesians, however, loyal to their Persian overlords, were unwilling to revolt, but faced with a foreign army in their midst, a few perhaps reluctantly guided the army up the Kayster Valley and across the Tmolos range into Sardis. While to cross the route from Ephesos to Sardis normally took three days, the army may have traveled faster, with sufficient speed to enter the satrapal capital without Persian opposition. With many of his troops at Miletos, Artaphrenes and the military force remaining in Sardis could only hold the towering acropolis, as Greeks plundered the lower city and, no doubt, the gold smelting and craft buildings,[30] and set fire to what they could inside and outside of the massive city wall (Charon of Lampsakos *FGrH* 262 F 10; Hdt. 5.101.1). Sardis lay in ruins and, as a crime against the gods, the Greeks set fire to the temple of Kuvava (Hdt.

5.102.1).[31] The plundering, looting, and burning may have lasted many days.[32]

When the opportunity arose, however, Artaphrenes commanded his Lydian and Persian soldiers down from the acropolis and into the city's agora, cutting through the destruction and the helter–skelter of Greek soldiers, and regained the central city as other satrapal troops finally appeared (Hdt. 5.101.2). The Greeks, apparently rather disorganized and fearing the Persians, fled into the Tmolos hills and under the cover of night began the long trek back to their ships at Koressos (Hdt. 5.101.3). Persian forces stationed in the distant regions but west of the Halys River had entered Sardis (Hdt. 5.102.1). Enraged over the Greek "rape" of Sardis and the destruction of Kuvava's temple, Artaphrenes commanded his enlarged forces to race towards Ephesos and capture the Greeks. At Ephesos, which remained loyal to the satrap and his king, the Persians attacked the fleeing Greeks who had turned and prepared for battle, and there the Persians killed many of them and their noble commanders, including the Eretrian general Eualkides. Those Greeks fortunate enough to reach their ships scattered in haste to their respective poleis. The Athenians, especially, separated from the Greek forces and flatly refused to aid the Ionians in spite of Aristagoras' urgent and frantic messages to stay (Hdt. 5.102.2-103.1).

Although the disaster and desertions at Ephesos marred the Ionian cause, the burning and looting of Sardis signaled to the Ionians that their rebellion could be successful. Actually they had no other choice but to rebel. The Persians would punish the rebels, whether they stopped then or continued. The events at Sardis, therefore, drove the rebels to exalt their victory and to sail along the Hellespontine and Propontic coasts as far as Byzantion and foster supportive rebellions throughout that region. Byzantion, for example, had not been a loyal vassal state.[33] The news of Sardis also spread rapidly throughout Karia, and a majority of Karian poleis and native tribes joined the "Ionian" war, including the previously reluctant polis of Kaunos (Hdt. 5.103.1-2).

The anxieties of the East Greeks generated by tyrants, taxes, and military service had not only produced the Milesian revolutionary movement in which the leader Aristagoras and his followers interacted, but also contemporaneously spawned the other revolutions, which by the late summer of 498 B.C. remained loosely coordinated, each polis and its general acting essentially independently. A revolutionary movement arose, however, still plagued by factionalism and parochialism. But the rebels had begun to believe their cause to be just—"freedom"-*eleutheria*—a doctrine not created out of a logographer's fancy or a simple ex-tyrant's personal desire but in order to resolve complex problematic issues. The "new order," consequently, ultimately produced in each participating polis historical traditions as well as anachronistic "tall tales" and fabricated stories, the numerous oral recollections of a series of independent events gathered by Herodotus: the interactions of Miletos, Chios, Samos, and Cyprus.

For Darius and Artaphrenes, nevertheless, the destruction of Sardis had triggered rebellions, from southern Kaunos to northern Byzantion, which totally disrupted their imperial control of Sparda and Daskyleion, and had spread rebellion throughout Skudra. The specter of massive rebellions throughout the empire, as in 522-1 B.C., loomed real. Cilicia, Phoenicia, Judah, and Egypt had to be controlled at all costs, as the Eretrian fleet had defeated the Cypriots in the Pamphylian Sea (Lysanias *FGrH* 426 F 1). That battle, more important than the destruction of Sardis, generated among the Greeks of Cyprus their rebellions against Darius in 497 B.C., rebellions independent of the revolutionary council in Miletos.[34] Factionalism also spread throughout that island as prince Onesilos led an anti-Persian group against his brother King Gorgos of Salamis and laid siege to the pro-Persian city of Amathos on the south–eastern coast, which, with the Phoenician city of Kition, refused to join the rebellion (Hdt. 5.104)

In the summer of 496 B.C., Darius ordered the Persian Artybios to attack the Cypriot rebels with a large fleet (Hdt. 5.108.1). Only then did Onesilos beseech the Ionian rebels for assistance. The Milesian revolutionary council, perhaps augmented by other Ionian generals, deliberated,[35] and realizing that military assistance to the Cypriot revolution would divert Persian troops from the Ionian region, the council voted to aid Onesilos and dispatched a sizable fleet to the eastern island. With the Ionians on Cyprus, the Persian military command in Cilicia under Artybios set sail for that island to reduce the rebellion and defeat the Ionian rebels (Hdt. 5.108.2). In sea battle, the Ionians gained victory, but on land the Persians defeated them and slew Onesilos. Before the war had ended, the Ionians deserted and sailed home. The Cypriot rebellion then crumbled and the Persians securely regained the entire island (5.109-116.1).[36] From Cyprus, the Persian Imperial Fleet of Egyptian, Phoenician, Cilician, and Cypriot ships would sail, unimpeded, against the Ionians. The Ionian adventure in Cyprus had failed to obtain its goals at the crucial time when the Persian troops from central Lydia had been systematically subjugating the rebellious East Greek poleis.

During the many months following the Greek raid upon Sardis, in the period of the Cypriot rebellion, imperial messengers crisscrossed the empire keeping Darius well informed of events, and brought the king's imperial orders to Artaphrenes and the Persian military commanders throughout Anatolia. No doubt during the turbulent summer of 497 B.C. Darius questioned Histiaios rigorously and at length as how best to suppress the rebellions,[37] and then ordered his Greek adviser to go to Sardis to assist Artaphrenes in directing the central phase of Persian reconquest (Hdt. 5.107).

It may have been at this time that several of the rebellious East Greek poleis contributed to the general Ionian cause quantities of electrum bullion to be cut and struck as staters, although evidence of this connection is lacking and only suspected.[38] The thirty examples of these staters of nine different obverse die types, uniform in style and in fabric and all struck upon the predominant Milesian weight standard (13.48-14.09 grms.), suggest that they were struck in one polis. Chios (sphinx), Lampsakos (protome of Pegasos), and Klazomenai (protome of winged boar) are certainly represented, and Samos (ox protome), Abydos (eagle), Dardanos (cock), Methymna on Lesbos (sow walking), Kyme (horse), and Priene (head of Athena) are plausibly represented, but Miletos the center and leader of the rebellion is noticeably absent. This had led Colin M. Kraay to consider that the entire series had been struck in the Milesian mint, with the different types representative of the contributing poleis or simply as control-marks selected by the Milesian officials in charge of minting.[39] Some of the bullion may have been looted from Sardis during the raid in the previous year, but, if the types do represent the contributing poleis, most of them had not participated in that venture and would not have shared in the booty. The bullion, therefore, came from their state treasuries and perhaps also from their sanctuaries. The staters would pay the revolution's costs. If the electrum issues are to be dated to these early years of the rebellion, we detect in the staters, in value a sizeable sum with each equal to twenty silver drachmae, a major and crucial financial effort to support the faltering East Greek military offensive campaigns. The drain upon the Milesian and other "Ionian" treasuries, the loss of military men and ships, and the destruction of the rural demesnes because of the general factors of war weakened the East Greeks with each succeeding year. With the final blow of Persian victory, the Ionians would suffer acutely.

During the campaign season of 497 B.C., the central phase of Persian reconquest commenced with significant inroads upon the rebellious East Greeks. Following the battle of Ephesos the year before, Darius dispatched his sons-in-law, the Persian generals Daurises and Hymaies, to join a third son-in-law, the faithful conspirator Otanes, in order to assist the king's half-brother Artaphrenes to divide systematically the regions of western Anatolia and to begin to sack each rebellious polis (Hdt. 5.116). While the Persian messengers raced along the Royal Road, Artaphrenes as supreme commander in the west may have acted immediately and by necessity hoping that the Great King would approve all of his decisions.[40]

Daurises headed for the Hellespont, and attacking and sacking Dardanos campaigned northward along the Asian coast to Abydos, Perkote, Lampsakos, Paisos, and then on toward Parion. The objectives were clear: to control the vital Troad and the Hellespont, to attempt to regain the Bosporos, and to renew control of Skudra. Daurises gained victory after victory, but with his attack upon Parion a messenger arrived, apparently from Artaphrenes, with news that the Karians had revolted and broken away, and that Daurises must leave the Propontis and march safely through loyal Lydia to attack Karia (Hdt. 5.117). Artaphrenes had judged wisely, for the Karians fiercely fought back and rather successfully against Daurises. Herodotus, unfortunately, omitted to relate why the Harpagid family failed to control Karia. Forewarned of the advancing army commanded by Daurises, the Karians rapidly mustered at the "White Monuments"[41] beside the Marsyas (modern Çine) River to meet the Persians advancing from the Maeander Valley. But the Persians advanced and, after a long and arduous battle, pushed the Karians southwest toward Miletos and to Labraunda where the Karians held ground, ambushed the Persians, and killed Daurises and two other senior Persian generals. Herakleides of Mylasa, brother of the former tyrant Oliatos, led the Karian counter-attack (Hdt. 5.118-121).

To aid Daurises in a pincer-movement in the Troad, Hymaies took the small polis of Kios on the southeastern bay of the Propontis but, upon learning of Daurises' hasty march toward Karia, Hymaies turned southward and then marched west toward the southern Hellespont and the Aiolian settlement at Ilion. Hymaies, under imperial orders, apparently sought to complete Daurises' military goals, yet illness struck him down before he could campaign farther (Hdt. 5.122).

Against the heart of Ionia and to renew the siege of Miletos, broken by the Greek raid upon Sardis, Darius had commanded Otanes to accompany Artaphrenes from Sardis down the Hermos Valley against Kyme and then Klazomenai (Hdt. 5.123). To the south, Lebedos, Kolophon, and Ephesos with their extensive Lydian inhabitants, including the Mermnad nobles, remained loyal to the Great King and enabled Artaphrenes to approach the Mykale ridge and its opposite Maeander Valley without opposition. The satrap's goals were to regain Myous, Priene, and Miletos. As the Persians, with their Lydian and other loyal Anatolian troops, marched southward, Aristagoras panicked, and summoning the Milesians attempted to persuade them to abandon their homeland. The rebel leader now realized the futility of his actions. In vain once again, Hekataios urged his fellow Milesians to build a fortress (teiche) on Leros, move there, and wait for a favorable time to return to Miletos. Aristagoras, abandoning his command in Miletos and turning it over to the noble Pythagoras, apparently a member of the Molpoi clan, then fled to his uncle's vassal estates in Thracian Myrkinos.[42]   There, Aristagoras, attempting to gain more territory for himself, was cut down by the independent Thracians (Hdt. 5.124.1-126.2).

The back of the Ionian resistance had been broken, and the Persians pursued only two other goals: the land assault against Miletos and the destruction of the Ionian fleet. Major though these goals may have been, with the internal disruption of the Milesian revolutionary council, the remaining resisting Ionians, while trying to sustain a military unity and offensive policy, could easily crumble as further Persian success in western Anatolia would increase factionalism and parochialism among the Ionians. Although Herodotus failed to note the succession of events, it appears that Artaphrenes had returned to Sardis and from his acropolitan palace directed the remaining campaigns and awaited the arrival of the Persian Imperial Fleet. At this point, Histiaios arrived in Sardis to be scrutinized at length by the satrap concerning why the Ionians had rebelled and what role had the Milesians taken against his imperial commands (Hdt. 6.1.1). Artaphrenes saw no value in allowing Histiaios to aid him, and the Milesian quickly perceived that he had neither a role nor a future in Sardis and that his only recourse was to flee under the cover of night for the safety of Chios (Hdt. 6.1.2-2.2). But the Chians distrusted him outright, and Histiaios gambled wrongly that the Milesians would welcome his advice. They, too, distrusted the former Persian agent, and Histiaios with little to no security tried once again to enter Chios but left for Mytilene, where he gained command of eight manned triremes willing to join him in independent piratical adventures along the Bosporos (Hdt. 6.3–6.5.3). Histiaios' attempts at diplomacy with Artaphrenes, with the Chians, and most important with the Milesians, had failed miserably. He was distrusted and not wanted by any group facing the last stages of the failing rebellion. The few Persians stationed in Sardis, who had supported Histiaios' diplomatic bid and who remained in touch with him, met swift death at Artaphrenes' orders (Hdt. 6.4.2). Assured of his command over Sparda and his successes in putting down the rebels, Artaphrenes asserted his strict satrapal rule. Stung bitterly by the rebellion, the satrap would allow no dissension nor allow anyone suspected of dissension to remain. His strong hand would continue to rule Sparda. By messenger, Artaphrenes informed his king that Histiaios was a traitor.[43]

With the Persian recontrol of Cyprus, the Ionian morale faltered and its strategic initiative wavered. To avoid the campaigns of Otanes and Artaphrenes, the central Ionian poleis with the exception of Miletos seem to have dispatched their ships and military forces to the major offshore islands. By the campaign season of 495 B.C., perhaps only distant Erythrai and heavily fortified and resistant Miletos remained of the important rebellious mainland territories and poleis.[44] The imperial strategy decisively directed by Artaphrenes focused upon Miletos alone. By land, the Persian army would lay siege to the city, and by sea, the Persian Imperial Fleet would attack the Greek navy (Hdt. 6.6). In haste and years too late, the rebellious generals, representing the remaining factions, which still maintained fleets at Chios and Samos, met with the Milesian revolutionary council. This time they managed to gather at the Panionion shrine some distance from Persian held Ephesos and along the difficult northern coast of the Mykale range. Any attempt to awaken the ancient Ionian religious spirit would help amidst the malaise of decaying morale. The representatives meeting (the probouloi) realized the futility of trying to fight the Persians on land and left the Milesians to defend their walls alone. The Greek fleet, however, could succeed if all went well, and prepared to meet the Persian Imperial Fleet in sight of Miletos' city walls not far from the small offshore island of Lade (Hdt. 6.7).

For Artaphrenes, the Athenian raids upon the Thracian Chersonese and the islands of Lemnos and Imbros were of little importance. In time the Persians would punish the Athenians. Darius' former vassal, the tyrant Miltiades, a noble Athenian, had some years earlier fled his realm in the Chersonese and now commanded the minor yet somewhat bothersome Athenian fleet. The Athenians seem not to have been concerned with the events at Miletos but only with their personal interests near the Hellespont and Miltiades' rule of the Chersonese (Hdt. 6.140).[45]

In the spring of 494 B.C., the Persian Imperial Fleet under the command of the Mede Datis set sail for Miletos, and reconfirmed Persian imperial power among the docile East Dorian Greeks of Knidos, Kos, and Halikarnassos.[46] By Herodotus' count, the Persians commanded 600 ships in stark contrast to the 353 Greek triremes, yet the Persians knew that even though they greatly outnumbered the Greeks, their naval forces were fundamentally inferior.[47] (Herodotus' figure of 600 Persian ships may be grossly incorrect, as the fleet may have been in reality much smaller.) Neither Cyrus nor Cambyses had developed an imperial fleet, and while Darius held Sparda, his important naval divisions had come from the Ionian maritime poleis. But to expand and defend his empire, Darius had to rely foremost upon the Phoenicians, who played a primary role in his Mediterranean fleet, and then upon the secondary fleets of the Cilicians, Cypriots, and Egyptians. In these troubled years he could not muster the Lykians, Karians, Ionians, and Hellespontines. Nevertheless, the Phoenicians, with centuries of sound naval experiences and traditions, thriving ports, and resources of suitable timber, were dependable. As rewards for their loyal naval services, the Phoenician city-states retained a degree of autonomy within the empire, as did the Cilicians. And for the battle at Lade, Datis by necessity had to rely upon the Cypriots who did remain loyal to the Great King.

Aware of their naval inferiority, the Persians banked upon the endemic Greek problems of factionalism and parochialism, and wisely gathered loyal vassals, the former Greek tyrants of the still rebellious poleis, to foster open factionalism among the Greeks and attempt to break up the temporarily united Greek fleet off Miletos in order to obtain victory over the reduced Greek forces (Hdt. 6.9.1-3). Darius' new orders sustained an old Achaemenid policy toward rebels who would put down arms and acknowledge Persian overlordship, a policy established by Cyrus at Sardis about forty years earlier. For all East Greeks who would end their resistance, the Persians promised no punishment. But if resistance continued, the Persians would be ruthless: burn their temples and homes, enchain them in slavery, cart their boys off for lives as eunuchs, transport their girls to Bactria, and populate Ionia with loyal subjects from the numerous imperial satrapies.

The tyrants' messengers sought out the pro-Persian factions which considered the king's offers but did not realize the rebellious factions were part of a large movement, and as each faction believed that it alone had been contacted, this aspect of Darius' strategy failed (Hdt. 6.10).

The Greeks, meanwhile, assembled at Lade and chose the competent general Dionysios from Phokaia to lead them. With patriotic words of "freedom," Dionysios rallied the Greeks yet warned them of the potential dangers of their weaknesses and disorder, of parochialism and factionalism. They all knew too well the consequences if they failed (Hdt. 6.11.1-2). At first, as with so many Greek adventures, enthusiasm soared high and for days the East Greeks submitted to the strenuous rigors of Dionysios' training maneuvers, but by the eighth day dissension arose amidst their ranks, they openly balked at Dionysios' commands, and the Samians began to worry about the reality of the Persian reprisals. Aiakes the son of the deposed tyrant of Samos, Syloson, who had fled to Persian during the affair of Myous in 499 B.C., sought out by messenger his supporting factions among the Samian fleet of 60 triremes at Lade (Hdt. 6.13.1). Then, finally in battle (late spring or early summer),[48] Dionysios' fears materialized: 49 Samian triremes responded to Aiakes' offer and left 11 anti-Persian triremes to face disaster. Then the entire fleet of 70 Lesbian ships deserted as did major contingents from the other poleis. Of the islanders, only the Chians held their position in support of the Milesian cause, approximately more than fifty-four percent of the East Greek fleet stayed, yet to be battered unmercifully at sea, and when trying to escape through Ephesian territory the Chians were attacked and killed by the loyal Ephesians (Hdt. 6.14-16). Exhausted and in despair, Dionysios with three captured imperial ships set sail for Sicily to escape the chains of defeat (Hdt. 6.16.1).

With a triumphant victory upon the sea (a victory which worried the Persians significantly that it would not occur or occur easily), the Persian armies set a massive siege upon the Milesian city walls, with siege engines, sappers and miners battering away upon the fortifications. The Ionian Revolt had been the child of the Milesians, and when the city fell the Persians ruthlessly punished the unfaithful rebels. Miletos lost its prime position within the Achaemenid Empire as established by special alliance with Cyrus. Darius enslaved the city (Hdt. 6.18). The Persians' warnings had been direct and clear, and were now carried out. The imperial armies slaughtered many of the men, and enchained many of the women and children for deportation to the east.[49] The city lay in

ruin[50] as the Persians stormed Apollo's oracular sanctuary at Didyma, looted its

treasuries, sent prizes off to Darius at Susa, and burned the holy temple (Hdt. 6.19.3). To

Ecbatana, the Persians shipped by caravan a bronze statue of Apollo (Paus. 1.16.3), and

to Susa a large bronze knuckle-bone weight (93.07 kg.).[51] Few nobles remained in

blackened Miletos to watch the Persians herd their Milesian slaves to Susa (Pliny NH

6.28.159) and loyal Karians from Pedasa move in and settle the Milesian hill regions (Hdt.

6.20). Outside the city's breached walls, the Persians remained encamped.

Persia's violent destruction of Miletos occurred not just because the "Ionian Revolt"

had been the child of the Milesians, but also because the Milesians had had a special

treaty of privileged vassalage status with the Great King, unlike the other rebellious

Persian subjugated Ionian poleis. Persian punishment, therefore, was excessively harsh,

as a warning to others not to rebel and as a specific punishment of the leading gentry and

their families who had incited the revolution. It was also a forewarning for the

Athenians. Normally the Persians did not practice the mass deportations of subjugated

communities as had the Neo-Assyrians, for the early Achaemenids held to the principles

of local national autonomy and religious tolerance. But when piqued, the Persians did

wield the stark principles of Assyrian deportation.[52] The uprooting of deportees

markedly weakened their national spirit and link with their homeland and also greatly

reduced the probability of national revival. Deportations were usually only partial, the

transportation of the leading citizens, the ranking magistrates and military personnel, as

well as skilled artisans. This event clearly marked the end of the Milesian Blütezeit, and

the Milesian artisans would apply their crafts to the Persian constructions in Susa. With

Milesian hostages in Elam, the Persians held in check the families and compatriots

remaining in Miletos. These would remain loyal to Persia and later, when allied with the

Athenians, would lead a pro-Persian movement in the 450's B.C.

Some Milesians, however, had fled to Samos. But there, factionalism between the

supporters of Aiakes, who had returned as Persian vassal and tyrant, and the nobles who

had resisted Persian control tore that island asunder. Those anti-Persian factions, both

Milesian and Samian, fearing further subjugation and possible enslavement, set sail for

distant Sicily and the city of Zankle upon the straits (Hdt. 6.22.1-25.1; Thuc. 6.4.5-6).[53]

The pro-Persian Samians, those who had responded to the Persian offers for amnesty, were once again governed by the Persian-appointed Aiakes. They restored their polis peacefully spared from the plunderings, burnings, and lootings, which the Persians had harshly inflicted upon Miletos (Hdt. 6.25.1). Other Milesians, nevertheless, painfully aware of the power of the Persian Empire, submitted to the new strictures of subjugation and vassalage, among them some of the aristocratic Molpoi who struggled to maintain the sacrifices at Didyma. From the list of eponymous Molpoi, the aisymnetai of Didyma and the leaders of the sacred confraternity, we note no break in the period of 494 and 493 B.C. We must also note that members of three or four aristocratic families served either before and after or during and after the revolt, including brothers of the rebellious tyrant Aristagoras, the son of Molpagoras.[54] Yet Miletos, sacked, deprived of her accumulated wealth, and seriously depopulated, would not regain her former maritime power. The heyday of Ionian commercial, colonial, and creative urban activities had ended. To quote George Huxley, "The fall of Miletos marks the end of early Ionia . . . the spring had gone from the year. At Lade, the Asiatic Ionians were condemned to a precarious existence between the naval power of Athens, and later of Sparta, on one side, and the great empire of Persia on the other." ". . . Lade symbolised a political failure whose origins lay far back in the Ionian past."[55]

Artaphrenes' masterful strategy to attack Miletos by sea and by land had succeeded. His fears that the Persian Imperial Fleet might not victoriously outmaneuver the smaller but more capable Greek fleet had been offset by diplomatic tactics which accentuated the factional rifts within the major revolutionary poleis as well as age-old parochialism, which had fostered hostilities among them, especially between Miletos and Samos. With the fall of Miletos, the remembrance of which would bring tears to the Athenians' eyes (Hdt. 6.21.2), Artaphrenes set about to restore firmly and effectively the rest of Ionia, Karia, Aiolis, the Hellespont, and the offshore islands claimed by King Darius as his. Karia quickly fell yet with some resistance (Hdt. 6.25.1), and a large Persian army commanded by the general Harpagos campaigned down the Kaikos Valley into Mysia and Aiolis (Hdt. 6.28.2).[56] Histiaios, however, still troubled the triumphant satrap. The ex-tyrant had left his second-in-command, the pirate Bisaltes, in Abydos, which once again had broken away from Persian control, and Histiaios, freewheeling amidst the confusion after the Battle of Lade, raided Chios and Thasos (Hdt. 6.26.1-28.1), then turned upon Lesbos. Motivated by the immediate necessity of self-preservation and personal profit, Histiaios had gathered Mytilenaians and other renegades from Ionia and Aiolis, and directed a raid upon the small mainland Aiolian town of Atarneus.[57] There, and by accident, he ran headlong into the army of Harpagos, which defeated his renegade forces and captured the hapless pirate leader. In Sardis, Artaphrenes and Harpagos ordered their soldiers to impale Histiaios, and then sent his embalmed head to Susa as a special gift for the Great King (Hdt. 6.28.2-30.1). But Darius (if we can trust Herodotus' account: 6.30.2), angered that his satrap had not sent Histiaios to him alive, still believed Histiaios a faithful vassal in spite of his raids upon Abydos, Thasos, Chios, Lesbos, and Atarneus, and ordered the head to be buried with honors.

In the spring of 493 B.C., the Persian Imperial Fleet set out from Miletos to subdue the remaining rebellious islands of Chios, Lesbos, and Tenedos.[58] Again successful, the Persians looted and burned, and systematically captured the inhabitants in order to punish the leaders and malcontents. Then the Persians turned to complete their recontrol of the mainland, where they continue to burn, loot, destroy, and enslave and castrate the handsome young boys and dispatch the beautiful young girls to the king (Hdt. 6.31-32).[59] Only the Samians, because of their double-cross of the Milesians, had escaped that punishment. From Ionia and apparently Erythrai, the Persians sailed toward the Thracian Chersonese to end Athenian interference there, then on to Perinthos, the several Thracian teichea along the Propontis, to Selymbria, and finally to the volatile and rebellious polis of Byzantion. Fearing the Persian wrath, many Byzantines and their neighboring Kalchedonians across the straits fled to Mesambria on the Black Sea. With Byzantion and Kalchedon in flames, the Persians set sail for Prokonnesos and Artake on the southern Propontic shores. Sometime earlier, the leaders of Kyzikos east of Artake had submitted to Oibares, the satrap of Daskyleion, and by means of a treaty of surrender (homologia)[60] vowed to be faithful vassals of the Great King (Hdt. 6.33.2). After subjugating the entire Propontic region, the Imperial Fleet returned to the Chersonese and destroyed the last outpost of resistance, Kardia (Hdt. 6.33). It had been the center for Miltiades' rule, and hereafter only one notice of the village appears in the records of the fifth century B.C.[61]

Artaphrenes ordered governmental representatives of each of the rebellious East Greek poleis to assemble at a meeting at which the new rules and regulations for order and restoration to the Persian Empire were dictated (cf. Hdt. 1.92, 1.169.2, 6.32).

Henceforth, Sardis would rule more resolutely than before in political, judicial, and military matters, and allow the Ionians no opportunity to rally at the now defunct Panionion council.[62] To counteract the factor of East Greek parochialism, which the satrap had played upon as a diplomatic aspect leading to the Ionian defeat, Artaphrenes ordered the poleis to contract alliances one with another, to submit to the satrapal court for arbitration in all disputes such as the Samian-Milesian struggle for control of Prienian territory, and, hereafter, no local wars, skirmishes or raids between poleis would be permitted (Hdt. 6.42.1). To reinstate the Great King's imperial rules for the collection of taxes from his vassal states, the "Ionian" territories were measured, their populations reduced by war considered among the factors for future agricultural production, and new tribute assessments levied (Hdt. 6.42.2). Throughout the territories, the rebellious generals who had led the fight against Persia were systematically deposed. By orders directly from King Darius carried to Sardis in the next year (492 B.C.), Mardonios, the son of the noble leader and conspirator Gobryas, who had wed Darius' daughter Artozostre, announced that tyrants and generals would no longer be permitted to govern but rather in their place aristocratic and oligarchic governments representative of their landed gentries. The battles, however, had taken their toll of many aristocrats, and then the systematic round-up of anti-Persian nobles, landed gentry, and others, had left in the reinstated poleis smaller groups manageable to rule from Sardis and cowed into renewing their vassalage obligations. In Samos, however, faithful to the Persians, Aiakes regained his office as tyrant (Hdt. 6.25), and on devastated Chios the Persians reinstated the tyrant Strattis (Hdt. 8.132). With the maritime facilities at Miletos destroyed, Darius and Artaphrenes needed secure and faithful governors in Samos and Chios, and apparently in Lesbos also, to rule the maritime islands and assist the Persian commanders of the Imperial Fleet who continued for at least a decade and a half to sail the eastern Aegean waters.

Urban centers lay devastated, houses and shops burned, temples and populations reduced. In the chorai, the landed gentry of the rural demesnes struggled to revive. The events of the revolt had greatly sapped the Ionian poleis of wealth and manpower, losses suffered by the aste and chorai alike. Economic depression spread throughout the coastal regions of western Anatolia, and the formerly brilliant, vibrant, and productive Ionian poleis fell into provincial languor. In Samos alone, the earlier vitality remained. The revolt had been the principal interest of the maritime poleis of Ionia, which had gained strength since the days of the fall of Phokaia and Teos by turning more extensively to the ports of Magna Graecia, Thrace, and the Black Sea in order to obtain grain to augment their own agricultural supplies. With the fall of Miletos, Samos gained the prime maritime role yet began to struggle with Athenian commercial interests in the north and in the eastern Mediterranean. During the next twelve to thirteen years, the former rebels from Karia, Ionia, Aiolis, and the Troad dutifully responded to the recurrent imperial demands for taxes and military service for the new phases of war. Darius had ordered Mardonios in 492 B.C. to gather in Ionia a Persian Imperial Fleet and the Imperial Army to attack, burn, and enslave Eretria and Athens (Hdt. 67.43.3-44.3).

II

The Punishment of Athens

Darius' orders to Mardonios were clear and direct: pillage, burn, and enslave rebellious Athens. Implicit in the king's commands were the imperial directives to control central Greece, Euboia, and Attica, and to consider Persian control of Sparta and the Peloponnesos. As with the subjugation of the rebellious nations in 522-520 B.C. and the subsequent conquests of Skudra and Hindush, Darius commanded a slow, methodical, and thorough conquest and provincial incorporation into the Empire. Mardonios would begin the slow penetration of Greece from the north. During the Milesian affair, Achaemenid control of Skudra had weakened greatly and two of several goals set before Mardonios were the recontrol of western Skudra and reunion with Persia's vassal state Macedonia (Hdt. 6.44-45). With a two-pronged military force, according to Herodotus' questionable figures a large land army of more than 20,000 men and a naval force of 300 ships, Mardonios attacked the rebellious island of Thasos, which fell quickly to his navy, and the Macedonians again recognized Darius' suzerainty. But, sailing around the Akte peninsula at Mt. Athos, Mardonios lost half of his fleet to northern storms, and then his army suffered a serious defeat at the hands of the Brygi tribe of western Skudra (492 B.C.).[63]

Mardonios remained long enough to subjugate the Brygi to vassalage, yet returned to Asia seriously wounded and in need of new forces. Darius' military strategy and diplomacy, which had for thirty years created a sound and powerful empire, now faltered amidst a series of strategic miscalculations. Mardonios' setback was purely temporary and the policy of a slow penetration of Greece from the north acutely sound. But the victor of Lade, and Mede Datis who temporarily replaced the ill Mardonios in command, advised Darius to abandon that policy and, instead, to dispatch a fleet directly across the Aegean to attack first Eretria and then Athens (Hdt. 6.46-120). In preparation, Persian heralds traveled throughout Greece demanding the recognition of Achaemenid suzerainty and the vassalage symbols of earth and water, while other heralds visited the coastal city-states and poleis throughout Darius' empire with the king's orders to prepare large ships and horse-transports for Datis' expedition. As the king's vassals complied with the orders, the Greek poleis placidly submitting to Darius' overlordship joined the Persian attack upon Athens. The island of Aigina, in sight of the Athenian ships at Phaleron Bay, offered the vassal's earth and water, escaped Datis' potentially destructive blows, and apparently sought new commercial privileges with the eastern Persian ports. And from Sparta, the exiled King Damaratos joined Darius' forces for the conquest of Greece. The parochialism which plagued the East Greeks also abounded in Greece proper.

In Cilicia, Datis and his second-in-command Artaphrenes, nephew of the king and son of the satrap of Sardis, mustered their fleet of ships and horse-transports and set sail for Ionia and Samos. If Herodotus' report is correct, the fleet included 600 triremes (6.95.2), yet a number one-half to one-third of that reported is more realistic.[64] From loyal Samos, Datis set sail for Naxos, and with an auspicious beginning to his expedition, captured and enchained many Naxians, and burned their city and its temples. Punishment for Naxian resistance in 499 B.C. had been properly wielded.[65] Datis then set sail for Eretria, and with Ionian and Aiolian troops aboard his fleet, entered Eretria's harbor, besieged the city, plundered it, burned its temples in revenge for the destruction of the temples in Sardis, and according to Darius' commands enchained the inhabitants for deportation to Susa.[66] Two leading Eretrian aristocrats, perhaps part of a great faction, had betrayed their city.[67] Factionalism also ran rife throughout the mainland Greek poleis. The destructions of Naxos and Eretria signaled warnings to the Athenians and others who had not cowed to Darius' demands that his imperial might would wield similar punishment.

Datis had fervently hoped that Athenian factionalism, and the Peisistratid faction in particular, would divide Athens' resistance to his inevitable conquest and promote the reinstatement of Hippias, then aboard his fleet, as Persian governor and tyrant of Athens. But the burning of Eretria had neither factionalized Athens nor weakened her resistance, and on the plain of Marathon Datis faced the Athenian levy and some Plataians drawn up to meet him. After numerous delays, the Persians waiting for the Peisistratid faction to gain control of Athens (which it never did) and the Athenians waiting for Spartan assistance (which came too late), the Athenians and Plataians attacked Datis' forces and won the battle.[68] Both Datis and Hippias, however, still hoped that the Athenians would surrender when the Persian Imperial Fleet sailed into Phaleron Bay. But the Athenians continued their unified resistance and mustered at Phaleron to confront Datis' fleet. Datis' initial strategic error had been to limit his forces to a naval attack and not continue Mardonios' slow penetration from the north. A northern attack would have gained Macedonian, Thessalian, and other Greek forces, Greeks who would have medized and served the king as military vassals. Datis' limited forces and Hippias' failure to generate rebellion within Athens brought about the failures at Marathon and Phaleron. The general could do nothing but return to Asia. In flight and in despair, Hippias died at Lemnos before reaching Sigeion (*Suda* sv Hippias), and Datis returned to Susa with only the Eretrians in chains. Athens had not been taken. The clash at Marathon demonstrated that the Athenian army could beat the Persians on land, something the Ionian nobles had failed to accomplish.

For Darius, the failure at Athens was only a temporary interruption within his greater imperial policy of a steady frontier advance into Europe and the conquest of Greece. New taxes would be levied and new armies would be raised. Throughout the empire, the heralds again announced Darius' imperial commands to equip an army, to provide ships and horses, and to supply the army with grain supplies (Hdt. 7.1.2).[69] For three years, 489-487 B.C., the subjected nations prepared to meet the king's demands, as imperial officers enrolled the landed gentry (the aristoi) for military service to invade Greece. The Persians had not only lost Athens but also their tenuous control of the western chain of Greek islands: Chalkis and Styra in Euboia, Keos, Kythnos, Seriphos and Siphnos (Hdt. 6.132-6). Paros west of Naxos, however, remained under Persian control.

The burdens of taxation and the extensive loss of military men since the siege against Naxos in 499 B.C. had become more than many subjects could bear. To overthrow these burdens, the Egyptians revolted in 486 B.C. (Hdt. 7.1.3). Sorely weakened, the Ionians could not resist Darius' demands. But the Egyptians, who had long served in the Persian Imperial Fleet, were relatively secure from Persia except through the Sinai passes, and struggled unsuccessfully for three years to shake off Persian overlordship. Egypt, far more crucial in wealth and manpower than rebellious Athens, demanded Darius' full attention. If Egypt could maintain her rebellion for more than three years or become independent, rebellions in the eastern and central satrapies would also erupt and, perhaps, destroy the empire.

Unfortunately for the empire, before Darius could suppress the revolt of Egypt, the Great King died in November of 486 B.C. Xerxes, the eldest son of the King and Queen Atossa, recently chosen by the Great King as his heir apparent amidst a bitter harem and palace quarrel (Hdt. 7.2-5.1), succeeded to the royal throne and in his second year as king quelled the revolt of Egypt. Leading the royal armies, Xerxes invaded Egypt and, by 9 January 484 B.C., recovered that satrapy, and appointed his own brother prince Achaemenes to satrapal power. In dealing harshly with the rebels, Xerxes confiscated properties from the temples and imposed new taxes upon the natives. The major restriction came with the abandonment of the toleration of Egypt as a distinct ethnic unity for which Cambyses and Darius had adopted the ageless native royal titles. Xerxes now ruled as an inflexible sovereign omitting the Egyptian royal titles and pronouncing forcefully a new title: "Xerxes the Great King."[70]

Trouble also erupted in Judah in 486 B.C. as noted all too briefly in Ezra 4:6, a rebellion which Xerxes quickly suppressed as he marched against Egypt.[71] Of this we know almost nothing except to suspect that the social and religious problems elaborated upon in the book of Malachai may shed a faint glimmer of light upon them; but, unfortunately, we know nothing of the outcome nor of the new imperial regulations which Xerxes may have imposed.[72]

Following victory over Egypt, King Xerxes then listened to the military plans of his cousin Mardonios for the immediate preparation for a third expedition against Athens (Hdt. 7.5-6). The gradual and methodical penetration of Greece from the north would laud Xerxes as an heroic Achaemenid king. The fulfillment of his predecessor's military goals and the conquest of new imperial satrapies would raise Xerxes' military and kingly stature to the rank of Cyrus, Cambyses, and his father Darius. At Persepolis and at Susa, Xerxes would also complete at great expense the construction of the sumptuous imperial

buildings, and order inscriptions carved into stone that he, Xerxes, had completed Darius'
work (XPa-f).   In addition, Xerxes would purify his father's imperial cult of
Zarathustrianism and set about to stamp out the early Iranian cults of the daevas alien
and incompatible with the worship of Ahuramazda and his military defender Mithra
(XPh).[73] The conquest and punishment of rebellious Athens, which had aided the rebel
Aristagoras and the burning of Sardis, would be no greater burden than these; and upon
Athens Xerxes himself would place the "yoke of vassalage" (Hdt. 7.8.1). Ruling nobles
from Thessaly,[74] and the Peisistratid faction from Athens[75] had traveled to the king at
Susa and had urged him to invade. They would be his vassals, as he would assure their
political rule (Hdt. 7.6.2). The positive aspects of Greek medism were reaping their
rewards for Xerxes.[76] While some Greeks feared Persian destruction if they resisted the
Great King, others sought his favors for their factional advantages.[77]

For four years, Xerxes and Mardonios prepared for the conquest of Greece (484-481
B.C.) and in the fifth year began the long and arduous march toward Athens (480 B.C.:
Hdt. 7.20). His subject nations had gathered ships, mustered their ranking cavalry and
infantry forces, prepared the horse-transports, and stockpiled the necessary grain
supplies (Hdt. 7.21). And for about three years, workers had been digging a canal through
the soft sandy marl at the base of the rocky Akte peninsula (Hdt. 7.22.1). Mardonios
would not risk rounding Mt. Athos again. From Sardis in the autumn of 481 B.C., Xerxes
dispatched heralds to Greece to demand once again the symbols of earth and water and
to establish hostelries for his personal expedition against Athens (Hdt. 7.32). But this
time he would not offer that amnesty to Athens and Sparta.[78] They were destined for
destruction. Confident of his plan, sanctioned by the grace of Ahuramazda whose sacred
chariot the king would accompany to Athens (Hdt. 7.40.4), Xerxes ordered that the Greek
spies caught at Sardis be shown the vast array of his military forces and then be released
to report to the Greeks the power of the Persian Empire (Hdt. 7.146-7). In the spring of
480 B.C., Xerxes commanded the entire Persian Imperial Fleet to muster offshore in the
harbors of Ionia and on the Sardian plain half of the regular troops of the Persian Army,
three of the six army corps, each about 60,000 strong.[79]

Xerxes' high hopes as recounted by Herodotus, however, failed to assess carefully
the flaws in the imperial military system, which would hinder and then halt the Persian
conquest of Greece. The recent wars in Ionia, Karia, Aiolis, the Troad, and Skudra had

taken many lives and had weakened the Imperial Army to the point that further losses in Greece would seriously overstrain the king's military forces. The wars in Cyprus and the Egyptian and Jewish rebellions accentuated acutely that military stress. To compound these problems, civil war had erupted in Babylonia, and further important military forces were lost. During his march from Susa to Sardis in 481 B.C., Xerxes had inflicted harsh blows upon Babylon and in political vengeance upon the rebellious Babylonians had destroyed their ancient and sacred ziggurat of Marduk-Bel.[80] In August of 482, revolution had erupted in Babylon as the noble Belshimanni arose, killed the Persian satrap Zopyros, and performed according to ritual custom the ancient akitu festival by grasping the hand of the god Marduk-Bel. Against this native pretender, who claimed the titles "King of Babylon" and "King of Lands," Xerxes dispatched his brother-in-law, the successful and powerful general Megabyzos, who promptly took the city. In retribution, the Persians carried off the solid gold eighteen-foot statue of the god, weighing almost eight hundred pounds, and melted it down as bullion. No longer grasping the hand of Marduk-Bel, and not performing the sacred akitu festival, Xerxes destroyed Babylon's theocratic monarchy, and the city lost its last major vestige of imperial significance.

The burdens of taxation and the Egyptian and Jewish rebellions had, indeed, helped to trigger the Babylonian rebellion, and perhaps other riots and rebellions for which, at present, we have no record. As punishment for the Babylonian nobles, the Persians seized their great landed estates and distributed them among the Persian aristocracy. Henceforth, the Persians ferociously taxed the Babylonians, now amalgamated into a new satrapy with the Assyrians (Hdt. 3.92, 7.63). Xerxes could now advance upon Greece with the proceeds of his Babylonian campaign in imperial coffers. For Xerxes and the empire, Babylonia was important and far more crucial than Cyprus, Egypt, or Ionia and Skudra. Wealthy Babylonia had remained the heart of the Persian Empire, its agricultural wealth extensive, and its manpower necessary to the military superiority of Achaemenid control. The violence heaped upon the city, as the Persians had struck against Miletos, Naxos, and Eretria, and the destruction of the ziggurat central to the sacred Babylonian akitu festival, boldly underscored the magnitude and the significance of the Babylonian rebellion and Xerxes' forceful suppression of the Babylonians. While Xerxes' forces gathered in Ionia and at Sardis during the early spring days of 480 B.C., as the warm breezes signaled the time to prepare the bridges for the crossing of the Hellespont (Hdt.

7.33-56), any major military failure during the campaign would end Xerxes' plans to conquer Greece and create the complex conditions of societal distortion throughout the empire and, perhaps, set off a chain reaction of rebellion.

It was also necessary to assure that the potentially recalcitrant Ionians, Egyptians, Jews, and Babylonians, recently rebellious and still smarting from newly imposed rules of harsh subjugation, would remain loyal and not thwart Xerxes' military efforts to subjugate the Greeks. If Herodotus' account is correct, the Persian general Artabanos earnestly advised his king not to deploy the Ionians because he questioned their political reliability.[81] But Xerxes rebutted Artabanos' arguments (Hdt. 7.51-2) and successfully maintained the stalwart military loyalty of his armed vassal contigents. From the inland regions of Sparda, Lydians marched with Mysians from the satrapy of Daskyleion in the infantry contingents commanded by the younger Artaphrenes (Aesch. *Pers.* 41; Hdt. 7.74.1). In the naval units, if Herodotus' account has historical merit, Lykians sailed with 50 ships (Hdt. 7.92), Karians with 70, and the East Dorians from their poleis with 30 (Hdt. 7.93). The mainland Ionians sailed with 100 ships (Aesch. *Pers.* 563; Hdt. 7.94), and nowhere in his account of this campaign did Herodotus mention any disloyalty. With the Ionians, the Aiolians sailed with 60 ships, the Pontic peoples with 100, while the Hellespontine Greeks were charged with guarding the bridge installations at Abydos (Hdt. 7.95.1-2). In comparison, the Ionian islanders furnished the Great King with only 17 ships, a mere token of their forces, which had battled at Lade fourteen years earlier (Hdt. 7.95.1). Xerxes assigned this combined Karian and Ionian fleet to the command of his cousin Ariabignes, the son of Darius and Gobryas' daughter (Hdt. 7.97; and fig. 12). If Herodotus' report of Artabanos' warnings was historical, the general's fears were unwarranted. The mainland Ionians remained loyal to their king and overlord. Xerxes eagerly engaged the Ionian fleet against the mainland Greeks and especially the Athenians (Hdt. 8.85.1), yet none defected or lagged in battle. In the course of the summer's campaign, only amidst the subject islanders did desertion arise, first a single Lemnian ship (Hdt. 8.11.3), then four Naxian ships (Hdt. 8.46.3),[82] and finally a single Tenian trireme (Hdt. 8.82.1). Ionian loyalty to Xerxes remained secure, and Themistokles' somewhat naive appeal to the Ionians after Thermopylae to revolt failed (Hdt. 8.22). Even the name of Tyrrhastiades of Kyme became buried in antiquity as one who had informed the king of outflanking strategies at Thermopylae (Diod. Sic. 11.8.5).

The landed nobles, the gentry of western Anatolia, serving among the vast infantry forces and sailing with their fleet of 410 ships, fought for their king. Although Herodotus reported that the Phoenicians accused the Ionians of treason for not having fought properly (8.90.1), this charge may have stemmed from either national jealousy or the ancient historian's leitmotif of Ionian discontent (cf. 8.10.2) and be of little or no historical value. Which Ionians they were, Herodotus did not state clearly. Only amidst the 17 islander ships did desertion arise, and then the defection of just five. In comparison, the excellent qualities of the Ionian fleet loyal to their king and battling the Greeks disturbed the mainland generals (Hdt. 8.22.2).

Across Skudra and Macedonia, Xerxes' land and naval forces proceeded without opposition. Thessaly quickly submitted to the king as did the other Greek regions of Malis, Locris, and all of Boiotia except the two small towns of Thespiai and Plataia.[83] It was already plain to both sides that the Greeks from the Peloponnesos had no intention of offering serious opposition to the Persians north of the Corinthian isthmus. The punishment of Athens and the conquest of northern and central Greece appeared certain. As Xerxes approached the crucial pass at Thermopylae, more than half of the European Greeks had submitted to him and Apollo's oracular shrine at Delphi had also sided with the king. Attica and Athens would fall easily, as they did, and once the king could control the Athenian fleet safely, he could then invade Argos by sea, which would declare itself openly pro-Persian, and the Persians would drive a wedge between Corinth and Sparta,' attack the isthmus by land, and defeat each of those two hostile poleis separately. Greek opposition at Cape Artemision crumbled rapidly as did opposition at Thermopylae.[84] Even the loss of many Persian ships to storms did not encourage the Spartans to alter their policy of defending the Peloponnesos at the isthmus rather than in Attica. Artemision, nevertheless, proved an invaluable experience to the Greeks; it dented the myth of Persian naval superiority. Yet the Greeks scurried in haste to the protective shores of Salamis Bay, as Xerxes' light, fast-sailing Phoenician triremes pursued the heavier Greek vessels. On land, as the Persians burned Thespiai and Plataia, Xerxes entered deserted Attica. Only a few Athenian zealots tried unsuccessfully to defend their acropolis. It, too, fell to the Persians, who systematically looted, burned, and destroyed Athens and its temples (Hdt.8.54). Victory was the king's.

The Persian Imperial Army controlled Attica, a pro-Persian government of

Peisistratids governed Athens, and the Persian Imperial Fleet lay anchored at Phaleron. Panic seized the Greek fleet, which had paused at Salamis only to evacuate the civilian population. That island was a veritable trap and all but the interested Athenians, Aiginetans, and Megarians were anxious to escape before Xerxes sprang it. Victory again seemed to be within his grasp, as it was amply clear that the Corinthians and Spartans were determined to abandon the Athenians. Had Xerxes taken no action, the few remaining Greek forces would have retreated to Corinth behind their isthmian wall. The Athenians, Megarians, and the Aiginetans would have been compelled to accept the terms of submission and vassalage; the Athenians and Aiginetans for a second time. With their forces incorporated in the Persian navy the isthmian wall would have been outflanked and the Persian army would have had but a few skirmishers to drive off (Hdt. 7.139). But Xerxes was intent upon conquering the Athenians and their fleet, to complete the submission of Athens to Persian rule, and to win another spectacular victory for his royal Achaemenid house.[85]

The opportunity for a brilliant success came in a note from the Athenian general Themistokles. The Greeks, he declared, were frightened and ready to flee, factionalism had shattered the Greek ranks, and he himself was willing to submit as a vassal for the reward of King's Friend, the highest honor at the Persian court. Xerxes believed Themistokles' message because it was not only plausible but also what he wanted to believe. Trouble was brewing in the empire and his presence in Asia was required. Nevertheless, dissensions among the Greek ranks, which Xerxes had counted upon, also ran rife. As the Spartans had abandoned their allies one after another, in haste each ally had made an alliance with the Persians and stressed pro-Persian sentiments earlier repressed. Now among the Greeks effectively blocked up in the Bay of Salamis the divisive factors of parochialism and factionalism continued to erupt. The Phoenician, Cypriot, and Ionian fleets with a triple line of ships blocked the eastern exit from Salamis while the Egyptian fleet of 200 ships sailed to block the western exit. The resisting Greeks, bottled up, would soon exhaust their supplies and mutual fears would quicken the pace of desertion from Salamis, as they had at Lade. Xerxes, therefore, ordered a direct attack upon the entrapped Greeks, who fought back desperately to escape. At first, the Persian attack succeeded, and Xerxes watched the Ionian Greeks badly beat the remaining Peloponnesian forces. But then the Aiginetans and Athenians broke through the imperial lines and attacked. At the day's end, the Persians had lost 200 ships, a third of their naval strength, against the Greek loss of 40.[86]

The Greek victory at Salamis checked the Persian advance. While the Persians lost none of their recently acquired Greek territories, their army and navy sorely needed reorganization. The combined forces in the wake of defeat required strong leadership, the army to succeed had to remain intact, and the navy could not suffer further reduction. The Greeks, on the other hand, encouraged by an unexpected victory, also realizing their losses, continued to fear that by the following year the Persians would complete their conquest. The battle of Salamis, however, was pivotal not just in the Persian defeat but in the series of strategic miscalculations, which Xerxes himself directed. He alone was responsible for the defeat by having ordered the offensive battle when a simple blockade would have been effective, and then he compounded his failure by becoming enraged and executing Phoenician captains for alleged cowardice.[87] Aware that his naval forces were perilously reduced, and sensitive to possible Ionian defection (Hdt. 8.97.1), Xerxes ordered his remaining Imperial Fleet to set sail for Kyme. Queen Artemisia's squadron proceeded independently, not for Kyme but for Ephesos' small harbor at Koressos, and transported several of Xerxes' harem-born sons with her to safety (Hdt. 8.103, 107). The army, now only one division, he dispatched with Mardonios in command to return to Thessaly for the winter. Xerxes' orders were for that army, in the following spring, to reoccupy Attica and to invade the Peloponnesos. The king himself retreated hurriedly by the land route to Sardis where he spent the next year keeping in touch with his scattered forces (Hdt. 8.117.2).

In Thessaly, Mardonios retained only one army division composed of the elite Immortals, Persians, Medes, Eastern Scythians, Bactrians, and Indians, an army of eastern national groups and almost exclusively Indo-Iranian. This division contained the king's best fighting forces from Asia in addition to half the troops of European Greece, and still outnumbered the resisting Greeks; yet Xerxes had significantly and seriously reduced Mardonios' army. Xerxes had commanded Artabazos the son of Pharnakes to march the second army to Skudra and guard the long Aegean coastal route by which the king could forward supplies to Mardonios. Xerxes commanded the third army under Tigranes to return to Ionia and guard western Anatolia.

Xerxes had blundered several times: by believing Themistokles' note (regardless of

Themistokles' actual intent), by attacking the Greeks at Salamis rather than waiting until they had factionalized further, by punishing the Phoenician captains and reducing his critically damaged Imperial Fleet, and by reducing Mardonios' land forces then cut off from the support of the Imperial Fleet and separated from Artabazos' and Tigranes' armies. The king's problems were further compounded by the development of rivalries among the Persian military leaders in Greece. When Xerxes returned to Asia, acute friction arose between Mardonios and Artabazos. And most significantly, the Persian losses at Artemision, Thermopylae, throughout Central Greece and Attica, and especially at Salamis, had significantly overtaxed Xerxes' military force. The empire could not sustain a new levy for troops, taxes, and grain supplies without increasing the factors of societal distortion to the level at which massive rebellions throughout the satrapies would again rise. Xerxes clearly realized that he himself had to command the interrupted and fractured Greek campaign from Sardis, where he could personally maintain better control of his empire. Yet in 479 B.C., as the Persian offensive in Greece continued to falter, the Samians, eager to survive, encouraged the Greeks and especially the Athenians with hollow arguments that, if aided, Ionia would revolt.

III

The Samian Affair

Following the disastrous events at Salamis, Herodotus' narrative of the series of continued Persian military clashes with mainland and East Greeks fell into three separate, disparate, and contrasting episodes while attempting to present an historical analysis. The events of Persians in Thessaly and Boiotia resound with strong oral traditions, which remain not only vivid but essentially correct. The events in Skudra are often disjointed and unclear. And events in Ionia are muddled and molded by later anachronistic claims by the Samians that they had acted as the saviors of Ionia and were the stalwart defenders and combatants for the liberation of Ionia and the restoration of *eleutheria*. The Samian "sell-out" at Lade became "covered up" by Herodotus' gullible acceptance in Samos of propaganda disseminated by the anti-Persian faction partially guilty of Ionia's fall in 494 B.C., and Ionia's quiescence during the harrowing years after the East Greek disaster at Lade.

This Samian faction spread the rumor that if the mainland Greeks would invade to liberate, the East Greeks would respond in revolution against King Xerxes safely ensconced in the imperial palace at Sardis; needless to say an extremely dangerous course of action. The mainland Greeks lacked both plans and ability in 479 B.C. to foster and accomplish the goal of revolution. Mainland Ionia lay secure in Persian military control. The Samian faction's intent was clear and simple: to overthrow the Persian enforced tyranny of Theomestor on the island of Samos and his supportive factions (Hdt. 9.90.1); nothing else.

The Persians, in turn, did not anticipate mainland Greek intervention in Ionia, yet remained exceedingly wary as the vague rumblings of rebellion, which emerged from time to time, cautioned them to consider the possibility of a new Ionian revolt. This was simply sound Persian policy. The loyal East Greek fleet of predominantly Samian ships had patrolled the Ionia and Aiolian coast during the winter of 480/79 B.C. and had kept secure guard for the Persian overlords should rebellion arise from non-loyal factions (Hdt. 8.130). Confident in their security of Ionia and the eastern islands, the Persian and East Greek commanders of the fleet stationed in the harbor of Samos planned further offensive strategy against the Greeks and awaited news of Mardonios' activities now that spring and a new campaign season were approaching (Hdt. 8.131.1).

The mainland Greek fleet of 110 ships at Aigina hesitated, reluctant to pursue the Persians farther east and to abandon the waters of Attica as Mardonios, still in Thessaly, would soon return to Athens in preparation for his land attack upon Corinth and Sparta. What rumors of Ionian rebellion may have circulated in reality (beyond the imagination of the Samians) clearly had not stirred the Greek fleet into action. Only when six Chians appeared did the Greeks at Aigina respond, and then with the utmost caution and fear. The Chians, who had earlier tried to overthrow Strattis the Persian appointed tyrant in Chios amidst typical factional strife, had failed. In desperation, they had sought Spartan assistance, but to no avail. Whether the six factionalists (stasiotai) had actually entreated the Spartans "to free Ionia" or whether that tag was purely Herodotean is impossible to ascertain. In any case, it had no affect upon the Spartans at home, and could only encourage the mainland Greek naval commanders to sail with them from Aigina. But the Greeks refused to go beyond Delos (Hdt. 8.132). Paros and Naxos to the south remained secure in Persian hands and the Persian fleet of Samians and Ionians lay ready in Samos' harbor seeking aggressive military action. If the Chians did plead for the liberation of Ionia and if rumors of rebellion had circulated, they were clearly not sufficient to encourage the Greek naval officers to advance beyond Delos. The mainland Greeks still feared, and rightfully, the Persian military forces in Thessaly and Skudra commanded by Mardonios and Artabazos and the Persian fleet at Samos.

The Greeks at Delos needed time to regain military strength. An expedition to Ionia at that time was simply foolhardy.[88] Twenty years had passed since 499 B.C. and the Ionian Revolt, and the mainland Greeks appear to have had little knowledge of conditions in Ionia, just as they had been ignorant of Xerxes' military might at Artemision, Thermopylae, and Salamis.[89] Beyond that, the Peloponnesians had long preferred to abandon Attica and hold the Corinthian isthmus (Hdt. 8.56, 74-5), and Sparta's command had also discouraged the pursuit of the Persians in Greece. The Spartan general Eurybiades spoke of military moderation (Hdt. 8.108), to which the Athenian Themistokles gracefully backed down from pleas of aggression (8.109). The victory at Salamis had not led to a hot pursuit of the Persians, nor did anyone in central or northern Greece doubt that the Persians remained lethal. The Greeks still feared both Mardonios and Artabazos and their armies.[90] As Daniel Gillis rightly noted: " . . . not even the awkward withdrawal of Xerxes' forces to the Hellespont (8.115) could outweigh the evidence that the reinforced Persian army was nearly invincible."[91]

Where the real Ionian danger lay was not in rebellion but in advice to the mainland Greeks to destroy the Persian bridges across the Hellespont. This Xerxes realized during his retreat across Skudra after his failure at Salamis; and the destruction of those bridges became a goal, which the Greeks themselves came to realize (Hdt. 8.98) as did Themistokles a bit later (Hdt. 8.108).

But then, a second appeal to the Greek navy materialized. This time three Samians made their way to the Greek fleet at Delos with a secret message from their faction opposed to the Persian supported tyrant Theomestor (Hdt. 9.90.1). Their argument, according to Herodotus' source, reiterated the general Ionian unrest and the notion that if attacked the Persians would be unable to maintain their control of Ionia (Hdt. 9.90.2). The Samian source maintained that the Persian fleet was neither able to sail nor to give battle (Hdt. 9.90.3). Yet a careful analysis of Herodotus' account of the naval events which followed fails to uncover any positive Ionian unrest verging upon rebellion or a marked inability of the Persian fleet at Samos either to sail or to give battle. What is blatantly apparent, however, is that a great number of Samians were actively supporting Theomestor, serving upon their ships in the Persian cause and, therefore, that the three Samian messengers represented a splinter faction, which seems to have acted for only a minority of Samians.

At Delos, according to Herodotus and his Samian source, the three messengers dramatically bound themselves in pledge (*pistin*) and oaths (*horkia*) to ally themselves militarily with the Greeks (*symmachiēs*: Hdt. 9.92.1). Thereupon, the Samian ship with two of the messengers sailed off to Samos while the third, Hegesistratos, remained, and set sail with the Spartan commander Latychidas and the Greek fleet for Samos on the following day (Hdt. 9.92.2, 96.1).

How strange that six Chians who represented the valiant Chian forces who battled to their deaths at Lade and Ephesos in 494 B.C. could not persuade the Greeks, while a small faction of double-dealing Samians who largely had abandoned their allies at Lade, whereupon the Persians had dealt their final blows upon the Ionian Revolt, could persuade the fearful Greeks to venture beyond Delos. The Chian and Samian reports were most probably not the only news that spring and summer of 479 B.C. to tell of conditions among the Ionians,[92] and the Greeks now on Delos may have assessed the conditions as not only better but more favorable than earlier when stationed at Aigina. Yet even though Herodotus saw through his Samian sources to blame Samos for earlier pride and private interests (6.13.2), the historian became captivated by the Samian account.[93] Herodotus, in referring to the Samian "false pretext" (*prophasios*), editorially described the Samians' decision at Lade as one based on self-interest, and not despair for Ionian military preparedness. Self-interest, of course, was not an outrageous motive, but in that context it contradicted Samian pretensions. The Samians were out to save their own skins (*kai ta idia*) and had betrayed the bulk of the East Greek fleet as soon as they had had a chance (*epeite taxista*).[94]

B. Mitchell recently examined Herodotus' account of Samos and Samian politics and neatly reconstructed the course of Samian events between Lade (494 B.C.) and Delos (479 B.C.).[95] At Lade, the Samian factions quarreled; the majority deserted the Ionian cause to bargain with the Persians and accepted Aiakes as tyrant (Hdt. 6.14.2). The loyalists, on the other hand, aristocrats who remained at Lade, ultimately escaped and fled to Zankle in Sicily before Aiakes' triumphal return to Samos (Hdt. 6.22–4).[96] By treachery and double-cross at Lade, the Samians had betrayed their fellow Ionians as well as compromised themselves with the Persians and Aiakes. In the following year, Mardonios replaced the tyrants throughout Sparda with aristocratic/oligarchic governments, but not on Chios or Samos. With Aiakes' death the Persians did not replace the tyrant but allowed his supportive faction of Samian aristocrats to gain political control of Samos. At Salamis, notably, the Samians lacked a tyrant, but since the Samians had remained exceedingly loyal throughout that campaign and fought particularly well for their Persian overlords, two leading Samian captains—Theomestor and Phylakes— received notable royal rewards, and Theomestor became tyrant of Samos (Hdt. 8.85.3). Yet not all of the Samians were pleased with this reversal of Persian policy and many refused to accept Theomestor, and quietly agitated for his removal until the events of Delos in the summer of 479 B.C. arose. This small but instrumental faction had not opposed Persian rule, but they did object to their removal from political power by Theomestor and his supportive factions.

Within this displaced minority faction, apparently, arose the realization that to gain mainland Greek support, in pledge and by oath they would join the liberating military alliance in order to overthrow Theomestor and regain power in Samos. This faction now generated the counter argument that Milesian inefficiency during the Ionian Revolt had occurred because of the poor leadership of Aristagoras *as tyrant* (which Herodotus continued to call the then Milesian commander, apparently from his Samian source; e.g. 5.49.1, 98.2), and because of the disunity of the Ionians in general. In these, the new Samian argument continued, lay the seeds of the failure at Lade, and not in Samian treachery. In a magnificent act of self-justification against the Ionian and Milesian recriminations of Samian double-cross at Lade, the anti-Theomestor faction, represented by Hegesistratos and his two associates at Delos, upon successfully gaining the coveted political power in Samos, would raise in that city's agora a stele inscribed with the names of the eleven aristocrats who as ship captains at Lade refused to desert the Ionian cause (Hdt. 6.14.2-3). Clearly, neither Aiakes, nor the succeeding pro-Persian aristocratic faction, nor Theomestor would have permitted the erection of that stele. It must have been erected, therefore, in the autumn of 479 B.C. or shortly thereafter. In this story, consequently, we can detect the strong hand of the aristocratic faction rising to victory in 479 B.C., a faction which remained loyal to its pledge and oath to the mainland Greek cause until 440 B.C. (Thuc. 1.115.2) and, until then, strongly opposed to tyranny and medism (Thuc. 1.115.4-5). In this faction lay the source of the "Samian Logos" adopted by Herodotus. The faction and its revisionist "history" also appealed to the growing desires of the Athenians who supported and sustained the anti-tyrannical and anti-Persian faction until they themselves clashed with the Samians in 440 B.C. Thus, Herodotus' account was acceptable to his Athenian audiences, which would not question its falsity.

What impressed the mainland Greeks on the island of Delos that summer of 479 B.C. was not just the eloquence and demeanor of the aristocrats, Hegesistratos the son of Aristagoras and his colleagues Lampon the son of Thrasykles and Athenagoras the son of Archestratidas, Samian landed gentry of the first rank (Hdt. 9.90-1), but their willingness to join the mainland Greek military alliance, that organization called by modern historians the Hellenic League.[97] To aid Chios, the League's fleet would have had to sail across open waters (cf. Hdt. 5.33.1) and be vulnerable to Persian attack, whereas to aid Samos would allow the Greeks sailing from Delos to round Mykonos (not a strong Persian outpost) and advance to the Milesian territory of the island of Ikaria and then to proceed to western Samos. Protection remained a key advantage to the Greeks, especially when the prize was Samos with its strategic position against the Persians. To have sailed to Chios would not have provided an important base strategically located, by which to pursue an attack upon Sparda. If Mardonios and Artabazos should gain an advantageous position in Greece, a retreat from Samos was far safer than from Chios. No doubt the Persians also understood this strategy, as they had moved their fleet from Kyme to Samos months earlier. Hegesistratos' request offered the Greeks, if successful, a prime eastern naval base: the harbor of Samos.

With victory at Salamis, the relatively few Greeks opposed to the Persians began to achieve a certain measure of unity, in contrast to parochialism and factionalism, a unity which had previously not existed nor would last very long. It was the first and last time in Greek history that their fundamental common opposition to Persian despotism generated a vague and still imprecise consciousness of community in race, language, religion, and customs (Hdt. 8.144). But the more fundamental powers of parochialism and factionalism would quickly return and destroy that brief common military action of the League, an action which spurred it to support the Samian rebellion in 479 B.C. As early as 481 B.C., after Xerxes had arrived in Sardis (Hdt. 7.145-6), some of the anti-Persian

Greeks had begun to assemble at the Hellenion at Sparta (Paus. 3.12.6; cf. Diod. Sic. 11.3) to exchange views of how to block the Persian advances and how to assure success. By means of oaths, the Hellenic Congress of the assembled poleis ended their rival and petty wars, agreed to send spies to Persia to assess Xerxes' power, and to send ambassadors to Argos, Syracuse, Corcyra, and Crete for additional military assistance. In addition, they had agreed that they would punish any of the Greeks who would submit to Xerxes without compulsion, specifically to his heralds who were then seeking oaths of vassalage and their symbols of earth and water. When the time should occur the members of the League would punish them, confiscate their properties, and deliver a tenth to Apollo's shrine at Delphi. In essence, the nature of that first oath warned the vulnerable Greeks not to submit to Persian suzerainty. The mainland Greeks still did not know the magnitude of Xerxes' forces, thus they bound themselves to assist one another with naval forces and land troops, each to the best of its ability. As yet, the League lacked an efficient organization for specifying the quota of forces from each member. The oath, nevertheless, did set into motion the means for the rudimentary military organization to wage war under the command of the Spartan generals (Hdt. 7.148-9, 158-62). By virtue of Sparta's superior military strength (Thuc. 1.18.2), the members of the League in common agreement gave the Spartan generals supreme command.

When the spies and ambassadors had returned in the spring of 480 B.C., the Congress reassembled and agreed to send military defensive expeditions to Tempe (Hdt. 7.173). Xerxes had just assembed his forces at Abydos in March-April (Hdt. 7.174). In a third session, the Congress agreed to send forces to Thermopylae and Artemision (Hdt. 7.175). The defense of Tempe had failed. Thereafter, the defensive strategy leading to Salamis and the events of the following year 479 B.C. at Aigina and Delos, arose from diplomatic negotiations between the Athenian and Spartan generals and not the League's Congress. The Congress, an assembly of ambassadors from each supporting polis, and each polis with a single vote and collectively a majority rule, essentially supported and followed the decisions of strategy and high policy made by the Spartan and Athenian Council of War. It had ordered the retreat from Artemision (Hdt. 8.18), to fight at Salamis (8.49, 56-63), and then almost to reverse that decision (8.74), not to sail to the Hellespont in the weeks after Salamis (8.108), to reject the Chian plea to sail eastward (8.132), and then with great vigor to support Hegesistratos' Samian request (9.90-2). To their Congress, the members of the League had earlier admitted the Tenian and Naxian deserters (8.46.3, 82). Months if not years later, the League would inscribe upon the bronze serpents, the League's votive tripod offered to Apollo at Delphi, the names of Naxos and Tenos as among those who "Fought the War" (Tod *GHI* 1^2 .19; *SIG*^{3} .31; ML *GHI* 27), and perhaps also inscribe the laudatory couplet "The saviors of Spacious Greece dedicated this [tripod] having rescued the poleis from hateful 'slavery' " (*doulosynēs*: Diod. Sic. 11.33.2).

As private citizens of the faction struggling to gain control of Samos, Hegesistratos and his colleagues offered their personal and their faction's pledge and oath to support the military alliance of the Hellenic League; but in time, when the polis would be taken, the oath would again be administered to incorporate greater Samos into the League (Hdt. 9.106.4). The three Samian aristrocrats had greatly impressed the Spartan and Athenian commanders, aristocrats and landed gentry in their own right, with the bond of aristocratic pledge and oath, actions among gentlemen of similar breeding and circumstances. At bottom lay the hope of gaining the strategically important harbor of Samos, at a time when courage supported the League's aggressive actions. Yet caution had to prevail. The War Council's dramatic decision to alter radically its military strategy from defensive to offensive action, nevertheless, marked a fundamental change in Greek policy toward Persia, especially since defensive campaigns still had to be fought against Mardonios and Artabazos. The Samian ruse that Ionia was about to rebel had worked, and had persuaded the War Council to advance, seize Samos, establish the anti-tyrannical and anti-Persian aristocratic faction there, and to proceed with offensive action against the Persian navy and army.

In Skudra, meanwhile in the autumn of 480 B.C., a series of unrelated events halted Artabazos' immediate return to Thessaly in order to support Mardonios' forthcoming military thrust once again upon Athens, and then upon Corinth and Sparta. Artabazos had accompanied King Xerxes safely across Skudra to the Hellespont. Well east of the strategic Persian garrison at Eion, the Greeks kindly welcomed their king and swore a new treaty which reaffirmed their friendship (*xeiniēn*) by the receipt of the royal gifts, a golden sword and a guilded tiara, and the exchange of vassalage oaths (Hdt. 8.120). But as the Persians reaffirmed their control of the eastern regions of that satrapy, several of the western Greek poleis rebelled.

Independent of events in Thessaly, Attica and the Peloponnesos, Potidaia, essentially remote astride the narrow neck of the Pallene peninsula, rebelled (Hdt. 8.126). This had little to do with Xerxes' recent hasty march through Skudra along the main road passing from western Terme to Eion along the Strymon River, and well to the north of Potidaia. It was essentially a rebellious action for autonomy at a time of ill-perceived Persian weakness, and especially at the moment when Xerxes and a large part of his forces commanded by Tigranes had crossed over into Anatolia, and when Artabazos and his forces in mid-December 480 B.C. were just beginning to return to rejoin Mardonios in Thessaly.   Potidaia, heavily fortified along its northern and landward side, could withstand a Persian siege, especially since Artabazos lacked ships to attack that city's vulnerable southern side. Not too far to the north, yet well south of the strategic main east-west route, the polis of Olynthos joined the rebellion. In counter-action Artabazos with his crack Parthian and Chorasmian troops, augmented by strong loyal Macedonia levies, promptly blockaded the Pallene isthmus, sealed off Potidaia, and then turned to besiege Olynthos. There, endemic internal factionalism generated treachery, whereby Artabazos, taking advantage of divide-and-conquer techniques, regained control of Olynthos and installed a garrison of loyalist Greeks from Torone at the southern tip of the Sithonia peninsula.

Returning to Potidaia, the Persians continued a long drawn out siege through three winter months and finally toppled that polis, yet with significant losses to their own forces.   In the spring of 479 B.C., therefore, Artabazos marched to Thessaly, joined Mardonios' formidable renewed campaign against Attica, and controlled the satrapies of Skudra and the newly emerging satrapy of Greece or Yauna, from Byzantion to Athens.

Xerxes ruled securely from the acropolitan palace in Sardis (Hdt. 9.108), and firmly in control of the crucial satrapy of Sparda remained in contact with Artabazos and his army as they progressed westward. Among the Ionia states, Tigranes' forces maintained control there. Under imperial command, the Persian fleet had departed in the spring of 479 B.C. from Kyme to the crucial harbor of Samos (Hdt. 8.130.1). About this time, heralds from Artabazos' camp reported to the Great King the Persian losses at Potidaia because of the abnormally high sea water generated by a local earthquake (Hdt. 8.126-9). Therefore, in an attempt to lessen the Persian ordeal upon his taxed army, Mardonios dispatched the Persian vassal King Alexander I of Macedon to Athens from their Thessalian winter camp (Hdt. 8.136.1; and fig. 19). To the Athenians, Alexander on behalf of the Persian king offered a treaty of vassalage (an homologia), the acceptance of subjugation but with generous terms, which included Xerxes' complete forgiveness of Athens' wrongs committed against Persia (including the breaking of the 507 B.C. vassalage oath, and the attack upon Sardis), Persian rebuilding of the destroyed Athenian temples, allowance for Athens to expand territorially at the expense of other Greek poleis, and a marked degree of local self-determination (Hdt. 8.140.1-2; cf. 8.144.2-3, 9.13.1). This new alliance, to replace that of 507 B.C., would raise Athens to the status of a semi-autonomous province within the Persian imperial structure, a status similar to that which Cyrus had offered Cilicia and Miletos, and Cambyses had offered the Phoenician harbor states. By this alliance, Mardonios expected to control the Athenian fleet and become master of the Greek waters in order to develop a superior military force over the mainland and Peloponnesian Greeks (Hdt. 8.136.2-3). With these terms, Alexander hoped to appeal strongly to the poorer Athenian classes for whom Mardonios' renewed invasion would only compound the miseries and losses of their few remaining possessions.[98] But the Athenians refused (Hdt. 8.143). Sparta, on the other hand, simply failed to react to the possible fall of Athens to Persia, as Greek parochialism began to disrupt the brief unity generated at Salamis. In this, the Persians had a strong chance for success.

As spring approached in 479 B.C., Mardonios prepared to invade Attica and then advance upon the Peloponnesos. His loyal Theban forces, however, advised him to remain in Boiotia to watch and wait as the Greeks factionalized (Hdt. 9.2.1). The Thebans wisely and correctly noted that time, accentuated by bribes—Persian gold diplomacy—rather than force of arms, would, once again, win over the recalcitrant Greeks, given their ethnic factional character (stasiōteōn: Hdt. 9.2.3). That Mardonios ignored sound Theban advice generated another strategic Persian military blunder (Hdt. 9.3.1).

Ten months after Xerxes had seized Athens (September 480 B.C.), in July of 479 B.C., Mardonios again occupied that city and firmly controlled Greece from Macedonia through Thessaly and Boiotia to Athens and her harbors of Piraeus and Phaleron (Hdt. 9.1). The Theban prediction of factionalism, a Greek constant, materialized as the Peloponnesians failed to support adequately the Athenian cause. The Athenians, consequently, fled once again to their ships and the island of Salamis (Hdt. 9.3.2).

From his seat of power in Athens, Mardonios repeated Xerxes' proposals of Athenian vassalage and local autonomy, with the hope that the medizing faction within the Athenian ranks would urge compliance (Hdt. 9.4.1-2). In response, Lykides, a member of the Athenian Boule and apparently the spokesman for the pro-Persian faction, urged consideration of the generous terms. But the other Athenians angered, and stoned Lykides to death (Hdt. 9.5.2).

Sparta, nevertheless, acted for her safety foremost and remained inactive, thus encouraging Mardonios' hopes for conquest following rampant parochialism and the failure of the Hellenic League (Hdt. 9.6.1). At the isthmus, the defensive wall was complete and would hold against Mardonios' land forces, especially now that Athens' fleet had escaped. Without that fleet, the Persians could not by-pass the isthmus route and attack Sparta by sea either through pro-Persian Argos or southern Lakonian Gytheion. On the other hand, the Spartans seem not to have considered fully the ramifications of a Persian commanded Athenian fleet, had Athens medized (Hdt. 9.8.1-2). The disillusioned Athenian ambassadors had even warned the Spartans in order to goad them into action that Athens might be compelled to submit (Hdt. 9.7).

The Spartans wasted time in vacillation until Peloponnesian allies convinced them of their folly, after which a startling Spartan complete reversal of attitude resulted in an order for Pausanias, the son of Kleombrotos and regent to the young King Pleistarchos, to march north against Mardonios (Hdt. 9.9-10). "At the very last second, fortune snatched victory from the Persians."[99] Xerxes firmly believed Mardonios would be victorious (Hdt. 1.130.3), as through a vast network of communications Persian messages crossed the Aegean from Sardis to Athens (Hdt. 1.130.4) by means of a line of Persian fire beacons dotting the Cycladic islands (Hdt. 9.3.1). But Mardonios, having wanted to hold and preserve Athens (Hdt. 9.12-13), turned and marched toward western Attica (burning and destroying as he proceeded) to entrench his army in southern Boiotia where loyal Thebans could secure his necessary supplies as he awaited confrontation by Pausanias (Hdt. 9.13.2-3). At Plataia, the Persian forces ultimately clashed with the Greek land forces, and again a series of Persian strategic military errors gave victory to the Greeks.

The conflict at Plataia was crucial. At Delos the Samians had rumored somewhat earlier that if the Greeks attacked and launched an all-out naval offensive, Ionia would

rebel against the Great King. The Samians implied that Tigranes' army could not hold

Ionia. These rumors, while essentially unfounded, did add to Mardonios' burden of

responsibility, especially at a time when a personal clash between Mardonios and

Artabazos may have been smoldering. The Greeks, on the other hand, plagued with inter-

state feuding, rivalries, distrust, and bad faith, could fall victim to Mardonios' divide-

and-conquer techniques, which would allow him to subdue systematically the Greek

poleis. Fearing just that, the Greeks rallied to swear a common oath at Plataia as a

formal insurance against factionalism and parochialism. Our ancient text (Lycurg.

Leocr. 81, c. 330 B.C.)[100] may not preserve the ipsissimae verbae but many scholars

argue that it does contain the essence of the Hellenic attempt at unity: "I will not hold

life dearer than freedom nor will I abandon my leaders whether they be alive or dead. I

will bury all allies killed in the battle. If I conquer the barbarians in war, I will

consecrate as a tithe all those who sided with the barbarian. I will not rebuild a single

one of the shrines which the barbarians have burned and razed but will allow them to

remain for posterity a memorial of the barbarian's impiety." Emotional and pietistic in

nature, elements which the Greeks could not overlook, the oath gave some structure to a

potentially fragmentary military alliance earlier formed at Sparta now forced by

necessity to oppose the Persians or fall to Persian subjugation.

After eleven days encamped at Plataia, Mardonios, vexed and angry (Hdt. 9.41; Plut.

Arist. 15.1), sought relief supplies, and feared reinforcements would bolster the Greek

army as the news reached him that the newly augmented fleet of the Hellenic League

had sailed for Samos. Yet he still had a severe disadvantage. Mardonios could not wait

for the Greek forces to falter, factionalize, and disappear. The news of the Greek attack

upon Samos demanded that he battle soon and achieve a decisive Persian victory in order

to force the Greek recall of their fleet at Samos. With both Greek and Persian rations

and water-supplies exhausted, a Persian victory now was absolutely necessary.

Athenians, determined to win in spite of Spartan obstinacy coupled with Spartan fear

of Athenian submission to Persia, triumphed with contingents, of other allied Greeks as

the Persian cavalry failed to outflank the Greek heavy infantry (Hdt. 9.21.3), as the

Persian light-armed infantry pitted itself against the Spartan contingents, which broke

through Persian lines to attack the Persian stockade (Hdt. 9.70), and as Mardonios, fatally entered the main line of battle. Persian strategic errors at Plataia marked the end of any hope for victory in Greece.[101] Even amidst battle, Artabazos had advised Mardonios to retire, to resort to bribery, to await Greek factionalism to spread, and above all not to resort to conflict.[102] But again, Mardonios the son of the key conspirator Gobryas, had rejected the plan and ordered battle with all speed (Hdt. 9.41). He and not Artabazos held the kratos or military leadership as commanded by the king (Hdt. 9.42.1), and his reaction was perhaps a sign of jealousy more than military conviction.[103]

The Greeks, too, had erred in trying to maintain an advanced position on the plain, and when their surprise attack upon the Persians failed they found their lines of supplies and their rear flanks open to Persian attack. That error could have cost the Greeks the battle. With food and water scarce, the Greek leaders had decided upon a retirement, which rapidly became a disorderly retreat, yet halted by the stubborn Spartan captains. Had the Greeks withdrawn, their coalition undoubtedly would have fractured, the Athenians would have submitted to the king, and the Peloponnesians would have retreated behind the isthmus wall. Mardonios could then have systematically subjugated the individual resistant poleis. The end of the war lay in sight with the eventual establishment of a satrapy of Yauna perhaps centered at Athens. As long as Mardonios was alive the Persians stood their ground, but with his death they fled in disorder (Hdt. 9.63-5).[104]

The Persian army need not have lost at Plataia, had Artabazos cooperated with Mardonios. As Mardonios' forces scattered amidst the Greek blows, Artabazos' army of almost equal force stood apart. Instead of entering the conflict as fresh Persian troops to sweep the Greeks back in rapid retreat into the Peloponnesos, Artabazos with a sizable force of men quickly turned and in stealth returned to Skudra. En route many of his men fell, cut down by hostile Thracians, or died from hunger and fatigue, before the remnant reached Byzantion and the boats to ferry them across to Asia and safety. The news of unrest in Samos had quickened Artabazos' retreat, and his arrival with Persian forces to assist Tigranes met Xerxes' pleasure (Hdt. 8.126.1). The Spartan refusal to pursue Artabazos had given the Persians an important respite (Hdt. 8.108).

Absolutely crucial to Mardonios' success or lack of success at Plataia had been the coordination of the Persian fleet at Samos with Tigranes' armies on the Asian mainland to retain control of Sparda, and their coordination with Mardonios and Artabazos' activities. From Sardis, Xerxes apparently obtained news through spies and messengers of all Persian and Greek activities and, we may assuredly suspect, monitored the military activities of 479 B.C. If Mardonios had gained victory, the Greeks would have been forced to return to Greece and guard the Peloponnesos, with the result that Tigranes would control Ionia as the Persian joint naval command at Samos. The admirals Mardontes the son of Bagaios, the Persian who had regained Sparda for Darius, Artayntes the son of Artachaies one of the commanders of the Athos canal project, and his grandson Ithamitres, would pursue the Hellenic League's fleet into its home waters. Therefore, as Mardonios and Artabazos arrived at Plataia, and the Hellenic League's fleet approached Samos (Hdt. 9.96.1), the Persian admirals in council determined not to engage the Greeks in battle but to abandon Samos temporarily and sail across the narrow straits and into the Milesian waters of the bay of the Maeander River in order to join Tigranes' army. Together they would fight the Greeks (Hdt. 9.96-7), regain Samos and the Cycladic islands, and support Mardonios' conquest of the Peloponnesos. Again, this was sound Persian strategy, as the Greeks then assembled at Samos were highly reluctant to pursue the Greeks into the Maeander and a Persian trap. Fearful of the Persian might, the Greeks debated whether to return home or to sail to the Hellespont and destroy the Persian bridges (Hdt. 9.98.1). Hegesistratos' faction, meanwhile, now held Samos as Theomestor's regime fell. Herodotus, unfortunately, omitted to note Theomestor's fate. But in sailing to Mykale, the Persian war council rendered a military decision which was the major tactical blunder of the forthcoming campaign: the council dismissed the Phoenician ships (Hdt. 9.96.1). Had the Phoenicians remained and had the Persian fleet sailed to do battle with the Greeks, the outcome of the battle might have been decidedly different.

It was probably mid-August, about the time that the annual northern Meltimi winds began to blow and clear the Aegean of the hot dry Sarocco winds from the Sahara, some six weeks after Mardonios' second occupation of Athens. Near the small stream of Gaeson on the southern slopes of Mt. Mykale, Tigranes systematically mustered and organized the Persian naval and military forces, the numbers of which are difficult to assess but which perhaps totalled about 6,000 military men (down from an earlier 10,000 because of constant losses), in addition to about 4,000 marines, and a fleet of about 100

ships. But fresh Persian reinforcements could be obtained across the mountain passes
from Sardis and possibly from up river at the Persian stronghold of Magnesia-on-the-
Maeander. The small Persian naval base at Myous perhaps also could assist Tigranes'
stand against the cautious Greeks. In all, about 10,000 awaited the Greeks to stand siege
and do battle.[105]

While the Greeks had not anticipated fighting the Persians on land but rather on the
sea where success might be assured, the Spartan commander-in-chief Latychidas altered
the War Council's plans. The League's forces perhaps totalled no more than 5,000 men,
about 2,500 regular marines in addition to about 1,000 archers and the rowers who
possibly were hoplites drafted into this naval effort. The Persians outnumbered the
Greeks, but man for man only the best trained Persian infantry forces could hold their
own against the Greek hoplites. But the Greek forces without cavalry troops anticipated
difficulties in trying to gain a coastal strip at Mykale against the increased forces
commanded by Tigranes. From Latychidas' view, the Hellenic League was to drive the
Persians out of Greece. At Mykale, consequently, the goal was not to defeat Tigranes'
land forces but to prevent the remnant of the Persian fleet from aiding Mardonios. The
Council, therefore, chose a very bold but arguable plan, an attack upon the Persian
stockade in order to destroy it and the Persian ships. Unless that Persian fleet was
destroyed, the Greeks serving under Latychidas risked being cut off from the mainland
when Mardonios and Artabazos would attack the Peloponnesos. But the Ionian discontent
with Persian rule had not spread substantially beyond Samos, and if successful at Mykale,
Latychidas could not rely upon the mainland Ionians to revolt except for the promise of
some of the Milesians. Chios and Lesbos, however, with the destruction of the Persian
fleet might join the League's forces. Ionian support of the Greek in 479 B.C. remained
purely emotional and unrealistic without their own military forces or mainland Greek
forces willing to invade Ionia. While the Ionians may have begun to realize the
precarious position of the Persian cause, even with Xerxes in Sardis, they were not
prepared to rally with the Greeks. These factors Latychidas and the League's Council
knew and planned to do little more than strike a crucial blow against the Persian fleet.
The attack would not be a liberation of Ionia. The Greeks, consequently, kept their fleet
prepared in case the Persians suddenly altered their plans and prepared to risk sea battle.

With the Greek advance upon Mykale, the Samians initiated stories, later adopted by

Herodotus, that earlier the Chians had failed to move the Hellenic League from Aigina while they had recently brought the fleet from Delos to armed conflict with Tigranes. They would also persuasively argue that at Mykale they played a major role in the Greek victory and the subsequent liberation of Ionia.[106] But in truth, the Samians who had fought loyally at Salamis, at Mykale did not rebel against their Persian commanders. Herodotus became exceedingly sympathetic toward the Samian propaganda, as it reflected aristocratic views similar to his own, anti-tyrannical and anti-Persian. Consequently, he interjected into his Mykale narrative the Samian view that the Persians had disarmed the Samians fearing their potential rebellion (9.99). But if truly disarmed (which we now must seriously question), the Samians did not rebel nor did they aid the attacking Greeks. In essence, the Samian forces at Mykale appear to have still served the pro-Persian faction earlier centered upon Theomestor and now displaced from power in Samos. Herodotus also wrote that the Persians had shifted the Milesians from the front lines to the rear, in anticipation of their rebellion (9.104). But this Herodotean report again reflects Greek propaganda, as a careful analysis of the Persian battle plan reveals the major role the Milesians played for their Persian commanders in guarding the pass from the southern coast across the Mykale ridge to the Kayster Valley and the Persian Royal Road from Ephesos to Sardis.[107]

The Samian report that they had liberated five hundred Athenian prisoners from the Persian camps clearly stems from later Samian propaganda intended to gain Athenian favor during the era of the Delian Confederacy (Hdt. 9.99.2). Similarly, the Milesian report that they misguided the Persians fleeing from Mykale (Hdt. 9.104) appears as Milesian propaganda to counter-balance the Samian report. For the Greeks at Mykale, the prize of victory would be the control of the Hellespont and the islands (including Chios and Lesbos), not the Ionian poleis on the mainland (Hdt. 9.101.3).[108] The Milesian factions in their asty and chora did nothing to aid the Greeks across the Maeander Bay.

At Mykale, Tigranes and the Persians initially held the military advantage over Latychidas and the Greeks. Yet the Greeks gained the victory. The Persian disaster stemmed from significant losses of manpower accumulated over the months since the spring of 480 B.C. when Xerxes had set out from Sardis for Athens, and a major loss of naval power. But at Mykale, Tigranes ordered a series of strategic moves which compounded the earlier Persian military miscalculations and blunders and produced failure. He should have kept the Persian fleet afloat in order to attack the Greeks, and by all means attempt to preserve the still important remnant of the Persian fleet. If by chance he were victorious, he could have sailed back into Greek waters to aid Mardonios. Instead, Tigranes ordered the ships beached, and put within a stockade of stones and tree trunks surrounded by a deep moat protected by his infantry. When the Greeks disembarked upon the shores of Mykale, consequently, they faced the Persian army lined up before the stockade. Herodotus reports that the Greeks attempted to foment Ionian rebellion, and this account may have some historical value, but the Greek enthusiasm for Ionian rebellion generated no plan or strategy for rebellion (Hdt. 9.98). What actually tipped the balance, however, was neither Persian nor Greek military strategy but the story, apparently based upon an accurate report, that Mardonios had met the Greeks at Plataia where the Greeks had killed that general, defeated his forces, and watched Artabazos hastily retreat toward Skudra (Hdt. 9.100.1).

The story spurred the Greeks on, and in heated land battle struggling against desperate Persian resistance, the Athenians broke through the Persian wicker wall of shields and pursued the Persians into the wooden stockade. Chaos erupted, some Persians fled, Ionian troops loyal up to that point then turned against their Persian commanders, and most of the Persians fought to the death, including the generals Tigranes and Mardontes. The Greeks gaining the stockade set fire to it and to the ships (Hdt. 9.102-106). Across the Mykale ridge, some of the Persians escaped toward Ephesos, including the commanders Artayntes and Ithamitres. Yet many of their soldiers also fell as the Greeks turned and pursued them (Hdt. 9.106.1).

Xerxes, surprised and astonished, received the bitter news. His brother, prince Masistes, described the debacle and blamed Artayntes' generalship for the disaster (Hdt. 9.107.2).[109] About 4,000 Persian and subject troops fell during the disaster, only about 2,000 survived, and similarly the Greek casualties mounted in number.[110] Yet the surviving Greeks quickly abandoned the Mykale beaches and, purposefully avoiding the Persian stronghold of Miletos, sailed hurriedly and cautiously back to Samos and security.

In Samos, the Hellenic League's War Council again met, this time to discuss its future actions in light of Greek victories at Plataia and Mykale, and the movement of Artabazos' army through northern Greece to Skudra and ultimately Sparda.[111] It was not a question of how to foment rebellion in Ionia or even if rebellion spontaneously arose how to protect the rebellious Ionian poleis, but rather how best to remove the East Greeks from Sparda and abandon mainland Ionia to the Persians, and how to transport the East Greeks to settlements in mainland Greece (Hdt. 9.106.2). Latychidas firmly presented Sparta's policy, that which his state had formulated c. 545 B.C. in reaction to Cyrus' occupation of Śfarda and the Ionian poleis. Sparta would give only empty-handed diplomatic protection, and continued her refusal to assist the Ionians militarily. To allow the mainland Ionians to join the Hellenic League would commit Sparta to a pledge of military protection, which she simply could not maintain. If, however, Samos recommitted her allegiance to the League, and Chios, Lesbos, and other islanders would also pledge their allegiance (Hdt. 9.106.4), then the Spartans would attack the Hellespont in order to destroy the Persian bridges and sever Skudra from Daskyleion and Sparda. This action would thwart Artabazos' return to Sardis and in the future enable the Thracians, independent of League assistance and military commitments from Sparta, to overthrow Persian subjugation.

Latychidas and the War Council, on behalf of the League, administered the formal oaths of allegiance to the Samian aristocrats, now in control of their island and the recognized government in power, to the aristocratic Chians and Lesbians free of their Persian supported tyrannies, and to a group of important but uncounted and unnamed other islanders. The oaths bound them, as they bound the earlier and charter members of the League, to serve with arms in the symmachia, to bind their oaths with pledges of fidelity (pisti) to remain faithful and not to desert their allies (Hdt. 9.106.4; Diod. Sic. 11.37.1; cf. Thuc. 1.89.2). The oath reaffirmed that which Hegesistratos and his colleagues swore on Delos months earlier (Hdt. 9.92.1), but more fundamentally bound the new island allies to the oaths and their provisions sworn to in 481 B.C. at Sparta. The military allies of the symmachy would end their rival and petty wars, would punish the recent medizers, and would supply naval forces and land troops to the military organization, each to the best of its ability (Hdt. 7.148-9, 158-62; Paus. 3.12.6; cf. Diod. Sic. 11.3). The remembrances of the Samian double-cross at Lade and the recent lessons of East Greeks fighting among the ranks of Tigranes' armies vividly remained. The clauses of service, fidelity, and non-desertion became the fundamental key elements binding the East Greek islanders to the military hegemony of the War Council bent upon success. Bound by these oaths, the enlarged fleet set sail for the Hellespont to destroy the Persian bridges (Hdt. 9.106.4).

Sparta's leadership of and military activity in the Hellenic League had been molded by her own social paradox. Since the Second Messenian War and the beginning of the sixth century B.C., a single class of aristocratic and military peers ruled over an extensive subject population of agriculturalists. To rule, therefore, the Spartan military functioned as a police force to control the enemy within, but was little prepared to fight the enemy without. To preserve their aristocratic elitism, the Spartans had structured their entire society and all its aspects for the fulfillment of that internal police duty. As a consequence of this policing condition, by c. 505 B.C., the Spartan efforts to structure and to maintain a Peloponnesian League, often requiring repeated warfare, effectively extended that policing action throughout the Peloponnesos. But her reluctant participation in the Hellenic League, thrust upon her by the Persian threat to invade the Peloponnesos in order to destroy Sparta's strongest ally Corinth and then Sparta itself, forced Sparta against her will to be drawn into an extensive and genuine military activity in the Aegean and in Ionia. That activity severely taxed Sparta's military forces and dangerously raised the necessity to incorporate non-equals into the military ranks of the aristocratic class. The action also generated unprecedented opportunities for ambitious Spartan kings, princes, and nobles to breach the traditional Spartan values, to seek honor and fame outside of Sparta, to gain wealth, and to altar Spartan xenophobia and the expulsion of foreigners. Problems internal to Lakonia and Spartan held Messenia forbade Spartan military assistance to the Ionian mainland poleis still guarded with Persian garrisons.[112]

Athens, on the other hand, began to assert her voice in the War Council to counterbalance Sparta's withdrawal from aggressive leadership. Despite strong Spartan opposition, the Athenians began in all haste and earnestness to refortify their asty and the port of Piraeus,[113] to seek aggressively overseas interests by encouraging the Ionians to enter a new phase of the war in the East against the Persians. Key to the advent of Athenian aggression and demand that the Hellenic League's forces sail for the Hellespont must have been urgent need for wheat and the Athenian necessity to begin the import of wheat in large quantities from the northern Black Sea emporia.[114]

In the late summer of 479 B.C., the Spartans, Athenians, and the other mainland Greeks could not seriously advance the argument that they foster Ionian rebellions against the Persians. A successful rebellion would necessitate the maintenance of large garrisons within almost every Ionian polis to fend off Persian attack, and such action would have committed the members of the Hellenic League to military duty in Ionia for an indefinite period of time (Hdt. 9.106.2). At bottom, the League's members could not regard such military action within the realm of practical policy. The only rational decision seemed to be the transportation of the Ionians en masse to Europe (Hdt. 9.106.3; Diod. Sic. 11.37.1-3).[115] But this Spartan argument contained no step by step program in regard to how this principle could be implemented, except to give the Ionians the lands of the pro-Persian Greeks in central and northern Greece, a suggestion which also implied Peloponnesian Argos, the pivotal region between Corinth and Sparta. But the Athenians, angered by this proposal, remained firm in opposition to this scheme. The arguments of common Athenian-Ionian ties, common blood and language, ties of religious rituals, and bonds of a way of life understood and shared apparently arose much later after the fact. In reality, the Athenians feared that their blackened and destroyed asty and its chora ravished by two years of Persian looting, plundering, and burning, would lose not only the just emerging concept of Athens' metropolitan center; but perhaps more important the Athenians weighed the economic factors foremost in their minds. If the Ionians moved to mainland Greece, the Athenians may have feared that the highly successful maritime Ionians developing new and neighboring poleis would be actively competing with their attempts to regain the Athenian mercantile ascendancy developed just before Xerxes' devastating invasion (Hdt. 9.106.3). By 480 B.C., Athens had almost eliminated Corinth as a major commercial rival and had begun to dominate the commercial lines to Magna Graecia. In 480 B.C., Athens fought Persia for the right of political self-determination, but in 479 B.C. had desperate need to gain access to the vital Black Sea grain routes and to redevelop Pireaus and the Athenian asty as commercial and craft centers. The Athenians simply could not allow the Ionians, and especially the Milesians, to regain their old colonial regions in the Black Sea. We may also suspect that the aristocratic Samians, at this time courting Athens' favors, were wary of the loss of the East Greek buffer between them and the Persians and also resisted any effort either in Ionia or in mainland Greece to renew mercantile rivalry with the Milesians.

In compromise, Latychidas dropped his proposal and agreed with the Athenians that the Hellenic League abandon any protective activities for the mainland Ionians. The compromise also included the joint decision to set sail with the Greek fleet for the Hellespont to destroy the Persian bridges. Why they did not know that the bridges had been removed and that only the cables remained at Sestos will always remain an historical puzzle. But the campaign to Abydos in the Troad across the Hellespont from European Sestos fervently underscored the first of many attempts by the Athenians to prevent future invasions of Europe by the Persians, a military theme which the Athenians reiterated often throughout the fifth century B.C. (Thuc. 1.89). The recovery of Sestos would then lead Athens to the recovery of Byzantion, the key emporium along the important trade routes to the profitable markets of the Black Sea.[116]

But at Abydos, when the Spartans realized that the bridges had been removed and that the cables were at Sestos, Latychidas pronounced the War Council's agreement completed. With the Peloponnesian ships and forces, the Spartan general returned home (Hdt. 9.114.2), probably some time before the beginning of September 479 B.C. The Athenians, however, now raised their aristocratic general Xanthippos to supreme command to direct the Athenian squadrons and the several unnamed and uncounted "Ionian allies," islanders and not mainlanders, toward a long methodical siege of the Persian garrison within fortified Sestos. The offensive campaign against Persia, begun at Mykale and continued at Sestos, bore witness to the rapid emergence of the Athenians as a leading military force acting independent of Sparta and the Hellenic League. With Latychidas' withdrawal from Abydos, the East Greeks and other fighting allies transferred their hegemony from Sparta to Athens and to Xanthippos' command of the naval forces of the Hellenic League. This, in retrospect, would be an important step in the following year when the Athenian commanders would organize on Delos a new naval symmachy independent of Spartan hegemony and the Hellenic League.

Xanthippos and many of the Athenians recognized the danger in the Persian control of the Thracian Chersonese and the militarily strategic position of Sestos linked by ferry to Abydos. By controlling Sestos, the Persians held the coastal road across southern Skudra linked by the other strong Persian fortresses at Doriskos on the Hebros River and western Eion on the Strymon River. With the fall of Abydos to the Athenians, the Persians throughout the Chersonese had gathered at Sestos for protection (Hdt. 9.115). The Greek arrival was unexpected, and the Persians taken unaware, as no preparation had been made for a long siege through a severe winter (Hdt. 9.116.3). Because the

Athenians were inexperienced and inefficient in siege techniques, weeks became months into the cold winter weather, and the problems of strife and rebellion arose as many within the Athenian ranks wished to return home (Hdt. 9.117). But Xanthippos and other Athenian commanders refused. Hunger forced many Persians to flee only to be killed by the rebellious Thracians from their pyrgoi (Hdt. 9.119.1). Finally, in the late winter, the Athenians broke through, captured the teichos (Hdt. 9.114.2-121; Thuc. 1.89.2; Diod. Sic. 11.37.4-5; Aristod 4.1) and nailed Artayktes, the garrison hyparchos (Hdt. 7.33, 78; 9.116.1) and brother-in-law of the king (Plut. *Them.* 13), to a board, and forced him to witness the stoning of his sons to death before his own death (Hdt. 9.120.4). In triumph, the Athenians sailed home with the cables; votive gifts for victory dedicated in their name to the goddess Athena on the acropolis and to Apollo at Delphi (Hdt. 9.121).[117] The fundamental purposes and the loyalties of the Hellenic League, so all important in the spring of 479 B.C., now in the spring of 478 had lost meaning. The war, however, had not been won by the timid, incompetent, and factional Greeks, but rather had been lost by repeated Persian military and diplomatic blunders.

In the spring of 478 B.C., King Xerxes, therefore, issued a vitally important imperial command: the Persians would abandon most of the Aegean coast of Anatolia and no longer expend money and military forces to continue the subjugation of rebellious peoples and East Greek poleis. To the king, his commanders, and his imperial advisors, Persian control of the key satrapies of Bactria, Sogdiana, Assyria, Across the River, and Egypt demanded intensive imperial attention and military control. Xerxes wisely decided that he could no longer commit his major military strengths to Greece or Ionia and endanger his imperial power in Egypt or the East.[118]

In reality, Persian military forces and manned ships never amounted to the numbers which Herodotus and the other ancient Greek authors reported, and in 478 B.C., Xerxes wisely turned to the more serious imperial goals than the domination of Yauna and Skudra. Pockets of peoples willing to remain under Persian rule, such as at Magnesia-on-the-Maeander, the Persians would guard, but volatile centers such as Miletos would be abandoned. For all Greeks, nevertheless, the fear of Persian domination remained vivid. As A.G. Woodhead succinctly noted: "Its territory vast, its wealth boundless, its armies invincible in numbers, and bravery, its kings shrewd and splendid—no wonder that the Greeks of the early fifth century trembled at the very name of Persia. The phrase is no mere literary flourish."[119] But the reality of Persian domination was not true in spite of the Greek belief that at Salamis the Greeks had devastated the Imperial Persian Fleet (Aesch. *Pers.* 548-590), an opinion which probably never entered the mind of anyone in Susa. The Persians had failed in Greece for good military reasons, and now the king would confine himself to defensible Asia. To give up his suzerainty over the hostile and volatile East Greeks was economically and militarily expedient. Xerxes had to maintain order within his Empire, to which Persian domination of the East Greeks was of very little importance. Egypt, in comparison, remained fundamentally more important, particularly in its tribute to the royal coffers. But it continued to plague Persia as a particular and constant distraction: military opposition to Cambyses in 525 B.C., revolution against Darius in 552 and again in 486 B.C., and then a costly and exhaustive rebellion in 460 B.C. But the Persian preoccupation with the control and recovery of Egypt turned to folly, much like the later Roman control of Britain; it exhausted the Persian financial and military efforts time and time again, and contributed little to the military strength of the empire. Beyond being important for its wealth, Egypt sustained the imperial theme that since the reign of the Assyrian King Esarhaddon (681-668 B.C.) Egypt had again entered the greater Near Eastern community, and that Cambyses' conquest of Egypt and that heroic adventure had to be sustained. As Aristotle suggested (*Rhet.* 1292a32), as long as the Persians were set upon recovering Egypt, they could barely generate any serious thoughts of renewing a full scale attack upon the East Greeks or the mainland Greeks.

In 478 B.C. the Persians would tacitly abandon many of the Eastern Greeks and Karians to the aggressive and offensive military advances of the mainland Greeks and the duplicity of the Athenians who anxiously yet eagerly intervened throughout the eastern coast of the Aegean, and would ultimately turn the propaganda of liberation into a new phase of imperial tyranny.

WESTERN ANATOLIA BY 478 B.C.

I

The East Greeks

"In winter, as you lie on a soft couch by the fire, full of good food, drinking sweet wine and munching on chickpeas, then you must ask questions such as these:

'Where do you come from?

Tell me, what is your age?

How old were you when the Mede came?' " (F 22)[1]

Cyrus had conquered Sardis. But it was not the fall of Sardis which shook Xenophanes of Kolophon who penned these words, it was the fall of the East Greeks to Persian rule. And because of Cyrus' conquest of Kolophon, Xenophanes fled Ionia at the age of twenty-five to live an exile's life in Sicily to the full age of ninety-one.[2]

When the Mede came, the blush of the highly expressive Ionian Blütezeit flourishing since the beginning of the sixth century B.C. markedly began to pale, and by the chaotic years of the "Milesian Affair" (499-494 B.C.) Ionia fell into despair and a cultural backwater. The creative Ionian spirit generated by the ambivalent intercourse with Lydia, which provided wealth, power, and artistic inspiration yet military and political threats to Ionian self-determination, had fallen underneath the heavy tread of Persian taxation of money and manpower for the imperial centers of Pasargadae, Persepolis, Susa, and Babylon, and the extensive satrapal necessities of Sardis.

The elements of the highly creative and expressive Ionian cultural achievements, which had gradually begun to emerge during the energetic age of Gyges' revitalization of Lydia, reached efflorescence during the successful and militarily antagonistic reigns of Kings Alyattes and Croesus during the first half of the sixth century B.C. Amidst the variety of East Greek poleis, each particularly distinct in its own ethnic and cultural complexities, yet each an aspect of the greater Ionian koine, Milesians specifically emerged to generate intellectual achievements which surpassed their contemporaries. The multiplicity of factors for that creativity are difficult to isolate and to analyze. Each aspect became intricately intertwined with the economic and social pressures during the last decades of the seventh and the early decades of the sixth century B.C., and together generated that innovative cultural revolution in all spheres of Ionian life. Similar factors had occurred elsewhere, for example at Corinth, but in Ionia the product of those factors created a cultural milieu hitherto unsurpassed. At Miletos, the generative combination of elements, of political and social strife (eris) which, in turn, spawned tyranny and factionalism (stasis), coupled vigorously with colonial and mercantile activities. These elements, in turn, were compounded with positive results brought about by the geographical restrictions of agricultural life for the resources and space of a successful ecological niche system limited by the Karian and Ionian mountains, the Lydian imperial and Karian tribal pressures upon that polis, and the rivalry of Myous and its harbor beyond at the head of the Gulf of the Maeander River. That accumulated creative spirit, however, may also be witnessed in the non–colonial and non–mercantile poleis of Kolophon and Ephesos, centers which remained essentially agricultural and highly influenced by Lydian and native Anatolian ethnic units and their particular and expressive cultural traits. In contrast, the colonial and mercantile city–states of Phoenicia failed to produce similar cultural achievements.

During the early seventh century B.C., the East Greek communities had lagged behind those of mainland Greece and their developing interrelations with Assyrian, Phoenician, and Egyptian centers, remained comparatively isolated from the Near Eastern influences, yet gradually developed within a cultural self–sufficiency.[3] The Kimmerians had disrupted the overland routes to Assyria, and the maritime routes between Corinth and Aigina and the Near Eastern ports by–passed the East Greeks except for the transitional centers on the island of Rhodes. By the mid–century, however, the Samians had become involved in the Near Eastern trade and led the introduction of the East Greeks to the greater cosmopolitan world of the eastern Mediterranean. At the end of the century, after the fall of Assyria, the Median and Babylonian stabilization of the Near East, and the revival of overland trade, the East Greek poleis along the border of Lydia, and especially Miletos, responded with their own colonial and mercantile adventures into Egypt, eastern Thrace, and the coastal regions of the Propontis and the southern Black Sea, and the farther reaches of Italy and the western Mediterranean. At that point, the Ionians began to foster an intellectual and artistic revolution, which brilliantly yet briefly surpassed all their contemporary societies, Greek and Near

Eastern. The revolution laid the foundations of rational thought and scientific inquiry, propagated the fundamentals of philosophy, natural science, history, and geography, and rendered major contributions to poetry, classical art, and architecture. With antecedents in the epic poetry of Homer, said to have been born in Smyrna, the intellectual activities of the Ionians, and especially the Milesians, for the first time in the history of man emerged center stage with emphasis upon the rationalization of man's mind in the investigation of the natural influences as divorced from the conceived influences of the supernatural and the irrational forces of magic and the anthropomorphic deities.[4]

In their creativity, the Ionians absorbed the multiplicity of Lydian and Anatolian influences, the stimulation and achievements of the mainland Greeks, and the practical and religiously oriented observations of the Egyptians and Babylonians, to generate an intellectual boldness of unique and influential systematic reflections of the external world, both earthly and heavenly. In the courts of the Ionian tyrants, at Miletos and Samos in particular, the peculiar and exceptional combination of societal elements provided liberal patronage for artists, poets, musicians, and architects of grandiose temples and complicated public works, and offered a vibrant intellectual world to the Presocratic cosmologists and philosophers. Their activities, in turn, enhanced the reputation of the tyrants.[5]

It was not just the tyrants who patronized the poets, musicians, and artists, but also the aristocrats, the landed gentry jockeying for social and political power within their respective socio-ecological niches, who generated the development of Ionian craft centers and increased the importation of exotic and ostentatious curios. An extraordinary symbiotic relationship developed, consequently, between the politically important and rich aristocrats, who often owned town houses in addition to their rural estates (Hdt. 5.29.1), and the urban craftsmen, the artisans and manual workers who created the Ionian arts. The artisans provided not only the essentials of life, the housing, clothing, shoes, weapons, and tools, but also the ceramics, statues, and temples of their poleis, yet were denied political status by the ruling elite who generally despised these banausoi or vulgar workmen, whether slaves, resident metics, or citizens (Xen. Oec. 4.2-3).[6] The landed-gentry were not the only buyers of ceramics; the others included men and women from all classes of society, foreign visitors and merchants, as well as the priests and priestesses of sanctuaries, and the administrators of the state. The aristocrats as patrons of the arts, however, set the pace in seeking new styles and the purchase of innovative designs.[7]

The craftsmen, however, also confident and independent in spirit, held positive attitudes toward their professions and distinctively began to make themselves known by signing their works.[8] In their workshops, fathers trained their sons, who in turn trained their sons in their families' crafts, often in two or three related occupations such as sculpture, bronze-casting, painting, and architecture, at the higher levels of quality, while utilitarian craftsmen usually did not diversify.[9] And often several skilled craftsmen worked together in the creativity of art, ceramics, and sculpture.[10]

In Ionia, ceramic shops offered for their local markets pottery decorated with distinctive "Orientalizing" patterns, the "Wild Goat Style," of goats and other animals surrounded by a variety of floral and geometric patterns, which suggest inspiration from eastern embroideries, yet adapted to an entirely particular Ionian style.[11] By the mid-sixth century B.C., Ionian ceramics and sculpture reached an acknowledged zenith of strong and substantial artistic traditions. In sculpture, the artists had assimilated the eastern static and hieratic conventions and styles modified by characteristic Greek directness, no less humor, with emphasis upon soft, plump bodies, yet with definite concern for abstract design, mass, and Ionian decorative patterns, specifically in the development of the large-scale clothed female figures.[12] In ceramics and sculpture, the particular stamp of Ionian art emphasized the pull of opposing values which varied in strength, "a deliberate and discriminate choice of the East Greeks themselves."[13] Strong decorative patterns based upon eastern conventions accentuated the definite approach for abstract forms, of mass and line, which G.M.A. Hanfmann stressed as "an eager inquisitive attitude to life."[14] Unlike Ionian ceramics which met fierce competition from Corinthian and then later Athenian wares and did not circulate beyond Ionia, Ionian sculpture in stone, bronze, and ivory from Smyrna, Ephesos, and Samos often excelled in quality that of the Greek mainland, and did exert a considerable influence upon Athenian sculpture.[15]

In architecture and the great temples at Ephesos, Didyma, and Samos, elaborate in size and Ionian decorative reliefs, the Ionian stone masons developed distinct forms of capitals and bases, with the same concern with superficial detail and elegance with which sculptors carved the female statues at Hera's temple at Samos and the row of seated females lining the sacred way to Milesian Didyma.[16] Floral and volute motifs adopted

from Near Eastern minor carvings on furniture begat a variety of Ionic and Aiolic volutes

springing from bands of leaves ringing column capitals. And to the column drums and

bases at Ephesos and Didyma, the Ionian sculptors added figural reliefs. For Herodotus,

the immense sixth century B.C. temple of Hera at Samos (c. 575 B.C.), designed by

Rhoikos and Theodoros, ranked as one of the three greatest building and engineering

feats in the Greek world (3.60.4). This temple, destroyed by fire, apparently during the

Persian attacks upon Samos in the reign of Cyrus, was included among the several

projects for restoration during the tyranny of Polykrates. But with his crucifixion at the

hands of the rebel Persian satrap Oroites of Sardis, the Samians, divided and weakened by

factionalism, failed to complete that project.[17] Similarly, the great Artemision at

Ephesos (temple D, c. 560-545 B.C.), an Ionian development of an earlier Anatolian cult

site to which Croesus lavishly contributed funds, was never properly finished.[18]

Fundamental to the flourishing of Ionian creativity lay the personal and socially

class-minded efforts of the aristocratic landed gentry and the tyrants, who arose from

that class, and their economic investments to demonstrate ostentatiously their wealth.

This jockeying for position within the poleis, as noted earlier, generated strife and

factionalism between the aristocratic groups, and also generated strong anti-aristocratic

sentiments especially among the poets, who penned their lyrical, elegiac, and iambic

lines often critical of noble and heroic ideals. This paradox, the aristocratic support and

economic investment in the Ionian Blütezeit and the poetic attacks upon aristocratic

ideals, nevertheless, persisted as a fundamental factor within Ionian culture. Together

they mark clearly the intense and rare combination of generative elements, often elusive

to identify precisely, which collectively constituted the Ionian spirit.

Ionian poets contemporary with the artists and philosophers developed new and often

radical approaches to older modes and materials. With Homer in the mid-eighth century

B.C., there had arisen a distinct Ionian concern for human spiritual and social

development within the particular East Greek community of the polis, and in association

with, but distinctly independent of, the ageless anthropomorphic gods. The Ionian polis,

strongly secular in its outlook, therefore, centered upon a humanism in contrast to the

god-centric and theologically motivated communities of the Near East. The professional

Ionian bards, who sang the Homeric epics at the request of their lords and honored guests

(*Od.* 1.325-7; 7.256-369, 487-521), gradually emerged in the early sixth century B.C. on the island of Chios within a guild of poets known as the Homeridai (*Hymn to Delian Apollo* 172-3; Thuc. 3.104.4-6). They stressed, as did Homer, the Ionian qualities of courtly sophistication and pleasant living, and the rise of aristocratic leadership. Their poems penetrated into the world of personal feelings and motives, of individuals as human beings rather than divine heroes, and of humanized deities.[19]

In the transition from the Homeric oral traditions[20] and the advent of written poetry in the seventh century B.C.,[21] other poets of that century and the sixth penned statements with strong anti-aristocratic biases critical of the Homeric epic-heroic values, and of the aristocrats themselves and their class values. This criticism heightened the social and political strife (eris) within the poleis, as the poets, often from aristocratic families themselves, took strong exception to the nobles' arrogance, luxury and outward display of wealth, and their ostentatious appearance in the cities' agorai. The sharpest attacks fell upon the aristocrats' improper exercise of authority, of violence, factionalism, and strife, whereas the poets stressed justice and fair-dealing, simple farmer's virtues, hard work, thrift, simplicity, cooperation, utility, and common sense. The new poets emphasized a deeply rooted conviction in the sense of identity and self-esteem.[22] Xenophanes, who feared the Persians, blamed the Lydians for introducing those detestable aristocratic values to his fellow Kolophonians once "rough with uncouth manners" (Ath. *Deip.* 12.526a). To this point, he penned: "They learned useless luxuries from the Lydians, while they were free from hateful tyranny, and they proceeded into the agora clad in all-purple dyed cloaks, not less than a thousand in all, boastfully rejoicing, with comely long-flowing locks drenched in the heavy aroma of unguents" (F 3).[23]

The Ionians, writing short poems for personal recitation or performances by choirs at religious festivals, accentuated their individualities and own consciousnesses in shifting from an emphasis upon Homeric "honor" per se to an emphasis upon a collective ability to defend the polis.[24] In the middle of the seventh century B.C., Kallinos of Ephesos summoned men to fight and protect their land and families amidst a world of Kimmerian and Trerian ravagings and the attacks of his fellow Ephesians upon Magnesia-on-the-Maeander.[25] The poets often wove their subtle stories to stress a moral, to express an emotion, or to convey a compassion, which far excelled the abilities of their contemporary painters and sculptors. Ionian poetry made demands upon the human emotions while art appealed to the sense of the dramatic and the beautiful.[26]

In the writings of Mimnermos of Kolophon, during the second half of the seventh century B.C., we can detect the distinct Ionian interests, a tendency towards voluptuousness and hedonism with an emphasis upon youth and pleasure as Mimnermos' only goals in life, and his pessimism on the brevity of youth and the unpleasantness of old age. His poems proclaim the joy of life, and the creed of pleasure as opposed to the older aristocratic heroic values in the Homeric epics. His hedonism stressed the universal principle that every individual held the right to enjoy his own life to the fullest.[27] "What joy would there be without golden Aphrodite?," he sang, yet noted "painful old age" when man becomes foul without and evil within (F 1).[28]

On the island of Lesbos, in the early sixth century B.C., Alkaios stressed the role of the citizens, as individuals collectively gathered for the well-being of their state. For Alkaios "not fine roofed houses, or well-built stone walls, not even canals and dockyards, make a polis, but men able to use their abilities" (F 28).[29] On Lesbos, his slightly younger contemporary, Sappho, sang in a voice of pure emotion, and sang the power of Eros to release the forces of her spirit: "Some say the fairest thing on this black earth is a troop of horsemen, others a band of foot soldiers, and still others a squadron of ships. But I say the fairest is she whom one loves" (F 38a). "The moon is set, and the Pleiades, it is midnight, and time is fleeting by; yet I lie alone" (F 111). "Love has shaken my soul, as a wind ripping down from the mountains through the oaks" (F 54).[30]

Amidst the last great flowering of Ionian culture, when the centers at Miletos, Ephesos, and Samos led the Greek world in architecture, sculpture, historical and philosophical investigation, Anakreon of Teos wrote his poems combining the vibrant elements of Ionian wit, sensuality, and technical virtuosity. The last of the great Ionian poets, Anakreon fled from the Persian soldiers first to Thracian Abdera and then to Polykrates' lavish court in Samos. But with the assassination of Polykrates at the hands of Oroites, Anakreon sailed to Athens where he lived for many years ([Plato] *Hipparchos* 228b). He too, in lines of love poetry, sang of secular eroticism, and shifted from the earlier poems for the landed gentry to poems of "courtly spirit" for tyrants and their patronage; not so much, C. J. Emlyn-Jones argued, as a change in spirit but "as a final consolidation of all that was characteristically Ionian."[31] "Oh boy child with girlish glance, I seek you, but you take no notice, not knowing that you hold the reins to my soul" (F 4). "For my words and tunes, boys would love me; for I sing what is pleasing and I know how to speak pleasing things" (F 72).[32] Then, perhaps following the fall of Teos at the hands of Harpagos and his Persian army, Anakreon lamented: " . . . I should live to see my fatherland in misery . . ." (F 37). "But alas! The crown of the polis (i.e. the wall) is destroyed" (F 65). "You Aristokleides, of all my gallant friends, I pity foremost; for in defending our fatherland from slavery (douleia) you lost your youth" (F 87).[33] And noting events perhaps before the fall of Sardis to Cyrus the Great and the quick submission of the Milesians to Persian suzerainty, Anakreon penned the acerbic line: "Once, long ago, the Milesians were brave" (F 99).[34]

From the lines of the Ionian poets emerge the voices of the poets themselves, speaking of their own persons, expressing their emotions and opinions, revealing themselves and their sentiments, and stressing their will to live. These personal facets, reflecting the social background of their home poleis, mirrored the universal standards of laws which ruled their fellow-men. In this, the poets contributed to the creation of new ideals for their poleis, and the emergence of the citizen, a new type of political individual also identified in the laws and recorded "constitutions" generated by the new rational and logical thinking. The very act of committing laws to stone or wood became popular in the early sixth century B.C. and added one more factor in the transition of the nature of law from the caprice of the aristocrats, who earlier altered it to suit their needs (Hesiod Erga 220-1, 264) to the responsibility of greater communal nevertheless still aristocratic decision. The progress of written laws, accelerated by the need for foundation charters for the expanding Ionian colonies, resulted in the emerging concept of law as the servant of the people rather than as the master of the state. Unlike the conquering Persians, the Ionians conceived the practical approach to law that men collectively, if only the broad and ruling aristocratic class, were fundamentally responsible for the state's legal procedures rather than the gods.[35]

From the island of Chios, the earliest extant laws inscribed on stone, by either the Ionians or the mainland Greeks, stressed the people collectively in legislative action, the rule of the demos, and the chief magistrates of that assembly, the demarchos and the basileus as aristocratic officials. More important, the inscription in its fragmentary state referred to the judicial functions of the law court presided over by the demarchos, and functions as outlined in the earlier ordinances (rhētras) of the demos.[36] The concept of law and court cases (dikai) impartially determined and unchanging without common consent by the ruling body arose within a political matrix of equality, at least among the landed gentry of the higher economic and social classes, and within a demos which fostered debate among those equals whether in assembly or in the courts where appeals (ekklētoi) to general and impartial principles of legal reasoning had also begun to develop. Law governed as the necessary arbiter if wrongs (adikētai) occurred within the complex social order. For the Chians who set up this stele (c. 575-550 B.C.) the source of authority rested in the assembly and not in the divine revelation of Ahura Mazda proclaimed by Darius and chiseled into stone at Naqsh-i Rustam and the "Ordinance of Good Regulations" (DNb). We can only wonder what legislative and judicial structures Thales may have had in mind when he urged the Ionians to gather at Teos to create a central administrative council (bouleutērion: Hdt. 1.170.3) to oppose Cyrus' forthcoming conquest.

The Ionian cultural revolution emphasized direct, empirical, and non-symbolical modes of thinking, challenged the earlier modes set by Ionian Homer and Boiotian Hesiod (whose father had fled from Aiolian Kyme), and also challenged the early Ionian cosmologists and philosophers themselves. Yet even within the oral and written traditions of Homer and Hesiod, where concepts were expressed in the language and personages of myth, the concepts were not in the modes of the Near Eastern mythopoeic[37] but distinct stages at which the mythology had become highly synthesized and largely transformed from active expressions of current religious beliefs into artistic genres. The strong similarities between Homer's heroic stories[38] and Hesiod's theogonic and cosmogonic stories[39] and the theogonic myths of the Near East[40] diminish in importance when compared to the radical changes emerging within the rational investigations, which broke with millennia old traditions and generated the origins of western science and philosophy.[41] Of Helen captive at Troy, Homer (c. 750-720 B.C.) sang of a heroine with emphasis upon her humanity, even though we can still detect within his epic poem her earlier solar imagery and mythopoeic fertility functions as a life-giving force entwined with stories of rape and recovery.[42] Homer's heroes and heroines marked the transition from myth to philosophy and, like Helen, his men possessed full personalities developing within emotional situations stimulating them to begin consciously to think, reason, rationalize, and feel human values, which became primarily relevant to Presocratic philosophy.[43]

In his *Theogony* (c. 680 B.C.), Hesiod attempted to created a complete, unified, and reasonable outline, a "just-so" story factually explaining how the universe came to be, not to record divine revelation or religious dogma but through experimentation and rational freedom to understand the world in order to control it. Both Homer and Hesiod had presented views that the world had been created and organized by the personal impulses of the powerful anthropomorphic deities, yet within their poems there arose the bases by which others would develop the attitude of the universe as a product of impersonal forces interacting in a predictable manner. Slightly later, in his *Erga*, Hesiod challenged Homer's heroic and aristocratic values by stressing justice for all classes of men, and the principles of how to thrive and be honest. While Homer had praised the early archaic-age nobles, Hesiod conflicted with them (*basilees:* 38, 248), the wealthy and powerful landed gentry who, holding large tracts of land, bitterly oppressed the poorer farmers.[44] Hesiod's primary powers of imagination, inspiration, and creativity set the stage for the later Ionian poets and Presocratic philosophers who, nevertheless, would challenge him just as Hesiod had challenged Homer.[45]

By the beginning of the sixth century B.C., there arose in Miletos in particular, a small group of men who began to investigate the universe not as Homer and Hesiod had, but in a distinctly new rational manner. They speculated upon the nature and origins of the universe without the anthropomorphic deities of epic mythology but with faith that in the chaos of the restless and unstable universe there existed permanence and unity which reason and the human mind could discern. The strife and factionalism of the Ionian polis and its complex ethos, which generated lyric, elegiac, and iambic poetry, law codes and the machinery of the collective assemblies and law courts, and which fostered the economic bases for the creative Ionian arts, sculpture, and architecture, also created the milieu of early Ionian philosophy. In this, the Ionians were unique in developing an intellectual and scientific outlook on their world, with specific concerns for geography, astronomy, meteorology, biology, ethnology, and politics. For these few, while countless others still rallied at the altars of their anthropomorphic deities, the absence of written authoritative and closely guarded theologies, composed by priestly ruling powers as means to perpetuate their social and political status, brought forth among these philosophers a freedom to interpret their traditional mythical heritage by means of rational and secular expressions of early scientific observation.   Unlike their Near Eastern contemporaries, Jews, Egyptians, Babylonians, and Persians, the Ionians could and did question the origins and shape of the world and the nature of its content, the origins of the heavenly bodies, of wind, thunder, and lightning, and the measurement of time, and anthropocentric questions of the origin of the animals and man.

Ionian science or actually philosophia, spiced by the Near Eastern traditions and records of practical observations and truly never free of the mythological,[46] reached a new intellectual plane among men as it focused upon the admiration of wisdom based upon knowledge (epistēmē) through contemplation and speculation (theoria) within the exploration and inquiry of nature and man's role in his universe. For the few, an orderly and systematic comprehension began gradually as they attempted to unravel the complexities of the description and explanation of natural phenomena, to a great degree stripped of magical beliefs, religious laws, and superstition. The Ionian philosophers formulated a distinction between the supernatural and the natural, between the animate and the inanimate, hitherto unknown among the Near Eastern religious, conservative, and normative laws, and the earlier Greek mythologies of Homer and Hesiod; and yet they remained religious men seeking a universal divine power which governed the rational universe.

In Miletos, Thales emerged as the first known Presocratic, reaching a prime of intellectual development about 585 B.C. (Hdt. 1.74.2) with knowledge of the Babylonian religious records of solar and lunar eclipses, perhaps obtained by the sage at Sardis, to predict, although probably not precisely, the solar eclipse of May 28th of that year. His motivation was clearly not religious but an acute curiosity in the celestial phenomenon itself, a practical yet revolutionary way of observing events in nature. And after visits to Egypt where he observed farmers measuring land, Thales speculated upon their applied rules to rationalize new methods of calculating areas of any shape. To the problems of land measurement and astrological charts, Thales applied reason in contemplating the theorem, as the particular and practical gave way to the pursuit of knowledge for its own sake. Thales, thereby, set his successors firmly within an Ionian and Milesian tradition of observation of reality in order to foster reason in the quest of truth. His curiosity and inquiry to know about things, which a century and a half later Herodotus would call historia (1.a), led to new philosophical and historical observations.[47]

The generative spirit of Thales' teachings quickly influenced Anaximander, another Milesian who reached his intellectual prime about 560 B.C., in two major creative efforts: a graphic view of the world and a detailed treatise on the nature of the universe. Perhaps influenced by contemporary Babylonian maps,[48] Anaximander devised a circular plan of the world with emphasis upon the distinct regions in roughly equal segments. The basis of his empirical knowledge of geography was apparently not solely Babylonian but gained from Greek seafarers' reports of Milesian commercial adventures in Egypt, Magna Graecia, Thrace, and the Black Sea, and the East Thracian and Black Sea colonial centers. In regard to the nature of the universe, Anaximander's treatise was among the earliest, and the broadest in scope and most imaginative, as he focused upon the apeiron, a term he invented for his new concept of the "indefinite," an unbounded spatial infinite in everlasting motion, reflective of definite legal and political preconceptions.[49] Immortal and deathless, the apeiron surrounds and guides all things; but, recalling the primeval mythos of "waters commingling as a single body," Anaximander explained a natural process devoid of personal motivation and the conflicts of the mythological gods. For him, the divine apeiron governed the entire universe subject to a single law, yet a universe in which the complexes of conflicting opposites (hot, cold, dry, moist, and others) generated the physical world of earth and sky, the celestial bodies, and by the heat of the sun living creatures arising from the watery slime. In contrast to Hesiod and others, Anaximander separated cosmogony from theogony in questioning how the universe came to be arranged as it is, how life arose within that order, and by emphasizing a natural cause of events rather than supernatural.[50] Many of the philosophical principles set down by Anaximander were continued by his associate and fellow citizen, the Milesian Anaximenes, especially in the investigation of the nature of the universe. But Anaximenes went beyond Anaximander who held that the apeiron was neither earth, air, fire, nor water, but a mixture of these. Anaximenes identified it with air.[51]

The Milesian philosophers had reached new and revolutionary conclusions about the nature of the universe in which they lived, but at a time, within the prime period of Anaximenes' teaching, when Cyrus' Persian armies approached Croesus' capital of Sardis. For the Milesians, the horrors of the fall and burning of Sardis and the subsequent

Persian attacks upon the other Ionian poleis, Priene, Myous, Phokaia, and Teos notably, had been softened by the quick Milesian abandonment of the treaty of vassalage with Croesus and the eager Milesian willingness to join forces with Cyrus and his Persian imperial system. The new treaty of privileged vassalage sworn to with religious oaths in recognition of Persian suzerainty enabled the Milesians to prosper as they had in years past. Their lands remained secure, the great rural estates untouched by the attacking Persian armies, and their city with its magnificent four harbors still bustled with craft activities, commercial enterprises, and continued philosophical investigations. But throughout the remaining East Greek territories on the mainland of Anatolia, individuals and then whole populations fled from the encroaching systematic Persian military advances. As Phokaians and Teians fled across the Aegean, from Kolophon Xenophanes left for Sicily and a long life in self-imposed exile.

Like the Milesians, Xenophanes continued the Ionian attacks upon the earlier anthropomorphic gods of Homer and Hesiod, gods who Xenophanes claimed barely rose above stealing, committing adultery, and deceiving one other in general wickedness (F 11-12). In contrast to his Near Eastern contemporaries who conceived of man in their gods' image, Xenophanes proclaimed that man had made his gods in his own image: "But mortals consider that the gods are born, and that they have clothes and speech and bodies like their own" (F 14). In his major attack upon the scores of anthropomorphic deities, Xenophanes penned: "The Ethiopians claim that their gods are snubbed-nosed and black while the Thracians claim that theirs have gray eyes and flame-red hair" (F 16). "If then, oxen, horses, and lions had hands and wished either to paint with their hands or to create works of art such as men do, then horses would paint their gods and make their shapes in horse-like forms, and oxen ox-like forms, in order that they have their own frame" (F 15). The effects of Ionian ethnography had altered the thinking of Xenophanes, as it would later affect the work of Milesian Hekataios and Halikarnassian Herodotus. But, while Xenophanes attacked anthropomorphism, he remained avidly religious in claiming that there existed "one god, the greatest among gods and men, in no way like mortals either in body or in mind" (F 23), a god who " . . . sees as a whole, thinks as a whole, and hears as a whole" (F 24). "Without toil, he shakes all things with the thought of his mind" (F 25). "Always he remains in the same place, not moving at all, nor is it fitting for him to go to different places at different times" (F 26).[52] Like Anaximander, Xenophanes sought new explanations for the nature of his universe without entirely leaving the world of his predecessors. But unlike Anaximenes, Xenophanes feared "the Mede" and fled.[53] Several years later, from Samos the philosopher Pythagoras would flee to Croton in southern Italy to escape Polykrates' tyranny, where he would continue his inquiry concerning nature and the principles of all things in numbers.[54]

The Persian capture of Sardis altered dramatically the long developing symbiotic relationship, although often violent in military conflict, between the Lydians and the East Greeks. The Persian demands for tribute and military service, by Cyrus and his military and satrapal officials, first from the mainland poleis and then the offshore islands resulted in significant changes. Paktyes' immediate rebellion against the Persian governor Tabalos in Sardis forced the Persians to deal ruthlessly with the Ionian rebels, first reducing the power of the Lydian landed gentry from a high powered cavalry force to the status of a rural landed gentry confined to agricultural activities, and then systematically subjugating the East Greeks, all save Miletos. The Persian general Mazares quelling that rebellion, destroyed Priene and enslaved its inhabitants, overran Myous, and pillaged Magnesia-on-the-Maeander. Campaigning against the coastal poleis, the Median general Harpagos reduced those centers from Kyme and Smyrna in the north to the Maeander River Valley in the south, and then set out to subjugate the southern Karians, Kaunians, and Lykians. Oroites, having replaced Tabalos as satrap of Sparda, eagerly tied all the East Greek, Lydian, and pockets of native Anatolian inhabitants to the Persian imperial system for his sovereign Achaemenid kings, Cyrus and Cambyses.

From Harpagos' onslaughts, the Phokaians and Teians fled en masse, disrupting significantly the social and political orders in their respective poleis. Even though some of them returned and developed, once again, their landed estates, and specifically the Teian pyrgoi, the craft and mercantile activities at Phokaia waned dramatically, the small harbors of Teos remained noticeably inactive, and the Teian asty became essentially insignificant during the later decades of the sixth century B.C. Thales' vision of a central Ionian council at Teos had failed, as had the frantic urgings of Bias of Priene for all Ionians to flee to Sardinia. Kolophon and Ephesos with significant numbers of Lydian nobles and exiled Mermnad families uprooted from Sardis settled in those predominantly agricultural poleis and intermingled with the recognizable and dominant native Anatolian ethnic groups still inhabiting those non-mercantile centers. Their quiescence during the late sixth and early fifth centuries B.C., and the several notable Ephesian military skirmishes against East Greeks, Eretrians, Athenians, and Chians, indicate a strong bond of loyalty between Ephesos and Persian Sardis. In the formerly productive East Greek centers, new crafts, sculpture, and major architectural projects all but ceased, as did work on the unfinished grand temples and other major public monuments. In offshore Klazomenai, however, the painting of black-figure sarcophagi continued within the protection of that island asty, but did wane.[55] Erythrai's fortune seemed tied to that of Chios, both protected from Persian advances by the Mimas Range, yet Erythrai too seems to have declined. The rapid crumbling of Ionian culture, the noticeable fading of the blush from the Ionian Blütezeit, came not just from Harpagos' systematic military campaigns against the resistant East Greek poleis, but also from the demands of Cyrus and Oroites for tribute in kind, for the imperial centers in the east, the satrapal offices at Sardis, and the local garrisons and governing offices, in addition to the firm demands for service in the imperial armies as Cyrus prepared for his conquest of Babylon. Oroites, also serving King Cambyses, continued the demands for tribute and military service during the years of that king's eastern and Egyptian campaigns.

The conquest of Sardis and the East Greek poleis marked the major turning point in the cultural development of western Anatolia and the Ionian artistic and philosophical advancements. The second turning point occurred in 522 B.C. with Oroites' rebellion, which violently disrupted Persian control of Sparda and the Ionian islands, as Oroites attacked Daskyleion and killed the satrap Mitrobates, invaded Cappadocia, and in a cruel act of duplicity crucified Polykrates in an attempt to gain the Samian regions of the Cyclades. This necessitated Darius' dispatch of Bagaios to order the Persian guards in Sardis to kill Oroites, and the king's command to Otanes to subdue and regain Cappadocia, Daskyleion, Sardis and East Greek poleis, including Samos, Chios, and apparently Lesbos. Not just Otanes' conquest of western Anatolia but the complexities of Darius' revitalization movement, throughout his empire and specifically in Sparda, systematically taxed the East Greek poleis with new demands for tribute and military service. With Darius' personal appointment of his half-brother Artaphrenes to the satrapal throne of Sardis, new Persian regulations bound the East Greeks more tightly than before to the imperial edicts, rules, and directives, from the larger satrapal or

provincial realm down to the individual poleis, rural villages, and ethnic units. Darius'
new imperial demands further curtailed the East Greek poleis and continued their
cultural and economic decline. Throughout the Greek regions of Sparda, the local Greek
governors raised by the Persian overlords to administer the poleis as hyparchoi, or
tyrants as the Greeks condemned them, did not generate the cultural advancements
which tryants elsewhere fostered, as in Corinth, Athens, and Samos for example, but
further entrenched their poleis within the complex bureaucratic and economic controls
from Susa and Sardis and halted the diplomatic and international political ties previously
developed in their assemblies and councils.

The loss of life at Sardis and in each East Greek polis can not be tallied, even
approximately, for either the campaigns of Cyrus, Mazares, and Harpagos or for the
campaigns of Bagaios and Otanes. Similarly, we cannot determine how many Lydians and
East Greeks died during Oroites' campaigns against Daskyleion and Cappadocia. Nor can
we measure the number of exiles fleeing to Thrace, Attica, Magna Graecia, and
elsewhere, or the numbers of East Greeks, Lydians, and native Anatolians transported to
distant regions of the Persian Empire, or the numbers of East Greek artisans employed
freely or by force at Pasargadae, Persepolis, Susa, and the other imperial palatial
centers.[56] But we may rather safely assume that the rapid waning of Ionian cultural life
during the second half of the sixth century B.C. occurred within a complex series of
factors and events, which stifled creative thinking and artistic expression, disrupted
mercantile activities, and produced a significant decline in the numbers of urban and
rural residents.

In contrast to our meager evidence for greater Sparda and Daskyleion, which
illustrates these dramatic changes, our evidence for Miletos indicates a continued
prosperity yet with the hallmarks of social decline. The physical development of Miletos,
its harbors, and the oracular temple of Apollo to Didyma, continued, as did the sculpting
of female statues to flank the long holy road to that sanctuary.[57] The special alliance
with Cyrus had enabled the Milesians to retain their former lands and economic
prosperity without the devastations of war suffered by the other poleis. The
ethnographic and geographic studies of Hekataios and the Milesian beginnings of
historical studies also indicate the continuance of philosophical studies and teachings at
that key Ionian center. Factionalism, however, had caused internal disruptions and

marked a gradual economic decline, especially among the landed estates, but less acute

than in the other poleis. If we can believe Athenaios (Deip. 12.524a), the factionalism

between the rich and the workers brought revolting atrocities to both sides: "At first the

poor workers (demos) prevailed and, after they had thrown the rich (ploutis) out, they

assembled the children of the fugitives on the threshing-floors, had oxen trample on them

and destroy them in the most terrible manner. Thereupon, the rich, again getting

control, tarred and burned to death all whom they could get hold of, along with the

children."[58] Under the strong and productive tyrannies of Histiaios and Aristagoras at

the end of the century, we can detect in Miletos, as in the other urban centers, the

several social, political, and economic factors unfavorable to the employment of artisans

and the continuation of crafts. The wealth which supported those activities, as well as

poetry and philosophy, came not from the resident metics or foreigners, but from the

wealthy aristocrats, nobles, or oligarchs whose economic standing and active political

roles and their patronage of the arts came from the agricultural produce of their landed

estates. The key factor to the creative Ionian spirit and the cultural revolution

throughout western Anatolia, therefore, rested securely upon the wealth of the Lydian

and the East Greek landed estates and the important roles played by the landed gentry

who fostered and invested in the development of Sfarda during the golden age of Croesus.

By means of this argument, we may also detect the reasons why at Ephesos, agricul-

tural, quiescent, and highly favored by the Lydian and Persian rulers, philosophical

discussion continued and flourished with Herakleitos about 540/30 B.C., and the poetic

traditions strongly intermingled with Lydian expressions continued with Hipponax several

decades earlier. Illustrative of his Lydian–Greek world of great estates, Hipponax wrote:

"With chariot and Thracian horses all white, he rushed on to Ilion's prygoi, but there

Rhesos palmus (i.e. the Lydian qalmluś) of the Aineians lay slain stripped of armor"

(F 66).[59] The dominant non-Greek traditions and influences at Ephesos strongly

associated with the cult of Artemis, in addition to the non-colonial and non-mercantile

role of that polis, and its non-military role among the events of Harpagos' conquest of

Ionia, Oroites' rebellion, and Bagaios and Otanes' counter-campaigns, left Ephesos with a

relatively strong aristocratic rule, political stability, and prestige. Amidst a vibrant

artistic output marked by orientalization, the Ephesians excelled in innovative

architectural forms at the Artemision, and within its foundation deposits, which we may date c. 600 B.C., appear examples of the first stages of Ionian coinage, rude dumps or flans, another Ionian or perhaps specifically Ephesian innovation which Croesus later adopted for his unparalleled development of Lydian bimetallic coinage.[60] The Ephesian landed gentry had apparently retained wealth and social and political stature, supported and encouraged the Ephesian artistic innovations, and did not encounter the economic decline experienced in Ionia.   Yet, uncomfortable with Hipponax, the tyrants Athenagoras and Komas banished the poet, who fled to offshore Klazomenai (Suda sv).

Philosophy, consequently, continued at Ephesos, as Herakleitos, rejecting the pronouncements of Anaximander and Pythagoras, established the sovereignty of thought in arguing that reason, the logos, ruled as the highest arbiter.[61] Herakleitos, a direct descendant of the ancient royal Ephesian house, held the aristocratic title basileus, which he surrendered to his brother along with its accompanying privileges to sit in the front row at games, to wear a cloak of royal purple, and to participate in the religious rites of Eleusinian Demeter (Strabo 14.1.3). In the life of Herakleitos we glimpse the quintessence of an Ionian noble, a member of the landed gentry, actively engaging in the Ionian cultural revolution, and representative of the social and political participation of the gentry in the basic roles and institutions of Ionian life. On the one hand, his poetry rings with Homeric sentiment: "For the aristoi choose one thing instead of all: everlasting fame among mortals; but the polloi glut themselves like cattle" (F 254).[62] On the other hand, he, too, attacked Hesiod and his Theogony (123-5): "Hesiod is the teacher of most men; who, they are sure, knew many things, but who did not recognize day and night, for it is one."[63] As with the Ionian sculptors, Herakleitos worked in terms not wholly distinct between the abstract and the concrete, and with his Ionian philosophical predecessors engaged in a direct confrontation with his world in which a logical order had begun to emerge. As with Xenophanes of neighboring Kolophon, Herakleitos argued: "Having listened not to me but to the logos, it is wise to agree (i.e. 'to bring the logos into conformity') that all things are one" (F 199). And with the Milesians, Herakleitos recognized a positive value in strife: "It is necessary to know that war is common, and that justice is strife (eris), and all things come to be through strife and necessity (chreōn)" (F 214).[64] Strife not only ensured the continual existence of the universe, it also explained change, as Herakleitos claimed: "War is the father of all and basileus of all, and some he shows as gods, others as men, some he makes slaves (doulous), others free (*eleutherous*)" (F 215). Herakleitos conceived his divine power to have in mind something like a "master plan" for the universe, perfectly executed and the equivalent of a perfect map, not unlike Anaximander's world map, or that of Hekataios.[65]   A contemporary of Herakleitos, Hekataios of Miletos also delved into a wide-range of interests, and like Herakleitos attempted to tidy up a mass of East Greek traditions within a system of rational principles (*FGrH* 1 F 1).   In similar manner, Hekataios apparently tackled and revised Anaximander's map, that bronze table of the whole earth with all the known seas and rivers (Hdt. 5.49.1), and it may have been Hekataios' map or his revision of Anaximander's that the Milesian Aristagoras carried to Sparta in 499 B.C.[66]

II

The Persian conquest and imperial control of Lydia and the several East Greek poleis altered markedly the full flower of Ionian life.   In some regions the social and economic decline progressed at a rapid rate, while in others, and specifically Miletos and Ephesos, and perhaps Kolophon, the changes while noticeable were significantly less acute.   But the most dramatic decline in urban vitality, and the extensive loss of life, especially among the landed gentry who served in the armed forces of their poleis and manned the war ships, occurred during the gruelling twenty years of the Ionian Revolutions, which erupted in 499 B.C. and lasted beyond the summer of 478 B.C.

The blows inflicted upon Ionia by the Persians during the 490's and the first phase of the revolution finalized the economic impoverishment of the East Greek regions as it also drastically reduced the numbers of both the urban inhabitants and the military landed gentry.   And the heaviest blows fell upon Miletos.   The revolution generated by Aristagoras and his supportive faction had begun as a maneuver to protect their political power.   When their plot to gain Persian favor by leading the imperial military forces to Naxos had failed, it unfortunately spawned a brief and unrealistic liberation movement throughout the East Greek centers.   The Ionians had not developed their Panionion council into a federated political power with a significant military force to check the superior land forces commanded by the Persians.   Factionalism and city-state parochialism endemic throughout the seventh and sixth centuries B.C. continued to thwart plans for federation and, more fundamentally, military success.   The Samians, long antagonistic toward the Milesians, to save their own political roles on Samos, readily abandoned Miletos and the other East Greek states, and allowed the Persian naval forces to defeat painfully the Ionian Revolution and then to wield destruction upon Miletos and Apollo's temple at Didyma, and to transport to the eastern provinces countless hapless Milesians.

Our ancient literary sources, and specifically Herodotus' *History*, fail to provide us with even the hint of accurate numbers of war casualties or precise descriptions of urban and rural devastations. The above analysis of Herodotus (chapter 8), nevertheless, does provide at least some indication of the magnitude of the warfare in addition to suggestions, truly just minimal descriptions, of the devastations to East Greeks, Lydians, Karians, and other western Anatolians, their homes, civic and religious monuments, and cultural activities.

In analyzing, once again, the Ionian Revolutions in three phases, we can begin to enumerate the recorded campaigns and their geographical areas, and consider the problems of skirmishes, prolonged injuries and illnesses which resulted in death, and the several other factors of military campaigns which added fatalities to the Lydian, Ionian, Aiolian, East Doric, and other western Anatolian groups which had fought either with the Persian armies and navies against the Ionian rebels and their mainland Greek allies, or with those Greeks against the Persians during that more than twenty year period. First, this analysis will provide, unfortunately, only a minimal conceptualization of the devastation and loss of life fundamentally important to our understanding of the dramatic and significant decline of western Anatolia during the first decades of the fifth century B.C. Second, it will enable us to perceive more fully the reasons why Xerxes willingly and wisely abandoned a devastated Ionian area in 478 B.C. in order to turn his attentions to more important satrapies within the empire.[67] Finally, it will allow us to assess more accurately the ease by which the members of the Hellenic League in 478 B.C. were able to occupy the coastal regions of Sparda without significant opposition from the Persians or even the clusters of loyalists such as at Ephesos and Kolophon. Resultant of this analysis, we can temper the ancient Athenian reports of military force, the propaganda of liberation of the East Greeks from the Persian Empire, and the sparse records of Athenian capture of booty from the Persians during the early years of the Athenian and Confederate campaigns along the coast of Persian Sparda. This analysis will also allow us to consider the devastations encountered by the rural landed estates and the loss of life to the landed gentry, as we may also consider the loss of urban lives and project into our analysis the consideration of significant destruction to the urban units, a marked reduction in crafts and trade, and a substantial decrease in the numbers of urban inhabitants. In regard to this point, J.M. Cook succinctly described the results of the Ionian Revolutions: " . . . when the archaeologist turns his attention to the fifth century in Ionia he seeks in vain. . . . Sculpture has virtually disappeared, while painting seems to have come to an end with the Clazomenian sarcophagi and the schools of vase decoration that were associated with them. There are no new city layouts rivalling that of Samos; and only one small temple of Miletos stands out as a meager creation of this century. The minor arts also were virtually at an end; and—whether in excavation or in surface reconnaissance—the archaeologist discovers scarcely any recognizable testimony of Ionic culture, or even of habitation, on the sites of the Ionic cities in this epoch. In material civilization the fifth century seems to have been the Dark Ages of Ionia."[68]

The litany of disasters is lengthy. Even before the outbreak of the Ionian Revolution in 499 B.C., military contingents of East Greeks campaigned with the Persians: King Darius to the Danube; Megabazos across Skudra to the borders of Macedonia; Otanes against rebellious Byzantion and Kalchedon, the regions of the Troad, and the islands of Lemnos and Imbros; and Megabates' significantly unsuccessful campaign against Naxos. Then the revolution erupted: the Milesian Iatragoras raided the Persians and their fleet at Myous; the Athenians and Eretrians with Ionian assistance raided Sardis at the same time that Artaphrenes' campaign had begun the siege of Miletos. In counter-attack, the Persians routed the Greeks at Sardis and waged a successful battle at Ephesos. Ionians may have assisted the Eretrians in their naval battles in the Pamphylian Sea; yet as the Ionian naval battles off Cyprus brought victories, the landed campaigns ended in defeat. Daurises campaigned from Abydos toward Parion, and then against the Karians. Hymaies campaigned in the Troad while Otanes and Artaphrenes attacked Kyme and Klazomenai, and then marched on into the Maeander Valley against Myous and Priene. At Lade, the Persians won the crucial battle. Chians died escaping through Ephesos, and the land and sea siege of Miletos ended in the ruthless punishment of the unfaithful rebels, the slaughter of Milesian men, and the enslavement of women and children deported to the east.[69] The city of Miletos lay sacked and burned, the temple of Apollo at Didyma ruined, its treasury looted, and to signify their victory the Persians carted off to Ecbatana the bronze statue of Apollo. Some of the Milesians fled to Samos, and with many Samians then fled to Zankle. The few who remained, including members of the aristocratic Molpoi, suffered further by the movement of Karians, neither urban nor wealthy in their background, from their rural villages into the Milesian plains. In the restoration of order throughout Ionia, Karia, Aiolis, the Hellespont, and the off-shore islands, prince Artaphrenes continued the Persian campaigns against resistant Karia; into Mysia and Aiolis under the command of Harpagos; against the piratical raids of Histiaios against the Aiolian town of Atarneus; into the Thracian Chersonese in order then to quell rebellious Byzantion and Kalchedon; and against Kyzikos. Only within Herodotus' brief description of the looting, burning, and systematic capture of the inhabitants of Chios, Lesbos, and Tenedos (6.31-2) do we begin to perceive the gory details of enslavement, the castration of boys, and the dispatch of girls to the king's eastern courts.

The new rules and taxation requirements instituted by Artaphrenes, and Darius' commands delivered by the general Mardonios, obviously increased the economic and political problems of the crushed and subjugated East Greeks. Only the agricultural regions of Lebedos, Kolophon, and Ephesos, and the important temples of Apollo of Klaros and Artemis at Ephesos, appear to have escaped the havoc inflicted.[70] Unfortunately our meager sources, literary, epigraphical, and archaeological, fail to enable us to assess precisely the continuance of urban and rural life in this region, and especially the continued importance of the prominent center of Ephesos. In this region we must suspect a significant pro-Persian sentiment, perhaps due to the presence of the Lydian nobles. Throughout this period, the Lydians of Sardis and its adjacent valleys appear to have remained faithful vassals of King Darius and to have aided in the Persian efforts to regain the coastal regions of Sparda and Daskyleion. The continued military service of the Lydians to their Persian lords may also have occurred at Ephesos and Kolophon and the adjacent region of Lebedos and the minor centers at Dios Hieron and Notion. But here, only the oblique statements of Herodotus lead us to this conclusion.

In the second phase of the Greek-Persian wars, directed toward the punishment of Athens of its repudiation of the vassalage alliance sworn to King Darius in 507 B.C. and then the Athenian participation in the attack and burning of Sardis in 498 B.C., further loss of life must be accounted. While Herodotus was again very vague in regard to which ethnic groups fought in the Persian campaigns from 492 to 484 B.C., we must consider the possibility of East Greek contingents serving Mardonios amid the ranks of the Imperial Army and Navy as he campaigned to Mt. Athos only to be seriously thwarted by storms and the harassing raids of the Thracian Brygi. Other East Greek contingents may also have served Datis as he besieged Naxos and Karystos, attacked and burned Eretria, and as he unsuccessfully campaigned on the plain of Marathon. Whether East Greeks served in the Persian army to quell the Jewish and Egyptian Revolt of 486-4 B.C., and other Asian military campaigns, we do not know, but that possibility is to be noted.

In the third phase of the wars, the evidence for wide-scale Ionian participation among the Persian forces, personally led by King Xerxes against Athens, confirms the Ionian military service (for whatever reason, fear or loyalty) under the Persian commanders. It also supports the suggestions that Ionians participated in the earlier Mt. Athos, Jewish and Egyptian campaigns, and lays stress upon the important point that armored nobles and other Ionians less wealthy served and died during the rigorous Persian campaigns of 480 and 479 B.C. in Europe. While Herodotus claims that the Persian general Artabanos questioned the Ionian loyalty to the king (7.51-2), that statement may be an Herodotean literary device, for the historian elsewhere notes that the Ionians affirmed their fidelity, neither defecting nor lagging behind (8.85.1), and at Salamis the Samians specifically fought to the point of special honor (8.85.3). Lydians and Mysians marched in rank with the infantry (Hdt. 7.74.1), as Lykians, Karians, and the East Dorians (according to Herodotus' questionable figures) manned 150 ships (7.92-3). The Pontic peoples set sail with 100 ships, the Aiolians with 60, and the mainland Ionians with 100 (Hdt. 7.94). Fourteen years earlier, at Lade, the mainland Ionians had entered into battle with 123 ships and had been sorely defeated (Hdt. 6.8). If Herodotus' figures reflect historical validity, the engagement of 100 ships to sail to Athens in 480 B.C. must represent a heavy military impressment of the Ionians significantly overburdened with earlier taxes and military service, and with considerable loss of manpower to be greatly accentuated by the forthcoming campaigns. This overburden of military service is further underscored by Herodotus' figures that at Lade 230 ships from Samos, Chios, and Lesbos had entered into that battle, before the desertions, but that in 480 B.C., the islanders manned only 17 ships (7.95.1), and among them the valiant and loyal Samians.

Xerxes' campaign across Skudra, Macedonia, and through Thessaly, undoubtedly generated minor skirmishes, and then certainly the major campaigns at Artemision and Thermopylae, and finally the crucial battle in the straits of Salamis. At that battle, Herodotus claimed 200 Persian ships perished, a loss which significantly reduced the Imperial Fleet (8.97.1), a point accentuated by Aeschylus' poetic interpretation of the Greek devastation inflicted upon the Imperial Persian Fleet *(Persae* 548-90).[71] Then, Mardonios' campaigns into Thessaly and back into Attica, Artabazos' Thracian campaign and battle against Potidaia and Olynthos, the final Persian defeat at Plataia, the battle at Mykale, and the burning of the Imperial Fleet, further emphasize the constant loss of Ionian lives and Ionian ships. Although the Persian military forces and manned ships never amounted to the numbers that Herodotus and the other ancient Greek authors attempted to count, the Persian Imperial Armies and Navy nevertheless were strong enough to continue the control of the greater part of the empire. Substantial losses of Ionian military forces, however, in particular of the landed gentry, and of ships, gravely marked the calamities throughout Ionia by 478 B.C. The events of Mykale did not mark a liberation or recovery for the Ionians but the further entrenched wasteland of the new Dark Age.

Perhaps no other ancient epigraphical or literary source reveals the plight of the Ionians during the decade or two after Xerxes' monumental expedition to Athens than the fragmentary inscriptions from Teos:

A. Whoever makes drugs that are poisonous (for use) against the Teians, either as a community *(xynon)*, or against an individual, that man is to die, both himself and his genos. Whoever prevents grain from being imported into the land *(gēn)* of Teos, either by craft or by cunning, either by sea or by (the) mainland; or, after it is imported, export it, that man is to die, both himself and his genos.

B. Whoever of the Teians, against the Public Examiner *(euthynos)* or the *aisymnetes* . . . . [disobeys] or rises in insurrection *(epanistaito)* . . . . he is to die, both himself and his genos. And in the future, whoever is *aisymnetes* in Teos or the land of Teos . . . . knowingly betrays . . . . the polis and the land of the Teians, or the men on the island[72] or on the sea (?) in the future (?) or in the Aroian guard-station *(peripolion* or township); or (whoever) in the future knowingly

commits treason or brigandage, or takes brigands under his protection, or knowingly commits piracy or takes pirates under his protection, (men) from the land of Teos or from the sea and cart off
plunder, or (whoever) knowingly conceives some evil plan against the
Teian community (with the assistance) of either Greeks or
barbarians, he is to die, both himself and his genos. Whoever serving
as *timiouchoi* (Public Officials) do not have the curse invoked when
by (the statue of the deity) Dynamis there is seated (the crowd for)
the agonistic festivals in (the months) Anthesterion, Herakleon, and
Dios, the curses shall apply to them. Whoever should take the stelae
upon which the curse is inscribed and either smashes them or paints
out the letters or makes them illegible, he is to die, both himself and
his family.[73]

The inscription does not note problems in the abstract, but rather vividly reveals the
problems of daily Teian life resultant of the cataclysmic series of events, especially
since 499 B.C., which brought political turmoil and acute economic depression to central
Ionia, and the demands of stringent punishments of death to the violators of the law and
to their families, demands which necessitated exacting curses. The chief problem lay in
the desperate need for grain, which the agricultural estates and other farms of Teos
could not supply to the state's significantly reduced population, supplies of grain which
Teians eagerly sought to import from whatever source they could, from the interior,
other coastal regions, or from overseas markets.[74] And the problems of insufficient
import was further marked by malicious speculation by some Teians in exporting what
had just been obtained and apparently for higher prices as the speculators found more
lucrative markets elsewhere, and very possibly in the neighboring Ionian poleis. This
acute demand for food compounded the political problems of insurrection, magisterial
betrayal, treason, brigandage and piracy (seen as distinctly different acts of malice),
widescale poisonings, and malevolent plans or cooperation by Teians with other Greeks no
less with Persians. The aristocratic magistrates, the timiouchoi, euthynoi, and
aisymnetai, who tried to govern their hapless state, through factionalism and strife
compounded by the severe economic depression and social upheavals, were also guilty of
many of the crimes plaguing the Teian polis. There is little reason not to believe that

these problems occurred elsewhere in Ionia, especially in devastated Miletos, while perhaps less so in Ephesos and possibly in Kolophon.

For reasons essentially unmeasureable, the major islands of Samos, Chios, and Lesbos continued to function remarkably better, perhaps because of continued political and economic development and the interests of their tyrants who survived Darius' orders of 493 B.C. to restore the traditional aristocracies. The islands did fare better, recovered and stabilized, and eagerly joined forces with the Hellenic League in the days after Mykale.

Any estimate of the extent of physical damage suffered by the mainland Ionian urban centers and the rural estates, farms, and villages, or of the numbers of men from the several economic and social classes killed in war related incidents, and the numbers of men, women, and children deported to distant parts of the Persian Empire, or the numbers of women and children killed in the general melée, cannot be precisely determined. But to understand more fully the events in Ionia during the fifth century B.C., whereby the offensive campaigns of the Delian Confederacy conflicted with the frontier of the Persian Empire, and occasionally forced the eruption of factionalism and civil war within several of the Ionian poleis, it is necessary to examine Ionia once again in yet other terms in order to focus upon the key problems of the landed gentry during the fifth century B.C., about which our meager literary and epigraphical sources provide a limited understanding.

In poetic style and symbolism, Aeschylus in his tragic *Persians* presented in Athens in 472 B.C. stressed the marked depopulation of the cities of Persia, empty never to be filled again, empty with the death of countless young men.[75] Most vivid are his poetic lines of the devastation inflicted upon the soldiers of Susa: "The great citadel of Susa empty of men" (119), "So the Persians' city can lament" (511-2), "Susa groans for its emptiness of men" (730), and ". . . emptiness brought to this citadel of Susa" (761). With similar poetic force, Aeschylus pronounced that the Persian royal house might fall, that rumors of revolution had spread (715), and that the Dowager Queen Atossa feared for her son and his empire (531). The Persian failures in Greece and the extensive loss of Persian infantry divisions and naval squadrons had seriously shaken an overtaxed empire. While we must mollify Aeschylus' heightened poetic sentiments written to accentuate the Athenian view of Xerxes' hybris in his attack upon the "freedom loving" Greeks, beneath the poetics and the poignant line ". . . all Asia's land moans in emptiness" (549) and the allusions to the emptiness of Susa rests the precise historical awareness by Aeschylus and his Athenian audiences of the countless loss of life to all who had participated. For Aeschylus, Susa represented the Persian Empire and his perception of the "groans for the emptiness of men" may, more directly, represent known Ionian groans and lamentations. Susa remained secure and prosperous unlike the stark and bleak Ionian poleis where the heaviest losses had fallen upon the armored troops, and the nobles and the landed gentry, who had fought under the Persian standards. At Persepolis, Darius had once described the Ionian shores as *by the bitter sea*, the salty waters of the Aegean (DPg), but now along those same shores families lamented the bitterness of war.

III

During the seventh and sixth centuries B.C., the East Greek poleis developing along the eastern frontier of the Lydian Empire encountered problems of individual stress and societal distortion as the East Greek, Lydian, Karian, and other Anatolian populations increased in numbers and in the demands upon the agricultural and other natural resources and, in turn, increased the techniques by which the peoples in their respective societal niches could expand and augment those resources. Within the government of each district political group, in transition between monarchy and aristocracy or as established aristocracy, members of the middle and upper economic classes, essentially the landed gentry, sought more living space and more resources for the sustenance of their lives. That pressure distinctly did not come from the ranks of the poor but rather from the discontented members of the middle and upper classes, whose collective individual stresses had begun to transform into the stage of societal distortion. In turn, the governments had to respond and seek means to alleviate the pressures, to revitalize the state in order to survive and continue rather than to falter and decline.[76]

Two courses of action lay before the ruling kings and aristocrats. One was to apply restraining pressures upon the members of the middle and upper classes and their overstrained niche–spaces by employing systematic methods of oppression, regimentation, bureaucracy, firm class regulation, rationing, and the imposition of strict caste subordination. This could increase the factionalism and strife latent or overt within the social system and result in revolution, which would produce either devastation or the positive steps by which a new government relieved the demands for space and resources through an intricate revitalization program. The other course of action was for the existing governments to relieve stress by finding new space and more resources through colonies, trade, and wars. The latter is precisely the course of action taken throughout Lydia and the East Greek poleis, and it, in turn, produced the Ionian cultural revolution of the early sixth century B.C., which illuminates the economic investments of the landed gentry in that cultural Blütezeit. Social oppression, however, was an inevitable consequence of a continued rise of populations, as the defenders of the achieved high way of life by necessity pushed against their competitors, an unpleasant social interaction noted in the anti-aristocratic lines of the Ionian poets.

In the poleis in which the niches of the middle and upper classes became crowded, trade inevitably developed. As a consequence of that trade, the populations continued to increase and grow denser, and generated new opportunities in the crafts which also increased as the members of the upper class sought more material prerogatives of their rank. An increased need and training of the military forces, and the acquisition of better arms and armor, further marked the advancement of trading poleis, and also of the activities of the military forces. Miletos, obviously, exemplified this niche analysis, yet other Ionian poleis, specifically Ephesos without colonization and overseas trade activities, also experienced a significant growth of the middle and upper classes. In the case of Ephesos, the movement of overland trade to Sardis and other urban centers, and the prime importance of the Artemision temple and its religious functions, provided the Ephesians with alternative methods by which to obtain resources. The limits of geographical space at Miletos, which accentuated the population crowding, did not occur to restrict the community at Ephesos, which did expand up the Kayster River Valley and into Magnesia-on-the-Maeander. Fundamental to these two diverse systems, nevertheless, were extensive numbers of aggressive landed gentry.

Within this ecological analysis of the social niche systems, the middle and upper classes were the first to feel the pressures of the growth of populations and crowding. As a result, the ruling classes, which had previously been sympathetic to the landless and non-wealthy urban dwellers, the banausoi or chairomachia, became selfish and oppressive. The social troubles identified as societal distortions, manifest in factionalism and the references to strife, become episodic rather than continuous, as the governments found methods by which to allocate peoples of the lower class to narrower social and economic niches. It is at this point that had we sufficient ancient sources, we might be able to detect the political machinations of the aristocratic factions which supported and elevated members of their own groups to the status of tyrant, a position clearly unlike that of the Persian appointed hyparchos. The high correlation of the self-generated tyrannies throughout the East Greek region intertwined with the hallmarks of the Ionian cultural revolution underscores the importance of the aristocracy in successfully seeking new resources and space, and in their crucial role in the development of armed military forces.

In 478 B.C., however, the earlier problems of the niche-system in Ionia had vastly changed. Twenty years and more of wars, rebellions, and campaigns abroad had significantly killed off members of the middle and upper classes, and of the lower class as well, and had eliminated the demands for space. The demands for resources, such as the dramatic Teian needs for grain, came not from the problems of local overcrowding but from the impoverishment of the farms complicated by the violent social disturbances among the agriculturalists. In 478, therefore, Xerxes withdrew his Persian garrisons, soldiers, and officers from the bleak and desolate coastal zone, into which the revived naval forces of the Hellenic League sailed and claimed to have "liberated" the East Greeks from Persian tyranny. In fact, the League simply swept up the sad Ionian remains abandoned by a wise king. The Mede had come and withdrawn.

IV

Lydians, Karians, and Lykians

"These were the groups which took part in ... [Xerxes'] expedition [against the Greeks] (7.61.1)." "The Lydians were armed very nearly in the Greek manner (7.74.1)." "The Mysians wore upon their heads helmets made after the fashion of their country and carried small shields; they used as javelins staves with one end hardened in the fire. The Mysians are Lydian colonists. . . ." (7.74.1-2)

Thus Herodotus described the landed Anatolian forces which invaded Athens in 480 B.C. But beyond these brief entries within his descriptive catalogue, the Halikarnassian historian focused predominantly upon the Greeks; consequently, we lose sight of the

Anatolian national forces bound to the satrapal governments of Sparda and Daskyleion. Our understanding of Persian control in western Anatolia during the fifth century B.C., therefore, rests upon scattered and meager literary, epigraphical, and archaeological sources, and an analysis of Persian imperial policies elsewhere within the greater Achaemenid Empire.

West of Mysia proper, throughout the Troad region of the satrapy of Daskyleion, surveyed in detail by J.M. Cook, the sparse archaeological evidence sketchily illuminates the changes occurring among the Greek settlements beginning about 700 B.C.,[77] amidst sparse native Anatolian settlements.[78] The Greek communities developed during the sixth century B.C. were marked by major architectural works c. 530 B.C.: a major temple at Neandreia, a single room (9.34 m. wide, 21.12 m. long) with a central row of seven elaborate Aiolic capitals;[79] at Assos, the notable hexastyle Doric temple with an Ionic frieze dedicated to the goddess Athena;[80] and the elaborate Ionic style terracotta plaques which graced a major building at Kebrene.[81] In the fifth century B.C., however, the urban Troad centers underwent a significant cultural decline which continued through the fourth century B.C.   This cultural shift is best noted at Ilion, within the well published archaeological records of the Troy VIII settlement.[82] Only at Kebrene is there evidence of a substantial and important fifth century urban center.

In eastern Mysia and the central region of the satrapy of Daskyleion, in comparison, the evidence is extremely sparse because of the lack of systematic archaeological survey. At Kyzikos the ruins still lie amidst groves of trees. Two mid-sixth century marble reliefs are all that remain, at present, of a major architectural project.[83] With the other Mysians, the Greek Kyzikines apparently had marched to Athens as loyal subjects of Megabazos, the satrap of Daskyleion. To Oibares, Megabazos' son, the Kyzikines had sworn their oaths of allegiance (Hdt. 6.33.3). South of Kyzikos, the archaeological exploration of the Lydo-Achaemenid acropolis at Daskyleion,[84] unlike the Greek poleis and centers in the Troad and at Kyzikos, reveals that that center retained a substantial Lydian and native Anatolian population, which flourished during the late sixth and throughout the fifth centuries B.C. as an important Achaemenid satrapal capital. We should, therefore, expect to find evidence for an extensive settlement of urban dwellings and estates of the landed gentry along the agriculturally rich plains which flank Daskyleion's acropolis and Lake Manyas' southern shore.[85] Surface sherds analyzed from atop the acropolis suggest an active local pottery industry and the importation of significant quantities of Corinthian and Attic wares, but they do not allow us to deduce any alteration in population.[86] Today, the region offers extensive woods and a broad lake for hunting and fishing and an abundance of wildfowl living among the marshes, as it no doubt offered the fifth century B.C. inhabitants.

At the end of the seventh century B.C., Lydian nobles serving King Sadyattes had settled Daskyleion (Nic. Dam. *FGrH* 90 F 63), from which point merchants traversing the northern caravan routes struck out across the plains for the Milesian colony at Kyzikos and the developing colonial and mercantile activities through the Propontis. By the reign of Croesus, Daskyleion had grown and become an integral part of the Lydian Empire (Hipponax F 104), a thriving Lydian center which the Persians conquered, incorporated into their imperial system, and elevated to the rank of capital city for *Tyaiy Drayahyā*, the satrapy of "The People who Live by the Sea."[87] Sometime thereafter, and perhaps during the satrapal rule of Mitrobates, masons and laborers fortified the acropolis with a late archaic circuit wall.[88] Yet with the chaos following the assassination of King Bardiya and Darius' usurpation of the Achaemenid throne, rebellion erupted within Sparda and Daskyleion, as Oroites, in what appears as a power play for wealth and position, attacked Daskyleion and murdered Mitrobates (Hdt. 3.126.2). Mitrobates, serving King Cambyses, may have supported Darius' claims to the throne, as perhaps did the satrap of Cappadocia, yet the evidence is not clear. Darius' victory in Parsa and Babylon, nevertheless, ushered in a new period of Achaemenid control, first the murder of the rebel Sardian satrap Oroites, and then the extensive reorganization of the Anatolian satrapies—Cappadocia, Sparda, Daskyleion, and semi-autonomous Cilicia—within the tightly knit system of imperial and satrapal rules, edicts, governors, garrisons, and bureaucrats.

To the satrapal throne at Daskyleion, Darius ultimately appointed Megabazos (Hdt. 6.33.3) as just reward for his military activities and successes in the conquest of western Skudra (Hdt. 4.143.1, 144.3; 5.1.1, 2.1-2, 10; 7.108.1), but not until several years after the revolutions in western Anatolia had been quelled and Darius had returned from his European campaign into Skudra and western Scythia. It was at Sardis, before Darius set off for Babylon c. 513 (?), that Megabazos returned from Skudra with the Paeonian hostages, met with the king, and by royal order transferred to Otanes the military command in the north-east Aegean and the straits (Hdt. 5.23-6). Bagaios had apparently been governing all of the western regions since the murder of Oroites, but of this Herodotus gives us little hint as to the problems which had developed since the summer of 522 B.C., or after the appointment of Megabazos to Daskyleion.

With the outbreak of the Milesian revolution in 499 B.C., the rebellions which spread throughout Karia, Ionia, and Aiolis, also spread among the coastal East Greek settlements of the Troad, and mark a break with Persian suzerainty at Daskyleion. Herodotus' brief statements are the first hint of disruption to Megabazos' satrapal rule of the Troad, and indicate that the main centers of rebellion extended along the crucial Hellespontine coast from Ilion, at the southern point where the Hellespont flows into the Aegean Sea, to Parion, at the northern point and the beginning of the expansive Propontis. Darius' son-in-law Daurises led the Persian forces against the central coastal region from Abydos to the borders of Parion (Hdt. 5.117), and with the king's imperial order to Daurises to campaign quickly into Karia, a second Persian army led by another son-in-law Hymaies invaded the central plains of Ilion (Hdt. 5.112). The Persian aims were clear: to suppress rebellion and to maintain the Hellespontine ferry-line between Abydos and Sestos and communication with settlements in Skudra. With the death of Hymaies, however, Herodotus does not refer to further problems in the Troad, and by the time of the battle at Lade, Megabazos' control of all of Daskyleion had again been secured.

The brief Herodotean statements and the archaeological records, which together indicate a decline in the material development of the coastal East Greek poleis in the Troad in addition to the decline in the numbers of military forces from those poleis, due to both military service for and rebellion against the Persians, enable us to consider a marked alteration in the lives of the landed gentry remaining throughout the Troad and apparently all of Daskyleion, including the satrapal center, during the first decade of the fifth century B.C. Continued demands by Megabazos and Darius for armed forces from the satrapy of Daskyleion to participate in the imperial campaigns were further compounded by Xerxes' orders for new troops to be levied for the expedition into Greece. In 480 B.C., Megabazos once again campaigned into Europe, this time with the Xerxes' fleet and in joint high command with the king's brother Achaemenes and with Prexaspes, the son of Aspathines—a close aid to Darius (Hdt. 7.97).[89] On land,

Megabazos' son Pherendates led the Sarangian troops (Hdt. 7.76.1). Unfortunately, we do not know who remained at Daskyleion to govern in Megabazos' absence, nor do we know the fate of Megabazos and his son, who seem not to have returned from Greece. Many others, Lydians, Greeks, and Anatolians, from the satrapy of Daskyleion, also may not have returned.

In the days after the disaster at Mykale, and before the king's departure for Susa and the East (Hdt. 9.108.2), Xerxes apparently issued several important decisions. One was to withdraw from the impoverished coastal zone held by the East Greeks. Another was the appointment of the general Artabazos to the satrapal throne of Daskyleion (Thuc. 1.129.1, 3)[90] not only as a reward for his loyalty and courage in escorting the king back to Asia in the autumn of 480 B.C., but also for his return to Asia in the autumn of 479 B.C. with the remnants of the defeated Persian armies. To secure Daskyleion as a major Persian military buffer against future Greek rebellion or aggression, Xerxes, therefore, entrusted that strategic acropolis to him. Artabazos was not only a good and loyal general having commanded the Parthians and Chorasmians in Greece (Hdt. 7.66.2), he was also Xerxes' older second cousin of royal blood, the son of Farnaka (Pharnakes: Hdt. 7.66.1; 8.126.1; 9.41.1; 66.1; 89.1), whose father Arsames was the king's great-grandfather. At Persepolis, Farnaka held the important post of chief economic official for King Darius (e.g. PFT 1793, 1795), where he transmitted royal edicts, issued orders on his own authority, and received extraordinary daily rations, and at the palace ranked with Gobryas, Darius' helper and the father of Mardonios who died at Plataia.[91] Artabazos, consequently, served Xerxes admirably, and established at Daskyleion a secure satrapal power, which he passed on to his descendants, his son Pharnabazos[92] and his grandson Pharnakes who governed at the outbreak of the Peloponnesian War (Thuc. 2.67.1) and who was apparently still alive in 414 B.C. (Ar. Aves 1028-30; Schol. 1028). Two years later, in 412 B.C., Artabazos' great-grandson Pharnabazos II was continuing his family's governance of Daskyleion (Thuc. 8.6.1), and continued it into the early fourth century B.C. (Xen. Hell. 4.1.1).

Of Daskyleion and the palace of Pharnabazos II, a vivid description was written by Xenophon in the early fourth century B.C. (Hell. 4.1.15-6): "scattered about the palace were many large villages (komai), with abundant supplies, and with excellent animals, some enclosed in paradises, and others in open spaces. A river flowed by full of all kinds of fish, in addition, there was wild fowl in abundance for those who knew how to catch it." In those villages, the descendants of the Lydians, Anatolians, and Persians, who had fought with Kings Darius and Xerxes against the East and mainland Greeks, continued to live.[93]

In 481-480 B.C., while Xerxes prepared at Sardis his great military expedition against Greece, from that satrapal palace his imperial heralds and messengers delivered to Daskyleion hundreds of documents exacting supplies and other war necessities from Megabazos, the peoples of Daskyleion, and the landed gentry dwelling in and around those villages.   Other documents may have emanated from Persepolis and Susa, or other imperial and satrapal centers.   The documents, either papyrus or parchment, have disintegrated in the course of time, but more than 300 complete or fragmentary clay sealings remain: 41 with seal impressions, some with Aramaic and Old Persian inscriptions, and one fragmentary Greek inscription.   Of the seals, the types found at Daskyleion are similar to those found at Persepolis: the king-hero fighting the horned and winged lion, and two winged and crowned man-bulls standing upright beneath the winged *xvarnah* disk; and several bear the king's personal seal and the royal proclamation: "I am Xerxes, King."[94] There is no reason, therefore, not to suspect that Daskyleion, too, bore substantial losses of men during the campaigns into Greece and Tigranes' battle at Mykale.

South of Ionia, the borders of Miletos give way to the serrated crest of Mt. Latmos, wild range of granite crags, and the small hilltop settlements and pastoral hamlets of Karia. Towering mountains, steep valleys, and immense forests of oak and pine dominate most of the region. And along the western coast settlements of Dorian Greeks clung to the shores.[95] The Persian wars had also brought to the eastern Dorians, the Karians, and the Lykians in the mountainous regions beyond, significant losses to their military forces.   As the Mysians and Lydians marched overland in 480 B.C. amidst Xerxes' infantry forces, naval squadrons of Dorians, Karians, and Lykians sailed with the Egyptians and Cypriots of the greater Persian Imperial Navy. According to Herodotus of Dorian Halikarnassos:

> "The Karians furnished 70 ships and were equipped as were the Greeks,
> and carried in addition scimitars and daggers" (7.93); "the Dorians of Asia
> furnished 30 ships, also armed like Greeks" (7.93); and "the Lykians

furnished 50 ships, their crews wearing greaves and breastplates, and bearing bows of cornel wood, reed arrows without feathers, and javelins. Their outer garment was of goat-skin, which hung from their shoulders; their head-dress a hat encircled with plumes; and the other weapons were daggers and scimitars" (7.92).

The eastern Dorians had settled the poleis of Iasos, Halikarnassos, Keramos, and (Old) Knidos[96] while, beyond, the Karians related to the Lydians and Mysians (Hdt. 1.171.6) and, farther east, the Lykians, dwelt in clusters of small mountain hamlets or villages in dendritic systems about small central place centers ruled by native and Median dynasts. Of those who sailed to Greece, many did not return. The expedition to Athens had reduced the numbers of armed warriors from Karia and Lykia, the descendants of armed soldiers who had earlier fought against the Persians in two major campaigns.

For the regions of Karia and Lykia, unfortunately, the archaeological surveys have not been sufficiently extensive to indicate a major transition of cultural and settlement decline at the end of the sixth century and the early decades of the fifth century B.C.[97] The statements of Herodotus, however, do indicate extensive Persian military campaigns throughout Karia during the last four decades of the sixth century B.C. in addition to stringent demands upon the Karians and the Lykians for military service in the imperial armies and navies. We may, therefore, strongly suspect throughout Karia and Lykia cultural decline and loss of population as witnessed in Ionia and in the Troad.

After the fall of the Ionians to the Persian armies in the 540's B.C., Harpagos had campaigned into Karia and Lykia. The Dorian poleis submitted with no opposition, except for a momentary resistance from the Knidians (Hdt. 1.174). Of the Karians, the Pedasians alone resisted Harpagos' occupation invasion, opposing him and thwarting his army from their fortified mountain stronghold at Lida; but in the course of time they, too, submitted (Hdt. 1.175). The native Anatolian Kaunians also readily submitted to Harpagos' onslaughts (Hdt. 1.171.1, 172); but at Xanthos in the heart of Lykia, a small band of Xanthians bravely resisted the inevitable. As the Persians finally overpowered the Xanthians, and breached the walls of their citadel, the Xanthians set fire to their buildings and possessions, and to the last man fought with sword in hand, not one escaping (Hdt. 1.176.2).

After the fall of Xanthos, the Persians resettled the Xanthos River Valley with "foreign immigrants" (epēlydes: Hdt. 1.176.3), settlers moved from the eastern satrapies of the empire and Medians of Harpagos' own clan, which held Xanthos and the Lykian regions as vassals loyal to the Persian throne. Eighty Xanthian families (histieōn) who, for some unknown reason yet perhaps dwelling in their highland summer homes, happened not to be in Xanthos, but returned and peacefully resettled in the valley as loyal subjects of their Harpagid dynastic lords, and the overlordship of the Achaemenid kings. Elsewhere, Cyrus had settled Hyrkanians in the Hermos River Valley, and apparently Assyrians from Nineveh at the small undeveloped settlement of Aphrodisias on the headwaters of the Morsynos branch of the Maeander River.[98] The Persians had adopted the Assyrian practice of the transplantation of ethnic groups throughout the empire in order to reduce rebellion and to increase imperial security. In Lykia, the Harpagid dynasty continued to serve their Persian lords faithfully.[99]

In the turmoil of the abortive attempt by the Milesians in 499 B.C. to revolt against Persia, the Karians joined the Ionians and failed. General Daurises invaded Karia and campaigned southward up the Marsyas River Valley into the rugged Karian highlands. At the White Pillars, a meeting place of the Karian federated tribes, the Karians decided once again to resist the Persian forces. The Karian dynast Pixodaros of Kindya (south of Dorian Iasos) argued to advance down the valley and meet the Persians on the northern shores of the Maeander River, and not to falter in the aggressive cause (Hdt. 5.118), but others persuaded the Karian forces to fight the Persians in the Marsyas Valley. Of this clash, Herodotus noted that ten thousand Karians died after fighting obstinately a long battle in which they were overcome by Persian odds (6.119.1; the number may be exaggerated but does represent significant losses). The Karians, still undaunted, again rallied at the Karian shrine of Zeus of Armies at Labraynda,[100] and with Milesian and allied soldiers rallying to their cause, the Karians attacked the Persians a second time, and suffered greater losses than in the earlier defeat, many of their army falling, with the Milesians forces hardest stricken (Hdt. 5.120). Yet, the Karians reassembled and for a third time attacked the Persian forces on the road to Pedasa, south-west of Kindya in the center of the Myndos peninsula, just north of Dorian Halikarnassos (Hdt. 8.104), Herakleides of Mylasa plotted the ambush of the Persians, and in killing Daurises and his generals Amorges, Sisimakes, and Myrsos, the son of Gyges, apparently the captain of a

Lydian division, he won that battle.

The Karians had taken every advantage they could to protect their settlements and dynastic rulers, whether it meant siding with the Persians or with the rebellious Ionians. At Myous several years earlier, Herakleides' brother Oliatos had been seized by the rebellious Milesians at the onset of their rebellion. At that point Oliatos, the son of Ibanollios, had been serving the Persian forces in the attack upon Naxos. Now, on the road to Pedasa, his brother Herakleides had joined with Milesians to fight the Persian forces. At Mylasa a second sacred precinct, the temple of Zeus Karios, also served as a common sanctuary for the federated Karian tribes, and in the heat of the Karian rebellion, the leading nobles of Mylasa rallied there for common cause. Yet, in spite of the Persian defeat near Pedasa, with the failure of the "Milesian Affair" at the battle of Lade, the Persians once again controlled all Karia, the native dynastic centers and the Dorian poleis. To reduce the potential Karian opposition to imperial rule, the Persians transported the Pedasians to the rural districts of Miletos along the Karian northern frontier and the rugged mountains of the Latmos ridge (Hdt. 6.20). The Pedasians had earlier resisted Harpagos' conquest, and in the Karian rebellion apparently had supported Herakleides and the ambush of the Persian troops. Unfortunately, Herodotus is silent in regard to the activities of the loyalist Harpagids and Xanthians dwelling in the Xanthos Valley, and whether they assisted the Persian suppression of Karia after the battle near Pedasa.

With the armies of Mardonios and Datis campaigning into Greece, squadrons of East Dorian, Karian, and Lykian ships may have sailed with those commanders just as later they joined Xerxes' great Persian Imperial Navy setting sail for Athens and the crucial straits of Salamis. The death and destruction in the early campaigns, at Salamis, and then at Mykale, doubtlessly reduced the armed forces of the Dorian poleis and the Karian and Lykian urban centers and hamlets. Radical changes in population and cultural resources, therefore, must have occurred in the southern regions, just as they had occurred elsewhere throughout Sparda and Daskyleion. This new period of poverty compounded by the strategic problems of Persian administration in the mountainous settlements were, apparently, primary factors in the king's decision to withdraw from the coastal zones and apparently later the Karian Marsyas River Valley, yet to hold the Maeander Valley from Magnesia-on-the-Maeander eastward as well as the central Lykian regions still subject to the loyalist Harpagids.

Xerxes' strategic decision to withdraw from the coastal zones of the Aegean and Hellespont enabled the satraps of Sparda and Daskyleion to reform their lines of defense along a new and more viable frontier. Satrapal garrisons and officers retrenched within the Lydian and Harpagid settlements of the interior in opposition to the East Greek poleis along the coastal zones of the Troad, the coastal edge of Aiolis and Ionia, and the Dorian poleis and Karian settlements of the western mountains and valleys of Karia. Within this zone, the significant losses to the armed landed gentry had resulted in the marked decline of the wealth bases, and the visible abridgements in crafts and mercantile activities. The military activities of the Hellenic League in 478 B.C. compounded by similar activities of the Delian Confederacy in 477 B.C. and later years, consequently, confirmed the new frontier of the Persian Empire in western Anatolia. But what the mainland Greeks "liberated" was a zone unable to provide either the fiscal tributes or the military services commanded earlier by Darius and Xerxes, and a zone which Xerxes realized would no longer be fundamental in importance or beneficial to his empire. The reduced man-power and fiscal tribute would not off-set the imperial costs of holding those coastal regions, not only impoverished but also consistently rebellious.

Although the Persians were withdrawing from the coastal regions, imperial and satrapal control of the Lydians settled on the interior plains of Sparda and Daskyleion remained firm, as did Lydian loyalty and service to King Xerxes and his empire. In that loyalty rested the key to Xerxes' conscious actions to withdraw only from the coastal zones but to remain resolutely entrenched east of the coastal ridges and mountains. Although Herodotus was, for the most part, silent in regard to Lydian affairs after the fall of Croesus, the several events he does mention, often in passing, enable us to reconstruct the steps in affirming Lydian loyalty and entrenching Persian control.

More than sixty-five years earlier, the Persian forces commanded by Cyrus had defeated the Lydian armies at Sardis, and following Paktyes' unsuccessful revolt, the Persians commanded by general Mazares again defeated Lydian armies on the plains of the Hermos Valley. Mazares, thereupon, systematically reduced the Lydian high powered cavalry forces, potentially rebellious, to a rural landed gentry subservient to Sardian military and satrapal controls. During the months of Harpagos' campaigns throughout Ionia and Karia, the Lydians, consequently, remained quiescent. Although we may suspect that while they served dutifully in Oroites' rebellion against Darius and his campaigns against the satrapies of Daskyleion and Cappadocia, following Bagaios' recontrol of Sardis, the Lydians throughout central Sparda were omitted by Herodotus as being the target of Otanes' campaigns in subduing Cappadocia, Daskyleion, and the East Greeks. Several years later, Darius himself securely held Sardis and ruled from the satrapal throne within the acropolitan palace, both before and after his expedition through eastern Skudra and into western Scythia. In spite of Herodotus' general silence regarding Lydian affairs, by means of his indication of Persia's secure control over the interior Lydian regions of Sparda (except for Oroites' brief rebellion), we may strongly suspect a continued firm loyalty of the Lydians to their Persian overlords.[101] That loyalty was again secured by the stringent controls established during the satrapal governance of prince Artaphrenes in conformance to Darius' orders for the multi-faceted and all pervasive reorganization of the empire. The records of Lydian artisans working upon Darius' palaces at Susa, Persepolis, and earlier at Pasargadae, and the reliefs of Spardians bearing encomium tribute carved upon the monumental staircases of Darius' great apadana audience hall at Persepolis further indicate the Persian integration of the Spardians into the imperial system (Plate 2).[102]

Continued Lydian loyalty, tribute, and military service to Artaphrenes and Darius during the turbulent years of the Ionian rebellions ignited by the Milesians and then Mardonios' first landed campaign against the Greeks must be strongly suspected in light of Herodotus' failure to note contrary activities. We may, therefore, also consider that Lydians served in the Persian armies during those events just as they formed a major component in Xerxes' armies marching toward Athens in 480 B.C. The king's residency in Sardis during the winter of 481/480 B.C. had not stirred Lydian rebellion or caused discontent. At Kelainai on the Cappadocian frontier of Sparda, and at the headwaters of the Maeander River (Hdt. 7.26.3), in the autumn of 481 B.C., Xerxes had gathered his Asian forces to which, by the time he set out from Sardis in the spring of 480 B.C., he had added the Lydian and Mysian contingents descriptively noted by Herodotus (7.74). There is no doubt that many of those Lydians died during the costly military Persian campaigns through Greece, at Athens, and on the battlefield of Plataia, just as many Lydians apparently had also died during early Persian campaigns. In the autumn of 478 B.C., Xerxes' imperial control of the Lydians dwelling in the interior plains and valleys of

Sparda and Daskyleion remained unquestionably secure, and with notable satrapal strength and vitality which continued throughout the fifth century B.C. Even as later kings lost this early firm control over Sparda, the satrapy remained secure and vibrant within.

Xerxes' decision to retrench his satrapal forces behind the coastal regions had been formulated in recognition of the fundamental factors which had placed his empire in 478 B.C. under acute stress: his sober realization of the extensive losses of imperial forces in the Greek wars and the unrest throughout the empire and the rebellious conditions in the key satrapies. The recognition of the poverty of the East Greeks was clearly a secondary factor, yet significant, in Xerxes' actions to withdraw in order to preserve the imperial system, but did signal a major shift in Achaemenid policy which would prove to be detrimental to Xerxes' rule. The withdrawal from the coast marked the abandonment of the Achaemenid policy to retain, at all cost, the lands conquered by one's predecessors and the policy to expand territorially the empire inherited. Xerxes' failure to add the Greek satrapy of Yauna to the imperial system had seriously weakened his royal image as a conquering and heroic king, and the withdrawal from the coast further revealed a military weakness within the empire which would continued unchecked. Although the king attempted to halt the expanding factors of societal distortion which fostered decay from within the empire, he could not. At the moment, the abandonment of the Greeks in western Anatolia seemed to be a small price to pay for the retention and preservation of the Achaemenid Empire, but forces irreversible within the empire had already seriously undermined the king's sovereign powers. The withdrawal from the coastal regions had encouraged further Greek rebellions throughout the Hellespontine and Bosporos regions, and although the Persian forces vigorously resisted the inevitable, the confederate forces in control of the Anatolian coastal regions had also begun the liberation of Skudra.

Achaemenid imperial policy had always focused upon the security of the central satrapies of Egypt, "Across the River," Assyria-Babylonia, Elam, Parsa, Media, Parthia, and Bactria, and would continue to regard those regions as more crucial and fundamental to the wealth and stability of the empire than the western fringe of Sparda. Consequently, the marks of major societal distortion noted by Aeschylus, the discontent with the king's leadership (*Persae* 531) and revolution (715), necessitated the king's presence in Susa rather than in distant Sardis, and a series of new imperial policies as steps toward the reconfirmation of royal power. At this point, unfortunately, our sources are too meager to provide substantial evidence for Xerxes' activities in the restabilization of the empire, yet what evidence remains suggests that Xerxes' activities after 478 B.C. failed to generate steps toward a revitalization of the empire.

The problems of harem intrigue and politics began to erupt and set a pattern continuous throughout the remaining history of Achaemenid rule. The king's brother Masistes had set out in a bold attempt to seize Bactria and separate the eastern satrapies from Xerxes' rule. Although he failed to succeed (Hdt. 9.108-13), revolution in Egypt would erupt in the 460's and seriously disrupt the empire. Because of the acute societal distortion, from 478 B.C. to his assassination in 465 B.C. in his own bed-chamber, Xerxes had to remain within the heartland of the empire making his annual tour of the central administrative and ritual centers: Susa, Persepolis, Ecbatana, and Babylon. No longer did the king and his armies venture forth to expand the frontiers of the Achaemenid Empire. Instead, the Greek forces commanded by the Athenians as the military alliance of the Delian Confederacy after 478 B.C. systematically eliminated the Persian garrisons and forces from most of the coastal regions of Skudra, Daskyleion, and Sparda, and penetrating into the regions of eastern Lykia, at the Eurymedon River in 465 B.C., inflicted a serious blow upon the Achaemenid imperial forces and Xerxes' leadership (see chapter 10). The Greek view formulated by Aeschylus, that Xerxes' hybris had seriously weakened the Achaemenid Empire, while essentially an artistic device for tragic intent, can be sustained by our limited analysis of the Achaemenid Empire from within.

Instead of instituting positive policies directed toward the reinstitution of strong imperial control, a redevelopment of secure military forces, and the demonstration of aggressive imperial activities within and without the empire, Xerxes turned to demonstrate his regal importance in the completion of the imperial centers of Persepolis and at Susa, and the magnificent structures designed and begun during Darius' reign. At Persepolis, significant and costly changes altered earlier plans for the construction of a new monumental staircase, a grandiose "Gate of All Nations," the completion of the apadana audience hall with specific attention paid to the superior reliefs of the east staircase, the construction of a second royal palace, the development of the spacious "Hall of One Thousand Columns," great storerooms (usually labeled the "Harem"), and other monumental gates and major buildings. While these illustrate the height of royal

Achaemenid art in its classical development, they also mark extraordinary burdens upon the imperial treasuries significantly drained earlier by the costs of the Greek wars. The plans for Persepolis and Susa were too ambitious for the decades after Mykale as they placed heavy burdens upon the imperial treasuries at a time when new imperial problems, first at the Eurymedon River and then in the rebellion of Egypt, materialized. The problems of the 460's, however, Xerxes did not perceive a decade or two earlier when he authorized the extravagant sums for the new constructions. The events in Greece and Sparda and the problems developing within the empire by 478 B.C., however, should have registered with the king more clearly than they did. It was a shortsightedness common to many rulers, and cost the Achaemenid Empire dearly.

The outcome of the "Samian Affair" in the autumn of 478 and the succeeding turbulent months of 478 B.C., therefore, initiated not a simple or directly resultant stage of revolutions throughout greater Ionia against the Persians, but rather a complicated series of economic, political, and social conditions which highly accentuated the crises of certain and acute societal distortion. Revolution was not the prime issue. Instead, the major issue was to find successful means by which to revitalize the particular poleis in order to prevent further economic disintegration, and to preserve and reorganize the social and political order. The important matters at hand rested fundamentally in the multiple problems of the East Greeks to reorganize and to define their new governments no longer supervised or controlled by the satrapal officials from Sardis or stationed within their poleis, or maintained by the military forces of the Persian garrisons. The withdrawal of the Persian officials and forces left the East Greek poleis for the first time since their conquest by Croesus, more than three-quartes of a century earlier, with the new problems of political organization without an imposing imperial suzerainty, either Lydian or Persian. But these new political problems had suddenly materialized at the moment that the numbers of the ruling aristocratic classes, the landed gentry who had long held control of the local political and social matters, were significantly reduced. Those remaining were struggling with the more fundamental problems of their agricultural estates, of revival, maintenance, and survival, in addition to the economic problems of their client tenants and slaves. The economic crises of the estates were further complicated by the economically disrupted urban centers, the aste, where craft and mercantile activities had plummeted, where urban population had also significantly decreased, and where new and greater dependencies upon the rural estates for food and grain were compounded by the problems of the lack of importation. During the generation between 499 and 479 B.C., the significant decline of the rural gentry and the concomitant decline of crafts and mercantilism, the remaining gentry and tenant farmers could not support and sustain the numbers of the urban populations. They, too, declined in number. Artisans moved elsewhere, to Persepolis and Susa, and other Persian centers offering jobs to skilled craftsmen. Others apparently moved elsewhere. Still others were impressed into non-combative military service for the Persians. And with a decline in food production, a decline in urban birthrate may also have occurred. Piracy and brigandage complicated these problems even further.

Any means towards the stabilization of the East Greek poleis was sought towards the positive goals of economic recovery, social stabilization, and political self-determination. With the reappearance of the ships of the Hellenic League in the early summer of 478 B.C., therefore, the governing aristocrats of the poleis along the eastern Aegean shores eagerly pledged their allegiance to the military Greek forces determined to protect the Greek speaking peoples from future military encounters with the Persians. While political liberation from the Persians became the rallying point for military aggression (Thuc. 1.95.1), the more fundamental and immediately crucial issues for the East Greek aristocrats of economic and political stablization had encouraged them to join the military alliance. Joining forces with the Hellenic League was the only immediate and viable means in the early summer of 478 B.C. to stem the multiple problems of acute societal distortion and to attempt to establish modes for successful revitalization of the poleis.[103] It was the necessary and the only step to be taken at that moment, a step unavoidable but also one soon to be regretted.

10

ATHENIAN INTERVENTION IN IONIA

With the coming of spring in 478 B.C., the Athenians again prepared to take the offensive, which they had instituted in their siege of Sestos. Their objectives are not clear, but the prevailing motivation seems to have been the opening of the Hellespont and the Bosporos for the access of wheat. The Persian campaigns in Attica had ruined two harvests (Hdt. 8.142) and the Athenians, returning to their burned out and destroyed farms and homes, struggled with the crises of grain shortages.[1] The second major concern centered upon the fear of a fourth Persian expedition against Greece with the intent of conquering Athens. In the spring of 478 B.C., these goals could not be accomplished by fomenting revolution in Ionia, but by restoring Athens and Attica to the potential for growth, which had been stemmed by the previous generation of Persian wars. The immediate and fundamental concerns of the Athenians to survive and to rebuild their city clearly preceded any lofty thoughts concerning the "liberation" of the Ionians from the Persian Empire and freedom for the East Greeks.

But as the Athenians stirred toward renewed military preparation, the Spartans again asserted their rights to lead the collective Greek forces of the Hellenic League. Their aims, too, were not the "liberation" of the Ionians but survival and the protection of their polis. Spartan foreign policy had been molded by two major national factors: to preserve aristocratic elitism by controlling the "enemy within," and by constructing a military Peloponnesian League to extend that police action throughout the Peloponnesos. In the spring of 478 B.C., therefore, the Spartans instructed their leading commander Latychidas to resume command of the Hellenic League rather than let it falter to Athenian direction, in order to extend Spartan foreign policy within two new aspects of national defense. The Spartans eagerly agitated for the punishment of the mainland Greeks who had medized and became King Xerxes' vassals. This aspect of their policy was a direct extension of their internal police action to sustain a defensive Peloponnesian League. To punish the medizers was the next phase of outward defense in order to protect the internal status quo. In turn, the Spartans ordered Pausanias to sail eastward with the other forces of the Hellenic League in order to maintain their control over that part of the military alliance and to keep the Athenians in check. This command was merely a fourth aspect of the basic Spartan internal and national defense system. This later aspect was, however, an extremely risky step as it would over-extend the Spartans just as had the offensive campaigns at Mykale. But with the first sign of a reversal of this policy, that is, the firm rejection of Spartan command by the maritime members of the Hellenic League, the Spartans would withdraw permanently from that phase of their foreign affairs. It was of prime importance for the Athenians and the islanders to open the Aegean to northern grain trade and to reduce the problems throughout the Aegean basin which would in any way hinder that trade, whether it be the rampant piracy and brigandage, which had spread during the chaotic years of recent wars, or Persian control of the Hellespont, Propontis, and Bosporos.

Early that spring, consequently, the naval forces of the Hellenic League set sail; one section with Latychidas and Themistokles towards Thessaly (Hdt. 6.72; Plut. *Them*. 20.1-2)[2] and the second section commanded by Pausanias in a lightning raid headed for Cyprus (Thuc. 1.94). In a more than terse statement, Thucydides recorded that Pausanias commanded a fleet which consisted of twenty ships from the Peloponnesos, thirty ships from Athens, and ships "from a multitude of other allies."[3] How many allied ships and their origin, Thucydides unfortunately failed to note. The evidence from Herodotus (see chapter 8.III), however, strongly indicates that the mainland Ionians did not participate; and in seeking an origin for the "multitude of the other allies" we should consider poleis of the Hellenic League as listed on the Delphic Serpent Column (ML *GHI* 27), in addition to the poleis of Samos, Chios, Lesbos and the "other islanders" which had joined the Hellenic League in the autumn of 479 B.C. (Hdt. 9.106.4).[4] As for the "other islanders" referred to by Herodotus, we are again not certain, but they doubtlessly included the western Cycladic island poleis listed on the Serpent Column: Keos, Kythnos, Siphnos, Melos, Tenos, and Naxos. Siphnos and Melos had not submitted to Persia while Keos and Kythnos had, yet had rebelled against the Great King and had joined the Greeks; and Naxos and Tenos, while loyal to the Persian cause, had experienced factionalism and at least some of their forces had supported the Greek campaigns. By 478 B.C., they all had joined the forces of the League. To this list we may add the island polis of Seriphos which had fought at Salamis (Hdt. 8.46.4, 48) and, with less assurance, the central Cycladic island poleis of Mykonos, Rhenaia, and Syros adjacent to Delos, islands which apparently had joined the League during the summer of 479 B.C. when the fleet had been stationed there before sailing to Samos. At that time, the previously Persian controlled island of Paros may also have rebelled and joined the League's forces,[5] and perhaps its southern neighbor Ios had also joined at that time. To the west of Samos, on the island of Ikaros, the small poleis of Therme and Oine, too, may also have joined the League, and perhaps during the period when the League occupied the polis of Samos. As for the number of their ships, we have no idea whether Thucydides' *plethos* ("a multitude") indicates more or less than thirty or fifty ships. The combined fleet, however, may well have been less than one hundred ships strong. The Athenians, therefore, sailed with a substantial number of ships but clearly did not constitute a majority of the fleet. They did, however, have in their confidence the island poleis, including their neighbors Aigina[6] and Chalkis, Eretria, and Styra on Euboia. These poleis had also rebelled against King Xerxes and had joined the Hellenic League. Later that summer, these same island poleis would enthusiastically support Athens in her conflict with Sparta. Consequently, the Athenian commander Aristeides sailing with Pausanias could sustain the aggressive and offensive military strategies and attitudes which the Athenians had demonstrated during the events of the previous autumn at Sestos.

The expedition to Cyprus suggests that earlier that spring a meeting of the Hellenic League had been called, either of all of the representatives or of the executive council, directed by Sparta, which had sent its representatives Latychidas and Pausanias in cooperation with Athens, represented by Themistokles and Aristeides. To attack Cyprus was a major decision, absolutely fundamental to the goal of gaining the Bosporos. The attack would not be to seize and control the great island but rather to destroy the remnant of the Persian Imperial Fleet based there and to prevent the return of Persian naval forces into the Aegean in a Persian attempt to block the Hellenic fleet or to prevent the Hellenic attempt to seize the Bosporos. Thucydides' statement that "they campaigned against Cyprus and *katestrepsanto* most of it" must be interpreted not as *subdued and subjected it* but rather *ruined* or *upset it*.[7] Cyprus remained firmly under Persian control, but the attacks did eliminate a Persian naval counter force for more than a decade (Diod. Sic. 11.60.5; Plut. *Kim.* 12.5).

The expedition against Cyprus was swift and decisive, after which the Hellenic forces immediately returned into Aegean waters and sailed to Byzantion on the Bosporos.[8] As with Sestos, Byzantion had been a key Persian garrison polis, which the

Hellenic League's forces quickly besieged and took. Persian control of Byzantion, however, had never been secure (Hdt. 5.25-8; 6.33), and we may suspect that the Greek Byzantines supported the forces of the Hellenic League, thus facilitating the siege and bringing that polis to rapid submission. Very clearly, the Hellenic League had to set out primarily to gain Byzantion and to open the Bosporos to the grain trade sorely needed. When the fall of Byzantion had occurred, Thucydides did not make clear, yet the argument presented by Meritt, Wade-Gery, and McGregor that it occurred about June of 478 B.C. is persuasive.[9]

As the League's fleet rapidly sailed from Cyprus to Byzantion, the Greeks once again demonstrated to the eastern islands and to their key allies of Samos, Chios, and Lesbos their support of the islanders' revolutions against Xerxes. The rapid movement of the fleet, however, certainly provided nothing more than a nominal and token gesture to the mainland Ionians that the League was interested at that time in the "liberation" of the East Greeks. But with the Persian withdrawal from the coast, we may strongly suspect that many of the major littoral poleis, encouraged by the presence, if only briefly, of the fleet for a second time, rallied to the League's cause. They may not have been able to support the League with manned ships and to participate in the siege of Persian garrison at Byzantion, yet many of the coastal poleis, suffering serious economic and political crises, compounded by the turmoil of the withdrawal of the Persian military forces and the developing internal instability, by necessity sought alliance with the League. The rampant conditions of societal distortion necessitated positive activities toward the revitalization of the East Greek poleis, a stability which only the League at that moment could offer. But once again, we have no evidence in regard to which poleis responded and joined the League in the early summer of 478 B.C. Yet, we may suspect that during the course of that summer, after the League's fleet had passed Ionia and its forces had taken Byzantion, more and more of the East Greek poleis came to the crucial decision that their future development could only be secured with the military support and protection of the Hellenic League. It was not a question of Greek "liberation" of the East Greeks, but rather of the East Greeks seeking alliance in the military organization. By the autumn of 478 B.C., great sections of the western littoral zone of Anatolia would have been eager to obtain the military security offered to them by the League in order that each East Greek polis, in turn, could begin to redevelop its government and its economy. The question was not freedom but rather the practical question of rebuilding the economically distressed states and restoring local and internal political stability. The sudden and rather unexpected withdrawal of the Persians and the benefits of Darius' reorganization of Sparda and Daskyleion had left the East Greeks in great derangement, and any offer for at least military stability, and especially with ethnic groups of a common language and cultural background, became positive goals to obtain, regardless of consequences yet unseen and not predictable. In this move of the East Greeks towards the League, the Athenians apparently developed their rhetorical arguments that the Athenians long had close ethnic and religious ties with the Ionians (Thuc. 1.95.1). Such arguments would clearly support the Athenian policies for aggression in the Bosporos, and the new phase of Athenian leadership in the Aegean.

The poleis and ethnic units of the littoral zone in question are difficult to isolate, and from a lack of information we are impeded in noting which poleis and units during the summer and early autumn of 478 B.C. actively turned to the Hellenic League for support. The assessments of Meritt, Wade-Gery, and McGregor, however, do offer at least a thoughtful if not always accurate survey of the coastal zone from the Karian region through the Troad and Bosporos regions, which allows us to begin to identify the centers which may have sought the League's protection.[10] With the passage of the Hellenic fleet sailing from Cyprus to Byzantion along the coast beginning with the great island of Rhodes and the Karic Chersonese, the following centers may be isolated (from the south-east to the north in geographical order):

1. on the island of Rhodes, the poleis of Ialysos, Lindos, and Kameiros, and the neighboring western island polis of Chalke;

2. on the Karic Chersonese, the Cherronesioi, the poleis of Knidos and Ayliatai (?), and the island of Kedreai;

3. Keramos in southern Karia on the Gulf of Kos;

4. on the Myndos peninsula, Halikarnassos, Termera, Myndos, Madnasa, and Karyanda;[11]

5. the island poleis of Kos, and Pelea also on Kos, the Kalydnioi, and Lepsimandos;

6. and the northern Karian poleis of Bargylia, Iasos, and Latmos on the border of the Ionian zone.

In the central region of the western Anatolian coast, the following Ionian poleis, central to the long developing history of the East Greeks, may also be listed:

1.   the Maeander Valley poleis of Miletos, Myous, and Priene;[12]

2.   the Kayster Valley poleis of Marathesion, Pygela, Isinda, and Ephesos;

3.   the southern Mimas-Korykos-Kaystrios Range poleis of Notion, Kolophon, Dios Hieron, Lebedos, Teos, and Hairai;

4.   on the western and northern Mimas Range, the poleis of Erythrai and Klazomenai;

5.   and north of the Hermos Valley, the Ionian-Aiolic polis of Phokaia.

The region of the Hermos Valley and the small village of Smyrna apparently remained secure under Persian control, as they formed an important littoral zone and outlet for the Hermos Valley region and the overland route from the capital satrapal city of Sardis through the Lydian village of Nymphaion across the low-rising Smyrnaian-Sardian pass to the coast and Smyrna. This, we may strongly suspect, was a zone which the Persians diligently attempted to retain. Similarly, the Persians also retained control of part of the territory of Myous and, apparently, the choric regions.[13] The Persians, in losing Ephesos, however, no longer controlled the terminus of the major road from Sardis to Ephesos, and the key Lydian and native Anatolian centers of Ephesos, and Kolophon and her important native shrine at Klaros. The Samian holdings on the mainland (the peraia) due east of the great Ionian island and centered upon the subsidiary village of Anaia (Thuc. 3.32.2), which may not have been controlled by Samos in 479 B.C., had seemingly in 478 B.C. been rejoined to its metropolis.

     In the southern region of Aiolis, north of Phokaia, the following cluster of poleis may also be included in this survey list:

1.   the major Aiolic polis of Kyme;

2.   the minor poleis of Myrina, Gryneion, Alaia, Pitane, and the offshore island of Elaiousa, which was actually part of the dendritic polis of Erythrai;

3.   and north of Pitane, the Chians held sections of Aiolis as their peraia centered upon the small coastal town of Atarneus.[14]

The Persians, however, still claimed control of sections of Myrina and Gryneion, and as at Myous apparently the choric regions and not the aste. And north of Atarneus, in the coastal and valley regions of the Kaikos River, the exiled King of Sparta Damaratos held the towns of Pergamum, Teuthrania, and Halisarna for his sovereign King Xerxes who had granted those towns to the exiled Spartan shortly before the expedition against Athens in

480 B.C. (Athen. *Deip.* 1.29). Nearby, the Eretrian Gongylos, who had medized in 490 B.C., held the centers of Gambreion and Palaigambreion and, apparently, the choric regions of Myrina and Gryneion (Xen. *Hell.* 2.1.6). At the head of the Gulf of Adramyttion, the important Lydian center once governed by the crown prince Croesus himself may also have remained secure under Persian control and bound to the satrapal system of strong vassalage holdings similar to those of Damaratos and Gongylos. This zone, often considered part of the peraia of Lesbos,[15] apparently had not been regained by the Lesbians and remained the important northern littoral center for the Persian satrapy of Sparda.

Along the southern coast of the Troad and within the Lesbian sphere of influence and regions often controlled by Lesbos as its peraia (Thuc. 3.50.2-3),[16] Aiolic centers along the western edges of the Ida Range apparently also turned to the League for assistance:

1.   the poleis of Gargara, Lamponeia, and Assos.

For the moment, the Persians continued their control of Kebrene, the only substantial and important fifth century settlement in the southern Troad.

On the western coast of the Troad, we may count the following:

1.   the major polis of Neandreia;

2.   the island polis of Tenedos at the southern approach to the Hellespont;

3.   and the Hellespontine coastal poleis of Sigeion, Dardanos, Abydos, Arisbe, Perkote, Palaiperkote, Lampsakos, and Paisos.

Yet, Persian control of sections of Perkote and Lampsakos, apparently choric regions, did continue. Along the northern coast of the Troad:

1.   the poleis of Parion, Priapos, Artake on the western coast of the Kyzikine peninsula, and Kyzikos;

2.   and the major island of Prokonnesos in the western Propontis, may also be counted.

It is doubtful that the centers along the Propontic coast east of Kyzikos had been withdrawn from the satrapal control of Daskyleion centered just south of Kyzikos.[17] Only Kalchedon across from Byzantion can be rather safely included, and perhaps as part of the military action of the League while besieging Byzantion.

This list of poleis and ethnic groups modified from those considered by Meritt, Wade-Gery, and McGregor is, at best, only an approximation of the extent of the littoral East Greek zone which turned to the Hellenic League for stability. Perhaps a more cautious and realistic list should include fewer centers, but at least this list does consider a zone which may be identified as a region with discrete geographical niches in marked distinction from the inland and, at the moment, inaccessible valleys of Karia, the rugged and inland regions of the Troad, and the northeastern coastal regions of the satrapy of Daskyleion. It also takes into account, more pointedly than that analysis of Meritt and his associates, the ancient sources which distinctly note the retention of Persian control in specific yet diffuse sections of this zone: at Myous, Smyrna and the Hermos Valley delta, at Myrina and Gryneion, the Kaikos Valley and its delta region, the gulf coastal region of Adramyttion, and at Perkote and Lampsakos. We, therefore, must modify Cawkwell's thesis of Xerxes' cognizant withdrawal of Persian garrisons and officers from this impoverished and unstable zone. The Persians did not abandon entirely their control of the Spardian coast, but did retain garrisons in several key regions, which could be governed more realistically than not, during this turbulent period. The areas over which the governments at Sardis and Daskyleion attempted to maintain military and political control, and rather successfully during the second quarter of the fifth century B.C., were the major east-west river valleys and their coastal outlets to the Aegean: the Maeander from Magnesia and the choric regions of Myous; the Hermos and the villages of Nymphaion and Smyrna; the Kaikos and its coastal choric regions of Myrina and Gryneion from the upriver centers of Pergamum, Teuthrania, and Halisarna; and the terminus of the inland route from Sardis to Adramyttion at the head of its gulf.

The geographical structure of the strategically important river valleys which traversed Sparda from its central core westward to the Aegean provided natural and militarily viable routes and means for continued Persian control, as did the inland route from Sardis northward past Bin Tepe to the modern Turkish cities of Akhisar and Turgutalp, which continued north to the plains west of Balıkesir, and then directly westward through the narrow valley to Adramyttion on the coast. From present day Balıkesir a northern valley route linked this ancient road to the satrapal center at Daskyleion. The attempt by Daskyleion to retain control of the choric regions of Perkote and Lampsakos across the rugged mountains of Mysia and the Troad, however, did present greater problems and, yet, that control was maintained. In the mid-fifth century B.C., Persian presence in the Troad just beyond Sigeion persisted as a major problem for that East Greek polis (*IG* 1^2.32; *SEG* X 13; Hill *Sources* B28).

The major loss suffered by the Persians by their withdrawal from the littoral regions of western Anatolia, and the subsequent gain of those regions by the allied Greeks, was the Greek military control of the Thracian Chersonese along the western shore of the Hellespont and the key polis and its garrison at Byzantion on the Bosporos. Perhaps only at Alopekonnesos on the western coast of the Thracian Chersonese did Persian forces hold out,[18] while the remaining poleis and centers of the Chersonese had fallen with, or shortly after, the Athenian occupation of Sestos and its important east-west ferry crossing to Abydos in the Troad. Between the Chersonese and Byzantion, however, the East Greek poleis and teiche along the northern coast of the Propontis may not yet have been affected by either the Athenian military activities during the winter of 479/8 B.C. or the attack upon Byzantion by the Hellenic League in the early summer of 478 B.C. After the fall of Byzantion, nevertheless, the forces of the League would probably have been interested in wrenching from the Persians the major port poleis of Selymbria and Perinthos to the west of Byzantion along that coast. In gaining those key poleis, the Greeks would have been able to establish firmer control and protection of Byzantion by occupying the eastern sections of the important Thracian coastal road just beyond that polis.

The series of successes achieved by the forces of the Hellenic League in the early summer of 478 B.C. could have reaffirmed the offensive military solidarity of the Greeks against Persia, but did not. By then, the goals of the two major military contingents and their leaders were in marked opposition: Sparta strove to defend her social and economic control in Lakonia and Messenia and the protective military defensive system of the Peloponnesian League, while Athens increasingly sought naval control of the Hellespont and the Bosporos, a strategy which had now expanded to the desire of naval control of the central Aegean. That brief moment of military unity generated in 481 B.C., when the League had been founded, had totally disintegrated. The Greek victories at Marathon, Salamis, and then capped at Plataia had also spawned a psychological factor among the Athenians. No longer would they be a third rate polis, overshadowed by Sparta, Corinth, and Aigina among several states. Athens and specifically its commander Themistokles now sought to develop an active and secure grain trade with the northern regions and the Black Sea ports and, in turn, to develop its urban center into a secured, walled asty for defense against future aggression—and specifically—should the Persians attack once again (Thuc. 1.89.3-93.2).[19] This strategy also necessitated the fortification of Athens' three deep water ports at the Piraeus (Thuc. 1.93.3-8).[20] This policy was not new and can be traced back to Themistokles' archonship in 493/2 B.C. and his initial development of the Piraeus, and to his activities in 479/8 B.C. to fortify the Athenian asty and its port. In this act of fortification, the Spartans detected a threat to their internal policies and the "policing of their enemy from within."

The developing animosities marking the opposition of the Athenians to the Spartans came to a crucial climax at Byzantion in that early summer of 478 B.C. The personal behavior of Pausanias of Sparta had strongly piqued the allies to reject vehemently his chief command of the Hellenic League at the very moment several other political and diplomatic factors were compounding that crisis. Unfortunately, the full picture of the crisis is extremely muddled.[21] Nevertheless, at the very moment of allied rejection of Pausanias, orders had arrived from the government in Sparta that he return home to stand trial for "insubordination" (Thuc. 1.95.2-3). By this coincidence of events, which perhaps were totally intertwined (within allied rejection lay the charges by the members of the League at Byzantion of Pausanias' "insubordination" to the joint allied command) the allies turned to the Athenians and urged Aristeides to assume chief command (Thuc. 1.95.1, 95.4).[22] Behind both the charges of "insubordination' and the rallying of the allies to Athenian leadership may well have been the activities and subterfuge of the Athenians themselves as covert steps toward control of the League and of the seas (Thuc. 1.95.2). The Spartans, nevertheless, strongly desiring a maintenance of their "protective policies" had dispatched a new commander, Dorkis, to replace the recalled Pausanias. But when Dorkis arrived in Byzantion, perhaps in August or early September of that summer,[23] Aristeides with the cooperation of the allies had already begun to take new and divergent steps toward a major reorganization of the Greek naval forces. In no manner would the allies, again perhaps goaded by the Athenians, accept Spartan command; and Dorkis, upon his arrival, was simply and absolutely rejected (Thuc. 1.95.6-7). At that point, the Spartans, in order to maintain their internal policies, abandoned their command of the Hellenic League (Thuc. 1.95.7). With Dorkis and his Spartan forces, the allies from the Peloponnesos apparently returned home, thus leaving at Byzantion the Athenians and the allies from the Aegean islands and whatever other eastern Greek allies had joined the League's naval forces at that point. This action had not dissolved the Hellenic League but had pointedly removed Spartan and Peloponnesian participation in its naval activities. Years later, Thucydides in the voice of the Mytilenaians would argue that the Spartans had abandoned the League's navy and, thus, had surrendered it to the Athenians who by necessity had to assume command (Thuc. 3.10.2).[24]

Following the removal of Pausanias from Byzantion, and the rejection of Dorkis' attempt for renewed Spartan command, with the allied Greek forces remaining at Byzantion, Aristeides outlined distinct steps for the establishment of a new naval organization. The organization of the Hellenic League had not been terminated nor was the concept of its naval force abandoned, even though, in essence, it had become inoperative. In the autumn of 478 B.C., consequently, Aristeides and the Athenians led the cooperative island and East Greeks to the successful establishment of a distinctly separate naval organization, the Delian Confederacy.[25] During the autumn and winter of 478/7 B.C., the Athenians thereupon sent messengers to the Greeks outside of the mainland of Greece, Greeks who would be receptive to the establishment of a new naval organization and who, also, were distinctly not allied to Sparta's Peloponnesian League. For the meetings to formulate the articles of alliance for the new Confederacy, Aristeides chose the sacred (Thuc. 3.104) and strategically important central island of Delos; and to that island the Athenians summoned representatives from the northern Sporades, the Cyclades in general (with the major exceptions of the southern islands of Melos and Thera), the Thracian Chalkidike, the coastal northern and southern regions of the Hellespont, the Propontis, and the Bosporos, the Troad, Aiolis, Ionia, and Karia to join the Athenians in the construction of this new alliance.[26] The East Greeks scattered along the western shores of Anatolia from the Karic Chersonese to Kalchedon, which had early that summer turned to the military protection of the Hellenic League, now turned to the Athenians and, in positive steps, toward the formation of the new military alliance, rallied to the Athenian invitations and sent representatives to the meetings on Delos. By the summer of 477 B.C., the articles had been agreed upon, the oaths of allegiance sworn, perhaps more island, northern and East Greek poleis had joined the alliance, and the military program of the Confederacy was set into action (*Ath. Pol.* 23.5). Had the naval alliance, which began to emerge in the autumn of 478 B.C., been a mere continuation of the earlier Hellenic League, the necessity for an oath would not have arisen. In that the new military confederates swore a new oath, confederates who included some of those who fought with the Hellenic League in addition to the new members who had subsequently sworn separate oaths, a new organization came into being. The oath on Delos marked the establishment of a new organization, one which was distinct from the still continuing Hellenic League.

According to Thucydides, the avowed purpose of the Delian Confederacy was to end Persian control of the Greek states (subject to Skudra, Daskyleion, and Sparda), and to exact from the captured Persian centers, garrisons, and fortresses material compensation for the losses suffered by the Greeks during the Persian campaigns of 480-478 B.C. (1.96.1, 3.10.3, 6.76.3-4). Yet beneath those valiant statements of aggression against the Great King's domain lay more fundamental goals: the security of wheat for the Athenians and the other members of the Confederacy, the elimination of piracy and brigandage throughout the Aegean and the Hellespont-Bosporos link to the Black Sea, and the development and expansion of Athenian military dominination of the Aegean. The acquisition of materials basic to the redevelopment and revitalization of the extensively destroyed Athenian polis, its rural estates, the homes beyond the asty's newly restored walls, and the burned out asty itself and its port were absolutely primary necessities, and were of far greater importance than the tertiary "liberation" of the East Greeks. Persian abandonment of the coastal zone had generated the necessity for the East Greeks to turn first to the Hellenic League and now, more distinctly and earnestly, to the creating of the Delian Confederacy whereby their own political and economic stability would be assured. The Athenians did little to liberate the East Greeks but to provide the easterners with the means by which they could initiate their own steps toward their goals to stem the forces of acute societal distortion and to establish positive methods by which to revitalize their crisis-ridden poleis. At the same time, the Athenians set out to achieve their goals for the revitalization of Attica, yet from the beginning both goals were at variance as the Athenians consistently demanded, for their own protection and redevelopment, that the Athenian requirements be placed before any others. In the blustery winter months of 478/7 B.C., however, the allied representatives gathering on the small island of Delos were not concerned with these variances only later perceptible; but with an eagerness and immediacy to achieve their own steps toward successful revitalization, rallied behind Aristeides and the collective allied decision that Athens command the new Confederacy. The quarternary factor present in 478/7 B.C., was Athens' domestic power structure as reinforced by her hegemonic goals in the Aegean in contrast and in growing conflict with Spartan hegemonic power throughout southern and central Greece.

From the outset, the Delian Confederacy took the form of a new military alliance, a symmachy, in which each allied polis held equal representation in the confederate Synod empowered to formulate policies and to enact directives.[27] Because of Athens' naval strength and her potential for leadership, consequently, the allied Greek poleis without question entrusted to her the hegemony of the new military organization.[28] Although the hegemon would have military command, equality in representation and in decision-making was to exist among the allies collectively, so that the hegemon could not give more weight to her own interests than to those of her allies as a group.[29] This system, however, altered rapidly.

At Delos, the hegemony unofficially bestowed upon Athens during the months before the first sessions of the Delian meetings (Thuc. 6.67.3), was finally officially reconfirmed. At Byzantion in the summer of that year, when Pausanias had received his summons to return to Sparta, the Aegean allies who were then serving with the Hellenic League's fleet and were campaigning from Byzantion, had by necessity turned to the Athenian commanders and had proposed that they assume leadership.[30] Thus, after the departure of Pausanias and before the arrival of Dorkis, the Athenian general Aristeides had agreed to become the chief officer of the naval forces. Encouraged by the Greeks who sought Athenian leadership, he had begun to discuss the new alliance and formulate plans for it.[31]

The rejection of Dorkis when he subsequently arrived at Byzantion, consequently, signified again that the allied Greek poleis still supported Athens and expected leadership of her. But this change in leadership and fundamental policy drew the poignant conclusion that a new organization was of utmost importance. Athens, now in command of the prime Greek naval force, considered it absolutely necessary to organize the allied members into a new alliance, which would clearly define Athens' command and her relationship with the collective member poleis. Distinct leadership was what Athens sought. Several years earlier, Themistokles had anticipated this desirability of a strong naval force commanded by Athens and its usefulness for Athens' future.[32]

Under the leadership of Aristeides, therefore, the Greeks began to lay the foundations of their new alliance. His personality and manner of associating with the other Greeks had been a great asset to Athens; and largely because of Aristeides, the allies of the new organization quite willingly accepted the Athenian hegemony, which Aristeides carefully and shrewdly negotiated (Diod. Sic. 11.46.4).[33] Similarly, the admiration which the Greeks held for Themistokles and his naval genius further developed that allied enthusiasm (Diod. Sic. 11.46.5). The primary reasons for which the East Greeks especially sought Athenian leadership were, however, Athens' naval strength and her current enthusiasm for carrying the war into Anatolia in order to obtain Athens' stated goals. Nevertheless, between 477 and 449 B.C., Athens transformed the Delian Confederacy from an alliance of independent states into an Empire. For the Aegean poleis, which had joined the Confederacy voluntarily yet by necessity, and which believed the concept of equality; sovereignty gave way to subjection (*douleia*).[34] Of this transformation, the allies complained bitterly as they considered it a violation of the Confederacy's principle of equality (Thuc. 1.99.2).

At the time of the establishment of the Confederacy, the poleis which had joined in solemn alliance were sovereign and independent, *eleutheria*.[35] To the ancient Greek, sovereignty was a political condition, which maintained that his polis be subject to her own laws and to be free from the subjection to the laws of another.[36] Each polis exercised unfettered authority over her citizens and property within her borders.[37] Sovereignty implied self-government, an independent system of taxation, an independent judicial system, and the rule of territory without foreign interference.[38] Membership in the Delian Confederacy, therefore, did not infringe upon the fundamental sovereignty of a polis. But the principles of this concept quickly changed.

For Aeschylus, who wrote the *Persians* presented to the Athenians in 472 B.C., sovereignty (*eleutheria*) of the fatherland entailed the freedom for one's children, wives, the shrines of the ancestral gods, and one's ancestors' graves. The loss of sovereignty, enslavement or subjugation (*douleia*), in contrast, connoted subjection to others.[39] Sovereignty, therefore, "kept Greece from seeing a day of slavery (*doulion*)."[40] The conditions upon which the Delian Confederacy was founded and which its Synod's existence was thought to protect were the maintenance of individual freedom, equal participation in the expenses of the symmachy, and permanent association with other member poleis.

For the ancient Greeks, the concept of freedom or sovereignty (eleutheria) possessed an absolute political quality as it represented a polis' independence from any foreign relationship which might in any manner direct or limit the policies of the state without prior consent of that state.[41] Absolute independence from foreign influence could also be denoted by the superlative eleutherotate (Thuc. 6.89.6, 7.69.2). This concept of eleutheria is well illustrated by Thucydides in his comments concerning the key Ionian island of Chios. From 479 to 412 B.C., Chios remained an independent polis within the Confederacy and directed its own political policies without being restricted by Athenian legislation, as did Samos and Lesbos yet for shorter periods of time. Nevertheless, Chios had agreed to the confederate Synod's ability to declare war, make peace treaties, and to obtain from that island tribute in the form of manned ships. During the last quarter of the fifth century B.C., however, Chios began to feel the pressures of political direction imposed by Athens, and the Chians distinctly interpreted those pressures as a loss of eleutheria. At the time of her rebellion against Athens in 412 B.C., therefore, Chios struggled to maintain her eleutheria (Thus. 8.45.4).[42]

As with the Delian Confederacy, an organization of poleis may be established without the sacrifice of a polis' sovereignty. Participation in the Confederacy could be compatible with the concept of sovereignty if the alliance was founded upon the basis of polis–equality.[43] If an alliance had such a basis—and thus provided a guarantee of non-intervention by one ally in the domestic affairs of another—sovereignty was preserved.[44] The sovereignty of a polis was evident in its ability to declare war, to make peace, and to join freely an alliance or confederation (Xen. Hell. 6.3.7-8). In joining an alliance, the domain of external policy became freely limited and with equality by the decisions of its Synod, especially concerning war, military participation, peace, and treaties (Ath. Pol. 23.5). In such an alliance of poleis, therefore, two basic and powerful forces exist: the determination to achieve the set goals of the voluntary union and, in contrast, the resistance against total integration within the confederation to the degree that sovereignty is lost. For collective security and the achievement of the positive measures of revitalization, several poleis may ally on terms of equality and joint participation to ward off a foreign danger. But they are also fundamentally reluctant to sacrifice further aspects of their sovereignty or to destroy that political equilibrium which had brought them together as sovereign contracting parties. The decision to create an association and solidarity for the anti-Persian cause did necessitate a new set of legal procedures and the subsequent abandonment of only certain individual prerogatives such as those concerning war, military preparation, peace, and treaties.

Poleis in alliance could surrender to their common Synod certain international prerogatives, but only if these were voluntarily surrendered and their loss did not impinge upon the domestic independence of the individual poleis. The member poleis did not continue as confederates if they became politically dependent upon a stronger polis which governed them, for they would remain confederates only while they were able to cooperate on the basis of equality in the operation of the organization. Thus, within the initial stages of the Delian Confederacy, the allied poleis retained their sovereignty, were linked by a treaty or an international agreement, the Confederate Charter, and had as their political agent the Confederate Synod. The conditions upon which the Confederacy was founded and which the allied poleis thought the Synod's existance was to protect, were the measures of the maintenance of the independence of the polis, equal participation in confederate policy formulation, financial participation in the expenses of the Confederacy, and a permanent military association with the other allied poleis. To this system, the several East Greek governments eagerly sent their representatives to Delos, with the initial decision to do so originating within the councils and assemblies of the aristocratic landed gentry. The Ionian aristocrats had agreed upon the fundamental element which had led to the formation of that Confederacy: the dispatch of representatives to join the new symmachy.

The basic power of the Confederacy lay with the individual poleis bound into a political unity by the very fact of their association. Political power, therefore, proceeded fundamentally from the component organizations (the poleis) to the higher association, from lower state niches to the higher niche of the symmachy. The articles of the organization, the basic principles of the associated poleis, consequently created the authority by which that association functioned. The individual poleis surrendered to the Confederacy only such parts of their inherent rights as were definitely required to promote and to achieve the specific objectives of the higher and broader organization. The poleis gave, rather than received, authority, as they were the source of that power. As each polis was capable of existing apart from the Confederacy (yet chose not to), the

Confederacy could not exist apart from the individual poleis (Arist. *Pol.* 1317b).

The authority given to Athens as hegemon was, therefore, only the mode of service and the means of guardianship for the welfare of the confederate community, the collective poleis. Obedience by an individual polis was simply a return for the provision of defense and protection toward the achievement of revitalization. Sovereignty was the inviolable property of each polis and limited to its will, a sovereignty defined by several criteria: the right of the polis to choose its own form of constitution, the right to determine its own internal state concerns, independent internal jurisdiction, voluntary union in the Confederacy, and participation in the confederate resolutions of the Synod which considered war, peace, and the contracts of surrender with non-allied powers.[45]

At Delos in the winter of 478/7 B.C., the confederate poleis established a symmachy, a permanent military-naval organization to continue the war against King Xerxes and the Persian Empire.[46] No aspect of the Confederacy's principal articles suggested at that time a loss of sovereignty,[47] as each polis could join the Confederacy, pay tribute, and still be independent.[48] That a polis could retain both its *eleutheria* and hold membership in the Delian Confederacy is well illustrated by the eastern islands of Samos, Chios, and Lesbos. While the other confederate poleis became subject to Athenian regulations and restrictions issued by the Athenian Boule and Demos, or were subjugated outright by Athenian military conquest, these three islands remained independent.[49] Yet, they too, utlimately became subject to the Athenian government. Their *eleutheria* was not the result of their having joined the Hellenic League during the days following the crisis at Mykale but rather the result of their particular abilities and willingness to maintain their contributions to the Confederacy in the form of manned ships in lieu of substituting payment of tribute monies upon Athens' demand. The naval strengths of these three islands and their geographic position readily made them excellent fortified sentinels, which the Athenians found necessary to sustain as independent allies. They were key naval outposts which served the Athenian interests admirably by guarding the western coastal zones of Anatolia and providing the East Greek poleis with protection against future military threats from Sparda, Daskyleion, and Susa, or from Sparta (*Ath. Pol.* 24.2; Thuc. 3.11.6). The naval force of each of the three islands was powerful, with promise of future growth, and if Athens would give special attention to these islands she could maintain a favorable relationship with each and continue to benefit from the strength of their navies. The loss of the fleet of any one of the three during the first thirty years of the Confederacy's activities would have been detrimental to Athens' control of the Aegean. Consequently, when the Samians (the first of the three) rebelled against Athens in 440 B.C., and subsequently lost their independence, the Samian naval forces had been vying for their own control of the eastern Aegean and the Anatolian coast in cooperation with the forces and government of Sardis, governed by the satrap Pissouthnes, and in marked opposition to Athens' military Empire restructured out of the Delian Confederacy (Thuc. 1.115.2-117; 8.76.4).

The factors of equality and *eleutheria* were for the East Greek aristocratic governments decisively new qualities in their desired alliance with the Athenians, factors which no longer ranked them as vassals to the Lydian and Persian kings but rather as participating members in parity within the Confederate Synod toward the policy making of the Confederacy. Unlike the Hellenic League in which, during the events of 479 B.C., the military council had assumed directive power, the Delian Confederacy and its Synod of equal representation, of ambassadors from each of the participating poleis in that symmachy, represented a distinctly new stage for the East Greek landed gentry in terms of their duties of military service and taxation payments to their military leaders. Similarly, the oath of allegiance to the Delian Confederacy also represented a distinctive new phase for the eastern aristocrats in their initial understanding of their duties, rights, and responsibilities. The ratification of the confederate articles drawn up by the participating ambassadors of the first Delian Synod occurred in the form of an exchange of oaths of parity, rather than of vassalage, between Athens and the allied members of the Delian Confederacy.[50] The only known clause of the oath is the article (*Ath. Pol.* 23.5): "To have the same enemy and the same friend." This article, common to many other oaths which bound states into an alliance during the fifth and fourth centuries B.C., indicates the prime offensive and defensive functions of the Confederacy.[51] The oath was the basis of the agreement of equality among the participating poleis, including Athens. Both Thucydides and Aristotle remarked that Athens' subjugation of an ally, with the ally's subsequent loss of independence, was a violation of that treaty.[52]

Several modern historians have interpreted the ancient sources as meaning that the exchange of oaths involved two distinct parties: Athens, as represented by Aristeides, and the remaining body of the allied poleis.[53] This, however, is not the proper interpretation of either the *Athenaion Politeia* or of Plutarch *Aristeides* 25.1. The former states that Aristeides swore the oath with the "Ionians" (the Greek poleis of the Confederacy) while the latter mentions that as chairman of that first Delian Synod Aristeides administered the oath to the poleis and that he was the Athenian representative to take that oath. The proper interpretation of these statements, therefore, seems to be not that an oath was sworn between two parties (Athens as the first and the allies as the second, and on a basis of less than parity) but that all the participating poleis, including Athens, swore the oath together, equally and on the basis of parity. The emphasis placed upon Aristeides was not intended to indicate that Athens as the hegemon and one party took the oath with all the other poleis constituting a second party, but simply to indicate Aristeides' role as chairman of the Synod. For Athens to have taken the oath as one party (and superior to the collective Synod) and all the allies as a second (and inferior as a collective body to the hegemon) would not have maintained the Confederacy's basic principle of parity, of equal representation and equal authority.[54]

The Delian Confederacy was a new military organization, an alliance of poleis permanently bound into a relationship of parity one with another, for at the time of organization, permanency seemed most desirable as the Persian Empire was immense, its political power and military strength seemed (at the moment) to be unlimited, and there was little if any reason in 478/7 B.C. to expect its disintegration. Permanency of the symmachy, therefore, was prime, and indicated by the symbolic throwing of iron into the sea.[55] Indeed, in 478/7 B.C. protection from the Persian Empire was a factor considered of utmost importance, and the permanency of the Confederacy emphatically implied that there could be no secession from the organization. The denial of secession among the rules of the Hellenic League and of the Peloponnesian League had clearly served as the model for the Delian Confederacy.[56] When the military council of the Hellenic League had admitted Samos, Chios, Lesbos, and the other "islanders," those new members had specifically pledged that they would abide by the oaths of allegiance and not secede from that League (Hdt. 9.106.4).

As long as the political and military power of the Persian Empire remained stable, and King Xerxes' rule secure, there was still the danger that Xerxes would again launch a renewed campaign of conquest in the Aegean. To this danger, the East Greek poleis remained exceedingly vulnerable. While the Persian danger existed, even in a diminished

form, the Greeks allied within the Confederacy remained united and prepared for joint

resistance; therefore, the obligations of the oaths existed without limitations of time,

and the secession of individual member poleis would not be recognized. In 428 B.C.,

when the people of Mytilene on the island of Lesbos revolted against the Athenian rule of

the Confederacy, the Mytilenaian delegate appealed to the confederate covenant and to

the Confederacy's intended purposes, and he claimed that the Mytilenaians had been

morally released from their obligations to the Confederacy when the war against Persia

had ceased (c. 450 B.C., and the Peace of Kallias) and when Athens had begun to deprive

the allies of their independence (Thuc. 3.10.4-11.4).

With the Athenian subjugation of first the allied polis of Naxos (c. 465 B.C.) and then

Thasos (463 B.C.), a new political concept came into existance, that of *autonomia*. While

Naxos and Thasos fell under the conditions of *douleia*, the still independent allies began

to develop the concept of *autonomia* to mark their political self-determination whereby

their independence was now contingent upon the good graces of the more powerful

Athens.[57] This new concept, Martin Ostwald has cogently argued, "developed in the

attempts of the weaker states to find constraints with which to inhibit the exercise of

power" by Athens over them.[58] It was, Ostwald further maintains, a word "coined by

Athenian allies in protest against the more unpleasant manifestations of the Athenian"

Empire. The concrete signs of *autonomia* were an allied polis' retention of her defensive

walls and her military fleet. In contrast, the loss of *autonomia* came about by the

destruction of those fortifications, the loss of the military ships, and Athenian coercions

of the subjugated state to pay a moneyed tribute. Although we can not be certain,

additional factors may also have marked that point at which *autonomia* ended: the

presence of Athenian military and imperial officials, the establishment of colonies and

klerouchies, the taking of hostages, the inforcement of loyalty oaths to Athens, and

Athenian jurisdiction over the allies.[59] The allied obligations to pay tribute, agreed upon

on Delos, did not deprive an ally of its *autonomia*, but if tribute was imposed and forcibly

collected then *autonomia* was lost and the allied state became subject to Athens, and as

a forced tributary subject (*hypēkoos*).

We may now further observe that the concept of *eleutheria* distinctly denoted the

parity relationship among the confederate allies in 478/7 B.C. But as Athens denied

Naxos, Thasos, and other allies their *eleutheria* and forcibly placed them within vassalage or *douleia* relationships, the allies developed the concept of *autonomia* in an avid attempt to preserve the waning parity relationships.

By the spring of 448 B.C., the principles of equality had given way to the political restrictions and regulations which subjected almost all the allied poleis to Athens' imperial control, with the resultant loss of *autonomia* for those poleis. The transition of each confederate polis (with the exceptions of the islands of Samos, Chios, and Lesbos, at least temporarily) was from *autonomia* to *douleia* by the very process of subjecting each polis to restrictions, which had been for the Athenians a matter of necessary political policy. The allies had generated disruptive tendencies amidst their objections to Athenian domination, and if the Confederacy was to continue, the Athenians had to curb those tendencies. In the course of the three decades between 477 and 447 B.C., the Athenians had imposed limitations of self-determination in government upon their allies, either singularly or collectively, in the form of new prescriptions, and new demands for the compliance of the allies as individuals to Athenian legislation concerning the Confederacy. Other restrictions took the form of the limitations of the power of jurisdiction, in the first instance or upon appeal; the requirement of troops to be furnished by member poleis without conditions and without their voice in the resolution of war; the installation of Athenian magistrates in allied poleis of the control of allied government or administration; and the establishment of Athenian garrisons and klerouchies in the allied poleis.[60] By 447 B.C., the Delian Confederacy had transformed into an Athenian Empire, structured not too dissimilar to the Persian Empire and its restrictions and regulations.

The origin of this transformation had been established during the days on Delos of that first organizational year, and under the leadership of Aristeides. The prominence of that Athenian general in the formation of the Confederacy as a new symmachy strongly suggests that he chaired the meetings of the new alliance during that first year.[61] By autumn of 478 B.C., Aristeides had held conferences with many of the island and perhaps Hellespontine allies, and had won them over to the plan of the new organization, and by his personal magnanimity had generated among them a willingness to desire and accept the hegemony of Athens (Diod. Sic. 11.44.2, 6). As chairman of the first meetings of the Synod, Aristeides had advised the allies to consider Delos as the center for the new

Confederacy and he further suggested that the Confederate Treasury should be kept there, in the temple of Apollo and under that god's divine protection (Diod. Sic. 11.47.1). As Athens held the hegemony of the alliance, during the first year, at least, it was Aristeides who submitted to the vote of the Synod the many directives necessary for the proper functioning to the symmachy.

At that time, Athens as hegemon was concerned basically with matters of military and naval command and with finances. The duty of Athens was to lead the liberation of the Greeks from the Persian Empire, and the allies, in turn, were to follow Athens in war. Although this leadership had been extended to Aristeides during the summer of 478 B.C., and Athens had begun to direct the allied naval forces which were to form the Delian Confederacy, a formal election was probably held at the first meetings on Delos to choose Athens officially as hegemon. The election would have been a mere formality enacted by the larger Synod of allied representatives then present to ratify the earlier offer extended by the smaller group of allies campaigning at Byzantion. Although a formality, this election was a necessary and fundamental step in the establishment of a new symmachy of Greek states to carry on the war against Persia, and of a symmachy distinct from the Hellenic League.

Athens' position as hegemon also gave her control of the Confederate Treasury, and of the assessment and collection of the tribute which each member polis would submit annually. For this, the Synod appointed Aristeides to draw up the individual assessments of tribute which each member polis was to contribute.[62] Aristeides was also to decide which poleis were to contribute, instead of payments in money, manned ships to the Confederate Fleet (Thuc. 1.99.3). Unfortunately, we do not know by what means a contribution of money was measured in the terms of manned ships, but we can assume that *each polis including Athens* was assessed a given amount,[63] reiterating the principle of equal representation and participation based upon the individual polis' ability to contribute, and that the second step was Aristeides' determination with his assisting staff to assign those poleis with significant military fleets an assessment in manned ships in lieu of money. Athens, therefore, would always contribute her share of the Treasury's naval funds in the form of manned ships, whereas ultimately each polis originally assessed tribute in the form of manned ships would convert, either by its desire or by Athens' command, to payments of tribute in coin. In charge of this fleet, the Synod appointed the Athenian generals, and in charge of the Confederate Treasury to supply funds for the operation of that fleet, the Synod also appointed Athenians as the Treasurers of the Confederacy, a board called the Hellenotamiai, "The Treasurers of the Greeks."[64]

Athens' hegemony was, in the first few years of the Confederacy's development, fundamentally in the nature of an executive power and distinctly not that of a sovereign commander. The Synod, during the first few years, retained the right to formulate policy and to enact the directives toward the accomplishment of the goals of its symmachy, while the power to execute those policies had been placed in the hands of the Athenian generals, yet subject to the Synod's ultimate decisions. The function of Athens as the executive power was, therefore, to administer for the Synod the military and naval forces of the alliance, for within the Synod, the Athenians had only a single vote and that equal to the vote of any other allied polis.   But by means of Athens' special responsibilities, voted upon by the Synod, and her prestigious position—essentially her large and successful fleet—Athens could rest assured that a majority of the allies would vote in accordance with Athenian desire, especially the smaller and militarily vulnerable poleis which greatly needed a strong supportive guide, and thus Athens immediately obtained the position of *prima inter pares*.[65]   The hegemony itself had made Athens "first among equals," a position proposed and voted upon in the first Synod.

Thucydides clearly indicates that the conduct of the war was not the only major concern for the Athenians, but that they also played an important role in the routine administration of confederate affairs (Thuc. 1.97.1). Athens' role as hegemon had firmly enabled her to preside at the meetings of the Synod, as Athens was the executive power and her representatives chaired the meetings the Athenian chairman held a distinct degree of probouleutic authority within the Synod.[66] Through the control of the agenda of that Synod, the Athenian delegate as chairman representing the Athenian Demos undertook to transform the Confederacy into an Athenian Empire. A second means of Athens' control of the Confederacy was her command of its armed forces, which enabled her to influence the vote of the lesser poleis. In a brief period of time, Athens was then able either to patronize or to intimidate those poleis (Thuc. 3.10.3-5). Because of the collective votes of those poleis, which formed a majority of the Synod, the opponents of Athenian policies, as a minority block, were unable to carry out effective opposition to the Athenian direction. As a result, individual allied poleis became subjugated by Athens and suffered a loss of their *autonomia*. The transformation of the alliance governed at first by the representative Synod and then by the sole direction of Athens is indicated by Thucydides' remark: "At *first* [Athens] led the allies who were 'independent' and deliberated with them in a common Synod" (1.97.1). The early regular meetings of the Delian Synod, most likely annual, quickly came to be little more than formal sessions for the confirmation of decisions reached by Athens alone and then presented *pro forma* to the Confederacy for approval by the members of the alliance.[67] The representative Synod for a time did continue to exist and to function, but with markedly diminished importance.

The crux of the matter lay in that the Synod was not created to legislate for the citizens of the member allied poleis, neither did it ever receive that authority, nor did Athens. The enactment of policy and directives by the Synod was, however, fundamental to the functioning of the Confederacy. The member poleis, therefore, regarded these as their prerogative; thus the usurpation of that prerogative by Athens became the fundamental factor in the discontent among the allied poleis. At the point when most of the allies had become subjected to the control of Athens, therefore, the Synod ceased to function. After 449 B.C., there is no evidence that the Synod met, for by that time its duties had been assumed by the Athenian Boule and Demos.

In 454 B.C., when the Treasury was transferred from the island of Delos to Athens' fortified city, there is evidence of a directive power still being executed by the Synod. Plutarch, in his biography of Aristeides, reported that at that time a debate occurred in the Synod concerning the Samian proposal to move the Treasury for protection against the Persians, a proposal which the representatives of the Synod had to approve as it was contrary to the Charter's agreements formulated and, thus, the Synod's prerogative to discuss and vote upon the matter.[68] But following the positive vote and the successful transfer of the Treasury to Athens, the meetings of the Synod, formerly at Delos, were now held in Athens, and apparently at the time of the quadrennial Great Panathenaia (the occasion for the revision of tribute assessments) and also at the annual Dionysia during the other years.[69]

The Synod now located in Athens may have continued to meet during the next few years, but if it did, it was essentially an unimportant and purely ceremonial body for action taken by Athens. After 449 B.C., it was the Athenian Boule and Demos rather than the Confederate Synod which issued the directives to the allied poleis. The regulations for judicial procedures for the allied poleis, the Athenian Judicial Decree which regulated internal allied judicial conduct and transferred to Athens the trials of capital crimes;[70] the Athenian Currency Decree which standardized the coinage, weights, and measures of the allies (ML *GHI* 45); and the Athenian decree proposed by Kleinias which regulated the collection of confederate tribute (ML *GHI* 46); were not only political directives to allied poleis but Athenian legislation for allied citizens. They are, therefore, definite indications of the transformation of Athenian hegemony into imperial power, compounded by the fact that there is no suggestion that the Confederation Synod ratified these decrees promulgated in the Athenian assembly. By 449 B.C., the allied poleis and their citizens, excepting those of Samos, Chios, and Lesbos, were subject to and subjugated by the legislation of the Athenian Boule and Demos.

As military leader, Athens rapidly gained the sole command of the Confederate Navy not only to continue the avowed war against King Xerxes and his Empire but also to maintain the military unity of the Confederacy. Allied poleis which did not comply with the Synod's directives or those of the hegemon were, therefore, severely reprimanded and, if necessary, militarily coerced into compliance. In this, there is no evidence that Athens ever consulted the Synod before using the Confederate Fleet to suppress a rebellious ally. As hegemon, Athens apparently considered herself to have been authorized from the outset of the Confederacy's activities, tacitly if not formally, to take immediate action against allied sedition, or any act contrary to the Confederacy's principles. Immediate action by the Confederate Fleet was, therefore, absolutely necessary to maintain unity and to suppress any dissension, especially any which might threaten to become widespread. The Confederacy simply could not afford to wait while a Synod was summoned and assembled at Delos to deal with rebellion. Internal sedition would have been extremely detrimental to the Confederacy while it maintained its defensive and offensive military unity against the Persian Empire. The military action which led to the several known suppressions of poleis was definitely decided upon and directed by the Athenians. As Thucydides implied, the decision for the military suppression of Samos in 440-439 B.C. was a decision clearly made by the Athenian

Demos.[71]

For the allied Greeks, the articles of Confederacy maintained their freedom through the confederate law, but in that law also existed the concept of mutual coercion, mutually agreed upon for the necessity of all. The ancient evidence indicates, however, that while the Athenians had one concept of "mutual coercion, mutually agreed upon" several of the militarily powerful allies had others.

At Olympia in 428 B.C., the Mytilenaian representative noted that the change from Confederacy to Empire had taken place after the mid–century. The allies had been able to retain a share of the deliberative directive functions of the Confederacy as long as the purpose of the Confederacy was maintained and as long as the allies were joined in common opposition against Persia. Thus, the Mytilenaians maintained (according to Thucydides): "So long as Athens led us *as equals*, we were eager to follow; but when we saw her becoming less interested in the war against Persia than in the subjection of the allies, we began to feel nervous. Since the system of many votes (majority rule) had made them (the allies) incapable of combining to protect themselves, all the allies except us and Chios were subjected; we, too, continued to serve in her (Athens') campaigns, the so–called 'free and autonomous allies'" (3.10.4-5). "Our (the Mytilenaian) autonomy was spared for reason of propaganda: Athens realized that opinion counts in power politics far more than force. We were standing witnesses to her character—surely allies who have an equal vote could not be forced to take part in campaigns unless the parties attacked were in the wrong—and at the same time, while she was using us—the strong to crush the weak—she was also reserving us to the last, knowing that the strong when isolated would no longer be strong" (3.11.3-4).[72]

At the time of the Confederacy's organization, Athens' new allies were extremely shortsighted. The enthusiasm generated by the creation of an aggressive military-naval alliance to defend the Greeks against the Persians, coupled with the anticipation of swift victories to follow those of Sestos and Byzantion, led many of the Greeks to join the Confederacy without carefully giving thought to future changes. In many respects the Confederacy in its first days was, as Alfred Zimmern stated, "a child of necessity and its creators did not know what they were doing."[73] But the original oath of 477 B.C. remained; and Athens insisted upon adherence to it while the allies insisted that any action contrary to their interests went beyond the oath and violated their eleutheria. In reply to such claims, Thucydides, in the voice of Perikles and for the Athenians, commented that the tyranny which Athens may have been unjust to assume could not without danger by relaxed (2.53.2).[74] And yet, the East Greek governments had to join the Confederacy by necessity, as they could not exist along the western frontier of the Persian Empire and, perhaps, suffer a new phase of Persian conquest, destruction, and subjugation, when the Confederacy offered them military defense, strategic offensive activities whereby they could continue to push Persia back, and a means by which to revitalize economic and political bases of their poleis. In turn, the foundation of the Delian Confederacy served as the major means by which the Athenians revitalized their polis following two years of marked societal distortion created by the Persian occupation and destruction of their urban center. For the East Greeks and for the Athenians the creation of the Delian Confederacy was an absolute necessity, without which neither of the two groups could have hoped to revive. Yet with the Athenian rapid domination of the Confederacy and transformation of it into an Empire, the East Greeks continued to experience the problem of societal distortion, and in order to obtain some measure of self-preservation began to react to Athens' "tyranny," which seemed rather similar to the so–called "despotic and tyrannical power" of the Persians, as expressed by Herodotus.

The enthusiasm generated on Delos during the winter months of 478/7 B.C. was, indeed, shortlived.[75] By c. 465 B.C., the large southern Aegean and allied island of Naxos—in 490 B.C., brutally subjugated by the Persians—had seceded from the Confederacy, was forcibly subjugated by the Athenians and the allied forces, and compelled to remain in the alliance.[76]

Thucydides' brief statement in regard to the Naxian revolt and its suppression occurs within his very brief discussion of the early activities of the Delian Confederacy, the excursus on the Pentekontaetia (1.89-117). Chapters 89-97 present the origin and organization of the Confederacy, and they are followed by a short account of the Confederacy's military operations during the first eleven years of the alliance. Chapter 98 tersely describes four examples of different types of allied military operations in the Aegean as part of the offensive campaigns against the Persian Empire toward the Confederacy's goals. The first example is the confederate attack upon the Persian fortress of Eion in western Skudra and the crucial junction of the Thracian east-west coastal road and the north–south river valley of the Strymon. Eion marks the first

confederate campaign and continues the theme of military aggression against Persian
garrisons, begun against Sestos and then Byzantion.[77] The second campaign is that
against the island of Skyros in the northern Sporades, as the first example of confederate
subjugation and then colonization of a territory not held by the Persians, yet hostile and
inhabited by pirates.[78] Skyros lay astride the trade lines from Attica to the Thracian
regions being seized from the satrapy of Skudra, but more important also upon the trade
line to the Hellespont and the Bosporos along which the revived grain trade would move.
The third campaign is that against the polis of Karystos on the southern tip of the great
island of Euboia. Karystos had medized in 490 B.C., and had not joined the Delian
Confederacy, and yet lay between the important military and mercantile route from
Attica to Skyros and the northern regions. Thucydides included this campaign as an
example of confederate attacks upon a sovereign Greek polis, neither Persian controlled
nor piratical but formerly having medized and not within the military structure of the
new symmachy, therefore being militarily forced by the Confederacy to join its
alliance.[79] This chapter ends with Thucydides' reference to the campaign against Naxos
as the first example of allied secession. His brief account unfortunately omitted the
causes for secession since his purpose was merely to cite the expedition against Naxos as
one of four types of military campaigns conducted by the confederate forces during the
first eleven years of the alliance's history.

What is noticeably absent in this all too brief chapter is reference to military
activities along the western coast of Anatolia. In fact, the "liberation of Ionia" theme,
all too stressed throughout the pages of Herodotus' History and mentioned by Thucydides
himself in chapter 1.95.1, is remarkably absent in the remainder of the Pentekontaetia
excursus. The answer to this problem of why Thucydides omitted in chapter 98 reference
to campaigns in Ionia is, however, simple. The military activities of the Hellenic League
in 478 B.C. had been continued by the Delian Confederacy in 477 B.C. and the several
years thereafter, and they had included the ongoing military support of the island Greeks
and of the East Greeks from southern Karia to Kalchedon. Yet, those eastern military
campaigns which we must strongly suspect occurred, while the campaigns against Eion,
Skyros, Karystos, and Naxos were also taking place, were not in themselves important
examples of military campaigns against the Persians, pirates, medizing poleis, or even
rebellious allies. With the Persian withdrawal from most of the coastal zone of Sparda

and Daskyleion, the East Greeks rather freely transferred from the Persian Empire to the Delian Confederacy without military struggle. It was, therefore, the East Greeks themselves who initiated the steps of their alliance with the Delian Confederacy rather than confederate military campaigns in the Troad, Aiolis, Ionia, or Karia, which brought those poleis mentioned above into the Confederacy, either in the winter of 478/7 B.C. or the subsequent years.

The secession of Naxos from the Confederacy and its subsequent subjugation must have generated some degree of alarm among those East Greek poleis, no less the other members of the alliance. The fall of Naxos was crucial to the future of each allied polis. Having mentioned Naxos, Thucydides proceeded to discuss the problem of secession in general (1.99); although he did not specifically refer to Naxos, his statements may be applied to an analysis of the preceding situation in Naxos and to the conditions there before the 466/5 B.C. revolution. The Athenian historian stated there were several motivations for revolution, and that (1.99.1) "The principal reasons were being in arrears in paying tribute and supplying ships and, in some cases, the refusal to serve." He continued (1.99.1-2): "The Athenians were exacting and offensive by applying their coercive measures to those unaccustomed or unwilling to suffer hardship. In other ways the Athenians were no longer equally agreeable as rulers, and did not share in expeditions *on terms of equality*." The failures of the allies to fulfill their obligations by supplying Athens and the Confederate Fleet with the necessary tribute and manned ships, in addition to several of the allies blatantly refusing to serve with the fleet, led to greater coercive measures by Athens as hegemon of the alliance. The military superiority of the Athenians and the contrasting weakness of the individual allies easily enabled the Athenians to subdue those in revolt, and as Thucydides also stated (1.99.2): "It was easy to bring to one's side those states in revolt."

Thucydides analyzed the conditions for such revolutions by noting the failure of the allied poleis to supply manned ships to the fleet and to pay tribute in compliance with the principal articles of the Confederacy. The statement that a cause for revolution was the failure to serve refers to poleis which were supplying manned ships, and may refer to the fact that ships—perhaps a whole allied contingent—returned home in the middle of a campaign.[80] Thucydides further commented that in regard to unequal sharing in the expeditions (1.99.3), "The allies themselves were responsible, for the majority of them, because of this same avoidance of military service in order not to be away from home, allowed themselves to be assessed to pay money as the proportionate expenditure in place of ships."

Plutarch, in his biography of Kimon, declared that (11.1) "The allies paid the money tribute but they did not furnish the men and ships as they were assessed, for they soon grew weary of the expeditions and they desired nothing of war, for they desired to farm and to live in quietness." The emphasis upon "refusal to serve" underscores the problem of the Confederate Fleet, for by 466/5 B.C. the allies no longer wished to participate in the symmachy's naval campaigns but to remain at home. Plutarch's discussion of the failure of the allies to supply ships occurs within a context which reveals that they were failing to meet their naval obligations stipulated among the confederate articles at a time when the need for military aggression was waning. He further commented that the allies (Kim. 11.1) "were free from [the threat of] the barbarians and were not exceedingly annoyed by them, and they neither manned their ships nor sent men." With the growing reluctance to support the fleet, Athens' enforcement of the Confederate obligations then became harsh. Plutarch also remarked that, as a result of the allies' reluctance (11.1), "The Athenian generals [other than Kimon] were forcing them to do these things, and by prosecuting them by indictments and punishing those defaulting, they made the Empire burdensome and offensive."[81]

The military activities of the Confederate Fleet during the first eleven years of its attempts to achieve the goals of the symmachy, no less the personally motivated goals of the Athenians, had been extremely successful in gaining control of much of Persian Skudra, and in retaining firmly the western littoral zone of Daskyleion and Sparda. By c. 466 B.C., the fleet had begun to campaign among the mountain ringed bays of rugged Karia to add to its numbers the non-Greek Karian dynastic centers, and then to push on toward the similar non-Greek centers in Lykia (Plut. Kim. 12.1). The marked success, which again accentuates the argument of cognizant Persian withdrawal from much of the coastal zone, directly increased Athenian enthusiasm and hegemonic control, which now had been transformed into stern and single-handed rule. Yet to stem the Confederacy's successes, Xerxes and his Persian military advisors began to contemplate and to design a new and fourth major naval expedition into the Aegean against the military forces of the Confederacy. But this information had not reached the confederates or the discontent

Naxians. If the Persians did succeed in sailing in force into the Aegean basin, Naxos lay in the mid-path of a Persian imperial attack upon Delos and Athens. But for the Naxians, their immediate problems dominated their secessionist actions.

The Eurymedon Campaign of 465 B.C. marked the point at which the allied Greek poleis of the Confederacy were essentially free from Persian military threat and annoyance,[82] as Thucydides' discussion concerning the causes of revolution occurs between the account of the confederate expedition against Naxos (466/5 B.C.) and the battle at the Eurymedon (465 B.C.). The allied reluctance to supply the Confederacy with ships and men, and even with money, was the fundamental factor which led to the revolution of Naxos and her secession. That reluctance to campaign, present in the mid-sixties of that century, continued as late as the thirties (Thuc. 3.10-1). From the remarks of Thucydides and Plutarch it is evident that the rigors of the campaigns directed by Athens against Persia no longer pleased the allies (Thuc. 1.99.3; Plut. Kim. 11.1). The victories at Salamis, Plataia, and Mykale had generated a marked enthusiasm among the Greeks who joined Aristeides on Delos, but as the Persian threat diminished so did the enthusiasm. And the decisive victory at the Eurymedon only sharply accentuated that diminution. As Athens continued her direction of the Confederacy, she also firmly insisted upon full payment of tribute from each allied polis and full delivery of every manned ship, properly equipped, and that hegemonic insistence produced various allied reactions. Some allies who had defaulted in their tribute agreed to pay, while others who had previously supplied manned ships preferred to convert their tribute back into values of money. But all had acted under Athenian compulsion.

The major allied complaint against Athens was that she did not share in the expeditions on terms of equality (Thuc. 1.99.2), a marked change in the principles of the Confederacy which had changed by 466 B.C. By then, the Athenians not only decided on their own authority on the nature of the campaigns, but also behaved in every manner not as hegemonic leaders but autocratic leaders and not just one of several equal contin-gents.[83] By now, the Athenian generals were prosecuting the allies with indictments for having defaulted in the fulfillment of their obligations and, thereupon, punished them. This, Plutarch noted (Kim. 11), made the Empire burdensome and offensive, and bitterness spread among the islands and the coastal regions of the Aegean Sea.

The Delian Confederacy had originally joined sovereign poleis into a permanent symmachy with no right of secession, an organization in which the member poleis were bound to the cooperative direction of the hegemon. At the outset, the poleis, which had banded with Athens and had given her the hegemony, had considered that their sovereignty would not diminish, as the allies maintained that the compact which they had adopted designed the Synod to form policy, and that each polis would have one and an equal vote to ratify that policy. The Synod was, therefore, to have been the judge of the extent of reserved powers (the powers not given to the hegemon as established in the confederate articles) and also was not bound to the hegemonic branch of the symmachy which would attempt to control the extent of reserved powers. The allied poleis seem to have believed that the Confederacy had generated an alliance of numerous states-in-trust which gave designated powers to the hegemon (the trustee) to execute. If the trustee power did not perform its duties according to the established compact, the right of the states-in-trust to object, consequently, came into existence. This theory of secession was, no doubt, a product of time and circumstance and apparently did not exist in 477 B.C. but developed as a result of allied discontent by the time of the Naxian revolution.   Athens, however, was clearly of a different mind.   Her reaction to the secession of Naxos was to preserve the Confederacy at all cost by enforcing the Delian Oath which delineated the symmachy as permanent and forever binding (*Ath. Pol.* 23.5). Secession, the Athenians argued, was a flagrant breach of that sacred oath.

The new money contributions to the Treasury received from the series of conversions of tribute in manned ships to money enabled the Athenians to build new ships, now firmly under their control. Athenian insistence upon the fulfillment of all obligations, coupled with Athens' rising naval superiority, progressively detracted from her popularity and began to generate the specter of Athenian tyranny. That allied disfavor with Athens further supported the Naxian contention that the Athenians had violated the confederate articles of agreement. As the Naxians argued that the Athenians had assumed greater political power than had been granted to her by the Synod, at that point Naxos seceded from the Confederacy and revolted against Athens. But the Naxian hopes to maintain their independence and to withdraw from the Confederacy were in vain. The displeasure of one member of the alliance, or even the displeasure of several, was not sufficient to defeat its hegemonic trustee or even to curtail its power. The Athenians, consequently, directed the Confederate Fleet against

Naxos and placed the island under siege.[84]

With capitulation, Naxos lost her *eleutheria*, described by Thucydides as subjugation (*edoulōthē:* 1.98.4). As the Athenians held the executive power of the Confederacy and directed the military operations through their control of the alliance, they found it politically necessary and expedient to use force as they thought fit in order to retain confederate unity and to maintain the Athenian position of power. As there was still fear of a fourth Persian expedition against Greece, which did materialize early in 465 B.C. yet was halted at the Eurymedon River, the whole defense of the Delian Confederacy had to be maintained.

The subjugation of Naxos, *douleia*, restricted Naxian sovereignty. In the fifth century B.C., the condition of *douleia* among the Greeks, as among the Greeks and their Persian overlords, indicated a political situation in which the party subjugated was no longer independent. *Douleia* denoted the condition of personal subjection in which the freedom of an individual or a polis was restricted by the loss of political and civil rights.[85] As the Persian control of Ionia had subjugated the East Greeks and had prevented their self-determination,[86] Athenian control of her confederate allies as it transformed into imperialism similarly restricted their political self-determination,[87] for the antithesis of *douleia* was *eleutheria*, the political condition of sovereignty.[88] *Eleutheria* denoted the total character of independence within a polis while *douleia* restricted self-rule and generated a loss of political independence,[89] and by c. 465 B.C. the Athenians had begun to determine single-handedly the degree of subjugation imposed upon any given ally, conditions of subjugation which did vary for the next sixteen years accordingly with each subjected allied polis.

Many years later, Plato defined the condition of *eleutheria* as the rule of law, and *douleia* as produced by the rule of men (*Leg.* 9.865b), and explained *douleia* as the change in the constitution of a polis which had been subverted by a political and military force which had transformed the rule of law into the rule of men. The dominant power, Plato continued, thereby restricted the earlier nature of the law and transferred the polis in question to the status of a subjugated state which no longer retained external or internal sovereignty. *Eleutheria.* as defined by Lysias, denoted the freedom of citizens and resident aliens within a polis in contrast to the lack of freedom of slaves who held no civic rights (13.66). This differentiating characteristic marked the political power of the rule of one person or state over another. And for Thucydides, *douleia* denoted a form of clientship or political subservience (1.8.3): "weaker people were willing to submit to dependence on the stronger, and the more powerful men, with their enlarged resources, were able to make the lesser communities (poleis) their subjects *(hypēkoous)*." Although Thucydides' reference was to the Bronze Age, it was also relevant to his contemporary condition and the understanding of *douleia* in the fifth century B.C. It was as Thucydides stressed "contrary to established custom" or more precisely *contrary to the established juridical order*.[90] Athenian subjugation of Naxos had violated Naxian *eleutheria* as it had also violated the principles of the Confederacy.

The subjugation of Naxos resulted in the loss of Naxian *autonomia* and the establishment of Athenian imperial control. This infringement of Naxian *autonomia* became the pattern by which other allied poleis later experienced similar loss of *autonomia*, losses which Thucydides discussed in greater detail (e.g. Thasos, Aigina, and Samos) and which reaffirm this definition of *douleia*. From these later examples we may suspect that the Athenians compelled the Naxians to surrender their war ships (as distinct from merchant ships) to Athenian control, to continue their tribute payments in money rather than in manned ships,[91] and to destroy their fortifications about the asty. The Athenians may also have established a military garrison at Naxos and perhaps, in addition, a klerouchy, a small outpost of Athenians who lived in Naxos and would act when necessary to support Athenian control.[92]

The Athenian subjugation of Naxos, however, did not entail the harsh enslavement or chattelism, *andrapodismos*, suffered by the Persians captured at Eion in 470/69 B.C. or by the Dolopian pirates enslaved on Skyros.[93] For any man to be reduced to the condition of *andrapodismos* meant that he not only lost all political and civil rights but all personal rights as well, and for Thucydides it was almost synonymous with death (5.9.9). The *douleia* suffered by the Naxians was not this chattelism, but rather political subjugation, and a loss of independence suffered which became a precedent for all future allied rebellions and subjections. The *douleia* imposed upon the Naxians was similar to the loss of sovereignty suffered by the people of Karystos forced to join the Confederacy,[94] of whom Thucydides remarked (1.98.4): "They came to terms by means of an homologia, the treaty of surrender."[95] By his use of homologia, Thucydides did not imply an agreement on equal terms, as often mistakenly interpreted, but rather the acceptance by the subjugated polis of the terms which Athens offered. During the Persian campaign to Eretria in 490 B.C., Karystos had joined the Persian forces as a vassal state, a position reaffirmed after the battle of Artemision in 480 B.C.; consequently, after the battle of Salamis, the Karystians suffered for their medism at the hands of the Greeks.[96] To clear the Aegean of Persian naval forces and to punish the Persian vassal poleis, Themistokles had sailed among the western Aegean islands and forced several poleis to render tribute to the naval forces of the Hellenic League. In 480 B.C., therefore, Karystos was forced to pay because of her pro-Persian sympathies.[97] In 478/7 B.C., consequently, Karystos maintained a policy of non-cooperation with the allied Greeks and refused to join the Delian Confederacy, a refusal which piqued Athens' patience. Karystos' medism, her fighting on the side of the King Xerxes' forces at Salamis, her reluctance to cooperate with the Hellenic League after that sea battle, and the more important factor that Karystos presented a potential threat to Euboia and to Attica were the factors which precipitated the confederate attack. Karystos, situated on the southern bay of Euboia, threatened the political stability of the other Euboian poleis, and raised Athenian fears of Karystos' potential threat to the well-being of the Confederacy. Karystos' potential to interfere with shipping routes around southern Euboia northward past Skyros to Byzantion or to Eion generated the Athenian necessity to eliminate the dangers to those trade and military routes by that seat of medism within the heart of the Confederacy. The military activities, however, clearly favored the strategic position of Athens and hardly fulfilled the expressed purposes of the Confederacy. The Athenians had to be assured that this subjected polis now allied within the Confederacy would no longer medize nor be opposed to the policies of either the Confederacy or Athens. Karystos did not retain her sovereignty as the Athenians apparently established checks upon her internal political functions, possibly in the form of a klerouchy.

Within Athens, it was the growing tendency, and rather quickly, for Athens as hegemon to usurp the entire supreme command of the Confederacy from its Synod, and specifically in the making of decisions about foreign affairs (Thuc. 1.97-99; 6.42; 7.57). This action clearly violated the basic element of the allied poleis, their *eleutheria*, or their independence in foreign affairs. On the other hand, Athens claimed de jure to be simply prima inter pares because she contributed the most to the Confederacy, and because she was the hegemon. But de facto, Athens formulated the confederate policies and then swiftly executed them. As Athens interfered in the internal affairs of the allied poleis, she violated their basic element of *eleutheria*, their self-imposed laws and freedom in political self-determination. Athens, therefore, provided not only the military leaders but also the administrators of the Confederacy, and later the magistrates to govern the Empire. For those administrators it was both tempting and necessary to call upon the military commanders to enforce the payment of contributions and the allegiance of the recalcitrant allied poleis. This compulsion, consequently, clearly became an infringement upon the sovereignty of the allies; and to overcome this resentment, Athens established in those recalcitrant poleis governments and constitutions, which supported her policies, even though such actions were flagrant violations of allied political self-determination ([Xen.] *Ath. Pol.* 3.10).

The transition from the Delian Confederacy to an Athenian Empire began at the end of the first decade of the alliance. The restrictions imposed upon errant allies, first Naxos and then others, were clear indications that Athens' personal control of the Confederacy had tightened. In the late fifties the pace of that transition quickened, and by the early forties, the transition was complete. Yet Athenian domination was never totally secure, as several allies refused to regard past subjugations of other allied poleis as indications of an absolute powerful Athenian control. Some of those allies subsequently sought to break from the Confederacy and to reject the Athenian demands. In most cases, however, they were not successful.

IONIAN DISCONTENT WITH ATHENIAN IMPERIALISM

Xerxes' return to Susa was not the triumph envisioned in 481 B.C. when he had departed for Sardis. The failures in Yauna, the developing problems in Skudra, and the reorganization and retrenchment of Sparda and Daskyleion marked Xerxes' losses of territories conquered by Darius and a significant alteration of royal leadership within the Persian Empire. While the Athenian sculptures shipped to Susa would remind the Persians that Xerxes had destroyed Athens and its acropolis[1] and had accomplished that goal of his father, they also knew of the Persian military failures and the significant losses of imperial forces. The military stability of the Achaemenid empire had been seriously shaken. Furthermore, potential rebellion existed among the Egyptians, bittered by Xerxes' harsh suppression of their 486-4 B.C. revolt and by further military losses incurred in Greece; and bitterness bred potential rebellion among the Babylonians for the same reasons.[2]

To insure imperial control in order to curb rebellion, Xerxes relied greatly upon members of his royal family to maintain order in the key satrapies. In Sparda, the Great King's uncle Artaphrenes I firmly governed, and was apparently succeeded by his own son Artaphrenes II (fig. 22). And in Daskyleion, Megabates, the Persian cousin of King Darius, faithfully served King Xerxes, and sometime in the second quarter of the fifth century was succeeded by the Persian noble Artabazos who also served King Artaxerxes I (fig. 23).

To the Athenians sitting in their theater of Dionysos in the early spring of 472 B.C., Aeschylus vividly presented the Greek view of Xerxes' hybris to the gods, at least to the Greek gods,[3] and the significant transformation of the Achaemenid Empire. As those same Athenians departed from that theater and passed through their agora, they were doubtlessly aware of the recently erected new sculptural complex which replaced the one taken to Susa and which bore the impassioned inscription: "A great light occurred for the Athenians when Aristogeiton and Harmodios slew Hipparchos . . . and established . . . for the fatherland."[4] Perhaps in their ears rang Aeschylus' cry (Persae 402-3): "Come, children of the Hellenes! Liberate your fatherland!" words which echoed earlier Athenian political songs[5] praising the tyrannicides for isonomia ("equality before the law") and the expulsion of the tyrant Hippias. The sculpture also reminded the Athenians that they had expelled Hippias at Marathon and the Persians who had supported him.[6] With parts of Xerxes' Hellespont–cables hanging upon a monument on the acropolis, the Athenians could see the evidence of their victories, and proudly bore the spirit which the men at Salamis had generated.

Scattered about the agora and upon the acropolis, other stone monuments bore epigrams lauding the battles of Marathon, Salamis, and Plataia, epigrams which complemented Aeschylus' encomia of the victorious Athenians at the battle of Salamis and that of the sculptural and monumental complexes.[7] One need only to look up from the southern slopes of the agora to the newly built north wall of the acropolis to see the careful alignment of column drums and architectural pieces of the acropolitan temples destroyed by the marauding Persians. The north wall itself was an Athenian monument to Athens' victory and freedom.[8]

In Athens, the unique combination of events, reactions, and collective activities generated a spirit which spawned both the Athenian democracy and imperialism;[9] fundamental to which were the fortification of the asty and its harbor at Piraeus (Thuc. 1.90-3) and the exalted belief in *eleutheria*.[10] During the 470's B.C., the victories over the barbarian generated a vibrant revitalization movement, an aggressive stage, directed not by one or two leaders and their followers but by leaders and the Athenian Demos, the Athenians collectively. The leaders molded the final products but the Demos, the broad base of Athenian landed gentry and the others who structured the powerful political body of that assembly, debated and acted upon every public decision. But without the polis' silver mines at Laureion, untouched by the Persians, much of the physical rebuilding of Athens would not have been possible. Athenian spirit and ships depended directly upon the state's silver revenues.

In Ionia, the mood was quite different. There were no new sculptures, either seized or recently carved, epigrams, walls, or aggressive spirit. The mood was one of neither jubilation nor caution and rebellion-alert. The complex internal problems of rebuilding dominated the actions of the Ionian landed gentry and their poleis. It was not freedom but rather the practical question of rebuilding the economically distressed poleis and restoring local and internal political stability which concerned them. During the Persian occupation, the rebellious poleis had lost their protective fortification walls, and for the

first three quarters of the fifth century B.C. the impoverished Ionians did not rebuild.
But with the presence of Persian garrisons marking the frontier zone between the East
Greek poleis allied with the Delian Confederacy and the satrapal military powers of
Sparda and Daskyleion, the poleis had no choice but to rely without reservation upon the
confederate fleet for military protection, especially as their aste remained unwalled.[11]
The only archaeologically attested rebuilding occurred at Miletos where parts of the asty
were redeveloped along the so-called Hippodamian plan,[12] yet the north-western section
of the city remained in ruin.[13] And at Didyma, apparently, the Molpoi had reorganized
sufficiently to gather funds for the rebuilding of the small Ionic temple to Apollo.

In Teos, the grain shortages had created numerous problems including piracy and
brigandage; problems perhaps more widespread throughout Ionia than our meager sources
suggest, problems which only compounded the psychological and military insecurities of
the breached walls. If in Attica, fifty years after the Persians had departed, many of the
rural demesnes and farms had only recently recovered (Thuc. 2.16), there is no reason to
suspect that the demesnes of the landed gentry throughout the Ionian chorai fared
better. In reality, they probably fared worse.

What security the Ionians held was that of the Delian Confederacy. While the events
of 479 and 478 B.C. left the Ionians with the necessity of joining that symmachy, the
articles of the Confederacy did offer them the hope of survival, revival, and security
within a military alliance of parity to which, in the spring of 477 B.C., the participating
members swore oaths.   The dichotomy of basic principles, however, rapidly arose:
Athens as hegemon was determined to achieve the set goals of the symmachy while, in
contrast, each allied polis would resist integration into the Confederacy to the degree
that its sovereignty would be lost. The particularism and parochialism, which had all too
often prevented the East Greek poleis from collectively opposing the Lydian and the
Persian Empires, unfortunately persisted, and allied collective action against Athenian
usurpation of power from the Confederate Synod rarely occurred. With the exception of
Miletos, the Persians were less disruptive of the political accommodations reached with
the East Greek poleis than were the Athenians.

During the first eleven years of the Confederacy's history, 477-466 B.C., the gradual
transformation of the principle of equality to the development of Athenian restrictions

occurred, restrictions which became the hallmarks of subjugation and vassalage. With the fall of the key Persian garrison at Eion (Hdt. 7.107; Thuc. 1.98.1) c. 470/69 B.C., admirably commanded by the Persian general Boges, the western frontier of the Persian Empire crumbled.[14] The Persian hyparchoi throughout western Skudra, along the coastal zone and not ensconced among the interior Thracian tribal regions,[15] also quickly fell. Only the central fortified garrison at Doriskos fervently held out, ably commanded by Maskames, the son of Megadostes (Hdt. 7.105-6; fig. 21). Unlike the Persian littoral garrisons among the East Greeks, Thracian Eion and Doriskos were maintained by Xerxes' officers, even though they had lost their key garrisons at Sestos and Byzantion and easy communication with Sardis. The fall of Eion also altered Persia's alliance with Macedonia, and ended Xerxes' military plans for the Persian reoccupation of regions beyond Skudra (Plato *Menex.* 241d). Maskames' control of Doriskos, however, did remain firm as did Persian control of the interior regions of the Hebros River valley.[16] The Teichos Basileion garrisoned by Persian troops since c. 513 B.C. (Hdt. 7.59.1) had gained strength with the occupation of Byzantion by the renegade Spartan Pausanias, c. 477-472/1 B.C. (?), which temporarily severed that crucial port from the Confederacy.[17] Following the expulsion of Pausanias from Byzantion, with the Athenian commander Kimon's forceful control of that important polis and then his naval expedition against Eion (*Oxy. Pap.* 13.1610. fr. 6), Maskames' position became uncertain. With Kimon's expedition against the Dolopian pirates occupying Skyros, c. 469/8 B.C., the Confederacy's northern naval routes became more secure and Persian control of eastern Skudra greatly threatened.[18] But the the annihilation of many of the Athenians and their allies c. 464 B.C. attempting to settle the Strymon Valley north of Eion at Drabeskos[19] (attacked by the united forces of interior western Thracian tribes and goaded on by the Macedonians and their King Alexander I),[20] Doriskos gained security. Yet, while Byzantion was again in confederate control, the confederated forces were having difficulties in the Hellespontine area, specifically near Sigeion at the Asian entrance to that crucial strait and perhaps at Kardia in the Thracian Chersonese along the western Hellespontine shore. Persian garrisons still held much of the Chersonese and at least thirteen Persian ships reinforced the Persian armies there. Kimon's confederate campaigns against those forces, however, defeated the Persians and drove out what forces remained (Plut. *Kim.* 14.1). Trouble had also erupted on the island of Thasos just south of central Thrace (Thuc. 1.100.2). The new pressures upon Maskames came not just from the confederated Greeks and the coastal zones, but from inland at the head of the Hermos Valley where the Eastern Thracian Odrysians were beginning to consolidate and ultimately to expand southward to the coast,[21] thus creating a pincer movement upon the Persian stronghold.

During those eventful eleven years, the East Greek poleis moved firmly into the ranks of the confederate forces battling the Persians, and perhaps some of their peoples were among the ten thousand "Athenians and their allies" who had settled north of Eion and among those slaughtered by the western Thracians at Drabeskos (Thuc. 4.102.2; Isoc. 8.86). Other confederate and Athenian ships doubtlessly made direct contact with each of the poleis which we have considered to be early if not original members of the Delian Confederacy. The campaigns to regain Byzantion, to destroy Eion, to eliminate the Dolopian pirates, and to check Karystos (c. 468-466 B.C.) furthered the Confederacy's goals,[22] just as the losses at Drabeskos, Sigeion, and Kardia (?) could be considered directly related to the confederate cry for liberty for the Greeks.

The campaign against Naxos, nevertheless, signaled the first overt Athenian step towards allied subjugation, certainly visible in hindsight when Thucydides wrote (1.98.4) that the confederate siege of the rebellious island was "contrary to established custom" (para to kathestēkos)[23] as this was the first allied polis to be subjugated "enslaved": protē te hautē polis xsymmachis . . . edoulōthē). The siege may have begun in 467, raged during 466, and may have lasted into the very early months of 465 B.C.[24] At that time, a second confederate fleet was sailing among the stark, rocky coasts of Karia, attacking walled settlements, burning temples, and campaigning beyond the Greek and Karian ethnic regions into Lykia and the settlements of the Median Harpagids.[25]

The Dorian Greeks of Karia's offshore islands were, however, far less enthusiastic for "liberation" and membership in the Delian Confederacy than their northern Ionian neighbors, but with Kimon's demonstration of military power the Athenians prevailed upon the Dorian Greek councilors to accept membership and participation in the Confederacy under Athenian hegemony. On the island of Kos, the ruling power of a Monarchos and Boule, cut off from the mainland of Karia and under military pressure, reluctantly joined the Confederacy but tenaciously opposed Athenian leadership and the growing concept of the Confederacy as a "Pan-Ionian Union." Kos avidly maintained its

Dorian uniqueness and its ties with the poleis of Rhodes and of Karian Knidos, a Dorian

pentapolis which celebrated the athletic festival of Apollo at Triopeion near Knidos.

Independent in spirit and not enthusiastic to join the campaign against the Persians, the

Koans had developed a commercial connexion with Karia and Persia, which they did not

want to sever.[26] The constant unrest in Karia, no doubt, arose from similar motivations.

Having given assistance to the allied "Ionian" poleis and having begun to attack the

Persian controlled settlements (Diod. Sic. 11.60.1), Kimon, with Ionian military

assistance, then began to attack Lykia (Diod. Sic. 11.60.4). A third contingent, which

included the Byzantines, campaigned along the Thracian Chersonese, and a fourth

struggled to control the Strymon Valley. Other contingents may have been elsewhere.

All this military action, however, had significantly overtaxed the allies who had served

among the confederate fleets and who had under the direst of economic conditions

contributed funds to the Confederate Treasury. Thus, in mid-campaign, some of the

allies simply refused to continue and set sail for home.

The immediate reasons for allied discontent and desertion in mid-campaign were, as

Thucydides noted (1.99), the overtaxation of military service and tribute (similar to the

earlier demands by the Persians and Lydian sovereigns), and the growing awareness of

Athenian control both contrary to established custom and no longer according to the

principles of parity. Again, these arguments may be those of Thucydides' research and

allied hindsight, but clearly are to be included among the origins of allied discontent,

which accelerated during the mid-fifth century B.C. into further allied rebellions against

Athenian command and control. The eruption of the Thasian rebellion in 465 B.C., for

example, came as a direct result of Athenian and allied intervention in the Strymon

Valley which impinged upon Thasian interests in the Pangaion Mountain district to the

east of that valley and perhaps confederate activities at Abdera farther east (Pind. Pap.

Oxy. 5.841:65-7). The Athenians had begun to intervene in Thasian interests in mainland

emporia and mining activities, a mainland peraia which the Thasians considered their

sovereign territory. At Naxos and at Thasos the principles of political self-determination

and sovereignty came into question. While our ancient records are silent in regard to the

reaction of the East Greek landed gentry who, in restoring and reviving their demesnes,

still controlled their aristocratic-oligarchic governments, we must suspect the

development of first caution and then marked suspicion in regard to the Athenian directives and motives.

For the allies of the Confederacy, the concept of a common past (Persia's military aggressions against them) and the desire for a common future (a military offensive campaign against Persia) gave rise to the early confederate consciousness of mission. The collective voluntary acts of consolidation, however, quickly gave way to the assertive demands of Athens based upon her military dominance, which became manifest in Athens' early economic and then political control of the imperial structure. The military alliance with a dominant hegemon had begun to evolve from the early steps of de facto imperialism ultimately into an institutionalized religious and juridical imperial system.

The economic distress and poverty among the East Greek poleis no doubt compounded the problem of allied discontent, yet for many Ionians the Confederacy still offered security and the gradual economic recovery sought. In contrast, only in relatively secure and economically sound Lykia could the Persian vassals, the loyal Harpagids, recover after Kimon's attacks and build three large stone buildings on the acropolis of Xanthos—monuments G, H, and F, magnificent sarcophagi, the forerunners of the great Lykian heroa of the fourth century B.C. Their reliefs, the generic symbols of dynastic power and commemorative narratives of contemporary events, were carved in Near Eastern traditions often blended with local Lykian and Anatolian elements distinctly not Greek.[27]

What Ionian discontent had arisen was for Kimon and the other Athenian commanders fortunately checked by Xerxes' final military decree: to dispatch the Persian Imperial Navy against the forces of the Delian Confederacy. The dread fear of Persian return to the Aegean, the possibility of Persian recontrol of the western Anatolian littoral, and whatever new goals Xerxes set for his generals cowed the confederate allies once again, but only temporarily, to support the Athenian hegemony. From the Phoenician port-cities, the Persian naval bases on Cyprus and in Cilicia, Xerxes' royal order dispatched a large fleet manned with imperial soldiers. Kimon, having attacked the Karian and Lykian cities, overthrowing their Persian garrisons, and demanding that the "liberated" cities join the Confederacy, had laid siege to the city of Phaselis on the far eastern border of Lykia and was threatening the Persian controlled region of Pamphylia.[28] To counter-attack Kimon's advances, Xerxes ordered the new

Persian expeditions. To the delta of the Eurymedon River in western Pamphylia, the Persian Imperial Fleet set sail, and upon arriving there awaited further Persian reinforcements from Cyprus.

With the fall of Phaselis to Kimon's besieging forces and pro-confederate diplomacy persuasively managed by the Chians sailing with Kimon, the confederate fleet departed for the Eurymedon. The ancient sources are unfortunately contradictory and confusing, and as with the ancient accounts of the earlier Greco-Persian wars, the numbers of ships for this campaign are unreliable.[29]

Kimon's forces, heady with victory, took the offensive and sailed against the Persian fleet which, without its needed reinforcements, withdrew into the river's delta. The Greeks boldly attacked, destroying the entire Persian Imperial Navy which Thucydides recorded as up to two hundred ships, and then Kimon landed his troops to take the Persian camp. Without delay, Kimon turned and sailed eastward and defeated the approaching Persian reinforcements off Hydros some forty-five kilometers east of the Eurymedon. In defeat, Ariomandes, the son of the great Persian hero and general Gobryas, had held supreme command, accompanied by Tithraustes in command of the Persian Fleet and Pherendates in command of the army stationed on land. From the Eurymedon delta these Persians could have assembled a large force, and when ready have invaded the Aegean. But the battles very early in 465 B.C. had been decisive.[30] Sometime during the next four years, two small confederate task forces, one of thirty ships commanded by Ephialtes and the second of fifty ships commanded by Perikles when sailing into the same region met no Persian opposition (Plut. *Kim.* 13.4).

In Athens, new monuments arose bearing epigrams to the victories at Eion and the Eurymedon. For the latter, Diodorus Siculus preserved the epigrammatic lines (11.62.3):

> From when the ocean first cleft Europe from the Asian mass,
>
> And fierce Ares held men's land in thrall,
>
> Was never yet achieved by mortal men,
>
> A deed of such a kind on continent and sea at once.[31]

As the two headed comet which appeared at the time of the battle of Salamis signaled divine portent and the resultant victory, so may the famed meteorite which fell at Aegospotami in the Hellespont, 468/7 B.C., have stirred the superstitious Greek minds and portended the forthcoming victories against Xerxes' forces.[32]

Kimon's victory at the Eurymedon accentuated Athenian hegemony against Xerxes' forces, eliminated any serious renewed Persian threat to the Aegean, and opened the eastern Mediterranean for future profitable confederate and Athenian offensives. For the confederate allies, however, the fall of Thasos in 463 B.C. (Thuc. 1.101.1-3) was, as Russell Meiggs noted, an "unambiguous sign of tyranny."[33] The lessons learned at Naxos were reconfirmed at Thasos, and in 463 B.C. the East Greek allies had significant reasons to question the merits of the Confederacy, which they had joined. At this point, the processes of Athenian imperialism can be clearly detected, processes which transformed the Confederacy into an Athenian Empire. The growth of Athenian imperialism had not begun with a defined program or set theories of imperialism but rather was the product of a series of successive programs culminating in the events of 449 B.C.[34]

In Susa, in contrast, the mood changed gravely as the disaster at the Eurymedon compounded the tremendous shock of the earlier disasters and now a disaster within Persia. The Naxian rebellion had encouraged Xerxes to mount the naval expedition, but with Naxos' capitulation Kimon had been able to attack at the Eurymedon before Ariomandes' preparations had been completed. Xerxes had, once again, been seriously humiliated. Every satrap knew the decisiveness of those defeats and the losses incurred by his satrapal forces. The imperial crises set into motion at the Eurymedon paralleled that of Cambyses' fateful expedition into Nubia in 522 B.C. Both military expeditions had significantly overtaxed the military forces conscripted from the satrapies and markedly increased the monetary tributes needed by the empire, and had generated internal rebellions, regicide, and assassinations which seriously disrupted the Empire.[35] The humiliation at the Eurymedon was more than the nobles and the royal court could bear, as the disaster temporarily stunned the Empire preparing for Greek attacks upon Cyprus, Cilicia, the Phoenician ports, Judah, and Egypt. The Hellenic League had attacked Cyprus in 478 B.C. and there was no reason not to expect the Delian Confederacy to attack as well. Cyprus had been the key center for the Persian Imperial Fleet which had sailed to the Eurymedon and defeat. Kimon, however, did not follow up his decisive victory by attacking Cyprus, as Persian forces from Doriskos and Daskyleion were causing significant trouble in eastern Thrace and at Sigeion. Rebellious Thasians, rich and with a significant fleet, were also strongly resisting the attacking confederate forces. Persian nobles in the Susian palaces, nevertheless, plotted the assassination of the Great King. They could no longer bear the humility, the overtaxation of tribute and man-power, defeat, and direct attacks upon their Mediterranean naval bases. Persian naval weakness could clearly foster rebellion throughout the Empire, in spite of firm control in Bactria, Egypt, Sparda, and Daskyleion for example, and of what success the Persians could maintain in Skudra.

Near the end of 465 B.C.,[36] in Susa's royal palaces, Artabanos, the son of Artasyras, an Hyrkanian, with the assistance of the royal eunuchs Spamitres and Mithridates (the king's own chamberlain who had held his lord's confidence but who was also a relative and close friend of Artabanos),[37] rallied to gain for Artabanos the royal throne (Diod. Sic. 11.69.1). Artabanos wielded the greatest influence in the court as he commanded the king's royal body guard. With the eunuchs' assistance, Artabanos slew the king in his royal bed chamber, and then set about to create dissension within the palace and to realize the assassinations of the crown prince Dareios and his brother, the soon to be Artaxerxes I. In convoluted intrigue, Artabanos manipulated Artaxerxes' murder of his older brother Dareios, as Artabanos claimed it had been Dareios who had killed Xerxes. Thus, with the assistance of the royal body guard commanded by Artabanos, Artaxerxes killed Dareios only to find himself confronted by Artabanos and his seven sons,[38] who now strove to assassinate that prince. But in a quick turnabout, Artaxerxes drove his dagger into Artabanos and in victory assumed the royal tiara (Diod. Sic. 11.69.2).[39] Upon his assumption to the Achaemenid throne, the new king prudently removed the portraits of his dead father and brother from the east and north staircases of the apadana at Persepolis where they stood in full view for all to see, and carefully placed them away from most eyes among the objects stored in the great treasury building beyond the apadana.[40] Xerxes and Dareios, however, the new king buried with royal honors.

From the last months of 465 B.C., when the regicide occurred, into the summer of 463 B.C., Artaxerxes I successfully struggled to secure his throne, to suppress rebellion, and to punish severely all those involved in Artabanos' plot. Like Darius I fifty-seven years earlier, Artaxerxes set in motion the forces of imperial reform and revitalization; not necessarily new reforms but rather a reinforcement of the older rules and regulations as established by Darius (Diod. Sic. 11.71.2). Artaxerxes' chief aim was to organize imperial affairs, to replace the hostile satraps with nobles loyal to his throne, and to reform the problems of revenues and the raising of military troops (Diod. Sic. 11.71.1-

2). The new king successfully relieved the societal distortion which had intensified after the Eurymedon disaster and the tensions of malefaction among the satrapies. To these ends, Artaxerxes was extremely successful, as Diodorus Siculus noted: " . . . in general, his administration of the entire empire was mild, he enjoyed the favor of the Persians to a high degree" (11.71.2).

For the Great King, Sparda and Daskyleion remained faithful and secure; and early in his reign, an event in Susa set in motion a new aggressive policy against the East Greek poleis. At the palace arrived the Athenian Themistokles, who in his newly learned Old Persian beseeched the king for refuge. As Histiaios generations earlier had advised Darius the Great in Susa on Ionian and Greek affairs, now Themistokles would similarly serve Artaxerxes I. For Themistokles' services to the Achaemenid Empire and his assistance in helping to control western Anatolia, the Great King awarded the Athenian general turned renegade landed estates in Magnesia-on-the-Maeander, Myous, Lampsakos, Perkote, and Skepsis.[41]

For the East Greek allies, the confederate victory at the Eurymedon reconfirmed Athenian hegemony of the Delian Confederacy and the military power that the Athenians had been building since 477 B.C. The East Greeks now fully realized the might, the political and military power of the Confederacy as governed by the Athenians. What Athenian tyranny may have appeared at Naxos and did appear at Thasos was linked and intertwined with Athenian hegemonic power. At the same time, the events of the twenty-four months following Artabanos' abortive revolution in Susa raised numerous questions and problems for the East Greeks. The revolution against Xerxes, the regicide, the revolution against Dareios, and the rise of Artaxerxes to power led first to further imperial reorganization and the reconfirmation of Darius' imperial policies and then to renewed Persian military aggression in the East Greek territories. What greatly disturbed the Athenians and their loyal East Greeks was the Great King's placing of Themistokles in the stronghold of Magnesia-on-the-Maeander and Persian seizure of choric regions of Myous, a minor but key naval port at the head of the important Maeander Gulf. Both operations became major threats to the stability of Ionia, confederate control and solidarity, and to Athenian hegemony in that region, as they signaled Persian advances in that valley and brought the Persians and their Greek vassals closer to the pro-Persian faction which was gaining power in Miletos, a faction which would gain control of that polis by 454 B.C.

Achaemenid opposition against Sigeion also continued as the Persians boldly seized choric regions of confederate Lampsakos and Perkote (if Plut. *Them.* 29.11 be historical), and in the late 450's again occurred, perhaps sporadically rather than continuously to threaten Sigeion directly *(IG* 1^2.32; *SEG* X. 13, possibly 451/0 B.C.). The military advances against Sigeion appear to have been a Persian attempt directed by the satraps of Daskyleion to gain military control of the Anatolian coast of the Hellespont. For the moment, the Bosporos was secure in confederate hands as Kalchedon and Byzantion were both firmly governed by pro-confederates. But if the Persians could threaten the trade lines up the Hellespont by holding the Anatolian coast, and attempting to make a link with Doriskos still firmly held by the Persian army, then a new phase of Persian aggression in the Troad regions of Daskyleion and in the remnant of eastern Skudra could begin. Similarly, the Persian movement into Myous marked the first known step of Persian aggression into the Ionian littoral regions since the withdrawal of the Persian garrisons by the suspected decree of King Xerxes in 478/7 B.C. Persian aggression in the Troad, continued occupation of Doriskos, and aggression in the Maeander Valley appear to have been aspects of Artaxerxes' major plans for imperial revitalization and his attempt to regain East Greek and Thracian territories lost or relinquished by his father. For the Great King and his Empire, however, military advances in western Anatolia came to a halt as rebellion erupted once again in Egypt.

Regicide and assassination, as always in ancient Persia, signaled satrapal rebellion, which King Artaxerxes attempted to prevent. But Egypt, burdened with Persian tax levies and demands for military forces, reacted against Artaxerxes just as it had against Darius I. The isolation of that satrapy, connected to the greater Achaemenid empire by only the Sinai routes and the Phoenician naval lines but threatened by the confederate fleet, gave the rebellious native Egyptians encouragement to see in the regicide of King Xerxes the opportunity to rebel against the Persians for a third time. For Diodorus Siculus, not our best source but our major source for these events, the Egyptians specifically expelled the Persian tax collectors upon their rebellion (11.71.3). But the major blow was the assassination of prince Achaemenes, and the raising up of the Libyan Prince Inaros to the pharaohship of a native revitalization movement, which seized control of the North and the Delta region. In this attempt to wrest Egypt from the

Achaemenid Empire, Inaros in 460 B.C. directly appealed to the forces of the Delian Confederacy for military assistance which came, an event which radically altered the Confederacy (Thuc. 1.104.1).

In Athens, a series of important events had preceded Inaros' appeal, events of the winter of 462/1 B.C.:[42] a major rift with the Spartans and the subsequent Athenian renouncement of the Hellenic alliance against Persia and, to counter-balance that military and diplomatic shift, the Athenian formulation of alliances with Argos and Thessaly, states at enmity with Sparta (Thuc. 1.102,4). Sparta apparently did not contest the Athenian withdrawal from the Hellenic League or that of the poleis which had also joined the Delian Confederacy. At the same time the Athenians realized the greater importance of the Confederacy as a military block against Sparta's allies, the Peloponnesian League. Thus, when Inaros' appeal arrived in the summer of 460 B.C.,[43] the Athenians were commanding a full force of 200 ships off Cyprus, apparently, as a major commitment to the confederate goals to reduce Persian power in the eastern Mediterranean and also the newly developed goals to gain Cyprus. Inaros' appeal, therefore, suddenly and dramatically opened up the possibility of confederate domination of the greater eastern Mediterranean; and the entire fleet immediately departed for Egypt (Thuc. 1.104.2; Isoc. *Peace* 86; Diod. Sic. 11.71.5, 74.3).

At this point, Athenian interests to exclude Phoenician trade from Egypt in order to open new rich grain markets for Athenian trade may have taken precedence over the confederate goal for the reduction of Persian military power. For Inaros, the fall of Memphis would give him the legitimacy and justification for his reign.

Inaros' early successes had encouraged the confederates to campaign in Cyprus, in Cilicia, in Phoenicia, and in Egypt, but at a time when the Athenians had become embroiled in the first steps of a major war on the Greek mainland (*IG* 1^2.929; ML *GHI* 33; Plato *Menex.* 241e; Diod. Sic. 11.75.1-2; Aristod. *FGrH* 104 F 11.3). Confederate operations had barely begun in Egypt when Athenians attacked Aigina (Thuc. 1.105.2) and several years later Boiotian Tanagra (Thuc. 1.108.1), and in doing so campaigned with a significant number of their "Ionian allies" (Thuc. 1.105.2, 107.5; Paus. 5.10.4; ML *GHI* 36). In these instances, the terms "Ionians" and "allies" do not refer specifically to Ionians from Anatolia but broadly to confederates.[44] Consequently, we do not know which "Ionian" poleis contributed to the mainland expeditions nor the number of "Ionian" men employed. Samians had quickly eliminated a small Persian fleet of fifteen ships on the Nile near Memphis (Thuc. 1.104.2; ML *GHI* 34),[45] so, we may suspect that the major island poleis, especially Samos, Chios, and Lesbos, and perhaps the major coastal poleis such as Erythrai and Miletos, participated in both the Egyptian campaign and on the mainland, along with several other confederates. This allied support of Athens depended totally upon success, and any serious military setback either in Greece or in Egypt would disrupt the Confederacy.

In Egypt, the Athenians and confederates had joined Inaros' forces in an attack upon the Persian garrison in the "White Tower" at Memphis, and it was there that the Samian fleet engaged the Persians; but of the following events Thucydides only tersely noted: "The Greeks stayed on in Egypt and there were 'actions of many types' " (1.109.1). On the Phoenician coast, the confederates seem to have taken Doros under Mt. Carmel and perhaps Kelenderis in Cilicia,[46] but as with many events in the 460's and 450's these activities lack historical and textual precision. Further military activity on Cyprus continued but to what degree we simply do not know. To counter the confederate forces, nevertheless, Artaxerxes dispatched in 457/6 B.C. the Persian Megabazos to Sparta, who, with money, attempted to persuade the Spartans to attack Attica, thus forcing the Athenians and confederates to withdraw from Egypt. At the moment, however, the Spartans were unable to attack because of serious local problems with the rebellious Messenian helots; and Megabazos had spent most of his money in vain (Thuc. 1.109.2-3; Diod. Sic. 11.74.5-6).

The greater problem lay in Greece as the Athenians and their allies became more and more entangled in a war which, as the years transpired, altered radically and took on new focus. Initial failures led to successes at Aigina and in the Megarid, but by 454 B.C. Sparta actively intervened (Thuc. 1.107.2-108.2) and in gaining hegemony in Boiotia directly threatened Attica.[47] The Athenians, nevertheless, quickly regained Boiotia, and then took control of Phokis and Lokris, by which they committed themselves and their allies to ever expanding degrees of military action (Thuc. 1.108.2-3; Diod. Sic. 11.82.1-2). Following a series of military victories in the early spring of 454 B.C., the Athenians led a spectacular expedition around the Peloponnesos, and with all confidence expected the mainland campaigns to end successfully (Thuc. 1.108.5). But both fronts rapidly disintegrated. A second Athenian expedition into the Corinthian Gulf led by Perikles ended in marked failure at the same time as did the Egyptian expedition. Artaxerxes had dispatched the Persian generals Megabyzos, the son of Zopyros, and Artabazos to attack rebellious Egypt with a large army, which Diodorus noted included 300,000 men and 300 ships (11.74.6, 77). At Memphis, the Persians had defeated the rebels, Athenians, and the confederates, and drove the Greeks into the Delta not too far to the north and for a year and a half shut them up on the island of Prosopitis (Thuc. 1.109.3-4; Aristod. *FGrH* 104 F 11.4). Finally, the Persians took the island and only a few men escaped through Libya to Cyrene. Meanwhile, a confederate relief fleet of 50 triremes had sailed into the eastern Delta to aid the Greeks, but it became entangled in the Delta's channels, and was easily destroyed by the Phoenician fleet, also with only a small number of soldiers escaping. In conclusion to this account, Thucydides noted: "So ended the great expedition against Egypt of the Athenians and their allies" (1.110.5).

To compound the Athenian and confederate problems, a rumor quickly spread that Artaxerxes had dispatched or was about to dispatch a major naval expedition which would invade the Aegean and threaten Delos. In a frantic move, the Samian ambassador to the Confederacy proposed that the treasury be quickly transferred to Athens for safety (Diod. Sic. 12.38.2, 40.1; Plut. *Per.* 12.1, *Arist.* 25.3).[48] The confederates agreed, but unwittingly also transferred to Athens the Synod, which when meeting there rapidly lost its directive powers to the growing Athenian legislative and imperial powers. Within a few years the Synod would cease to meet.

While the details of the Greek mainland war are extremely more complex and detailed, it is important not to focus on the plight of the Athenians but rather of the "Ionian allies" in this two front "war." The events of 460-454 B.C. had once again acutely overtaxed all the confederates in military service and tribute, and had rapidly accentuated Ionian societal distortion. For the great sentinal islands (Samos, Chios, and Lesbos) the principles of parity would continue, but for the lesser island and Anatolian poleis including, as we shall see, Erythrai and Miletos the violations of the principles of parity and the rapid imposition of aspects and institutions of vassalage generated political opposition among the Ionian landed gentries towards the Athenians and their confederate hegemony. This opposition occurred shortly after the initiation of Artaxerxes' new aggressive policy against the East Greek poleis, specifically in the Maeander River Valley. To counteract the growth of Athenian political intervention in

Ionia, consequently, significant groups of landed gentry turned to the Persian Empire for assistance in the support of their rebellions against Athens and secessions from the Confederacy. At some point, perhaps between 465 and 454 B.C., anti-Athenian factions which had turned to Persian assistance gained control of the aste and the governments of Erythrai and Miletos.

These key Ionian rebellions, the important marks of Ionian discontent with the rising tide of Athenian imperialism, evolved from an integral series of factors which had arisen at Naxos and then in Egypt and the Greek mainland, and others which had been developing simultaneously.

Following the Eurymedon victory, 465 B.C., several allied poleis had begun to provide their military services to the Confederacy not in terms of their original assessment in manned ships but in coinage.[49] The initiation for this substitution came not from Athens but from the poleis which sought to relieve the demands upon their forces, for Thucydides implied that the major reason for that significant transformation had developed within from the increased Athenian claims for continued military service, and at a time when Athenian intervention on the basis of self-interest had increased to the level of tyrannical and imperial subjugation. For Thucydides, to pay a monied phoros, tribute to the Confederacy denoting the status of hypēkoos, indicated subjugation (Thuc. 2.9.4), just as it had for Aeschylus in 472 B.C. (Pers. 234, 242). To achieve the goals of the Confederacy in 460-59 B.C., the Athenians required extensive service at Cyprus, in Phoenicia, in Egypt, and on the Greek mainland, but the use of confederate forces at Aigina and in Boiotia had distinctly overextended the original principles of the Confederacy. We unfortunately do not know by what argument the Athenians requested or required confederate forces to campaign on the mainland. But more than an over-extension of service since the subjugation of Naxos, which had just preceded the Eurymedon victory, we can begin to detect the introduction by Athens of Athenian imperial magistrates to assist the hegemon in controlling rebellious, potentially volatile, and crucial poleis throughout the confederate regions ([Xen.] Ath. Pol. 1.19; Ath. Pol. 24.3b-25.1a). As with the other events of this period, c. 466-454 B.C., our historical information for the development of the magistracies unfortunately lacks clarity, yet the following suggestions are plausible.

With the subjugation of Naxos and then Thasos, the Athenians began to place

Athenians as archons, imperial magistrates elected not by the confederate synod but by the Athenian Demos, in the large confederate poleis.[50] Our limited evidence indicates that few were ultimately placed in the smaller and pro-Athenian poleis, and possibly none at all in the very small and complacent poleis. Their duties were to govern in the poleis according to Athenian goals and demands, to counsel and to obtain the cooperation of the local government, and where necessary, especially after rebellion, to establish a new government favorable to Athens. The archons also supervised the collection of the phoros and presided over the prosecution of minor judicial cases. As part of their functions, the Athenian archons performed supervisory duties similar to those of the Persian appointed hyparchoi; therefore, for the Ionian poleis the new Athenian imperialism began distinctly to resemble Persian imperialism.

After 458 B.C., the Athenians may have introduced the second imperial magistracy, the Episkopoi. They were overseers and legal advisors who advised the subjected allied poleis in the reorganization of their governments often along democratic principles and procedures compatible with the Athenians. After this initial formation of the new governments, the Episkopoi periodically toured their respective territories to assure that all allied governments were functioning in the interests of Athens, their imperial center. Unlike other imperial officers, the Episkopoi were not stationed permanently in one polis. They were scattered throughout the Confederacy with imperial duties which were general and supervisory with bases, apparently, in the major allied poleis. But their duties demanded that they travel about the Confederacy, probably within a specific area under supervision, and often return to Athens in order to report directly to the Athenian government. They were neither military commanders nor police officials but rather civilian imperial officers who exercised their influence through persuasion, the assistance of allied citizen "friends" of Athens (the Proxenoi), the articles and regulations of Athenian laws concerning the Confederacy, and the Athenian armed forces. This office not only paralleled that of the Achaemenid King's Eyes, but strongly suggests that the Athenians adopted the form for it directly from the Persians.[51] With the Athenian constitutional change in 458 B.C., which allowed members of the Zeugital rank of the Demos to be eligible for selection to archonships (*Ath. Pol.* 26.2), we may find the advent of the imperial Episkopoi. As the need for more domestic and imperial archons sharply increased the Athenians by necessity had to expand the pool of men who could be selected. At some point, the imperial archons numbered 700 as did the domestic archons (*Ath. Pol.* 24.3). By necessity, the Athenian leaders had to expand the democratic procedures in order to obtain and maintain their imperial goals.

In some poleis, the Athenians established permanent garrisons supervised by garrison commanders, the Phrourarchoi. The garrison troops provided the necessary occupation forces to maintain subjection to the regulations of Athens, and if archons were not present the Phrourarchoi held the imperial judicial functions. A fourth class of imperial magistrate were the Heralds (Kerykes) who traveled from one polis to another to announce the provisions of new laws and decrees of the Athenian Boule and Demos to the confederates. In some cases, the new regulations were inscribed on stone stelae erected in the agorai of the allied poleis or set up before their civic temples. As with the other imperial magistracies, the offices of Phrourarchos and Keryx paralleled similar Persian satrapal offices and the Achaemenid institutions of imperialism. By 453/2 B.C. (?), the Archons, Episkopoi, and Phrourarchoi had been established (*IG* 1^3.14) among the allied confederate states which, in addition to autonomous Samos, Chios, and Lesbos, numbered about 214.[52]

With the Athenian fears of another Persian campaign similar to that at the Eurymedon, Athens drove the confederate forces on to Cyprus, Phoenicia, and Egypt, but in doing so accentuated the processes of imperialism which rapidly eroded the fundamental principles of the Confederacy. That imperial transformation, consequently, developed the concept of autonomia as a firm legalistic argument, a concept which began to develop with the fall of Thasos. As confederate parity was transformed into imperial vassalage, Athens stressed the concept of "Athens and her allies" to emphasize the principal of parity but at a time when Erythrai and Miletos rebelled to salvage their political self-determination. In both Ionian aste, the rebellions arose out of factionalism or stasis, internal political rivalries arising within the minority group of the landed gentry. It was not the demos in either instance which generated the respective staseis but the aristoi or oligoi, those who held land and power.[53] As the Persian overtaxation of Egypt had fomented the revolution there, so Athenian overtaxation of the confederate allies fostered the revolutions of Erythrai and Miletos.

At Erythrai, sometime before the spring of 453 B.C., the faction in opposition to the Athenian imperial control of the Confederacy and measures to subjugate the allies seized the asty. In exile, a loyalist pro-Athenian faction gathered within a choric dendritic system. At Boutheia in the Mimas peninsula north of the Eyrthraian asty, the pro-Athenian faction formed a tribute-paying association to pay to the confederate Treasury at least one half of the assessed tribute. The dendritic syntely may have included, in addition to Boutheia, the choric centers of Polichna, Ptelion, Sidoussa, and the off-shore island center of Elaiousa.[54] In the summer of 452 B.C., however, the Athenian and confederate forces took the asty of Erythrai, expelled the pro-Persian faction, and raised to political power the members of the loyalist faction. The members of the pro-Persian faction, overthrown and in exile, probably in Sparda, were labeled by the Athenians tyrants, a pejorative term for the opposition. And for the pro-Athenian faction the victorious Athenians issued from their Boule and Demos a series of stringent regulations, which the loyalist faction now governing Erythrai was forced to accept.[55]

Upon seizing a rebellious allied polis, the first step for the Athenians was to issue an homologia, a contract drawn up by the victorious power which outlined the conditions of surrender. The terms were occasionally open to negotiation, but at the discretion of, Athens, and were sometimes unilateral and unconditional. The enactment of an homologia marked the beginning of a polis' servitude to Athens, its *douleia*. Although the ancient literary sources fail to note the rebellion of Erythrai or Miletos and the ensuing homologiai, the pattern established by the Athenians strongly suggests the Athenian promulgation of an homologia for the loyalist Erythraian faction gaining local political control of its polis and its asty.[56] The pro-Persian faction had definitely fled the region. While we do not know precisely the terms of surrender enacted, such conditions were applicable included the destruction of fortification walls, the handing over of ships, and the delivery of hostages from the families raised to power. The destruction of walls ended the polis' independence, the loss of ships marked the renunciation of the polis' military power, and the submission of hostages tacitly led to the readiness of the subjected people to accept further Athenian demands as would be outlined in the oaths of allegiance and articles of regulations, such as those of the Athenian decree for the Erythraians, *IG* 1[3].14, promulgated, it seems, in the summer of 452 B.C.

The ancient Athenian copy of that decree has long been lost and the early nineteenth century transcription by Fauvel transmitted by Boeckh presented numerous problems including that of precise dating. Because the original text of *IG* 1[3].14 can no longer be studied, it is difficult to edit and to restore Boeckh's text; nevertheless, following the recent edition by Englemann and Merkelbach several articles of that decree can be recovered to a greater degree than not.

The most notable directive issued, not by the confederate Synod, but by the Athenian Boule and Demos as the emerging imperial power, was the reorganization of the Erythraian government in parallel structure to the then present Athenian democratic government. The Athenians outlined an Erythraian Demos and a Boule, the latter to consist of 120 men, citizens over 30 years of age, selected by lot. Several years earlier, perhaps before 454 B.C., the political and judicial structure of Erythrai consisted of boards of prytaneis, councillors who held office in rotating succession; a boule council; a small court of nine jurists, one chosen from each of the nine Erythraian tribal phylae; and a larger court of not less than 61 members. Over the polis, the Boule governed according to the law (nomoi) and civic decrees (psephismata).[57] While the Athenian regulations did not radically alter this political organization, the obvious point is that the Athenians and not the Erythraians outlined the form of the new Boule. While the Boule was to be in accord with the Erythraian people, the Athenians demanded that it also be in accord with them and their allies. In the oath of loyalty, also outlined by the Athenians, the Erythraian Bouleutai were to govern most justly for the Erythraian people and for the Athenians and their allies as well. The key issue was to prevent the return of the pro-Persian faction, and in governing Erythrai the Bouleutai would be carefully supervised by the Athenian Episkopoi and the Phrourarchos.

The subjection of the Erythraian people to the demands of the Athenian government was further underscored by the requirements of a difficult to reconstruct passage of that decree. To Athens at each Athenian Great Panathenaic Festival, apparently starting in the summer of 450 B.C., the Erythraians were to bring offerings of a value not less than 300 drachmae, at least part of which the Athenian "Directors of the Sacrifices" would distribute to the Erythraians present in Athens. By this article, the Athenians set in motion the process which subordinated Erythrai to the Athenian religious structure. To include Erythrai within that structure connoted a marked degree of metropolitan demands of a socially related group. In this, Athens began to construct a new concept for the Confederacy. By transforming it into an empire the Athenians promoted this rule, and shortly later other rules, to alter the military alliance into a religious federation or amphictyony.   In the minds of the Athenians, the Confederacy had distinctly become a sphere, *the territory of the Athenian symmachy*, with particular military, religious, and imperial structures; a sphere from which Erythraians convicted in the Erythraian courts of murder and in exile would be excluded.   The emerging empire rapidly became an imperial nation of peoples subject to Athenian rules, demands, and religious ties.   It was never a question of state and citizens, but of an amphictyonic empire of Athenians and subjects.

Of the Milesians and their relationship with the Confederacy and Athenian leadership, we have no information until the period c. 454 B.C. when the oligarchic faction in Miletos also rebelled against the Athenians and seceded from the Confederacy.   In the spring of 453 B.C., the rebellion was still underway, and is noted by three disparate and apparently unrelated factions loyal to the Athenians and living in exile, outside of the asty of Miletos and its central chora, in the distant reaches of the island of Leros, in the border fortress of Teichioussa,[58] and as "Neopolitai in Miletos in the White Promontory north of Halikarnassos."[59]   By the evidence of the Athenian Tribute Lists, it appears that the small poleis at the head of the Maeander Gulf—Latmos and Bolbai—had joined both the asty and the chora of neighboring Myous and the asty of Miletos, and had joined the massive Persian penetration into that gulf.   As against Erythrai to the north-west, the Athenians also directed confederate forces against Miletos, Latmos, Bolbai, and at least seven other small Karian poleis which, we suspect, had also rebelled (to the south: Ouranion, Lapsimanda, Amyranda, Oula, Tarbanes, Idyma, and Erines).[60]   It is possible that other poleis had rebelled and were also subject to Athenian military action.   By the spring of 452 B.C., however, the eight Karian poleis from Bolbai south had been regained; and in the spring of 451 B.C., the pro-Persian faction which earlier had seized the Milesian asty had fled into exile, apparently to Sparda, and the loyalist factions scattered about were placed in power by the Athenian generals and imperial magistrates.   In that year, the Milesians paid their tribute without the qualifying rubrics of exile,[61] and both Latmos and the asty of Myous contributed funds to the Confederacy.

For the loyalist Milesians returning to the asty, the Athenians first promulgated an homologia, and then a decree containing an oath of allegiance to be sworn to the Athenians.   Unfortunately, that oath-decree is lost, but what do survive are eight fragments of a second Athenian decree, promulgated perhaps in 449/8 B.C., which

contains additional regulations imposed by the Athenians upon the Milesians, an imperial

decree which bears the bold heading: "Regulations for the Milesians. Resolved by the

Boule and the Demos . . . " (IG 1^3.21).[62] For the Athenians, the Erythraian and Milesian

revolutions had raised the reality of Persian imperial intrusion into the Aegean. The

earlier revolutions of Naxos and Thasos had clearly indicated that to be successful, the

Erythraian and Milesian oligarchs could not have rebelled without foreign support. The

Milesians needed military aid, and Persian military assistance from the garrison centers

of Magnesia-on-the-Maeander and Myous could easily have been sent to the Milesian

oligarchs.

For the Milesians who remained, Athenian subjugation was a stark reality with which

they had to contend. The Milesians lost their political self-determination and their

autonomous judicial procedures. They were now subject to Athenian law and imperial

magisterial governance. Although the inscription is extremely fragmentary and with

extensive lacunae, and any restoration can only approximate the sense of the articles

therein, we may consider the following aspects of Athenian subjugation of the

Milesians. As with the Erythraians, the Milesians were to act in the best interests of the

Athenians, but at this point the Athenians had dropped the concept of "The Athenians and

their allies." Any Milesian who did not act in accord with the Athenian regulations would

be atimos, deprived of his civic rights, and his money would be deposited in the Milesian

public treasury, yet a tithe of that money would be given to the cult of Athena in

Athens. The Athenian religious strictures had taken on a new form. The five Athenian

imperial Archons stationed in Miletos were to receive on behalf of the state the court

fees from those judicial actions, however dikai, public law suits, were to be heard not in

the Milesian courts but in the Athenian. For those suits, the Archons were to conduct

the initial hearings, the anakriseis. In Athens, the Athenian jurors would be paid from

those court fees.

As in all similar cases, the Athenian judicial regulations for the Milesians were to be

inscribed upon a special stele set up in Miletos. They were regulations which demanded

Milesian obedience, and in no manner were the Milesians to destroy or obliterate the

letters of that stele or alter the laws inscribed thereon. If a Milesian did violate the law,

the Athenian Supervisors or Epimeletai were to bring that Milesian before the Athenian civic archons within five days, and then before an Athenian court. The law also referred to the exiled faction which had seized power. Exiles who returned to Miletos would have their property confiscated according to the decrees of the Athenians, and the polis of the Milesians was to give compensation in gold and in silver for the properties confiscated at the previously established rate for which the evidence is now lacking. The laws had been established according to Athenian directive, and in the future the Milesians were forbidden to promulgate civic regulations contrary to the established law.

The Athenian regulations further demanded that public law cases concerning the tax, the eisphora, and the illegal fugitives were to be brought before the local courts, and it was now the responsibility of the wealthy and landed Milesian families, the oikoi, to bring those cases to the attention of the courts and the appropriate magistrates. But if the Milesians did not confiscate the properties of fugitives and properly carry out the court trials, the Athenians announced that the five imperial Athenian Archons would deliver a graphe, a private case, against each returned exile.

To affirm strict adherence to their regulations, the Athenians then insisted that each Milesian male citizen swear the oath of allegiance to the five Athenian imperial Archons. Violators would be prosecuted, sent to Athens for trial, and their property confiscated. The Athenians invariably reserved the right to intervene. In regard to the special problem in the Milesian village of Arnasos, the Athenian Boule announced that it would rule. Similarly, it would be in charge of the Athenian occupation troops temporarily stationed in Miletos, and in time the Athenian generals would establish an Athenian garrison in the polis.

Although this inscription is too fragmentary for a precise determination of its provisions, it is evident that several of the articles deal with the establishment and the functioning of a special court in Athens to try Milesians. The defendants were apparently those accused of rebellion, that is of treason, against the Athenians, and others who would be accused of the same in the future. Such cases would be sent to Athens by the Athenian imperial Archons stationed in Miletos, a judicial step which followed the preliminary hearings, the anakriseis, by the same imperial magistrates. The crime of treason demanded the punishment of atimia and the confiscation of property with an assessment of tithes to be awarded to Athens' patron deity. For these trials, the Athenians established a complex judicial machinery, two archons and their colleagues and a court, which suggests that the Athenians anticipated a crowded court docket.

Military domination, economic exploitation, and ideological bases for hegemony or sovereignty had occurred in the earlier Lydian and Persian Empires; but the Athenians, perhaps for the first time, institutionalized imperialism by means of discreet judicial procedures. Treason and sedition, as noted in the Naxian and Thasian rebellions against Athenian control and in the articles of the Athenian decrees for Erythrai and Miletos, were apparently far more rampant than the ancient evidence indicates. And treason and sedition undermined the evolving Athenian imperial structure.

To mark the judicial regulations, the Athenians ordered two inscriptions to be erected in Miletos as visible signs of Athenian imperial control: the lost inscription bearing the oath of allegiance and a copy of the articles of IG 1^3.21. All the articles would be enforced by the Athenians stationed in Miletos. In addition to the Athenian imperial magistrates in residence, Athenian occupation troops remained perhaps temporarily in that asty supplementary to the permanent Athenian garrison also established there, and the latter would continue Athens' military surveillance of that crucial Ionian polis.

The regulations of Athenian control over the political self–determination of the Eythraian and Milesian factions loyal to Athens and the Confederacy clearly mark several of the many major steps whereby the Athenians subjugated their military allies "contrary to custom" (Thuc. 1.98.4). Most strikingly, we must note, the regulations had not been promulgated for the revolutionary oligarchs who had repudiated their alliance with Athens and the Confederacy and, in turn, had joined forces with the Persian Empire, but for those in exile who had remained loyal to the alliance and had continued to pay their assessed tribute to the confederate treasury. The evidence of SIG^3.57 (DGE 727; Tod GHI 1^2.35; ML GHI 43), the Milesian Law against Tyrants, indicates that the Milesian oligarchic rebels had not returned nor would they be allowed to do so, as the articles of this inscription placed the rebels in perpetual damnation, just as the Athenian regulations prevented the return of the rebellious Erythraians. The stringent Athenian regulations, therefore, were carefully promulgated to prevent a second Milesian rebellion such as had occurred with that group of disgruntled oligarchs (cf. [Xen.] Ath. Pol. 3.11).

The origins of the two Ionian rebellions are to be directly placed within the historical development of the growing Athenian control over the Confederacy, which restricted the early concepts of autonomy and the principles of parity upon which the alliance had been founded. The change had begun with the fall of Naxos early in 465 B.C. and had accelerated by the early 450's with the marked overextension of confederate military activities in Egypt, Cyprus, Phoenicia, and in Greece. The principle of parity established in 478/7 B.C. had given way to inequity and recognition of the development of Athenian imperial controls. The Erythraian and Milesian oligarchs, consequently, violently reacted and in abrogating the earlier established principles of the Confederacy did so because the Athenians had usurped their role as hegemon of a parity alliance and were strongly asserting a dominant rule which had placed the loyalist Erythraians and Milesians in a clearly subservient role which ranked them as subject vassals. It was that violent and duplicitous transition, spearheaded by the Athenians, against which the oligarchs had rebelled and, consequently, turned to Persian suzerainty. Regardless of what had happened in Miletos in 494 B.C., by the mid-450's, the oligarchs in Miletos, in severing their alliance with the Delian Confederacy, could expect Persian encouragement and cooperation in that rebellion. Oligarchic rebellion in Erythrai and Miletos found favor from the officials at Sardis and at Susa, and favorable arrangements offered by the Persians for their new subjects. Regardless of what had transpired earlier, the Persians invariably received former enemies who sought Persian protection and lavished upon them favorable conditions for their new roles within the Achaemenid imperial system. The life of the Erythraian and Milesian oligarchs under Persian rule would not be restricted as were the lives of the Erythraians and Milesians who had remained and who lived under the stringent regulations devised by the Athenian Demos. Within the satrapy of Sparda, or elsewhere within the Persian Empire, the exiled oligarchs could retain a greater degree of self-determination than the pro-confederate loyalists who returned to the war torn poleis of Erythrai and Miletos.

In principle, each of the thematic imperial regulations established by the democratic Athenian Boule and Demos for the Erythraians and Milesians paralleled the thematic regulations of vassalage as established by the earlier Lydian and Persian imperial structures. Athens' regulations inscribed upon the stone stelae boldly pronounced the Athenian regulations of subjugation for the loyalist Erythraians and Milesians formerly bound to the Athenians by the terms of parity and cooperative military alliance. Within this act of Athenian transformation of confederate freedom to imperial tyranny, we can detect the reasons why factions of the Erythaian and Milesian landed gentry rebelled against the Athenians.[63]   For socio–political security and benefits, the oligarchic factions rebelled against the Athenians and turned to the secure and regularized satrapal government of Sparda and the suzerainty of King Artaxerxes I.

IONIA UNDER ATHENIAN IMPERIALISM

The fall of Erythrai and Miletos marked a distinct phase toward the finalization of Athenian imperial control. New Athenian regulations subjugating the East Greek governments also directly affected individuals with terms which specifically inflicted harsh blows upon the landed gentry. To regain their hold on those confederates and to compensate for the disaster in Egypt, the Athenians had quickly rebuilt their armed strength. The critical military overextension in 454 B.C., by which they had suffered greatly, absolutely necessitated a halt in the mainland offensive and the contract with the Spartans in the spring of 451 B.C. of a five year military truce (Thuc. 1.112.1; Diod. Sic. 11.86.1).[1] With that blunder of mainland warfare temporarily rectified, the Athenians then concentrated upon maintaining confederate solidarity by again attacking Persia. That was the enemy which had fomented the rebellions in Ionia and Karia and which was still, in 451 B.C., applying military pressure upon Sigeion in the Troad. This new objective was to counter decisively Artaxerxes' attempts to reclaim the Anatolian littoral by dispatching Kimon with the Athenian and confederate fleet to seize Cyprus. This time, the Athenian imperial resolution was unqualified. That island had long been the vulnerable zone within the Persian Empire, which the Athenians calculated, if taken, would force the Persians to remove their forces from western Anatolia. That tactic had been tried earlier but unsuccessfully during the Ionian Revolt, the aftermath of the Greek victory at Mykale, and after the Eurymedon. As with that last campaign in the late 460's, Athenian control in 450 B.C. of Persian Cyprus would open the eastern regions of Persian Cilicia, Phoenicia, and Egypt to the imperialistic Athenians in the name of and at the expense of the East Greeks and the other confederates.[2]

This campaign, unfortunately, can not be satisfactorily recovered beyond the all too brief, yet reliable, account presented by Thucydides (1.112.1–4).[3] To Cyprus, he recorded, Kimon commanded a fleet of 200 ships. Once there, he immediately dispatched 60 to Egypt in response to an appeal from the anti-Persian forces now led by the rebel Amyrtaios who, after the Persian crucifixion of Inaros, was still holding part of the Delta. With the remaining 140 ships, the Athenians then besieged the Cypriote city of Kition where the enemy mortally wounded Kimon. Without his leadership and with food supplies exhausted, the Athenians and their allies consequently abandoned that siege and sailed on to the port of Salamis. There in a fierce double encounter, the Athenians held their own and soundly defeated the Imperial Persian fleet and land forces of Phoenicians, Cilicians, and Cypriotes.

To commemorate this new phase of victorious offensive activity, the Athenians subsequently raised another epigram (Diod. Sic. 11.62.3):

> On Cyprus isle these men slew many Medes.
>
> They captured on the sea a hundred ships.
>
> Phoenicians were their crews and deeply Asia mourned for them,
>
> by both arms smitten in the shock of war.[4]

The Persians, suffering extensive military losses on Cyprus and struggling with continued native unrest and Greek intervention in Egypt, found their military control in the eastern Mediterranean critically disrupted. These demonstrable crises in the summer of 450 B.C., consequently, significantly threatened the stability of the Great King's key satrapies from Egypt to Cilicia, and especially Syrian "Across the River" adjacent to the Assyrian (-Babylonian) satrapy of the Mesopotamian Valley.

Artaxerxes' response, as reported by Diodorus Siculus (12.4.5), has long stimulated a major historical controversy. But to explain satisfactorily why the Athenians then abandoned Cyprus and Egypt, and why Athenian and confederate warships no longer sailed east of Lykia, or Persian warships west of Cilicia and Pamphylia, the only convincing reason is to accept Diodorus' statement that Artaxerxes sought peace. That account, unfortunately not the most reliable, stated that Artaxerxes had dispatched to his generals on Cyprus and to the satraps of that region the terms of peace which he would permit them to settle upon with the Greeks. Thus to Athens the Persian generals Megabyzos and Artabazos, the victors at Memphis and the Delta, sent Persian ambassadors with the king's message, which the Athenians found acceptable. In response, the Athenian Demos dispatched to the east a plenipotentiary embassy led by the high priest of Eleusis, the aristocrat Kallias. Unfortunately, Diodorus failed to note whether Kallias and his associates traveled only as far as Cyprus or on to the king's court at Susa; and Herodotus' oblique reference to a Kallias in Susa (7.151) is much too insufficient to determine just where this Kallias finalized the treaty.[5] Regardless, the Great King would have had to review the terms if they had differed in any way from his original concessions, and upon review to approve them.

Concerning the terms agreed upon, the 1940 study by H.T. Wade-Gery remains essentially basic;[6] but rather than accept the embellishments of the fourth century B.C. writers as he did, let us return to the text offered by Diodorus which, as it is, makes sense without those embellishments and amidst the all too many pages of modern scholarship.[7] Diodorus' Athenian version of the treaty states:

> All the Greek poleis of Asia are to be autonomous; the Persian satraps are not to come nearer to the sea than a three days' journey and no Persian warship is to sail inside of Phaselis [the Lykian polis on the Pamphylian coast] and the Kyanean Rocks [at the northern entrance to the Bosporos]; and if those terms are observed by the King and his generals, the Athenians are not to send troops into the territory over which King Artaxerxes rules.

In this, the Great King offered two principles: autonomy for the East Greek poleis and non-aggression between the Athenians and the Persians. Artaxerxes renounced his claim of sovereignty over the East Greek poleis and affirmed that his satraps would not campaign west of the Sardian plain, the three day march from Sardis to coastal Ephesos (Hdt. 5.100). Nor would the Persian Imperial Fleet sail out of Persian waters into the Greek Bosporos or into the Greek waters of Lykia. In turn, the Athenians would respect Artaxerxes' sovereignty over the Persian Empire and halt further aggression. But in reality, the East Greek poleis did not become autonomous. They rapidly became subject to numerous imperial restrictions set out by the Athenians. Sovereignty existed only on aristocratic Samos, Chios, and Lesbos.

In essence, what the treaty formalized was Xerxes' order in 479 B.C. to withdraw from the western Anatolian littoral and ended Artaxerxes' recent campaigns to regain coastal territories in the Troad, Karia, and Ionia. In western Anatolia, the simple price Artaxerxes paid was to convert his recently revived offensive strategy into a stabilized power of defense. And in the eastern Mediterranean, the Persian Empire remained secure under the Great King's imperial powers. For the Athenians, it confirmed their desire for imperial stability and solidarity, particularly in Ionia. With treaties concluded with Sparta and Persia, the Athenians could now turn to their primary problem that with the conclusion of the war with Persia, the fundamental raison d'être of the Delian

Confederacy, had ceased.[8] But rather than disband the Confederacy and lose vital economic and imperial status, the Athenians rapidly and systematically converted it into an amphityonic empire.[9]

Artaxerxes' overtures for peace apparently arrived in Athens during the autumn of 450 B.C., with the detailed negotiations held during the winter of 450/49 B.C. Kallias, consequently, must have returned home sometime in the spring of 449 B.C. At that point, Perikles, as the leading general and political power in the direction of imperial policy, proposed to the Athenian Demos a series of measures, which would transform the Confederacy into an amphictyonic Athenian Empire. It was a bold and decisive act (Plut. Per. 17).[10] He proposed to invite all the Greek poleis, regardless of size, to send deputies to a common congress to be held in Athens. The agenda contained three major items which directly related to the long Greco-Persian conflict. The first raised the question of the temples destroyed during Xerxes' occupation of Greece and the problem that the Oath of Plataia had contained a specific clause, which prohibited their being rebuilt. What Perikles now wanted discussed were the bases of that earlier agreement of the Hellenic League, which had stood all too briefly in concerted opposition against Persia, but which had formulated religious vows, and which could not be easily dismissed, that the Greeks would leave as perpetual monuments the ruined temples. For Athens as the center of a confederate imperial force, the acropolis and much of Attica remained without impressive monuments worthy of Athens' new imperial status. But in raising this item for discussion, Perikles not only actively revived the long defunct Hellenic League but usurped Sparta's leadership in that organization and its war council.

The second item also dealt with religious matters, specifically the sacrifices owed to the gods on behalf of the Greeks promised at the time they had fought Xerxes' forces. As all oaths generated deep and significant undercurrents of reverence towards the divine powers, Perikles linked the failure to fulfill those vows with the equally important religious factor of the destroyed temples. We must suspect that Perikles had something very specific in mind, which he avidly felt had not been fulfilled by the Spartan leadership during those battle-torn years of 481-479 B.C. The third item also asserted Athenian leadership of the Greeks. That, Perikles pointed out, was the keeping of the peace on the seas, that all might sail without fear. The congress could consider, therefore, that the Athenians' fait accompli had cleared the Aegean of pirates and

Persians, and through the recent treaty with King Artaxerxes had assured the Greeks that the Persians would not enter the Confederacy's proscribed territory.

In assembly, the Athenian Demos voted its acceptance of Perikles' proposal and immediately set in motion the mechanics by which the congress would convene (Plut. *Per.* 17.2). The assembly chose twenty men from its own, Athenians specifically over the age of fifty, men who would have ranked among the Greek victors against Xerxes; and dispatched them in groups of five throughout the Confederacy, but rather than to the poleis of the entire Greek mainland sent them only to those within the territory of the Spartan dominated Delphic Amphictyony.[11] They significantly avoided the Peloponnesos except for northern Achaia. Thus, when Perikles proposed to invite all of the Greek poleis, he or the Athenian assembly in the course of debate specifically excluded Sparta and her allies of the Peloponnesian League. All members of the Delian Confederacy, nevertheless, were carefully included. The first group of heralds set out to invite "the Ionians and the Dorians in Asia and the islands between Lesbos and Rhodes," and the second "the Hellespont and Thrace as far as Byzantion."

This decision infuriated the Spartans who immediately intervened and, censuring the congress, acted upon the members of the Delphic amphictyonic league not to attend. As the Delphic Amphictyony included the medizing amphictyons of Boiotia, the Lokroi, the Oitaioi of the Malian Gulf, the Achaioi Phthiotai, and the Thessalians, Sparta may have become angered at their being included in matters of the Hellenic League from which she had adamantly tried to exclude medizing poleis and peoples (cf. Plut. *Them.* 20.3-4).

Spartan censure, however, failed to cancel the meeting of the deputies from the Delian Confederacy, in what appears to be the last meeting of the Confederate Synod. The proposals for agenda items one through three were obviously discussed and immediately acted upon. In Athens, specifically, plans for rebuilding the temples, and the Parthenon in particular, were worked out; and, we must assume, the sacrifices were given. That Synod must also have ratified by fiat the Athenian plan for the military safety of the seas. Whether the confederate deputies objected to the Athenian methods, especially the deputies from Ionia, we do not know; but as Athens cowed a majority of the small and vulnerable poleis, about 68 percent of the Confederacy, into tacit acceptance of imperial rule, a majority in favor of Athenian action could be easily obtained. We are, consequently, aware of little dissent except in Kolophon and Kos.

With the conclusion of the Delian Congress, Perikles and the Athenian political leadership in conjunction with the Demos sought new means by which to continue the structure of the Confederacy. The treaty with Persia had transformed it from an offensive to a defensive military alliance, but had also raised the specter that it had constitutionally terminated that alliance. To prevent wide-scale rebellion, to ensure the continued payments of tribute, and to sustain Athenian naval control over the entire confederate territory, the Athenian leadership thereupon significantly altered the military confederacy into a religious alliance, which blended numerous Greek ethnic and dialectic groups from Thrace to Karia, the Bosporos to the Cyclades, and even Karian and Lykian non-Greeks into a federation, and which bound them all to a widely expanded concept of a "Pan-Ionian" religious union.[12] The new amphictyony clearly built upon the long dormant yet still viable concept of the Panionion at Mykale and the ancient Pan-Ionian cult to Apollo on Delos (Thuc. 1.96.2). Years earlier, Aristeides and the Athenians had wisely chosen Delos at which to structure the Confederacy, and now Perikles and other Athenians would transfer that amphictyony to Athens, yet still maintain the Delian interrelationships as the foundation for the new concept. Athens as a center for "Pan-Ionianism" had significantly increased to the point of marked realization several decades earlier when Kimon returned from Skyros in 468 B.C. with the bones of some hapless ancient whom he identified as Theseus, the national hero and mythological ancestral father of not only the Athenians but also the eastern Ionians.[13] Theseus now played a major role in the Athenian Panathenaia.[14] By the mid-century, the Pan-Ionian poem the *Ionika* by Panyassis of Halikarnassos strongly reconfirmed those vivid oral traditions, and stressed once again the important religious link between Athens and the eastern Ionian poleis as being that of a metropolis with colonists overseas.[15] That metropolis-colony relationship, regardless of what political animosities would have arisen or would yet arise, firmly bound the colonists to the metropolis by religious ties which could not be severed, and now ties focused upon the tomb of Theseus in the Athenian agora and the transfer of confederate functions from Delos to Athens. Therefore, when the Samian proposal in 454 B.C. arose to relocate the Treasury and, thus, the Synod in Athens for security, the Athenians were able to impose their city's protectorship under the tutelage of the goddess Athena Polias and Theseus' heroism upon the confederation and yet continue at a diminished level Delian Apollo's role as cult deity.[16] Bound by the Oath of

Plataia not to rebuild the temples, especially Athena's Parthenon, Perikles had ingeniously summoned the deputies of the confederate poleis to discuss new methods by which to modify those earlier religious restrictions. Perikles raised the issue of military defense, the basic constitutional principle of the Confederacy, by requesting a reconfirmation of the Athenian protection of the seas, but also raised the religious issues pertinent to the formation of the amphictyony about the sacrifices long overdue and the foundations of temples. Through religious and mythological means, the Athenians usurped the directive powers of the defunct Synod and attempted to reconsolidate their allies into a cohesive imperial amphictyonic union rather than merely continue the policy of military defense against the Persians.[17] Thus, through religion and the amphictyony, the Athenians reinforced the Delian Oath's clauses of permanency and non-secession, two major factors in the transformation of the military alliance based upon parity to the imperial system of Athenian suzerainty over "allied" subjugation and the processes of vassalage. The foundation of the new Parthenon two years later, after extensive architectural planning and preparation,[18] became the center of the amphictyony. This new union significantly joined the disparate groups with permanent religious relationships, which superseded the sustained military and tributary relationships.

With that transformational step initiated, the Athenians then set into motion other steps for the development of the imperial amphictyony. Of the next two or three steps, our knowledge rests upon the notes of several Hellenistic and Roman era scholiasts of which only a scrap of papyrus remains, and caution in regard to its restoration must prevail.[19] In the late spring of 449 B.C. just thirty years after the clash at Plataia and Mykale, the Athenians made preparations to build the Parthenon and a new acropolitan gateway, the Propylaia, in accord with Perikles' proposals.[20] The funds for those projects came from the annual tribute of the confederate poleis. At the Panathenaia, the Hellenotamiai brought those funds to the acropolis, dedicated them to Athena, and then placed them in the Athenian treasury. Five thousand talents (thirty million drachmae) collected from the allied poleis were set aside immediately for the new buildings and, in time, an additional three thousand talents (eighteen million drachmae) from the same source would also be expended. The distinction between the confederate and Athenian treasuries had hazed and dimmed as the concept of a single fiscal unit became reality. In the epigraphical financial records for the Parthenon, beginning in

447/6 B.C., the confederate reserve had been amalgamated with Athena's treasury some time before the foundation for the new temple had been laid.[21]

In further reference to Perikles' proposals contained in the "Congress Decree" (Plut. *Per.* 17), one of the scholiasts noted, in order that the Athenians control the seas, the Athenian Boule would be in charge of the old triremes to make them safe and to build new triremes annually.

The Athenians had asserted their military and political control over the allied confederates and had formed an imperial amphictyony. Additional measures, however, were needed to complete their judicial and economic control.

In the late summer or early autumn of 449 B.C., after the enactment of the second decree of Athenian regulations for Miletos, the Athenian Klearchos proposed to the Demos the stringent articles of the Judicial Decree.[22] Klearchos outlined new judicial procedures to punish allies in violation of Athenian imperial regulations. His proposal entailing articles of judicial procedure, earlier applied specifically to Erythrai and Miletos, now regulated not just an individual rebellious polis but rather the entire confederate empire, each polis and each individual in those poleis. The articles went beyond the public domain into the private. Following that spring meeting of the Synod, the Athenians had abandoned joint action with the allies. The confederates no longer drafted policy but rather the Athenian government legislated imperial regulations, which summarily denied every confederate polis (except Samos, Chios, and Lesbos) her judicial autonomy. Klearchos' decree became one of several general decrees or *koina psephismata* which fundamentally structured the Athenian empire.[23] While several allied poleis had lost their *autonomia* because of rebellions and resultant subjugations, the Athenian Judicial Decree deprived almost all the confederates of their autonomia, and did so by a single act of Athenian legislation.

In reaction, a majority of allied poleis seemingly accepted this legislation without military reaction and openly continued to cooperate with Athens as they benefited economically from the empire, secure as it was from piracy and war. The Judicial Decree, nevertheless, marked the loss of *autonomia*, of independent jurisdiction and categorically denied the earlier assumed sovereignty. Klearchos proposed, in order to govern the empire, that the case of law suits demanding exile, death, or the loss of civil rights (atimia), there was to be immediate referral to Athens' courts.[24] Capital cases would be tried there and not in the local allied courts. While murder and most cases of treason could be clearly attested, some aspects of treason, sedition, and other public crimes subject to atimia composed a wide category into which any resistance to Athenian imperialism would be grounds for trial and punishment.

In order to check allied sedition, the Athenian imperial magistrates stationed in the allied aste initiated the first step, whereby they singularly held the summary hearing for the sole purpose of determining whether the action was admissible. In this, the magistrate possessed no discretionary power, but if his findings were positive, he introduced the suit directly to the Athenian courts.[25] As his claims were based upon Athenian law and not local law, he did not have the power to create new actions by his own authority, but only the power to fulfill the legislation of the Athenian government. Athens' imperial jurisdiction, consequently, bound the entire empire to the rule of her imperial magistrates, her generals and the fleet, and her imperial regulations. When necessary, any malcontent would face the imperial magistrate representing the Athenian state as both litigant and prosecutor, and then be tried in Athens.

Once determined by the Athenian courts, the Demos reorganized, the punishments of exile and death were relatively simple processes to execute. In exile, the allied citizen was banished not only from his native polis but from the entire empire, an imperial territory which the Athenians conceived as a nation, an amphictyony rather than a state.[26] But exile, no less death and the loss of civil rights, were restrictions of civic rights within the allied polis and could not refer to the Athenian Empire until such legislation by Klearchos was enacted which extended Athenian judicial control. Following the Congress Decree and the establishment of the amphictyony, therefore, any inhabitant of an allied polis could be prosecuted and the punishments formerly imposed upon Athenian citizens inflicted upon allied citizens. In this, the Athenian judicial system acted as the supreme juridical body for the empire, with the Athenians paradoxically using their state's democratic procedures to rule an empire. Exile, consequently, was a severe punishment as the banished found himself removed from his polis-centered kin, religious and political group, and the empire–centered religious union, without which he found great difficulty in establishing himself in another Greek state. Total loss of civil rights demanded the general confiscation of property, the extension of atimia to the family, the perpetual banishment from the polis, and eventual death if the convicted returned. Atimia as a suspension of "citizen rights" prevented participation in legal rights, religious rites, and offertory rites including funeral rites: an exclusion from all forms of state and cult life.[27] For Ionians, refuge in Persia, in contrast, offered stability, often land, and a future of prosperity.

Conviction for murder, treason, or sedition[28] usually resulted in punishment by exile or death, and the Athenian imperial decrees bear witness to the demand of death for murder and imply the prohibition of treason and sedition on pain of exile. Death was obligatory in the case of murder and was also a penalty for treason, although the Athenian jurors had to determine just what constituted treason. In each case, however, imposition of the death penalty, or even fines exceeding 500 drachmae, could be considered only by the "plurality of the Demos," the assembly sitting as the courts. The punishment of atimia ranged from exile and total loss of civil rights to partial civic restriction. The severity with which it was applied often depended upon the nature of the crime and the political relationship of the polis to Athens when the crime was committed.[29] Atimia did not necessarily involve the withdrawal of all protection, but did necessarily involve a loss of honor and possibly political privileges, and in some cases the confiscation of property.[30] The punishment imposed also depended upon whether an actual crime had been committed or whether the imperial magistrates were levying the charge in order to eliminate malcontents.

The original purpose of the Delian Confederacy was to facilitate offensive military action against the Persian Empire. When the purpose ended with the peace treaty, rather than disband that structure, the Athenians altered the alliance into an amphictyonic empire. In this restructuring and revitalization, the institutionalization of judicial and subsequent imperial procedures were key elements. Klearchos' Judicial Decree, therefore, represented the internal momentum of the institution, and the historical fact of that institution. Treason and sedition noted in the Naxian and Thasian rebellions, and in the regulations promulgated for Erythrai and Miletos were, apparently, far more rampant than the evidence indicates. Military controls, economic regulations, and the revitalization of the Confederacy-cum-Empire about the Athenian cults of Athena Polias, Athena Nike, and Athena Parthenos in the rising Parthenon and its quadrennial Panathenaic Festival,[31] all structured an amphictyonic empire but did not prevent treason or sedition. A judicial institution as proposed by Klearchos, therefore, outlined the necessary procedures whereby the Athenians in the first instance intervened in the judicial self-determination of their subjects and gave to the Athenian law courts the power to punish actions hostile to Athenian imperial control or even intent. In Athens, the Athenians, needless to say, ruled upon the cases favorably in light of their imperial goals. They believed that it was necessary to rule or to be ruled. While it was possible to believe in the peaceful coexistence or in independent political units, for the initial Confederacy was built upon just such concepts, the Athenians also believed that they had to rule and overrode the Confederacy not only by pure military force but by institutional momentum. Their experience reveals that in addition to military, economic, and cultural imperialism there was institutional imperialism, fueled by the internal momentum of several institutions, the Judicial Decree and the subsequent Currency Decree.

Eight battered epigraphical fragments of the Currency Decree unfortunately resist a secure restoration of their articles. The recent edition by Erhard Erxleben, based upon the earlier studies of Mario Segré, nevertheless, does offer realization of the processes of those detailed Athenian democratic and judicial procedures for the implementation of new imperial regulations.[32] The articles, proposed and voted upon in the Athenian assembly by the Demos, outlined new restrictions for the subjected allies. They also noted the implementation of those regulations with the assistance of the Athenian domestic and imperial magistrates and the full functioning of the democratically structured Athenian judicial system, with direct reference to Klearchos' Judicial Decree (#8), and with specific concerns for the Athenian cults of Athena, and Athena and Hephaistos. Unfortunately the entire preamble of the decree is missing, but the decree's contents indicate that it was proposed shortly after Klearchos' proposal had been enacted as law.

By this imperial legislative action, the Demos directed the Hellenotamiai, the Athenian Treasurers of the Confederacy, to register all the allied poleis which minted silver coinage, and to register notice of that coinage. If the Hellenotamiai failed to do so correctly, they were subject to trial in the Athenian courts according to the prescribed Athenian judicial system and, if found guilty, were fined and exiled (#1). In turn, the Athenian imperial magistrates stationed within the allied poleis were directed to implement the decree's regulations. If any one of them failed to do so, or if any other Athenian resident in the allied poleis, or if any citizens of those allied poleis failed to act in accordance with the articles of the decree, he was atimos, his property confiscated and deposited in the Athenian public treasury, and a tithe given to Athena (#2). In most cases, the Athenian imperial magistrates implemented the regulations, but in those poleis where there were none, then the magistrates of each allied polis was ordered to do so. If the magistrates of those poleis failed to comply with that order, they also came to trial in Athens on the charge of treason with the penalty of atimia (#3).

The first order was to collect from the subjected allied poleis the foreign silver coinage from their mints and any other sources, and to submit that coinage to the Athenian mint. No less than half was to be reminted immediately as Athenian silver coinage, the famous "owls." The Athenian imperial magistrates with the cooperation of the allied governments collected the coinage and submitted it to Athens, and for that process, the Athenians collected a three percent (?) charge. In Athens and at the mint, the Athenian domestic Epistatai or Superintendents supervised the exchange, and if they failed they, too, were held liable to punishment. They also saw to it that the silver from the premium on exchange was struck as Athenian coins and immediately delivered either to the Athenian generals or to the Athenian Financial Receivers, the Apodektai. But before the new coinage was delivered to the allied poleis, the Athenian assembly reviewed the amounts and voted upon the sum, which they would deliver to the Athenian cult of Athena and Hephaistos, a new cult in the agora and part of the recent program for the building of temples in Athens (#4).[33] Athena and her consort, the patron deities of the Athenian mint, consequently, benefited at the expense of the allies.

The decree further noted that if any Athenian in the assembly should propose or put to a vote a resolution counter to what had just been resolved, he would be indicted immediately by the Athenian Judicial Board of Eleven, which would condemn him to death. If a legal objection occurred, however, the case went before the Athenian courts (#5).

Following the acceptance of the decree, the Athenian Demos then selected four imperial Heralds and dispatched them to the allied poleis to announce the regulations: one each to the poleis on the islands, to the Hellespont, to Thrace, and to Ionia including Aiolis and Karia. The generals then assigned the terrritories and provided the necessary transportation. But should any of the generals fail to carry out his duties, he was to be found guilty at his euthyna, or review of office upon the conclusion of his annually elected term,[34] and fined 1000 drachmae (#6).

Once notified of the regulations, the magistrates of the allied poleis recorded the decree and ordered that a copy be inscribed upon a stone stele set up in their agora, just as the Athenian Epistatai set up a copy before their mint. But as a concession, the Athenians agreed that if an allied polis objected to this, their government would pay for the inscription and its placement. Apparently Kos, long in opposition to the Athenians, did object, and there a stone cutter prepared the stele, supervised by the imperial Herald who conducted that aspect of the negotiations (#7).

To assure the permanency of the decree, the assembly further resolved that the Secretary of the Athenian Boule would add to the annual oath of the democratically selected Boule the following clause:

> If someone strikes silver coins in the poleis or does not use the Athenian
> coins, measures, or weights but foreign coins, measures, and weights, let
> him be brought to charges before the Boule according to our decree
> which Klearchos proposed (#8).

And again, the litigiously minded Demos reiterated the regulations that the inhabitants of the allied poleis were to surrender their domestic coins in exchange for Athenian currency, the "money of the land." If anyone desired not to exchange his silver, he could keep it but was forbidden to use it (#9).

When the allied individuals brought forth their money, the Athenian Epistatai registered each one, and then transferred the foreign money to the Athenian mint (#10). They also kept accounts and posted them publicly upon white boards also set up before the Athenian mint. Anyone who wished, could freely and easily examine the imperial records. The Epistatai also drew up other detailed records of the total sum of the foreign silver and indicated the sums separately by region, and then again by each allied polis (#11).

The Currency Decree not only curtailed the political self-determination of allied governments, it also set laws directly affecting individuals. Through it, the Athenians gained economic domination of the confederate territory by creating a common currency and related system of weights and measures. For them, it produced a monetary uniformity, which eliminated a variety of weight systems and enabled the Hellenotamiai and other Athenian treasurers to operate within a standard fiscal system. The idea was not new. Some poleis had not developed mints, and many others had ceased minting during the 470's. They had found Athenian currency not only financially stable but also desirable in their markets for most economic transitions. Consequently, a widescale adoption of Athenian silver coins had occurred,[35] especially among the island poleis securely linking the major trade routes for the Athenians in the Aegean. But along the western littoral of Anatolia, and in central Ionia, several significant local mints were still functioning when the Athenians promulgated their currency demands. As it had been standard Athenian practice to shut down the mints of rebellious allies subjugated or of poleis and peoples forcefully brought into the Confederacy (such as Skyros,[36] Karystos,[37] Thasos,[38] Aigina,[39] and Erythrai[40]), the new measures affected all the confederate poleis in similar terms of forceful subjection. Only the few allies minting electrum and the autonomous islands of Samos, Chios, and Lesbos were exempt.

Lacking gold and electrum deposits other than those they controlled in the Thracian Pangaion mountains, the Athenians fostered the production of electrum, especially the staters of Kyzikos. While the Athenian silver tetradrachms dominated the markets of the Aegean islands and the north, in the eastern and especially Black Sea markets electrum and not silver coins were demanded.[41] Electrum staters and fractional "sixths," therefore, continued to circulate, to supply the coffers of the Hellenotamiai, and to accumulate on the Athenian acropolis.[42] With Carthaginian control of the Iberian silver mines[43] and the disastrous inundation of the Siphnian mines in the late sixth century B.C.,[44] Athens alone controlled the remaining silver resources in the Aegean,[45] and her own mines of Laureion and those of the Pangaion.[46] From these, the Athenian minters struck currency with a fineness in silver and measurement[47] and established an important token value of that currency over the intrinsic value of the variety of now-banned local coinages.

Athens' grand patron deity Athena, honored annually and especially quadrennially at the Great Panathenaia, soon found her image struck upon every Athenian "owl" and in almost every allied market, money pouch, and cheek, and upon all of the required payments of tribute. To this Athena, beginning in the spring of 453 B.C., the Athenian Hellenotamiai offered annually one-sixtieth of the tribute collected, an aparche or First-Fruit Offering from the phoros.[48] A holy dedication, this gift had no Delian precedent or synodial directive. It, too, came about as one of many Athenian legislative acts in the complex construction of the amphictyony.

Mint by mint, the Athenians imposed the regulations, leaving only four to provide the coveted electrum.

Northern Kyzikos, with two excellent yet unfortified harbors, jutted from the southern shore and prospered with rejuvenated Greek trade in the Propontis (Thuc. 8.107). From Thasos and the Pangaion, from Daskyleion and the Scythian Crimea, imported gold alloyed with silver generated the quantities of electrum staters, "sixths," and "twelfths" vital to commerce in the Black Sea, and especially to Athens.[49] Under either Persian domination or Athenian, Kyzikos' position would have remained secure. But the Kyzikenes carefully sought that diplomacy by which they would prosper most, and their minters struck a series of electrum staters to laud Athens. They not only copied the sculptural complex in the Athenian agora of the "Tyrannicides" Harmodios and Aristogeiton but also issued a series of staters with the portrait of Athena Parthenos in her triple-crested helmet and Athena's symbolic owl, and still other Athenian mythological motifs, the goddess Gaia holding the infant Erechthonios, Kekrops with the olive branch of Athens, and Triptolemos in his winged dragon-chariot.[50]

The new currency regulations, however, did affect Parion, Lampsakos, Abydos, and Dardanos. Parion, apparently, ceased to strike her drachmae and fractions, which had conformed to the prominent eastern Chian standard of weights and which were minted essentially for local commerce.[51]

From Lampsakos, electrum staters struck on a reduced Chian standard struggled unsuccessfully with the Kyzikenes circulating in the northern regions, and occasionally even traveled to Athens as confederate tribute. Hampered by Athenian control of Thraco-Thasian gold and by Kyzikos' domination of eastern gold, Lampsakos had reduced the gold percentage in her electrum from 40-60% to about 30%.[52] Kyzikos similarly had altered the gold percentage in her staters, perhaps because of the demands upon her mint for greater production, but possibly also because of the shortage of gold.[53] But the decree did halt Lampsakene minting of the silver drachmae and fractions struck according to the Persian weight standard. The Persian Empire and Themistokles' choric estates in Lampsakos had significantly affected the Lampsakene markets, and the exchange of their famed wine necessitated local transactions between the Persian silver sigloi and the Lampsakene silver.[54]

Abydos, across from Sestos, had also issued Persian weight silver drachmae and fractions. From their local mines the Abydenoi seemingly dug small quantities of gold, which they probably sold to Lampsakos.[55] From Dardanos, Persian weight silver drachmae and fractions, intended only for local transactions, also ceased with the Abydian silver.[56]

Unaffected by the currency regulations, or any Athenian imperial regulations, the cities of Lesbos significantly remained autonomous; and at Mytilene the mint continued to strike electrum 'sixths' on the important commercial Phokaic weight standard.[57]

In 451/0 B.C., Athens, fearful of civil unrest in Ionia, had gathered at Lesbos a special naval force to halt Persian incursions.[58] Kimon, returned from exile under ostracism, had feverishly worked to create both good will and an effective defense apparatus throughout the Confederacy. He wished to quell discord among the aristocratic poleis, which had been restless since Ephialtes' democratic reforms in Athens of 462 B.C.,[59] and perpetuated by the repeated annual election of Perikles as general and his consequently all-pervasive influence. While Persia threatened the Hellespont, Kimon recognized that sedition threatened Ionia, goaded on by Sardis.

Kyme, to the north of Ionia, subject to the regulations halted its minor issues of small fractions for local use only, which had adhered to the Aiginetic weight standard.[60] Phokaia, however, exempt from the silver regulations continued her electrum 'sixths' and fractions, which served well Athenian need for the 'yellow alloy' so much in demand in the Black Sea and eastern markets. In Athens' treasuries, this extraordinary electrum, essentially unnegotiable in Attica, was accumulated and noted annually in the auditor's credit columns.[61]

Farther to the south, Klazomenai had reorganized her mint in 479-8 B.C. and issued silver struck according to the Milesian weight standard, drachmae and fractions.[62] But coincidental with the growth of Athens' monetary dominance over the Aegean and Ionia, Klazomenai abandoned the Milesian standard and began about 460 B.C. striking fractional denominations on the Athenian standard. An Attic weight diobol plus a surviving Milesian weight didrachma equalled in weight an Attic didrachma. Similarly, a Milesian drachma and an Attic obol together equalled a single Attic drachma, and an Attic hemiobol plus a Milesian triobol weighed the same as an Attic triobol. Significantly, Klazomenai had adopted c. 460 B.C. the Athenian 'owls' and eastern electrum to serve her international trade and the local treasuries' necessities. But in 449 B.C., the Athenians closed that mint.

Erythrai, however, had not remained so calm. Overshadowed by Chios looming across the western straits, and reluctant to become embroiled in Athens' enveloping commerce and monetary systems, Erythrai had retained a modified Persian system of weights and measures for its silver drachmae and fractions,[63] and continued to trade with the inland regions of Sparda. This standard of weights remained unique in Ionia; it was significantly heavier than the Attic drachma (c. 4.69 grms.) yet significantly lighter than Sparda's silver siglos (c. 5.57 grms.). Thus, between two economic worlds, Erythrai struggled to produce a coinage acceptable to a myriad of markets and upon the scales of shrewd merchants. With Erythrai militarily subject to Athens' rule in 453-2 B.C., the Athenian troops and Episkopoi had seized her mint. Athens demanded the Erythraian adoption of Laureion's "owls" and active participation in the amphictyonic rites centered around Athena's holy acropolis, now guarding the Confederate Treasury as well as the soon to be defunct Confederate Synod. (In Miletos, the mint had long ceased to operate.[64])

Between the summer of 451 and the spring of 450 B.C., Kolophon, midway between Erythrai and Miletos, revolted. Even while in the Confederacy, Kolophon had continued her active trade inland to Sparda along the Kayster River. Her coins utilized the Persian standards of weights and measures, and the landed gentry seethed with discontent as Athens' tyranny more and more controlled the Confederacy. In rebellion, the mint continued producing silver drachmae and hemi- and quarter-obol pieces, unmindful of Athens' currency regulations. But in 446 B.C., Kolophon, reduced by the imperial forces, returned to Athens' fold. Subjected and under strict regulations, Kolophon's mint closed (IG 1³. 37; SEG X.17; ATL 2.D15). [65]

Teos to the north of Kolophon and Ephesos to the south remained loyal to the Confederacy and immune to Sardis' subversive schemes. Teos, harassed with internal discord, piracy, and grain shortages, had, nevertheless, issued significant numbers of staters and fractions struck on the waning Aiginetic standard.[66] Ephesos, like Teos, also came to rely heavily upon the Confederacy's protection and upon the benefits of trade with the other members, and had struck a sparse series of tetradrachmae and smaller pieces on the Milesian standard.[67] Both mints closed according to the regulations.

Offshore, Chios and Samos, remaining bastions against Persian intrigue, actively and faithfully supported the Confederacy and cooperated with Athens in driving the Persians from Ionia and Karia. While sedition, rebellion, and economic decline disrupted the Ionian mainland, Chios, especially, prospered. In eastern Thrace, in the Hellespont, and in Ionia, her silver didrachmae rapidly replaced Aigina's coinage in international trade and even rivalled Athens' "owls." Upon the merchants' and bankers' scales, Chian didrachmae balanced with the Chian weights of Parion, Lampsakos (electrum), Phokaia, and Klazomenai; and with only slight adjustments or with exchange discount rates, they often balanced with the Thracian weights (vaguely "heavy" Chian or "light" Attic); with the "heavy" Attic weight standard; with the Persian weights of Abydos, Dardanos, Erythrai and Kolophon; and with the Aiginetic weights of Kyme and Teos. Chios even equated thirty of her didrachmae with one electrum Kyzikene or one gold Persian daric.[68]

Thus, the powerful and important Ionian community of aristocratic Chios wisely perceived the advantages of Confederacy and diligently cooperated with Athens to avoid conflict.[69] In turn, Athens' reliance upon Chios as one of the three able military sentinels (along with Samos and Lesbos) guarding the Anatolian coast dictated judicious dealing with the three sentinels. Athens avoided any restrictive measures which might threaten their coveted autonomy, and allowed the three islands to prosper competitively. While the Athenian "owls" triumphed over Aigina's silver "turtles," the considerably lesser Chian silver "sphinxes" mastered the northeastern markets, much to Athens' unhappiness.

Samos, too, avidly supported Athens' confederate hegemony. Warfare and its ensuing prosperity added to the Samian monetary needs, and Samian currency had improved in both quality and quantity. From every available source, Samos gathered silver, disregarding metallic uniformity, and struck her tetradrachmae and fractions which mingled with the similar Milesian weights of Ephesos. With a slight discount, the Samian tetradrachmae balanced three Attic drachmae.[70] To her currency's reverse dies in 460/59 B.C., Samos added the triumphal olive branch beside Hera's beloved ox, a symbol of Samian liberation and affluence.

Unfortunately, the Samians had halted the reconstruction of the famed Heraion sometime about 480 B.C.[71] Into Karia, to the Eurymedon, at Cyprus, and eastward into

Egypt, Samians fought with Athenians to reduce Persian power. Into the markets of the Great King's Empire, Samian silver circulated during the second quarter of the century.[72] Samos, like Athens and the others, sought valuable Egyptian grain; evidence indicates how shrewdly the Persians and Egyptians tested the Samian currency used for payment.

Panicked in the summer of 454 B.C. by the disasters in the Delta and in the Corinthian Gulf, and by the rumors that the Persian Imperial Fleet would embark upon the Aegean, the Samian ambassador was the one who proposed the confederate evacuation of Delos and the deposition of the Treasury on Athenian soil. By the following February, the Samian population was bitterly divided: the so-called "democrats" remained loyal to Athens; the aristocrats regretted the hasty move from Delos and Athens' rapid aggrandizement ever since. During the Heraic Festival and the "Holy Wedding," the aristocrats seized the unguarded asty, thereupon commemorating their coup by wreathing the currency's ox with an ornamental collar, issuing quantities of the triumphant aristocratic issues, and beginning to count the years of aristocratic rule.[73]

In Karia, from Iasos to Kaunos, the poleis which had joined the Confederacy also became enmeshed in Aegean commerce and adopted the Athenian, Chian, and Samian currencies for trade. By mid-century, only Knidos and Kos were still maintaining independent mints. Knidos, periodically issued drachmae on the Aiginetic standard, but with the enactment of the Currency Decree closed her mint.[74] Kos, however, tenaciously continued the triple-sigloi in honor of Triopian Apollo, for Athens' ascendancy in Karia grated upon the independent spirits of the Dorian Greeks. Kos, like Kolophon, avidly maintained her commercial connections with the Persians and other peoples of Sparda and refused to obey the Athenian demands that her mint be closed. Through force, Athens compelled Kos to do so, but only temporarily, for during the period 446/5 - 443/2 B.C. Kos rebelled and severed her ties with Athens, and perhaps briefly reopened her mint and resumed the striking of the triple-sigloi. But by the spring of 442 B.C., Athenian imperialism crushed that island.[75]

The Athenian Currency Decree rapidly imposed a sovereign monetary system upon allied poleis, which possessed established currencies of their own. On one level, the purpose was to facilitate trade through the development of a uniform system of measurements by eliminating from the unified territory of the confederate empire the widely disparate weight systems of different tetradrachmae, staters, drachmae, and fractions fluctuating significantly within only broad limits for their respective standards.   (In Kos, the commemorative Persian triple-sigloi, with wear, weighed between 15.25 and 16.89 grms., and clustered about 16.30-16.75 grms. At Karian Knidos, the minters struck Aiginetic drachmae with weights between 5.98 and 6.54 grms., which clustered about 6.10-6.25 grms.   Samos struck Samian weight tetradrachmae between 11.85 and 13.53 grms., which grouped about 12.70-13.15 grms., and peaked at 13.00-13.05 grms.   In Kolophon, the Persian weight drachmae ranged from 4.74 to 5.63 grms., and clustered about 5.30-5.45 grms.   And from Teos, the Aiginetic staters classed between 10.85 and 12.16 grms., gathering about 11.60-11.97 grms.)

In contrast, the Athenian laureate "owls" weighed between 16.70 and 17.40 grms., with a cluster at 17.00-17.25 grms. (more narrowly at 17.12-17.20 grms.).   Perhaps only the Chian silver currency achieved an exactness in weight and a wide acceptability to rival the Athenian "owls."   Chian staters ranged between 7.74 and 7.90 grms., became acceptable in the eastern and Persian markets, and structured the basis for the wide-scale Chian standard utilized in Ionia and the Hellespont .

The accuracy in weight of the Athenian "owls" and the Chian "sphinxes" eliminated the need for merchants, bankers, and treasurers to weigh coins; altered the whole attitude toward coinage from that which saw it as an effect of intrinsic value to that which saw it as an object of only token value; and led to a substantial adoption even in Greek and eastern markets beyond the realm of the currency regulations. Athens' "owls," however, were produced in far greater quantity than the Chian silver staters and achieved a far wider international acceptability.   The Athenian silver currency and the electrum issues of Kyzikos together dominated commercial activity in the greater Aegean and the Black Sea; the silver currency of Chios and Samos and the electrum of Lampsakos, Mytilene, and Phokaia exchanged only as second best.

But most of all, the Currency Decree was an imperialistic measure which subjugated the allies by seeking hard profit for the Athenians. It created a market for the thousands of talents of silver transported from Delos to Athens which were being converted into the currency of an empire.   The imperial pride focusing upon the imperial goddess and her Panathenaic festivals also focused upon her portrait and emblems struck upon the coins which the subjected allies by law were required to contribute.

The regulations of the Currency Decree, however, soon proved inadequate. Within only two years, Kleinias was proposing additional measures, for the Hellenotamiai, had encountered difficulties with their audits. Too often, pouches arrived in Athens containing less than the assessed tribute. The confused records and audits, reported in 448 B.C., could not be permitted. The Hellenotamiai, therefore, demanded more control and, in 447 B.C., it was granted.[76]

Once again, the imperial Heralds delivered to the allies Athens' imperial regulations regarding confederate matters. This time, Athens required the allies to submit not only their assessed tribute but also a separate sealed record of their contributions. The sealed record and the account of the actual contribution were expected to coincide. Deficiencies were promptly noted, counter-records carefully kept, and indictments swiftly issued for malpractice and fraud.[77]

In strong imperial terms, Kleinias proposed "in order that the phoros may be collected year by year, and be brought to Athens, the Athenian Boule, the imperial Archons in the allied poleis, and the Episkopoi are to be in charge." The Hellenotamiai, specifically now responsible only to the Athenians, had demanded regulation in order to combat corruption in the tribute collection process. The regulations were aimed not at poleis or their governments but individuals, not rebels but malefactors, both allied and Athenian. If injustices occurred, indictments were given, and fine penalties levied in the Athenian courts; and the Athenians insisted upon new legal contracts with their subjected poleis (the *xsymbola* of line 11)[78] in order to prevent fraud. The regulations were not needed, as some have suggested, because allied poleis in the wake of the treaty with King Artaxerxes were reneging on their tribute obligations and chafing under Athenian hegemony,[79] but rather because extensive corruption had arisen within the system.

But more important than the problems of imperial corruption, both allied and Athenian, was the reference by Kleinias to earlier agreements or demands that the allies offer to the Athenians a cow or a panoply of armor, and that if any individual be found guilty of malpractice the same imperial judicial procedures occur (lines 41-4). The contribution of either to the Athenian metropolis marked each polis as subject and of colonial status, as such contributions were delivered for the Athenian Great Panathenaic festivals.[80]

The foundations of the new Parthenon, set down in 447 B.C., supported a national center of the amphictyony, which the Athenians molded out of the Delian Confederacy. The quadrennial Great Panathenaia received confederate youths bearing the sacrificial cows, panoplies, and hydriai filled with tribute[81] and bound first the rebellious states restored to the empire with the status of Athenian colonies ethnically and religiously tied to the Ionian metropolis Athens, and then allied poleis rebellious and non-rebellious, except Samos, Chios and Lesbos. Not Pheidias' great chryselephantine statue of Athena Parthenos but the Erechtheion's ancient olive wood statue of Athenia Polias nearby served as the religious focal point of the amphicytony,[82] as allies voluntarily developed local cults of "Athena the Protectrix," and "Athena of the Athenians."[83] Athenian imperial magistrates, garrison troops, klerouchs, and colonists scattered throughout the Confederacy also supported similar cults. The legislation of the Currency Decree prohibiting the use of local or foreign silver and demanding the use of Athenian coins not only structured a new token-monetary system but propagated Athena's amphictyonic image throughout the empire.

The crucial problem of Athens' empire, however, rested in the failure of the amphictyonic confederation to be active rather than passive, with no inherent bond other than Athenian imperial legislations which subjected rather than maintained the initial principles of parity and the preservation of autonomy. Imperialism signaled for the ruling landed gentries vassalage. Fundamentally, as Thucydides suggested (8.48.5), the desire of allies for political autonomy determined protest, separatism, and decentralization movements in marked rejection of economic, social, and religious benefits and relationships.[84]

THE FRONTIER OF IMPERIALISM

Empires are dangerous possessions, as Perikles admitted (Thuc. 2.63.2). For King Xerxes' Achaemenid Empire, the rapid succession of military failures at Salamis, Plataia, and Mykale dramatically transformed the preceding Stage #2, offensive$_1$, imperial aggression and expansion, into the first phases of Stage #3, defensive$_2$. That transition occurred as the Persian military leaders delineated their imperial borders and from the western Anatolian littoral withdrew their land and naval forces, garrisons, and imperial magistrates. The Ionians, by necessity, responded in turn to their own acute needs for political and economic stability and sought the Athenian military protection gained by joining the Delian Confederacy. For Xerxes and his generals, the later failure at the Eurymedon River reconfirmed those defensive$_2$ actions. Although the victories at the Egyptian Delta could have altered Persia's status (Stage #3), the Persians failed to be aggressive and instead reinforced their defense of Egypt and Syria. Kimon's renewed aggression against Cyprus, therefore, won for the Athenians victory and the Peace of Kallias. Persia, in turn, continued to endure the defensive$_2$ activities of Stage #3.

For the Athenians, in contrast, the events at Eion had rapidly transformed their Delian Confederacy from Stage #1 (defensive$_1$) to Stage #2 (offensive$_1$), to be succeeded by a series of progressive imperial steps. The fall of Naxos signaled the initial phase of the alteration from Confederacy to Empire, and the fall of Thasos confirmed that imperial tyranny. With recovery from the disasters at the Delta, in major part due to Persia's failure to counter-attack, the Athenians consequently marked the Peace of Kallias with a series of blatant imperial acts of legislation. The Athenian democracy, ironically yet in normal reaction to imperial successes, issued Klearchos' proposal for the Athenian Judicial Decree and shortly thereafter the Currency Decree. Two years later, the Athenian Demos capped those imperial events of 449 B.C. by accepting Kleinias' proposals to regulate the collection of tribute from their imperially bound confederates.

For the Ionians, the conflicting imperial events generated yet another contrastable transformation in our paradigmatic scheme. Following the Greek defeat of the Persians at Mykale (479 B.C.), the Ionians entered the initial phases of a new Stage #1, defensive$_1$ (β). King Xerxes' royal edict to withdraw Persian forces, garrisons, and magistrates to

an inland imperial frontier between the Ionian coast and the royal Achaemenid
Hauptstadt of Sardis (with the major exception at Smyrna) left the coastal poleis
extremely vulnerable to the wiles, dangers, and crises of the turmoil and confusion of the
several critical years after 479 B.C.. Within this disruptive matrix, the Ionians and the
Athenians collectively and consciously spawned at Delos the new military alliance, in
part to protect the Ionians in order to give solace to their vulnerability as realized by
both the Ionians and the Athenians, and, as the ancient propaganda permits, "to liberate"
the Ionians of the geographical regions (the complex of ecological niches) to be
defended.   Intertwined throughout every aspect of Ionian life—political turmoil,
economic failures, and devastating shortages of food, acute disruption of the societal
functions, and the destruction of urban walls, each compounded by perplexing religious
uncertainties—the devastating loss of life by war and the critical decline of population
throughout Sparda and its neighboring satrapy of Daskyleion marked with no uncertain
terms and with vivid bluntness the inability of the Ionians to defend themselves.

The critical transition from Stage #3 B, the last phases of $defensive_2$ to the new
Stage #1, $defensive_1$ (β^n), necessitated if not demanded a marked alteration within
Ionia, the important process of revitalization to enable the Ionians to achieve some
measure of success; and that revitalization came from the Athenians in response to
Xerxes' imperial withdrawal and the local Ionian social and economic depression. In
response to the Athenian overtures to lead and to develop the Delian Confederacy, the
Ionian landed gentry in their fervent attempts to stabilize, restore, and revive their
demesnes and poleis rallied in support of Athenian hegemony, and in particular to
Aristeides' personal leadership of the Confederacy.

As the Ionian poleis transformed, each socio-political unit attempting to regain
political centralization and positive internal functioning sought to combat the various
centrifugal forces of personal interest or individualism in conflict with the collective
aristocratic/oligarchic political body (e.g. Teos: ML *GHI* 30). Military failures had
outweighed success because of military weaknesses and an acute decline in manpower
specifically among the ranks of the landed gentry who structured the councils and
assemblies of their respective poleis. Consequently, the same socio-political ranks of the
gentry as well as the non-landed classes (perhaps about 10% of the population) within the
aste urban centers suffered noticeable losses of necessary and fundamental resources,

further accentuated by unfavorable balances of trade. Such failures or negative alterations, no doubt, occurred among the religious and philosophical standards of each community, which resulted in a search for the return of old or the establishment of new standards. By focusing upon the Pan-Ionian center on Delos and the establishment of a successful new "Ionian" military alliance, a conscious transferral occurred from the earlier goals and values generated at the then defunct Panionion religious center on Mt. Mykale to those generated on Delos. From the outset, Athenian interest to protect Ionia was based upon presumed historical relationships, and the Delian Confederacy was founded upon traditions and Athens' traditional role.

The same societal pressures generated by these crises also affected the lower classes and non-landed but without perceptible overt reactions. Poverty, a decline in population, and societal problems could be absorbed by the lower classes without significant perceptible change but not by the elite who occupied distinctly different and broader ecological niches. The Ionian attempt at revitalization during the 470's and the 460's B.C. came about as the response by the landed gentry to the social and physical crises or challenges in order to regain and to preserve their status, wealth, and leadership (e.g. the Milesian Molpoi). The revitalization processes, however, were unsuccessful, as the Ionian Stage #1, defensive$_1$ (β^n) system was rapidly absorbed by a dominant offensive system (Y), the growth of the Athenian imperial processes, whereby the various Ionian societal systems lost their self-identities and became part of Y, the Athenian Empire. The revolutions in Erythrai, Miletos, and Kolophon, however, did mark notable yet also unsuccessful attempts by the aristocratic/oligarchic factions to break away from the Athenian Y and to create poleis in alliance with Persia. The goals, however, were not to have substituted a Persian imperial Y for the Athenian imperial Y but to attain semi-autonomous rank within Persian Sparda such as Miletos had held between 545 and 494 B.C. The identity and integrity of the ruling aristocratic/oligarchic gentry would be maintained similar to the identity and integrity of the Karian and Lykian nobility in their respective centers. The revolutionary failures, however, occurred not just because of superior Athenian forces but more because of internal Ionian factionalism which arose within the ranks of the markedly reduced and distressed gentry. The non-landed classes, least of all, were not instrumental in fostering that factionalism, but rather it was the aristocrats/oligarchs who controlled their governments and social life. They formed the poleis' limited military forces, were the major agents of economic activity, and were in control of their communities' religious life (e.g. ML *GHI* 43). Strife (eris) and conflict (stasis) persisted as normal events of Ionian life as the leading factions of the aristocrats/oligarchs within the poleis struggled to control ecological niches which in the mid-fifth century B.C. could no longer support them.[1]

Ionian poverty is strongly noted among the records of the Athenian Tribute Lists in which the payments to Athens are remarkably low. The Milesian syntely never submitted more than 10 talents (450/49 B.C.) and no other central Ionian polis as much. And within seven years, the Milesians were submitting only 5 talents. The Erythraian syntely in 448/7 B.C. submitted between 9 talents, also reduced to 7 after 444/3 B.C. The Ephesians submitted between 7½ and 6 talents, the Teians 6, and the Kolophonians 3 to 1½. Only Kyme on the border of Aiolis submitted 12 talents in 452/1 and 451/0 B.C., but that sum was lowered to 9 in 448/7 B.C.[2] Hairai, Lebedos, and Phokaia submitted from 3 to 1 talents while the poleis of Pygale, Priene, Myous, Karian Latmos, and Myrina near Kyme paid 1½ to 1 talents.[3] The others submitted far less. Within the Athenian Empire, the Ionian district ranked among the least prosperous. The Milesian inscription noting the political expulsion of the unsuccessful revolutionists (ML *GHI* 43) emphasizes further the poverty of Miletos, as attested by the small sums of 100 silver staters rewarded to any Milesian who should slay the outlawed revolutionary oligarchs and their descendants, and the fines of 100 and 150 staters imposed upon the Milesian magistrates for any neglect of their duties in punishing the revolutionists with compulsory death sentences.

The long-term depopulation of the Ionians, and specifically the gentry, the burden of tribute to the Athenians, and the Ionian failure in economic competition accentuated by the emergence of Athens as the dominant imperial and commercial power marked the Ionian decline to a low provincial status.[4] The internal disruption was further compounded by factionalism and strife generated by the Persian attempts in the mid-century to regain territories in the Troad and especially to regain the Maeander Valley in a drive to return Miletos to the Persian imperial system. The persistence of the prygoi, such as at Teos, Erythrai, Smyrna, and Miletos show how well-established the landed gentry, natural allies of the Persians, were. Factionalism was not only the business of the landed gentry but also one of their characteristic forms of behavior, as several small groups of powerful gentry struggled at loggerheads, stimulated by Athenian and Persian foreign intervention.[5]

Factionalism in the fifth-century B.C. was further complicated by a series of significant legal factors. The poleis had long developed constitutions and law codes, which the political factions had to manipulate and gain control of in order to legitimize and secure their own political position. Many of the constitutional systems, while controlled by the aristocratic/oligarchic gentry, often tended to represent more broadly based political systems which are to be identified imprecisely as "democracy," or rather as a greater political consciousness among a broader base of citizens. Rather than perceived as an extension of political power from the upper classes to the lower, it is best perceived as divisions of the ruling gentry, some limiting ruling power and others extending it to broader groups of gentry and other landed citizenry. This perception, therefore, minimizes the participation of the urban non-landed who appear to be a minor and almost insignificant political factor. Herodotus' Ionian "democracies" (6.43.3) had remained aristocratic-oligarchies with, from time to time, one or more factions appealing to broader bases of citizen support. Oligarchy was the prevalent political form while the Athenian democracy was unusual in the general trend of government. Factionalism in Ionia resulted not from class struggle,[6] a conflict between the oligoi and the demos, but rather from the conflict between the oligoi and the leaders of the demos, the *prostatai tou demou*.[7] The use of hoplite armies and naval forces during the Ionian Revolts had required the services of a large proportion of the citizenry, but after 479 B.C. both the armed forces and the citizenry had critically declined in numbers. The broader based factions which ultimately succeeded to power in Erythrai and Miletos, for example, were nevertheless politically reinforced by contact with the successful democratic forces of military Athens.[8] As Athenian imperial intervention stimulated factionalism so did Persian intervention, as both acted toward a resolution in favor of one or another faction.

Beyond the Ionian littoral of western Anatolia, the Lydian gentry were similarly settled in rural clusters or ribbons of villages along the river valleys and about the central urban center of Sardis, but unfortunately our ancient sources are silent whether factionalism also occurred in Sparda and Daskyleion. As limited degrees of strife and factionalism are attested throughout the fifth century B.C. in other Persian satrapies such as Egypt, Syrian "Across the River" and its subdivision Judah, Assyria (Babylonia), and Bactria, we may justly assume that a limited degree of factionalism did occur throughout western Anatolia as well. Yet three major factors apparently checked crises from erupting as violently as those in Ionian Erythrai, Miletos, and Kolophon: one, the paucity of major urban centers such as the East Greek aste nodes; two, the firm Persian control of the western satrapies from the imperial centers at Sardis and Daskyleion as demonstrated, for example, by the later satraps of Sparda Pissouthnes and Tissaphernes; and three, a marked decline in the power and numbers of the Lydian landed gentry due to the series of Persian-Lydian wars since 545 B.C. Yet even at a markedly reduced number, the Lydian and Ionian landed gentry (as well as the Aiolian and Karian) still provided in the mid-fifth century B.C. the key to the processes of Athenian and Persian imperialism and the conflict between the two imperial forces and their institutions, as the gentry still remained fundamental to political organization, social stratification, social interaction, and economic activity.

Each ethnic cluster, Lydian, East Greek, and Karian, continued fundamentally as a religious association in addition to its socio-politico-economic condition. In the fifth-century, with the decline in urban nodes, the ethnos or tribal system continued amidst a population thinly scattered yet still united politically, in customs and religion, and governed periodically by means of assemblies or religious festivals not at the urban aste but within the rural dendritic systems, such as identified in Erythrai and Miletos.[9] In several Ionian poleis, however, the asty still forcibly maintained itself as the political center of at least portions of the ethnos, just as the urban centers of Daskyleion and Sardis maintained their control through established and complex dendritic systems among the Lydian and other native Anatolian groups with their respective political units. While so-called "democracies" or broadly based aristocratic/oligarchic governments often arose in aste-poleis systems, aristocracies/oligarchies continued among the ethnos systems. The Ionian and Lydian landed gentry famed for horse raising actually had fought poorly in land-warfare, and proved unable to defend themselves against the Persian invaders. What military strength the sixth-century Ionians and Lydians did muster was, by the mid-fifth century, radically reduced.

This notably irregular pattern of urban and rural settlement- and demesne-clustering produced a marked variable-density of cities and towns from the East Greek littoral zone to the inland Lydian zone of Sparda and Daskyleion. The East Greek urban nodes centralized poleis along the coast with a "high degree" of East Greek and Anatolian villages within dendritic nodule systems, which diminished as the coastal agricultural zone transformed inland into the low lying north-south ridges. East of those ridges lay the "low degree" Lydian villages and demesnes within complex dendritic systems along the inland valleys. The border between the East Greek and Lydian agricultural zones, therefore, remained fluid and often shifted as village nodules and demesnes were transferred from the Athenian imperial sphere to the Persian, or from the Persian imperial sphere to the Athenian. Once the Persians had withdrawn from most of the East Greek littoral zone, the latter transferral occurred, however, at a far slower rate than Athenian to Persian transfer because of the rather constant power of the Persian landed forces entrenched within Lydian Sparda and Daskyleion. Athenian imperial power rested upon naval forces while Persia's strength consisted of land forces. Where the Persians often did gain in transversing the fluid border within that frontier of imperialism was along the east-west river valleys in the East Greek littoral zones where the Persians fostered factionalism and rebellion against the Athenian imperial system, and seized land, sometimes permanently, sometimes temporarily, consequently leaving it in turmoil. After the initial Athenian success of bringing East Greek poleis into the Delian Confederacy, and then forcing Karian centers to join, the Athenians and the confederates did not gain significant new territories in western Anatolia from the satrapal systems of Sparda and Daskyleion, except for several Greek poleis in the eastern Propontic region, notably Kios and Astakos. Only after Perikles' expedition in 437 B.C. into the Black Sea did several Propontic and Pontic poleis join the Confederacy.[10] The inhabitants of those remote and non-Persian states, nevertheless, joined for purposes other than those originally stated in 478/7 B.C., and essentially for the economic benefits and political stability which the Confederacy offered, and in fear of the Athenians. The Athenians, however, argued that they relied little on force (Thuc. 1.77.1-4) but rather on the processes of law (IG 1^3.40 : 5-10; Isoc. 4.113).

In contrast, Persia's major gains were in southern Ionia, Karia, and Lykia. By 438 B.C., the loss of more than 40 states in the Karian District resulted in the official Athenian imperial merger of the Ionian and Karian Districts for the tribute records of 438/7 B.C.[11] By 433/2 B.C., 56 allied poleis, tyrannies, ethnic and dynastic groups in southern Ionia, throughout Karia, and the multi-state of the Lykian syntely (ATL 1.446), almost 23% of the confederate states, had defected to Persia without Athenian resistance. They were not large urban nodes but village nodules, nevertheless politically sovereign units, the largest being Karian Keramos which had paid 1½ talents annually.[12] In total, these Karian and Lykian allies had contributed only slightly more than 21 talents 2792 drachmae, and because of their ambivalency, their remoteness in rugged Karian valleys and highlands, and because of Persian imperial progress, the Athenians tacitly ignored their defections. For Athens, to secure the Hellespont and the vital grain trade took precedence over regaining Persian Karia where only 15 coastal states remained within the Athenian Empire.[13]

North of Karia, in comparison, the Persian attempt to regain the Maeander Valley from the inland stronghold of Magnesia to the confederate poleis of Myous, Latmos, Priene, and Miletos, resulted in failure. The mid-century campaign to recontrol Miletos and its important harbors met fierce Athenian resistance and ultimately Athenian success, and with the Peace of Kallias the littoral zone remained within the Athenian Empire. Yet the Athenians did not attempt to push inland to seize the important Persian center of Magnesia, or to gain the great landed demesnes held by Themistokles and his family. Similarly, in the coastal regions of the Kayster Valley, the Persian attempts to foment rebellion in Kolophon also failed because of Athenian resistance and success. And Ephesos, with a large proportion of native Anatolians, rather similar to the various ethnic populations in Kolophon, remained secure under Athenian imperialism. By the spring of 445 B.C., however, the Athenians removed the Ionian poleis of Isinda, Marathesion, and Pygela from the Ephesian syntely and entered their tributes among the Athenian records separately (*ATL* 1.276). Such action appears to have been the Athenian attempt to strengthen imperial control along the Ionian coast south of Ephesos.

At the coastal regions of the Hermos Valley, the Persians also did not regain territories, yet did hold the small but insignificant center of Smyrna on the coast at the end of the major road from Sardis across the inland ridges past the Lydian village of Nymphaion. The Ionian Revolts had devastated the population,[14] and in the fifth century Smyrna had become a small, insignificant village controlled by the Persians. Its harbor had become useless. In the fourth century B.C., some influential gentryman or Persian lord holding important demesnes in the area lived in a complex of heavily walled buildings, a fortified manor with an open courtyard adjoining and a number of lightly walled outer buildings as barns and other farm structures.[15] The Persian assistance to Kolophon, therefore, apparently had moved from Smyrna directly south rather than westward down the Kayster Valley, and thus by-passed Athenian controlled Ephesos. Persian control of Smyrna and its small coastal region, consequently, remained firm. And Larisa in the Hermos Valley, inland from the river's marshy delta and the territories of Phokaia, the Persians also securely held. While the Athenians attempted to assess Larisa a tribute of 3 talents in the special assessment of 425 B.C.,[16] the Persians retained full control. Although our archaeological evidence for the Persian control of Sparda is still meager, it is only at Larisa (c. 540 B.C.) that we have any evidence of palace construction in the royal style noted at Pasargadae, Persepolis, Susa, and the several other eastern sites.[17] And not far from Phokaia, the Persians also build a rock cut tomb in their royal style, but perhaps not until the end of the fifth or the early fourth century B.C.[18] The low degree of Persianization of Sparda is accentuated by the realization that the Persians did not compete for Lydian or Ionian ecological niches but were easily accommodated within regions of decreased population as the ruling elite distinct from the Lydian and Ionian landed gentry.

With rebellion latent in Miletos and with the destruction of Smyrna, the only major port in Ionia which the Athenians could safely utilize in the mid-century was that of rich and important Kyme, secure from potential Persian pressures. Yet beyond the northern regions of Kyme and the Aiolic village of Pitane, the coastal region north of the Kaikos Valley and the inland Pergamene plain to the important Lydian center at Adramyttion continued to remain under Persian control. Only at the very small polis or rather village of Astyra on the coast west of Adramyttion did the Athenians gain control, and perhaps not in the mid-century but during the first or second decade of the confederate campaigns.

The broad frontier between the East Greek poleis hugging the Anatolian littoral and the Lydian Hauptstadt of Sardis rested squarely among the important inland choric regions and their rural centers where the conflict between the Persian and Athenian Empires took place. Yet the processes and the institutions of those imperialisms appeared significantly similar. As the Persians withdrew from the coastal zones, the Athenians gradually replaced the Persian institutions with their own, a replacement which they fully set in motion by the mid-century. Only briefly, for about twenty years after 478 B.C., were the East Greek poleis free of imperial institutions, a freedom which, nevertheless, accentuated their political and military crises during that turbulent generation. In time, Athenian imperial magistrates replaced the Persian satrapal and imperial magistrates, Athenian garrisons[19] replaced Persian garrisons, and the crucial demesnes governed by Persian, Median, Lydian and Greek nobles in exile were paralleled by the occurrence of private Athenian possession of East Greek demesnes.[20]   At some point in mid-century, the Athenians developed the policy of settling Athenian citizens on land confiscated from the imperial allies, a confiscation which significantly weakened the resources of the Ionian poleis. The Ionians had to accept the settlements and in turn the Athenians lowered the tribute assessments.[21]   Athenian imperial legislation drafted by the Boule and Demos simply replaced the Great King's imperial edicts and the satrapal regulations from Sparda and Daskyleion. Tribute formerly paid to the Persian treasuries now flowed first to Delos and by the mid-century to Athens, and both tributes were based upon Artaphrenes' assessment of the agricultural potential of the Ionian landed gentry and their poleis (Hdt. 6.42.2). The major difference, however, was the military means by which each imperial system controlled the East Greek poleis. The Persian system relied extensively upon land troops and a limited by significant naval force.   With the destruction of that naval force at the battle of Mykale, however, King Xerxes was forced by necessity to withdraw from the vulnerable littoral zones. The Athenian imperial system in comparison relied extensively upon its significant and superior naval force and a critically limited number of land forces scattered among the Ionian poleis. The Persian armies, consequently, maintained a secure inland frontier and from time to time penetrated the Athenian imperial sphere.   The limited Athenian land forces, in comparison, seriously prevented the Athenians from gaining territories beyond the littoral zones where their naval forces could be successfully effective. Within urban nodes, the aste of Erythrai, Miletos, and Kolophon, the Persians regained allied vassals, yet within the complex and significant dendritic systems of the choric centers and the demesnes of the rural gentry the Athenians retained imperial control. But in each case, Erythraian Boutheia, Pteleon, Sidoussa, Polichna, and Elaiousa; Milesian Leros, Teichioussa, and the White Promontory; and Kolophonian valley in the region of confederate Notion were coastal and readily accessible to the Athenian naval forces.

These complex processes of Athenian and Persian imperialisms can be further

detected among the events of the Samian Revolution of 440–439 B.C. (Thuc. 1.115-7).[22]
Important to that affair were three factors: (1) Samos' attempt to gain the long contest
control of mainland Ionian territories at Priene allied to Athens, (2) the contemporary
civil conflict within Samos, and (3) the alliance of an oligarchic faction (the *dunatotatoi*
or the chief influential leaders) with the Persian military power at Sardis eager to disrupt
Athenian imperialism. While the Samian oligarchic faction desired Priene's mainland
territories, the so-called "democratic faction" or the *prostatai tou demou* sought
Athenian intervention to overthrow the *dunatotatoi*. Consequently, when Athens
ultimately subjugated Samos and raised the *prostatai tou demou* to power, the oligarchs
in exile on the Anatolian mainland rallied, and in political coalition with other oligarchs
remaining on Samos allied with Pissouthnes, the Persian satrap of Sardis (fig. 22). This
complex affair further illustrates the faltering of Athenian imperialism when civil
factionalism divided an Ionic polis. While the successful, if only temporary, ruling
faction (oligarchic, "democratic," or pro-Persian) held the polis' central urban node (the
asty), the faction in rivalry for political control organized either in the polis' choric
districts or in the case of the island poleis in the mainland choric territories.

Throughout his *History* Thucydides further noted oligarchs in exile in the rural
districts or in the mainland rural territories outside of the central urban node where the
ruling faction was "democratic," pro-Athenian, and enmeshed within the Athenian
imperial system. Those oligarchs in the eastern Aegean islands, such as at Samos, or in
Ionian, northern Aiolian, or southern Karian poleis, in order to regain political control of
the central urban nodes and to succeed in their rebellions against imperial Athens, often
sought Persian or later Spartan assistance. By 427 B.C., for example, the Samian
oligarchs had centered at the rural village of Anaia near Ephesos (Thuc. 3.32.3) where
they approached the Spartan general Alkidas. In the previous days, Alkidas (Thuc. 3.29.2)
had sailed to Embaton in Erythrai and then to Myonnesos in Teos (Thuc. 3.32.1), both
villages within their respective poleis but away from their central urban nodes, and he
sailed there apparently to link up with their oligarchic factions. Furthermore, at Anaia,
other Ionian oligarchic exiles advised the Spartan Alkidas to seize poleis in Ionia or the
polis of Kyme in order to bring Ionia into revolution against Athens (Thuc. 2.31.1).
Similarly, in 424 B.C., from the island of Lesbos, Mytilenaian and other Lesbian oligarchs
also in exile gathered on the mainland and sought to hire Peloponnesian mercenaries to

aid their revolt against Athens (Thuc. 4.52.2). In their attempt to succeed, they seized first the village of Rhoiteion north of Troy and then the southern Athenian allied polis of Antandros (Thuc. 4.52.3), for their plan was to seize the mainland area north of the island of Lesbos, territories taken by the Athenian military forces in 427 B.C. (Thuc. 3.50.3). Thucydides then noted (4.75.1) that the oligarchic Mytilenaian dominance of Antandros menaced "democratic" Lesbos and the Athenian Empire just as the Samian oligarchs at Anaia had menaced Samos (Thuc. 3.9.2, 3.32.2, 4.75.1).

This division between the oligarchic, anti-Athenian rural districts and the so-called "democratic," pro-Athenian central urban nodes was also apparent in Thrace when the Spartan general Brasidas campaigned successfully in the rural districts but could not budge the central urban nodes of Sane and Dion in 424 B.C. (Thuc. 4.109.4). And the Persian support of apparently oligarchic exiles is reported among the events of the exiles from the central island of Delos in 422 B.C., who settled on the Anatolian coast across from Lesbos, Persian territory given to the Delian exiles by Pharnakes II, the satrap of Daskyleion (Thuc. 5.1; fig. 23).

One of the clearest instances of these factors at work may be seen in the division of the polis of Ionian Kolophon in 427 B.C. (Thuc. 3.34.1) again caused by factionalism and Persian intervention. In this case the central urban node was held by the oligarchs and guarded by the Persian general Itamenes and his troops, while the Athenian imperial forces held the Kolophonian port of Notion, some distance south of the central urban node. Further factionalism, nevertheless, disrupted Notion, as the anti-Athenian faction of oligarchs there allied with Pissouthnes and, supported by Arkadian and Persian mercenaries, joined in political union with the ruling faction in Kolophon. In reaction, the democratic faction in Notion (Thuc. 3.34.2), part there and part in exile, actively sought Athenian military assistance, and successfully regained Notion (Thuc. 3.34.4) as a "democratic" pro-Athenian center, to which exiled Kolophonian "democrats" scattered among the other Ionian poleis were summoned.[23]

The distinct separation and function of the two units of the polis, the rural district or chora, on the one hand and the central urban node, the asty, on the other, have been observed at Lampsakos, Myous, and Perkote. While these poleis paid tribute to Athens, Themistokles as vassal of King Artaxerxes I also held parts of these poleis as Persian imperial estates, and from their resources and that of Persian Magnesia-on-the-Maeander paid his imperial tribute to his sovereign king. It is now possible to identify the payments to Athens as being from the factions dwelling in the primate central urban nodes, and the payments to the Persian king as being from Themistokles who held the rural agricultural estates and manors as chora-dendritic systems. Lampsakos, Myous, and Perkote, as royal estates given to Themistokles, were only three among numerous royal Persian estates in western Anatolia, no less throughout the Achaemenid Empire. Members of the king's royal family, and the other leaders of the king's noble tribe, the Achaemenians, held vassalage estates in their tribal territories of Parsa, and as the Persian king utilized those nobles as satraps and other imperial bureaucrats throughout the Empire, the king gave to their relatives and tribal nobles estates or manors within the satrapies and, in particular, western Anatolia. They were agricultural estates and manors very similar to the towered and fortified manors which have been noted in Miletos, Teos, and Erythrai, and similar to the towered manors, the pyrgoi, in Ionian Smyrna, which remained part of the Persian Empire through the fifth century B.C.

Throughout fifth century B.C. Ionia, acculturation can now be clearly observed. Rural manorial districts of the Ionian poleis, when separated from their central urban nodes and the imperial controls of the Athenian Empire easily re-allied with the Persian government of Sardis and became, yet in several cases only temporarily, part of the Persian Empire. Their political structures and economic systems were similar to those of the satrapy of Sardis. Furthermore, we find an overt interest by the Persian King and his satraps in the development of agricultural land in western Anatolia. The Athenian government, in contrast, inflicted a harsh duplicity: subjugating the Ionians in the name of liberation and demanding annual tribute but not caring about the development of either the rural manorial territories in Ionia or the central urban nodes which usually remained loyal to the imperial Athenians. In contrast to the building projects in Ionia during the second half of the sixth century B.C. under Persian occupation, the fifth century Ionians liberated yet controlled by the Athenians did not refortify their urban centers, build markets, harbors, temples, civic buildings, or give contracts for monumental sculpture. In general, with the exception of limited rebuilding in Miletos, the central urban nodes in fifth century B.C. Ionia were severely economically depressed areas. And here, a lack of accultration between the Athenians and the Ionian Greeks occurred, in spite of the Athenian imperial propaganda which we read in the pages of

Herodotus and Thucydides, in the imperial Athenian inscriptions, or find portrayed on the frieze and the metopes of the Athenian Parthenon.[24]

When considering the nature of the frontier between the Athenian and Persian Empires in Ionia during the fifth century B.C., we are now able to perceive the complexities. While Ionian poleis allied with the Athenian Empire remained loyal to Athens' direction, the border of a given polis was apparently definite   Yet when factionalism separated the central urban node from the rural districts, in some instances the rural districts often allied with the Persian Empire while in other instances the urban centers allied.   The border then shifted from relatively defined polis divisions to relatively less defined borders between the rural demesnes and their subsidiary and dependent agricultural units.   Rural Ionian Greeks and the local indigenous Anatolian peoples residing in those rural districts, consequently, easily acculturated into the Persian Empire. The vassalage agricultural systems of rural Ionia and Persia, Persian interest and development of those agricultural systems, and the political conservativism and similarities of the aristocratic and oligarchic East Greeks, the landed gentry, and the aristocratic Persians fostered those processes of acculturation. In contrast, the imperial Athenians related to the *prostatai tou demou,* and the few mercantile and non-landed inhabitants of the Ionian urban centers, who, estranged from the oligarchic rural estates, turned to the military and political protection of Athens. As Pseudo-Xenophon stated simply *(Ath. Pol.* 3.10):   "Likes prefer likes."   The democratic basis to Athenian imperialism fostered those so called "democracies" in the East Greek urban centers, appealed to those East Greeks living in the central urban nodes, and gave those factions political control in opposition to the rebellious and pro-Persian conservative oligarchs. In two notable instances, however, namely Erythrai and Miletos in the late 450's, the central urban nodes allied with Persia and were governed by local East Greeks as tyrants locally appointed but assisted with Persian aid. The chora, in these two cases, controlled by the rival rural oligarchs, remained loyal to Athens, but the oligarchs' loyalty came from their desires to regain control of the urban nodes and their governments, to overthrow the pro-Persian tyrannies simply as other examples of political factionalism, and not through a strong political or economic desire to remain allied with Athens. In these cases, the rival factions' alliances with Athens served to foster the political goals of those factions, and little more. What is also apparent in those two examples is that the tyrannies in the central urban nodes retained land connections with Sardis and the Persian Empire, while the exiled factions and the Athenian naval forces remained allied by maritime connections.

A third variation to this division of the formal Ionian polis and its factionalism was the alliance of the rural districts with Sparta and her military forces in Ionia, an alliance which produced an intermediate zone between the Athenian controlled central urban node and the formal territories of the Persian Empire. This later Spartan intervention within Ionian affairs complicated further the frontiers, for while the rural territories allied to Sparta were anti-Athenian, there is no indication of overt alliance with Persia; yet it may have been covert. Sparta had not allied with Persia nor were her actions pro-Persian; in fact a state of war existed between Sparta and Persia until their treaties of 412-411 B.C.[25] And in the first two treaties of 412 between Sparta and Persia (Thuc. 8.18, 37) the Persians noted the distinction between the Persian chora and the Greek poleis, while the third treaty of 411 (Thuc. 8.58) referred only to the chora.

We can now define the Ionian frontier as a physical space in which cultural groups (Lydian, Persian, and Athenian imperial, in addition to the East Greek socio-politico-economic units, all with distinct identities) came into conflict. The frontier was a broad zone of the Lydian, Persian, Athenian, and ultimately Spartan antagonists and the East Greek poleis (their urban and rural regions) and several local indigenous enclaves, in Karia and Lykia the assimilation of Anatolian populations into the Persian satrapal system had occurred with a marked retention of their indigenous native character and with a far greater degree of exclusion than in Ionia. There, the indigenous (non-Greek native) populations within the East Greek poleis lost much of their sub-identities, yet could still be noted at Ephesos, Kolophon, Smyrna, Erythrai, Teos, and Miletos to a marked degree.   In Ionia, nevertheless, a higher degree of social inclusion, of acculturation, occurred than in Karia and Lykia or in Aiolis. In contrast, Persian Sparda remained greatly Hellenized yet barely Persianized.

Within this frontier and imperial zone of conflict existed a second series of groups with separate sub-identities that interacted notably with the Persians and the Athenians, and within that interaction did not lose their sub-identities as central urban nodes, rural territories, and dendritic and primate variations thereof.   In defining this eastern imperial frontier it is necessary to consider not only the problems of the external frontier but also those of the internal frontier, in regard to Lydian, Persian, and East Greek fortified and non-fortified manors of the landed gentry in addition to the political, military, and economic boundaries between the imperial structures, and most notably the Athenian and Persian Empires. The fluid frontier between the Persian and the Athenian Empires existed not as a geographical boundary of a discrete border with fixed points of demarcation but rather as village units and their agricultural territories on both sides of a frontier zone pierced by roads and mountain passes. The frontier existed not of areas but rather of a network of the demesnes of the landed gentry strung together by the routes of communication.

This analysis of the two conflicting empires, as they had evolved by the mid-fifth century, reveals several patterns of development and institutions in their respective empires. Imperialism is that set of policies which aims at the creation, the organization, and the maintainence of a harmonious and mutually beneficial relationship between diverse political groups. That is, imperialism structures a geographical unit of a vast size, composed of various distinct political units which are subject to the direction of the imperial center. In the case of Persian imperialism, numerous Iranian tribes and tribal kingdoms, established Near Eastern states (e.g. Chaldea, Lydia, Judah, and Egypt), scores of Phoenician and East Greek city-states, and several client kingdoms were incorporated into the Persian Empire. Central direction was provided by the sovereign, the Persian King of Kings. In comparison, Athenian imperialism united about 252 Greek poleis that had joined the Delian Confederacy and that became subject to Athens' military, political, economic, judicial, and ideological will.

In another way imperialism may be envisaged as an obligation imposed upon the superior force, in essence a philosophical justification of that institution which presupposes an ethical or ideological factor which the conqueror transfers to the conquered. While most of the elements of Persian and Athenian imperialism had existed in earlier imperialisms, there were qualitative differences in the Persian and Athenian structures. Military domination, economic exploitation, and ideological bases for hegemony occurred earlier. But with the extensive sources for the institutionalization of both imperial structures, and a comparison of those imperial institutions, we can now understand the conflict of the two empires more clearly.

For the allies of the Delian Confederacy, the concept of a common past (Persia's military aggressions against them) and the desire for a common future (a military offensive campaign against Persia for the security of wheat importation, the elimination of piracy and brigandage, yet stated in terms of freedom for the Greeks and just retribution from the Persians) formulated the early confederate consciousness of mission. Persia's consciousness of mission was also formulated upon the principles of its common past (the Zarathustrian concept that Ahura Mazda had given the king all the kingdoms of the world to maintain) and the desire for a common future (the protection of the empire, strict obedience of vassals and vassal states, and military offensive campaigns to maintain that protection and obedience).

Empires can be created by either or both of two means: by voluntary association or by forceful annexation. It is the former upon which the Athenian Empire was based. Initially, each associate poleis was independent, was allowed its own political self-determination, and was co-equal in the cooperative military alliance. Those collective voluntary acts of coordination quickly gave way to the demands of Athens. Those demands, based upon her military dominance, resulted in Athens' economic and then political control of the allied structure. Consequently, the foundation of Athens' power can be studied in terms of the institutions that defined her relationship to the subjected poleis. We can, therefore, demonstrate the steps by which military alliance with a dominant partner was transformed from a de facto imperialism into an institutionalized imperial system.

The Persian Empire, by contrast, was based upon forceful annexation. Following Cyrus' consolidation of the tribal kingdom of Anshan in Parsa and the conquest of the Median Empire, Cyrus sought to build an empire. His first goal was to incorporate the territorial additions using the earlier organization of the Medes as adopted from Assyrian and Urartian models. His second goal was the further conquest of Iranian tribes and tribal kingdoms in the plateau regions of Parthia, Hyrkania, Areia, Sogdiana, and Bactria, which bore common ethnic similarities—aristocratic vassalage, agricultural and herding economies, and fundamental Iranian religious values and institutions which were also common in Media. By 545 B.C., Cyrus' armies had marched westward conquering the Urartian kingdom and then Lydia, itself a combination of a centralized Lydian Empire, Lykian and Phrygian tribal kingdoms, and East Greek poleis. Cyrus' conquest of the Chaldean Empire completed the initial stages of Persian forceful annexation of territories, and were followed by Cambyses' and Darius' conquests of centralized Egypt, the tribal kingdoms of Thrace, and the emerging kingdoms of the Indus Valley.

In each step of Persian imperialism, conquest brought the imposition of imperial control by the king upon the subject peoples and nations. Political control required not only military dominance over, and military service from the subject peoples, but also the subject people's support of the empire in the form of tribute from subjects and gifts from allied client vassals. The demands of the king, enforced by his armies, consolidated the nations. While vassal kingdoms, such as Cilicia, retained domestic political self-determination, the subject peoples and kingdoms lost that right. Theoretically, the empire could not have existed without the king, who personally united the kingdoms subject to him which recognized him as the Great King, the King of Kings. The center of Persian imperialism was the king and his set of subordinate officials within the empire.

In 520 B.C., however, Darius altered the structure and transformed Persia's de facto empire into an institutionalized one. Because Darius had killed the legitimate king, Bardiya, it became necessary to restructure the Persian Empire; and through the institutionalization of that empire Darius confirmed the imperial position that he had gained illegitimately by force. Consequently, the foundation of Darius' imperial power can also be studied in the terms of the imperial institutions that regulated the relationships of the subjected kingdoms, tribes, and city-states. And fundamental to Darius' control was the important role played by the landed gentry and the basic units of their agricultural demesnes, for this study, the landed gentry throughout western Anatolia. The gentry and their demesnes lay as the basic imperial institution, an agricultural foundation that substantially supported both the Persian and the Athenian Empires.

The critical processes of revitalization, therefore, have prime relevancy for the development and institutionalization of empires. With regard to the specific cases of revitalization, King Gyges' revolution and control of Lydia, King Darius' revolution and control of Persia, and Aristeides' break with the Hellenic League and the establishment of the Delian Confederacy, each was a deliberate, organized, and conscious effort by the members of those respective societies to construct rapidly a more satisfying state than existed during the preceding periods of societal distortion. Each revitalization movement demanded and obtained a successful leadership that resolved the problems of stress and distortion that the previous leadership had not. Each leader, however, could not function alone, and had to have a substantial base of support from the elite, the landed gentry.

The formalizing of Persian and Athenian imperialism into institutions presents an opportunity to study not only the social structures but also (1) the internal momentum involved in institutionalization and (2) the ways in which imperialism made sense and worked in the lives of the people affected. The institutions are in effect the form of thought or action taken by the prevalent and permanent forces at work in the interactions of the Persians and Athenians with their respective subjected peoples. Similarly, the institutions also fixed the confines and imposed the forms of the activities of the subjects and their political systems. Yet in both cases, the empire was an imperfect agent of order and of purpose in an evolving society. At the point of its inception, both intent and chance played active roles, and the imperial structure imposed a pattern of conduct upon the activities of members and imposed its compulsion upon the course of unanticipated events. As antithetical complements, the institutions and human actions continually remade each other.

At one level, Darius' intent to regain the rebellious poleis of Ionia and to subject Athens was aimed at the preservation of Persian imperial solidarity. At a second level, Darius had to suppress rebellion—any rebellion—in order to preserve the imperial power which he had usurped. To retain the royal tiara, he was virtually compelled to institutionalize his imperial position. At a third level, King Xerxes recognized the impracticality of controlling the East Greek poleis along the western Anatolian littoral. The Greek intent of collective independent poleis directed by Athenian hegemony generated a cooperative military alliance to assure East Greek independence from Persian imperialism. But this intent changed as East Greek liberation occurred and Athens' hegemony demanded of the allies total allegiance to the military adventure. Chance altered the Greek intent as Athens restructured the Delian Confederacy by means of imperial institutions and transformed the military confederation into an empire. Similarly, chance altered Persia's intent as Persia's army during the reign of Xerxes lost almost one-third of its military power in defeat at Plataia and lost much of its naval force at the same time at Mykale. Xerxes' final attempt to crush the confederate navy and the Confederacy faltered further at the Battle of the Eurymedon.

Internal rebellion in Egypt, therefore, forced Xerxes' successor, his son Artaxerxes I, to sue for peace from Athens. Athenian naval supremacy and Persian lack of naval power had culminated in the confederate fleet's victories in Cyprus.

In contrast to the institutionalization of the Persian Empire, that of the Athenians began at the beginning of the second decade of military activity and built upon the institutionalization of the cooperative Confederacy as established in 478/7 B.C. To create a new military alliance, each allied state including Athens affirmed the constitutional oath of allegiance which strictly bound it to the articles of the Confederate Charter: to appoint and to accept Athens as military hegemon, to contribute to the treasury, and to uphold and to maintain the equality of each state in the Synod and the sovereignty of each. The oath also upheld confederate permanency, which the Athenians interpreted as irrevocable, binding, and a firm judicial statement of non-secession. Without the oath the Charter remained ineffectual for the oath provided a religious bond which would prevent rebellion, secession, and separatist movements among the allies.

In such an alliance two basic and powerful forces existed: the determination to achieve the set goals of the voluntary union and, in contrast, the resistance against total integration within the confederation to the degree that sovereignty was lost. While no aspect of the Charter suggested a loss of a polis' independence, Athens quickly violated the principle of equality, demanded strict adherence to the clause of permanency, and considered her hegemony an imperial power *ex officio* rather than leadership *in camera*. From the outset, the Athenians attacked Persian fortresses, eliminated pockets of hostile pirates, liberated Greeks and Greek poleis, secured the sea lanes for their commercial advantages, reduced hostile Greeks, and directed the war for their parochial gains. But Athenian victories over the Persians also produced confederate discontent with Athenian hegemony. The enthusiasm generated on Delos had deteriorated. Discontent with the burdens of a prolonged war and Athenian direction of the Confederacy for Athenian advantages spurred the allies to declare that the Athenians had violated the constitutional "equality of poleis," and that since the Charter was now violated they could secede from the legally defunct alliance now bound together only by Athens' formidable military power. With such arguments, the Greeks of the allied polis of Naxos seceded. While Naxos and later other rich and powerful allied poleis seceded, the

Athenians quickly directed the confederate fleet against those rebels, insisted upon their return to the Confederacy, and subjugated them with Athenian laws (distinctly not synodal) and often with military occupation. Consequently, the de jure structure of the Confederacy became a de facto military structure, and with the subjection of Naxos Athens began the formal institutionalization of imperialism to prevent rebellion and to control confederate territory.

For the Greeks of Ionia, Karia, the Hellespont, and Thrace, Persian rule had produced economic benefits and an international peace by exchanged agreements that had created a productive Pax Persica. Persian taxes were not oppressive and Persian enforced tyrannies had been replaced with more broadly based governments such as aristocracies and oligarchies, the rule of law rather than arbitrary practice. But should East Greeks rebel, the Persian destructions of Miletos and Naxos in the 490's served as examples of Persian severity. Few Greeks realized that Xerxes' military affectiveness would diminish. In turn, the Persian palace officials, realizing Xerxes' political weakness, assassinated the Great King and raised the royal prince Artaxerxes to the throne to revive Persia's aggressive policy against the East Greeks and the Athenians. And Artaxerxes' ambassadors, armed with Persian gold and silver, did persuade confederates to rebel. Supported by gold, the Ionian poleis of Erythrai, Miletos, Latmos, and Myous, and then Kolophon seceded and rejoined the Persian Empire. They too, however, succumbed to the forces of Athens.

While rebellions and Persian subversions threatened Athenian control of the Confederacy, Persia's failures in foreign policy diminished her opposition. And while Athenians feared further confederate rebellions as Athens' imperial tyranny increased and as eastern allies no longer objected to Persia's domination, King Artaxerxes was forced to sue for peace and the Athenian government shrewdly contracted a peace treaty with Persia. In so doing, the Athenians by-passed the synodal directives, usurped the confederate prerogative of the making of peace, and ended the raison d'être of the alliance. The Synod became defunct as the Athenian government assumed its power and issued legislation which not only regulated allied governments but allied citizens as well. Of a military alliance of 252 members, only Samos, Chios, Lesbos, and ultimately Aigina retained their political self-determination in addition to Athens.

With further imperial crises generated in the period 449-439 B.C., the Athenians increased their indissoluble consolidation of empire, as events of the Boiotian and Euboian wars in 446 B.C. (Thuc. 1.113-4) placed Attica in the most direct and imminent military danger since 479 B.C. Following the subjugation of autonomous Samos in 439 B.C., the Athenians still touted the concept of symmachy (*IG* 1^3.48; ML *GHI* 56:19) yet blatantly referred to members of that military alliance as *the poleis which the Athenians control* (*IG* 1^3.27:14-5; *SEG* X .19 and *IG* 1^3. 19:9-10; *SEG* X .23). Athenian imperial tyranny, of which Thucydides unabashedly wrote at the end of the century (1.124.3; 2.63.2; 3.37.2; 6.85.1), was becoming a perception which many, including Herodotus (5.90-3), Sophocles (*Oedipus*),[26] and Aristophanes (*Eq.* 1111-2), would utter loudly.[27] The Athenian intellectual climate was changing, admitting imperial force, and vehemently criticizing Ionian behavior. Herodotus, writing in cynical terms, inferred that the Ionians were weak, for the majority of them had submitted to Persian subjugation (1.169-170). Not only had the Ionians lost their wars with Persia but were now charged with having dragged Athens into those conflicts. The Ionian actions, he argued, had been irresponsible, and as medism was the easier course of events, the Ionians were chastized. Echoing Herodotus, Thucydides also censured the Ionians for having submitted to Kings Darius and Xerxes and having "chosen *douleia*, subjugation for themselves" (6.82.4).

In fear of the massive Persian empire and their own subjugation, the Athenians had built their empire and, in one of the greatest of historical ironies, in fear of that Athenian Empire (Thuc. 1.23.6),[28] the Spartans waged war, defeated Athens, and dismembered her empire.

APPENDIX I

Herodotus' Use of Folklore Motif

This exclusive list illustrates Herodotus' use of folklore motif. Entries marked with an asterisk have special pertinency to the Herodotean themes discussed in chapter 5. S. Thompson *Motif-Index of Folk-Literature* 6 vols. (Bloomington 1966), hereafter T *M-I*.

*Accidental death through misdirected weapon, Hdt. 3.64; T *M-I* N337.

Ambiguous oracle, Hdt. 1.53, 66; T *M-I* M305.

Animal assistance, Hdt. 1.23, 78, 80, 84, 2.75, 140.1, 3.39-42, 111; T *M-I* B268, 268.6, 300, 401, 405, 431.2, 548.21, 551, 847, K632, 632.1.

Cheating by substitution of worthless articles, Hdt. 3.56; T *M-I* K476.

Deaf and dumb speak, Hdt. 1.88; T *M-I* F1041.22.

Dreams, prophecy, destruction or evil, Hdt. 1.34, 107, 108, 209-210, 2.139, 311, 3.124; T *M-I* D1810.83, 1812.5.1.2, M302.7

Enemies invited to banquet and killed, Hdt. 1.106, 2.100, 107; T *M-I* K811.1.

Exposed or abandoned child rescued, Hdt. 1.109-113; T *M-I* A131, R131.3.1.

Fish follows or fails to follow music, Hdt. 1.141; T *M-I* B767.1, J1909.1.

*Horse indicates election of king, Hdt. 3.84; T *M-I* H171.3.

Leader suckled by an animal, Hdt. 1.22.3; T *M-I* A5111-2.2.1.

King's daughter placed in a brothel to catch a thief, Hdt. 2.121; T *M-I* K425.

*Missing ears, Hdt. 3.69; T *M-I* F511.2.4, D702.1, D712.1.

*Punishment for desecration of holy places and sacrilege, Hdt. 1.19, 105, 167, 2.11, 3.29-30, 149; T *M-I* Q222, 551.6.

*Recognition by unique ability to bend bow, Hdt. 3.21, 4.5, 7-10; T *M-I* H31.2, P11.4. Cf. Homer *Odyssey* 21; J. Gray *The Krt Text in the Literature of Ras Shamra* (Leiden 1964).

Relative's flesh eaten unwittingly, Hdt. 1.119, 123, 128-9; T *M-I* G61, K940.1.

Transformation to gain access to enemy's camp, Hdt. 1.155.7, 3.155-160; T *M-I* D641.2.

APPENDIX II

The Population of Ionia in the
Mid-Fifth Century B.C.

Norman J. G. Pounds, "The Urbanization of the Classical World," *Annals of the Association of American Geographers* 59.1 (March 1969), 135-57, suggested that for ancient Greek agricultural poleis in the mid-fifth century B.C., the tribute rate paid to the Treasury of the Delian Confederacy of one talent may represent a populace of 750. Following Pounds' suggestion, Keramos may have had approximately 1125 inhabitants.

Using Pounds' suggestions further and the data of the 454/3 B.C. Athenian Tribute List, we find in a Confederacy of at least 211 poleis (including Athens, Samos, Chios, and Lesbos) the possibility that 167 poleis may have had populations below 3000 (79% of the poleis). This included 124 poleis which ranked below one talent per annum tribute, thus below a suggested population of 750; 23 poleis which paid 1 to 2 talents of 750-1500 inhabitants; 16 poleis which paid 2 to 3 talents or 1500-2250 inhabitants; and 4 poleis which paid 3 to 4 talents or 2250-3000 inhabitants. Figures above 5 talents per annum may reflect trade and/or craft-industry and not a purely agricultural economic structure.

Ionian polis	tribute	inhabitants
Kyme	12 talents	9000
Miletos	10	7500
Ephesos	7½	5625
Erythrai	7	5250
Teos	6	4500
Hairai	3	2250
Phokaia	3	2250
Kolophon	3	2250
Lebedos	3	2250
Myous	1½	1125

Klazomenai	1 ½		1125
Hessioi	1		750
Karian Latmos	1		750
Myrina beyond Kyme	1		750
Priene	1		750
Pygale	1		750
Marathesion	½		375
Troad Gargara	4500	drachmae	563
Maiandros	4000		500
Notion	2000		250
Isinda	1000		125
Pitane	1000		125
Dios Hieron	1000		125
Gryneion	1000		125
Elaia beyond Myrina	1000		125
Aiolian Astyra	500		63

The komai of the Erythraian syntely (map 5)

Boutheia	1000	125
Elaiousa	100	13
Polichna	1000	125
Ptelion	100	13
Sidousa	500	63

In comparison, A. W. Gomme *The Population of Ancient Athens* (Oxford 1933), Table 1, 26, suggested for Athens, Piraeus, and their urban environs in 431 B.C., a population of 315,000 citizens, metics, and slaves. A. French *The Growth of the Athenian Economy* (London 1964), 139, suggested that the total population of all Attica, c. 430 B.C., exceeded 300,000 free and non-free inhabitants. Lydian Sardis during the reign of King Croesus may have had 20-50,000 inhabitants (chapter 2 note 91); and in the sixth century B.C., one-quarter of a million free inhabitants may have dwelt within all of the East Greek poleis (chapter 3 note 57). In 1951, most modern Greek villages included less than 2,000 inhabitants (chapter 7 note 106).

APPENDIX III

Greek Epigraphical Sources

$IG\, 1^2$ to $IG\, 1^3$

IG	$1^2.10$	=	IG	$1^3.14$
	$1^2.11$			$1^3.15$
	$1^2.12$			$1^3.15$
	$1^2.13a$			$1^3.15$
	$1^2.14$			$1^3.37$
	$1^2.15$			$1^3.37$
	$1^2.16$			$1^3.10$
	$1^2.22$			$1^3.21$
	$1^2.23$			$1^3.18$
	$1^2.25$			$1^3.36$
	$1^2.26$			$1^3.9$
	$1^2.27$			$1^3.27$
	$1^2.28a$			$1^3.19$
	$1^2.30$			$1^3.18$
	$1^2.32$			$1^3.17$
	$1^2.39$			$1^3.40$
	$1^2.50$			$1^3.48$
	$1^2.55$			$1^3.55$
	$1^2.66$			$1^3.34$
	$1^2.90$			$1^3.76$
	$1^2.115$			$1^3.104$
	$1^2.141$			$1^3.45, 157, 211, 212, 213$

NOTES

Introduction

[1] Barbier de Meynard and Pavet de Courteille, trans. C. Pellat, Mas῾ūdī *Les Prairies d'Or* (Paris 1962, vol. 1; 1965, vol. 2). Trans. G. Herrmann, *The Iranian Revival* (Oxford 1977), 122.

[2] G. V. Sumner, "A Note on Thucydides 1.2.6," *CP* 54 (1959), 116-8; H. W. Stubbs, "Thucydides 1.2.6," *CQ* 22 (1972), 74-7; M.H.B. Marshall, "Urban Settlement in the Second Chapter of Thucydides," *CQ* 25 (1975), 26-40.

[3] H. Bengtson, "Die 'Ionier' in der Überlieferung des Alten Orients," *Philologus* 92 (1937), 148-55; C.Töttössy, "Graeco—Indo-Iranica," *AAH* 25 (1977), 129-31.

[4] W. B. Fisher (ed.), *The Cambridge History of Iran* 1, *The Land of Iran* (Cambridge 1968), 9, fig. 7 - p. 19.

[5] H. Goblot, *Les qanats: Une technique d'acquisition de l'eau* (Paris 1979), 69-71.

[6] N. F. Miller, "Economy and Environment of Malyan, a Third Millennium B. C. Urban Center in Southern Iran" (Ph.D. dissertation, Univ. of Michigan 1982).

[7] J. A. Cramer, *A Geographical and Historical Description of Asia Minor* (Amsterdam 1971; reprint of 1832 ed.), 323-475.

Chapter 1. The Processes of Ancient Imperialism

[1] T. S. Kuhn, *The Structure of Scientific Revolutions*, 2nd ed. (Chicago 1970), 4-27; see J. Galtung, "A Structural Theory of Imperialism," *Journal of Peace Research* 8 (1971), 81-117; M. I. Finley, "Empire in the Greco-Roman World," *Greece & Rome* 2nd. s. 25 (1978), 1-15.

[2] One must also consider the imperial powers of Macedon and the Odrysians when one studies Thrace.

[3] R. Meiggs, *The Athenian Empire* (Oxford 1972), 24.

[4] W. Schuller, *Die Stadt als Tyrann: Athens Herrschaft über seine Bundesgenossen* (Konstanz 1978).

[5] A. Goetze in C. H. Kraeling and R. M. Adams (eds.), *The City Invincible* (Chicago 1960), 173: ". . . we have to piece together from single occurrences an integrated picture of the whole." When there is no systematic presentation in the material which one receives then one must build a paradigm, a stronger concept than the term theory, as it provides a theoretical framework, a vocabulary of conceptual terms, and a picture of the nature of the real-world activities to be analyzed. A new paradigm redefines the scope of the subject and points up the most interesting problems to be solved—a deep and important theory which renovates a field of study. J. Wilson, *City Invincible*, 149: ". . . little pieces here and there and build them into a concept rather than a structure above ground without any foundations underneath."

[6] K. Raaflaub, "Beute, Vergeltung, Freiheit?" *Chiron* 9 (1979), 1-22.

[7] Similarly, few Athenian red-figure vases found their way to fifth century B.C. Sardis. I am grateful to Professor C. Greenewalt Jr. of the Sardis Expedition (Dept. of Classics, University of California, Berkeley) for this information.

[8] J. M. Balcer, "Separatism and Anti-Separatism in the Athenian Empire (478-433 B.C.)," *Historia* 23 (1974), 21-39.

[9]Aigina, *IG* 4.29, 33; Chalkis, *IG* 11.9.934; Kos, W. R. Paton, and E. L. Hicks, *The Inscriptions of Cos* (Oxford 1891), 160, no. 148; Samos, *SEG* 1.375, cf. *SEG* 1.376; G. F. Hill, *Sources for Greek History*, new ed. (Oxford 1951), B. 96(a) (b ii) (c) (d i); J. P. Barron, "Religious Propaganda of the Delian League," *JHS* 84 (1964), 35-48.

[10]C. Starr, *The Economic and Social Growth of Early Greece. 800-500 B.C.* (New York 1977), 40-1, 166; M. M. Austin and P. Vidal-Naquet, *Economic and Social History of Ancient Greece* (London 1977), 53-6.

[11]J. M. Balcer, "Miletos (*IG* 1^2.22 [1^3.21]) and the Structures of Alliances," in W. Schuller (ed.), *Studien zum Attischen Seebund (Xenia: Konstanzer althistorische Vorträge und Forschungen; Heft 8)* (Konstanz 1984), 11-30.

[12]A. F. C. Wallace, "Revitalization Movements," *American Anthropologist* 58 (April 1956), 264-80.

[13]The process of cognitive dissonance: L. Festinger, *A Theory of Cognitive Dissonance* (Stanford 1957); J. W. Brehm and A. R. Cohen, *Explorations in Cognitive Dissonance* (New York 1962); Festinger, *When Prophecy Fails* (New York 1964 ed.), 12: "when people are committed to a belief and a course of action, clear disconfirming evidence may simply result in deepened conviction and increased proselyting. But there does seem to be a point at which the disconfirming evidence has mounted sufficiently to cause the belief to be rejected."

[14]F. Sjöqvist, *Sicily and the Greeks* (Ann Arbor 1973), 3: "The interpretation and historical evaluation of (ancient literary legends) have, in recent times, caused a lively discussion. . . . The two poles between which the discussion oscillates are clearly opposed to one another. On one side, one tries to vindicate the historicity of the myth and to consider it a "genuine" one, while, on the other side, the saga is considered an aetiological legend, invented in later times to serve political and ideological purposes during the period of the historical Greek colonization." For example, note the literary legends in Herodotus (p. 9).

[15]A. Giovannini and G. Gottlieb, "Thukydides und die Anfänge der athenischen Arche," *Sitzungsberichte der Heidelberger Akademie der Wissenschaften Philosophisch-historische Klasse* 7 (1980), 7-45; a curious piece well argued but not convincing that Thucydides' (1.96) organization of the Delian Confederacy was simply a rehearsal of Herodotus' organization of the Hellenic League (7.145.1). The existence of an oath at Delos created a Confederacy distinct from the League.

[16]Wallace, "Revitalization Movements," *American Anthropologist* 58 (1956), 279.

[17]H. T. Wade-Gery, "Thucydides the Son of Melesias," *JHS* 52 (1932), 205-27; also in *Essays in Greek History* (Oxford 1958), 239-70.

[18]*An Inquiry into the Human Prospect* (New York 1974), 135.

[19]Compare Theodor Mommsen and his comments about the *Res Gestae Divi Augusti.*

[20]J. M. Balcer, "Alexander's Burning of Persepolis," *Iranica Antiqua* 64 (1979), 96-105.

[21]J. M. Balcer, review of Meiggs, *Athenian Empire* in *American Historical Review* 78 (1973), 661-2.

[22]J. M. Balcer, "The Greeks and the Ancient Near East," *Indiana Social Studies Quarterly* 32 (1979), 11-27.

Chapter 2. Lydia Before the Persians

[1]Marmor Parium, *FGrH* 239 F42: "Cyrus King of the Persians took Sardis and overthrew Croesus," in 541/0 B.C. (?). G. M. A. Hanfmann, "Greece and Lydia: The Impact of Hellenic Culture," *Le Rayonnement des Civilisations grecque et romaine sur*

les cultures périphériques (Paris 1965), 492; C. Segal, "Croesus on the Pyre: Herodotus and Bacchylides," Wiener Studien 84 (1971), 39-51; M. Mallowan, "Cyrus the Great (558-529 B.C.)," Iran 10 (1972), 7-12; P. Filippani-Ronconi, "La conception sacrée de la royauté iranienne," Acta Iranica 1 (Leiden 1974), 90-101; G.V. Tsereteli, "The Achaemenid State and the World Civilization," Acta Iranica 1, 102-7; G. Widengren, "La royauté de l'Iran antique," Acta Iranica 1, 84-9; J. Wolski, "La constitution de l'empire d'Iran et son rôle dans l'histoire de l'antiquité," Acta Iranica 1, 71-83; J. Cargill, "The Nabonidus Chronicle and the Fall of Lydia," AJAH 2 (1977), 97-116; H. Erbse, "Über Herodots Kroisoslogos," Ausgewählte Schriften zur Klassischen Philologie (Berlin 1979), 180-202.

[2] D.G. Mitten, "A New Look at Ancient Sardis," BA 29 (1966), 42-4.

[3] G. M. A. Hanfmann, "Prehistoric Sardis," in G. Mylonas (ed.), Studies Presented to David M. Robinson 1 (St. Louis 1951), 160-83; "Lydiaka," HSCP 63 (1958), 65-88; Sardis und Lydia: Akademie der Wissenschaften und Literatur, Mainz 6 (Wiesbaden 1960), 507-11; L. A. Borsay, "Lydia: Its Land and History" (Ph.D. dissertation, University of Pittsburgh 1965); J. G. MacQueen, "Geography and History in Western Asia Minor in the Second Millennium B.C.," Anatolian Studies 18 (1968), 168-86; D.G. Mitten and G. Yüğrüm, "The Gygean Lake, 1969: Eski Balikhane, Preliminary Report," HSCP 75 (1971), 191-5; G. M. A. Hanfmann, Letters from Sardis (Cambridge, Mass. 1972), 194-5, 206-7, 210-12, 218-9, 235, 241, 260-1, figs. 156-62; J.G. MacQueen, "The First Arrival of Indo-European Elements in Greece: Some Observations from Anatolia," in Acta of the 2nd International Colloquium on Aegean Prehistory (Athens 1972), 142-5; Ph. H. J. Houwink ten Cate, "Anatolian Evidence for Relations with the West in the Late Bronze Age," in R. A. Crossland and A. Birchall (eds.), Bronze Age Migrations in the Aegean (London 1973), 143-53, 158-61; J. D. Muhly, "Hittites and Achaeans: Ahhijawā Redomitus," Historia 23 (1974), 129-45; G. M. A. Hanfmann and J. C. Waldbaum, A Survey of Sardis and the Major Monuments outside the City Walls (Cambridge, Mass. 1975), 5-6; J. Mellaart, The Archaeology of Turkey (London 1978), 105.

[4] J. G. MacQueen, The Hittites (London 1975), 50-3, 56-9.

[5] A. M. Snodgrass, The Dark Ages of Greece (Edinburgh 1971), 313-7, 360-401; V.R. d'A. Desborough, The Greek Dark Ages (London 1972), 19-25.

[6] Hom. Il. 2.864-6, cf. 3.401, 10.431, 18.291; Hdt. 7.77; Strabo 12.8.12, 13.4.8 (cf. 12.8.3 rejection); Pliny HN 5.11; App. 1.8; E. Littman, Sardis, 6.1, Lydian Inscriptions (Leiden 1916), 84: "the Lydian word Müim . . . perhaps derived from Maion . . . may be an epichoric name for the Lydians." G. M. A. Hanfmann, "Archaeology in Homeric Asia Minor," AJA 52 (1948), 135-55; K. Bittel, Grundzüge der Vor- und Frühgeschichte Kleinasiens (Tübingen 1950), 16-89; J. G. Pedley, Sardis in the Age of Croesus (Norman 1968), 24-31.

[7] Hdt. 1.7; Nic. Dam. FGrH 90 F 46. The eponymous Tylon was later identified with the Greek Herakles, thus Heraklid. R. Schubert, Geschichte der Könige von Lydien (Breslau 1884); B. Radet, La Lydie et le monde grec au temps des Mermnades (Paris 1893); L. Alexander, The Kings of Lydia (Princeton 1913); P. Naster, "De laatste Lydische Herakliden," Philologische Studien 7 (1935-6), 3-16; O. Seel, "Herakliden und Mermnaden," in Navicula Chiloniensis: Studia Philologa Felici Jacoby Professori Chiloniensi Emerito Octogenario Oblata (Leiden 1956), 37-65; H. Diller, "Zwei Erzahlungen des Lyders Xanthos," in Navicula Chiloniensis 66-78; Hanfmann, "Lydiaka," HSCP 63 (1958), 70; Sardis und Lydia 510 and n. 2, 512; J. L. Myres, Herodotus: Father of History (Chicago 1971; reprint), 138-9.

[8] Sagen, which in reference to Lydia the Greeks labeled myths (Dion. Halik. Ant. Rom. 1.27.1; Strabo 12.8.19) and Cicero (de Officiis 3.9) called fabulae, more precisely identify the tales as both legend and myth, with degrees of underlying historical kernels; Pedley, Sardis 30-7; P. Thompson, The Voice of the Past: Oral History (New York 1978), 1, 19, 24. The complexity of the Greco-Lydian Sagen is indicated by the multiple names attributed to the last Tylonid king: Kandaules, Myrsilus, Adyttes-Sadyattes (Hdt. 1.8; Nic. Dam. FGrH 90 F 44, 45, 47; Pliny HN 35.55). L. Radermacher, Mythos und Sage bei den Griechen (Baden 1938), 11-137; W. Aly, Volksmärchen, Sage und Novelle bei Herodot

und seinen Zeitgenossen (Göttingen 1969 edition); J. M. Cook, "Greek Settlement in the Eastern Aegean and Asia Minor," *CAH* (3rd ed.) 2.2 (Cambridge 1975), 799-800.

[9]Sagen sources collected in J. Pedley, *Ancient Literary Sources on Sardis* (Cambridge, Mass. 1972), F 1-7, 9-14, 18-9, 26-38, 43-4, 46-8.

[10]D. G. Hogarth, "Lydia and Ionia," *CAH* (1st ed.) 3 (Cambridge 1929), 506-7.

[11]In contrast to Pedley, *Sardis* 44, who noted: "rise to power of Gyges ... not ... clear." Hanfmann, *Sardis und Lydien* 515; S.C. Humphreys, *Anthropology and the Greeks* (Boston 1978), 29-30. D. Hegyi, "Notes on the Origin of Greek Tyrannis," *AAH* 13 (1965), 311; incorrectly stated: "Gyges crushed the power of the local dynasties, broke their independence; he limited the political influence of landed nobility, and transformed Lydia into a monarchy with a strictly concentrated despotic character."

[12]Hanfmann and Waldbaum, *Survey of Sardis* 22.

[13]A. Ramage and N. H. Ramage, "The Siting of Lydian Burial Mounds," in *Studies Presented to George M. A. Hanfmann* (Cambridge, Mass. 1971), 143-60, esp. fig. 1, "Distribution Map of Lydian Mounds"; G. M. A. Hanfmann, *From Croesus to Constantine* (Ann Arbor 1975), 2 and fig. 3 (from Ramage and Ramage above); R. Gusmani, *Lydisches Wörterbuch* (Heidelberg 1964), 19-20. See C. H. Greenewalt Jr., *Ritual Dinners in Early Historic Sardis: University of California Classical Studies* 17 (Berkeley 1976); N.H. Ramage, "A Lydian Funerary Banquet," *Anatolian Studies* 29 (1979), 91-5.

[14]Hom., *Il.* 16.670-5; R. Gusmani, "Der lydische Name der Kybele," *Kadmos* 8 (1969), 158-61; G. M. A. Hanfmann and N. H. Ramage, *Sculpture from Sardis: The Finds through 1975* (Cambridge, Mass. 1978), 23.

[15]M. Braun, *History and Romance in Graeco-Oriental Literature* (Oxford 1938), 13-8; H. T. Bossert, *Altanatolien* (Berlin 1942), pls. 557-9; O. K. Armayor, "Sesostris and Herodotus' Autopsy of Thrace, Colchis, Inland Asia Minor, and the Levant," *HSCP* 84 (1980), 67-73.

[16]H. T. Bossert, *Asia* (Istanbul 1946), 70-5; O.R. Gurney, *The Hittites* (Harmondsworth 1952), 135; S. Lloyd, *Early Anatolia* (Harmondsworth 1956), 144-5; Hanfmann, *Sardis und Lydien* 508 and n. 1; four km. east of Manisa rather than the Niobe rock in town now shown to tourists. Bossert, *Altanatolien* pls. 154-6, false Niobe; pls. 560-2, real Mother Goddess; G. M. A. Hanfmann and M. B. Balmuth, "The Image of an Anatolian Goddess at Sardis," *Jahrbuch für Kleinasiatische Forschung* 2 (1965), 261-9; A. Henrichs, "Despoina Kybele: Ein Beitrag zur religiösen Namenkunde," *HSCP* 80 (1976), 253-86; I.M. Diakonoff, "On Cybele and Attis in Phrygia and Lydia," *AAH* 25 (1977), 333-40; D.H. French, "Archaeology, Prehistory and Religion," in S. Şahin et al., *Studien zur Religion und Kultur Kleinasiens* 1 (Leiden 1978), 375-83.

[17]Hom. *Il.* 20.385; Hdt. 1.84; Strabo 13.4.6; Plut. *Quaestiones Romanae* 53 (277D); Eustathius *Commentarii ad Homeri Iliadem* 366.15-20.

[18]Hanfmann and Waldbaum, *Survey of Sardis* 5. I regret not having seen G.M.A. Hanfmann, *Sardis from Prehistoric to Roman Times* (Cambridge, Mass. 1983).

[19]Bossert, *Asia*; A. Heubeck, *Praegraeca: Erlanger Forschungen* 12 (Erlangen 1961), 71-3; R.R. Dyer, "Asia/*Aswia and Archilochus Fr. 23," *Parola Passato* 101 (1965), 115-32.

[20]Bittel, *Grundzüge der Kleinasiens* 96-7; S. Heinhold-Krahmer, *Arzawa: Untersuchungen zu seiner Geschichte nach den hethitischen Quellen* (Heidelberg 1977), 1-6.

[21]Hanfmann, *Croesus to Constantine* 2-5.

[22]Ibid. Çeltiki fig. 6, Sart Mustafa fig. 4.

[23]*Metamorphoses* 8.618-723; Hanfmann, *Croesus to Constantine* 3.

[24]In earlier studies ["Imperialism and Stasis in Fifth Century B.C. Ionia," in *Arktouros: Hellenic Studies presented to Bernard M.W. Knox* (Berlin 1979), 261-8; and "Fifth Century B.C. Ionia: A Feudal Frontier Redefined," in *The Frontier: Comparative Studies* 3 (Norman, forthcoming)] I referred to this phenomenon as feudalism. Herein I explain its function as the preferred suzerainty.

[25]A. Heubeck, *Lydiaka: Erlanger Forschungen, Reihe A: Geisteswissenschaften* 9 (1959), 16; Gusmani, *Lydisches Wörterbuch* 179-80. Hom. *Il.* 13.793 noted Palmys, a member of an Anatolian royal family.

[26]Hipponax F 3, 4, 34-5; Tzetzes *Chil.* 5.456; C. Roebuck, *Ionian Trade and Colonization* (New York 1959), 52 and n. 57; S. Mazzarino, *Fra Oriente e Occidente* (Florence 1947), 182-3, 370 n. 514; R. Drews, *Basileus: The Evidence for Kingship in Geometric Greece* (New Haven 1983), 129-31.

[27]Roebuck, *Ionian Trade* 52-3, stressed Phrygia's role as a transmitter of Near Eastern materials into Lydia; while O. W. Muscarella, "The Archaeological Evidence for Relations between Greece and Iran in the First Millennium B.C., *"Journal of the Ancient Near Eastern Society of Columbia University"* 9 (1977), 31-47, argued for sea routes rather than land. G. L. Huxley, "Titles of Midas," *GRBS* 2 (1959), 85-99.

[28]Hdt. 1.84.3. The archaeological evidence uncovered on the acropolis indicates a date of development c. 700 B.C., but this may be due to the loss of evidence by the extensive erosion of the Hyde.

[29]Hanfmann, *Letters*, HoB: 44-5, 47 181, fig. 134; PN: 249, figs. 176-7.

[30]Hanfmann, *Sardis und Lydien* 524; Hanfmann and Waldbaum, *Survey of Sardis* 28-9; A. Ramage, *Lydian Houses and Architectural Terracottas* (Cambridge, Mass. 1978).

[31]Hdt. 1.8.1; Nic. Dam. *FGrH* 90 F 44-7; Herodoros *FGrH* 31 F 49; Paus. 4.21.5; Alexander *Anth.* Palat. 7.709.

[32]Pedley, *Sardis* 34; Ramage and Ramage, "Siting of Lydian Burial Mounds," *Studies Presented to Hanfmann* 158-60.

[33]W. Ramsay, *The Historical Geography of Asia Minor* (London 1890), 23-4; Bittel, *Grundzüge der Kleinasiens*, fig. 49 climate, fig. 50 vegetation, fig. 51 rainfall; J. M. Cook, *The Greeks in Ionia and the East* (New York 1963), 17-8, 28; Hanfmann, *Sardis und Lydien* 499-502; Hanfmann and Waldbaum, *Survey of Sardis* 19.

[34]Today, 4 cbm. rain in the summer to 160 cbm. in the winter; Hanfmann, *Sardis und Lydien* 502-3.

[35]Gusmani, *Lydisches Wörterbuch* 74.

[36]A Lydian myrrh, bákkaris (Hipponax F 19: Simonides F 14.2) or brénthion (Hesychius sv; Pollux 6.104). The lydions present at Gordion and the Ionian sites begin to appear in the second quarter of the sixth century B.C. and continue well into the fifth; and imitations thereof occur in Greece and Magna Graecia; Roebuck, *Ionian Trade* 56 and n.70. Mitten, "A New Look at Ancient Sardis," *BA* 29 (1966), 48.

[37]Textiles: *Schol. Ar. Ach.* 112; *Schol. Ar. Pax* 1174; Pliny *HN* 7.56; Hyginus *Fables* 274. Sheep: Archilochos F 23. Horses: Hdt. 1.78.1. Metalwork: Daimachos *FGrH* 65 F 4. Leather: Sappho F 17.1-3; Hipponax F 24.2, 24.3; cf. Hdt. 1.55. Wine: Hipponax F 102; Roebuck, *Ionian Trade* 55-7.

[38]Roebuck, *Ionian Trade*, 58.

[39]Ibid. 52.

[40]Bossert, *Asia* 79-80; E. Richardson, *The Etruscans* (Chicago 1964), 6; J.-Chr. Billingmeier, "Troy, Taruiša, and the Etruscans," *Talanta* 8-9 (1977), 5-10. Herodotus'

Sagen (1.7) suggest a period just after the Trojan War, in the reign of Atys the son of Manes.

[41]Schubert, *Geschichte der Könige von Lydien*; Radet, *La Lydie et le monde grec*; Alexander, *Kings of Lydia*; Naster, "De laatste Lydische Nerakliden," *Philologische Studien 7* (1935-36), 12, 16.

[42]Bossert, *Altanatolien* 23-7; Bittel, *Grundzüge der Kleinasiens* 94-6; R. S. Young, "The Nomadic Impact: Gordion," in M. J. Mellink (ed.), *Dark Ages and Nomads c. 1000 B.C. Studies in Iranian and Anatolian Archaeology* (Istanbul 1964), 52-7.

[43]G. Neumann, *Untersuchungen zum Weiterleben hethitischen und luwischen Sprachgutes in hellenistischer und römischer Zeit* (Wiesbaden 1961), 69-71; Gugu from the Hittite ḫuḫḫa-, "grandfather." V. V. Struve, "Chronology of the Sixth Century B.C. and the Work of Herodotus," *VDI* (1952), 60-78 [in Russian] noted the chronological problems in Herodotus' text in regard to the dating of the Lydian reigns. Struve suggested the date c. 654 B.C. for the death of Gyges, 66-7.

[44]M. Cogan and H. Tadmor, "Gyges and Assurbanipal," *Orientalia* 46 (1977), 65-85; A. J. Spalinger, "The Date of Gyges and its Historical Implications," *JAOS* 98 (1978), 400-9.

[45]Bittel, *Grundzüge Kleinasiens* 90-4; A. R. Burn, *The Lyric Age of Greece* (New York 1960), 100-6.

[46]Bittel, *Grundzüge der Kleinasiens* 97-100; R. Young, "Gordion: Problems of Western Phrygia," *Le Rayonnement des Civilisations grecque et romaine sur les cultures périphériques* (Paris 1965), 481-5.

[47]R. S. Young, "Progress at Gordion, 1951-1952," *University Museum Bulletin* 17.4 (Dec. 1953), 25-9, 39.

[48]A. T. Olmstead, "The Assyrians in Asia Minor," in *Anatolian Studies Presented to Sir William Mitchell Ramsay* (Manchester 1923), 283-96; Hanfmann, *Sardis und Lydien* 514; Mitten, "A New Look at Ancient Sardis," *BA* 29 (1966), 44-5.

[49]A. T. Olmstead, *History of Assyria* (New York 1923), 421-3; Hanfmann, *Sardis und Lydien*, 514; H. W. F. Saggs, *The Greatness that was Babylon* (New York 1962), 129-30; G. L. Huxley, *The Early Ionians* (London 1966) 54, 72; Pedley, *Sardis* 44-50; D. Frankel, *The Ancient Kingdom of Urartu* (London 1979).

[50]Roebuck, *Ionian Trade* 45.

[51]Pedley, *Ancient Literary Sources* 21, noted on Mita's death (Strabo 1.3.21) that Jerome reported 696 and Africanus 676 B.C. In conformity with Hanfmann's lower dates for the Kimmerian raids, I have chosen the latter.

[52]R. Young, "The Campaign of 1955 at Gordion: Preliminary Report," *AJA* 60 (1956), 263 n. 24.

[53]Roebuck, *Ionian Trade* 44 n. 17; Snodgrass, *Dark Ages* 348; Phrygian power established c. 725 B.C., 350.

[54]Pedley, *Ancient Literary Sources* F 292, Rassam Cylinder; Ramage, *Lydian Houses* 2, notes c. 645 B.C. burnt strata in Section HoB.

[55]Magnes of Smyrna noted Amazonian (Kimmerian) hippomachian raids upon Gyges' Lydia, in Nic. Dam. *FGrH* 90 F 62; Hogarth, "Lydia and Ionia," *CAH* (1st ed.) 3.510; Dygdamis in the Mykale area, C. B. Wells, *Royal Correspondence in the Hellenistic Period* (London 1934), nn. 7, 14-7.

[56]Huxley, *Early Ionians* 54 n. 78; Ath. Deip. 525c noted Ephesians; Strabo 14.1.40 noted Milesians; either version is possible.

[57] Arist. F 478; Steph. Byz. sv Antandros; cf. Pliny *HN* 5.123.

[58] Kallinos (Diehl F 3); Roebuck, *Ionian Trade* 53 n. 59; Huxley, *Early Ionians* 53-4.

[59] Kallisthenes *FGrH* 124 F 29; G. M. A. Hanfmann, "The Third Campaign at Sardis (1960)," *BASOR* 162 (1961), 8-49.

[60] Nic. Dam. *FGrH* 90 F 62.

[61] Humphreys, *Anthropology and the Greeks* 45-75; in reference to K. Polanyi, "Ports of Trade in Early Societies," *Journal of Economic History* 23 (1963), 30-45; also in G. Dalton (ed.), *Primitive, Archaic and Modern Economies* (Garden City 1968), 238-60.

[62] Diehl F 13; Paus. 9.29.4.

[63] Huxley, *Early Ionia* 53.

[64] Diehl F 3; C. M. Bowra, "Xenophanes, Fragment 3," *CQ* 35 (1941), 119-26. See the sixth century B.C. Samian nobleman with long hair and similarly dressed, E. Buschor, *Altsamische Standbilder* (Berlin 1934), pls. 160-2.

[65] F. Jacoby, "Zu den älteren griechischen Elegikern: II. Zu Mimnermos," *Hermes* 53 (1918), 296.

[66] R. Fleisher, *Artemis von Ephesos und verwandte Kultstatuen aus Anatolien und Syrien* (Leiden 1973).

[67] Hanfmann, *Letters* 148, 153-5, figs. 107-12.

[68] Balcer, "The Greeks and the Ancient Near East," *Indiana Social Science Quarterly* 32 (1979), 19.

[69] Gurney, *Hittites* 63-79, 102-3; Hanfmann, "Greece and Lydia," *Rayonnement des Civilisations* 492-3; MacQueen, *Hittites* 57-9, 112-7.

[70] MacQueen, *Hittites* 59.

[71] V. Korošec, *Hethitische Staatsverträge* (Leipzig 1931), 65-92; E. Neufeld, *The Hittite Laws* (London 1951); G. Mendenhall, *Law and Covenant in Israel and the Ancient Near East* (Pittsburgh 1955), 29-34; R. Werner, *Hethitische Gerichtsprotokolle: Studien zu den Boğazköy-Texten* 4 (Wiesbaden 1967); N. Oettinger, *Die militärischen Eide der Hethiter: Studien zu den Boğazköy-Texten* 22 (Wiesbaden 1976).

[72] Nic. Dam. *FGrH* 90 F 47.8; Naster, "De laatste Lydische Herakliden," *Philologische Studien* 7 (1935-36), 12, 16; Hanfmann, *Sardis und Lydien* 511; Pedley, *Ancient Literary Sources* 16.

[73] Pedley, *Sardis* 34, incorrectly attributed this to Nicolas of Damascus.

[74] Hegyi, "Notes on the Origin of Greek Tyrannis," *AAH* 13 (1965), 311; R. Drews, "The First Tyrants in Greece," *Historia* 21 (1972), 138; see M. Bloch, *Feudal Society* (Chicago 1961), 443.

[75] Sovereignty also in terms of the synonymous tyrannos (Hdt. 1.7, 14) and basileus (Hdt. 1.11, 12, 13); R. Nordin, "Aisymnetie und Tyrannis," *Klio* 5 (1905), 392-409.

[76] Pedley, *Ancient Literary Sources* 7, incorrectly translated servitutem as serfdom rather than vassalage.

[77] J. A. S. Evans, "Herodotus and the Gyges Drama," *Athenaeum* 43, n.s. 33 (1955), 333-6; A. E. Raubitschek, "Gyges in Herodotus," *Classical World* 48 (1955), 48-50; A. A. Mosshammer, *The Chronicle of Eusebius and Greek Chronographic Tradition* (Lewisburg 1979), 105-12.

[78] Hdt. 1.15; Huxley, *Early Ionians* 75; Pedley, *Sardis* 50-1; Mellaart, *Archaeology of Turkey* 105.

[79] Pedley, *Sardis* 51-2.

[80] Hdt. 1.17, 18.3; Roebuck, *Ionian Trade* 45; Burn, *Lyric Age* 210-3; Huxley, *Early Ionians* 76; Pedley, *Sardis* 52-7; Mellaart, *Archaeology of Turkey* 105-6.

[81] Mimnermos Diehl F 2; Hdt. 1.16.2; Nic. Dam. *FGrH* 90 F 64; J. M. Cook, "Old Smyrna, 1948-1951," *BSA* 53-4 (1958-9), 23-7; J. K. Anderson, "Old Smyrna: The Corinthian Pottery," *BSA* 53-4 (1958-59), 148; Mitten, "A New Look at Ancient Sardis," *BA* 29 (1966), 46-50.

[82] Huxley, *Early Ionians* 77.

[83] Bittel, *Grundzüge der Kleinasiens* 100-1; Huxley, *Early Ionians* 78; Pedley, *Sardis* 54-5; Mellaart, *Archaeology of Turkey* 105-6.

[84] Hdt. 1.74.3, incorrectly identified him as Labynetos; R. P. Dougherty, *Nabonidus and Belshazzar: A Study of the Closing Events of the Neo-Babylonian Empire* (New Haven 1929), 32-42; H. Tadmor, "The Inscriptions of Nabunaid: Historical Arrangement," *Assyriological Studies* 16 (Chicago 1965), 351-63.

[85] Pedley, *Sardis* 58-70, 123-9; Hanfmann, *Letters* 109, 118-20, 142-3, 183-7, figs. 88-9.

[86] Croesus controlled mines between Pergamum and Atarneus, Strabo 14.5.28. Mt. Sipylos, Strabo 14.5.28; and near Atarneus [Arist.] *de. Mir. Ausc.* 52 (834A).

[87] Hanfmann, *Sardis und Lydien* 515; M. Miller, "The Herodotean Croesus," *Klio* 41 (1963), 58-94.

[88] Hdt. 1.26; Ael. 3.26; Polyainos 6.50. The *Suda* sv Aristarchos noted that c. 560-50 B.C., the Ephesians invited the Athenian Aristarchos to Ephesos to reorganize the government that brought that polis five good years. Tyranny, however, returned before Cyrus' invasion, *Suda* sv Hipponax.

[89] A. Bammer, *Die Architektur des jüngeren Artemision von Ephesos* (Wiesbaden 1972), 6-9.

[90] D. J. Wiseman, *Chronicles of Chaldean Kings (626-556 B.C.) in the British Museum* (London 1956), 40-2.

[91] G. M. A. Hanfmann, "On the Palace of Croesus," in U. Höckmann and A. Krug (eds.), *Festschrift für Frank Brommer* (Mainz 1977), 145-54, pl. 41; M. J. Mellink, "Archaeology in Asia Minor," *AJA* 82 (1978), 329-30, fig. 8; "Archaeology in Asia Minor," *AJA* 83 (1979), 340, pl. 56, fig. 12-3; "Archaeology in Asia Minor," *AJA* 85 (1981), 473-4.

[92] Hanfmann, *Sardis und Lydien*, 524; Hanfmann and Waldbaum, *Survey*, 23.

[93] S. Kiyonaga, "The Date of the Beginnings of Coinage in Asia Minor," *RSN* 52 (1973), 5-16; L. Weidauer, *Probleme der frühen Elektronprägung* (Friburg 1975); M. J. Price review of Weidauer, *Probleme* in *NC* 7th. s. 16 (1976), 273-5; A. M. Snodgrass, *Archaic Greece: The Age of Experiment* (London 1980), 134-5; D. Kagan, "The Dates of the Earliest Coins," *AJA* 86 (1982), 1-18.

[94] M. S. Balmuth, "Remarks on the Appearance of the Earliest Coins," in *Studies Presented to George M. A. Hanfmann*, 1-7; J. Price and N. Waggoner, *Archaic Greek Silver Coinage: The 'Asyut' Hoard* (Dorchester 1975), 122-3; Humphreys, *Anthropology and the Greeks*, 46.

[95] Hdt. 5.14.2, 15.2, 100; 6.43.2; 7.62.2, 67.1, 88.2, 96.1-2, 148.4, 208.1; 8.3.1-2; 9.26.4, 27.2, 77.3, 112. Thuc. 1.38.2, 128.7; 2.11.3, 87, 95.3; 3.98.1, 105.3; 4.91; 5.7.2,

47.7; 7.15.1, 50.2, 58.3, 80.7.

[96]Thuc. 1.25.1, 38.2; 8.89.2.

[97]Hdt. 4.153; 7.149.2; 9.10.2.

[98]Heubeck, *Praegraeca*, 68-70; P. Gauthier, "Les tyrants dans le morte Grec antique," *REG* 81 (1968), 555-61; Drews, "The First Tyrants in Greece," *Historia* 21 (1972), 129-44; A. Ferrill, "Herodotus on Tyranny," *Historia* 27 (1978), 385-97; K. Kinzl (ed.), *Die ältere Tyrannis bis zu den Perserkriegen* (Darmstadt 1979); see D. W. W. Wormell, "Studies in Greek Tyranny: I - The Cypselids," *Hermathena*, 66 (1945), 1-24; *pace* K. Waters, *Herodotus on Tyrants and Despots* (Wiesbaden 1971), 1-3.

[99]J. Sundwall, *Die einheimischer Namen der Lykier, Klio Beiheft* 11 (Leipzig 1913), 220-1; Hegyi, "Notes on the Origin of Greek Tyrannis," *AAH* 13 (1965), 317.

Chapter 3. Ionia before the Persians

[1]R. Redfield *et al.*, "Memorandum for the Study of Acculturation," *American Anthropologist* 38 (1936), 149; see also B. J. Siegel *et al.*, "Acculturation Formulation," *American Anthropologist* 56 (1954), 973-1002.

[2]Hanfmann, *Letters* 188, 192, fig. 142. Isolated Submycenaean and Protogeometric sherds (all questionable) found at Babylon and Nineveh do not prove the arrival of Greeks there; G. M. A. Hanfmann, "Ionia, Leader or Follower?", *HSCP* 61 (1953), 11 n. 56. LH IIIB pottery at Maşat Höyük, 312 km. northeast of Ankara; T. Özgüç, "Excavations at the Hittite Site, Maşat Höyük: Palace, Archives, Mycenaean Pottery," *AJA* 84 (1980), 309. G. Kleiner, *Alt-Milet* (Wiesbaden 1966), 8, 11-4; *Die Ruinen von Milet* (Berlin 1968), 24-5.

[3]Hanfmann, "Ionia, Leader or Follower?," *HSCP* 61 (1953), 3-5; F. Cassola, *La Ionia nel Mondo Miceneo* (Naples 1957); Snodgrass, *Dark Age* 66-8; Desborough, *Greek Dark Ages* 179-84; J. N. Coldstream, *Geometric Greece* (London 1977), 51; J. Chadwick, "The Ionian Name," in *Greece and the Eastern Mediterranean in Ancient History and Prehistory, Studies Presented to F. Schachermeyr* (Berlin 1977), 106-9; P. Alin, "Mycenaean Decline—Some Problems and Thoughts," in *Greece and the Eastern Mediterranean* 31-9.

[4]Hanfmann, "Ionia, Leader or Follower?," *HSCP* 61 (1953), 5-7; Snodgrass, *Dark Age* 332; J. T. Hooker, *Mycenaean Greece* (London 1976), 115.

[5]M. Nilsson, *The Mycenaean Origin of Greek Mythology* (Berkeley 1932), 54-5; Homeric *Sagen* canonized (by tradition) in Smyrna and Chios originated as a full epic cycle in the Argolid during the LH IIIB period, ibid. 24-5; G. S. Kirk, *Homer and the Epic* (Cambridge 1965), 73-4; J. A. Notopoulos, "Homer, Hesiod and the Achaean Heritage of Oral Poetry," *Hesperia* 29 (1960), 177-97, stressed the introduction of mainland Achaean (LBA) oral poetry into Geometric Ionia through "Homer."

[6]C. J. Emlyn-Jones, *The Ionians and Hellenism* (London 1980), 4-5.

[7]T. Lenschau, "Zur Geschichte Ioniens," *Klio* 13 (1913), 175-83; M. B. Sakellariou, *La migration grecque en Ionie* (Athens 1958); P. Amandry, "La Grèce d'Asie et l'Anatolie du 8e au 6e siècle avant Jésus-Christ," *Anatolica* 2 (1968), 87-102; Snodgrass, *Dark Age* 44, 55, 66-7.

[8]Snodgrass, *Dark Age* 67; Cook, "Greek Settlement in the Eastern Aegean," *CAH* (3rd ed.) 2.2, 779-82.

[9]Snodgrass, *Dark Age* 90; Cook, "Greek Settlement in the Eastern Aegean," *CAH* (3rd ed.) 2.2, 776-9.

[10]V. Ehrenberg, "When did the *Polis* Rise?," *JHS* 57 (1937), 147-59; C. G. Starr, "The Early Greek State," *Parola Passato* 12 (1957), 97-108; J. M. Cook, "Old Smyrna, 1948-

1951," *BSA* 53-4 (1958-9), 1-34; R. V. Nicholls, "Old Smyrna: The Iron Age Fortifications and Associated Remains on the City Perimeter," *BSA* 53-4 (1958-9), 35-137; C. G. Thomas, "Homer and the Polis," *Parola Passato* 21 (1966), 5-14; F. Gschnitzer, "Stadt und Stamm bei Homer," *Chiron* 1 (1971), 1-17; A. Snodgrass, "An Historical Homeric Society," *JHS* 94 (1974), 114-25; A. M. Snodgrass, *Archaeology and the Rise of the Greek State* (Cambridge 1977); C. G. Thomas, "The Territorial Imperative of the Polis," *Ancient World* 2 (1979), 35-9.

[11] Hanfmann, "Ionia, Leader or Follower?", *HSCP* 61 (1953), 3, at the sanctuary of Zeus Labranda in Karia, two inscribed clay tablets have been found, each with one side in Karian script and the other in an unknown alphabet related to "Cypro-Minoan." Non-Greek inscriptions at Smyrna; J. M. Cook, "Archaeology in Greece, 1948-1949," *JHS* 70 (1950), 10; "Archaeology in Greece," 1949-1950," *JHS* 71 (1951), 249 fig. 9; H. Gallet de la Santerre, "Chronique des Fouilles en 1950: Asie Mineure," *BCH* 75 (1951), 128-9. Kleiner, *Alt-Milet* 14-25; V. Ševoroškin, "Karisch, Lydisch, Lykisch," *Klio* 50 (1968), 53-69; Cook, "Greek Settlements in the Eastern Aegean," *CAH* (3rd. ed) 2.2, 790-96.

[12] C. G. Yavis, *Greek Altars: Origins and Typology* (St. Louis 1949), 54-139, Ephesos 98-9, Miletos 102-5, and Didyma (Paus. 5.13.11) 208-9; A. Bammer, "Recent Excavations at the Altar of Artemis in Ephesus," *Archaeology* 27 (1974), 202-5; A. Bammer, F. Brein, P. Wolff, "Das Tieropfer am Artemisaltar von Ephesos," in S. Şahin, *Studien zur Religion und Kultur Kleinasiens* 1, 107-57.

[13] Pace Roebuck, *Ionian Trade* 17-8.

[14] Littman, *Sardis* 6.1, *Lydian Inscriptions*; J. Friedrich, *Kleinasiatische Sprach-denkmäler* (Berlin 1932), 108-23; C. D. Buck, *The Greek Dialects* (Chicago 1955), 141-9, 184-96; L. H. Jeffery, *The Local Scripts of Archaic Greece* (Oxford 1961), 325-62; Gusmani, *Lydisches Wörterbuch*; G. Neumann, "Ein weiteres Fragment der Synagogen-Inschrift aus Sardeis," *Kadmos* 7 (1968), 94-5; R. Gusmani, *Neue epichorische Schriftzeugnisse aus Sardis* (Cambridge, Mass. 1975).

[15] A thesis basically similar to Roebuck, *Ionian Trade* 29-34, but with a rejection of his claim (p. 24) of a strong sense of Ionian unity. Burn, *Lyric Age*, a sound but traditional survey of the seventh and sixth centuries B.C.; Emlyn-Jones, *Ionians and Hellenism*, a good current study of archaic Ionian cultural achievements.

[16] Roebuck, *Ionian Trade* 6; Snodgrass, *Dark Age* 91.

[17] Hanfmann, "Ionia, Leader or Follower?", *HSCP* 61 (1953), 11-5; Roebuck, *Ionian Trade* 16.

[18] J. Sundwall, "Zu den karischen Inschriften und den darin vorkommenden Namen," *Klio* 11 (1911), 464-80; G. Bockisch, "Die Karer und ihre Dynasten," *Klio* 51 (1969), 117-75.

[19] Coldstream, *Geometric* Greece 258.

[20] D. C. Kurtz and J. Boardman, *Greek Burial Customs* (Ithaca 1971), 176-7, and fig. 32 (Larisa); G. Bean, *Aegean Turkey* (New York 1967), 183-4, and fig. 43.

[21] Ramage and Ramage, "The Siting of Lydian Burial Mounds," *Studies Presented to George M. A. Hanfmann* 143-60.

[22] Snodgrass, *Dark Age* 157-8, 186, 189. At Karian Iasos, for example, cist inhumation and pithos burials also occurred, 97, 258.

[23] Ibid. 332.

[24] W. Judeich, "Zur ionischen Wanderung," *Rheinisches Museum* 82 (1933) 305-14.

[25] Cook, *Greeks in Ionia* 32; Snodgrass, *Dark Age* 298, 329, 369, 380, 415-6; Coldstream, *Geometric Greece* 261-2.

[26] *CIG* 3081; Y. Bequignon, "Les 'Pyrgoi' de Teos," *RA* 28 (1928), 185-208; D. W. S. Hunt, "Feudal Survivals in Ionia," *JHS* 67 (1947), 68-76.

[27] Humphreys, *Anthropology and the Greeks* 198-201.

[28] F. Barth, "Ecologic Relationships of Ethnic Groups in Swat, North Pakistan," *American Anthropologist* 58 (1956), 1079-88; *Ethnic Groups and Boundaries* (Bergen 1969), 9-20; I. Hodder (ed.), *The Spatial Organisation of Culture* (London 1978), 3-24, 93-111, 155-78, 199-269; G. E. Hutchinson, *An Introduction to Population Ecology* (New Haven 1978), 152-212; P. Colinvaux, "In the Grand Scheme of Things Every Species has its 'Niche'," *Science Digest* 87 (1980), 72-7.

[29] C. Renfrew, "Trade as Action at a Distance," in J. A. Sabloff and C. C. Lamberg-Karlovsky (eds.), *Ancient Civilization and Trade* (Albuquerque 1975), 7; J. K. Davis, *People of the Mediterranean* (London 1977), 20-1.

[30] Snodgrass, *Dark Age* 335, 337.

[31] Ibid. 192, 195-6, 387, 414; Humphreys, *Anthropology and the Greeks* 194-202.

[32] Mazzarino, *Fra Oriente e Occidente* 194-5, and n. 547.

[33] Hom. *Il.* 6.191-5, Glaukos married into the royal family of Lydia.

[34] M. I. Finley, *The World of Odysseus* 2nd ed. (London 1977), 60-1.

[35] Snodgrass, *Dark Age* 297-8; Coldstream, *Geometric Greece* 260.

[36] P. Walcot, *Hesiod and the Near East* (Cardiff 1966), 106-8, 115-8; *Greek Peasants, Ancient and Modern* (Manchester 1970), 23-4.

[37] U. von Wilamowitz-Möllendorf, "Panionion," *Sitzungsberichte der königlich-preussischen Akademie der Wissenschaft* 25 (1906), 45-6; Coldstream, *Geometric Greece* 246, 265-8.

[38] Roebuck, *Ionian Trade* 43.

[39] Coldstream, *Geometric Greece* 267.

[40] Ibid. 268.

[41] Ibid. 262-3. In contrast, Hanfmann, "Ionia, Leader or Follower?," *HSCP* 61 (1953), 12-5, considered a Ripe Geometric koine, early eighth century B.C., in Rhodes, Knidos, Kos, Miletos, Samos, Ephesos, Chios, Smyrna, and Phokaia; into Aiolic Pitane and Myrina by sea travel.

[42] G. L. Huxley, "Mimnermus and Pylos," *GRBS* 2 (1959), 103-7; M. Moggi, *I sinecismi interstatali Greci* 1 (Pisa 1976), 40-3.

[43] Burn, *Lyric Age* 98-100; Coldstream, *Geometric Greece* 247, 263.

[44] Coldstream, ibid. 268.

[45] Roebuck, *Ionian Trade* 15; Coldstream, *Geometric Greece* 303-4, 314.

[46] Coldstream, ibid. 341-6.

[47] Roebuck, *Ionian Trade* 33, 59.

[48] Hogarth, "Lydia and Ionia," *CAH* (1st ed.) 3.509.

[49] R. M. Cook, "Amasis and the Greeks in Egypt," *JHS* 57 (1937) 227-37.

[50] Roebuck, *Ionian Trade* V-1, noted a paradox: the natural advantages of Ionian land and the political failure of its inhabitants. My analysis eliminates Roebuck's paradox.

[51] Humphreys, *Anthropology and the Greeks* 130-4. Walcot, *Greek Peasants*, see the comparative sociological and anthropological bibliography 120-3. *Oikos* as a unit: B. Bravo, "Une lettre sur plomb de Berezan: Colonisation et modes de contact dans le Pont," *Dialogues d'histoire ancienne* 1 (1974), 111-87; J. Chadwick, "The Berezan Lead Letter," *Proceedings of the Cambridge Philological Society* 199 (1973), 35-7; W. Donlan, *The Aristocratic Ideal in Ancient Greece* (Lawrence 1980), 2-3.

[52] C. Smith (ed.), *Regional Analysis:* 1 *Economic Systems* (New York 1976), 6, 12, 34; *pace* C. Doxiades, *Ekistics* (New York 1968), 132-50, who confused the issues. See D. L. Clarke, "A Provisional Model of an Iron Age Society and its Settlement System," in D. L. Clarke (ed.), *Models in Archaeology* (London 1972), 801-69; also in D. L. Clarke, *Analytical Archaeologist* (London 1979), 363-433; I. Hodder, "Spatial Studies in Archaeology," *Progress in Human Geography* 1 (1977), 33-64.

[53] A. Momigliano and S. C. Humphreys, "The Social Structure of the Ancient City," *Annuali della Scuola normale Superiore di Pisa* ser. 3.4 (1974), 331-67.

[54] Roebuck, *Ionian Trade* 79-137; J. Boardman, *The Greeks Overseas* (Harmondsworth 1964), 236, 240, 245-53.

[55] Boardman, ibid. 72-5, 129-57.

[56] P. Ebner, "Il mercato dei metalli preziosi nel secolo d'oro dei Focei (640-545 B.C.)," *Parola Passato* 21 (1966), 111-27; G. Pugliesi Carratelli, "Greci d'Asia in Occidente tra il secolo VII e il VI," *Parola Passato* 21 (1966), 155-63; G. Vallet and F. Villard, "Les Phocéens en Mediterranée occidentale à l'époque archaïque et la fondation de Hyélè," *Parola Passato* (1966), 166-90.

[57] Roebuck, *Ionian Trade* 21.

[58] Mazzarino, *Fra Oriente e Occidente* 194-5, and n. 547, Mermnads living in Kolophon; Lydians dwelling in Miletos, 195-6; and at Ephesos 196-7.

[59] C. Talamo, "Per la storia di Colofone in età arcaica," *Parola Passato* 28 (1973), 343-75.

[60] E. Akurgal, "The Early Period and Golden Age of Ionia," *AJA* 66 (1962), 373.

[61] Huxley, *Early Ionians* 112.

[62] Roebuck suggested that archaic Erythrai lay perhaps 2 km. west of the modern spa of Cesme on the south side of the gulf, and only later shifted to the fourth century B.C. site usually noted (*ATL* 1. 485-7); *Ionian Trade* 14-5. This suggested location would have placed Erythrai closer to Chios and farther from the East Greek poleis of Teos and Klazomenai, and the Lydian occupation of Smyrna.

[63] The Hermos River emptied into the gulf closer to ancient Phokaia than at present, and enabled Phokaia to serve as the communication terminus for Sardis following that river valley, and serve as an easier communication route than crossing the Kemal Pasha (Bel Kave) pass to Smyrna; Roebuck, *Ionian Trade* 14.

[64] E. Langlotz, *Die kulturelle und künstlerische Hellenisierung der Küsten des Mittelmeers durch die Stadt Phokaia* (Cologne 1966). Phokaia's northern colonial adventures at Propontic Lampsakos and Black Sea Amisos were overshadowed by Milesian activities.

[65] J. M. Birmingham, "The Overland Route Across Anatolia in the Eighth and Seventh Centuries B.C.," *Anatolian Studies* 11 (1961), 185-95. Aristotle F 611.37, noted Mita married a Greek princess from Kyme. Hdt. 1.14.2, noted Mita offered his throne to Apollo at Delphi, and was the first foreigner to offer gifts to Delphi.

[66]D. H. F. Gray, review of C. W. Blegen et al., Troy 4 (Princeton 1958), in JHS 82 (1962), 197, citing comments of J. Boardman.

[67]H. Diels, Die Fragmente der Vorsokratiker 1 (Berlin 1934), T 10-1 (Arist. Pol. 1259a6). Thales' father Hexamyos (T 3) was Karian of noble descent and a member of the Thelidai family (Diog. Laert. 1.27).

[68]Roebuck, Ionian Trade 41, 60.

[69]Ibid. 33, 35, 68; Burn, Lyric Age 107-22; Snodgrass, Dark Age 297; "T. S. Noonan, "The Origins of the Greek Colony at Panticapaeum," AJA 77 (1973), 77-81; Coldstream Geometric Greece 261.

[70]A. G. Dunham, A History of Miletos (London 1915), 70-6; F. Jacoby, "Zu den älteren griechischen Elegikern: II. Zu Mimnermos," Hermes 53 (1918), 262-307; Roebuck, Ionian Trade 13-4, 135-6; Huxley, Early Ionians 53.

[71]Hdt. 1.18-20, 5.92; Nic. Dam. FGrH 90 F 59; Arist. Pol. 1284a, 1311a; É. Will, Korinthiaka (Paris 1955), 367-8, 543, 548-52; A. Andrewes, The Greek Tyrants (London 1956), 118; H. Berve, Die Tyrannis bei den Greichen, 1 (Munich 1967), 100; 2 (Munich 1967), 578-9; C. Mossé, La Tyrannie dans la Grèce antique (Paris 1969), 11-4.

[72]Pedley, Sardis 53.

[73]Nordin, "Aisymnetei und Tyrannis," Klio 5 (1905), 392-409; M. White, "Greek Tyranny," Phoenix 9 (1955), 1-18; É. Will, "Les Tyrannies dans la Grèce antique," REG 69 (1956), 439-44; P. Oliva, "La tyrannie premiere forme de l'état en Grèce, et son role historique" La Pensée 66 (1956), 102-13; "Die Bedeutung der frühgriechischen Tyrannis," Klio 38 (1960), 81-6.

[74]Suda sv Pythagoras.

[75]L. R. Farnell, The Cults of the Greek States 4 (Oxford 1907), 224-5.

[76]Ibid. 226-8; Coldstream, Geometric Greece 261.

[77]Drews, "The First Tyrants in Greece," Historia 21 (1972), 129-44; Ferrill, "Herodotus on Tyranny," Historia 27 (1978), 385-97.

[78]Humphreys, Anthropology and the Greeks 222.

[79]von Wilamowitz-Mollendorf, "Panionion," Sitz. königlich-preussischen Akad. Wissen. 25 (106), 45-54; T. Lenschau, "Die Gründung Ioniens und der Bund am Panionion," Klio 36 (1944), 201-37; C. Roebuck, "The Early Ionian League," CP 50 (1955), 26-40; F. Cassola, "La struttura della lega ionica," Labeo 4 (1958), 153-71; G. Fogazza, "Per una storia della lega ionica," Parola Passato 28 (1973), 157-69; G. Maddoli, "Erodoto e i Ioni: per l'interpretazione di 1.143," Parola Passato 34 (1979), 256-66.

[80]Humphreys, Anthropology and the Greeks 54-5.

[81]Dunham, Miletos 75-6; Huxley, Early Ionians 110.

[82]Barth, "Ecologic Relationships," American Anthropologist 58 (1956), 1079; J.G. Pedley, "Carians in Sardis," JHS 94 (1974), 96-9.

Chapter 4. The Persian Conquest of Śfarda

[1]Tadmor, "The Inscriptions of Nabunaid: Historical Arrangement," Assyriological Studies 16 (1965), 352; R. Drews, "The Fall of Astyages and Herodotus' Chronology of the Eastern Kingdoms," Historia 18 (1969), 4; M. A. Dandamayev, "Politische und wirtschaftliche Geschichte," in G. Walser (ed.), Beiträge zur Achämenidengeschichte (Wiesbaden 1972), 16. G. Harris, "Ionia under Persia: 547-477 B.C.—A Political History" (Ph.D. dissertation, Northwestern University 1971).

[2] J. V. Prášek, *Geschichte der Meder und Perser bis zur makedonischen Eroberung* 1 (Gotha 1906), 2 (Gotha 1910); C. Huart, *Ancient Persia and Iranian Civilization* (New York 1927); R. W. Rogers, *A History of Ancient Persia* (New York 1929); A. Christensen, "Die Iranier," *Kulturgeschichte des alten Orients* 3.1 (Munich 1933); *Les Gestes des rois dans les traditions de l'Iran antique* (Paris 1936); M. Ehtécham, *L'Iran sous les achéménides* (Fribourg 1946); A. T. Olmstead, *History of the Persian Empire* (Chicago 1948); R. Ghirshman, *Iran* (Harmondsworth 1954), 119-34; R. N. Frye, *The Heritage of Persia* (Cleveland 1963); W. Culican, *The Medes and Persians* (New York 1965); E. Herzfeld, *The Persian Empire* (Wiesbaden 1968); J. Harmatta, "The Rise of the Old Persian Empire," *AAH* 19 (1971), 3-15; Mallowan, "Cyrus the Great," *Iran* 10 (1972), 1-18; M. A. Dandamaev, *Persien unter den Ersten Achämeniden (6. Jahrhundert v. Chr.)* (Wiesbaden 1976). I regret I was not able to consult the study by J. M. Cook, *The Persian Empire* (New York 1982), which appeared after the preparation of this monograph.

[3] There is no evidence that Cyrus first attempted diplomatic measures and invited Croesus to be his vassal over western Sfarda as Huart, *Ancient Persia* 38, suggested. Cyrus deliberately conquered Media, Sfarda, and Babylonia; as Cambyses conquered Egypt; and Darius conquered Thrace (Skudra) and north-western India. Both Darius and Xerxes sought to conquer mainland Greece but failed.

[4] Mallowan, "Cyrus the Great," *Iran* 10 (1972), 6-7; J. Cargill, "The Nabonidus Chronicle and the Fall of Lydia," *AJAH* 2 (1977), 97-116; J. A. S. Evans, "What Happened to Croesus?," *CJ* 74 (1978), 34-40.

[5] D. Lewis, *Sparta and Persia* (Leiden 1977), 62.

[6] Mallowan, "Cyrus the Great," *Iran* 10 (1972), 4.

[7] The tittle-tattle and harem gossip of Ktesias is usually unreliable and this single reference to Barene remains suspect.

[8] Segal, "Croesus on the Pyre: Herodotus and Bacchylides," *Wiener Studien* 84 (1971), 39-51.

[9] Mallowan, "Cyrus the Great," *Iran* 10 (1972), 6.

[10] T. S. Brown, "Aristodicus of Cyme and the Branchidae," *AJP* 99 (1978), 64-78.

[11] B. M. Mitchell, "Herodotus and Samos," *JHS* 95 (1975), 75-91. See also M. White, "The Duration of the Samian Tyranny," *JHS* 74 (1954), 36; T. J. Cadoux, "The Duration of the Samian Tyranny," *JHS* 76 (1956), 106.

[12] Andrewes, *Greek Tyrants* 117-22; White, "Duration of the Samian Tyranny," *JHS* 74 (1954), 36; H. Immerwahr, "The Samian Stories of Herodotus," *CJ* 52 (1957), 312-22; H. -J. Diesner, "Die Gestalt des Tyrannen Polykrates bei Herodot," *AAH* 7 (1959), 211-9; J. Boardman, "Chian and Early Ionic Architecture," *Antiquaries Journal* 39 (1959), 200-2; H. -J. Diesner, *Griechische Tyrannis und griechische Tyrannen* (Berlin 1960), 16-21; J. Labarbe, "Un décalage de 40 ans dans la Chronologie de Polycrate," *AC* 31 (1962), 153-88; J. Barron, "The Sixth-Century Tyranny at Samos," *CQ* 14 (1964), 210-29; *The Silver Coins of Samos* (London 1966), 33-9; Berve, *Tyrannis* 1, 107-14; 2. 582-7; N. G. L. Hammond, *A History of Greece to 322 B.C.*, 2nd ed. (Oxford 1967), 198-9; M. Miller, *The Thalassocracies: Studies in Chronography* 2 (Albany 1971), 22-37; J. Labarbe, "Un Putsch dans la Grèce antique: Polycrate et ses frères à la conquête du pouvoir," *Ancient Society* 5 (1974), 21-42. Andrewes, *Greek Tyrants* 120 and Berve, *Tyrannis* 1.108, argued that Polykrates initially rebelled against Persia. The evidence noted by Herodotus, however, does not favor a rebellion c. 532 B.C. and then an alliance in 525 B.C. with Persia. Huxley, *Early Ionians* 125-9, considered that Polykrates arranged secret negotiations with Cambyses before their invasion of Egypt.

[13] C. M. Bowra, "Polycrates of Rhodes," *CJ* 29 (1934), 375-80; Wells, *Royal Correspondence* 48-9; C. M. Bowra, *Greek Lyric Poetry* (Oxford 1961), 249-50.

[14]B. Soyez, "Le Phénicien Thalès et le synecisme de l'Ionie," *AC* 43 (1974), 74-82; Moggi, *I sinecisme interstatali Greci* 95-100.

[15]V. Ehrenberg, "Freedom-Ideal and Reality," in *The Living Heritage of Greek Antiquity* (The Hague 1967), 132-46.

[16]J. A. Davidson, "The First Greek Triremes," *CQ* 41 (1947), 18-24.

[17]Mossé, *La Tyrannie dans la Grèce antique* 18.

[18]A. R. Burn, *Persia and the Greeks: The Defense of the West*, 546-478 B.C. (New York 1962), 44.

[19]Vassalage, lordship, suzerainty, and sovereignty are terms preferable to "feudalism," which retains distinct late medieval European legal arrangements.

[20]Mazzarino, *Fra Oriente e Occidente* 370 n. 514.

[21]C. Roebuck, "Tribal Organization in Ionia," *TAPA* 92 (1961), 495-506; M. P. Nilsson *Cults, Myths, Oracles and Politics in Ancient Greece* (New York 1972 ed.), 142-9; E. Beneviste, *Indo-European Language and Society* (Coral Gables 1973), 239-61.

[22]Xen. *Cyr.* 1.2.5.; Strabo 15.3.1; observations confirmed by H. von Gall, "Persische und medische Stämme," *AMI* 5 (1972), 261-83. Strabo 8.7.1; Plato *Tim.* 24a; Plut. *Solon* 23; reflect an early Iranian class arrangement noted in the Avestan *Gāthās*, priests, warriors, and agriculturalists. A fourth class, artisans, arose in the Sasanian era. This basic Indo-European motif is essentially unimportant in this analysis. E. Beneviste, "Les classes sociales dans la tradition avestique," *Journal Asiatique* 221 (1932), 117-34; G. Dumézil *L'idéologie tripartie des Indo-Européens* (Brussels 1958); Harmatta, "The Rise of the Old Persian Empire," *AAH* 19 (1971), 9-14; R. Ghirshman, "Les tribus perses et leur formation tripartie," *CRAI* (1973), 210-1; Beneviste, *Indo-European Language* 227-8; P. R. Helm, "Herodotus' *Mēdikos Logos* and Median History," *Iran* 19 (1981), 85-90.

[23]J. Harmatta, "Migrations of the Indo-Iranian Tribes," *AAH* 26 (1978), 185-94.

[24]M. D. Sahlins, *Tribesmen* (Englewood Cliffs 1968), VII-VIII, 15-7.

[25]C. S. Littleton, *The New Comparative Mythology* (Berkeley 1966), 25-8; M. C. Root, *The King and Kingship in Achaemenid Art* (Leiden 1979), 29-32.

[26]G. G. Cameron, *History of Early Iran* (Chicago 1936), 170-227; Wiseman, *Chronicles of Chaldean Kings* B.M. 21901: 23-30, 47-8, 614-10 B.C. (44-5); 13-9, 36, 39; Dandamayev, "Politische und wirtschaftliche Geschichte," *Beiträge zur Achämenidengeschichte* 15-6; W. Hinz, *The Lost World of Elam* (London 1972), 138-61; N. V. Aroutiounian, "Problèmes concernant de dernière période de l'histoire d'Urartu," *AAH* 22 (1974), 415-28; J. Reade, "Elam and the Elamites in Assyrian Sculpture," *AMI* 9 (1976), 97-105; R. Zadok, "On the Connections between Iran and Babylonia in the Sixth Century B. C.," *Iran* 14 (1976), 61-78; W. Hinz, *Darius und die Perser* 1 (Baden-Baden 1976), 58.

[27]R. N. Frye, "The Institutions," *Beiträge zur Achämenidengeschichte*, 84-5.

[28]Sahlins, *Tribesmen* 20-1; P. Briant, *Etat et pasteurs au Moyen-Orient ancien* (Cambridge 1982), 57-112.

[29][Arist.] *Oec.* 1344b; Ehtécham, *L'Iran* 18-41; see B. Spooner, "Iranian Kinship and Marriage," *Iran* 4 (1966), 51-6.

[30]P. Kübler, "Die persische Politik gegenüber dem Griechentum in der Pentekontaetia" (Unpublished inaugural dissertation, Ruprecht-Karl-Universität, Heidelberg 1950), 16.

[31] T. C. Young Jr., "A Comparative Ceramic Chronology for Western Iran, 1500-500 B.C.," *Iran* 3 (1965), 53-86; "The Iranian Migration into the Zagros," *Iran* 5 (1967), 27; see also Ghirshman, *Iran* 73-126.

[32] Young, "Iranian Migration," *Iran* 5 (1967), 27; P. R. S. Moorey, "Towards a Chronology for the 'Luristan Bronzes'," *Iran* 9 (1971), 113-30; "Some Elaborately Decorated Bronze Quiver Plaques made in Luristan, c. 750-650 B.C.," *Iran* 13 (1975), 19-30.

[33] R. Ghirshman, "Review-Article" of I. M. Diakonov *Istoria Midii—Histoire de la Médie* [in Russian] (Moscow 1956), in *Bibliotheca Orientalis* 25 (1958), 257-61; Young, "Iranian Migration," *Iran* 5 (1967), 27, 29, 33. The foreign influences within Iron Age II represent the main Iranian migrations and Median consolidation east of the Alvand region before the ninth century B.C., 30-1.

[34] C. Goff, "Excavations at Bābā Jān, 1968," *Iran* 8 (1970), 155.

[35] For maps of Iron Age III Median sites refer to D. Stronach, "Excavations at Tepe Nūsh-i Jān, 1967," *Iran* 7 (1969), 1 fig. 1; T. C. Young Jr., "Excavations at Godin Tappeh 1973," *Proceedings of the IInd Annual Symposium on Archaeological Research in Iran, 1973* (Teheran 1974), 84 fig. 1. R. H. Dyson, "Problems of Protohistoric Iran as seen from Hasanlu," *JNES* 24 (1965), 193-217; C. Burney, *From Village to Empire: Introduction to Near Eastern Archaeology* (Oxford 1977), 201-3.

[36] T. C. Young Jr., "Godin Tepe," in "Survey of Excavations," *Iran* 6 (1968), 160-1; *Excavations at Godin Tepe: First Progress Report* (Toronto 1969); "Godin Tepe," in "Survey of Excavations in Iran during 1968-69," *Iran* 8 (1970), 175-6; "Godin Tepe," in "Survey of Excavations in Iran during 1970-71," *Iran* 10 (1972), 184-6; T. C. Young Jr. and L. D. Levine, *Excavations of the Godin Project: Second Progress Report* (Toronto 1974).

[37] Mellink (ed.), *Dark Ages and Nomads*; Young, "Iranian Migration," *Iran* 5 (1967), 34 n. 97; C. G. Meade, "Luristan in the First Half of the First Millennium B.C.," *Iran* 6 (1968), 105-34; P. Calmeyer, *Datierbare Bronzen aus Luristan und Kirmanshah* (Berlin 1969); Moorey, "Towards a Chronology," *Iran* 9 (1971), 113-30; "Some Elaborately Decorated Bronze Quiver Plaques," *Iran* 13 (1975), 19-30.

[38] D. Stronach, "Tepe Nūsh-i Jān," in "Survey of Excavations," *Iran* 6 (1968), 162; "Tepe Nushi Jan: A Mound in Media," *The Metropolitan Museum of Art Bulletin* 27 (Nov. 1968), 177-86; "Excavations at Tepe Nūsh-i Jān, 1967," *Iran* 7 (1969), 1-20; A. D. H. Bivar, "A Hoard of Ingot-Currency of the Median Period from Nūsh-i Jān, near Malayir," *Iran* 9 (1971), 97-111; D. Stronach "Tepe Nūsh-i Jān," in "Survey of Excavations in Iran, 1969-70," *Iran* 9 (1971), 175; M. Roaf and D. Stronach, "Tepe Nūsh-i Jān, 1970: Second Interim Report," *Iran* 11 (1973), 129-40; D. Stronach, "Tappeh Nuši Jān: A Case for Building Rites in 7th/6th Century B.C. Media?," *Proceedings of the IInd Annual Symposium on Archaeological Research in Iran, 1973* (Teheran 1974), 223-38; "A Fourth Season of Excavations at Tappah Nuši Jān," *Proceedings of the IIIrd Annual Symposium on Archaeological Research in Iran, 1974* (Teheran 1975), 203-12; "Tepe Nush-i Jan" in "Survey of Excavations in Iran—1973-4," *Iran* 13 (1975), 187-8; Roaf and Stronach, "Excavations at Tepe Nush-i Jan," *Iran* 16 (1978), 1-28; Stronach, "Tepe Nush-i Jan," in "Survey of Excavations in Iran—1977," *Iran* 16 (1978), 195.

[39] I am grateful to my colleague, William M. Sumner, Department of Anthropology, The Ohio State University, for his personal observations of settlement patterns in the Marv-Dasht; see also his "Cultural Development in the Kur River Basin, Iran: An Archaeological Analysis of Settlement Patterns" (Ph.D. dissertation, University of Pennsylvania 1972), 50-1, 194, 203, 248-9, 252, 263-9, figs. 16-7. Sumner discovered the site of Elamite Anshan, confirmed by E. Reiner, "The Location of Anshan," *Revue d'Assyriologie* 67 (1973), 57-62; see J. Hansman, "Elamites, Achaemenians and Anshan," *Iran* 10 (1972), 101-25; A. S. Shahbazi, "From Pārsa to Taxt-e Jamšīd," *AMI* 10 (1977), 197-9.

[40] C. Goff Meade, "Bābā Jān," in "Survey of Excavations in Iran during 1966-67," *Iran* 6 (1968), 157-8; "Excavations at Bābā Jān 1967: Second Preliminary Report," *Iran* 7

(1969), 115-30; C. Goff, "Excavations at Bābā Jān, 1968," *Iran* 8 (1970), 141-56; "Excavations at Baba Jan: The Architecture of the East Mound, Levels II and III," *Iran* 15 (1977), 103-40; "Excavations at Baba Jan: The Pottery and Metal from Levels III and II," *Iran* 16 (1978), 29-68.

[41]Masjid-i Sulaiman and Bard-i Nishandeh, reported by R. Ghirshman, "Masjid-i-Solaiman, Résidence des premiers Achéménides," *Syria* 27 (1950), 205-20; as early Persian sites are of the fifth century B.C., D. Stronach, "Achaemenid Village I at Susa and the Persian Migration to Fars," *Iraq* 36 (1974), 239-48.

[42]C. C. Lamberg-Karlovsky, "Tepe Yahya," *Iran* 12 (1974), 228-31; J. Hansman, "An Achaemenian Stronghold," *Acta Iranica* (1975), 289-309; H. W. Bailey, "Nasā and Fasā," *Acta Iranica* 3 (1975), 309-12; M. Dandamayev, "The Dynasty of the Achaemenids in the Early Period," *AAH* 25 (1977), 39-42.

[43]B.C. Brundage, "Feudalism in Ancient Mesopotamia and Iran: The Medes and Persians," in R. Coulbourn (ed.), *Feudalism in History* (Princeton 1956), 108-10.

[44]M. H. Fried, "On the Evolution of Social Stratification and the State," in S. Diamond (ed.), *Culture in History* (New York 1960), 713-31.

[45]Hdt. 5.52, 8.98; Ramsay, *Historical Geography* 27-43; W. M. Calder, "The Royal Road in Herodotus," *CR* 39 (1925), 7-11; Birmingham, "Overland Route across Anatolia," *Anatolian Studies* 11 (1961), 185-95; W. Hinz, *Darius und der Perser* 2 (Baden-Baden 1979), 119-22. In May of 1974, Victor W. von Hagen, Leader of the Persian Royal Road Expedition, set out to explore the road from Susa to Sardis. His reports include: "Along the First Road," *Geographical Magazine* 46.9 (June 1974), 456-61; "Horror of the Tomissa Crossing," ibid 48.5 (February 1976); "Clue to a Tigris Source," ibid 48.6 (March 1976), 365-68. I have not been able to obtain a copy of his *La Strada dei Cancelli d'Oro* (Milan 1978). See also W. Kleiss, "Ein Abschnitt der achämenidischen Königsstrasse von Pasargadae und Persepolis nach Susa, bei Naqsh-i Rustam," *AMI* 14 (1981), 45-53.

[46]Xen. *Cyr.* 7.4.1-2; A. Erzen, *Kilikien bis zum Ende Perserherrschaft* (Leipzig 1940), 97-120; J. D. Bing, "A History of Cilicia during the Assyrian Period" (Ph.D. dissertation, Indiana University 1969).

[47]Boardman, *Greeks Overseas* 122; and L. H. Jeffery, *Archaic Greece* (London 1976), 220; for example, considered a marked decline of Greek trade with Egypt until c. 480 B.C. See M. M. Austin, *Greece and Egypt in the Archaic Age, Proceedings of the Cambridge Philological Society*, Suppl. 2 (1970), 7, 20, 33-4.

[48]W. Caskel, "Arabia," in H. Bengtson, *The Greeks and the Persians* (London 1969), 409-19.

[49]Mallowan, "Cyrus the Great," *Iran* 10 (1972), 3.

[50]Boardman, *Greeks Overseas* 77-9.

[51]M. A. Dandamayev, "Social Stratification in Babylonia (7th-4th Centuries B.C.), *AAH* 22 (1974), 433-44.

[52]C. C. Torrey, "The Chronicler's History of the Return under Cyrus," *AJSL* 37 (1920-21), 81-100; W. H. Dubberstein, "Critical Note: The Chronology of Cyrus and Cambyses," *AJSL* 55 (1938), 417-9; S. Smith, *Isaiah Chapters XL-LV: Schweich Lectures* 1940 (London 1944); E. J. Bickerman, "The Edict of Cyrus in Ezra 1," *JBL* 65 (1946), 249-75; K. Galling, "Von Naboned zu Darius: Studien zur chaldäischen und persischen Geschichte," *Zeitschrift des deutschen Palästina-Vereins* 69 (1953), 42-64; 70 (1954), 4-32; G. G. Cameron, "Ancient Persia," in R. C. Dentan (ed.), *The Idea of History in the Ancient Near East* (New Haven 1955), 79-97; Wiseman, *Chronicles of the Chaldean Kings*; P. R. Ackroyd, "Two Old Testament Historical Problems of the Early Persian Period," *JNES* 16 (1957), 13-27; M. Smith, "II Isaiah and the Persians," *JAOS* 83 (1963), 415-21; J. L. McKenzie (ed.), *The Anchor Bible: Second Isaiah* (Garden City 1968), XXIV-XXX, LXVI-LXVII, 15-35; "The oracles of Deutero-Isaiah are very probably to be dated at or shortly

after the date of Cyrus' conquest of Lydia, when the magnitude of Persian power and Persian ambitions had become apparent" (p. XXVIII); R. D. Barnett, "ᶜAnath, Baᶜal and Pasargadae," in *Mélanges de l'Université Saint-Joseph* 45 (Beirut 1969), 407-22; J. Harmatta, "Les modèles littéraires de l'édit babylonien de Cyrus," *Acta Iranica* 1 (1974), 29-44; G. G. Cameron, "Cyrus the 'Father' and Babylonia," *Acta Iranica* 1 (1974), 45-8; L. Vanden Berghe, "Cyrus le Grand et le Rayonnement de la civilisation iranienne," *Acta Iranica* 1 (1974), 60-7; A. Pagliaro, "Cyrus et l'Empire Perse," *Acta Iranica* 2 (1974), 2-23.

[53] II Chron. 36:22-3; Ezek. 27:10 D. Ben-Gurion, "Cyrus, King of Persia," *Acta Iranica* 1 (1974), 127-34; A. Netzer, "Some Notes on the Characterization of Cyrus the Great in Jewish and Judea-Persian Writings," *Acta Iranica* 2 (1974), 35-52.

[54] A. Cizek, "From Historical Truth to the Literary Convention: The Life of Cyrus the Great viewed by Herodotus, Ctesias and Xenophon," *AC* 44 (1975), 531-52; analyzed the Greek interpretations of Cyrus as *res vera* and *res gesta* transforming into res *ficta historia*, or *logos* into *mythos*. For example, he argued that Herodotus represented the tragedy of Cyrus in an interpretation of his life and feats according to the conventions of Dionysian ritual intrinsic to Aeschylean drama. Ktesias, in contrast, wrote according to the romantic pattern, characteristic of the decline of Attic tragedy when post-Euripidean epigonism stressed the over-doing effects of the picturesque and improbably were associated with the taste for genre scenes. Xenophon, Cizek noted, wrote an illustration of a Socratic model, ethical, and pedagogical. As S. J. Pease, "Xenophon's Cyropaedia, 'The Compleat General'," *CJ* 29 (1934), 436-40; noted, Xenophon's admiration of Cyrus stressed reverence, justice, and self-control. This is also apparent in Plato *Epistle* 2.311A: "Men are accustomed to refer to Periander of Corinth and Thales of Miletos together, and Perikles and Anaxagoras, and Croesus too and Solon as wise men with Cyrus the ruler." A. Bauer, *Die Kyros-Sage und Verwandtes* (Vienna 1882), 5-10, 19-26; R. Drews, "Sargon, Cyrus and Mesopotamian Folk History," *JNES* 33 (1974), 387-93.

[55] J. B. Pritchard (ed.), *Ancient Near Eastern Texts Relating to the Old Testament* 2nd ed. (Princeton 1955), 315-6; W. Eilers, "Le Téxte cunéiforme du Cylindre de Cyrus," *Acta Iranica* 2 (1974), 25-34.

[56] C. C. Torrey, "The Bilingual Inscription from Sardis," *AJSL* 34 (1917-1918), 185-98; A. Cowley, *Aramaic Papyri of the Fifth Century B.C.* (Oxford 1923); R. P. Dougherty, "Writing upon Parchment and Papyrus among the Babylonians and Assyrians," *JAOS* 48 (1928), 109-35; G. R. Driver, *Aramaic Documents of the Fifth Century B.C.* (Oxford 1954); K. Balkan, "Inscribed Bullae from Daskyleion-Ergili," *Anatolia* 4 (1959), 123-8; F. Altheim and R. Stiehl, *Die aramäische Sprache unter den Achaimeniden* (Frankfurt am Main 1963); P. Grelot, *Documents araméens d'Égypte* (Paris 1972); H. Metzger, E. Laroche, A. Dupont-Gommer, "La Stéle trilinque récemment découverte au Létoon de Xanthos," *CRAI* (1974), 82-149.

[57] E. R. Service, *Origins of the State and Civilization* (New York 1975). 8-21.

[58] M. Dandamayev, "Achaemenid Babylonia," in *Ancient Mesopotamia* (Moscow 1969), 296-7.

[59] J. M. Balcer, "The Athenian Episkopos and the Achaemenid 'King's Eye'," *AJP* 98 (1977), 252-63; and bibliography therein, also see C. Autran, "L'Oeil du Roi: concept politico-administratif commun à l'Iran, à la Chine et à l'Hellade," *Humanitas* 3 (1950/51), 287-91.

Chapter 5. Darius' Reorganization of the Persian Empire

[1] *FGrH* 1; L. Pearson, *Early Ionian Historians* (Oxford 1939), 25-106; G. Nenci, *Hecataei Milesii Fragmenta* (Florence 1954); Dandamaev, *Persien unter den Ersten Achämeniden* 122-4; V. Hunter, *Past and Process in Herodotus and Thucydides* (Princeton 1982), 310-3.

[2] *FGrH* 765; often utilized by Nicolas of Damascus, *FGrH* 90 F 66-8; Pearson, *Early Ionian Historians* 109-37; H. Diller," Zwei Erzählungen des Lydiers Xanthos," in *Navicula*

Chiloniensis 66-78.

[3]*FGrH* 4; 687a; Thuc. 1.97.2; Pearson, *Early Ionian Historians* 139-50.

[4]*FGrH* 262; 687b; Pearson, *Early Ionian Historians* 152-233.

[5]A. M. Pizzagalli, "L'Epica Iranica e gli scrittori Greci," *Atene e Roma* 10 (1942), 33-43; R. Drews, *The Greek Accounts of Eastern History* (Washington D. C. 1973), 22-32.

[6]*FGrH* 687 F 2; M. Moggi, "Autori Greci di Persiká I: Dionysio di Mileto," *Annali della Scuola Normale Superiore di Pisa* 2 (1972), 433-68; Drews, *Greek Accounts* 20-1; P. Tozzi, *La rivolta ionica* (Pisa 1978), 33-5; see Panyassis *Ionika*, legends and stories of the colonization of Ionia; V. J. Matthews, *Panyassis of Halikarnassos: Text and Commentary* (Leiden 1974).

[7]Kübler, "Die persische Politik," #411, son of Megabyzos #245, and Amytis #20, grandson of Zopyros #410.

[8]J. Wells, "The Persian Friends of Herodotus," *JHS* 27 (1907), 37-47; "The Persian Friends of Herodotus," *Studies in Herodotus* (Oxford 1923), 95-111.

[9]Cf. Cyrus' dream of Darius' rule Hdt. 1.209, the omen 3.76.9, and the thunderclap 3.86.2, as other examples of literary devices to explain dramatically the usurpation. C. F. Lehmann-Haupt, "Dareios und sein Ross," *Klio* 18 (1923), 59-64; Bittel, *Grundzüge der Kleinasiens* fig. 46, a gold winged daemon, the Persian *xvarnah*, with fine wings, found at Sardis, may have been a prototype to Hdt. 1.209-211.1, a Leitmotif of Darius' usurpation, Darius with wings over Asia and Europe. A. Farkas, "The Horse and Rider in Achaemenid Art," *Persica* 4 (1969), 57-76. See Appendix I: "Herodotus' Use of Folklore Motif."

[10]R. Schmitt, "Medisches und Persisches Sprachgut bei Herodot," *ZDMG* 117 (1967), 119-45. Classicists have long misunderstood the point, Burn, *Persia and the Greeks* 6; Hdt. "did not know the [Persian] language." J. Myres, *Herodotus* (Chicago 1971 edition), 159; "his etymologies of Persian names are fanceful," 1.131, 139, 6.98. R. Schmitt, "The Medo-Persian Names of Herodotus in the Light of the New Evidence from Persepolis," *AAH* 24 (1976), 25-35; "Die Verfassungsdebatte bei Herodot 3, 80-82 und die Etymologie des Dareios-Namens," *Historia* 26 (1977), 243-4; O. K. Armayor, "Herodotus' Persian Vocabulary," *Ancient World* 1 (1978), 147-56.

[11]J. V. Prášek, "Hekataios als Herodots Quelle zur Geschichte Vorderasiens," *Klio* 4 (1904), 196-8; F. J. Tritsch, "Harpy Tomb," *JHS* 62 (1942), 42-9; A. S. Shahbazi, *Irano-Lycian Monuments* (Teheran 1975), 69-70.

[12]L. Pearson, "Credulity and Scepticism in Herodotus," *TAPA* 72 (1941), 335-55; A. Leo Oppenheim, "The Interpretation of Dreams in the Ancient Near East," *Transactions of the American Philosophical Society* n.s. 46 (1956), 179-371; A. Momigliano, "The Place of Herodotus in the History of Historiography," in *Studies in Historiography* (New York 1966), 127-41; P. Frisch, *Die Träume bei Herodot* (Meisenheim am Glan 1968); D. Hegyi, "Historical Authenticity of Herodotus in the Persian 'Logoi'," *AAH* 17 (1969), 73-87; R. Drews, "Herodotus' Other Logoi," *AJP* 91 (1970), 181-91; C. W. Fornara, *Herodotus: An Interpretative Essay* (Oxford 1971), 36, 60-5; R. Rtskhiladze, "La spécificité de l'Orient dans les 'Histoires' d' Hérodote," *AAH* 22 (1974), 487-94; D. Lateiner, "No Laughing Matter: A Literary Tactic in Herodotus," *TAPA* 107 (1977), 175-82; O. K. Armayor, "The Homeric Influence on Herodotus' Story of the Labyrinth," *Classical Bulletin* 54 (1977-78), 68-72; "Herodotus' Catalogues of the Persian Empire in Light of the Monuments and the Greek Literary Tradition," *TAPA* 108 (1978), 1-9; O. Murray, *Early Greece* (Atlantic Highlands 1980), 31; D. Lateiner, "A Note on ΔΙΚΑΣ ΔΙΔΟΝΑΙ in Herodotus," *CQ* 30 (1980), 30-2.

[13]H. Immerwahr, *Form and Thought in Herodotus* (Cleveland 1966), 33-4; Myers, *Herodotus* 160.

[14]Hdt. 3.27-38; Diod. Sic. 1.46; Strabo 17.2.25; Plut. *de Iside et Osiridi* 44C; F. K. Kienitz, *Die politische Geschichte Ägyptens* (Berlin 1953), 55-60; M. F. Gyles, *Pharaonic*

Policies and Administration: 663 to 323 B.C. (Chapel Hill 1959), 38-40; P. Salmon, *La politique Égyptienne d'Athènes (VIe et V^e siecles avant J.-C.)*, (Brussels 1965), 61 n. 8; E. Bresciani, "Egypt and the Persian Empire," in H. Bengtson, *Greeks and Persians* 334-6; J. Perrot, "Le Palais de Darius le Grand à Shush," *Proceedings of the IInd Annual Symposium on Archaeological Research in Iran, Nov. 1973* (Teheran 1974), 91-101; Root *King and Kingship* 39, 68-72, 123-8; M. A. Dandamayev and V. G. Lukonin, *The Culture and Economic-System of Ancient Iran* [in Russian] (Moscow 1980), 104-5.

[15] My "The Date of Herodotus IV.1: Darius' Scythian Expedition," *HSCP* 76 (1972), 99-132, failed to note Hdt. 5.25.1. We must return to a date c. 513 B.C. R. Schmitt, "Die achaimenidische Satrapie TAYAIY DRAYAHYĀ," *Historia* 21 (1972); H.-J. Schnitzler, "Der Sakenfeldzug Dareios' des Grossen," *Antike und Universalgeschichte: Festschrift für Hans Erich Stier* (Münster 1972), 52-71; Dandamaev, *Persien unter den Ersten Achämeniden* 131: J. Harmatta, "Darius' 514/513 Expedition against the Sakā Tigraxaudā," *AAH* 24 (1976), 15-24, offered a new reading for DB OP V; S. Parlato, "La cosiddetta campagna scitica di Dario," *Annali, Istituto Orientale de Napoli* 41 (1981), 213-50.

[16] M. White, "Herodotus' Starting Point," *Phoenix* 23 (1969), 39-48.

[17] Immerwahr, *Form and Thought* 5-7.

[18] Ibid. 169-70; B. N. Alexanderson, "Darius in the *Persians*," *Eranos* 65 (1967), 1-11; H. Bellen, "Der Rachegedanke in der griechische-persichen Auseinanderzetzung," *Chiron* 4 (1974), 43-67.

[19] F. H. Weissbach, *Babylonische Miszellen* (Leipzig 1903), no. 10, pp. 24-6; Olmstead, *History of the Persian Empire* 116; A. Demandt, "Die Ohren des falschen Smerdis," *Iranica Antiqua* 9 (1972), 94; Dandamaev, *Persien unter den Ersten Achämeniden* 76-7.

[20] A. E. Cowley, *Aramaic Papyri of the Fifth Century B.C.* (Oxford 1923), nos. 62-65, pp. 164-71, 248-71; Olmstead, *History of the Persian Empire* 223; E. N. von Voigtlander, *The Bisitun Inscription of Darius the Great: Babylonian Version* (London 1978), 67.

[21] von Voigtlander, *Bisitun Inscription* 63-6, BE 3627 (Berlin VA Bab. 1502) and Bab. 41446. Not a close copy of Bisitun Babylonian text but closer to the Elamite and Old Persian. There are omissions of words and phrases found in the other texts. Bab. 41446 may not be a fragment of BE 3627, but a second inscription at Babylon engraved upon the front and back of three free standing steles.

[22] U. Seidl, "Ein Relief Dareios' I. in Babylon," *AMI* 9 (1976), 125-30, pls. 34, 37.

[23] von Voigtlander, *Bisitun Inscription* 65.

[24] Darius Bisitun Old Persian 70 (hereafter DB OP; Elamite = E, Babylonian = B). Not in B, E #1 or #2. An Elamite version was engraved as DB1 on the sculpture, above Dba and to the left of DBa OP. There was no B version of DB1; von Voigtlander, *Bisitun Inscription* 62. R. P. Dougherty, "Writing upon Parchment and Papyrus among the Babylonians and Assyrians," *JAOS* 48 (1928), 109-35; J. Lewy, "The Problems Inherent in Section 70 of the Bisitun Inscription," *HUCA* 25 (1954), 169-208; I. M. Diakonoff, "On the Interpretation of §70 of the Bisitun Inscription (Elamite Version)," *AAH* 17 (1969), 105-7.

[25] Dandamaev, *Persien unter den Ersten Achämeniden* 125.

[26] R. G. Kent, *Old Persian* 2nd ed. (New Haven 1953), 116-34; hereafter DB OP. von Voigtlander, *Bisitun Inscription* 54-62; hereafter B, with reference to edited sections. F. Vallat, "Corpus des inscriptions royales en Élamite achémenide, Thèse présentée pour l'obtention du Doctorat de IIIe cycle (Paris 1977); hereafter E. Hdt. 7.11, combined both royal lines (Darius, Hystaspes, Arsames, Ariaramnes, Teispes, Cyrus II, Cambyses I, and Achaemenes) and omitted Cambyses II, Cyrus I, and Bardiya; cf. Manetho *FGrH* 609 F 2; Strabo 15.3.24. The first text at Bisitun was the Elamite (1), then the Babylonian. The Old Persian text [which preceded the copying of Elamite (2)] is a translation of either the Babylonian or Elamite version. The Babylonian and Elamite versions tend to divide

the military action by campaigns, the Old Persian by battles. The Babylonian version is more extensive than the Elamite and includes casualty statistics and other details which the scribe composing the Elamite version considered unnecessary wordiness of the Babylonian text, but unfortunately often essential information. The Bisitun Babylonian version and the Babylon Palace variation stress Babylon and Babylonia, and often Elam. Frequent Aramaicisms appear in the Babylonian text of which only the preamble (B 1-14) are polished and its material arranged well. The voice is that of Darius and von Voigtlander argued a copy of the king's proclamation upon his accession in Babylon, following the fall of Nebuchadrezzar IV. von Voigtlander's observation is that the Babylonian text is prime and the original dictation, *Bisitun Inscription* 6-7. L. W. King and R. C. Thompson, *The Sculptures and Inscription of Darius the Great on the Rock of Behistun in Persia* (London 1907); F. H. Weissbach, *Die Keilinschriften der Achämeniden* (Leipzig 1911), 9-74; G. G. Cameron, "A Photograph of Darius' Sculptures at Behistan," *JNES* 2 (1943), 115-6; "Darius Carved History on Ageless Rock," *National Geographic Magazine* 98.6 (Dec. 1950), 825-44; M. Miller, "The Earlier Persian Dates in Herodotus," *Klio* 37 (1959), 29-52; G. G. Cameron, "The Monument of King Darius at Bisitun," *Archaeology* 13 (1960), 162-71; "The Elamite Version of the Bisitun Inscriptions," *JCS* 14 (1960), 59-68; H. Luschey, "Studien zu dem Darius-Relief in Bisitun," *AMI* 1 (1968), 63-94, pl. 25-42.

[27] DB B 1: "I am Darius, the King, son of Hystaspes..."; OP 1: "I am Darius, the Great King, an Achaemenid...", without reference to Hystaspes until OP 2 as in B and E 2; E follows OP with alteration of word order. R. G. Kent, "Old Persian Texts," *JNES* 1 (1942), 415-23.

[28] A. T. Olmstead, "Darius and his Behistun Inscription," *AJSL* 55 (1938), 399; G. G. Cameron, "Darius and Xerxes in Babylonia," *AJSL* 58 (1941), 315; Olmstead, *History of the Persian Empire* 92.

[29] DB E and OP 35-6; B 28-9.

[30] Kent, *Old Persian*, Darius Susa (DS) E 3b:12-5; Xerxes Persepolis F 3:15-27. F. Vallat, "Table Élamite de Darius 1er," *Revue d'Assyriologie* 64 (1970), 149-60, lines 9-11; "Deux Nouvelles 'Chartes de Fondation' d'un Palais de Darius 1er à Suse," *Syria* 48 (1971), 57, E lines 8-14.

[31] W. Hinz, "Zu den elamischen Burgbau-Inschriften Darius I. aus Susa," *AAH* 19 (1971), 17-24; M.-J. Stève, "Inscriptions des Achéménides à Suse," *Studia Iranica* 3 (1974), 169.

[32] M.-J. Stève, "Inscriptions de Achéménides à Suse," *Studia Iranica* 4 (1975), 24.

[33] DB E 62-3, not in OP or B.

[34] Pritchard (ed.), *Ancient Near Eastern Texts* 2nd ed., 315-6; J. Harmatta, "The Literary Patterns of the Babylonian Edict of Cyrus," *AAH* 19 (1971), 217-31.

[35] Kent *Old Persian*: A theme reiterated in the OP texts, Darius Persepolis d, e, h; Naqsh-i Rustam a; Susa a, d, e, f, i, j, k, l, m, o, p, s, t; Suez c; Elevand; and Hamadan.

[36] DB E and OP 10-4; B 10-3.

[37] Dandamaev, *Persien unter den Ersten Achämeniden* 101-7.

[38] G. G. Cameron, "The Persian Satrapies and Related Matters," *JNES* 32 (1973), 47-56, noted that the lists of Darius and Xerxes at Bisitun, Persepolis, Naqsh-i Rustam, Susa, and the Suez Canal inscriptions are not lists of provinces or of administrative satrapies but rather of various groups of people whom they thought worthy of specific mention, and cannot be correlated with the satrapal list of Hdt. 3.89-115, which must come from a different source. R. Schmitt, "Der Numerusgebrauch bei Länder- und Völkernamen im Altperischen," *AAH* 25 (1977), 91-9.

[39] DB E and OP 10-2; B 10-1. E and OP omit Babylonia and Elam given in B.

[40]DB E and OP 11; B 10. W. Schulze, "Der Tod des Kambyses," *Sitzungs. königlich-pruessischen Akademie Wissen, Berlin (Phil-hist. Klasse),* (1912), 685-703; E. Herzfeld, "Der Tod des Kambyses," *BSOAS* 8 (1935-7), 589-97; J. Puhvel, "The Death of Cambyses and Hittite Parallels," *Studia Classica et Orientalia Antonio Pagliaro Oblata* 3 (Rome 1969), 169-75; see Herodotus' treatment of the "suicide" of King Kleomenes I of Sparta (6.75), D. Harvey, "Leonidas the Regicide?," *Arktouros,* 253-60.

[41]DB E and OP 10-1; B 10. Bardiya's "missing ears" is a basic folklore motif, S. Thompson, *Motif-Index of Folk-Literature* rev. ed. (Bloomington 1955-8), sv "Ears," F511.2.4; D702.1, D712.1; S. Thompson and J. Balys, *The Oral Tales of India* (Bloomington 1958), H41, H56, K1311. See Appendix I: "Herodotus' Use of Folklore Motif." J. Wiesehöfer, *Der Aufstand Gaumātas und die Anfänge Dareios' I.* (Bonn 1978), argued Gaumata was the pretender Pseudo-Bardiya or Smerdis.

[42]O. Klima, "Gaumāta der Magier," *Archiv Orientální* 31 (1963), 119-21; E. J. Bickerman and H. Tadmor, "Darius I, Pseudo-Smerdis and the Magi," *Athenaeum* 56 (1978), 245, 249, 261.

[43]DB E and OP 16-20; B 15-9; Dandamayev and Lukonin, *Culture and Economic-System of Ancient Iran* 105-6.

[44]OP 16 notes the name of the "pretender" as Nidintu-Bel the son of Ainaira; B 15 states the son of Kinzer, a *zazakku* or high tax official; E 16 states the son of Hanara. A Babylonian treaty dated 3 October 522 B.C. bears the name of Nebuchadrezzar III; Dandamaev, *Persien unter den Ersten Achämeniden* 132 and nn. 548-9; Cameron, "Darius and Xerxes in Babylonia," *AJSL* 58 (1941), 316-8.

[45]DB B, not E or OP. Ghirshman, *Iran* 140, noted: "The text seems to belittle the extent of the sedition. The truth was far otherwise. Practically the whole of the Empire was embroiled in the revolts; even Persis was not spared. . . ." Dandamaev, *Persien unter den Ersten Achämeniden* 128-34.

[46]Only E 15 glosses Assina with "an Elamite man."

[47]DB E and OP 52, 56, 57, 62; B 45, 46, 48, 50. A. Poebel, "Chronology of Darius' First Year of Reign," *AJSL* 55 (1938), 142-65, 285-314; W. Hinz, "Das erste Jahr des Grosskönigs Dareios," *ZDMG* 42 (1938), 136-73; A. Poebel, "The Names and Order of the Old Persian and Elamite Months during the Achaemenian Period," *AJSL* 55 (1938), 130-41; R. A. Parker, "Persian and Egyptian Chronology," *AJSL* 58 (1941), 285-301; R. T. Hallock, "The 'One Year' of Darius I," *JNES* 19 (1960), 36-9; L. Trümpelmann, "Zur Entstehungsgeschichte des Monumentes Dareios' I. von Bisutun und zur Datierung der Einführung der altpersischen Schrift," *Archäologischer Anzeiger* 82 (1967), 296; placed the 'one year' following the overthrow of Assina, which Dandamaev, *Persien unter den Ersten Achämeniden* 59-60 accepted; *pace* Hallock. A. S. Shahbazi, "The 'One Year' of Darius Re-Examined," *BSOAS* 35 (1972), 609-14.

[48]DB E and OP 21-48; B 20-38.

[49]DB E and OP 20-1; B 21. B notes the Elamites themselves killed the "pretender" of their own volition. OP omits this.

[50]DB E and OP 24-5, 31-2; B 22, 25. B notes the 47 nobles, omitted in OP. E 25 is closer to B than OP, especially lines E 20-1 = B 47 but not 48a.

[51]DB E and OP 26-8; B 23; and Babylon BE 3627 (Berlin VA Bab. 1502), col. 1. E 26 states Dardashi "installed in Media," not in OP or B.

[52]DB E and OP 33; B 26.

[53]The date omitted in DB E and OP is given in B 26, V. Tashritu.

[54]DB OP 35-7; B 28-30. E and OP state Hyrkania while B gives Margiana. Hyrkania may be an error, or a glaring omission of details, as the suppression of the Parthian

rebellion was followed by the suppression of the Margianian rebellion. In B 32, the confusion is compounded further by Darius' concluding statement that with the fall of Parthia and Margiana, "this is what I did in Bactria and Margiana," E, OP and Babylon F 3627, col. 2 omit "and Margiana."

[55] DB E and OP 38-9; B 31-2; Babylon F 3627, col. 2.

[56] D. Stronach, *Pasargadae* (Oxford 1978).

[57] A. B. Tilia, *Studies and Restorations at Persepolis and Other Sites of Fārs* 2 (Rome 1978), 73-91.

[58] DB E and OP 40-4; B 33-6; E 41, line 5 follows B line 73; Babylon F 3627, col. 2.

[59] DB OP 45-8; B 37-8. B gives interpolative and clarific details omitted in OP. E 45 follows B 37, then OP.

[60] B 37 mentions the Sattagdian rebellion by name, a detail omitted in OP 46. E 46 states Arachosia. Dandamaev, *Persien unter den Ersten Achämeniden* 130, failed to note the Babylonian text which states the suppression of the rebellion in Sattagydia. He, therefore, argued that Darius on route to India in 512 B.C. then went against Sattagydia.

[61] DB OP 49-51; B 39-40. E follows OP, except in 50 which follows B 39. Cameron, "Darius and Xerxes in Babylonia," *AJSL* 58 (1941), 318-9.

[62] DB OP 50; E and B 39.

[63] DB E and OP 22; B 21.

[64] DB OP 68; B 54; E 68 variation of OP and B. F. Gschnitzer, *Die sieben Perser und das Königtum des Dareios: Ein Beitrag zur Achaimenidengeschichte und zur Herodot-analyse* (Heidelberg 1977); A. S. Shahbazi, "An Achaemenid Symbol: II. Farnah '(God given) Fortune'," *AMI* 13 (1980), 125-6.

[65] DB E and OP 11, 42; B 10, 34; Olmstead, *History of the Persian Empire* 111; Kent *Old Persian* 194; Dandamaev, *Persien unter den Ersten Achämeniden* 179, 184-6.

[66] DB E and OP 29-30; B 24.

[67] DB E and OP 33; B 26.

[68] DB E and OP 31-2; B 25.

[69] DB E and OP 36; B 29.

[70] DB B 35-6; omitted in E and OP.

[71] DB E and OP 21; B 20.

[72] E 29, Issila in "Assyria," not in B.

[73] DB E and OP 38; B 31.

[74] Olmstead, *History of the Persian Empire* 108-10; "Darius and his Behistun Inscription," *AJSL* 55 (1938), 392-416; Dandamaev, *Persien unter den Ersten Achämeniden* 108-28, esp. 120 n. 502. Dandamayev carefully noted that Darius gave no patronymic nor date for the uprising of Gaumata, as he had for the other usurpers, 119. J. Beloch, *Griechische Geschichte* 2.1 (Strassburg 1914), 4 n. 1, raised the same question. M. Meuleau, "Mesopotamia," in Bengtson, *Greeks and the Persians* 357; H. Rosen, "Herodotus Reconsidered," *Giornale di metafisica* 18 (1963), 205-13.

[75] Darius' propaganda to discredit Bardiya included the story that he lacked ears (Hdt. 3.69) and another that he was a eunuch (Plato *Epist.* 7.332a; *Leg.* 3.695b-c), to indicate

that he was deformed and not worthy to be king. Darius similarly marred the rebel Fravartish, the Median king (DB E and OP 32, B 25) and Cissantakhma, the Sagartian king (DB E and OP 33, B 26). At Bisitun, the left side of Bardiya's head is unfortunately severely damaged and we are unable to establish whether the ear was there. A. H. Krappe, "Solomon and Ashmodai," *AJP* 45 (1933), 260–8; the *ears of Smerdis* is a typical oriental harem story. See note 41 above, and Appendix I, "Herodotus' Use of Folklore Motif."

[76] OP Bardiya Greek > Smerdis: Greek nasalization of OP plosive (cf. OP Bagabukshu>Gr. Megabyzos), sporadic augmentation of sibilant (cf. Gr. mikros>smikros), retention of liquid plus stop cluster (cf. Aeschylus Mardos/Mardis), and with regularized Greek nominative inflectional ending.

[77] F. J. Groten, "Herodotus' Use of Variant Versions," *Phoenix* 17 (1963), 79–87; Immerwahr, *Form and Thought* 21-2, 32, 168-70.

[78] H. H. Bacon, *Barbarians in Greek Tragedy* (New Haven 1961), 41; Aeschylus' research on the genealogy of the Persian kings (*Pers.* 765-81) was the product of research and not invention. The Greek and Roman world, however, accepted Herodotus' romantic version and not that of Aeschylus: Plato *Epist.* 7.332a; *Leg.* 695b; Justin 1.9.4; Polyainos 7.11.2. Both Sophocles (*OT* 387) and Euripides (*Or.* 1498) used the Old Persian word *magos* as priestly impostor, apparently reflecting Herodotus' own statements (3.61-87); see M. Smith, *Jesus the Magician* (New York 1978), 71, who wrongly noted that "in the drama of the later fifth century *magos* can mean 'quack'."

[79] E. J. Bickerman review of M. A. Dandamaev, *Persien unter den Ersten Achämeniden* in *Athenaeum* 56 (1978), 413-5; Bickerman and Tadmor, "Darius I, Pseudo-Smerdis and the Magi," *Athenaeum* 56 (1978), 239-61.

[80] Earlier arguments include: F. W. König, *Der falsche Bardija: Dareios der Grosse und die Lügenkönige* (Vienna 1938); A. Poebel, "The Duration of the Reign of Smerdis, the Magian, and the Reigns of Nebuchadnezzar III and Nebuchadnezzar IV," *AJSL* 56 (1939), 121-45; W. B. Henning, "The Murder of the Magi," *Journal of the Royal Asiatic Society* (1944), 135-44; Klima, "Gaumata der Magier," *Archiv Orientální* 31 (1963) 119-21; Dandamayev, "Politische und wirtschaftliche Geschichte," *Beiträge zur Achämeniden-geschichte* 16-7, "starb Kambyses unter mysteriösen Umständen."

[81] Hansman, "An Achaemenian Stronghold," *Acta Iranica* 2nd. s. 6 (1975), 289-309; Bailey, "Nasā und Fasā" *Acta Iranica* 2nd s. 6 (1975), 309-12; Dandamaev, *Persien unter den Ersten Achämeniden* 91-4.

[82] Dubberstein, "The Chronology of Cyrus and Cambyses," *AJSL* 55 (1938), 417-9; Drews, "The Fall of Astyages and Herodotus' Chronology of the Eastern Kingdoms," *Historia* 18 1969), 5.

[83] Herodotus' romantic and tragic story (3.27-30, 61-4) of the revenge of the Egyptian god Apis is valueless; A. Hübner, "Zum Tod des Kambyses," *Zeitschrift für vergleichende Sprachforschung* 68 (1944), 57.

[84] DB OP col. 5 which was not added to either the Elamite or the Babylonian texts: F. H. Weissbach, "Die fünfte Kolumne der Grossen Bisutun-Inschrift," *Zeitschrift für Assyriologie* 46 (1940), 53-82; R. G. Kent, "Old Persian Texts: Darius' Behistan Inscription, Column V," *JNES* 2 (1943), 105-14; "Old Persian Texts. V: Darius' Behistan Inscription, Column V: A Correction," *JNES* 3 (1944), 232-3; W. Eilers, "The End of the Behistan Inscription," *JNES* 7 (1948), 106-10; G. G. Cameron, "The Old Persian Text of the Bisitun Inscription," *JCS* 5 (1951), 47-54; R. G. Kent, "Cameron's Old Persian Readings at Bisitun: Restorations and Notes," *JCS* 5 (1951), 55-7; V. V. Struve, "The Dating of the Behistun Inscription," *VDI* (1952), 26-48 [in Russian], erred in dating Column 5 to Darius' fifth year, 517 B.C. The portrait of Gobryas appears on both the Bisitun and Naqsh-i Rustam reliefs, and at the latter with the inscription (OP DNc-d): "Gobryas, a Patischorian, spear-bearer of Darius the King. Aspathines, bowbearer, holds the battle-ax of Darius the King,"; see Hdt. 3.69, 78; DB OP col. 5, sect. 68. Dandamayev incorrectly claimed the bowbearer to be Intaphernes, *Persien unter den*

Ersten Achämeniden 8. R. G. Kent, "IX. Naqsh-i-Rustam D," *JNES* 4 (1945), 233; W. Schwenzner, "Gobryas," *Klio* 18 (1923), R. P. Dougherty, *Nabonidus and Belshazzar: Yale Oriental Series* 15 (New Haven 1929), 170-2, 187-8, 199.

[85] O. Leuze, *Die Satrapieneinteilung in Syrien und im Zweistromlande von 520-320* (Halle 1935), 36-42; G. Posener, *La Première Domination Perse en Égypte* (Cairo 1936); R. Parker, "Darius and his Egyptian Campaign," *AJSL* 58 (1941), 377; "Persian and Egyptian Chronology," *AJSL* 58 (1941), 285-301; Kent, "Old Persian Texts," *JNES* 1 (1942), 415-23; G. G. Cameron, "Darius, Egypt, and the Lands beyond the Sea," *JNES* 2 (1943), 307-13; A. T. Olmstead, "Tattenai, Governor of Across the River," *JNES* 3 (1944), 46; E. Bresciani, "La satrapia d' Egitto," *Studi classici e orientali* 7 (1958), 132-88; Salmon, *La politique Égyptienne* 61-5; M. Mayrhofer, "Aus dem perserzeitlichen Ägypten," *Anzeiger der phil.-hist. Klasse der Österreichischen Akademie der Wissenschaften* 109 (1972), 317-20.

[86] Hdt. 4.166; Polyainos 7.11.7.

[87] R. de Vaux, "Les décrets de Cyrus et de Darius sur la reconstruction du Temple," *Revue biblique* 46 (1937), 29-57; K. Galling, "Syrien in der Politik der Achämeniden bis zum Aufstand des Megabyzos 448 v. Chr.," *Der Alte Orient* 36 (1937), 42-4; Olmstead, "Darius and his Behistun Inscription," *AJSL* 55 (1938), 409-12; J. Morgenstern, "Two Prophecies from 520-516 B.C.," *HUCA* 22 (1949), 365-83, 400-31; claimed Darius established Zerubbabel to the throne. That is contrary to the evidence outlined herein. S. A. Cook, "The Age of Zerubbabel," in H. H. Rowley (ed.), *Studies in Old Testament Prophecy Presented to Theodore H. Robinson* (Edinburgh 1950), 19-36; P. R. Ackroyd, "Two Old Testament Historical Problems of the Early Persian Period," *JNES* 17 (1958), 13-22; D. W. Thomas, "The Sixth Century B.C.: A Creative Epoch in the History of Israel," *Journal of Semitic Studies* 6 (1961), 33-46; K. Galling, *Studien zur Geschichte Israels im persischen Zeitalter* (Tübingen 1964), 61-77, 127-48; G. Sauer, "Serubbabel in der Sicht Haggias und Sacharjas," in *Das Ferne und Nahe Wort: Festschrift für Leonhard Rost* (Berlin 1967), 199-207; T. A. Busink, *Der Tempel von Jerusalem von Salomo bis Herodes*, 2, *von Ezechiel bis Middot* (Leiden 1980), 794-841.

[88] B. Meissner, "Die Achämenidenkönige und das Judentum," *Sitzungs. preuss. Akademie Wissenshaft, Berlin (Phil.-hist. Klasse)* (1938), 6-26; E. J. Bickerman, "The Edict of Cyrus in Ezra 1," *JBL* 65 (1946), 249-75; F. M. Heichelheim, "Ezra's Palestine and Periclean Athens," *Zeitschrift für Religions und Geistesgeschichte* 3 (1951), 251-3; J. M. Myers (ed. and trans.), *Anchor Bible: Ezra. Nehemiah* (Garden City 1965), XXV-XXX, 43-6, 50-4; M. Smith, "Palestinian Judaism in the Persian Period," in Bengtson, *Greeks and the Persians* 386-401; C. C. Torrey, *Ezra Studies* (New York 1970), 115-35, 184-99, 306; M. Smith, *Palestinian Parties and Politics that Shaped the Old Testament* (New York 1971), 103-17; H. Kreissig, *Die sozialökonomische Situation in Juda zur Achämenidenzeit* (Berlin 1973), 35-9.

[89] Aryandes dispatched expeditions against Cyrenaica and held the urban center of Barka; Hdt. 4.167, 200-5. The Bisitun sculpture portrays the nine rebellious "kings" mentioned in the texts: OP DBb-j, in addition to Skunkha OP DBk.

[90] W. W. How and J. Wells, *A Commentary on Herodotus* 1 (Oxford 1928), 300-1: "H. puts together without any real chronology, independent narratives, of which he knows only that they all belong to the early years of Darius." A. T. Olmstead, "Persia and the Greek Frontier Problem," *CP* 34 (1939), 308; Burn, *Lyric Age* 314-8; D. Gillis, *Collaboration with the Persians* (Wiesbaden 1979), 7, erred greatly in stating: "There is no hint of [Ionian] unrest or revolt at Cambyses' death or during the ensuing palace struggle (3.140). On the contrary, the Ionians with their neighbors loyally pay tribute to Darius when he emerges as King (3.90)."

[91] DB OP col. 5: sect. 71 (5:1-14) revolt of Elam; sect. 74 (5:20-30) Eastern Scythia.

[92] Strabo 14.1.16-7; Aelian *VH* 4.4; Diogenian 5.14; *Suda* sv chlamys. Berve, *Die Tyrannis* 1, 583. Herodotus' account of these events is confused and unreliable, and perhaps fits more readily into the pattern of poetic form and thought as analyzed by Immerwahr (see n. 13) than historical cause and effect. As argued, Herodotus followed

the propagandistic version of the events of 522-520 B.C. as offered by Darius at Bisitun, and this emphasized Herodotus' dramatic intent. Of the subsequent events at Samos, even Herodotus found his sources in marked contradiction and unbelievable. Into his Samian logos, Herodotus then introduced the Scythian theme (3.134) apparently to heighten his dramatic effect. Herodotus' account and his vague chronological outline is further disrupted by the insertion of the Babylonian revolt (which one we do not know) at the same time as Otanes' expedition against Samos, 3.150. Herodotus' stress upon the Babylonian revolt was not due only to his literary form but also due to the emphasis placed upon that revolt by his informant Zopyrus, 3.160. Darius' campaign to Sardis and to Scythia, Herodotus noted occurred "following the taking of Babylon," 4.1.1; and the confusion has now been settled (see chapter 5 n. 15 that Scythia referred to the eastern regions and not to European Scythia). The Libyan expedition is also marred by Zopyros' information (4.43). Darius' campaign against Egypt and to punish Aryandes (4.166) began in November 519 B.C. Darius' expedition against the European Scythians and his return to Sardis occurred sometime c. 513 B.C.

[93] Wallace, "Revitalization Movements," *American Anthropologist* 58 (1956), 274.

[94] Ibid. 275.

[95] I. C. Jarvie, *The Revolution in Anthropology* (Chicago 1969), 81-6, 100.

[96] P. J. Junge, *Dareios I. König der Perser* (Leipzig 1944), 43-67; J. Harmatta, "The Rise of the Old Persian Empire," *AAH* 19 (1971), 14-5; E. Leach, *Custom, Law, and Terrorist Violence* (Edinburgh 1977), 18: ". . . instead of the ruler dominating the individual by virtue of a legitimate authority delegated from society (or from God) we have the criminal terrorist dominating society by virtue of an illegitimate authority delegated by a factional group of revolutionaries, the inverted ruler has become a criminal, though not of course in his own estimation." "The deviant characteristics of the hero and of the criminal are essentially the same" (p. 27).

[97] DB E and OP 11; B 10. Poebel, "The Duration of Smerdis," *AJSL* 56 (1939). 123, a bibliography of fourteen tablets dated to the reign of Barzia; Cameron, "Darius and Xerxes in Babylonia," *AJSL* 58 (1941), 314-6; R. A. Parker and W. Dubberstein, *Babylonian Chronology 626 B.C.-A.D. 75* (Providence 1956), 14-5; Zadok, "On the Connections between Iran and Babylonia—Sixth Century B.C.," *Iran* 14 (1976), 74-6; Dandamaev, *Persien unter den Ersten Achämeniden* 126-8., nn. 526-33.

[98] S. V. Pallis, *The Babylonian Akītu Festival* (Copenhagen 1926); Dougherty, *Nabonidus and Belshazzer* 173, 198-9.

[99] Dandamaev, *Persien unter den Ersten Achämeniden* 144-65; an argument reflective of DB E and OP 68; B 54; and noted in I Esdras 3:1, 7, 14; is supported by Plato *Epist.* 7.332a: The nobles "participated jointly in the affairs of state and in power;" and Plut. *Mor.* 490A, Darius shared power with his brothers and his friends. This argument was earlier but briefly stated by B. Skladanek, "The Structure of the Persian State," *Acta Iranica* 1 (1974), 119.

[100] I. Gershevitch, *The Avestan Hymn to Mithra* (Cambridge 1959), 14, 296-9, and n. 145.

[101] W. Spiegelberg, *The Credibility of Herodotus' Account of Egypt in Light of the Egyptian Monuments* (Oxford 1927); A. Klasens, "Egypte onder Perzen en Grieken-Romeinen—Cambyses en Egypte," *Vooraziatisch-Egyptisch Gezelschap*, "Ex Oriente Lux," Jaarbericht 65 (1946), 339-49; K. M. T. Atkinson, "The Legitimacy of Cambyses and Darius as Kings of Egypt," *JAOS* 76 (1956), 168; T. W. Africa, "Herodotus and Diodorus on Egypt," *JNES* 22 (1963), 254-8; J. A. Wilson, *Herodotus in Egypt* (Leiden 1970), 8; Dandamaev, "La politique religieuse des Achemenides," *Acta Iranica* 1 (1975), 193-200, Cambyses' actions in Egypt were not religious but political in order to reduce the influence of the temples; Root, *King and Kingship* 123-8; Dandamayev and Lukonin, *Culture and Economic-System of Ancient Iran* 105. See Appendix I. "Herodotus' Use of Folklore Motif."

[102]Cambyses' death remains obscure (see note 40). The meaning of the words of the Bisitun texts imply either "natural death" or "suicide." Herodotus' romantic account does not correct the problem (3.64). Regicide may rest behind both accounts.

[103]"Democracy" meant not an Athenian form but the roll of all of the aristocratic leaders, see Hdt. 5.92.1; 6.43; Diod. Sic. 10.25.2; G. Walser, "La notion de l'État chez les Grecs et les Achéménides," in *Assimilation et Résistance à la Culture Greco-Romaine dans le Monde Ancient Travaux du VIe Congrès International d'Études Classiques, Madrid 1974* (Bucharest 1976), 227-31; not an historical Persian debate but a contemporary Greek philosophical discussion concerning the ideal polis.

[104]Kent, *Old Persian*; "Old Persian Texts: VI. Darius' Naqsh-i-Rustam B Inscription," *JNES* 4 (1945), 39-51; "VIII. Addenda on Naqsh-i-Rustam B," *JNES* 4 (1945), 232-3.

[105]DB OP 35; B 28.

[106]DB OP 25.

[107]DB OP 29.

[108]DB OP 38.

[109]DB OP 41.

[110]DB OP 45.

[111]DB OP 26.

[112]DB OP 33.

[113]E. E. Herzfeld, *Am Tor von Asien: Feldsdenkmäle aus Irans Heldenzeit* (Berlin 1920), pls. 9-10; Root, *King and Kingship* 58-61, 184-226; see H. J. Kantor, "Narration in Egyptian Art," *AJA* 61 (1957), 44-54; A. Perkins, "Narration in Babylonian Art," *AJA* 61 (1957), 54-62; H. G. Güterbock, "Narration in Anatolian, Syrian and Assyrian Art," *AJA* 61 (1957), 62-71.

[114]I. M. D'jakonov, "The Origin of the 'Old Persian' Writing System and the Ancient Oriental Epigraphic and Annalistic Traditions," in M. Boyce and I. Gershevitch (eds.), *W. B. Henning Memorial Volume* (London 1970), 98-124.

[115]F. Sarre and E. Herzfeld, *Iranische Felsreliefs* (Berlin 1910), illust. 86; Herzfeld, *Am Tor von Asien* pls. 1-2; see also pl. 3, an Old-Babylonian relief, and pl. 29, relief of Ardashir at Tag-i Bustan; N. C. Debevoise, "The Rock Reliefs of Ancient Iran," *JNES* 1 (1942), 76-105; H. H. von der Osten, *Die Welt der Perser* (Stuttgart 1956), pl. 11; see relief of Naram-Sin at Darband-i-Gawr pl. 9; E. Porada, *The Art of Ancient Iran* (Baden-Baden 1964), fig. 15, pp. 40-1; C. Nylander, *The Deep Well* (London 1969), 71-85, pl. 3, figs. 8-9; see fig. 10 of King Khosroe Parvez at Tag-i Bostan, pl. 4; H. Luschey, "Zum Problem der Stilentwicklung in der Achämenidischen und Sasanidischen Reliefkunst," *Iranica Antique* 11 (1975), 113-33; Root, *King and Kingship* 196-201, pl. 49.

[116]Aesch. *Pers.* 536; Root, *King and Kingship* 116-8, 164-9; see Appendix I: "Herodotus' Use of Folklore Motif."

[117]A. S. Shahbazi, "An Achaemenid Symbol," *AMI* 7 (1974), 135-44; there is no inscription at Bisitun to identify the winged figure; see R. Ghirshman, "La frontalité dans l'art iranien et ses origines," *CRAI* (1975), 51-60; E. Porada review of Ann Farkas, *Achaemenid Sculptures* Leiden 1974 in *Art Bulletin* 58 (1976), 612-3; Shahbazi, "An Achaemenid Symbol: II. Farnah '(God given) Fortune'," *AMI* 13 (1980), 119-47; M. Boyce, *A History of Zoroastrianism* 2 (Leiden 1982), 96-7, 100-5. J. Duchesne-Guillemin, *Zoroastrianism: Symbols and Values* (New York 1970), 140-1, *xvarnah* the basis of the aureoles of saints of Buddhism, Christianity, and Islam, the emanation of sun, the heavenly fire, a luminous life-force which is communicated to men, a fluid transmitted primarily to the head. This Aeschylus understood, and in his *Persians* produced in 472

B.C., he stressed the importance of the spirit of the dead preceding king, as at the tombs at Naqsh-i Rustam. Aeschylus discussed the role of Darius and his daemon or *xvarnah* (620, 633, 640) as something more than human about the former king, the dead king who embodied the daemon of the royal house (*vith*); A. J. Podlecki (trans. and comm.), *Aeschylus: The Persians* (Englewood Cliffs 1970), 2, 15.

[118] A. S. Shahbazi, personal letter, 27 February 1980; G. Azarpay, "Crowns and some Royal Insignia in Early Iran," *Iranica Antiqua* 9 (1972), 108-15; H. von Gall, "Die Kopfbedeckung des persischen Ornats bei den Achämeniden," *AMI* 7 (1974), 145-61; M. Boyce, "Iconoclasm among the Zoroastrians," in J. Neusner (ed.), *Christianity, Judaism and other Greco-Roman Cults: Studies for Morton Smith at Sixty* 4 (Leiden 1975), 93-111; P. Calmeyer, "Zur Genese altiranischer Motive: 'Personliche Krone' und Diadem," *AMI* 9 (1976), 45-63; "Vom Reisehut zur Kaiserkrone: Stand der Archäologische Forschung zu den Iranischen Kronen," *AMI* 10 (1977), 168-90.

[119] Plut. *Arta.* 3.1; D. Stronach, "Excavations at Pasargadae: Third Preliminary Report," *Iran* 3 (1965), 17; L. Trümpelmann, "Das Heiligtum von Pasargadae," *Studia Iranica* 6 (1977), 7-16; C. Nylander, "Achaemenid Imperial Art," in M. T. Larsen (ed.), *Power and Propaganda: A Symposium on Ancient Empires* (Copenhagen 1979), 345-59.

[120] J. de Mecquenem, "La Ziq-Kurat," *Gazette des Beaux Arts* 18 (1937), 201-14; P. Scheil, "Esagil," *Memoires de l'Academie des Inscriptions et Belles-Lettres* 39 (1914), 293-308.

[121] A. W. Lawrence, "The Acropolis and Persepolis," *JHS* 71 (1951), 111-9; E. F. Schmidt, *Persepolis* 3 vols. (Chicago 1953-1970); R. D. Barnett, "Persepolis," *Iraq* 19 (1957), 55-77; A. U. Pope, "Persepolis as a Ritual City," *Archaeology* 10 (1957), 123-30; R. Ghirshman, "Notes iraniennes VII, à propos de Persepolis," *Artibus Asiae* 20 (1957), 265-78; G. Woodcock, "Persia and Persepolis," *History Today* 17 (1967), 236-41, 301-7; D. N. Wilbur, *Persepolis* (London 1969); W. Lentz, W. Schlosser, and G. Gropp, "Persepolis—Weitere Beiträge zur Funtionsbestimmung," *ZDMG* (1971), 254-68; F. Krefter, *Persepolis Rekonstruktionen* (Berlin 1971); A. B. Tilia, *Studies and Restorations at Persepolis and other Sites of Fārs* 1 (Rome 1972); R. N. Frye, "Persepolis Again," *JNES* 33 (1974), 383-6; G. Gnoli, "Politique religieuse et conception de la royauté sous les Achaménides," *Acta Iranica* 2 (1974), 117-90; C. Nylander, "Al-Bērunī and Persepolis," *Acta Iranica* 1 (1974), 137-50; A. Farkas, *Achaemenid Sculpture* (Leiden 1974); H. von Gall, "Das persische Königszeit und die Hallenarchitektur in Iran und Griechenland," *Festschrift für Frank Brommer* 119-32; A. B. Tilia, *Studies and Restorations at Persepolis* 2 (Rome 1978).

[122] H. L. Ginsberg, "King of Kings' and 'Lord of Kingdoms'," *AJSL* 57 (1940), 71-4; J. G. Griffiths, "Βασιλεὺς Βασιλέων: Remarks on the History of a Title," *CP* 48 (1953), 145-54.

[123] G. Azarpay, "Crowns and some Royal Insignia in Early Iran," *Iranica Antiqua* 9 (1972), 108-15; P. Calmeyer, "The Subject of the Achaemenid Tomb Reliefs," *Proceedings of the IIIrd Annual Symposium on Archaeological Research in Iran, Nov. 1974* (Teheran 1975), 233-42; W. Kleiss and P. Calmeyer, "Das unvollendete Achämenidische Felsgrab bei Persepolis," *AMI* 8 (1975), 81-98; Calmeyer, "Zur Genese altiranischer Motive," *AMI* 8 (1975), 99-113; H. von Gall, "Die Grosskönigliche Kopfbedeckung bei den Achämeniden," *Proceedings of the IIIrd Annual Symposium on Archaeological Research in Iran, Nov. 1974* (Teheran 1975), 219-32.

[124] A. L. Oppenheim, "Akkadian pul(u)ḫ(t)u and Melammu," *JAOS* 63 (1943), 31-4; Schmidt, *Persepolis* 3 (Chicago 1970), 80-5, 108-18. In the Sasanian period the king was *particeps siderum, frater solis et lunae*, "companion of the stars, brother of the sun and the moon," Amm. Marc. 17.5.3; H. P. L'Orange, *Studies on the Iconography of Cosmic Kingship in the Ancient World* (Oslo 1953), chapter 9, "The Astral Movement of the Achaemenian Throne," 80-7. The king as cosmocrator is analogous to the heavenly bodies, with the sun (here Ahura Mazda) in the shield of the world or "word ring," Tert. *Apoll.* 16.9, *Solem . . . in suo clypeo*.

[125] Edith Porada, interview held at J. Pierpont Morgan Library, New York, New York,

23 March 1978. Starting with Darius, the Persian king appeared on seals from Anatolia as the hero fighting the supernatural lion, bull, and dragon. The king as hero transgressed the human aspect into the supernatural as he fought the evil foe. The king on the seals appears in close relationship to the king on the Persian gold and silver coinage minted only in western Anatolia. The king is not the "theocratic" king/hero as at Persepolis but rather the warrior-frontier-conflict king, a king in Anatolia where theocracy was not the norm. Iranian kingship for the East Greek poleis was that of the king "in conflict," a concept of "status minor regis" or "status secundus regis." E. Porada, *Corpus of Ancient Near Eastern Seals in North America Collections: The Collection of the Pierpont Morgan Library* (Washington D. C. 1948), 1 text, 101-2; J. Boardman, "Pyramidal Stamp Seals in the Persian Empire," *Iran* 8 (1970), 30-4; Root, *King and Kingship* 303-8.

[126] W. Hartner and R. Ettinghausen, "The Conquering Lion, the Life cycle of a Symbol," *Oriens* 17 (1964), 161-71; W. Hartner, "The Earliest History of the Constellations in the Near East, and the Motif of the Lion-Bull Combat," *JNES* 24 (1965), 1-16, suggested that the bull-lion conflict symbolized the first rays of Taurus ascending in conflict with Leo. I am not convinced by this argument as we do not know the fixed symbolism or either the Achaemenid or Assyro-Babylonian zodiac for this period. D. J. Wiseman, *Cylinder Seals of Western Asia* (London 1958), #100-2, 104-6, 110.

[127] W. Lentz, "Has the Function of Persepolis been fully Recognized so Far?", *The Memorial Volume: Vth International Congress of Iranian Art and Archaeology* 1 (Teheran 1972), 289-90.

[128] C. W. McEwan, *The Oriental Origin of Hellenistic Kingship: Studies in Ancient Oriental Civilization*, 13 (Chicago 1934); C. J. Gadd, *Ideas of Divine Rule in the Ancient East* (London 1948), 33-62 H. Frankfort, *Kingship and the Gods* (Chicago 1984) 231-48; J. L. Myers, "Persia, Greece and Israel," *Palestine Exploration Quarterly* 85 (1953), 8-22; B. Segall, "Notes on the Iconography of Cosmic Kingship," *The Art Bulletin* 38 (1956), 75-80; G. Widengren, "The Sacral Kingship of Iran," *Numen Suppl.* 4 (Leiden 1959), 242-57; H. W. F. Saggs, *The Greatness that was Babylon* (New York 1962), 359-72; A. L. Oppenheim, *Ancient Mesopotamia* (Chicago 1964), 99-104; R. N. Frye, "The Charisma of Kingship in Ancient Iran," *Iranica Antiqua* 4 (1964), 36-54; J. Duschesne-Guillemin, "Religion et Politique, de Cyrus à Xerxès," *Persica* 3 (1967/68), 1-9; H. Ringgren, *Religions of the Ancient Near East* (Philadelphia 1973), 99-107; C. Herrenschmidt, "Désignation de l'Empire et concepts politiques de Darius 1er d'après ses inscriptions en vieux-perse," *Studia Iranica* 5 (1976), 33-65; "Les créations d'Ahuramazda. Essai sur la royauté perse impériale," *Studia Iranica* 6 (1977), 17-58; "La religion des Achèménides: État de la question," *Studia Iranica* 9 (1980), 325-39.

[129] Hesychios sv ouranos noted the Persian royal palace as heaven; see L'Orange *Studies on the Iconography of Cosmic Kingship* 21-8, 134-7.

[130] R. Levy (trans.), *The Epic of Kings: Shah-Nama, the National Epic of Persia by Ferdowsi* (London 1967); see H. Lewy, "The Babylonian Background of the Kay Kāus Legend," *Archiv Orientální* 17 (1949), 28-109; R. C. Zaehner, "Zoroastrian Survivals in Iranian Folklore," *Iran* 3 (1965), 87-96.

[131] Pritchard (ed.), *Ancient Near Eastern Texts* 119.

[132] Genesis 37:2-4; E. A. Speiser (trans. and comm.), *The Anchor Bible: Genesis* (Garden City 1964), 292-4.

[133] Exodus 2:1-10.

[134] Horse motif: Arr. *An.* 6.29.7; Strabo 15.3.7; see Nepos *de Reg.* 1.2. The horse as a symbol of profane and sacred contests is prominent throughout the Vedic literature, see *The Rig Veda*, trans. D. O'Flaherty (Harmondsworth 1981), 85-8. See also "Appendix I: "Herodotus' Use of Folklore Motif."

[135] A. Christensen, *Les Gestes des rois* (Paris 1936), 106-8.

[136] E. A. Havelock, "Prologue to Greek Literacy," in *Lectures in Memory of Louise*

Taft Semple, 2nd. s. (Cincinnati 1971); C. J. Bleeker, "Wer war Zarathustra?," *Persica* 7 (1975-8), 25-41.

[137] *City Invincible* 175.

[138] Ginsberg, "'King of Kings' and "Lord of Kingdoms'," *AJSL* 57 (1940), 71; from Assyrian *shar sharrani* (see Tiglath-Pileser I, c. 1117 B.C.: Prism col. 1.1.30), the Sasanian *Shahanshah* or *Rex Regum* of Amm. Marc. 17.5.3, found Greek variations as "Despot of Despots," Aesch. *Pers.* 666, and "Lord of Lords" *Suppl.* 524. There were no Sumero-Akkadian or Old Babylonian equivalents. See Diod. Sic. 1.55. E. Campanile, "Ant. Pers. xšāyaθiya xšāyaθiyānām," *Studi Linguistici in onore di Tristano Bolelli* (Pisa 1974), 110-8.

[139] M. Mayrhofer, "Die Rekonstruktion des Medischen," *Anzeiger der phil.-hist. Klasse der Österreichischen Akademie der Wissenschaften* (1968), 1-22.

[140] Herrenschmidt, "Les Créations d'Ahuramazda," *Studia Iranica* 6 (1977), 17-58.

[141] M. Boyce, *A History of Zoroastrianism* 1 (Leiden 1975), 4-5.

[142] Gershevitch, *Avestan Hymn to Mithra*, 296-9.

[143] Boyce, *Zoroastrianism* 1, 52-3.

[144] A. D. H. Bivar, "Religious Subjects on Achaemenid Seals," in J. R. Hennells (ed.), *Mithraic Studies* 1 (Manchester 1975), 95.

[145] G. Dumézil, *Mitra-Varuṇa: Essai sur deux représentations indo-européennes de la Souveraineté* (Paris 1940), 45-50, 66-9, 73-4; Boyce, *Zoroastrianism* 24-5.

[146] D. Stronach, "A Circular Symbol on the Tomb of Cyrus," *Iran* 9 (1971), 155-8; now (in personal conversation, 27 December 1981) denies this attribution to Mithra, yet there is no evidence of Cyrus' devotion to Ahura Mazda. W. Eilers, "The Name of Cyrus," *Acta Iranica* 3 (1974), 3-9; J. Duchesne-Guillemin, "Le Dieu de Cyrus," *Acta Iranica* 3 (1974), 11-21; A. Closs, "Vorzarathustrische Religionen in Iran und in den Randgebieten als Hintergrund des Zarathustrischen und des spätern Mazdaismus," *Acta Iranica* 3 (1974), 111-21; Boyce, *History of Zoroastrianism* 2, 41-69; see V. V. Strouve, "The Religion of the Achaemenides and Zoroastrianism," *Cahiers d' Histoire Mondiale* 5 (1959-60), 529-45.

[147] R. Ghirshman, "Les Daivadana," *AAH* 24 (1976), 3-14.

[148] Aesch. *Pers.* 170-2; Hdt. 3.84, 7.8, 13, 53; Xen. *Cyr.* 3.1.8, 8.5.22; *An.* 1.4.6; Ezra 7:14; Esther 1:14; Ktesias *FGrH* 688 F 13; Dan. 3.3. Widengren, "The Sacral Kingship of Iran," *Numen Suppl.* 4 (1959), 242-5; Frye, *Heritage of Persia* 91-3. The "horse trick motif" (Hdt. 3.85-7) arose in Iran. Widengren (244) noted an ancient Indo-Iranian custom which, during an interregnum, the king selected by an omen given by the sun god through his special horse. But in the case of Persia in 522 B.C., no interregnum existed except in the official propaganda disseminated by Darius.

[149] Timokrates 129, silver footed stools; D. B. Thompson, "The Persian Spoils in Athens," *The Aegean and the Near East: Studies Presented to Heddy Goldman* (Locust Valley 1956), 286-90.

[150] Tilia, *Studies at Persepolis* 2, 56; also M. Kervan, D. Stronach, F. Vallat, J. Yoyotte, "Une statue de Darius découverte à Suse," *Journal asiatique* 260 (1972), 235-66; J. Perrot and D. Ladiray, "La Porte de Darius à Suse," *Cahiers de la Délégation archéologique Francaise en Iran* 4 (1974), 43-56; D. Stronach, "La Statue de Darius le Grand découverte à Suse," ibid. 61-72; M. Roaf, "The Subject Peoples on the Base of the Statue of Darius," ibid. 73-160; F. Vallat, "Les textes cunéiformes de la Statue de Darius," ibid. 161-70; J. Yoyette, "Les inscriptions hiéroglyphiques de la Statue de Darius à Suse," ibid. 181-3.

[151] Aesch. *Pers.* 661; Xen. *An.* 2.5.2-3; see Plut. *Them.* 29.7, King Damaratos and the

upright tiara. Fillet or diadem, Xen. *Cyr.* 8.3.13; Curtius 3.3.19; Amm. Marc. 18.5.6, 8.5; see Aristophanes *Aves* 847.

[152]The apadana bas-reliefs removed to the treasury; Tilia, *Studies and Restorations at Persepolis* 1 175-240, fig. 5; Frye, "Persepolis Again," *JNES* 33 (1974), 383-6; are of King Xerxes and his heir Dareios, whom Artaxerxes I overthrew. Farkas, *Achaemenid Sculpture* 51-3, 55-6; A. S. Shahbazi, "The Persepolis 'Treasury Reliefs' Once More," *AMI* 9 (1976), 151-6.

[153]Aeschylus also called Darius *Ballen (Pers.* 657-8), the king, the ancient king; a Phrygian term for king (Hesychius sv) with an oriental sound for Greek ears. Perhaps from Bel(?); also Soph. *Poimenes* F 472.

[154]Aesch. *Pers.* 152, 499, 588, 694-6; *Agam.* 920; Hdt. 7.136; Eurip. *Orest.* 1507; *Troad.* 1020-1; Xen. *Cyr.* 4.4.10, 13; Nepos *Conon* 3.3; Strabo 11.13.9. Feodora Prinzessin von Sachsen-Meiningen, "Proskynesis in Iran," in F. Altheim (ed.), *Geschichte der Hunnen* 2 (Berlin 1960), 128; E. J. Bickerman, "A propos d'un passage de Chares de Mytilène," *Parola Passato* 91 (1963), 241-55; R. N. Frye, "Gestures of Deference to Royalty in Ancient Iran," *Iranica Antiqua* 9 (1972), 102-7.

[155]Note the important free standing fire altars at Pasargadae, Stronach, *Pasargadae* 138-41; and at Naqsh-i Rustam, Schmidt, *Persepolis* 3, fig. 3.A, pp. 11-2; note the Median ritual center at Nush-i Jan. E. Benveniste, *Les Mages dans l'ancient Iran* (Paris 1938): M. Dandamayev, "New Data on the Religion of Persia at the turn of the Sixth and Fifth Centuries B.C." [in Russian], *VDI* 128 (1974), 28-9.

[156]Gershevitch, *Avestan Hymn to Mithra* #95-6.

[157]B. Goldman, "Persian Fire Temples or Tombs?" *JNES* 24 (1965), 305-8; D. Stronach, "Urartian and Achaemenian Tower Temples," *JNES* 26 (1967), 278-88; Schmidt, *Persepolis* 3 (Chicago 1970), 17-49; Stronach, *Pasargadae*, 117-35.

[158]W. Röllig, "Politische Heiraten im Alten Orient," *Saeculum* 25 (1974), 11-23.

[159]Hellanikos of Lesbos *FGrH* 687a F 7a and 7b.

[160]In April of 503 B.C., Darius gave a great gift of 2000 liters of wine and 100 sheep to his daughter, Artystone; G. G. Cameron, "Darius' Daughter and the Persepolis Inscriptions," *JNES* 1 (1942), 214-8; W. Hinz, "Achämenidische Hofverwaltung," *Zeitschrift für Assyriologie* 61 (1971), 288-98; M. Mayrhofer, "Alltagsleben und Verwaltung in Persepolis," *Anzeiger der phil.-hist. Klasse Öster. Akademie der Wissenschaft* 109 (1972), 195.

[161]M. W. Mather and J. W. Hewitt (eds.), *Xenophon's Anabasis: Books I-IV* (Norman 1962), 227.

[162]H. Heydemann, "Ellas ed Asia sul Vaso dei Persiani nel Museo di Napoli," *Annali dell'Istituto di Correspondenza Archeologica* 45 (1873), 20-52; C. Anti, "Il vaso di Dario e i Persiani di Frinico," *Archeologica Classica* 4 (1952), 23-45; J. H. Oliver, *Demokratia, the Gods and the Free World* (Baltimore 1960), 118-20, pl. 1.

[163]A. Momigliano, "Tradizione e invenzione in Ctesia," *Atene e Roma* 12 (1931), 15-44; J. A. Bowman, "Studies in Ctesias," (Ph.D. dissertation, Northwestern University 1938); J. M. Bigwood, "Ctesias of Cnidus" (Ph.D. dissertation, Harvard 1964); N. G. Wilson, "The Composition of Photius," *GRBS* 9 (1968), 451-5; "Two Notes: II. Photius' Bibliotheca," *GRBS* 12 (1971), 559-60; P. Lemerle, *Le premier humanisme Byzantin* (Paris 1971), 177-204; F. W. König, *Die Persika des Ktesias von Knidos* (Graz 1972); T. Hägg, "Photius at Work," *GRBS* 14 (1973), 213-22; J. M. Bigwood, "Ctesias' Account of the Revolt of Inarus," *Phoenix* 30 (1976), 1-25; "Ctesias as Historian of the Persian Wars," *Phoenix* 32 (1978), 19-41.

Chapter 6. Sparda and the Empire

[1] Aesch. *Pers.* 61, 762-5, 929-30; Hdt. 1.95, 130; Xen. *Cyr.* 7.2.11; Plato *Alk.* 1.121; Plut. *Arist.* 9.5, referred to the Persian Empire as "Asia in Europe."

[2] O. Szemerenyi, *Four Old Iranian Ethnic Names: Scythian-Skudra-Sogdian-Saka* (Vienna 1980), 26: "the province of the Skudra . . . was essentially European Turkey and the Eastern Part of modern Bulgaria, that part of the Eastern Balkans which on maps of the ancient world goes by the name of Thrace; in all probability it did not include any part of Macedonia."

[3] R. G. Kent, "More Old Persian Inscriptions," *JAOS* 54 (1934), 34-52; "The Restoration of Order by Dareios," *JAOS* 58 (1938), 112-21; R. G. Kent, "Old Persian Texts," *JNES* 1 (1942), 415-21; M.-J. Steve, "Inscriptions des Achéménides à Suse," *Studia Iranica* 3 (1974), 7-28; F. Vallat, "Deux Inscriptions Élamites de Darius 1er (DSf et DSz)," *Studia Iranica* 1 (1972), 3-13.

[4] Dandamayev, "Politische und wirtschaftliche Geschichte," *Beiträge zur Achämenidengeschichte* 17.

[5] A. T. Olmstead, "Wearing the Hat," *American Journal of Theology* 24 (1920), 94-5; W. Eilers "Vom Reisehut zur Kaiserkrone: A. Das Wortfeld," *AMI* 10 (1977), 153-68.

[6] Olmstead, "Persia and the Greek Frontier Problem," *CP* 34 (1939), 307; P. J. Junge, "Satrapie und Natio: Reichsverwaltung und Reichspolitik im Staate Dareios' I," *Klio* 34 (1941), 1-55; Dandamayev, "Politische und wirtschaftliche Geschichte," *Beiträge zur Achämenidengeschichte* 19-20.

[7] Ehtécham, *L'Iran* 127-31, for example, considered Herodotus' list of satrapies to correspond exactly to Darius' imperial organization; H. Castritius, "Die Okkupation Thrakiens durch die Perser und der Sturz des athenischen Tyrannen Hippias," *Chiron* 2 (1972), 1-15; Dandamayev and Lukonin, *Culture and Economic System of Ancient Iran* 109-11.

[8] G. Treuber, *Geschichte der Lykier* (Stuttgart 1887), 95-116; W. Schwabacher, "Lycian Coin-Portraits," in *Essays in Greek Coinage Presented to Stanley Robinson* (Oxford 1968), 111-24; A. S. Shahbazi, *The Irano-Lycian Monuments* (Teheran 1975); P. H. J. Houwink ten Cate, *The Luwian Population Groups of Lycia and Cilicia Aspera during the Hellenistic Period* (Leiden 1965), VIII-X, 1-12, 42.

[9] H. Matzat, "Über die Glaubwürdigkeit der geographischen Angaben Herodots," *Hermes* 6 (1872), 455-60; C. Hignett, *Xerxes' Invasion of Greece* (Oxford 1963), 82.

[10] Frye, *Heritage of Persia* 101-2; Myers, *Herodotus* 160.

[11] W. H. Roscher, "Das Alter der Weltkarte in 'Hippokrates' περὶ ἑβδομάδων und die Reichskarte des Darius Hystaspis," *Philologus* 70 (1911), 529-38; Huxley, *Early Ionia* 74, 101, 137-8; Dandamayev, "Politische und wirstschaftliche Geschichte," *Beiträge zur Achämenidengeschichte* 43-5.

[12] Hdt. 4.44; Arist. *Pol.* 8.13.1. The conquest of Hindush may have occurred c. 512 B.C., but this date is very uncertain; Dandamaev, *Persien unter den Ersten Achämeniden* 131. Cyrus conquered the eastern territories up to the Indian frontier, Dandamayev and Lukonin, *Culture and Economic-System of Ancient Iran* 104; and with the death of Darius' father Hystaspes I c. 514/3 B.C., who controlled the eastern zones for his son, Darius would then have campaigned to recontrol the area (1) not gained by Cyrus, and (2) perhaps unsettled following Hystaspes' death. See V. G. Childe, "India and the West before Darius," *Antiquity* 13 (1939), 5-15.

[13] Torrey, *Ezra Studies* 296; Hanfmann, *Letters* 3-4.

[14] Vitruvius 2.8.9-10; Pliny *HN* 35.172; Arrian *An.* 1.17.3-6; Hanfmann, *Letters* 249-50; "On the Palace of Croesus," *Festschrift für Frank Brommer* 145-52.

[15] Of the six co-conspirators, Intaphernes, unfit for high office, perished in disgrace (Hdt. 3.118-9). Yet the six families received special honors, a tradition into the Seleucid, Arsacid, and Sasanian periods. Their qualities included: virtue (Hdt. 1.138), fidelity to the king (Xen. *Cyr* 8.5.25-7), respect for law and custom (Hdt. 1.169, 7.136), bravery (DNa 4), humanitarianism (Hdt. 1.134), and justice (Hdt. 5.16-25, 7.194; Diod. Sic. 15.10). Dandamayev, "Politische und wirtschaftliche Geschichte," *Beiträge zur Achämenidengeschichte* 19. Boyce, *History of Zoroastrianism* 2, 92-4.

[16] Prāsek, *Geschichte der Meder und Perser* 2, 131; Dandamayev, "Politische und wirtschafliche Geschichte," *Beiträge zur Achämenidengeschichte* 52-4.

[17] K. M. T. Atkinson, "The Legitimacy of Cambyses and Darius as Kings of Egypt," *JAOS* 76 (1956), 167-77.

[18] A. Ramage, "City Area: Pactolus North," in G. M. A. Hanfmann, "The Tenth Campaign at Sardis," *BASOR* 191 (1968), 10-3; Hanfmann, *Letters* 221-2, 228, figs. 169-70; *Sculpture* 21, 33-4, stuccoed and gaily painted, the four lions roaring eastward toward the rising sun.

[19] Hanfmann, *Survey* 53-87.

[20] Dandamayev, "Politische und wirtschaftlichte", *Beiträge zur Achämenidengeschichte* 21; Frye, "Institutions," *Beiträge zur Achämenidengeschichte* 85; Dandamayev and Lukonin, *Culture and Economic-System of Ancient Iran* 114-27.

[21] Dandamayev, "Politische und wirtschaftliche Geschichte," *Beiträge zur Achämenidengeschichte* 21-4; H. Bengtson, "Syria under the Persians," *Greeks and Persians* 402-4.

[22] W. Schwenzner, "Gobryas," *Klio* 18 (1923), 41-58, 226-52; O. Leuze, *Die Satrapieneinteilung in Syrien und im Zweistromlande von 520-320* (Halle 1935), 25-36, 43-99; Dandamaev, *Persien unter den Ersten Achämeniden* 100 n. 397.

[23] Hdt. 3.136, 7.44, 96, 98, 100, 8.67; Diod. Sic. 16.41-5; Arrian *An.* 2.13.7, 2.15.6; S. Frankenstein, "The Phoenicians in the Far West: A Function of Neo-Assyrian Imperialism," *Power and Propaganda* 263-94.

[24] Clermont-Ganneau, "Le Paradeisos royal achéménide de Sidon," *Revue biblique* 30 (1921), 106-9; D. Harden, *The Phoenicians* 2nd. ed. (New York 1963), fig. 12; W. Fauth, "Der königliche Gärtner und Jäger im Paradeisos," *Persica* 8 (1979), 1-53.

[25] A. A. Sarfaraz, "Borazjān," in "Survey of Excavations in Iran 1971-1972," *Iran* 11 (1973), 188-9; A. B. Tilia, "Discovery of an Achaemenian Palace near Takht-i Rustam to the North of the Terrace of Persepolis," *Iran* 12 (1974), 200-4.

[26] ML *GHI* 12, line 4; G. Widengren, *Der Feudalismus im alten Iran* (Cologne 1969), 12-108, carefully demonstrated the meaning of *bandaka* as "Dienstmann" or "Diener" in the sense of vassal and *doulos*. Beneviste, *Indo-European Language and Society* 289-94; Chadwick, "The Berezan Lead Letter," *Proceedings of the Cambridge Philological Society* 199 n.s. 19 (1973), 35-7, Anaxagoras has my property (line 6) — *kai dōlōs kai dōlas koikias* ("slaves, both male and female, and houses"). C. G. Thomas, "On the Origin of the Institution of Slavery," *Ancient World* 1 (1978), 109-10; D. S. Wiesen, "Herodotus and the Modern Debate over Race and Slavery," *Ancient World* 3 (1980), 3-16.

[27] R. Gusmani, "Onomastica iranica nei testi epicorici lidi," in *Umanità e Storia: Scritti in onore de Adelchi Attisani* 2 (Naples 1971), 4; from OP *bandakasha-; W. Hinz, *Altiranisches Sprachgut der Nebenüberlieferungen* (Wiesbaden 1975), 63.

[28] Xen. *Hell.* 4.1.5; Diod. Sic. 12.27; Polyainos 7.11.7.

[29] LXX I Esdras 6:27, *eparchos*; P. Krumbholz, *De Asiae Minoris Satrapis Persicis* (Leipzig 1883), 4-5, n.1.

[30]Bengtson, "Syria," *Greeks and Persians* 404.

[31]Pearson, *Early Ionian Historians* 25-8; E. Herzfeld, *Persian Empire, Studies in Geography and Ethnology of the Ancient Near East* (Wiesbaden 1969), 288-92.

[32]E. S. G. Robinson, "Greek Coins Acquired by the British Museum (1938-48)," *NC* 6th s. 8 (1948), pL 5.8-8a; Schwabacher, "Lycian Coin-Portraits," in *Essays in Greek Coinage* 111-24; Shahbazi, *Irano-Lycian Monuments* pls. 26, 33.

[33]W. J. Martin, "Tribut und Tributleistungen bei den Assyrien," *Studia Orientalia* 8 (1936), 3-50; N. B. Jankowska," Some Problems of the Economy of the Assyrian Empire," in Diakonoff (ed.), *Ancient Mesopotamia* (Moscow 1969), 253-76; also in *VDI* (1956), 28-46 [in Russian]; P. Briant, "Appareils d'Etat et developpement des Forces productives au Moyen-Orient ancien: le cas de l'Empire achéménide," *La Pensée* 217/8 (1981), 9-23.

[34]Hanfmann, *Letters* 88; *Croesus to Constantine* 15; M. B. Nicol, "Dorudzan," *Iran* 5 (1967), 137-8; the Royal Road at Persepolis is 4.76 m. wide. Dandamayev and Lukonin, *Culture and Economic-System of Ancient Iran* 118-22.

[35]R. Hallock, *The Persepolis Fortification Tablets* (Chicago 1969), 6, 40-5.

[36]Richard T. Hallock, interview, Oriental Institute, University of Chicago, 31 March 1978; *PFT* p. 2; J. M. Balcer review-article of J. Hofstetter, *Die Griechen in Persien* Berlin 1978, in *Bibliotheca Orientalis* 36 (1979), 276-80. Elamite *marrish* ("measure") was written in Greek *marig* or **mariks*, cf. Arist. *HA* 8.9.1, *maris*; apparently derived from Old Iranian **mari-* or **vari-*, and perhaps **mariks-* in Old Persian; Hinz, *Altiranisches Sprachgut* 160-1; OP **maribara-*. The Samian lunate gamma has often been incorrectly transliterated as a sigma.

[37]G. Cousin and G. Deschamps, "Lettre de Darius, fil d'Hystaspes," *BCH* 13 (1889), 529-42; M. van den Hout, "Studies in Early Greek Letter-Writing II," *Mnemosyne* 2 (1949), 141-52; F. W. Schehl, "Darius' Letter to Gadatas," *AJA* 54 (1950), 265; F. Lochner-Huttenbach, "Brief des Königs Darius an den Satrapen Gadatas," in W. Brandenstein and M. Mayrhofer, *Handbuch des Altpersischen* (Wiesbaden 1964), 91-8. Gadatas was not a satrap but rather a local official or *hyparchos*, Xen. *Cyr.* 5.3.10 is in error.

[38]Also noted at Persepolis, I. Gershevitch, "Amber at Persepolis," *Studia classica et orientalia Antonino Pagliaro Oblata* (Rome 1969), 198.

[39]Aesch. *Pers.* 978-81; Xen. *An.* 2.4.8, 3.4.13, 3.5.17, 4.3.4; *Cyr.* 8.2.10-1, 8.6, 16; *Oec.* 4.8; Aristophanes *Acharn.* 91-124; Plut. *Arta.* 12.1; W. Dittenberger, *Orientis Graeci inscriptiones selectae* (Leipzig 1905), #264.4-8, 390.7, 391.7-10, 392.10-5; Balcer, "The Athenian Episkopos and the Achaemenid 'King's Eye'," *AJP* 98 (1977), 252-63.

[40]W. Brandenstein, "Der persische Satz bei Aristophanes, 'Αχαρνῆς, Vers 100," *Wiener Zeitschrift für d. Kunde Süd.-u Ostasiens* 8 (1964), 43-58; Brandenstein and Mayrhofer, *Handbuch des Altpersischen* 91.

[41]Drews, *Greek Accounts of Eastern History* 34-5.

[42]W. K. Pritchett, *The Greek State at War* 1 (Berkeley 1974), 129-30.

[43]Hanfmann, *Letters* 11.

[44]J. Hofstetter, *Die Griechen in Persien* (Berlin 1978), #221, p. 131; J. Wiesehofer, "Die 'Freunde' und 'Wohltäter' des Grosskönigs," *Studia Iranica* 9 (1980), 7-21.

[45]Hofstetter, *Die Griechen* #77, pp. 45-6.

[46]Ibid. #154, pp. 87-8; G. Walser, "Griechen am Hofe des Grosskönigs," *Festgabe Hans von Greyerz* (Bern 1976), 189-202.

[47] E. Drioton and J. Vandier, *L'Egypte* (Paris 1952), 600-2, 619; Lewis, *Sparta and Persia* 24; note Neh. 11:23-4.

[48] Walser, "Griechen am Hofe des Grosskönigs," *Festgabe Hans von Greyerz* 189-202; Hinz, "Achämenidische Hofverwaltung," *Zeitschrift für Assyriologie* 61 (1971), 260-311; Mayrhofer, "Alttagsleben und Verwaltung in Persepolis," *Öster. Akad. der Wissenschaft* 109 (1972), 192-202; Hofstetter, *Die Griechen;* R. T. Hallock, "The Elamite Texts from Persepolis," in H. Franke (ed.), *Akten des vierundswanzigsten international Orientalisten-Kongresses, München* (Wiesbaden 1959), 177-9.

[49] G. G. Cameron, *Persepolis Treasury Tablets* (Chicago 1948).

[50] G. G. Cameron, "The Oriental Institute Archaeological Report on the Near East," *AJSL* 50 (1933-4), 272; J. Friedrich, "Ein phrygisches Siegel und ein phrygisches Tontäfelchen," *Kadmos* 4 (1965), 154-6; Cameron, "The Persian Satrapies and Related Matters," *JNES* 32 (1973), 52-3. The location of the Phrygian tablet is no longer known.

[51] Note also Harpalos, an Ionian engineer and bridge builder, in the service of King Xerxes, Hofstetter, *Die Griechen* #130, p.74.

[52] G. F. Seibt, *Griechische Söldner im Achaimenidenreich* (Bonn 1977).

[53] G. M. A. Richter, "Greeks in Persia," *AJA* 50 (1946), 15-30; J. P. Guépin, "Greek Artists under Achaemenid Rule," *Persica* 1 (1963-64), 34-52; C. Nylander, "Old Persian and Greek Stonecutting and the Chronology of Achaemenian Monuments I," *AJA* 69 (1965), 49-56; H. J. Etienne, *The Chisel in Greek Sculpture* (Leiden 1968); C. Nylander, *Ionians at Pasargadae* (Uppsala 1971); "Anatolians in Susa—and Persepolis (?)," *Acta Iranica* 3 (1975), 317-23; Root, *King and Kingship* 7-15.

[54] G. P. Carratelli, "Greek Inscriptions of the Middle East," *East and West* 16 (1966), 31-6.

[55] M. Mayrhofer, *Onomastica Persepolitana* (Vienna 1973), 8.1717, 1294, 1296; Gerschevitch, "Amber at Persepolis," *Studia Classica et Orientalia* 167-251; Hinz, "Achämenidische Hofverwaltung," *Zeitschrift für Assyriologie* 61 (1971), 269-311.

[56] Eretrians also to Susa (Hdt. 6.20; Plato *Menex.* 240a-b; *Leg.* 3.698c); Libyans to Bactria (Hdt. 4.165, 167, 204); and Karians under Darius III to the Tigris (Arrian *An.* 3.8.5, 3.11.5); F. Grosso, "Gli Eretriesi deportati in Persia," *Rivista di filologia e di istruzione classica* 86 (1958), 350-75; R. J. Penella, "Scopelianus and the Eretrians in Cissia," *Athenaeum* 52 (1974), 295-300.

[57] Strabo 13.4.13; A. Keramopoullos 'Ο Κῦρος καὶ τὸ 'Υρκάνιον πεδίον, *Athena* 16 (1904), 161-88; L. Robert, "Hyrcania," *Hellenica* 6 (1948), 16-26.

[58] G. G. Cameron, "Ancient Persia," in *The Idea of History* 92-3; M. Meuleau, "Mesopotamia under Persian Rule," in Bengtson, *Greeks and Persians* 358; M. Dandamayev, "Achaemenid Babylonia," *Ancient Mesopotamia* 297.

[59] Duchesne-Guillemin, "Le Dieu de Cyrus," *Acta Iranica* 3 (1974), 18; P. Gignoux, "Le dieu Baga en Iran," *AAH* 25 (1977), 119-27.

[60] Cameron, "Darius and Xerxes in Babylonia," *AJSL* 58 (1941), 314-25; G. G. Cameron, "The Elamite Version of the Bisitun Inscriptions," *JCS* 14 (1960), 63-4; M. Mayrhofer, "Xerxès-le-Grand," *Acta Iranica* 1 (1974), 108-16 Dandamaev, *Persien unter den Ersten Achämeniden* 204-7, 215-41. The thesis of R. J. Littman, "The Religious Policy of Xerxes and the Book of Esther," *Jewish Quarterly Review* 65 (1975), 145-55, is untenable.

[61] T. Jacobsen, *City Invincible* 178-80.

[62] *FGrH* 680 F11; S. Burstein, *The Babyloniaca of Berossus* (Malibu 1978), 3.5.2.

[63] Strabo 15.3.15; L. Robert, "Une nouvelle Inscription grecque de Sardes: Réglement de l'autorité perse relatif à un culte de Zeus," *CRAI* (1975), 306-30.

[64] Boardman, *Greeks Overseas* 111.

[65] E. Laroche, "Koubaba, déesse anatolienne, et le probleme des origines de Cybèle," in *Éléments orientaux dans la religion Grecque ancienne* (Paris 1960), 113-28; R. D. Barnett, "Some Contacts between Greek and Oriental Religions," in *Éléments orientaux dans la religion Grecque ancienne* (Paris 1960), 143-53; G. M. A. Hanfmann and J. C. Waldbaum, "Kybele and Artemis: Two Anatolian Goddesses at Sardis," *Archaeology* 22 (1969), 264-9; Hanfmann, *Letters* 133-4.

[66] P. Ermann, "Men, Herr von Axiotta," in S. Şahin, *Studien zur Religion und Kultur Kleinasiens* 1, 415-23.

[67] Littman, *Lydian Inscriptions Sardis* 6.6, p. 85; J. Keil, "Die Kulte Lydiens," in *Anatolian Studies Presented to Sir William Mitchell Ramsay* (Manchester 1923), 239-66; Hanfmann, *Letters* figs. 35, 113.

[68] Olmstead, "Persia and the Greek Frontier Problem," *CP* 34 (1939), 306.

[69] In my earlier article, "The Date of Herodotus IV. 1: Darius' Scythian Expedition," *HSCP* 76 (1972), 99-132; I erred in failing to note Hdt. 5.25. The date proposed, 519 B.C., is incorrect, and I return to c. 514-511 B.C.

[70] Theopompos (?) claimed that Philip II of Macedon mounted a successful invasion of Scythia in 339 B.C. for the sole purpose of replenishing his treasury, Justin 9.1-2; Orosius 3.13.1-4; A. Momigliano, "Della spedizione scitica di Filippo, alla spedizione scitica di Dario," *Athenaeum* 11 (1933), 336-59; see G. Dumézil, "Note sur un Roman Scythique d'Hérodote: Skyles," *Acta Iranica* 1 (1975), 215-22.

[71] Pelasgians Hom. *Il.* 1.594 "vulgar tongue," cf. 2.867 Karian "barbaric;" Hdt. 2.51, 6.137-40; Antandros, a Pelasgian town, Hdt. 7.42; J. A. R. Munro, "Pelasgians and Ionians," *JHS* 54 (1934), 109-28.

[72] Dandamayev, "Politische und wirtschaftliche Geschichte," *Beiträge zur Achämenidengeschichte* 48-9.

[73] PW *RE* sv Boryza, Thynias; see also E. Unger, "Die Dariusstele am Tearos," *Archäologischer Anzeiger* (1915), 3-18.

[74] Found in the Gherla district of Roumania by János Hermatta in 1937, "A Recently Discovered Old Persian Inscription," *AAH* 2 (1953), 1-16; W. Hinz, "Die Quellen," *Beiträge zur Achämenidengeschichte* 6-7.

[75] Hallock *PFT* pp. 50-3; #852, 1006, 1010, 1056, 1057, 1085, 1171, 1172, 1176, 1186, 1215, 1278, 1363, 1575, 1813, 1819, 1820, 1823, 1847, 1946, 1947, 1954, 1955, 1957, 1987, 2055, 2069.

[76] Mayrhofer, *Onomastica Persepolitana* 8.387; Aesch. *Pers.* 14, 247; *Agam.* 282; Hdt. 1.120.2, 3.34.1, 77.2, 84.2, 118.2, 126, 5.14, 8.98; express messengers *PFT* 1334, 1335, 1672; in comparison to slow Xen. *Cyr.* 5.5.1, 8.4.2, 8.6.17-8; *An.* 1.6.11, 8.28; *Hell.* 2.17, 1.9, 3.1.1. Lewis, *Sparta and Persia* 2-3, n. 2, the envoy Artaphrenes "of royal stock and descended from a family of experience in western matters," from Susa to Sparta, see Thuc. 2.57.1, a Peloponnesian envoy bound for Susa. C. Nylander, ΑΣΣΥΡΙΑ ΓΡΑΜΜΑΤΑ : Remarks on the 21st Letter of Themistokles," *Opuscula Atheniensia* 8 (1968), 122-36, incorrectly believed this spurious letter referred to Old Persian; an error repeated by R. J. Lenardon, *The Saga of Themistocles* (London 1978), in his uncritical study of the twenty-one epistles attributed to Themistokles.

[77] Strabo 15.2.8; J. Lewy, "The Problems Inherent in Section 70 of the Bisitun Inscription," *HUCA* 25 (1954), 173-7, 185-6; B. Porten, *Archives from Elephantine* (Berkeley 1968), 56-7.

[78]W. Hinz, "Die Einfuhrung der altpersischen Schrift," *ZDMG* 102 (1952), 28-38; J. Harmatta, "The Bisitun Inscription and the Introduction of the Old Persian Cuneiform Script," *AAH* 14 (1966), 255-83; G. Windfuhr, "Notes on the Old Persian Signs," *Indo-Iranian Journal* 12 (1970), 121-5; R. T. Hallock, "On the Old Persian Signs," *JNES* 29 (1970), 52-5; G. Cohen, "Origin of Persian Cuneiform," *Comments on Etymology* 6 (1976), 1-11; M. Mayrhofer, "Überlegungen zur Entstehung der altpersischen Keilschrift," *BSOAS* 42 (1979), 290-6.

[79]II Kings 18:26; F. Altheim and R. Stiehl, *Die aramäische Sprache unter den Achaimeniden* (Frankfurt am Main 1963); W. Hinz, *Neue Wege im Altpersische* (Wiesbaden 1973), 39-52; J. A. Delaunay, "L'Araméen d'Empire et les débuts de l'écriture en Asie centrale," *Acta Iranica* 2 (1974), 219-46.

[80]J. D. Whitehead, "Early Aramaic Epistolography" (Ph.D. dissertation, University of Chicago 1974), 279.

[81]A. Poebel, "The King of the Persepolis Tablets: The Nineteenth Year of Artaxerxes I," *AJSL* 56 (1939), 301-4; R. T. Hallock, "Darius I, the King of the Persepolis Tablets," *JNES* 1 (1942), 230-2.

[82]Skins: Hdt. 5.58; Nic. Dam. *FGrH* 90 F 1; Ktesias discovered lists of Median Kings "in the royal leather records," *FGrH* 688 F5.4; Diod. Sic. 2.32.4; papyrus Hdt. 1.123, 124, 125, 3.128; *skytalē* Plut. *Arta.* 6.3. R. P. Dougherty, "Writing upon Parchment and Papyrus among the Babylonians and Assyrians," *JAOS* 48 (1928), 109-35; J. Starcky, "Une tablette araméenne de l'an 34 de Nebuchadonosor," *Syria* 37 (1960), 99-115; Hinz "Achämenidische Hofverwaltung," *Zeitschrift für Assyriologie* 61 (1971), 308-11.

[83]R. A. Bowman, *Aramaic Ritual Texts from Persepolis* (Chicago 1970); R. G. Wasson, "The Soma of the Rig Veda: What was it?," *JAOS* 91 (1971), 169-86; D. H. H. Ingalls, "Remarks on Mr. Wasson's Soma," *JAOS* 91 (1971), 188-91; P. Bernard, "Les mortiers et pilons inscrits de Persepolis," *Studia Iranica* 1 (1972), 165-76; B. A. Levine, "Aramaic Texts from Persepolis," *JAOS* 92 (1972), 70-9; J. Naveh and S. Shaked, "Ritual Texts or Treasury Documents?," *Orientalia* 42 (1973), 445-57; I. Gershevitch, "An Iranist's View of the Soma Controversy," in P. Gignoux and A. Tafazzoli (eds.), *Mémorial Jean de Menasce* (Louvain 1974), 52-75; J. A. Delaunay, "A propos des Aramaic 'Ritual texts from Persepolis' de R. A. Bowman," *Acta Iranica* 2 (1974), 193-217; W. Hinz, "Zu den Mörsen und Stösseln aus Persepolis," *Acta Iranica* 1 (1975), 371-85.

[84]J. Kutsher and J. Polotsky, "An Aramaic Scroll from the Fifth Century B.C.E.," *Kedem* 2 (1945), 66-74 [in Hebrew]; G. R. Driver, *Aramaic Documents of the Fifth Century B.C.*, 1st ed. (Oxford 1954), 2nd ed. (Oxford 1957); J. Lewy, review of Driver *Aramaic Documents in Jewish Quarterly Review* 45 (1954-5), 289-95; P. Grelot, *Documents araméens d'Egypte* (Paris 1972); Whitehead, "Early Aramaic Epistolography"; J. A. Fitzmyer, "Some Notes on Aramaic Epistolography," *JBL* 93 (1974), 201-25; J. C. Greenfield, "On Some Iranian Terms in the Elephantine Papyri," *AAH* 25 (1977), 113-8; see also A. H. Sayce, *Aramaic Papyri Discovered at Assuan* (London 1906); A. Dupont-Sommer, "L'Óstracon araméen d'Assour," *Syria* 24 (1944-5), 24-61; "Un papyrus araméen d'époque saite découvert à Saqqara," *Semitica* 1 (1948), 43-68; *Les Araméens* (Paris 1949), 80-97; J. Harmatta, "Irano-Aramaica," *AAH* 7 (1959), 337-409; Porten, *Archives from Elephantine*; Y. Muffs, *Studies in the Aramaic Legal Documents from Elephantine* (Leiden 1969).

[85]The Persepolis Fortification Tablets date to 509-494 B.C.; the Treasury Tablets to 492-458 B.C. W. Hinz, "'Glückwunsch' aus Persepolis," in *Mémorial Jean de Menasce* (Louvain 1974), 125-9; J. A. Delaunay, "Remarques sur quelques noms de personne des archives élamites de Persepolis, "*Studia Iranica* 5 (1976), 9-31; E. Lipiński, Western Semites in Persepolis," *AAH* 25 (1977), 101-12; R. T. Hallock, "The Use of Seals on the Persepolis Fortification Tablets," *Bibliotheca Mesopotamica* 6 (1977), 127-33.

[86]Whitehead, "Early Aramaic Epistolography," 59-68.

[87]R. T. Hallock, "Darius I, the King of the Persepolis Tablets," *JNES* 1 (1942), 230-2; "New Light from Persepolis," *JNES* 9 (1950), 237-52; G. G. Cameron, "Persepolis

Treasury Tablets Old and New," *JNES* 17 (1958), 161-76; R. T. Hallock, "A New Look at the Persepolis Treasury Tablets," *JNES* 19 (1960), 90-100; G. G. Cameron, "New Tablets from the Persepolis Treasury," *JNES* 24 (1965), 167-92; M Mayrhofer, "Aus dem perserzeitlichen Ägypten," *Anzeiger der. phil.-hist. Klasse der Österreichischen Akademie der Wissenschaften* 109 (1972), 317-20; R. T. Hallock, "The Persepolis Fortification Archive," *Orientalia* 42 (1973), 320-3; "The Evidence of the Persepolis Tablets," *Cambridge History of Iran* 2 (Cambridge forthcoming).

[88] Cameron, *Persepolis Treasury Tablets* 27-9; Driver, *Aramaic Documents* 2nd ed., 4; C. Starr, "A Sixth-Century Athenian Tetradrachm used to Seal a Clay Tablet from Persepolis," *NC* 136 (1976), 219-22 (= *PFT* 2053); Hallock, "The Use of Seals on the Persepolis Fortification Tablets," *Bibliotheca Mesopotamica* 6 (1977), 127-33.

[89] M. J. Mellink, "Archaeology in Asia Minor," *AJA* 59 (1955), 235-6; K. Balkan, "Inscribed Bullae from Daskyleion-Ergili," *Anatolia* 4 (1959), 123-8; R. Schmitt, *Altpersische Siegel-Inschriften* (Vienna 1981), SXf-g, 32-3.

[90] von Voigtlander, *Bisitun Inscription* 8.

[91] Windfuhr, "Notes on the Old Persian Signs," *Indo-Iranian Journal* 12 (1970), 121-5; Hinz, *Neue Wege im Altpersischen* 15-23; P. Lecoq, "La Langue des inscriptions Achéménides," *Acta Iranica* 2 (1974), 55-62; "Le problème de l'écriture cunéiforme vieux-perse," *Acta Iranica* 3 (1974), 25-107; before Cameron's readings of DB OP 70, scholars considered the "invention" to have been Aramaic, see V. V. Struve, "The Reform of the Written Language under Darius I," *VDI* (1951), 186-91 [in Russian].

[92] C. C. Torrey, "The Bilingual Inscription from Sardis," *AJSL* 34 (1917-8), 185-98; Bossert, *Altanatolien* pl. 198; H. Donner and W. Röllig, *Kanaanäische und Aramäische Inschriften* 1 (Wiesbaden 1962), #260; 2 (Wiesbaden 1964), 305-9.

[93] Xen. An. 7.8.25; A. D. H. Bivar, "A Satrap of Cyrus the Younger," *NC* 7th s., 1 (1961), 119-20; Shahbazi, *Irano-Lycian Monuments* 120-1, fig. 6 and pl. 75; W. A. P. Childs, *The City-Reliefs of Lycia* (Princeton 1978).

[94] J. Imbert, "L'épigramme grecque du Stèle de Xanthe," *REG* 7 (1894), M. Lidzbarski, "Aramaische Inschriften aus Kappadocien," *Ephemeris für semitische Epigraphif* 1 (1900-2), 59-74, 319-26; C. C. Torrey, "An Aramaic Inscription from Cilicia, in the Museum of Yale University," *JAOS* 35 (1915-17), 370-4; F. W. König, *Die Stele von Xanthos* (Vienna 1936); F. J. Tritsch, "The Harpy Tomb at Xanthos," *JHS* 62 (1942), 39-50; G. E. Bean, "Notes and Inscriptions from Caunos," *JHS* 73 (1953), 10-35; *JHS* (1954), 85-110; E. S. G. Robinson review of A. B. Brett, *Museum of Fine Arts, Boston. Catalogue of Greek Coins* (Boston 1955), in *AJA* 60 (1956), 298-9; Donner and Röllig, *Kanaanäische und Aramäische Inschriften*; P. Coupel and P. Demargue, *Fouilles de Xanthos 3. Le Monument des Néréides* (Paris 1969): J. Bousquet, "Arbinas, fils de Gergis, dynastie de Xanthos," *CRAI* (1975), 138-50; H. Metzger, E. Laroche, and A. Dupont-Sommer, "La Stéle trilingue récesument découverte au Létoon de Xanthos," *CRAI* (1974), 82-93, 115-25, 132-49; M. Mayrhofer, "Kleinasien zwischen Agonie des Perserreiches und Hellenistischen Fruhling," *Anzeiger der phil.-hist. Klasse der Österreichischen Akademie der Wissenschaften* 112 (1975), 274-82; E. Badian, "A Document of Artaxerxes IV?," in K. H. Kinzl (ed.), *Greece and the Eastern Mediterranean in Ancient History and Prehistory* (Berlin 1977), 40-50; J. Teixidor, "The Aramaic Text in the Trilingual Stele from Xanthos," *JNES* 37 (1978), 181-5, retains the date 358 B.C. for Artaxerxes III Ochus; J. Borchhardt, "Eine Doppelaxtstele aus Limyra," in Şahin, *Studien zur Religion und Kultur* 183-91; W. A. P. Childs, "The Authorship of the Inscribed Pillar of Xanthos," *Anatolian Studies* 29 (1979), 97-102; H. Metzger, *Fouilles de Xanthos: 6, La Stèle trilingue du Létōon* (Paris 1979).

[95] Hdt. 7.30.2, stele set up by Croesus on the eastern Lydian border with Phrygia to mark the boundary, a stele apparently inscribed in Lydian; see Unger, "Die Dariusstele am Tearos," *Archäologischer Anzeiger* (1915), 3-18.

[96] F. M. Cross Jr., "An Aramaic Inscription from Daskyleion," *BASOR* 184 (1966), 8-9; R. S. Hanson, "Aramaic Funerary and Boundary Inscriptions from Asia Minor," *BASOR* 192 (1968), 3.

[97] S. Waszynski, "De l'authenticité de la correspondance de Pausanias avec Xerxes," *Eos* 6 (1900), 113-7; A. T. Olmstead, "A Persian Letter in Thucydides," *AJSL* 49 (1933), 154-61; C. W. Fornara, "Some Aspects of the Career of Pausanias of Sparta," *Historia* 15 (1966), 257-71; D. J. Stewart, "Thucydides, Pausanias, and Alcibiades," *CJ* 61 (1966), 145-52; M. Lang, "Scapegoat Pausanias," *CJ* 63 (1967), 79-85; A. Y. Parshikov, "Pausanias and the Political Struggles in Sparta," *VDI* 1 (1968), 126-38 [in Russian]; J. M. Balcer, "The Medizing of the Regent Pausanias," *Actes du Premier Congrès international des Études Balkaniques et sud-est Européenes* 2 (Sofia 1969), 105-14; A. Blamire, "Pausanias and Persia," *GRBS* 11 (1970), 295-305.

[98] Frye, "Institutions," *Beiträge zur Achämenidengeschichte* 88-9.

[99] *PFT* #1404, 1321.

[100] E. J. Bickerman, "The Edict of Cyrus in Ezra 1," *JBL* 65 (1946), 249-75; Hinz, *Darius* 1, 114, would substitute Ahura Mazda for Yhwh.

[101] Porten, *Archives from Elephantine* 29.

[102] Ehtécham *L'Iran* 85-6; A. E. Speiser, *City Invincible* 159; Meuleau in Bengtson, *Greeks and Persians* 380-1.

[103] Boyce, *Zoroastrianism* 1, 190; A. S. Shahbazi, "The 'Traditional Date of Zoroaster' Explained," *BSOAS* 40 (1977), 25-35.

[104] S. Insler, *The Gāthās of Zarathustra: Acta Iranica* 3rd. s., 1 (1975).

[105] Aesch. *Pers.* 584-5, 919, cf. 95; Ezra 7:12-26; Xen. *An.* 9.13. A. T. Olmstead, "Darius as Lawgiver," *AJSL* 51 (1935), 247-9.

[106] Xen. *Oec.* 14.6; Plato *Epist.* 7.332b; Diod. Sic. 1.95.4-5; W. Spiegelberg, *Die sogennante demotische Chronik* (Leipzig 1914), 30-1; N. J. Reich, "The Codification of the Egyptian Laws by Darius and the Origin of the 'Demotic Chronicle'," *Mizraim* 1 (1933), 178-85; M. F. Gyles, *Pharaonic Policies and Administration, 663 to 323 B.C.* (Chapel Hill 1959), 40, 70, 81-2; E. Bresciani, "Egypt and the Persian Empire," in Bengtson, *Greeks and Persians* 338.

Chapter 7. Vassalage and the Landed Gentry

[1] Arist. *Oec.* 1354b (2.1.4); Diod. Sic. 10.25.2; Ehtéchem, *L'Iran* 91-105; Mazzarino, *Fra Oriente e Occidente* 191-252; H. S. Nyberg, "Das Reich der Achämeniden," *Historia Mundi* 3 (1954), 75-97; Frye, *Heritage of Persia* 106-10; V. Martin, "La politique des Achéménides. L'exploration prélude de la conquête," *Museum Helveticum* 22 (1965), 38-48; Dandamayev and Lukonin, *Culture and Economic-System of Ancient Iran* 141-62.

[2] Aesch. *Pers.* 586-7; Xen. *Hell.* 3.4.21; *An.* 1.1.8; *Cyr.* 8.6.23; Ktesias *FGrH* 688 F53-4; B. D. Meritt, "Inscriptions of Colophon," *AJP* 56 (1935), 374-6, Ins. 2, line 34.

[3] Porten, *Archives from Elephantine* 58-9.

[4] J. A. S. Evans, "Herodotus and the Ionian Revolt," *Historia* 25 (1976),36.

[5] P. Briant, "Des Achéménides aux rois hellénistiques: continuités et ruptures," *Annali della Scuola Normale Superiore di Pisa* 9 (1979), 1375-1414; "Conquête territoriale et stratégie idéologique: Alexandre le Grand et l'idéologie monarchique achéménide," *Prace Historyczne* 63 (1980), 37-83.

[6] Whitehead, "Early Aramaic Epistography."

[7] Bresciani, "Egypt and the Persian Empire," in Bengtson, *Greeks and Persians* 341-4; Grelot, *Documents araméens d'Égypte* #1, pp. 71-6.

[8]Grelot, ibid. #2 pp. 75-8.

[9]Ibid. #54-5, pp. 267-75.

[10]Muffs, *Studies in Aramaic Legal Documents from Elephantine* 11-3, 186-93.

[11]A. E. Cowley, *Aramaic Papyrus of the 5th Century B.C.* (Oxford 1923); Porten, *Archives from Elephantine* 52.

[12]Driver, *Aramaic Documents* 10-6, #1:2, 2:2, 6:2; Porten, *Archives from Elephantine* 53.

[13]Whitehead, "Early Aramaic Epistography."

[14]H. F. Lutz, "An Agreement between a Babylonian feudal lord and his retainer in the reign of Darius II," *The University of California Publications in Semitic Philology* 9 (1928), 269-77; G. Cardascia, *Le ḫaṭru et les collectivités en Babylonie, d'après les archives de la maison Muraŝû: Mémoire présenté à l'Ecole des Hautes Etudes* (Paris 1946); *Les Archives des Maraŝû* (Paris 1951); E. Ebeling, "Die Rüstung eines babylonischen Panzerreiters nach einem Vertrage aus der Zeit Darius II," *Zeitschrift für Assyriologie* 16 (1952), 203-13; B. C. Brundage, "Feudalism in Ancient Mesopotamia and Iran," *Feudalism in History* 108-10; G. Widengren, "Recherches sur le féodalisme l'Iran antique," *Orientalia Suecana* 5 (1956), 79-182; G. Cardascia, "Le fief dans la Babylonie achéménide," *Recueil de la Société Jean Bodin* 1.2 (Brussels 1958), 55-88; M. A. Dandamajew, "Die Lehnsbeziehungen in Babylonien unter den erster Achämeniden," in *Festschrift fur Wilhelm Eilers* (Wiesbaden 1967), 37-42; D. B. Weisberg, *Guild Structure and Political Allegiance in Early Achaemenid Mesopotamia* (New Haven 1967); M. Dandamayev, "Achaemenid Babylonia," in *Ancient Mesopotamia* 296-311; M. W. Stolper, "Management and Politics in Later Achaemenid Babylonia: New Texts from the Murasu Archive," 2 vols. (Ph.D. dissertation, University of Michigan 1974); R. Zadok, "Nippur in the Achaemenid Period: Geographical and Ethnical Aspects," (Ph.D. dissertation, Hebrew University, Jerusalem 1974); G. Ries, *Die neubabylonische Bodenpachtformulare* (Berlin 1976); M. W. Stolper review of Ries, *Die neubabylonische Bodenpachtformulare* in *Bibliotheca Orientalis* 35 (1978), 230-3; M. W. Stolper, "The Genealogy of the Muraŝû Family," *JCS* 28 (1976), 189-200.

[15]A. T. Clay, "Aramaic Indorsements on the Documents of the Muraŝû Sons," *Old Testament and Semitic Studies in Memory of William Rainey Harper* 1 (Chicago 1908), 287-321.

[16]D. Sidersky, "L'onomastique hébraïque des Tablettes de Nippur," *Revue des Études juives* 87 (1929), 178-99; M. D. Coogan, "Patterns in Jewish Personal Names in the Diaspora," *Journal for the Study of Judaism* 4 (1973), 184-91; "Life in the Diaspora: Jews at Nippur in the Fifth Century B.C.," *Biblical Archaeologist* 37 (1974), 6-12; M. W. Stolper, "A Note on Yahwestic Personal Names in the Muraŝû Texts," *BASOR* 222 (1976), 258; G. Wallis, "Jüdische Bürger in Babylonien während der Achämeniden-Zeit," *Persica* 9 (1980), 129-188.

[17]G. Hüsing, *Poruŝātiŝ und das achamanidische Lehenswesen* (Vienna 1933).

[18]Zadok, "Nippur in the Achaemenid Period," XV-XXXVII.

[19]Cardascia, "Le fief dans la Babylonie achéménide," *Recueil de la Société Jean Bodin* 63-7; Stolper, "Management and Politics in Later Achaemenid Babylonia," 52-3; Zadok, "Nippur in the Achaemenid Period," XXXV.

[20]Throughout this monograph I have avoided the commonly used "feudalism" to denote the relationship of the vassals to the king. Instead, I have used suzerainty and vassalage, but they too are imprecise, as they, like "feudalism," connote the legal relationships of free and equal men of the western medieval period, and their benefits of beneficium or later feodum; F. L. Ganshof, *Feudalism* 2nd ed. (New York 1961), 106-11. While the Persian vassals were not chattel slaves, the literal concept of *doulos*, they were also not free and equal but clearly subservient to the king and to the king's

authority. Consequently, this is a non-issue for Pollux *Onomasticon* 3.83; D. Lotze, Μεταξὺ 'Ελευθέρων καὶ Δούλων (Berlin 1959); and W. L. Westermann, "Between Slavery and Freedom," *American Historical Review* 50 (1945), 213-27.

[21]*Chōrion:* Hdt. 3.86.1; 4.92, 113.2-3; cf. 1.196.1; 2.75.1, 122.3; 6.137.4; 8.25.2; *phrouria:* Hdt. 2.30.3; 6.26.1; 7.59.1. P. Briant, "Contrainte militaire, dépendance rurale et exploitation des territoires en Asie achéménide," *Index: Quaderni camerti di studi romanistici* 8 (1978-9), 49-85; "Communautes rurales, forces productives et mode de production tributaire en Asie Achéménide," *Zaman* 2-3 (1980), 75-100.

[22]Keramopoullos, 'Ο Κῦρος καὶ τὸ 'Υρκάνιον πεδίον,*Athena* 16 (1904), 161-88.

[23]L. Robert, "Hyrcania," *Hellenica* 6 (1948), 16-26; "Types mónetaires à Hypaipa," *Revue Numismatique* 6th. s., 28 (1976), 37-8.

[24]Briant, "Contrainte militaire," *Index* 8 (1978/9), 62.

[25]Hdt. 3.125; Xen. *Hell.* 3.1.25-7; 3.2.12; 4.1.15-6; 4.1.33; *An.* 1.2.7; 4.4.2; 4.4.7; *Oec.* 4; Plut. *Them.* 30; *Alk.* 24; Nepos *Agesil.* 3.1.

[26]Briant, "Contrainte militaire," *Index* 8 (1978/9), 69.

[27]G. Cardascia, "Armée et fiscalité dans la Babylonie Achéménide," in *Armées et fiscalité dans le monde Antique* (Paris 1977), 3-10.

[28]J.-P. Vernant, "Remarques sur la lutte de classe dans la Grecè ancienne," *Eirene* 4 (1965), 5-19; W. K. Lacey, *The Family in Classical Greece* (Ithaca 1968); R. J. Littman, "Kingship in Athens," *Ancient Society* 10 (1979), 5-31; G. E. M. de Ste Croix, *The Class Struggle in the Ancient Greek World* (London 1981), 114-33.

[29]There is no reason to consider Pythios' wealth was derived from trade, even Herodotus' figures of two thousand silver talents and three million and nine hundred and ninety-three thousand gold darics are accurate, as did Hunt, "Feudal Survivals in Ionia," *JHS* 67 (1947), 74.

[30]Hofstetter, *Die Griechen* #123, 124, 125, pp. 70-2.

[31]Ibid. #77, pp. 44-5; #116, p. 68; #274, pp. 157-8.

[32]Nepos *Alc.* 9.3; *ATL* 1. 256-7, 478, "fifty talents . . . seems impossibly large, but for the wealth of the temple" (Strabo 13.3.5). Nepos *Milt.* 3.1-6, that Darius gave to each Greek tyrant who participated in the Danube expedition a city in that territory of Asia Minor from which they came, appears to be a confusion of Hdt. 4. 137, yet underscores the vassalage role of each tyrant to the king.

[33]Thuc. 6.59.3; J. K. Davies, *Athenian Propertied Families* (Oxford 1971), #11793; III-IV, VII, IXC, 445-8, 450, 452; Hofstetter, *Die Griechen* #154, pp. 87-8; #8, pp. 7-8; #157, p. 89.

[34]Hofstetter, *Die Griechen* #246, pp. 143-5.

[35]Thuc. 1.138.5; Diod. Sic. 11.57.7-58.1; Nepos *Them.* 10.2; Strabo 13.1.12; 14.1.10; Plut. *Them.* 29.7 = Neanthes *FGrH* 84 F 17; Phanias *FHG* II. 29; *Them.* 30; Them 31.1-3 = Theopompos *FGrH* 115 F 87; Athen. *Deip.* 1.29, 1.54; Aristodem. 10.5; *Schol.* Aristophanes *Eq.* 84 = Neanthes F 17; *Suda* sv Themistokles; Paus. 1.26.4; Passis *FGrH* 480 F 1; Steph. Byz. sv Lampsakos; Davies, *Athenian Propertied Families* #6669, 211-20; Hofstetter *Die Griechen* #305, pp. 171-6; Podlecki, *Life of Themistocles* 42, 104, 106, 117-8, 129.

[36]Brandenstein and Mayrhofer, *Handbuch des Altpersischen* 132.

[37]Soph. *Helenes Gamos* F 184; *Troilos* F 577; H. Bacon, *Barbarians in Greek Tragedy*

(New Haven 1961), 69.

[38]E. F. M. Agricola, *De Aristidis censu* (Berlin 1900); O. Murray, Ο ΑΡΧΑΙΟΣ ΔΑΣΜΟΣ , *Historia* 15 (1966), 142-56.

[39]Hekataios' information (Strabo 1.1.11) may have originated with Anaximander and his "geographical studies" based upon bronze maps made centuries earlier in Babylonia.

[40]M. I. Finley, *The Ancient Economy* (London 1973), 95-6.

[41]Mermnad: Hdt. 1.14.1; 1.91.1; Median: Hdt. 1.96.2, 100.1, 109.4, 111.2, 112.3; Achaemenid: Hdt. 3.14.9, 81.1; 7.35, 52.2.

[42]Variant titles: *tagos*, Aesch. *Pers.* 21-3; 323-4; cf. Arist. F 497-8; archons, Aesch. *Pers.* 24; I Esdras 3:14; Xen. *Oec.* 4.8.9; *kōmarchoi*, LXX Esther 2:3; Xen. *An.* 4.5.10; M. T. W. Arnheim, *Aristocracy in Greek Society* (London 1977), 58.

[43]Ehtécham, *L'Iran* 118.

[44]Histiaios' arguments at the Danube Bridge (Hdt. 4.137) are repeated by Aristagoras at Sparta (Hdt. 5.49). L. Solmsen, "Speeches in Herodotus' Account of the Ionian Revolt," *AJP* 64 (1943), 194-207; the "speeches are . . . the means by which Herodotus expresses his personal impressions, views, and judgments on the events which he reports" (p. 207); *pace* D. Hereward, "Miltiades' Speech at the Bridge," *Proceedings of the Classical Association* 52 (1955), 24-5; "Miltiades' Speech at the Bridge," *Kodaigaku: Palaeologia* 6 (1957/8), 113-23; J. de Romilly, "Le classement de constitutions d'Hérodote à Aristote," *REG* 72 (1959), 81-99; *pace* P. T. Brannan, "Herodotus and History: the Constitutional Debate Preceding Darius' accession," *Traditio* 19 (1963), 427-38; K. Kinzl, *Miltiades-Forschungen* (Vienna 1968), 27-50; K. Bringmann, "Die Verfassungsdebatte bei Herodot 3, 80-82 und Dareios' Aufstieg zur Königsherrschaft," *Hermes* 104 (1976), 266-79; J. Bleicken, "Zur Entstehung der Verfassungstypologie im. 5. Jahrhundert v. Chr. (Monarchie, Aristokratie, Demokratie)," *Historia* 28 (1979), 148-72, a product of the second half of the fifth-century and its political theory (156).

[45]K. H. Waters, *Herodotus: On Tyrants and Despots* (Wiesbaden 1971), 5-7; note Immerwahr, *Form and Thought* 13, "the ultimate aim of Hdt. is never the individual story by itself, but always in relation to others."

[46]Finley, *Ancient Economy* 48-50, who quotes the views of Georg Lukács (R. Livingstone trans.), *History and Class Consciousness* (Cambridge, Mass. 1971), 55-9; see Vernant, "Remarques sur la lutte des classes," *Eirene* 4 (1965), 5-19.

[47]A. M. Snodgrass, *Arms and Armour of the Greeks* (London 1967), 49, 58-61, 67, 77-81; P. A. L. Greenhalgh, *Early Greek Warfare* (Cambridge 1973), 143-5.

[48]E. Meyer, *Geschichte des Altertums* 4.1 (Stuttgart 1944), 33, 56; Widengren, "Recherches sur le féodalisme l'Iran antique," *Orientalia Suecana* 5 (1956), 79-100.

[49]*Bandaka* = "possession" or "property," Kent, *Old Persian* 199; an adjective for officials and royal servants; Aesch. *Pers.* 242; Aristotle de *Mundo* 398a30; Nic. Dam. *FGrH* 90 F 66.5; Xen. *An.* 2.5.38; Gadatas was not a satrap (Xen. *Cyr.* 5.3.10), as is often claimed.

[50]Ebeling, "Die Rüstung eines babylonischen Panzerreiters," *Zeitschrift für Assyriologie* 16 (1952), 203-13.

[51]*CIG* 3081; Hunt, "Feudal Survivals in Ionia," *JHS* 67 (1947), 68-76; Hanfmann, "Ionia, Leader or Follower?," *HSCP* 61 (1953), 3; M. Weber (R. I. Frank trans.), *Agrarian Sociology of Ancient Civilizations* (London 1976), 152; see I. T. Sanders, *Rainbow in the Rock: The People of Rural Greece* (Cambridge 1962), 64; the Turks held land during the Ottoman period and gave grant-fiefs or estates called Ciftliks in Turkish, compare ancient Damnion *teichos* (below), the Turkish feudal estate of Eski Ergeli.

[52]L. Robert, *Noms indigenès dans l'Asie-Mineure gréco-romaine* 1 (Paris 1963), 14-6; Sundwall, *Die einheimischen Namen der Lykier, Klio Beiheft* 11 (Leipzig 1913), 59.

[53]Hipponax F 66; *GDI* 5636:4-9; Hesychios sv *pyrgos: promacheōn, teichos*; sv *pergamion, dēmion* (small estate or township); Hunt, "Feudal Survivals," *JHS* 67 (1947), 70 n. 13; J. M. Cook, *The Troad* (Oxford 1973), 192, sixteenth century A.D. Turkish settlement Bergaz or Birgos derived from *pyrgos*.

[54]A. Bon, "Les ruines antiques dans l'île de Thasos et en particulier les tours helléniques," *BCH* 54 (1930), 147-94; J. H. Young, "Studies in South Attica: Country Estates at Sounion," *Hesperia* 25 (1956), 122-46; "Ancient Towers on the Island of Siphnos," *AJA* 60 (1956), 51-5; M. Dufková and J. Pečírka, "Excavations of Farms and Farmhouses in the Chora of Chersonesus in the Crimea," *Eirene* 8 (1970), 123-74; J. Pečírka, "Homestead Farms in Classical and Hellenistic Greece," in M. I. Finley (ed.), *Problèmes de la terre en Grèce ancienne* (Paris 1973), 113-47; J. E. Jones, "Town and Country Houses in Attica in Classical Times," in H. Mussche, P. Spitaels, F. Goemaere-De Poerck (eds.), *Miscellanea Graeca* 1, *Thorikos and the Laurion in Archaic and Classical Times* (Ghent 1975), 116-22, fig. 18-9, 23.5; R. E. Wycherley, *The Stones of Athens* (Princeton 1978), fig. 70 (5).

[55]R. Martin, *L'Urbanisme dans la Grèce antique* (Paris 1956), 22.

[56]Davis, *People of the Mediterranean* 254.

[57]C. W. J. Eliot, *Coastal Demes of Attica* (Toronto 1962), 3-4.

[58]G. Bean, *Aegean Turkey: An Archaeological Guide* (New York 1967), 136-46.

[59]J. M. Balcer, "The Early Silver Coinage of Teos," *RSN* 47 (1968), 5-50, pls. XI-XIX.

[60]Jeffery, *Local Scripts of Archaic Greece* 226; J. M. Balcer, Phokaia and Teos: A Monetary Alliance," *RSN* 49 (1970), 25-34, pls. 3-8.

[61]Hekataios *FGrH* 1 T 5-6; Tozzi, *La rivolta ionica* 93, n.93; mid-fourth or post Alexander inscription in honor of Hekataios notes Milesian relationship with Leros in the time of Aristagoras' attempt to fortify, Hdt. 5.125.

[62]C. Fornara, *Archaic Times to the End of the Peloponnesian War* (Baltimore 1977), 62.

[63]G. De Sanctis, "I Molpi di Mileto," *Studi in onore di Pietro Bonfante* 2 (Milan 1930), 669-80; F. Sokolowski, *Lois Sacrées de l'Asie Mineure* (Paris 1955), #50; S. Luria, "Kureten, Molpen, Aisymneten," *AAH* 11 (1963), 31-6.

[64]*DGE* 701 [G. Hill *Sources in Greek History* (Oxford 1951), B116]; H. Engelmann and R. Merkelbach, *Die Inschriften von Erythrai und Klazomenai* 1 (Bonn 1972), 22-32.

[65]J. M. Cook and G. E. Bean," The Carian Coast III," *BSA* 52 (1957), 109-10.

[66]Ibid. 134-5.

[67]Skylax 67; Steph. Byz. sv. Daunion Teichos; *ATL* 1. 260-1, 480, fig. 189; Hekataios *Periegesis* B F 233: "Abarnos: *Polis* and *chora* and *akra* of Parian;" for *teichea* around Daunon *Teichos* note Hdt. 6.33.1.

[68]Didyma *teichē* ("Twin Forts"): Skylax 67; Polybius 5.77.8; *ATL* 1 262-3, 481-2, fig. 189.

[69]Aeschines 3.83; [Dem.] 7.37; Dem. 9.15, 10.8; also called Ganos: Skylax 67; Hellanikos *FGrH* 4 F 62; Xen. An. 7.5.6-8; *ATL* 1. 398-9, 545-6, fig. 189.

[70]Skylax 67; Hekataios *FGrH* 1 F 156; Hdt. 7.112.1; *ATL* 1, 372-3, 533-4.

[71]ATL 1. 236-7, 470.

[72]ATL 1. 258-9, 479.

[73]N. J. G. Pounds, "The Urbanization of the Classical World," *Annals of the Association of American Geographers* 59 (1969), 140-3; note the reservations of Finley, *Ancient Economy* 124 n. 3, 204-5, which are too facile. See Appendix II, "The Population of Ionia in the Mid-Fifth Century B.C."

[74]ATL 1. 236-7, 470.

[75]Steph. Byz. sv; *ATL* 1. 345-5, 525-6.

[76]S. Casson, "A Greek Settlement in Thrace," *Antiquity* 7 (1933), 324-8.

[77]Hdt. 7.59.2, 105-6; Dem. 9.15, 10.8; Aeschines 3.82; Livy 31.16.4.

[78]Hdt. 7.107; Thuc. 1.98.1; *Pap. Oxy.* 13, 1610 (= Ephoros *FGrH* 70 F 191); Ion *FGrH* 392 F 13; Dem. 23.199; Aeschines 2.184; Diod. Sic. 11.60.2; Plut. *Kim.* 7.1-8.2; Paus. 8.8.9; Nepos *Cim.* 2.2; Polyainos 7.24.

[79]Also called Heraion *teichos* in relationship to Damnion *teichos:* Hdt. 4.90; Xen. *An.* 7.5.8; Dem. 3.4; Nepos *Alc.* 7.4; *ATL* 1.481-2.

[80]Widegren, "Recherches sur le féodalisme," *Orientalia Suecana* 5 (1956), 118.

[81]Gusmani, "Onomastica iranica nei testi epicorici lidi," in *Umanità e Storia* 6-7.

[82]M. I. Finley, *Ancient Slavery and Modern Ideology* (New York 1980), 67-92.

[83]Cf. Hdt. 9.109.3, 116.2.

[84]Dandamajew, "Die Lehnsbeziehungen," *Festschrift für W. Eilers* 37-42; A. W. Gomme, *A Historical Commentary on Thucydides* 1 (Oxford 1959), 290-2; followed by *ATL* 3.292; wrongly argued that the fiefs (*sic*) of Themistokles and Gongylos were "but empty show."

[85]Hinz, "Achämenidische Hofverwaltung," *Zeitschrift für Assyriologie* 61 (1971), 289.

[86]A Hellenistic inscription, inscribed on the inner wall of the western chamber of the temple of Artemis at Sardis, records a vassalage tenure as a direct personal concession from the king, which compares to Achaemenid vassalage and earlier Assyrian land contracts. The Hellenistic inscription contains articles of special condition to provide for the contingency of the resumption of land by the king; K. T. M. Atkinson," A Hellenistic Land-Conveyance: The Estate of Mnesimachus in the Plain of Sardis," *Historia* 21 (1972), 45-74. Hanfmann and Waldbaum, *Survey* 22: " 'the village (kome) of Tobalmoura in the Sardian plain on the hill of Ilos ... villages of Tandos and Kombdilipia ... Periasasostra in the water of Morstas ... Nagrioa; village of Ilos in Attoudda'. It had at Tabolmoura a squire's house (*aule*), and outside the house were houses (oikiai) of serfs (*lāon*) and slaves and two gardens requiring fifteen *artabas* of seed and slaves dwelling at that place: four slaves are named for Tobalmoura. In addition to revenues payable in gold staters, wine vessels are mentioned as revenue payable in kind."

[87]S. A. B. Mercer, "The Oath in Cuneiform Inscriptions," *AJSL* 29 (1913), 65-94; D. J. McCarthy, *Treaty and Covenant: A Study in Form in the Ancient Oriental Documents and in the Old Testament* (Rome 1963); Ries, *Die neubabylonischen Bodenpachtformulare.*

[88]Hdt. 7.135, 151; Xen. *An.* 1.9.8, 9.10, 3.5.16, 4.4.6; Cyr. 7.4.3, 9; J. Duchesne-Guillemin, *Zoroastre: Étude critique avec une traduction commentée des Gāthā* (Paris 1948), 3, 25-8; M. Lorenz, "Zarathustras Friedenbotschaft," *Acta Iranica* 3 (1974), 123-32.

[89]Olmstead, *History of the Persian Empire* 71; Frye, *Heritage of Persia* 109, suggested a system of subinfeudation through sub-grants, but that suggestion missed the

centralized role of the king, something akin to Liege Lordship; P. J. Junge, "Hazaraptiš," *Klio* 33 (1940), 13-38.

[90] Hdt. 5.105 is naive and without historical merit. Olmstead, "Persia and the Greek Frontier Problem," *CP* 34 (1939), 308-9; M. McGregor, "The Pro-Persian Party at Athens," *HSCP* Suppl. 1 (1940), 71-95; C. A. Robinson Jr., "Athenian Politics 510-486," *AJP* 66 (1945), 243-54; F. E. Adcock, "Development of Ancient Greek Diplomacy," *AC* 17 (1948), 4; A. E. Raubitschek, "Treaties between Persia and Athens," *GRBS* 5 (1964), 151-9; Solomon, *Politique Égyptienne d'Athènes* 70-1; F. Schachermeyr, "Athen als Stadt des Grosskönigs," *Grazer Beiträge* 1 (1973), 211-10; L. L. Orlin, "Athens and Persia ca. 507 B.C.: A Neglected Perspective," in *Michigan Oriental Studies in Honor of George G. Cameron* (Ann Arbor 1976), 255-66, suggested Athens sought a *symmachia* while Artaphrenes sought vassalage.

[91] Gershevitch, *Avestan Hymn to Mithra*.

[92] P. Thieme, "The Concept of Mithra in Aryan Belief," in J. R. Hinnells (ed.), *Mithraic Studies* 1 (Manchester 1975), 21-39; W. Lentz, commentary upon Thieme, ibid. 133; R. Frye, "Mithra in Iranian History," ibid. 62-7; M. Boyce, "On Mithra, Lord of Fire," *Acta Iranica* 1 (1975), 69-76; tenets of modern Zoroastrianism in Yazd, Iran; Boyce, *A Persian Stronghold of Zoroastrianism* (Oxford 1977), 31.

[93] Gershevitch, *Avestan Hymn to Mithra* VII, 3, 7, 26-8.

[94] Duchesne-Guillemin, *Zoroastre* 8; A. D. H. Bivar, "Religious Subjects on Achaemenid Seals," *Mithraic Studies* 1, 90-105; "Document and Symbol in the Art of the Achaemenids," *Acta Iranica* 1 (1975), 60-7. During the reign of Artaxerxes II (405-359 B.C.) Iranian anthropomorphic statues began to appear. At Bisitun, the winged figure can not be Ahura Mazda, as often claimed. Boyce, *History of Zoroastrianism* 2, 105-6.

[95] *Yasna* 48:6; Ehtécham, *L'Iran* 185-6; Duchesne-Guillemin, *Zoroastre* 147; G. G. Cameron, "Zoroaster the Herdsman," *Indo-Iranian Journal* 10 (1968), 261-81.

[96] W. Wüst, "Bestand die Zoroastrische Urgenmeinde aus Ekstatikern und Rinderhirten der Steppe?," *Archiv für Religionswissenschaft* 36 (1939), 234-49.

[97] Gershevitch, *Avestan Hymn to Mithra* 32-5.

[98] M. B. Rowton, "The Woodlands of Ancient Western Asia," *JNES* 26 (1967), 261-77; J. D. Hughes, *Ecology in Ancient Civilization* (Albuquerque 1975), 68-80.

[99] Neh. 2:8; Xen. An. 1.2.8-9; Ktesias *FGrH* 688 F 34a; Cicero de Sen. 59; Diod. Sic. 14.80.2; Plut. de Solertia animalium 21; E. Semple, *The Geography of the Ancient Mediterranean* (New York 1931), 479-83.

[100] Boyce, *Persian Stronghold of Zoroastrianism* 143.

[101] R. Redfield, *Peasant Society and Culture* (Chicago 1956), 27; Walcot, *Greek Peasants*.

[102] P. Briant, "Dörfer und Dorfgemeinschaften im achämenidischen und hellenistischen Asien," *Jahrbuch für Wirtschaftsgeschichte* 4 (1975), 115-33.

[103] Finley, *Ancient Economy* 48, 95, 97.

[104] J. Pečírka, "Land Tenure and the Development of the Athenian Polis," *Geras: Studies Presented to G. Thompson* (Prague 1963), 183-201; D. Asheri, "Laws of Inheritance, Distribution of Land, and Political Constitutions in Ancient Greece," *Historia* 12 (1963), 1-21; F. Cassola, "Sull'alienabilità del suolo nel mondo Greco," *Labeo* 11 (1965), 206-19; M. I. Finley, "The Alienability of Land in Ancient Greece: A Point of View," *Eirene* 7 (1968), 25-32; Weber, *Agrarian Sociology* 42-3, 46, 148-51, 179; M. M. Austin and P. Vidal-Naquet, *Economic and Social History of Ancient Greece* (London 1977), 41; Davis, *Mediterranean People* 45-7, 51.

[105] Finley, *Ancient Economy* 99; see C. W. J. Eliot," Where did the Alkmaionidai Live?," *Historia* 16 (1967), 279–86.

[106] Walcot, *Greek Peasants* 24 and n. 1; Sanders, *Rainbow in the Rock* 9, 1951 census: 44.6% of modern Greeks lived in 5,473 communes or local political units, of less than 2,000 inhabitants. P. 60, average peasant holding was less than 10 acres, too small an area to support an average family of 5 people; 37% of the farms were less than 2.5 acres; 51% comprised 2.5 to 12.5 acres; "people have a strong trait of localism." P. 66, size of farms in Thessaly averaged just over 11 acres, less than 10 in Macedonia, Thrace, and Central Greece; just over 5 acres in Epirus and the Peloponnesos; less than five on the islands. Renfrew, "Trade as Action at a Distance," *Ancient Civilization and Trade* 8, 14–5, 27; villages up to 4,000 persons were possible, and similar to early neolithic Jericho and Çatal Hüyük, but less than agricultural towns of South Italy today. C. A. Doxiades, *Ekistics* 31 (1971), 4–21, for classical Greece a *polis* area was 1471 sq. km. See also, E. Friedl, *Vasilika: A Village in Modern Greece* (New York 1962); J. F. Kolars, *Tradition, Season, and Change in a Turkish Village* (Chicago 1963); W. G. East, *The Geography Behind History* (New York 1967), 76, 98; J. L. Bintliff, "New Approaches to Human Geography. Prehistoric Greece: A Case Study," in F. W. Carter (ed.), *An Historical Geography of the Balkans* (London 1977), 60, 88–90, 109, fig. 24.

[107] C. W. J. Eliot, *Coastal Demes of Attika* (Toronto 1962), 3–4.

[108] G. P. R. Métraux, "Western Greek Land Use and City Planning in the Archaic Period" (Ph.D. dissertation, Harvard 1972).

[109] J. M. Wagstaff, "A Note on Settlement Numbers in Ancient Greece," *JHS* 95 (1975), 163–8; see N. J. G. Pounds, *Historical Geography of Europe 450 B.C. - A.D. 1330* (Cambridge 1973), 30; Martin, *L'Urbanisme* 44–7.

[110] C. Müller (ed.), *Geographi Graeci Minores* (Paris 1882), 1.99, 1.101.

[111] Dandamayev, "Politische und wirtschaftliche Geschichte," *Beiträge zur Achämenid-engeschichte* 33–42; M. H. Jameson, "Agriculture and Slavery in Classical Athens," *CJ* 73 (1977/78), 122–46.

[112] J. M. Balcer, "The Persian Occupation of Thrace, 519–491 B.C.: The Economic Effects," *Actes du IIe Congrès international des Études du Sud-Est Européen* 2 (Athens 1972), 241–58.

[113] Austin and Vidal-Naquet, *Economic and Social History* 42–3; R. J. Hopper *Trade and Industry in Classical Greece* (London 1979), 40–1, 46, 62–3. This view of the chora and the asty is in marked difference to R. Redfield, *The Primitive World and its Transformation* (Ithaca 1953), 34, 55.

[114] J. Hasebroek, *Trade and Politics in Ancient Greece* (New York 1965 reprint), 97–182.

[115] A. W. Gomme, "The Citizenship Law of 451-0," *Essays in Greek History and Literature* (Oxford 1937), 86–8; M. F. McGregor, "Athenian Policy, at Home and Abroad," *Lectures in Memory of Louise Taft Semple* 2 (Cincinnati 1967), 1–8; Humphreys, *Anthropology and the Greeks* 76–106, 194–202, 212–7.

[116] Arnheim, *Aristocracy in Greek Society* 11–2.

[117] S. M. Burstein, *Outpost of Hellenism: The Emergence of Heraclea on the Black Sea* (Berkeley 1974); I. S. Sventsitskaya, "The Status of the Dependent Population in Asia Minor in the Fifth and Fourth Centuries B.C.," *VDI* (1967), 80–6 [in Russian], persuasively argued that the Mariandynoi were not helots or serfs but rather native tribes subject to the ruling Greek aristocracy.

[118] Weber, *Agrarian Sociology* 186–7.

[119] Hopper, *Trade and Industry* 148, 152.

[120]Hdt. 5.99.2; Ath. *Deip.* 8.348; I. T. Hill, *The Ancient City of Athens* (Chicago 1969 reprint), 31, 82; J. Travlos, *Pictorial Dictionary of Ancient Athens* (New York 1971), 392-400.

[121]Finley, *Ancient Economy* 22 125, 152; Weber, *Agrarian Sociology* 48-9; Austin and Vidal-Naquet, *Economic and Social History* 6-7, 112-8.

[122]Aristoph. *Plutos* 904; Xen. *Mem.* 3.7.6; [Xen.] *Vect.* 4.6; Plato *Leg.* 643e, 918d, cf. 919d; cf. Plut. *Per.* 12; Hopper, *Trade and Industry* 64, 126, 131-2.

Chapter 8. The "Ionian" Revolutions.

[1]Thuc. 3.65, 82; A. E. Wardman, "Herodotus on the Cause of the Greco-Persian Wars," *AJP* 82 (1961), 147-8; C. Hignett, *Xerxes' Invasion of Greece* (Oxford 1963), 3-25, pointedly noted that Herodotus and Aeschylus are the only important ancient sources for the Persian Wars; K. H. Waters, "The Purpose of Dramatisation in Herodotus," *Historia* 15 (1966), 157-71; D. Hegyi, "The Historical Background of the Ionian Revolt," *AAH* 14 (1966), 285-6, correctly noted: "In the contemporary sources there is no trace to the effect that in the first half century of the Persian rule some kind of collective consciousness would have developed in the circle of the Greeks of Asia Minor, which would have set them as 'Greeks' against the oppressing 'Persians.' [It was not with] the manifestation of some sort of a collective 'people's or national' consciousness, but with identical political and social interests of the tyrannoi, the leaders of the Greek poleis . . ."; M. Moggi, "La tradizione delle guerre persiane in Platone," *Studi Classici e Orientali* 17 (1968), 213-26; J. de Romilly, "Guerre et paix entre cities," in J. P. Vernant *Problèmes de la guerre en Grèce ancienne* (Paris 1968), 207, 215-6; D. J. Mosley, "Diplomacy and Disunion in Ancient Greece," *Phoenix* 25 (1971), 319, "Disunion was perhaps the besetting sin of ancient Greece."

[2]I approach Herodotus books 5 and 6 cautiously, and essentially follow G. A. H. Chapman, "Herodotus and Histiaeus' Role in the Ionian Revolt," *Historia* 21 (1972), 546-68; and his comments upon J. A. S. Evans, "Histiaeus and Aristagoras: Notes on the Ionian Revolt," *AJP* 84 (1963), 113-28; and A. Blamire, "Herodotus and Histaeus," *CQ* 9 (1959), 142-54; and Chapman's rejection of M. Lang, "Herodotus and the Ionian Revolt," *Historia* 17 (1968), 24-36; a rejection earlier persuasively argued by K. H. Waters, "Herodotus and the Ionian Revolt," *Historia* 19 (1970), 504-8. P. Tozzi, *La rivolta ionica* (Pisa 1978), provides the most thorough account of the events, of the ancient sources, and the numismatic and epigraphic evidence. D. Gillis, *Collaboration with Persia* (Wiesbaden 1979) is an interesting but Pro-Greek view of the war, essentially an uncritical recount of Herodotus' narrative. P. B. Manville, "Aristagoras and Histiaios: The Leadership Struggle in the Ionian Revolt," *CQ* 27 (1977), 80-91, returns to the self-seeking motives of Aristagoras and Histiaios, both against Persians and against each other, for power and influence, as rivals and enemies. His approach is a literal interpretation of Herodotus, the "tatooed man," the speeches, and the independent personal roles. Manville failed to understand Milesian tyranny as vassalage (*doulos*) and not monarchy on a throne (*sic*, p.85). Most valuable is the recent study of D. Lateiner, "The Failure of the Ionian Revolt," *Historia* 31 (1982), 129-60.

[3]Chapman, "Herodotus and Histiaeus' Role," *Historia* 21 (1972), 551, 553-5; Practice of personal rewards, Syloson Hdt. 3.140, Zopyros, 3.160, Demokedes 3.130.3, Mandrokles 4.88, Pythios 7.29, Maskames 7.105-6; Evans, "Histiaeus and Aristagoras," *AJP* 84 (1963), 114-6; Blamire, "Herodotus and Histaeus," *CQ* 9 (1959), 142-5.

[4]M. Cary, "The Ionian Revolt," *CAH* 1st ed., 4, 214.

[5]The "massacre of the Persian ambassadors" logos (Hdt. 5.18-22.1) is fanciful.

[6]Megabazos' warning to Darius of Histiaios' fortification of Myrkinos (Hdt. 5.23) is anachronistic; Chapman, "Herodotus and Histiaeus' Role," *Historia* 21 (1972), 555-8.

[7]Dunham, *Miletos* 90.

[8]Thrasyboulos: Hdt. 1.20-3; 5.92; Ar. Pol. 1305a15-8; post-Thrasyboulos: Hdt. 5.28; SIG [3]. 57:1; Athen. Deip. 523F-534B; Plut. Q.G. 32.

[9]J. Pečírka, "Die Landgüter der Milesier," Jahrbuch für Wirtschaftsgeschichte 2 (1971), 55-61.

[10]J. Plescia, "Herodotus and the Case for Eris (Strife)," Parola Passato 27 (1972), 301-11; see also D. Loenen, Polemos: een Studie over oorlog in de griekse oudheid (Amsterdam 1953), in Mededelingen der koninklijke nederlandse Akademie van Wetenschappen, afd. Letterkunde, n.r., d.16, no. 3; D. Daube, Civil Disobedience in Antiquity (Edinburgh 1972), 123-4; G. Daverio Rocchi, "Aristocrazia genetica ed organizzazione politica arcaica," Parola Passato 28 (1973), 92-116.

[11]M. I. Finley, "The Freedom of the Citizen in the Greek World," Talanta 7 (1976), 7.

[12]Hesychios sv Oinitēs; P. Chiller, Ἐπιγραφαὶ, Ῥόδον, Θήρας, Νάξου, Ἀρκαδίας, Ἀρχαιολογικὴ Ἐφημερίς (1914), 133-4; S. Luria, "Ein milesischer Männerbund im Lichte ethnologischer Parallelen," Philologus 83 (1928), 113-36; W. Zschietzschmann, "Branchidae," Studies Presented to David Moore Robinson 2. 1039-43; Sokolowski, Lois Sacrées de l'Asie Mineure 129-35.

[13]Hdt. 5.30.1; Tozzi, La rivolta ionica 98. The eponymous Molpos Aristagoras 506/5 B.C. was the son of Kleidikos and not the tyrant. Histiaios was the son of Lysagoras, neither being eponymous Molpos, but the suffix—agoras strongly suggests Lysagoras ranked among them. G. Kawerau and A. Rehm, Das Delphinion im Milet (Berlin 1914); F. Jacoby, Atthis: The Local Chronicles of Ancient Athens (Oxford 1949), 180, 359 n.27; E. Bickerman, Chronology of the Ancient World (London 1968), 67.

[14]Hdt's report of numbers of Persian ships and infantry forces throughout the Persian Wars is incredible, and even the moderate estimates given by the fourth century writers cannot be accepted with confidence. In most instances I note Hdt's figures but with this caveat. F. Maurice, "The Size of the Army of Xerxes in the Invasion of Greece 480 B.C.," JHS 50 (1930), 210-35; Hignett, Xerxes' Invasion 345-55.

[15]Hdt. 5.33.4, that Megabates himself warned Naxos appears as an anachronistic and erroneous statement.

[16]G. De Sanctis, "Aristagora di Mileto," Rivista di filologia 59 (1931), 48-72, placed the Ionian Revolt as the particular work of Aristagoras.

[17]The story of the "Man with the Tatooed Head" (Hdt. 5.35.2) and Histiaios' plans to aid the rebellion (5.35.3-4) are also anachronistic and erroneous. Huxley, Early Ionians 145; Chapman, "Herodotus and Histiaeus," Historia 21 (1972), 552, 559 and n.65.

[18]Tozzi, La rivolta ionica 25-7, 227-30. "Iōnes" in Hdt. signifies not just the twelve major poleis but all Greeks in Anatolia including Aiolians, and peoples of the Troad, Karia, and Cyprus. Samos, Chios, and Lesbos comprised a separate geo-political unit usually not included in "Ionia." Aesch. Pers. 882-3; Arist. Pol. 1284a38; Ath. Pol. 24.2; Plut. Arist. 23.4; yet Thuc. 9.9.4 considered Ionia to include Lesbos and the Doric islands.

[19]If Hdt's account is reliable confusion arises why Kleomenes believed it necessary to attack Susa, a three month march from Sardis, rather than just aid the coastal rebellion and perhaps attack Sardis. As Huxley, Early Ionians 147 suggested, all Aristagoras could reasonably expect was a Spartan naval (?) and infantry support in Ionia. J. Larsen, "Sparta and the Ionian Revolt," CP 37 (1932), 136-50, "domestic conditions in Greece made Spartan intervention in the Ionian Revolt impossible" (p.150).

[20]E. Vanderpool, "Some Ostraka from the Athenian Agora," Hesperia Suppl. 8 (1949), 400-1; not listed in Davies, Athenian Propertied Families or in Hofstetter, Die Griechen.

[21]See my case study "Athenian Politics: The Ten Years after Marathon," in Panathenaia: Studies in Athenian Life and Thought in the Classical Age (Lawrence 1979), 27-49; the curious view of P. Musiolek, "Themistokles and Athen," AAH 6 (1958), 301-19;

J. H. Schreiner, "Thucydides 1.93 and Themistokles during the 490's," *Symbolae Osloensis* 44 (1969), 38.

[22]Hdt. 6.132, fifty Athenian ships against Aigina. D. Hegyi, "Athens and Aigina on the Eve of the Battle of Marathon," *AAH* 13 (1965), 171-81.

[23]Tozzi, *La rivolta ionica* 157-8, considered much of Hdt's narrative of Aristagoras in Sparta and in Athens as anachronistic, reflective of the dualism of the Pentekontaetia. Gillis, *Collaboration* 16 accepted the Herodotean narrative.

[24]Contrary to Burn, *Persia and the Greeks* 193, who argued that the tribute of 400 talents from the first Persian nomos became unbearable and that "Ionia was evidently seething with discontent." The actual East Greek portion of the 400 talents was relatively small and no greater than the Ionians openly accepted to pay to the Delian Confederacy. Croesus, Cyrus, Darius, and Athens never returned to local Ionian circulation any of the collected funds.

[25]Jeffery, *Archaic Greece* 220.

[26]I can not support Hegyi's thesis that the Ionians revolted not against Darius and the Persian Empire but against his harsh satrap Artaphrenes, "Historical Background," *AAH* 14 (1966), 285-302.

[27]Evans, "Histiaeus and Aristagoras," *AJP* 84 (1963), 118, the dawning consciousness of the differences between the imperial barbarians and the Greeks is meaningless.

[28]*Pace* Huxley, *Early Ionians* 146.

[29]The "war" was not a "decisive struggle between theocracy, mysticism, and ecstasy supported by Persians in Anatolia and secularism of Hellenic civilization" as claimed by Max Weber citing Eduard Meyer, *Agrarian Sociology* 187.

[30]PN, PC and HoB: G. M. A. Hanfmann and A. H. Detweiler, "From the Heights of Sardis," *Archaeology* 14 (1961), 7-8; Hanfmann, "The Fourth Campaign at Sardis (1961)," *BASOR* 116 (1962), 1-15; Tozzi, *La rivolta ionica* 77 n.11.

[31]Hanfmann and Detweiler, "New Exploration of Sardis," *Archaeology* 12 (1959), 53.

[32]G. B. Grundy, *The Great Persian War* (London 1901), 97-8; Tozzi, *La rivolta ionica* 167 n.155.

[33]Burn, *Persia and the Greeks* 201-2.

[34]Ibid. 200.

[35]There is no textual evidence in Hdt. 5.108.2, that the Panionion Council met to consider Onesilos' appeal. The phrase *to koinon tōn Iōnōn* (Hdt. 5.109.3) within an Ionian speech reportedly given in Cyprus remains highly suspect to which we must give little historical credence. Tozzi, *La rivolta ionica* 154 rightly suggested that the Council was not the Panionion but simply an Ionian symmachy (Hdt. 5.120; 6.13.1).

[36]Tozzi, *La rivolta ionica* 75-7, nn. 2-10, n.23-4, 31.

[37]Hdt. 5.106. Chapman, "Herodotus and Histiaeus," *Historia* 21 (1972), 551-3, 559. Hdt.'s source was apparently Persian but the text is the historian's recreation of what he thought took place.

[38]T. Reinach, *L'Anarchie monétaire et ses remèdes chez les anciens grecs* (Paris 1911); P. Gardner, "The Coinage of the Ionian Revolt," *JHS* 31 (1911), 151-60; "Note on the Coinage of the Ionian Revolt," *JHS* 33 (1913), 105; M. O. B. Caspari, "The Ionian Confederacy," *JHS* 35 (1915), 173-88; "A Survey of Greek Federal Coinage," *JHS* 37 (1917), 168-83; G. Nenci, "La monetazione della revolta ionica nei suoi aspetti economici e politici," in *Studi in onore di Amintore Fanfani 1: Antichità e alto medioevo* (Milan

1962), 71-83; J. A. Dengate, "The Coinage of Klazomenai" (Ph.D. dissertation, University of Pennsylvania 1967); "A Mint for the Coinage of the Ionian Revolt," *AJA* 72 (1968), 164; Meiggs, *The Athenian Empire* 27-8, 441-2; Tozzi, *La rivolta ionica* 81-92.

[39] C. M. Kraay, *Archaic and Classical Greek Coins* (London 1976), 30. Chios (Kraay 30 n.2) and Klazomenai (Dengate, "A Mint for the Coinage," *AJA* 72 [1968]), have also been considered as central mints. Meiggs' suggestion of independent mints appears unlikely.

[40] Tozzi, *La rivolta ionica* 178.

[41] R. P. Harper, "II. What does Gerga Mean?," in Şahin, *Studien zur Religion und Kultur Kleinasiens* 1, 386-8.

[42] Evans, "Histiaeus and Aristagoras," *AJP* 84 (1963), 117.

[43] T. S. Brown, "Aeneas Tacitus, Herodotus and the Ionian Revolt," *Historia* 30 (1981), 385-93.

[44] Burn, *Persia and the Greeks* 209, and others, maintained Phokaia, Teos, Priene, and Myous still remained outside of Persian recontrol, but there is no textual reason except for the vague statement of Hdt. 6.6 to support that difficult geographical contention. Even Erythrai may have fallen by 495 B.C.

[45] D. Mustili, "L'occupazione ateniese di lemnos e gli scavi di Hephaistia," in *Studi offerte A. E. Ciaceri* (Genoa 1940), 149-58.

[46] Burn, *Persia and the Greeks* 218, 236.

[47] H. Hauben, "The King of the Sidonians and the Persian Imperial Fleet," *Ancient Society* 1 (1970), 1-8.

[48] R. Van Compernolle, "La date de la bataille navale de Lade," *AC* 27 (1958), 383-9.

[49] The polis was not empty of Milesians, pace Hdt. 6.22.1. On the fall note Diod. Sic. 10.25.2, 6.18-20, 32; Paus. 8.46.3; on Milesians to Sogdiana note Strabo 11.11.4, 17.1.43; Curt. 7.5.28.

[50] The western quarter of Miletos was not rebuilt after 494 B.C., Tozzi, *La rivolta ionica* 205 n. 128; see also 78 nn. 12-14, 79 n. 18; on Didyma 79 n. 19. J. M. Bigwood, "Ctesias as Historian of the Persian Wars," *Phoenix* 32 (1978), 36-41.

[51] Jeffery, *Local Scripts of Archaic Greece* 343 n. 30.

[52] B. Obed, *Mass Deportations and Deportees in the Neo-Assyrian Empire* (Wiesbaden 1979); D. Ambaglio, "Il motivo della deportazione in Erodoto," *Rendiconti Istituto Lombardo* 109 (1975), 378-83.

[53] C. H. Dodd, "The Samians at Zankle Messana," *JHS* 28 (1908), 56-76; H. E. Gielow, "Die Silberprägung von Dankle-Messana," *Mitteilungen der bayerischen numismatischen Gesellschaft* 48 (1930), 36-68; E. S. G. Robinson, "Rhegion, Zankle-Messana and the Samians," *JHS* 46 (1946), 13-20; Barron, *The Silver Coins of Samos* 40-5.

[54] Tozzi, *La rivolta ionica* 98. 1). Pythomandros I, his son Artemon 500/499 B.C., and Artemon's sons Pythomandros II 488/7 and Diagores 483/2 B.C. 2). Hegestratos' sons, Nympharetos 503/2 and Timokrates 485/4 B.C. 3). Molpagores' sons Daphnis 498/7 and Leonax 492/1. Grandsons (? or 4). Hekataios 497/6, Theodoros 491/0, and Molpagores 487/6 B.C.

[55] Huxley, *Early Ionians* 152-3.

[56] Hdt. 6.28.2 specifically referred to Harpagos as a "Persian man," yet he may be an Harpagid descendant of the Mede Harpagos who conquered Lykia; a simple literary

transformation similar to Datis the Mede becoming Persian (*Schol.* Arist. *Pax* 289) and Mardonios the Persian becoming a Mede (Nepos *Paus.* 1.2).

[57]Chapman, "Herodotus and Histiaeus," *Historia* 21 (1972), 565-6.

[58]G. C. Whittick, "Σαγηνεύουσι δὲ τόνδε τὸν τρόπον: Herodotus VI.31," *AC* 22 (1953), 27-31.

[59]For archaeological evidence of destruction at Larisa see Tozzi, *La rivolta ionica* 80 n. 30; for Iasos 78 nn. 15, 17.

[60]J. M. Balcer, *The Athenian Regulations for Chalkis: Studies in Athenian Imperial Law* (Wiesbaden 1978), 55-65.

[61]*IG* 1^2.928 (*SEG* X.405), line 35, yet not certain, c. 465 B.C.; but not in *IG* 1^2.375 (*SEG* X. 302), c. 445/4 or 3 (?) B.C. and not in *ATL* 1.

[62]F. Cassola, "La struttura della lega ionica," *Labeo* 4 (1958), 153-71, in the early fourth century B.C., the League revived and continued to function into the Roman era.

[63]This section is greatly dependent upon the important study of A. T. Olmstead, "Persia and the Greek Frontier Problem," *CP* 34 (1939), 305-22. Less directly, it reflects the studies of Hignett, *Xerxes' Invasion* and P. Green, *Xerxes at Salamis* (New York 1970). Because the story has been rehearsed all too often, and my analysis is both brief and subjective, I have omitted the copious references to the supportive secondary literature. See also A. T. Olmstead, "Oriental Imperialism," *American Historical Review* 22 (1918), 755-62; Burn, *Persia and the Greeks;* C. G. Starr, "Why did the Greeks defeat the Persians?," *Parola Passato* 17 (1962), 321-32; J. Wolski, "Les Grecs et les Ioniens au temps des Guerres médiques," *Eos* 58 (1969), 33-49; Podlecki, *Life of Themistocles.* Thucydides noted that the Corinthians in 432 B.C. claimed that the Persian invasion of Athens had failed primarily because of fundamental mistakes (1.69.5).

[64]Hignett, *Xerxes' Invasion* 345-50; K. Kraft, "Bemerkungen zu den Perserkriegen," *Hermes* 92 (1964), 153-8; C. Blinkenberg, *Die lindische Tempelchronik* (Bonn 1915), Ṣ 32, pp. 26-9, this is uncertain as the name of the Persian [st]rategos can be restored as Datis, Artaphrenes, or another. Datis is only a possibility in a difficult text, yet 43 (D) while questionable in regard to origin does note Datis the *nauarchos* of Darius, line 26.

[65]R. R. Holloway, "The Crown of Naxos," *American Numismatic Society Museum Notes* 10 (1962), 1-8.

[66]Professor Pierre Ducrey, University of Lausanne, and excavator of Eretria, in a personal letter, dated 21 November 1978, noted: "What I know about the 'Perserschutt' is very little. Personally I have never seen any sure trace of this famous destruction layer."

[67]Hdt. 6.101; Paus. 7.10.2; Euphorbos (Hofstetter *Die Griechen* #109, p. 65) and Philagros (#255, p. 149) leading men of the asty to whom Darius gave great grants of land for their services, Plut. *de Garr.* 15 = *Mor.* 510B.

[68]F. Schachermeyr, "Marathon und die persische Politik," *Historische Zeitschrift* 172 (1951), 1-35; W. K. Pritchett, *Marathon: University of California Publications in Classical Archaeology* 4.2 (Berkeley 1960), 137-75; N. G. L. Hammond, "The Campaign and Battle of Marathon," *JHS* 88 (1968), 13-57; accepted Hdt.'s figures for troops, 31-3; G. L. Cawkwell, "The Power of Persia," *Arepo* 1 (1968), 3; A. T. Hodge, "Marathon: The Persians' Voyage," *TAPA* 105 (1975), 155-73; P. Bicknell, "The Command Structure and Generals of the Marathon Campaign," *AC* 39 (1970), 427-42; A. W. Gomme, "Herodotus and Marathon," *More Essays in Greek History and Literature* (Oxford 1962), 29-37, from *Phoenix* 6 (1952), 77-83, rejected the Herodotean indication of Athenian factionalism during the Marathon period, p. 37, and suspected an Ionian report to the Athenians that "the cavalry are away" as the signal to the Athenians to attack.

[69]Olmstead, "Persia and the Greek Frontier Problem," *CP* 34 (1939), 313; and *History of the Persian Empire* 227, noted: In June of 486 B.C., the Babylonian Nabu-ittanu

reported home that Shatamaksu and Nubagaza, the majordomo, had informed him that according to the King's Law he must pay a new toll on the barley, wheat, and mustard that he was bringing through the storehouse on a Babylonian canal. They told him: "It was determined, before the judge it was recorded" (*Vorderasiatische Sprachdenkmaler* III, no. 159).

[70] Posener, *La première domination Perse en Égypt* nos. 43-77; Olmstead, *History of the Persian Empire* 235-7. To establish firm Persian command in Egypt, Xerxes appointed his brother Achaimenes to the satrapal throne, as the former satrap Pherendates had apparently been killed in the revolt.

[71] J. M. Myers, *The Anchor Bible: Ezra. Nehemiah* (Garden City 1965), 36-7; J. Morgenstern, "Jerusalem - 485 B.C.," *HUCA* 27 (1956), 100-79; "Jerusalem - 485 B.C. (continued)," *HUCA* 28 (1957), 15-47; "Jerusalem - 485 B.C. (concluded," *HUCA* 31 (1960), 1-29; "Further Light from the Book of Isaiah upon the Catastrophe of 485 B.C.," *HUCA* 37 (1966), 1-28; Busink, *Der Tempel von Jerusalem* 2, 842-52.

[72] M. Noth, *The History of Israel* (New York 1958), 316; J. Bright, *A History of Israel* (Philadelphia 1959), 360, commented: "The view of J. Morgenstern that a major rebellion in 485 led to the destruction of Jerusalem and the Temple and the massacre or enslavement of much of the population, although penetratingly developed, is too largely inferential." P. R. Ackroyd, *Israel under Babylon and Persia* (Oxford 1970), 173.

[73] W. T. in der Smitten, "Xerxes und die Daeva," *Bibliotheca Orientalis* 30 (1973), 368a-369b.

[74] Pindar *Pyth.* 10.71-2 (cf. Hdt. 3.96, 7.108); F. Hiller von Gaertringen, "Das Königtum bei den Thessalern," in *Aus der Anomia* (Berlin 1890), 1-16; M. Nilsson, *Mycenaean Origins of Greek Mythology* (Berkeley 1932), 233-4; H. D. Westlake, "The Medism of Thessaly," *JHS* 56 (1936), 12-24; F. Hermann, "Die Silbermünzen von Larissa in Thessalien," *Zeitschrift für Numismatik* 35 (1924), 3-18.

[75] Themistokles' faction in Athens had begun a systematic attack through ostracism to uproot the medizing Peisistratid faction, Balcer, "Athenian Politics," *Panathenaia* 27-49; see also B. D. Meritt, "Greek Inscriptions: An Early Archon List," *Hesperia* 8 (1939), 59-65; M. McGregor, "The Pro-Persian Party at Athens," *HSCP Suppl.* 1 (1940), 71-95; C. A. Robinson Jr., "Athenian Politics, 510-486 B.C.," *AJP* 66 (1945), 243-54.

[76] J. Wolski, "Μηδισμός et son importance en Grece a l'epoque des guerres Mediques," *Historia* 22 (1973), 3-15; Gillis, *Collaboration with Persia*; D. Graf, "Medism: Greek Collaboration with Achaemenid Persia" (Ph.D. dissertation, University of Michigan 1979).

[77] "Medism" entailed the swearing of oaths with the Persians (horkiatomei), Plut. *Them.* 21.7.

[78] Hdt. confused the issue (7.133.1-2) by writing that Persian heralds had commanded Athens and Sparta to submit. The Athenians and Spartans had thrown the heralds into a well and a pit. Hdt. then tantalizingly noted that not these events of the well and pit, but "another reason" brought the war and Persian punishment. I, for one, should like to know that "other reason." K. Kraft, "Bemerkungen zu dem Perserkriegen," *Hermes* 92 (1964), 144-53; R. Sealey, "The Pit and the Well: The Persian Heralds of 491 B.C.," *CJ* 72 (1976), 13-20.

[79] Olmstead, "Persia and the Greek Frontier Problem," *CP* 34 (1939), 314.

[80] Cameron, "Darius and Xerxes in Babylonia," *AJSL* 58 (1941), 314-25; Olmstead, *History of the Persian Empire* 237 and n. 23; J. M. Bigwood, "Ctesias' Description of Babylon," *AJAH* 3 (1978), 32-51.

[81] Artabanos' counsel not to lead the Ionians against their *patria* appears to be an Herodotean anachronism (7.51.2).

[82] Hignett, *Xerxes' Invasion* 14.

[83] Herrmann, "Die Silbermünzen von Larissa in Thessalien," *Zeitschrift für Numismatik* 35 (1924), 3-18; G. A. Papantonios, "Ὁ Μηδισμὸς τῶν Θεσσαλῶν, τῶν Βοιωτῶν καὶ τῶν Φωκέων," *Platon* 15, (1956), 18-30; D. Müller, "Von Doriskos nach Therme, Der Weg des Xerxes-Heeres durch Thrakien und Ostmakedonien," *Chiron* 5 (1975), 1-11; N. G. L. Hammond, "The Extent of Persian Occupation in Thrace," *Chiron* 10 (1980), 53-61.

[84] J. F. Lazenby, "The Strategy of the Greeks in the Opening Campaign of the Persian War," *Hermes* 92 (1964), 264-84; H. Hörhager, "Zu den Flottenoperation am Kap Artemision," *Chiron* 3 (1973), 43-59.

[85] F. Schachermeyr, "Athen als Stadt der Grosskönig," *Grazer Beiträge* 1 (1973), 211-20.

[86] N. G. L. Hammond, "The Battle of Salamis," *JHS* 76 (1956), 32-54; R. Lattimore, "Aeschylus on the Defeat of Xerxes," *Classical Studies in Honor of William Abbott Oldfather* (Urbana 1943), 82-93; W. Marg, "Zur Strategie der Schlact bei Salamis," *Hermes* 90 (1962), 116-9; A. Ferrill, "Herodotus and the Strategy and Tactics of the Invasion of Xerxes," *American Historical Review* 72 (1966), 102-15; H. Bengtson, "Zur Vorgeschichte der Schlact bei Salamis," *Chiron* 1 (1971), 89-94; F. J. Frost, "A Note on Xerxes at Salamis," *Historia* 22 (1973), 118-9.

[87] Hdt. 8.90, 100; cf. 8.92, 9.32; Diod. Sic. 11.19.4; Hignett, *Xerxes' Invasion* 245-6.

[88] Gillis, *Collaboration with the Persians* 33.

[89] Grundy, *The Great Persian War* 434-5.

[90] Gillis, *Collaboration with the Persians* 72-3.

[91] Ibid., 77.

[92] Grundy, *The Great Persian War* 522.

[93] Lateiner, "The Failure of the Ionian Revolt," *Historia* 31 (1982), 151-60.

[94] I am most grateful to Prof. Donald Lateiner for these comments, transmitted by letter, 26 November 1980.

[95] B. Mitchell, "Herodotus and Samos," *JHS* 95 (1975), 75-91.

[96] We simply do not know where the Samians went after their expulsion from Zankle, c. 489/8 B.C. Barron, *Silver Coins of Samos* 45, that they returned to Samos whence Aiakes had been expelled, cited Hdt. 6.43.3 as evidence, yet Barron's historical argument is incorrect.

[97] U. Kahrstedt, "Sparta und Persien," *Hermes* 56 (1921), 320-5; W. Judeich, "Griechische Politik und persische Politik im V. Jahrhundert v. Chr.," *Hermes* 58 (1923), 1-19; P. A. Brunt, "The Hellenic League against Persia," *Historia* 2 (1953/4), 135-62.

[98] Olmstead, "Persia and the Greek Frontier Problem," *CP* 34 (1939), 319.

[99] Ibid. 320.

[100] Isoc. *Panegyrikos* 4.156; Lyk. *Leokr.* 81; Diod. Sic. 11.29.3; Tod *GHI* 2. 240; G. Daux, "Le Serment de Platees," *Revue archeologique* 17 (1941), 176-83; "Serments amphictioniques et serment de Platees," *Studies Presented to D. M. Robinson* 2, 775-82; Brunt, "The Hellenic League," *Historia* 2 (1953/4), 135-62; A. E. Raubitschek, "The Covenant of Plataea," *TAPA* 91 (1960), 178-83; P. Siewert, *Der Eid von Plataiai* (Munich 1972). Theopompos *FGrH* 115 F 153 branded the oath as a forgery, and numerous current scholars have followed that approach; see C. Habicht, "Falsche Urkunden zur Geschichte Athens im Zeitalter der Perserkriege," *Hermes* 89 (1961), 1-35.

[101]Grundy, *The Great Persian War* 549, 554-5.

[102]Aristeides suppressed Athenian factionalism at Plataia, an oligarchic group determined to overthrow the "democratic" faction (Plut. *Arist.* 13).

[103]Cf. Theban theme Hdt. 9.41.4, perhaps a literary motif and not historical; R. Lattimore, "The Wise Advisor in Herodotus," *CP* 34 (1939), 24-35. See also Hdt. 8.126.1 and 9.41.1: Artabazos held in highest esteem by Xerxes.

[104]Grundy, *The Great Persian War* 16; Green, *Xerxes at Salamis* 256-7; I reject Diod. Sic. 11.35.2-3, that Plataia and Mykale occurred on the same day.

[105]Grundy, *The Great Persian War* 526; Hignett, *Xerxes' Invasion* 252-3; Green, *Xerxes at Salamis* 278-80.

[106]Mitchell, "Herodotus and Samos," *JHS* 95 (1975), 90-1.

[107]Gillis, *Collaboration with the Persians* 35, accepted Herodotus' account.

[108]Grundy, *The Great Persian War* 527.

[109]Xeinagoras of Halikarnassos, the son of Prexileos, who literally saved Masistes' life at Mykale, gained highest honors from King Xerxes who appointed him ruler (*ērxe*) of all Cilicia as the king's gift for saving his brother's life (Hdt. 9.107.3).

[110]Green, *Xerxes at Salamis* 283.

[111]Meiggs, *Athenian Empire* 413-4. Thuc.'s reference to "allies from Ionia and the Hellespont, who had already revolted from the king" contrasts with Hdt.'s statement. Thuc., at this point, may reflect events of 478 B.C., Meiggs 35. Hdt.'s version is more convincing.

[112]M. I. Finley, "Sparta," in J. P. Vernant (ed.), *Problèmes de la guerre en Grèce ancienne* (Paris 1968), 159-60.

[113]Thuc. 1.89.3, 93.2; R. E. Wycherly, *The Stones of Athens* (Princeton 1978), 9-15.

[114]T. S. Noonan, "Grain Trade of the Northern Black Sea in Antiquity," *AJP* 94 (1973), 232-6. While the ancient sources do not suggest this, and traditionalists would question this assumption, I know of no valid counter-argument.

[115]Grundy, *The Great Persian War* 529.

[116]Hdt. 9.106; Diod. Sic. 11.37.1-3; Grundy, *The Great Persian War* 530; Hignett, *Xerxes' Invasion* 259-61; Green, *Xerxes at Salamis* 283-5.

[117]Delphi Tod *GHI* 1^2.18; ML *GHI* 25; Athens A. E. Raubitschek, *Dedications from the Athenian Acropolis* (Cambridge, Mass. 1949), #172; Meiggs, *Athenian Empire* 36, 416-7.

[118]Cawkwell, "The Power of Persia," *Arepo* 1 (1968), 1-5.

[119]A. G. Woodhead, *Thucydides on the Nature of Power* (Cambridge, Mass. 1970), 134.

Chapter 9. Western Anatolia by 478 B.C.

[1]J. M. Edmonds, *Elegy and Iambus* (Loeb edition) 1 (Cambridge, Mass. 1931).

[2]Ibid. F 7; Lucian *Macr.*

[3]R. M. Cook, "Ionia and Greece in the Eighth and Seventh Centuries B.C.," *JHS* 66 (1946), 80-7.

[4]Emlyn-Jones, *The Ionians and Hellenism.*

[5]J. Boardman, *Pre-Classical: From Crete to Archaic Greece* (Harmondsworth 1967), 152.

[6]Hdt. 2.167; Aristophanes *Achar.* 478, *Ekkles.* 252-3, *Ran.* 840, *Eq.* 19, 129, 1315; Xen. *Oec.* 4.2, 6.5; Plato *Rep.* 495d-e, 590c; Andok. 1.146; Arist. *Pol.* 1258b35-9, 1337b8-14; Dem. 18.258-9, 18.261; A. Burford, *Craftsmen in Greek and Roman Society* (London 1972), 12, 15, 23, 25.

[7]T. B. L. Webster, *Potter and Patron in Classical Athens* (London 1972), 295-8.

[8]Burford, *Craftsmen* 20, 27.

[9]Ibid. 84-6.

[10]Ibid. 95.

[11]Boardman, *Pre-Classical* 94-5.

[12]Emlyn-Jones, *Ionians and Hellenism* 36-40.

[13]Boardman, *Pre-Classical* 169.

[14]Hanfmann, "Ionia: Leader of Follower?," *HSCP* 61 (1953), 23.

[15]E. Bushor, *Altsamische Standbilder* II (Berlin 1934), 24; G. M. A. Richter, *Archaic Greek Art* (New York 1949), 110; *Korai: Archaic Greek Maidens* (London 1968), no. 55; Emlyn-Jones, *Ionians and Hellenism* 40-5.

[16]Richter, *Archaic Greek Art* 110-2; *Korai*, Ephesos - #82-5, figs. 263-9; Miletos - #63, 70-1, 94-7, figs. 207-8, 210, 228-9, 291-300; M. J. Mellink, "Archaelogy in Asia Minor," *AJA* 80 (1976), 278-9; "Archaeology in Asia Minor," *AJA* 82 (1978), 325.

[17]R. A. Tomlinson, *Greek Sanctuaries* (London 1976), 124-7; A. W. Lawrence, *Greek Architecture* (Harmondsworth 1957), 92-3, 132-6; W. B. Dinsmoor, *The Architecture of Ancient Greece* (New York 1975 edition), 124-5.

[18]E. S. G. Robinson, "Coins from the Ephesian Artemision Reconsidered," *JHS* 71 (1951), 156-67; Dinsmoor, *Architecture of Ancient Greece* 127-35; Tomlinson, *Greek Sanctuaries* 127-32.

[19]G. S. Kirk, *Homer and the Epic* (Cambridge 1965), 54-62; C. G. Thomas, "The Roots of Homeric Kingship," *Historia* 15 (1966), 404-5; Kirk, "The Homeric Poems as History," *CAH* 3rd ed. 2.2, 820-50.

[20]J. A. Davidson, "Pisistratus and Homer," *TAPA* 86 (1955), 1-21; G. S. Kirk, "Homer and Modern Oral Poetry: Some Confusions," *CQ* 10 (1960), 271-81; *The Songs of Homer* (Cambridge 1962); *Homer and the Epic* (Cambridge 1965); J. B. Hainsworth, *The Flexibility of the Homeric Formula* (Oxford 1968); *Homer, Greece and Rome: New Surveys in the Classics* No. 3 (Oxford 1969); Kirk, *Homer and the Oral Tradition* (Cambridge 1976). B. M. W. Knox in his 1981 Martin Lectures argued for written Homeric texts. We look forward to studying carefully the forthcoming printed text.

[21]Jeffery, *Local Scripts of Archaic Greece* 43-50, 57-64.

[22]W. Donlan, "The Tradition of Anti-Aristocratic Thought in Early Greek Poetry," *Historia* 22 (1973), 145-54; S. G. Farron, "The Odyssey as an Anti-Aristocratic Statement," *Studies in Antiquity* 1 (1979-80), 59-101.

[23]Edmonds, *Elegy and Iambus* 1, F 3; cf. *Schol. Aesch. Pers.* 42 ["soft-living Lydians"]: They live softly, thus Anakreon's phrase—"Lydian-like persons"—meaning "luxurious;" J. M. Edmonds, *Lyra Graeca* 2 (Cambridge, Mass. 1964), F 134; C. M. Bowra,

"Xenophanes, Fragment 3," CQ 35 (1941), 119-26.

[24] Emlyn-Jones, Ionians and Hellenism 89-91.

[25] Edmonds, Elegy and Iambus 1, T and F 1-4.

[26] B. Snell, The Discovery of the Mind: The Greek Origins of European Thought (Oxford 1953), 42-70; Boardman, Pre-Classical 147.

[27] F. Jacoby, "Zu den älteren griechischen Elegikern: II Zu Mimnermos," Hermes 53 (1918), 262-307; H. Fränkel, Early Greek Poetry and Philosophy (New York 1975), 207-14.

[28] Edmonds, Elegy and Iambus 1, F 1.

[29] Edmonds, Lyra Graeca 1, F 28; E. Lobel and D. Page (eds.), Poetarum Lesbiorum Fragmenta (Oxford 1955); D. L. Page, Sappho and Alcaeus (Oxford 1955); C. M. Bowra, Greek Lyric Poetry 2nd ed. (Oxford 1961), 130-240.

[30] Edmonds, Elegy and Iambus 1, F 27a.1-4, 50, 90; Fränkel, Early Greek Poetry 170-88.

[31] B. Gentili (ed.), Anacreon (Rome 1958); Bowra, Greek Lyric Poetry 268-307; Fränkel, Early Greek Poetry 291-303.

[32] Edmonds, Lyra Graeca 2, F 4, 72; Hdt. 1.135; Xen. Cyr. 2.2.28, claimed the Persians learned pederasty from the Greeks; K. Dover, Greek Homosexuality (London 1978), 201 n. 9; but in a world of eunuchs, pederasty did not have to be introduced.

[33] Edmonds, Lyra Graeca 2, F 37, 65, 87.

[34] Ibid. F 99; also quoted by Aristophanes Ploutos 1009.

[35] Jeffery, Local Scripts of Archaic Greece 20; W. Jaeger, Paideia 1 (New York 1965), 115-7; Emlyn-Jones, Ionians and Hellenism 106-8.

[36] Tod GHI 1^2.1; ML GHI 8; L. H. Jeffery, "The Courts of Justice in Archaic Chios," BSA 51 (1956), 157-67; I avoid the restoration of J. H. Oliver, "Text of the So-Called Constitution of Chios from the First Half of the Sixth Century B.C.," AJP 80 (1959), 296-301.

[37] H. Frankfort et al., Before Philosophy (Harmondsworth 1949, 262: "The cosmologies of mythopoeic thought are basically revelations received in a confrontation with a cosmic 'Thou'. Revelation transcends reason."

[38] R. Carpenter, Folk Tale, Fiction and Saga in the Homeric Epic (Berkeley 1946), 136-56; Pritchard, Ancient Near Eastern Texts 142-9; J. Gray, The Krt Text in the Literature of Ras Shamra: A Social Myth of Ancient Canaan 2nd ed. (Leiden 1964).

[39] R. Barnett, "The Epic of Kumarbi and the Theogony of Hesiod," JHS 65 (1945), 100-1; H. Güterbock, the Hittite Version of the Hurrian Kumarbi Myths: Oriental Forerunners of Hesiod," AJA 52 (1948), 123-34; R. Barnett, "Ancient Oriental Influences on Archaic Greece," in The Aegean and the Near East: Studies Presented to Hetty Goldman (Locust Valley 1956), 212-38; P. Walcott, "The Text of Hesiod's Theogony and the Hittite Epic of Kumarbi," CQ 50 (1956), 198-206; Hesiod and the Near East (Cardiff 1966), 1-54.

[40] A. Heidel, The Babylonian Genesis (Chicago 1951); E. A. Speiser, Anchor Bible: Genesis (Garden City 1964), 3-20; D. Thompson, "The Possible Hittite Sources for Hesiod's 'Theogony'," Parola Passato 22 (1967), 241-51; W. Burkert, Structure and History in Greek Mythology and Ritual (Berkeley 1979), 18-22.

[41] G. S. Kirk and J. E. Raven, Presocratic Philosophers (Cambridge 1966), 8-9.

[42]L. L. Clader, *Helen: The Evolution from Divine to Heroic in Greek Epic Tradition* (Leiden 1976).

[43]G. S. Kirk, *The Nature of Greek Myths* (Harmondsworth 1974), 287-9.

[44]C. G. Starr, "The Decline of the Early Greek Kings," *Historia* 10 (1961), 129-38; P. Oliva, ΠΑΤΡΙΚΗ ΒΑΣΙΛΕΙΑ, ΓΕΡΑΣ: *Studies Presented to George Thomson on the Occasion of his 60th Birthday* (Prague 1963), 171-81; C. G. Thomas, ΠΑΤΡΙΚΗ ΒΑΣΙΛΕΙΑ: Η ΥΠΟΛΗΨΙΣ, *Historia* 15 (1966), 368-9; "The Roots of Homeric Kingship," *Historia* 15 (1966), 387-407.

[45]H. T. Wade-Gery, "Hesiod," *Phoenix* 3 (1949), 81-93; also in *Essays in Greek History* 1-16; J. M. Robinson, *An Introduction to Early Greek Philosophy* (Boston 1968), 3-21.

[46]W. K. C. Gutherie, *A History of Greek Philosophy* 1 (Cambridge 1962), 31-5; Jaeger, *Paideia* 155-6; M. L. West, *Early Greek Philosophy and the Orient* (Oxford 1971), attempted to link firmly Presocratic thought with early Indo-Iranian cosmological and theogonical doctrines but based his arguments largely upon Sasanian era sources which can not be accepted as secure evidence for the pre-Achaemenid period nor the early Achaemenid period, and their influence upon the Aegean intellectuals.

[47]Gutherie, *History of Greek Philosophy* 45-72; Kirk and Raven, *Presocratic Philosophers* 74-98; K. Freeman, *Companion to the Pre-Socratic Philosophers* (Cambridge, Mass. 1966), 49-55.

[48]C. H. Kahn, *Anaximander and the Origins of Greek Cosmology* (New York 1960), pl. 1, Babylonian Map of the World, sixth to fourth centuries B.C. (B.M. 92687); W. Burkert, "Iranisches bei Anaximandros," *Rheinisches Museum* 106 (1963), 97-134.

[49]P. Seligman, *The 'Apeiron' of Anaximander* (London 1962).

[50]G. Vlastos, "Equality and Justice in the Early Greek Cosmogonies," *CP* 48 (1947), 157-78; W. K. C. Guthrie, "The Presocratic World-Picture," *Harvard Theological Review* 45 (1952), 87-104; O. Gigon, "Die Theologie der Vorsokratiker," *La Notion du Divin depuis Homère jusqu'à Platon: Fondation Hardt, Entretiens sur l'Antiquité Classique* 1 (Geneva 1954), 127-55; C. H. Kahn, *Anaximander and the Origins of Greek Cosmology* (New York 1960); Gutherie, *History of Greek Philosophy* 72-115; F. M. Cornford, *Before and After Socrates* (Cambridge 1962), 16-20; K. Freeman, *Companion to the Pre-socratic Philosophies* (Cambridge, Mass. 1966), 55-64; Kirk and Raven, *Presocratic Philosophers* 99-142; Robinson, *Introduction to Early Greek Philosophy* 23-40; Fränkel, *Early Greek Poetry* 252-79.

[51]Gutherie, *History of Greek Philosophy* 115-40; Kirk and Raven, *Presocratic Philosophers* 143-62; Freeman, *Companion to Pre-socratic Philosophies* 64-73; Robinson, *Introduction to Early Greek Philosophy* 41-50.

[52]W. Jaeger, *The Theology of the Early Greek Philosophers* (Oxford 1947), 18-54.

[53]Edmonds, *Elegy and Iambus* 1, F 11, 12; Guthrie, *History of Greek Philosophy* 360-402; Cornford, *Before and After Socrates* 16; Kirk and Raven, *Presocratic Philosophies* 163-81; Robinson, *Introduction to Early Greek Philosophy* 50-6; Fränkel, *Early Greek Poetry* 325-37.

[54]Robinson, *Introduction to Early Greek Philosophy* 57-84; G. E. R. Lloyd, *Early Greek Science: Thales to Aristotle* (London 1970), 24.

[55]K. F. Johansen, "Clazomenian Sarcophagus Studies," *Acta Archaeologica* 13 (1942), 1-64; G. M. A. Richter, *Archaic Greek Art: Against its Historical Background* (New York 1949), 112-3; J. Boardman, *Athenian Black Figure Vases* (New York 1974), 65.

[56]W. Hinz, "The Elamite Version of the Record of Darius's Palace at Susa," *JNES* 9 (1950), 1-7; R. Ghirshman, *Village Perse-achéménide, Memoires de la Mission archéologique en Iran* 36 (Paris 1954); "L'Apadana de Suse," *Iranica Antiqua* 3 (1963), 148-

54; C. Nylander, "Old Persian and Greek Stonecutting and the Chronology of Achaemenian Monuments: Achaemenian Problems I," *AJA* 69 (1965), 49-55; "The Toothed Chisel in Pasargadae: Further Notes on Old Persian Stonecutting," *AJA* 70 (1966), 373-7; F. Vallat, "Deux Nouvelles 'Chartes de Fondation' d'un Palais de Darius Ier a Suse," *Syria* 48 (1971), 58; C. Nylander, *Ionians at Pasargadae* (Uppsala 1971); anon. "Recherches dans le secteur est du tepe de l'Apadana," *Cahiers de la Délégation archéologique Francaise en Iran* 4 (1974).

[57] B. Housoullier, "Offrande à Apollo Didyméen," *Mémoires, Délégation française en Perse* 7 (1905), 155-65; T. Wiegand, *Achter vorläufiger Bericht über die von den Staatlichen Museen in Milet und Didyma* (Berlin 1924); Richter, *Archaic Greek Art* 107-10; G. Gruben, "Das archaische Didymaeion," *Jahrbuch des deutschen archäologischen Instituts* 78 (1963), 78-182; Tomlinson, *Greek Sanctuaries* 132-6; J. Boardman, *Greek Sculpture: The Archaic Period* (New York 1978), 70, 89.

[58] Emlyn-Jones, *Ionians and Hellenism* 30-1.

[59] A. D. Knox, *Herodes, Cercidas and the Greek Choliambic Poets* (Loeb edition), (London 1953), Hipponax F 2-71; O. Masson, *Les Fragments du poète Hipponax: Edition critique et commentée* (Paris 1962), 31-2.

[60] Robinson, "Coins from the Ephesian Artemision," *JHS* 71 (1951), 156-67; Emlyn-Jones, *Ionians and Hellenism* 143-4.

[61] A. N. Zoumpos, *Herakleitos von Ephesos als Staatsmann und Gesetzgeber* (Athens 1956): P. Wheelright, *Heraclitus* (Princeton 1959); M. Heidegger and E. Fink, *Heraclitus Seminar 1966/67* (University, Ala. 1970); G. S. Kirk, *Heraclitus: The Cosmic Fragments* (Cambridge 1970); West, *Early Greek Philosophy* 111-202, rejected the "logos-doctrine," 124-9. His argument for Zarathustrian influence is strong, 165-202; but fails to identify the mode of intellectual exchange. Before Darius' reign, Zarathustrian ideas remained within the Iranian highland. Darius' references to Zarathustrian principles in the Bisitun text were new to the populace of Mesopotamia as they were modes for legitimatization. There is no evidence for Median or Persian magi in western Anatolia during the sixth century B.C., or the Median diaspora resultant of Cyrus' conquest of Media as West suggested (241). C. H. Kahn, *The Art and Thought of Heraclitus* (Cambridge 1979); J. Sallis and K. Maly (eds.), *Heraclitean Fragments: A Companion Volume to the Heidegger/Fink Seminar on Heraclitus* (University, Ala. 1980)

[62] Kirk and Raven, *Presocratic Philosophies* 213.

[63] E. Hussey, *The Presocratics* (London 1972), 42, F 57.

[64] West, *Early Greek Philosophy* 137-8.

[65] R. Fertonani, "Ecateo di Mileto e il suo razionalismo," *Parola Passato* 7 (1952), 18-29.

[66] Jaeger, *Paideia* 157-8; see A. E. M. Johnston, "The Earliest Preserved Greek Map: A New Ionian Coin Type," *JHS* 87 (1967), 86-94.

[67] Cawkwell, "The Power of Persia," *Arepo* 1 (1968), 1-5.

[68] J. M. Cook, "The Problem of Classical Ionia," *Proceedings of the Cambridge Philological Society* 7 (1961), 9; A. Rumpf, "Zu den klazomenischen Denkmälern," *Jahrbuch des deutschen archäologischen Institut* 48 (1933), 55-83; R. M. Cook, "A Terracotta Sarcophagus in the Fitzwilliam Museum," *JHS* 56 (1936), 58-63; W. Voigtländer, "Quellhaus und Naiskos im Didymaeion nach den Perserkriegen," *Istanbuler Mitteilungen* 22 (1972), 93-112.

[69] M. J. Mellink, "Archaelogy in Asia Minor," *AJA* 78 (1974), 123.

[70] P. Tozzi, "Per la storia della politica religiosa degli Achemenidi: distruzioni persiane di templi greci agli inizi del V secolo," *Rivista Storica Italiana* 89 (1977), 18-32.

[71]A. S. F. Gow, "Notes on the Persae of Aeschylus," *JHS* 48 (1928), 133-59; R. Lattimore, "Aeschylus on the Defeat of Xerxes," in *Classical Studies in Honor of William Abbott Oldfather* (Urbana 1943), 82-93; H. D. Broadhead, *The Persae of Aeschylus* (Cambridge 1960), XV-XLVIII: H.D. Edinger, "Vocabulary and Imagery in Aeschylus' Persians," (Ph.D. dissertation, Princeton University 1961); H. C. Avery, "Dramatic Devices in Aeschylus' *Persians*," *AJP* 85 (1964), 173-84; B. Alexanderson, "Darius in the Persians," *Eranos* 65 (1967), 1-11.

[72]Perhaps the small island of Apsis also called Arkonnesos, lying between Teos and Lebedos to the east (Strabo 14.1.29) within the greater polis of Teos. Compare Erythrai and Miletos with island dependencies.

[73]*SIG* [3]. 37-8; Schwyzer *DGE* 710; Buck, *Greek Dialects* 3; Tod *GHI* 1[2].23; ML *GHI* 30; see P. Herrmann, "Teos und Abdera im 5. Jahrhundert v. Chr.," *Chiron* 11 (1981), 1-30.

[74]Tod *GHI* 1[2]. p. 29, noted "the dependence of Teos" upon foreign grain, which ML *GHI* p. 65 expanded, and considered the Teian need for grain a permanent aspect of Ionian dependency upon imported grain. Meiggs and Lewis failed to take into account the significant decline of Teian population which, without a drastic alteration in local grain production, would not have necessitated import.

[75]*Pers.* 61, 119, 512, 549, 718, 730, 761, 992-3, 925.

[76]T. F. Carney, *The Shape of the Past: Models and Antiquity* (Lawrence 1975), 93-106, 236-43, 260-3, fig. 5.6 (p. 261); P. Colinvaux, "An Ecologists' View of History," *Yale Review* 64 (1975), 357-69; "The Human Breeding Strategy," *Nature* 261 (June 1976), 356-7; *The Fates of Nations* (New York 1980), 58-105.

[77]J. M. Cook, *The Troad* (Oxford 1973); Dardanos 58-9, Ophryneion 75-7, Rhoiteion 80-7, Ilion (Troy VIII) 85, 98, neighboring Kara Tepe 113, Hanay Tepe 212-3, 'Upshan' Tepe 129, Ballı Dağ 136-7, Yenişehir 163-5, Sigeion 175-7, Neandria 206-7, Kolone and Larisa 217-8, Hamaxitos 231-5, Lamponeia 263, Antandros 270, Berytis 277, Kebren 332, Gergis 348.

[78]Cook, *Troad*; Dardanos 58-9, Ophryneion 75-7, Rhoiteion 80-7, Ilion (Troy VIII) 85, 98, neighboring Yenişehir 163-5, Assos 239-46, Lamponeia 263, Berytis 277, Kebren 332.

[79]R. Koldewey, *Neandria* (Berlin 1891); Lawrence, *Greek Architecture* 131-2, fig. 74; Å. Åkerström, *Die architektonischen Terrakotten Kleinasiens* (Lund 1966), 8-13.

[80]Richter, *Archaic Greek Art* 117; Lawrence, *Greek Architecture* 119, pl. 38A; Åkerström, *Die architektonischen Terrakotten* 13-21.

[81]Åkerström, *Die architektonischen Terrakotten* 7; Cook, *Troad* 336-7.

[82]C. W. Blegen, C. G. Boulter, J. L. Caskey, M. Rawson, *Troy: Settlements VIIa, VIIb and VIII 4.1 Text* (Princeton 1958), 247-50.

[83]F.W. Hasluck, *Cyzicus* (Cambridge 1910); Richter, *Archaic Greek Art* 114-5; E. Akurgal, *Ancient Civilizations and Ruins of Turkey* (Istanbul 1973), 47.

[84]The mound of Hisar Kalesi near Ergili. R. G. Kent, "Old Persian Texts: IV. The Lists of Provinces," *JNES* 2 (1943), 302 n. 12.

[85]J. A. R. Munro, "Dascylium," *JHS* 32 (1912), 57-67; M. J. Mellink, "Archaeology in Asia Minor," *AJA* 59 (1955), 235-6; E. Akurgal, "Les Fouilles de Daskyleion," *Anatolia* 1 (1956), 20-4; J. M. Cook, "Greek Archaeology in Western Asia Minor," *Archaeological Reports for 1959-1960* (1960), 34-5; Akurgal, *Ancient Civilizations* 41, 47, pl. 20.
A distinct rough and rugged zone separates the agricultural plains of the Troad from the broad, soft rolling and very fertile plains of northern Mysia and the region of Daskyleion. The plains of Daskyleion are extremely rich in agricultural production today, and the acropolis juts out of the plain at a point where a good flowing small river enters into the large Lake Minyas which abounds with a fantastic mosquito population living

amidst a broad swampy bird sanctuary. Malaria may have been an ancient problem. Archaeological excavations have uncovered Hellenistic ashular walls interspersed with re-used marble blocks (late-fifth century B.C.) bearing string courses of fine bead and reel, and dominant egg and dart designs; a long zig-zag wall which ultimately intersected with a Roman building. Full excavation would be most rewarding.

[86]My thanks to my colleague Professor Shirley J. Schwarz who analyzed the sherds (which we left at Daskyleion), 21 August 1978:

		Types	
Types	1.	Attic BF 6-5th C.	12 sherds
	2.	Hellenistic Fine Ware	17
	3.	Red Glaze Roman Fine Ware	17
	4.	Late Roman Red Provincial	4
	5.	Amphora - Red Mixed	12
	6.	Brick	8
	7.	Local Red Ware	10
	8.	Local Grey Ware	10
	9.	Black painted, Late Roman (?)	3

The top of the acropolis is very flat and is now used for the growing of wheat. Three trenches have been excavated into the southern great slope. The three other sides are sheer and form a perfect acropolis.

[87]Hdt. 3.120.2; Thuc. 1.129.1; R. Schmitt, "Die achaimenidische Satrapie," *Historia* 21 (1972), 522-7.

[88]Cook, "Greek Archaeology in Western Asia Minor," *Archaeological Reports* (1960), 34, noted a settlement from the beginning of the seventh century B.C. marked by Subgeometric, Proto-Corinthian, Orientalizing, and monochrome ceramics.

[89]Upon the royal reliefs at Bisitun and Naqsh-i Rustam, Aspathines stands behind Darius and carries the royal bow and battle-ax. Behind Aspathines stands Gobryas (DNc-d). In 480 B.C., also joining Megabazos was Ariabignes (Hdt. 7.97), the son of King Darius by Gobyras' daughter.

[90]While the correspondence between Pausanias and Xerxes (Thuc. 1.128-32) were late fifth-century forgeries, see chapter 6 n. 97, the satrapal role of Artabazos at Daskyleion should not be disputed.

[91]R. Hallock, "The Evidence of the Persepolis Tablets," to appear in *The Cambridge History of Iran* 2 (Cambridge forthcoming); typescript courtesy of Dr. Hallock, pp. 2-4

[92]There is no reason to believe the Artabazos in supreme command of the Persian fleet at Cyprus in 450 B.C. (Diod. Sic. 12.3-4) was Artabazos the son of Pharnakes, as Lewis, *Sparta and Persia* 52 suggested. I suggest Pharnabazos governed at the mid-century.

[93]On the basis of a high degree of sixth and fifth century B.C. sherds of Greek ceramics several scholars speak of a Greek settlement at Daskyleion. Beyond the sherds, we have no positive evidence that Greeks dwelt at Daskyleion before the end of the fifth century B.C.

[94]K. Balkan, "Inscribed Bullae from Daskyleion-Ergili," *Anatolia* 4 (1959), 123-8; R. Schmitt, *Altpersische Siegel-Inschriften* (Vienna 1981), 32-3, SXf-g.

[95]S. Haynes, *Land of the Chimaera: An Archaeological Excursion in the South-West of Turkey* (London 1974).

[96]G. E. Bean, *Turkey Beyond the Maeander* (London 1971), 20, 53.

[97]W. Eilers "Kleinasiatisches," *ZDMG* 94 (1940), 189-233; G. E. Bean and J. M. Cook, "The Cnidia," *BSA* 47 (1952), 171-212; P. M. Fraser and G. E. Bean, *The Rhodian Peraea and Islands* (Oxford 1954); Bean and Cook, "The Halicarnassus Peninsula," *BSA* 50 (1955),

85-171; "The Carian Coast III," *BSA* 52 (1957), 58-146; R. Shafer, "A Break in the Carian Dam," *AC* 34 (1965), 398-424; W. Radt, *Siedlungen und Bauten auf der Halbinsel von Halikarnassos, Beiheft 3 der Istanbuler Mitteilungen* (Tübingen 1970); Bean, *Turkey Beyond the Maeander.*

[98]Bean, *Turkey Beyond the Maeander* 221.

[99]G. E. Bean and T. B. Mitford, *Journeys in Rough Cilicia in 1962 and 1963* (Vienna 1965); G. E. Bean, *Turkey's Southern Shore* (New York 1968); G. E. Bean and T. B. Mitford, *Journeys in Rough Cilicia 1964-1968: Ergänzungsbände zu den Tituli Asiae Minoris,* Nr. 3 (Vienna 1970); G. E. Bean, *Journeys in Northern Lycia 1965-1967: Ergänzungsbände zu den Tituli Asiae Minoris,* Nr. 5 (Vienna 1971); *Lycian Turkey: An Archaeological Guide* (London 1978); T. R. Bryce, "The Other Pericles," *Historia* 29 (1980), 377-81.

[100]G. Säflund, "Karische Inschriften aus Labranda," *Opuscula Atheniensa* 1 (1953), 199-205; c. 350 B.C.

[101]The pattern of Lydian settlements during the fifth century B.C. has not, to date, been plotted; yet we may suspect that the Seleucid settlements during the third century B.C. may indicate an earlier settlement pattern. W. M. Calder and G. E. Bean, *A Classical Map of Asia Minor* (London 1958); G. M. Cohen, *The Seleucid Colonies: Studies in Founding, Administration and Organization* (Wiesbaden 1978).

[102]G. Walser, *Audienz beim persischen Grosskönig* (Zürich 1965); *Die Volkerschaften auf den Reliefs von Persepolis* (Berlin 1966).

[103]Carney, *Shape of the Past* 180, "Confronted by attack by an apparatus state (as in the Persian Wars), the city-state's only recourse was to league together for mutual protection (as in the Delian League). The head of the league thus came to control pooled resources of such magnitude as to produce step-level change in her own economy (Athens built docks and a fleet, of unprecedented and unapproachable size). Thus league members became subjects of an empire (The Athenian Empire) and involved in a mobilized economy." This statement points out the major issues involved but fails in its attempt to mold the factors into a workable historical model by not understanding the precise steps by which the East Greeks turned to mainland Greek assistance in 478 and 477 B.C.

Chapter 10. Athenian Intervention in Ionia

[1]Noonan, "The Grain Trade of the Northern Black Sea," *AJP* 94 (1973), 231-42; R. J. Seager and C. J. Tuplin, "The Freedom of the Greeks of Asia: On the Origins of a Concept and the Creation of a Slogan," *JHS* 100 (1980), 141-54.

[2]F. J. Frost, *Plutarch's Themistocles* (Princeton 1980), 178-9.

[3]Diod. Sic. 11.44.2, stated 50 Peloponnesian ships, 30 Athenian ships, and omitted reference to the allies. This record should be ignored, Meiggs, *Athenian Empire* 38 n.1, 447-58.

[4]*ATL* 3.95-100, yet the "three categories of names" is not convincing; Raaflaub, "Beute, Vergeltung, Freiheit?," *Chiron* 9 (1979), 12-3.

[5]*ATL* 3.189-90, 198.

[6]D. MacDowell, "Aegina and the Delian League," *JHS* 80 (1960), 118-21; T. J. Figueira, "Aeginetan Membership in the Peloponnesian League," *CP* 76 (1981), 1-24.

[7]Diod. Sic. 11.44.2, "The Greeks freed those poleis which still had Persian garrisons." For Meiggs, *Athenian Empire* 56-8, the expedition was "puzzling" and a Greek attempt to gain control of the island, but I see no sound reason to accept that argument.

[8]Thuc. 1.94.2; Diod. Sic. 11.44.2-3; Nepos *Paus.* 2.1-2; Paus. 3.4.9; Simonides F 89;

Plut. *Kim.* 6.3; Raaflaub, "Beute, Vergeltung, Freiheit?," *Chiron* 9 (1979), 20: "Asien war persisches Territorium, die Grenze verlief am Bosporus," is not correct. The border was, more correctly, the Strymon River marked by the Persian frontier fortress at Eion, thus the 470/69 B.C. "first confederate expedition" (Thuc. 1.98).

[9] *ATL* 3.175, 192.

[10] *ATL* 3.194-224; Balcer, "Separatism and Anti-Separatism in the Athenian Empire," *Historia* 23 (1974), 21 n. l; Meiggs, *Athenian Empire* 50-67.

[11] I reject the suggestion by Meritt *et al.* (*ATL*) to include Amynanda and Pyrnos as their locations are not secure; see Bean, *Turkey Beyond the Maeander* end map. I also reject Syangela as being too far inland.

[12] The inland position of Maiandros may have remained, at this time, under Persian control.

[13] J. M. Balcer, "Imperialism and Stasis in Fifth Century B.C. Ionia: A Frontier Redefined," *Arktouros* 261-8.

[14] The location of Karene is not secure, *ATL* 1.495-6.

[15] *ATL* 3.196. This would eliminate Astyra, at this time, from the East Greek group joining the Hellenic League.

[16] *ATL* 2. A9. III. 125-37.

[17] This eliminates Kios and Astakos.

[18] *ATL* 3.205-6.

[19] Thuc. 1.69.1; Diod. Sic. 11.39-40.4; *Ath. Pol.* 23.4; Plut. *Them.* 19.1-3; Nepos *Them.* 6.2-7.

[20] Diod. Sic. 11.41-3; Plut. *Them.* 19.3-4; Nepos *Them.* 6.1; Aristod. 5.4; Ar. *Eq.* 813-6, 884-5; Plato *Gorg.* 455d-e.

[21] Meiggs, *Athenian Empire* 39; see also chapter 11 n. 17.

[22] Hdt. 8.130; Thuc. 1.95, 130; Diod. Sic. 11.44.5-6, 46.4-5; Plut. *Arist.* 23.4, *Kim.* 6.3-4; Nep. *Arist.* 2.2-3; Aristod. *FGrH* 104 F 7.

[23] *ATL* 3.175, 225.

[24] Thucydides' statement at the end of 1.95.7—[The Spartans] . . . thought that the Athenians were competent to take the leadership and were friendly to them at the time."—is incompatible with Herodotus' narrative of events (esp. 8.3.2) and to Thucydides' previous statements. We must reject it as a later aspect of Athenian propaganda, Meiggs, *Athenian Empire* 5, 40-1. I. Hahn, "Aspekte der spartanischen Aussenpolitik im V. JH.," *AAH* 17 (1969), 285-96; on Thuc. 1.77.1, see R. I. Winton, Φιλοδικεῖν δοκοῦμεν : Law and Paradox in the Athenian Empire," *Museum Helveticum* 37 (1980), 89-97. R. Sealey, "On the Athenian Concept of Law," *CJ* 77 (1982), 289-302.

[25] *ATL* 3.191-3.

[26] Hdt. 8.3.2, 9.120; Thuc. 1.75.2, 89, 95.2-6, 96.1, 6.76.3; Xen. *de Vect.* 5.5; Dem. 3.24; Andok. 3.37-8; Plut. *Arist.* 24-25.1, *Kim.* 6.3, 9; Nepos *Arist.* 2.2-3; Aristod. *FGrH* 104 F7; Polyainos 1.34.2. W. Kolbe, "Die Anfänge der attischen Arché," *Hermes* 73 (1938), 249-68; J. Larsen, "The Constitution and Original Purpose of the Delian League," *HSCP* 51 (1940), 175-213; B. D. Meritt, "The Early Years of the Delian League," *Proceedings of the Classical Association* 43 (1946), 10-1; *ATL* 3.183-243; G. E. M. de Ste Croix, "The Character of the Athenian Empire," *Historia* 3 (1954-5), 1-41; H. D. Meyer,

"Vorgeschichte und Gründung des delisch-attischen Seebundes," *Historia* 12 (1963), 405–46; R. Sealey, "The Origin of the Delian League," *Ancient Society and Institutions* (New York 1967), 233–56; H. G. L. Hammond, "The Origins and the Nature of the Athenian Alliance of 478/7 B.C.," *JHS* 87 (1967), 41–61; H. Papp, "Zum Verhältnis Athens zu seinen Bündern im attische–delischen Seebund," *Historia* 17 (1969), 425–43; A. Jackson, "The Original Purpose of the Delian League," *Historia* 18 (1969), 12–6; Meiggs, *Athenian Empire* 42–67; A. French, "Athenian Ambitions and the Delian Alliance," *Phoenix* 33 (1979), 134–41; N. D. Robertson, "The True Nature of the 'Delian League'," *AJAH* 5 (1980), 64–96; "The True Nature of the 'Delian League II'," *AJAH* 5 (1980), 110–33. Thuc. 1.96.1, 3.10.3, 6.76.3–4. Athenian raids upon the Persian fortresses at Sestos and Byzantion during the year before the meeting on Delos had raised disputes over the captured booty and the Athenians now sought better means to continue the plundering; Plut. *Kim.* 9.3–6 (Ion *FGrH* 394 F 13); Polyainos 1.34.2; Raaflaub, "Beute, Vergeltung, Freiheit?," *Chiron* 9 (1979), 1–22.

[27]Thuc. 1.96.2, 3.11.4, *isopsēphous*; Diod. Sic. 11.47.1; W. Caldwell, *Hellenic Conceptions of Peace, Studies in History, Economics and Public Law* 84 (New York 1919), 68–9. Thuc. 1.97.1, 98.4, 5.18.5; the fact that a new oath was taken created a new confederation distinct from the Hellenic League. This negates Giovannini and Gottlieb "Thukydides und die Anfänge der athenischen Arche," *Sitzungsberichte der Heidelberger Akademie der Wissenschaften. Philosophisch-historische Klasse* (1980), 7. Abhandlung 7–45. N. G. L. Hammond argued incorrectly for a bicameral organization without legal parity between Athens and the allies, *A History of Greece to 322 B.C.* 256–7; and "The Origins and Nature of the Athenian Alliance," *JHS* 86 (1967), 50–2, 58–61. See now P. Culham, "The Delian League: Bicameral or Unicameral?", *AJAH* 3 (1978), 27–31.

[28]Hdt. 7.3.2; Thuc. 1.95.1–2, 96.1, 97.1, 6.67.3, 82.3; Xen. *de Vect.* 5.5–6; Nep. *Arist.* 2.2–3; Aristod. *FGrH* 104 F 7.

[29]The hegemony Athens obtained was basically the command of the confederate forces which may be interpreted as military "leader," "guide," or "director" (see chapter 2 n. 95). Hegemony was also compared to the command obtained by leaders of colonies and political parties, Thuc. 1.25.1, 38.2, 8.89.2. The power of hegemony was associated with the power to "rule," Hdt. 4.153, 7.149.2, 9.10.2. Thucydides noted that in 478 the Athenians had rid themselves of the rule and hegemony of the Lacedaemonians, 6.82.3. Thuc. 1.120.1: "It is the duty of hegemons, while equitably considering their particular interests, to have special regard for the common good, for in other matters they are honored above all."

[30]Thuc. 1.95.1–2, 128.3. Although the identity of the "allies" is not known, they probably included Lesbos, Chios, and Samos. See chapter 6 n. 97.

[31]*ATL* 3.225.

[32]Thuc. 1.75.2; Plut. *Them.* 2.4, 4.4, 10, 19.3, 20.1–2; Nep. *Them.* 2.2–5; J. de Romilly, *Thucydide et l'impérialisme athénien* (Paris 1947), 59–62. S. Dow, "The Purported Decree of Themistokles: Stele and Inscription," *AJA* 66 (1962), 352–68; M. Jameson, "A Revised Text of the Decree of Themistokles from Troizen," *Hesperia* 31 (1962), 310–5; "The Provisions for Mobilization in the Decree of Themistokles," *Historia* 12 (1963), 385–404; M. Chambers, "The Significance of the Themistokles' Decree," *Philologus* 3 (1967), 157–69; P. Karavites, "Realities and Appearances, 490–480 B.C.," *Historia* 26 (1977), 129–47; G. M. E. Williams," The Image of the Alkmeonidai between 490 B.C. and 487/6 B.C.," *Historia* 29 (1980), 106–10.

[33]Meiggs, *Athenian Empire* 42 and n. 4. We must use the *Letters of Themistokles* with great caution and avoid an uncritical acceptance.

[34]R. Christensen, "De jure et condicione sociorum Atheniensium quaestio historica," in *Opuscula philologica ad Ioannem Nicolaum Madvigium* (Copenhagen 1876), 2–6; J. Stahl, *De Sociorum atheniesium judiciis commentatio* (Münster 1881), 2–4; *hupékoos* in contrast to *xsymmachias autonomoi* Thuc. 7.57.3, or simply *autonomos* 6.69.3, 7.57.7, or *panu eleutherōs xsymmachountas* 6.85.2. Thucydides designated two imperial (post foundation) categories: A. ship contributors 6.85.2, 7.57.4–5, as autonomous 1.39.2,

3.10.1, 10.6, 10.11; B. tribute contributors 2.9.4, 7.57.4, 57.5, subjected *douleia* 3.10.5, cf. [Xen.] *Ath. Pol.* 1.10; Isok. 12.63.

[35]Hdt. 8.132.1, 9.90.1-2; Thuc. 1.89.2, 95.1, 97.1, 3.10.1-3, 5.18.5; *Ath. Pol.* 23.5; Plut. *Arist.* 25.1; cf. Diod. Sic. 11.34.2, 4.

[36]*Schol.* Thuc. 2.29.2; I. Bekker, *Anecdota Graeca* I (Berlin 1814), 466; Cicero *Epis. ad. Attic.* 6.2.4.

[37]Hdt. 1.95-6, 8.140a; Thuc. 5.18.2, 77.5, 79.1; Xen. *Hell.* 5.2.14; G. Ténékidès, *La Notion juridique d'indépendance et la tradition hellénique* (Athens 1954), 7; C. Périphanakis, *La Théorie grecque du Droit et le Classicisme actuel* (Athens 1946).

[38]Thuc. 5.18.2; Xen. *Hell.* 5.2.14; *Ath. Pol.* 24.2.

[39]Aesch. *Pers.* 234, 242, cf. 402-5.

[40]B. D. Meritt, "The Marathon Epigrams Again," *AJP* 83 (1962), 296.

[41]Ténékidès, *La Notion juridique* 10; M. Ostwald, *Autonomia: Its Genesis and Early History. American Classical Studies* 11 (1982), 46.

[42]T. Quinn, "Political Groups at Chios: 412 B.C.," *Historia* 18 (1969), 22-30.

[43]Hdt. 7.104; Ténékidès, *La Notion juridique* 25.

[44]Fifth and fourth century alliances based upon equality included: 420, Athens, Argos, Mantinea, and Elis, Thuc. 5.47; 395, Athens, Corinth, Argos, and Boiotia, Xen. *Hell.* 4.2.13-7; 369, Athens and Sparta, *Hell.* 7.1.14; 362, Mantinea, Elis, Achaia, Athens, and Sparta, *Hell.* 7.5.3; and 339, Athens and Thebes, Aeschines 3.143.

[45]Thalheim PW *RE* sv Autonomia 2.2606.

[46]*Ath. Pol.* 23.5; Plut. *Arist.* 25.1. E. Bickerman, "Remarques sur le droit des gens dans la Grèce classique," *Revue internationale des droits de l'antiquité: Mélanges Ferdinand DeVissher* 4 (1950), 99-116; F. Wüst, "Amphiktyonie, Eidgenossenschaft, Symmachie," *Historia* 3 (1955), 149-53.

[47]Contrary to the view of V. Ehrenberg, *The Greek State* (Oxford 1940), 115, who claimed: "the mere fact of a phoros was felt as an infringement of autonomy."

[48]Thuc. 5.18.5; Xen. *Hell.* 3.4.25. H. T. Wade-Gery, "The Peace of Kallias," *Essays in Greek History* (Oxford 1958), 212, argued that the Peace of Kallias stated that the Greek states in Ionia were to pay tribute to Persia and to be autonomous. H. Schäfer, "Die Autonomie-klausel des Kalliasfriedens," *Probleme der alten Geschichte* (Göttingen 1963), 253-68, also considered this point.

[49]Thuc. 1.19, 3.10.5; Arist. *Pol.* 1284a38; *Ath. Pol.* 24.2. The autonomy held by Aigina between 445 and 432 B.C., during which time she contributed money as tribute, is a fourth example that poleis could be and were members of the alliance and autonomous; Thuc. 1.67.2, 139.1, 140.3; *ATL* 1.218.

[50]*Ath. Pol.* 23.5; Plut. *Arist.* 25.1; cf. *IG* 1².90:18 (Tod *GHI* 1².68; *SEG* X.89; Bengtson *SV* 2.187); Xen. *Hell.* 2.2.20 (Bengtson *SV* 2.211); 5.30.26 (Bengtson *SV* 2.253); P. Herrmann, *Der römische Kaisereid* (Göttingen 1968), 21-5.

[51]The Treaty between Athens and Boiotia in 422 B.C., *SEG* X.89 (Tod *GHI* 1².68; *ATL* 1. T74), lines 17-8; the Treaty between Sparta and Athens in 404 B.C., Xen. *Hell.* 2.2.20; Treaty between Gortyn and Lappa during the second century B.C., *GDI* 5018, lines 6-7. Cf. Thuc. 1.44.1; Athens purposely did not include this article in her treaty with Corcyra. J. Larsen, "The Constitution of the Peloponnesian League," *CP* 28 (1933), 270-5. G. M. E. de Ste Croix, *The Origins of the Peloponnesian War* (London 1972), 298-307, similarly considered the Delian charter oath as reciprocal (de Ste Croix's Type B), yet

incorrectly considered the Confederacy as bicameral (as did Hammond, "Origins and Nature of the Athenian Alliance," *JHS* 87 [1967], 41-61), and argued that *isopsēphos* (Thuc. 3.11.4) was merely "metaphorical." De Ste Croix unconvincingly denied the basis of "equality."

[52]Thuc. 1.98.4; Arist. *Pol.* 1284a38.

[53]Larsen, "Constitution and Original Purpose of the Delian League," *HSCP* 51 (1940), 183; *ATL* 3.230; Meiggs, *Athenian Empire* 44-6.

[54]Equal representation, Thuc. 1.96.1, 3.10.3; equality in synodal deliberations, Thuc. 1.97.1.

[55]Hdt. 9.106.4; *Ath. Pol.* 23.5; Plut. *Arist.* 25.1-3; note that the symbolic throwing of iron ingots into the sea indicated a permanency of the alliance for which the oath was sworn. Cf. the oath sworn by the Phokaians in 545 B.C., Hdt. 1.165; also note Horace *Epode* 16.25-6.

[56]Thuc. 1.71.5-6; Larsen, "The Constitution of the Peloponnesian League," *CP* 28 (1933), 265-70.

[57]Ostwald, *Autonomia* 20-1, 39, 46.

[58]Ibid. 1.

[59]Ibid. 41-2.

[60]Cf. Thuc. 4.82, 132.3; 5.33, 79.1; Xen. *Hell.* 6.3.7-9, 5.3-5; 5.1.34, 36; 6.3.14, 3.18, 4.2; [Dem.] 55.26; Diod. Sic. 15.20.2-3, 38.2.

[61]*Ath. Pol.* 23.4-5; Diod. Sic. 11.47.1-2; Plut. *Arist.* 23.4, 24.

[62]Thuc. 1.96.1; 5.18.5; *Ath. Pol.* 23.5; Dem. 23.209; Aeschin. 3.258; Andok. 4.11; Diod. Sic. 11.47.1-2; Plut. *Arist.* 24.3-4, 26.3; Nepos *Arist.* 3.1; Paus. 8.52.2; *ATL* 3.234-43; S. K. Eddy, "ΕΠΙΦΟΡΑ in the Tribute Quota Lists," *AJP* 89 (1968), 129-43; D. Blackman, "The Athenian Navy and Allied Naval Contributions in the Pentecontaetia," *GRBS* 10 (1969), 180-216; A. French, "The Tribute of the Allies," *Historia* 21 (1972), 1-20.

[63]Thucydides' 460 talents (1.96), therefore, included Athens' assessment in coin before the conversion to manned ships.

[64]Thuc. 1.96.2; Andok. 3.38; Xen. *de Vect.* 5.5; Antiphon 5.69-71; A. G. Woodhead, "The Institution of the Hellenotamiae," *JHS* 79 (1959), 149-52.

[65]*ATL* 3.III.iv.

[66]*ATL* 3.228 n. 10.

[67]Thuc. 1.96.2; Gomme *HCT* 1.280, Ostwald, *Autonomia* 23: Thuc. (1.97.1) anachronistically used the term *autonomōn*.

[68]Plut. *Arist.* 25.3: "For by deliberating to transfer the money from Delos to Athens contrary to the Charter (*syntheke*) as proposed by the Samians, Aristeides spoke that it was not just, but that it was advantageous." Plutarch, the only source for this synodal discussion, stated that the proposal was made by Aristeides. As Aristeides was probably long dead by 454 B.C., the passage is suspect. The authors of the *ATL* 3.262 remarked that either the passage is historical, in which case it may refer to some earlier occasion, or is unhistorical only in part, in which case the mention of Aristeides should be eliminated. Another consideration may be that not Aristeides but someone else made the statement. Meritt, Wade-Gery, and McGregor preferred this view. The original directive enacted to establish the Treasury at Delos was reported by Diod. Sic. 11.47.1. W. Pritchett, "The Transfer of the Delian Treasury," *Historia* 18 (1969), 17-21, questioned the traditional date 454 B.C., and the *ATL*. To place this event before Eurymedon as

Pritchett did, is unconvincing; and ignores the question of the *aparche* in 454/3 B.C. On the illegality of the proposal compare Thuc. 1.97 *para to kathestēkos*.

[69]*ATL* 3.138, 140.

[70]Balcer, *Athenian Regulations for Chalkis*, 119–42.

[71]Thuc. 1.115.2-117; Diod. Sic. 12.27.1; Plut. *Per.* 24.1.

[72]The paraphrase of the two passages is that of the *ATL* 3.138-9, with my insertions in parentheses.

[73]A. Zimmern, *The Greek Commonwealth* (New York 1931), 186.

[74]Cf. Thuc. 3.37.2; Isok. 7.29; Arist. *Pol.* 1274a7.

[75]Thuc. 1.96; *Ath. Pol.* 23.2-5; Diod. Sic. 11.47.

[76]P. Deane, *Thucydides' Dates 465-431 B.C.* (Don Mills 1972), 9-13; M. P. Milton, "The Date of Thucydides' Synchronism of the Siege of Naxos with Themistokles' Flight," *Historia* 28 (1979), 257-75.

[77]A. G. Woodhead, "The Second Capture of Sestos," *Proceedings of the Cambridge Philological Society* 181 (1950-51), 9-12; J. Smart, "Kimon's Capture of Eion," *JHS* 87 (1967), 136-8.

[78]A. Podlecki, "Cimon, Skyros and 'Theseus' Bones,' " *JHS* 91 (1971), 141-3; J. M. Balcer, "The Archaic Silver Coinage of Skyros and the Forgeries of Konstantinos Christodoulos," *RSN* 57 (1978), 69-101.

[79]Thucydides stated that the campaigns were conducted by the Athenians. This was to imply Athenian military leadership over the forces of the allies, 1.98.1-3; G. Lombardo, *Cimone: riconstuzione della biografia e discussioni storiografiche* (Rome 1934), 62-77.

[80]This does not refer to "the failure to send land-troops," for the assessment of Aristeides was in terms of ships or money, Thuc. 1.96.1. The *lipostration* does not specifically refer to land troops refusing to serve but can also indicate refusal of naval forces to continue to serve. Allied poleis that sent ships to the confederate fleet manned their ships, at least in the early period of the alliance, and the refusal to serve must refer to them. G. Smith's argument ("Athenian Casualty Lists," *CP* 14 [1919], 353) that military service was required from the allies cannot be accepted as a valid interpretation of *lipostration*. She argued that it was reasonable to suppose a quota was fixed for each ally by the Athenian executive power of the Confederacy and that types of troops were specified. Plutarch's (*Kim.* 11.1) comment that the allies "neither manned their ships nor sent men" does not refer to *lipostration*. Thucydides' statement in 1.99 emphasized naval operations, whereas Plutarch indicated a failure to send military forces. The context of Plutarch's statement indicates a condition of the sixties and very possibly was in reference to land troops similar to those which served at Tanagra.

Although allies of the Confederacy served at the inland battle of Tanagra, 454 B.C. (Thuc. 1.107.6-108.1; Diod. Sic. 11.80.2-6; Plut. *Kim.* 17.4-8) which was the first recorded instance in which allies were used in battle against a Greek enemy of Athens and not of the entire Confederacy, it is difficult to consider the possibility of any requirement of the allies to supply land forces from the outset of the Confederacy. Pausanias (5.10.4) recorded an inscription at Olympia which noted Argives, Athenians, and Ionians fighting at Tanagra. The reference to "Ionians" is a term for the members of the Confederacy, *Ath. Pol.* 23.5. It is not known who these "Ionians" were, their citizenship, the number of these "Ionians," or the reasons for their fighting with Athens at Tanagra. The use of allied land forces at Tanagra does not necessarily indicate that allied poleis were to supply land forces and this requirement may have been a clause in the charter of the Confederacy. The military activities of the "Ionians" at Tanagra were completely outside the stated purposes of the Confederacy. It may be assumed, therefore, that the "Ionians" at Tanagra were there not because of the regulations of the Confederacy as established in 478/7 B.C., but rather because of the political transactions between the Ionians and the Athenians during the years before Tanagra.

[81]H. Robertson, *Administration of Justice in the Athenian Empire* (Toronto 1924), 27-8, n. 1.

[82]Thuc. 1.100.1; *Pap. Oxy.* 13.1610 F 191 (= Ephoros *FGrH* 70 F 191); Diod. Sic. 11.60.6-62; Plut. *Cim.* 12-13.3; M. White, "Some Agiad Dates," *JHS* 84 (1964), 147.

[83]Gomme *HCT* 1.283.

[84]Plut. *Them.* 25.2; Nep. *Them.* 8.6; Aristod. 10.3.

[85]Thuc. 1.55.1, 103.1; 2.78.4; 3.73; 4.118.7; 6.27.2; 7.85.4, 8.15.2, 28.4. Gomme *HCT* 1. 282; *ATL* 3.155-7; Schuller, *Die Herrschaft der Athener* 104-6.

[86]Thuc. 6.77.1, 82.3; 8.48.5.

[87]Thuc. 1.68.3, 69.1, 121.5, 124.3; 3.10.3-5, 13.6, 63.3; 4.96.1, 87.3, 92.4; 5.86, 92, 100; 6.76.2, 76.4, 77.1.

[88]Thuc. 2.78.4; 4.118.7.

[89]Thuc. 2.63.1, 3; 3.46.5; Isok. 9.202e; cf. [Xen.] *Ath. Pol.* 1.9, "political subjection." Arist. *Pol.* 1255b21: "statesmanship is the government of free and equal men." Xen. *Ath. Pol.* 1.8: "For the *Demos* would not want a good ruling state under which it is enslaved, it wants to be *eleutheros* and to rule. Bad government is of little concern to it;" cf. Arist. *Pol.* 1319b27. Arist. *Pol.* 1279a7: "The state is a partnership of free men;" also 1255b19, 1280a7, 1292b4, 19956. *Nic. Eth.* 9.12.1; based on equality "equal citizens have many things in common," *Nic. Eth.* 8.11.8 and *Pol.* 1255b21; to rule by law Eur. *Suppl.* 403-8, 441; Plato *Prot.* 326d; cf. Arist. *Pol.* 1255b, 1275a, 1283b, 1291b, 1317a; and equality of law, Plato *Pol.* 276a, 301a.

[90]Thuc. 1.99.4, a violation of autonomy and independence. *Schol. Thuc.* 1.99.4: "contrary to the mores and decorum." Thuc. 3.56.2: "in accordance with the law which has universal sanction". Thuc. 4.97.3: "for it was an established custom of them all, when invading one another's country to abstain from the sanctuaries therein." *Schol.* Thuc. 4.97.3; "within the law, lawful, legal, keeping within the law." Thuc. 7.67.2: "contrary to their established usage [in military activities];" cf. Aesch. *Eum.* 706; *Pers.* 385. Hdt. 1.64.1, 196.3, 209.5; 2.121, 177.2; 3.89.1, 159.2; 5.25.1, 38.2, 74.1, 92, 94.1; 6.36.1, 43.1, 65.1, 131.1; 7.105, 106.1; 8.85.3; 9.90.1. Arist. *Pol.* 1324b7; Diod. Sic. 11.47.

[91]This point remains questionable, A. G. Woodhead, "West's Panel of Ship-Payers," ΦΟΡΟΣ (Locust Valley 1974), 176 and n. 31, 177.

[92]M. Wagner, *Zur Geschichte der attischen Kleruchien* (Tübingen 1914), 46-7; H. Nesselhauf, "Untersuchungen zur Geschichte der delisch-attischen Symmachie," *Klio* 30 (1933), 128-9; F. Hampl, "Poleis ohne Territorium," *Klio* 32 (1939), 13; *ATL* 3.157.

[93]Thuc. 1.98.1-2; *Pap. Oxy.* 13.1610 F 6 (= Ephoros *FGrH* 70 F 191); *Schol.* Aeschin. 2.31. Plut. *Kim.* 8.3-6. The enslavement of the Lacedaemonian helots was termed *douleia* rather than *andrapodismos* (Thuc. 5.23.3), as Thucydides' reference to their enslavement during the Messenian Wars presented a connotation of political conquest, 1.101.2.

[94]Thuc. 1.76.2, 115.1, 144.2; Diod. Sic. 12.7, 26.2, 28.4.

[95]Hdt. 9.105; How and Wells, *Commentary on Herodotus* 2, 332; White "Some Agiad Dates," *JHS* 84 (1964), 147.

[96]Hdt. 6.99.2; 8.66.2.

[97]Hdt. 8.112.2, 121.1; 9.105.

Chapter 11: Ionian Discontent with Athenian Imperialism

[1]Arr. *An.* 3.16.7; Paus. 1.8.5; returned to Athens in 331 B.C. by Alexander III. Aulus Gellius noted (7.17.1) that Xerxes also took to Susa an Athenian library. On Aulus Gellius, B. Baldwin, *Studies in Aulus Gellius* (Lawrence 1975), noted (9-10, 86-7) that he was an honest plodder, always "citing a reputable source" and studied in metropolitan libraries, taking considerable time in gathering and assembling materials which would otherwise be little known or altogether lost. His work is "an intellectual junk heap or a magpie's nest."

[2]J. M. Bigwood, "Ctesias of Cnidus" (Ph.D. dissertation, Harvard 1964), 156-64; Cameron, "Darius and Xerxes in Babylonia," *AJSL* 58 (1941), 319-25; Olmstead, *History of the Persian Empire* 236-7; F. M. T. de Liagre Böhl, "Die babylonischen Prätendenten zur Zeit Xerxes," *Bibliotheca Orientalis* 19 (1962), 110-4.

[3]J. Vogt, "Die Hellenisierung der Perser in der Trägodie des Aischylos: Religiöse Dichtung und historisches Zeugnis," in *Antike und Universalgeschichte: Festschrift für Hans Erich Stier* (Münster 1972), 131-45.

[4]*SEG* X.320; Simonides F 76; Marmor Parium *FGrH* 239 F 54; Lucian *Philops* 18; B. D. Meritt, "Greek Inscriptions," *Hesperia* 5 (1936), 355-8, [*isonomon* pa]*trida* is conjecture. M. Hirsch, "Die athenischen Tyrannenmörder in Geschichtsschreibung und Volkslegende," *Klio* 20 (1926), 129-67; H. Friedel, "Der Tyrannenmord in Gesetzbegung und Volksmeinung der Griechen," *Würzburger Studien zur Altertumswissenschaft* (Stuttgart 1937); K. Schefold, "Die Tyrannenmörder," *Museum Helveticum* 1 (1944), 189-202; S. Brunnsåker, *The Tyrant-Slayers of Kritios and Nesiotes* (Lund 1955); B. B. Shefton, "Some Iconographic Remarks on the 'Tyrannicides,'" *AJA* 64 (1960), 173-9; C. W. Fornara, "The Cult of Harmodius and Aristogeiton," *Philologus* 114 (1970), 155-80; Wycherly, *Stones of Athens* 73-4.

[5]D. Page, *Poetae Melici Graeci* (Oxford 1962), nos. 893-6; V. Ehrenberg, "Das Harmodioslied," *Wiener Studien* 69 (1956), 57-69; see A. E. Raubitschek, "Das Datislied," in K. Schauenburg (ed.), *Charities, Studien zur Altertumswissenschaft* (Bonn 1957), 234-42.

[6]V. Ehrenberg, "The Origins of Democracy," *Historia* 1 (1950), 515-48; C. Kardara, "On Theseus and the Tyrannicides," *AJA* 55 (1951), 293-300; "The Tyrannicides Once More," *AJA* 64 (1960), 281; C. M. Bowra, *Greek Lyric Poetry* 2nd ed. (Oxford 1961), 373-6; A. J. Podlecki, "The Political Significance of the Athenian 'Tyrannicide-Cult,'" *Historia* 15 (1966), 129-41; M. Ostwald, *Nomos and the Beginnings of Athenian Democracy* (Oxford 1969), 96-136, 182-5; M. Moggi, "I furti di Statue attribuiti a Serse e le relative restituzioni," *Annali della Scuola Normale Superiore di Pisa: Classe de Lettere e Filosofia* 3.3 (1973), 1-42; J. H. Kroll, "Wappenmünzen, Gorgoneia, Owls," *Museum Notes* 26 (1981), 26-8.

[7]A. Raubitschek, "Two Monuments Erected after the Victory of Marathon," *AJA* 44 (1940), 53-9; F. Jacoby, "Some Athenian Epigrams from the Persian Wars," *Hesperia* 14 (1945), 156-211; W. Peek, "Aus der Werkstatt," *Studies Presented to David Moore Robinson* 2, 305-12; B. D. Meritt, "Epigrams from the Battle of Marathon," *The Aegean and the Near East: Studies Presented to Hetty Goldman* (Locust Valley 1956), 268-80; P. Amandry, "Sur les 'Épigrammes de Marathon'," in F. Eckstein (ed.), Θεωρία: *Festschrift für W.-H. Schuchhardt* (Baden-Baden 1960), 1-8; W. Peek, "Zur den Perser Epigrammen," *Hermes* 88 (1960), 494-98; B.D. Meritt," The Marathon Epigrams Again," *AJP* 83 (1962), 294-8; K.-W. Welwei, "Die 'Marathon-Epigramme' von der athenischen Agora," *Historia* 19 (1970), 295-305; W. C. West III, "Saviours of Greece," *GRBS* 11 (1970), 271-82; M. L. Lang, "Again the 'Marathon' Epigram," ΦΟΡΟΣ 80.

[8]Wycherly, *Stones of Athens* 106.

[9]H. Strasburger, "Herodot und das perikleische Athen," *Historia* 4 (1955), 1-25; F. D. Harvey, "The Political Sympathies of Herodotus," *Historia* 15 (1966), 254-5; J. Bleicken, "Zur Entstehung der Verfassungstypologie im 5. Jahrhundert v. Chr.," *Historia* 28 (1979), 163-71.

[10]K.A. Raaflaub, "Athens 'Ideologie der Macht' und die Freiheit des Tyrannen," in W. Schuller (ed.), *Studien zum Attischen Seebund (Xenia: Konstanzer althistorische Vorträge und Forschungen;* Heft 8), (Konstanz 1984), 45-86.

[11]Miletos (Hdt. 6.18), Thasos (Hdt. 6.46); Pritchett, *Greek State at War* 1, 61-5.

[12]Arist. *Pol.* 1267b, 1330b23; G. Kleiner, *Die Ruinen von Milet* (Berlin 1968), 24-32; J.R. McCredie, "Hippodamos of Miletos," in D.G. Mitten, D.G. Pedley, and J.A. Scott (eds.), *Studies Presented to George M.A. Hanfmann* (Cambridge, Mass. 1971), 95-100.

[13]Kleiner, *Die Ruinen von Milet* 24-32.

[14]*Pap. Oxy.* 13.1610 F 6 (= Ephoros *FGrH* 70 F 191); Diod. Sic. 11.60.2; Plut. *Kim.* 7-8.2; Nepos *Cim.* 2.2; *Schol.* Aeschin. 2.31; Aeschin. 3.183-5; Paus. 8.8.9; Smart, "Kimon's Capture of Eion," *JHS* 87 (1967), 136-8; C.M. Danov, *Altthrakien* (Berlin 1976), 279.

[15]Pindar F 36.65-7 (*Pap. Oxy.* 5.841); J.N. Svoronos, "L'Hellénisme primitif de la Macédoine prouvé par la numismatique et l'or du Pangée," *Journal international d'Archeologie numismatique* 19 (1918-1919), 1-261; T.D. Ziatkovskaia, "The South-Thracian Tribal Federation in the Sixth and Fifth Centuries B.C.," *VDI* 2 (1967), 147-58 [in Russian].

[16]D. Müller, "Von Doriskos nach Therme. Der Weg des Xerxes-Heeres durch Thrakien und Ostmakedonien," *Chiron* 5 (1975), 2-3; N.G.L. Hammond, "The Extent of Persian Occupation in Thrace," *Chiron* 10 (1980), 53-61.

[17]Justin 9.1.3; Fornara, "Some Aspects of the Career of Pausanias of Sparta," *Historia* 15 (1966), 261-71.

[18]Thuc. 1.98.2; *Pap. Oxy.* 13.1610 (= Ephoros *FGrH* 70 F 191, fr. 6); Diod. Sic. 11.60.2; Plut. *Theseus* 36.1-2; *Kim.* 8.3-7; Podlecki, "Cimon, Skyros and 'Theseus' Bones,' " *JHS* 91 (1971), 141-3.

[19]*IG* 1^2.928 (*SEG* X.405); B.D. Meritt, "An Athenian Casualty List," *Hesperia* 25 (1956), 375-7; Thuc. 1.100.3; 4.102.2; Diod. Sic. 11.70.5; 12.68.2; Paus. 1.29.4-5; Plut. *Kim.* 14.1; Nepos *Cim.* 2.2; *ATL* 3.106-10; Deane, *Thucydides' Dates* 13-5; Danov, *Altthrakien* 279; Milton, "The Date of Thucydides' Synchronism of the Siege of Naxos with Themistokles," *Historia* 28 (1979), 258. Milton's persuasive argument demands a reassessment of the dates assigned to events during the second quarter of the fifth century. Deane's study offers such a reassessment. Few dates, however, are secure.

[20]Hdt. 5.17.2; Plut. *Kim.* 14.3; P. Franke, "Geschichte, Politik und Münzpragung von frühen Makedonien," *Jahrbuch für Numismatik und Geltgeschichte* 3-4 (1952-3), 109. Whether King Alexander I of Macedon acted according to pro-Persian diplomacy is questionable, yet it was clearly anti-Athenian to block Athenian intervention in the eastern Macedonian frontier.

[21]A. Höck, "Das Odrysenreich in Thrakien," *Hermes* 26 (1891), 76-117; Danov, *Altthrakien* 222-36, 282-317.

[22]Hdt. 9.105; Thuc. 1.98.3. G. d'Aspremont Lynden, "L'Empire d'Athènes et la démocratie sociale de Périclès," *Lettres d'humanité* 5 (1946), 86; G. Busolt, *Griechische Staatskunde* 4.1.1 (Munich 1926), 1272, suggested Athens established a klerouchy at Karystos.

[23]Thuc. 1.98.4; *Schol.* Thuc. 1.98.4; cf. Thuc. 4.97.3, 7.67.2; also Arist. *Pol.* 1284a38: "They [the Athenians] humbled these [Samos, Chios, and Lesbos] contrary to the alliance;" and Thuc. 3.10.6, a reference to "when all members were under the same treaty."

[24]Milton, "The Date of Thucydides' Synchronism," *Historia* 28 (1979), 262.

[25]Pap. Oxy. 13.1610 F 8 (= Ephoros *FGrH* 70 F 191); Diod. Sic. 11.60.1-7; Plut. *Kim.* 12.1-5; Frontinus 3.2.5.

[26]R. Meiggs, "The Crisis of Athenian Imperialism," *HSCP* 67 (1963), 6-8; J.P. Barron, "The Fifth-Century Diskoboloi of Kos," in C. Kraay and G. Jenkins (eds.), *Essays in Greek Coinage Presented to Stanley Robinson* (Oxford 1968), 75-89.

[27]P. Roos, *The Rock-Tombs of Caunus* I: *The Architecture, Studies in Mediterranean Archaeology* 34.1 (Göteborg 1972); W. A. P. Childs, *The City-Reliefs of Lycia* (Princeton 1978), X, 4-5, 107.

[28]Pap. Oxy. 13.1610 F 191.56-61 (= Ephoros *FGrH* 70 F 191); Diod. Sic. 11.60.1, 60.4; Plut. *Kim.* 12.1, 3-4; Frontinus 3.2.5; W. Peek, "Die Kämpfe am Eurymedon," *HSCP Suppl.* 1 (1940), 97-120; Meiggs, *Athenian Empire* 56-8, 73-86; C.R. Rubincam, "A Note on Oxyrhinchus Papyrus 1610," *Phoenix* 30 (1976), 357-66.

[29]Thuc. 1.100.1; *Pap. Oxy.* 13.1610 (=Ephoros *FGrH* 70 F 191); Diod. Sic. 11.60.3-62; Plut. *Kim.* 12-13.3; Nepos *Cim.* 2.2-3; Paus. 1.29.14, 10.15.4; Aristod. 11.2, 46.2, 49.2; Justin 2.15.20; Polyainos 2.15.20; Lykourgos 72; Plut. *Kim.* 9, half of the booty went to the confederate treasury on Delos, the other half to the Athenians who spent those funds on the great south wall of the acropolis, R. Carpenter, *The Architects of the Parthenon* (Baltimore 1970), 165-7; J. S. Boersma, *Athenian Building Policy from 561/0 to 405/4 B.C.* (Groningen 1970), 52-3.

[30]Milton, "The Date of Thucydides' Synchronism," *Historia* 28 (1979), 267-8.

[31]Trans. A. French, *The Athenian Half-Century* (Sidney 1971), 38.

[32]Marmor Parium *FGrH* 239 F 57; P. J. Bicknell, "The Comet of 480 B.C. and the Owls of Athens," *New Zealand Numismatic Journal* 14.3 (1977), 18-21; "Again the Comet of 480 and the Owl of Athens," *New Zealand Numismatic Journal* 15.2 (1980), 62-3.

[33]Meiggs, *Athenian Empire* 84-6; Deane, *Thucydides' Dates* 15-7.

[34]M. I. Finley, "The Fifth-Century Athenian Empire," in P. S. A. Garnsey and C. R. Whittaker (eds.), *Imperialism in the Ancient World* (Cambridge 1978), 103.

[35]Olmstead, *History of the Persian Empire* 289.

[36]Pap. Oxy. 13.1610 F 191.128-32 (= Ephoros *FGrH* 70 F 191); Diod. Sic. 11.69, 11.71.1; Prášek, *Geschichte der Meder und Perser* 2, 160.

[37]Kübler, "Die persische Politik," Spamitres K-356, variant Aspamitres (K-[103]+), Mithridates K-255.

[38]Justin 3.1.2; after Darius' "Gang of Seven," as noted on Bisitun, Seven became a basic Persian Group, and revived during the Sasanian period as the King's seven trusted officials.

[39]Artapanos, variant Artapanes; Ktesias *FGrH* 688 F 29-30; *Pap. Oxy.* 13.1610 F 15-6 (= Ephoros *FGrH* 70 F 191); Arist. *Pol.* 1311b34, placed the assassination of Dareios before that of Xerxes; Diod. Sic. 11.69, 71.1-3; Justin 3.1.1-9.

[40]Frye, "Persepolis Again," *JNES* 33 (1974), 383-6; Tilia, *Studies and Restorations at Persepolis and Other Sites* 1, 175-240; A. S. Shahbazi, "The Persepolis 'Treasury Reliefs' Once More," *AMI* 9 (1976), 151-6.

[41]Diod. Sic. 11.57-8.1; Plut. *Them.* 29.5, 31.1-3; Nepos *Them.* 10.2-3; Aristod. 10.5; Podlecki, *Life of Themistocles* 41-2, Themistokles held some kind of office, perhaps prytanis, obtained 50 talents per year from his estates, and issued small denomination coins to pay troops in his private employ.

[42]Deane, *Thucydides' Dates* 21-2; Meiggs, *Athenian Empire* 92-128.

[43]A. Momigliano, "La spedizione ateniese in Egitto," *Aegyptus* 10 (1929), 190-206; J. Barns, "Cimon and the First Athenian Expedition to Cyprus," *Historia* 2 (1953), 163-76; A. Argentati, "La spedizione in Egitto (459-454 ? a.C) nel quadro della politica estera ateniese," *Acme* 6 (1953), 379-404; J. Scharf, "Die erste ägyptische Expedition der Athener," *Historia* 3 (1954/5), 308-25; P. Salmon, *La Politique Egyptienne d'Athenes* (Brussels 1965), 90-192; J. M. Libourel, "The Athenian Disaster in Egypt," *AJP* 92 (1971), 605-15; Bigwood, "Ctesias' Account of the Revolt of Inarus," *Phoenix* 30 (1976), 1-25.

[44]"Ionians" as a fifth century B.C. term for the Delian Confederacy, Thuc. 1.96.1; *Ath. Pol.* 23.5; note *ATL* 3.227; Gomme *HCT* 1. 271.

[45]Jeffery, *Local Scripts of Archaic Greece* 331, 342; pl. 63, no. 21: "For this deed, there are at hand many witnesses, since on the Nile Furious Ares established battle in the islands about beloved Memphis,<a war>of the Medes and the Greeks, and the Samians took fifteen Phoenician Ships."

[46]*ATL* 3.9-11; Meiggs, *Athenian Empire* 102, 420-1.

[47]Deane, *Thucydides' Dates* 46-62.

[48]Plutarch *Arist.* 25.3, noted that the move of the Treasury was "contrary to the charter," which indeed it was until the Samian proposal had been properly discussed and voted upon in the Synod. This can not be interpreted as an Athenian breach of the covenant. Plutarch was simply noting that such a move was contrary to the charter and implied "unless properly discussed."

[49]*ATL* 3.28.

[50]Meiggs, *Athenian Empire* 90; Finley, "The Fifth-Century Athenian Empire," in Garnsey and Whittaker, *Imperialism* 112-3.

[51]Balcer, "The Athenian Episkopos and the Achaemenid's 'King's Eye'," *AJP* 98 (1977), 252-63.

[52]J. M. Balcer, "Imperial Magistrates in the Athenian Empire," *Historia* 25 (1976), 257-87; M. H. Hansen, "Seven Hundred *Archai* in Classical Athens," *GRBS* 21 (1980), 151-73.

[53]Loenen, *Stasis* 7-8; Lincott, *Violence, Civil Strife and Revolution* 90-103.

[54]*ATL* 1.248-9, 272; *ATL* 2.79; *ATL* 3.21, 266; Engelmann and Merkelbach, *Die Inschriften von Erythrai und Klazomenai* 1, 33-7; L. I. Highby, "The Erythrai Decree," *Klio Beiheft* 36 (1936); B. D. Meritt, "Attic Inscriptions of the Fifth Century (Athens and Erythrai)," *Hesperia* 14 (1945), 82-3; "Greek Inscriptions (77. Erythrai and Athens)," *Hesperia* 15 (1946), 246-9. IG 1^2.11 and 12/13a do not relate to *IG* 1^3.14 but probably belong to the 440's rather than to 452 B.C. (?), and indicate a second rebellion c. 446/5-445/4 B.C. as suggested by the absence of tribute, *ATL* 1.272; R. Sealey, "Notes on Tribute-Quota Lists 5, 6, and 7 of the Athenian Empire," *Phoenix* 24 (1970), 17.

[55]*IG* 1^3.14 = Engelmann and Merkelbach, *Inschriften von Erythrai and Klazomenai* 38-47; this text supersedes ML *GHI* 40; Bengtson *SV* 2.134; *ATL* 2. D10. Traditionally dated 453/2 B.C. but uncertain, Engelmann and Merkelbach 41.

[56]Balcer, *Athenian Regulations for Chalkis* 55-65.

[57]Engelmann and Merkelbach, *Inschriften von Erythrai und Klazomenai* 1, 22-32.

[58]*ATL* 1.342-3; *ATL* 2. List 1, Col. VI: 19-22; J. L. Benson, *Ancient Leros* (Durham 1963), 45-8.

[59]B. D. Meritt, "The Tribute Quota List of 454/3 B.C.," *Hesperia* 41 (1972), 403-17; Col. III: 18-20.

[60]*ATL* 1: Bolbai, Lapsimandros, Erines, Amynanda, Paktyes-Idyma, Ouranion, Oula, Tarbanes; *ATL* 2. List 2, Col. I: 11-18; *ATL* 3.6-9; Meiggs, *Athenian Empire* 118, 238.

[61]*ATL* 2. List 3, Col. II: 28.

[62]Balcer, "Miletos (*IG* 1^2.22 [1^3.21]) and the Structures of Alliances," in W. Schuller (ed.), *Studien zum Attischen Seebund* (*Xenia: Konstanzer althistorische Vorträge und Forschungen*; Heft 8) (Konstanz 1984), 11-30. G. Glotz, "Une inscription de Milet," *CRAI* (1906), 511-29; J. H. Oliver, "The Athenian Decree Concerning Miletos in 450/49 B.C.," *TAPA* 66 (1935), 177-98; A. J. Earp, "Athens and Miletos ca. 450 B.C.," *Phoenix* 8 (1954), 142-7; Sokolowski, *Lois Sacrées de l'Asie Mineure* 129-35; Barron, "Milesian Politics and Athenian Propaganda, c. 460-440 B.C.," *JHS* 82 (1962), 1-6; P. Herrmann, "Zu den Beziehungen zwischen Athen and Milet im 5. Jahrhundert," *Klio* 52 (1970), 163-73; C. Fornara, "The Date of the 'Regulations for Miletos'," *AJP* 92 (1971), 473-5; H.-J. Gehrke, "Zur Geschichte Milets in der Mitte des 5. Jahrhunderts v. Chr.," *Historia* 29 (1980), 17-31; H. B. Mattingly, "The Athenian Decree for Miletos (IG 1^2.22+ = ATL II, D11): A Postscript," *Historia* 30 (1981), 113-7.

[63]Some scholars, however, deny this, such as J. D. Smart, "Review Article: The Athenian Empire," *Phoenix* 31 (1977), 245-57; in review of Meiggs, *Athenian Empire* and W. Schuller, *Die Herrschaft der Athener im Ersten Attischen Seebund* (Berlin 1974).

Chapter 12. Ionia under Athenian Imperialism

[1]Deane, *Thucydides' Dates* 63-4; Meiggs, *Athenian Empire* 125. Kyme, Phokaia, and Teos are also missing from the collected fragments of the 453 and 452 B.C. tribute lists. They may have been inscribed upon the missing fragments. Knowledge of conditions there are not sufficient to warrant speculation about revolutions.

[2]E. F. Bloedow, "Corn Supply and Athenian Imperialism," *AC* 44 (1975), 20-9.

[3]Phanodemos *FGrH* 325 F 23 (Plut. *Kim.* 18-19.2) gave a much embellished story; and Diod. Sic. 12.3-4 a third version. Meiggs, *Athenian Empire* 126-8; Diodorus may have confused Ephoros' history of Eurymedon with this campaign against Cyprus. S. T. Parker, "The Objectives and Strategy of Cimon's Expedition to Cyprus," *AJP* 97 (1976), 30-8.

[4]Trans. French, *The Athenian Half-Century* 38.

[5]Meiggs, *Athenian Empire* 92-3, 487-95.

[6]"The Peace of Kallias," in *Athenian Studies Presented to W. S. Ferguson: HSCP Suppl.* 1 (1940), 121-56; also in *Essays in Greek History* 201-32.

[7]J. H. Oliver, "The Peace of Callias and the Pontic Expedition of Pericles," *Historia* 6 (1957), 255; A. Andrewes, "Thucydides and the Persians," *Historia* 10 (1961), 15-8; R. Meiggs, "The Crisis of Athenian Imperialism," *HSCP* 67 (1963), 10-7; K. Kraft, "Bemerkungen zu den Perserkriegen," *Hermes* 92 (1964), 158-71; A. E. Raubitschek, "Treaties between Persia and Athens," *GRBS* 5 (1964), 151-9; S. K. Eddy, "On the Peace of Callias," *CP* 65 (1970), 8-14; C. L. Murison, "The Peace of Callias: Its Historical Context," *Phoenix* 25 (1971), 12-31, rejected Wade-Gery's thesis; as did C. Schrader, *La Paz de Calias: Testimonios e Interpretacion* (Barcelona 1976); Meiggs, *Athenian Empire* 129-51, 487-95; A. R. Hands, "In Favor of a Peace of Kallias," *Mnemosyne* Ser. 4.28 (1975), 193-5; W. E. Thompson, "The Peace of Callias in the Fourth Century," *Historia* 30 (1981), 164-77; J. Walsh, "The Authenticity and the Dates for the Peace of Callias and the Congress Decree," *Chiron* 11 (1981), 31-63, returns to Eddy's thesis. The fifth century use of *autonomous* in this treaty is questionable, Ostwald, *Autonomia* 25-6.

[8]Meiggs, *Athenian Empire* 150 argued that, at this point, the Athenians demanded the defortification of Ionian poleis. I see, however, no evidence for the reconstruction of fortifications after 479 B.C.

[9]W. A. Laidlaw, *Delos* (Oxford 1933), 63; Wüst, "Amphiktyonie, Eidgenossenschaft, Symmachie," *Historia* 3 (1954/5), 129-53.

[10]In Balcer, "Separatism and Anti-Separatism," *Historia* 23 (1974), 35-9, this is analyzed in detail. G. W. Philaretos, "Un congrès à Athènes sous Périclès pour la liberté des mers et la paix," *L'Acropole Revue Mensuelle* 1 (1920), 104-11; K. Dienelt, *Die Friedenspolitik des Perikles* (Vienna 1958), 22; A. E. Raubitschek, "The Peace Policy of Pericles," *AJA* 70 (1966), 37-42; R. Seager, "The Congress Decree: Some Doubts and Hypotheses," *Historia* 18 (1969), 129-41; F. Schachermeyr, *Perikles* (Stuttgart 1969), 135-6; *Geistesgeschichte der Perikleischen Zeit* (Stuttgart 1971), 30-1; A. B. Bosworth, "The Congress Decree: Another Hypothesis," *Historia* 20 (1971), 600-16; B. R. MacDonald, "The Authenticity of the Congress Decree," *Historia* 31 (1982), 120-3.

[11]*IG* 1³.9; Tod *GHI* 1².39; *SEG* X.18; Bengtson *SV* 142; B. D. Meritt, "Athens and the Amphiktyonic League," *AJP* 69 (1948), 312-4; A. Wilhelm, "IG 1²26," *Mnemosyne* 2 (1949), 286-93; B. D. Meritt, "Athens and the Amphiktyonic League," *AJP* 75 (1954), 369-73; M. Sordi, "La posizione di Delfi a dell' Anfizionia nel decennio tra Tanagra e Coronea," *Rivista di Filologia* 86 (1958), 48-65; G. Zeilhofer, *Sparta, Delphoi und die Amphiktyonen im 5. Jahrhundert vor Christus* (Erlangen 1961), 43-56.

[12]Kimon brought many Greeks and non-Greeks into the Confederacy, *Pap. Oxy.* 13.1610 (= Ephoros *FGrH* 70 F 191); Diod. Sic. 11.60.3-4; *ATL* 1.334-5, *Lykioi kai synteleis*, 446/5 B.C. payment; Gomme *HCT* 1. 290; S. Perlman, "Panhellenism, the Polis and Imperialism," *Historia* 25 (1976), 1-30.

[13]Plut. *Kim.* 8.5-7; *Thes.* 26.1-4; *Paus.* 1.17.6; W. R. Connor, "Theseus in Classical Athens," in A. Ward (ed.), *The Quest for Theseus* (New York 1970), 143-74; Podlecki, "Cimon, Skyros and 'Theseus' Bones,'" *JHS* 91 (1971), 141-3.

[14]Plut. *Thes.* 24.3; Paus. 8.2.1; *Schol.* Plato *Parm.* 127a; J. A. Davidson, "Notes on the Panathenaia," *JHS* 78 (1958), 23-41.

[15]Matthews, *Panyassis of Halikarnassos* 26-31, F24 K, F25 K, and F29, 115-25, 135-7.

[16]B. D. Meritt, and H. Wade-Gery, "The Dating of Documents to the Mid-Fifth Century—I," *JHS* 82 (1962), 69-71; Barron, "Religious Propaganda of the Delian League," *JHS* 84 (1964), 35-48; Raubitschek, "The Peace Policy of Pericles," *AJA* 70 (1966), 37-41; W. K. Pritchett, "The Transfer of the Delian Treasury," *Historia* 18 (1969), 21.

[17]H. T. Wade-Gery, "Thucydides the son of Melesias," *JHS* 52 (1932), 217; also in *Essays in Greek History* 254-5; V. Ehrenberg, "The Foundation of Thurii," *AJP* 69 (1948), 163; *ATL* 3.105; A. E. Raubitschek, "Theopompos on Thucydides, son of Melesias," *Phoenix* 14 (1960), 81-95; F. J. Frost, "Pericles, Thucydides, Son of Melesias, and Athenian Politics before the War," *Historia* 13 (1964), 385-99; Raubitschek, "Peace Policy of Pericles," *AJA* 70 (1966), 37-41.

[18]T. L. Shear Jr., "The Early Projects of the Periklean Building Program" (Ph.D. dissertation, Princeton University 1967).

[19]*Schol.* Dem. 22.13-4; U. Wilcken, "Der Anonymus Argentinensis," *Hermes* 42 (1907), 374-418; H. T. Wade-Gery and B. D. Meritt, "Athenian Resources in 449 and 431 B.C.," *Hesperia* 26 (1957), 163-88.

[20]A. W. Gomme, "Thucydides ii.13.3: An Answer to Professor Meritt," *Historia* 3 (1954/5), 333-8.

[21]*IG* 1².339-53 with *SEG* X. 246-56; *IG* 1².354-62 with *SEG* X. 257-63; Meiggs, *Athenian Empire* 130.

[22]Balcer, *Athenian Regulations for Chalkis* 102-42.

[23]*ATL* 3.142; B. D. Meritt, "Greek Inscriptions," *Hesperia* 13 (1944), 216-7.

[24] Balcer, *Athenian Regulations for Chalkis* 118–42; *IG* 1³.40, lines 76–9 of Archestratos' rider.

[25] Aesch. *Eum.* 360–4; Xen. *Sym.* 5.2; Plato *Chrm.* 176c; Isaeus 6.12-3, 15; R. Bonner, *Evidence in Athenian Courts* (Chicago 1905), 49; G. Calhoun, "Athenian Magistrates and Special Pleas," *CP* 14 (1919), 338–50; U. Paoli, *Studi sul processo attico* (Padua 1933), 66, 83; R. Bonner and G. Smith, *Administration of Justice from Homer to Aristotle* 2 (Chicago 1938), 250-3; A. Dorjahn, "On the Athenian Anakrisis," *CP* 36 (1941), 182-5; H. Wolff, "The Origin of Judicial Litigation among the Greeks," *Traditio* 4 (1946), 67-9; W. Jones, *The Law and Legal Theory of the Greeks* (Oxford 1956), 299; D. MacDowell, *The Law in Classical Athens* (London 1978), 239-42.

[26] *IG* 1³.55: B 11-4 (restoration); E. Balogh, *Political Refugees in Ancient Greece* (Witwatersrand 1943), 24-6, nn. 69-71; D. MacDowell, *Athenian Homicide Law in the Age of the Orators* (Manchester 1963), 113-22.

[27] [Lys.] 6.24-5; Aeschin. 1.19-21, 28; *IG* 1³.104: 26-9; U. Kahrstedt, *Staatsgebiet und Staatsangehörige in Athen* (Stuttgart 1934), 106-11.

[28] Lys. 13.67; Dem. 8.66, 19.137; L. Losada, *The Fifth Column in the Peloponnesian War* (Leiden 1972); G. Starr, *Political Intelligence in Classical Greece* (Leiden 1974), 16-7.

[29] U. Paoli, *Studi di diritto attico* (Florence 1930), 304-39.

[30] P. Vinogradoff, *Outlines of Historical Jurisprudence* 2 (Oxford 1922), 189; MacDowell, *Law in Classical Athens* 73-5.

[31] R. Meiggs, "The Political Implication of the Parthenon," *Greece & Rome Suppl.* to 10 (1963), 36-45.

[32] M. Segré, "La legge ateniese sull'unificazione della moneta," *Clara Rhodos* 9 (1938), 151-78; E. S. G. Robinson, "The Athenian Currency Decree and the Coinage of the Allies," *Hesperia Suppl.* 8 (1949), 324-40; E. Erxleben, "Das Münzgesetz des delisch-attischen Seebundes I," *Archiv für Papyrusforschung* 19 (1969), 91-139; II, 20 (1970), 66-132; III, 21 (1971), 145-62.

[33] Plato *Critias* 109C, 112B; Cic. de *Nat. Deor.* 1.83; Paus. 1.14.6; B. D. Meritt, "Perikles, the Athenian Mint, and the Hephaisteion," *Proceedings of the American Philosophical Society* 119 (1975), 267-74.

[34] MacDowell, *Law in Classical Athens* 170-2.

[35] C. G. Starr, *Athenian Coinage: 480-449 B.C.* (Oxford 1970); S. Eddy critical review of Starr in *AJP* 94 (1973), 308-10; G. K. Jenkins, *Ancient Greek Coins* (London 1972), 77-83; C. M. Kraay, *Archaic and Classical Greek Coins* (London 1976), 63-74.

[36] Balcer, "Late Archaic Coinage of Skyros," *RSN* 57 (1978), 69-101; and the cogent down-dating of the Asyut Hoard (Price and Waggoner, *Archaic Greek Coinage: The "Asyut" Hoard*) noted by H. A. Cahn, "Asiut: Kritische Bemerkungen zu einer Schatzfundpublikation," *RSN* 56 (1977), 279-87; and C. M. Kraay, Review-Article, "The Asyut Hoard: Some Comments on Chronology," *NC* ser. 7.17 (1977), 189-98.

[37] Kraay, *Archaic and Classical Greek Coins* 92.

[38] Thuc. 1.98.4; Ar. *Vesp.* 354-5; Plut. *Them.* 25.2; Nepos *Them.* 25.2; *Cim.* 2.5; Kraay, *Archaic and Classical Greek Coins* 149-50.

[39] Thuc. 1.105.2-4, 108.4; Diod. Sic. 11.70.2-3, 78.3-4; Kraay, *Archaic and Classical Greek Coins* 47.

[40] See n. 63.

[41] Kraay, *Archaic and Classical Greek Coins* 260-7.

[42] Kyzikene electrum staters and "sixths" simply called gold among the 453 B.C. treasury records of the Hellenotamiai, Meritt, "The Tribute Quota-List of 454/3 B.C., *Hesperia* 41 (1972), 416.

[43] A. Schulten (ed.), *Avieno Ora Maritima* (Barcelona 1955), v.291-8, p. 116 (text 4th century A.D., re. 520 B.C.); *Tartessos* (Hamburg 1950), 72-9; G. Bonsor, *Tartesse* (New York 1922), 33-4.

[44] Hdt. 3.57, 59; T. Bent, "On the Gold and Silver Mines of Siphnos," *JHS* 6 (1885), 195-8; R. Hopper, "The Mines and Miners of Ancient Athens," *Greece & Rome* 8 (1961), 141-3.

[45] Troad, G. Hill, *A Handbook of Greek and Roman Coins* (London 1899), 20-1; Kea, *British Naval Intelligence Division, Geographic Handbook Series, Greece: Regional Geography* 3 (London 1945), 447.

[46] Pangaion, *Ath. Pol.* 15.2; Laureion, Hdt. 7.144; Aesch. *Pers.* 238; Thuc. 1.14; *Ath. Pol.* 22.7; Plut. *Them.* 4; E. Ardaillon, *Les Mines du Laurion dans l'antiquité* (Paris 1897); G. Marinos and W. Petraschek, *Laurium* (Athens 1956), [in Greek]; G. Calhoun, "Ancient Athenian Mining," *Journal of Economic and Business History* 3 (1931), 333-61; M. Cary, "Sources of Silver for the Greek World," *Mélanges Gustave Glotz* 1 (Paris 1932), 133-42; A. Momigliano, "Sull'amministrazione del Minere del Laurio," *Athenaeum* 10 (1932), 247-58; S. Lauffer, *Die Bergwerksklaven von Laureion, Akademie der Wissenschaften und Literatur in Mainz* 12 (Wiesbaden 1955).

[47] The ores from the ancient shafts of Laureion contained between 5 and 11% lead, which became a valuable product in itself; a minuscule trace of gold which was never exploited, approximately 0.13 grms Troy weight per ton of lead; and the silver at 1.86 kgrms per ton of lead which the Athenians managed to refine to 97.8% pure; Marinos and Petraschek, *Laurium* 12-23, 223-5. Laureion's mines also yielded rich quantities of cinnabar and ochre, in addition to lead and silver. Theophrastos *Lap.* 8.51.7; Pliny *HN* 23.12.158; Vitruvius 7.7; Dioscoridos 5.108; C. M. Kraay, "Gold and Copper Traces in Early Greek Silver," *Archaeometry* 1 (1958), 1-5.

[48] Meritt, "The Tribute Quota List of 454/3 B.C.," *Hesperia* 41 (1972), 415.

[49] J. P. Guépin, "Le cours du Cyzicène," *AC* 34 (1965), 200; M. Laloux, "La circulation des monnaies d'électrum de Cyzique," *Revue Belge de Numismatique* 117 (1971), 31-69; Kraay, *Archaic and Classical Greek Coins* 260-7.

[50] L. Lacroux, "A propos des monnaies de Cyzique et de la legende d'Oreste," *AC* 15 (1946), 218-21; Jenkins, *Ancient Greek Coins* 96-7.

[51] J. Babelon, *Traité de Monnaies Grecque et Romaines* 1^2 (Paris 1910), 387-9; P. Gardner, *History of Ancient Coinage* (Oxford 1918), 171.

[52] A. Baldwin, *The Electrum Coinage of Lampsakos* (New York 1914), 1-14, and 14, n. 2.

[53] J. Johnston, "An International Managed Currency in the Fifth Century," *Hermathena* 47 (1932), 137.

[54] Thuc. 1.138.5; Diod. Sic. 11.57.7; Plut. *Them.* 29.10; Strabo 13.1.12; H. Gaebler, "Die Silberprägung von Lampsakos," *Nomisma* 12 (1933), 12-20; Kraay, *Archaic and Classical Greek Coins* 244-5.

[55] Xen. *Hell.* 4.8.37; Strabo 13.1.23; Pliny *NH* 37.193; J. P. Six, "Die Münzen von Abydos," *Zeitschrift für Numismatik* 3 (1876), 237-8; E. S. G. Robinson, "Some Electrum and Gold Greek Coins," *Centennial Publication of the American Numismatic Society* (New York 1958), 593; Kraay, *Archaic and Classical Greek Coins* 245.

[56]Babelon, Traité 1[2].373-6; B. V. Head, Historia Numorum (Oxford 1911), 544.

[57]E. Babelon, "L'Étalon phocaique," Revue numismatique 3 (1895), 20-4; Head Historia Numorum 557-9; P. Gardner, "Coinage of the Athenian Empire," JHS 33 (1913), 163-4; History of Ancient Coinage 173; see T. J. Quinn, "Political Groups in Lesbos during the Peloponnesian War," Historia 20 (1971), 405-16.

[58]IG 1[2].30+23; C. P. Loughran and A. E. Raubitschek, "Three Attic Proxeny Decrees," Hesperia 16 (1947), 79; SEG X. 20; M. B. Walbank, "Honors for Parianos of Issa and his Sons Athenodoros and Ikesios," Hesperia 42 (1973), 334-9; H. B. Mattingly, "The Athenian Proxeny Decree, IG 1[2].30+23 (SEG 10.20)," Phoenix 29 (1975), 284-6.

[59]R. Sealey, "Ephialtes," CP 59 (1964), 11-22; F. Kiechle, "Athens Politik nach der Abwehr der Perser," Historische Zeitschrift 204 (1967), 265-304.

[60]Babelon, Traité 1[2].331-8; Head, Historia Numorum 552-3.

[61]F. Bodenstedt, "Studien zur Elektronprägung von Phokaia und Mytilene," RSN 52 (1973), 17-51; Weidauer, Probleme der frühen Elektronprägung; F. Bodenstedt, Phokäisches Elektron-Geld von 600-326 v. Chr. (Mainz 1976).

[62]J. A. Dengate, "The Coinage of Klazomenai" (Ph.D. dissertation, University of Pennsylvania 1967), 17-135.

[63]Babelon, Traité 1[2].303; Head, Historia Numorum 578; Gardner, History of Ancient Coinage 167; Kraay, Archaic and Classical Greek Coins 244.

[64]Babelon, Traité 1[2].270; Gardiner, "Coinage of the Athenian Empire," JHS 33 (1913), 165.

[65]L. Robert, "Décrits de Kolophon," Revue Philologique s. 3.10 (1936), 158-70; J. Milne, Kolophon and its Coinage: Numismatic Notes and Monographs 96 (New York 1941); E. S. G. Robinson, review-notice of Milne, Kolophon in Numismatic Literature 5 (Oct. 1948), 133-4; C. M. Kraay, "Monnaies provenant du site de Colophon," RSN 42 (1962/63), 9; Archaic and Classical Greek Coinage 244.

[66]Balcer, "The Early Silver Coinage of Teos," RSN 47 (1968), 5-50; Kraay, Archaic and Classical Greek Coins 243.

[67]B. V. Head, "On the Chronological Sequence of the Coins of Ephesus," NC n.s. 20 (1880), 85-105; "Coinage of Ephesus," NC 3.1 (1881), 13-4; Babelon, Traité 1[2].53-9; Head, Historia Numorum 572; Kraay, Archaic and Classical Greek Coins 244.

[68]ML GHI 117; Head, Historia Numorum 599-600; Gardner, "Coinage of the Athenian Empire," JHS 33 (1913), 161-7; A. Baldwin, "The Electrum and Silver Coins of Chios," American Journal of Numismatics 48 (1914), pl. 4.11; J. Mavrogordato, "A Chronological Arrangement of the Coins of Chios," NC 4.15 (1915), pl. 18.5; A. S. Hemmy, "The Weight-Standards of Ancient Greece and Persia," Iraq 5 (1938), 65-80; J. Boardman, "Excavations at Pindakas in Chios," BSA 53/4 (1958/9), 308 and n. 23; Kraay, Archaic and Classical Greek Coins 242-3, 260, mistakenly stated that Chios and Samos (241, 332) were subject to the Currency Decree's regulations. Meiggs and Lewis GHI 116, incorrectly stated that Chios had issued silver dekadrachms. This is to read didrachms.

[69]W. E. Thompson, "The Chian Coinage in Thucydides and Xenophon," NC s. 7.11 (1971), 323-4; see T. J. Quinn, "Political Groups at Chios: 412 B.C.," Historia 18 (1969), 22-30; Athens and Samos, Lesbos and Chios 478-404 B.C. (Manchester 1981).

[70]C. M. Kraay and V. M. Emeleus, The Composition of Greek Silver Coins (Oxford 1962), 24; Barron, The Silver Coinage of Samos 11, 49-59, 80-92; Kraay, Archaic and Classical Greek Coins 240-2, 332-4.

[71]Barron, Silver Coinage of Samos 34, 55.

[72]Ibid. 88-9.

[73]Ibid. 48-62; Jenkins, *Ancient Greek Coins* 91; R. P. Legon, "Samos in the Delian League," *Historia* 21 (1972), 145-58.

[74]H. A. Cahn, *Knidos: Die Münzen des sechsten und des fünften Jahrhunderts v. Chr.* (Berlin 1970), 44-55.

[75]A. Georgiades and W. K. Pritchett, "The Koan Fragment of the Athenian Monetary Decree," *BCH* 89 (1965), 400-40; Barron, "The Fifth-Century Diskoboloi of Kos," *Essays in Greek Coinage Presented to Stanley Robinson* 88-9; Jenkins, *Ancient Greek Coins* 90-1; Kraay, *Archaic and Classical Greek Coins* 245-6.

[76]*IG* 1³.34; *SEG* X. 31; *ATL* 2. D7; ML *GHI* 46; B. Hill and B. D. Meritt, "An Early Decree Concerning Tribute," *Hesperia* 13 (1944), 1-15.

[77]W. Wallace, "The Public Seal of Athens," *Phoenix* 3 (1949), 70-3; R. Bonner, "The Use and Effect of Attic Seals," *CP* 3 (1908), 399-407; D. Lewis, "The Public Seal of Athens," *Phoenix* 9 (1955), 32-4.

[78]This concept of contract appears in *IG* 1³.10:6-11; Thuc. 1.77; *IG* 2².141:18-25; Dem. 7.11; and is not to be interpreted as "seal" as in Hill and Meritt, "An Early Decree," *Hesperia* 13 (1944), 11.

[79]Hill and Meritt, ibid. 15; Meiggs, *Athenian Empire* 165.

[80]ML *GHI* 49:11-12; also p. 131 #5 and p. 121; A. J. Graham, *Colony and Mother City in Ancient Greece* (Manchester 1964), 62.

[81]*IG* 1³.36 (*ATL* 1.123 fig. 178, D8. fr. 2; 2. D8).

[82]C. J. Herington, *Athena Parthenos and Athena Polias* (Manchester 1955); "Athena in Athenian Literature and Cult," *Greece & Rome Suppl.* to 10 (1963), 61-73.

[83]Aigina: *IG* 4. 29; Chalkis: *IG* 12. 9. 934 (cf. Aelian *VH* 6.1); Kos: Paton and Hicks, *The Inscriptions of Cos* 148, 160; Samos: *SEG* I. 375, *IGA* 8; Barron, "Religious Propaganda," *JHS* 84 (1964), 35-48.

[84]G. E. M. de Ste Croix, "The Character of the Athenian Empire," *Historia* 3 (1954/5), 1-41; D. W. Bradeen, "The Popularity of the Athenian Empire," *Historia* 9 (1960), 257-69; T. J. Quinn, "Thucydides and the Unpopularity of the Athenian Empire," *Historia* 13 (1964), 257-66; H. Papp, "Zum Verhältnis Athens zu seinen Bündnern im attisch-delischen Seebund," *Historia* 17 (1969), 425-43; J. T. Chambers, "The Fourth-Century Athenians' View of their Fifth-Century Empire," *Parola Passato* 30 (1975), 177-91.

Chapter 13. The Frontier of Imperialism

[1]R. H. Whittaker and S. A. Levin, *Niche Theory and Application* (Stroudsburg 1975), 1-3, 418-22; Lintott, *Violence, Civil Strife and Revolution* 30.

[2]Miletos *ATL* 1.342; Erythrai 272; Ephesos 276; Teos 422; Kolophon 316; Kyme 324.

[3]Hairai *ATL* 1.222; Lebedos 328; Phokaia 436; Pygale 390; Priene 388; Myous 346; Latmos 328; Myrina 348.

[4]Emlyn-Jones, *Ionians and Hellenism* 165-6.

[5]Lintott, *Violence, Civil Strife and Revolution* 34, 58.

[6]M. O. Wason, *Class struggles in Ancient Greece* (London 1947); C. Parain, "Les caractères spécifique de la lutte de classes dans l'Antiquité classique," *La Pensée* 108 (1963), 3-25; de Ste Croix, *The Class Struggle in the Ancient Greek World* 283-93.

[7]W. Schuller, "Zur Entstehung der griechischen Demokratie ausserhalb Athens," in H. Sund and M. Timmermann (eds.), *Auf den Weg Gebracht* (Konstanz 1979), 433–47.

[8]Lintott, *Violence, Civil Strife and Revolution* 82.

[9]Snodgrass, *Archaic Greece* 33, 42.

[10]Plut. *Per.* 20.1-2; *ATL* 3.114-7, would date the expedition earlier, c. 450 B.C. For the date c. 437 B.C., see Kagan, *Outbreak of the Peloponnesian War* 387-9.

[11]*ATL* 2. List 17, p. 23; 3.212.

[12]*ATL* 1.306, 500. See Appendix II: "The Population of Ionia in the Mid-Fifth Century B.C."

[13]Iasos *ATL* 1.286; Madnasa 334; Myndos 348; Pele 372; Halikarnassos 224; Syngela 414; Keramos 306; Auliatai 242; Knidos 314; Rhodian Chersonese 440; Karbasyanda 296; Kaunos 304; Pasanda 370; Krya 320; and Phaselis 434.

[14]Tozzi, *La rivolta ionica* 80 and n. 32.

[15]Bean, *Aegean Turkey* 50; Cook, "Old Smyrna," *BSA* 53-4 (1958-9), 30.

[16]*ATL* 1.328-9.

[17] J. Boehlau and K. Schefold, *Larisa am Hermos* 1 (*Die Bauten*) (Berlin 1940), 84, n. 1; K. Schefold, *Die Griechen und ihre Nachbarn* (Berlin 1967), 232-3, pl. 263; H. von Gall, "Das persische Königszeit und die Hallenarchitektur in Iran und Griechenland," *Festschrift für Frank Brommer* (Mainz 1977), 121-3, fig. 3.

[18]Bean, *Aegean Turkey* 124-5; note also the undated Persian-style (?) "Pyramid" tomb at Sardis, G. M. A. Hanfmann, "The Fourth Campaign at Sardis (1961)," *BASOR* 166 (1962), 28-30; G. M. A. Hanfmann and J. C. Waldbaum, "The Eleventh and Twelfth Campaigns at Sardis (1968,1969)," *BASOR* 199 (1970), 36-8.

[19]Garrisons at Erythrai and Miletos; Kyzikos, Eupolis *Poleis* F 233; Byzantion, Ar. *Vesp.* 235-7; Samos, Thuc. 1.115.2-5; A. S. Nease, "Garrisons in the Athenian Empire," *Phoenix* 3 (1949), 102-11.

[20]J. Cargill, *The Second Athenian League* (Berkeley 1981), 146-50.

[21]Hairai from 3 to 1 talent in 446 B.C., *ATL* 1.222; Dios Hieron from 1000 to 500 drachmae in 446-4 B.C., 266; Erythrai from 9 to 7 talents in 446-5 B.C., 272; Kyme from 12 to 9 talents in 450-48 B.C., 324; Kolophon from 3 to 1½ talents in 450-46 B.C., 316; Phokaia from 3 to 2 talents in 446-3 B.C., 436; and Lebedos from 3 to 1 talent in 446/5 B.C., 328; Meiggs, *Athenian Empire* 121, 125.

[22]Gomme, *HCT* 1, 353-60; Kagan, *Outbreak of the Peloponnesian War* 170-8; Meiggs *Athenian Empire* 188-95; Legon, "Samos in the Delian League," *Historia* 21 (1972), 145-58; C. W. Fornara, "On the Chronology of the Samian War," *JHS* 99 (1979), 7-18; D. M. Lewis, "Additional Note," *JHS* 99 (1979), 18-9; W. Schuller, "Die Einführung der Demokratie auf Samos im 5. Jahrhundert v. Chr.," *Klio* 63 (1981), 281-8.

[23]Notion (*ATL* 1.358-9) and Kolophon (*ATL* 1.316-7) paid their tribute to Athens separately as two distinct poleis. In 450 B.C., when Kolophon revolted against Athens, Notion remained loyal (*IG* 1².14/15: ML *GHI* 47; D. Bradeen and M. McGregor, *Studies in Fifth-Century Attic Epigraphy* [Norman 1973], 94-9).

[24]E. B. Harrison, "Athena and Athens in the East Pediment of the Parthenon," *AJA* 71 (1967), 27-58; Perlman, "Panhellenism, the Polis and Imperialism," *Historia* 25 (1976), 1-30.

[25]S. van de Maele, "Le Livre VIII de Thucydide et la Politique de Sparte en Asie Mineure (412-411 av. J.-C.)," *Phoenix* 25 (1971), 32-50; Lewis, *Sparta and Persia* 62.

[26]B. M. W. Knox, *Oedipus at Thebes* (New Haven 1957), 99-106.

[27]W. R. Connor, "Tyrannis Polis," in J. H. D'Arms and J. W. Eadie (eds.), *Ancient and Modern: Essays in Honor of Gerald F. Else* (Ann Arbor 1977), 95-109; K. Raaflaub, "Polis Tyrannos: Zur Entstehung einer politischen Metapher," *Arktouros* 237-52.

[28]J. de Romilly, "La crainte dans l'oeuvre de Thucydide," *Classica et Mediaevalia* 17 (1956), 119-27; R. Sealey, "Thucydides, Herodotus, and the Causes of War," *CQ* 51 (1957), 1-12; T. E. Wick, "A Note on Thucydides I, 23.6," *AC* 44 (1975), 176-83.

BIBLIOGRAPHY

Abbott, E., "The Early History of the Delian League." *CR* 3 (1889). 387-90.

Ackroyd, Peter R., *Israel under Babylon and Persia*. Oxford 1970.

_____, "Two Old Testament Historical Problems of the Early Persian Period." *JNES* 17 (1958). 13-27.

Adams, C. J., ed., *Iranian Civilization and Culture. Essays in Honour of the 2.500th Anniversary of the Founding of the Persian Empire*. Montreal 1972.

Adcock, Frank E., "The Development of Ancient Greek Diplomacy." *AC* 17 (1948). 1-12.

_____, "Some Aspects of Ancient Greek Diplomacy." *Proceedings of the Classical Association of England and Wales* 21 (1942). 92-116.

Åkerström, Åke, *Die architektonischen Terrakotten Kleinasiens*. Lund 1966.

Africa, Thomas W., "Herodotus and Diodorus on Egypt." *JNES* 22 (1963). 254-58.

Agricola, Ernest F. M., *De Aristidis censu*. Berlin 1900.

Akurgal, Ekrem, *Ancient Civilizations and Ruins of Turkey*. Istanbul 1973.

_____, "The Early Period and the Golden Age of Ionia." *AJA* 66 (1962). 369-79.

_____, "Les Fouilles de Daskyleion." *Anatolia* 1 (1956). 20-4.

Alexander, Leigh, *The Kings of Lydia*. Princeton 1913.

Alexanderson, Bengt N., "Darius in the *Persians*." *Eranos* 65 (1967). 1-11.

Ålin, P., "Mycenaean Decline—Some Problems and Thoughts," 106-9. Edited by K. Kinzl, *Greece and the Eastern Mediterranean in Ancient History and Prehistory, Studies presented to F. Schachermeyr*. Berlin 1977.

Altheim, Franz, "Alexander und Zarathustra." *Gymnasium* 58 (1951). 123-9.

Altheim, Franz and Stiehl, R., *Die aramäische Sprache unter den Achaimeniden*. Frankfurt am Main 1963.

Aly, Wolf, *Volksmärchen, Sage und Novelle bei Herodot und seinen Zeitgenossen*. Göttingen 1921.

Amandry, Pierre, "Sur les Épigrammes de Marathon," 1-8. Θεωρία: *Festschrift für W.-H. Schuchhardt*. Edited by Felix Eckstein. Baden-Baden 1960.

_____, "La Grèce d'Asie et l'Anatolie du 8e au 6e siècle avant Jésus-Christ." *Anatolica* 2 (1968). 87-102.

Ambaglio, Delfino, "Il motivo della deportazione in Erodoto." *Rendiconti, Istituto Lombardo*. 109 (1975). 378-83.

Anderson, J. K., "Old Smyrna: The Corinthian Pottery." *BSA* 53-4 (1958-59). 138-51.

Andrewes, Anthony, *The Greek Tyrants*. London 1956.

_____, "Thucydides and the Persians." *Historia* 10 (1961). 1-18.

Anti, C., "Il vaso di Dario e i Persiani di Frinico." *Archeologica Classica* 4 (1952). 23–45.

Ardaillon, E., *Les Mines du Laurion dans l'antiquité*. Paris 1897.

Argentati, Argentina, "La spedizione in Egitto (459-454 ? a.C.) nel quadro della politica estera ateniese." *Acme* 6 (1953). 379–404.

Armayor, O. Kimbell, "Herodotus' Catalogues of the Persian Empire in Light of the Monuments and the Greek Literary Tradition." *TAPA* 108 (1978). 1–9.

_____, "Herodotus' Persian Vocabulary." *Ancient World* 1 (1978). 147–56.

_____, "The Homeric Influence on Herodotus' Story of the Labyrinth." *Classical Bulletin* 54 (1977-78). 68–72.

_____, "Sesostris and Herodotus' Autopsy of Thrace, Colchis, Inland Asia Minor, and the Levant." *HSCP* 84 (1980). 51–74.

Arnheim, M. T. W., *Aristocracy in Greek Society*. London 1977.

Aroutiounian. N. V., "Problèmes concernant da dernière périod de l'histoire d'Urartu." *AAH* 22 (1974). 415–28.

Asheri, David, "Distribuzioni di terre nell'antica Grecia." *Memorie dell'accademia delle scienza di Torino* Ser. 4a, n. 10 (1966).

_____, "Laws of Inheritance, Distribution of Land, and Political Constitutions in Ancient Greece." *Historia* 12 (1963). 1–21.

Atkinson, K. M. T., "The Legitimacy of Cambyses and Darius as Kings of Egypt." *JAOS* 76 (1956). 167–77.

Atkinson, K. T. M., "A Hellenistic Land–Conveyance: The Estate of Mnesimachus in the Plain of Sardis." *Historia* 21 (1972). 45–74.

Austin, M. M., *Greece and Egypt in the Archaic Age*. Proceedings of the Cambridge Philological Society, Suppl. 2 (1970).

Austin, M. M. and Vidal-Naquet, P., *Economic and Social History of Ancient Greece*. London 1977.

Autran, C., "L' 'oeil du roi': concept politico-administratif commun à l'Iran, à la Chine et à l'Hellade." *Humanitas* 3 (1950/51). 287–91.

Avery, Harry C., "Dramatic Devices in Aeschylus' *Persians*." *AJP* 85 (1964). 173–84.

Azarpay, Guitty, "Crowns and Some Royal Insignia in Early Iran." *Iranica Antiqua* 9 (1972). 108–15.

Babelon, Ernest, *Traité de monnaies grecque et romaines*. 4 Vols. Paris 1910.

_____, "Études sur les monnaies primitives d'Asie Minor: l'Étalon phocaïque." *Revue numismatique* 3rd s. 8 (1895). 1–44.

Bacon, Helen H., *Barbarians in Greek Tragedy*. New Haven 1961.

Badi^c, Amir Mehdi, *Les Grecs et les Barbares*. Vol. 1 Lausanne 1963; Vol. 2 Lausanne 1966.

Badian, Ernst, "A Document of Artaxerxes IV?," 40–50. Edited by Konrad H. Kinzl, *Greece and the Eastern Mediterranean in Ancient History and Prehistory*. Berlin 1977.

Bailey, H. W., "Nasā and Fasā." *Acta Iranica* 2nd. s. 6 (Leiden 1975). 309-12.

Balcer, Jack Martin, "Alexander's Burning of Persepolis." *Iranica Antiqua* 13 (1978). 119-33.

_____, "The Athenian Episkopos and the Achaemenid 'King's Eye'." *AJP* 98 (1977). 252-63.

_____, *The Athenian Regulations for Chalkis: Studies in Athenian Imperial Law*. Wiesbaden 1978.

_____, "The Date of Herodotus iv.1: Darius' Scythian Expedition." *HSCP* 76 (1972). 99-132.

_____, "The Early Silver Coinage of Teos." *RSN* 47 (1968). 5-50.

_____, "Fifth Century B.C. Ionia: A Frontier Redefined." *Comparative Frontier Studies: An Interdisciplinary Newsletter* 13 (1979). 2-3.

_____, "The Greeks and the Ancient Near East." *The Indiana Social Studies Quarterly* 32 (1979). 11-27.

_____, "Imperial Magistrates in the Athenian Empire." *Historia* 25 (1976). 257-87.

_____, "The Late Archaic Coinage of Skyros and the Forgeries of Konstantinos Christodoulos." *RSN* 57 (1978). 69-101.

_____, "The Medizing of the Regent Pausanias." *Actes du Premier Congrès international des Études Balkaniques et sud-est Européennes*. Vol. 2, Sofia 1969, 105-14.

_____, "The Persian Occupation of Thrace, 519-491 B.C.: The Economic Effects." *Actes du IIe Congrès international des Études du sud-est Européennes*. Vol. 2. Athens 1972, 241-58.

_____, "Phokaia and Teos: A Monetary Alliance." *RSN* 49 (1970). 25-34.

_____, Review of Josef Hofstetter, *Die Griechen in Persien*. Berlin 1978, in *Bibliotheca Orientalis*. 36 (1979). 276-80.

_____, Review of Russell Meiggs, *The Athenian Empire*. Oxford 1972, in *American Historical Review* 78 (1973). 661-2.

_____, "Separatism and Anti-Separatism in the Athenian Empire (478-433 B.C.)." *Historia* 23 (1974). 21-39.

_____, "Imperialism and Stasis in Fifth Century B.C. Ionia." 261-8. Edited by G. W. Bowersock, W. Burkhart, and M. Putnam, *Arktouros: Hellenic Studies presented to Bernard M. W. Knox on the occasion of his 65th Birthday*. Berlin 1979.

_____, "Athenian Politics: The Ten Years After Marathon," 27-49. Edited by T. E. Gregory and A. J. Podlecki, *Panathenaia: Studies in Athenian Life and Thought in the Classical Age*. Lawrence 1979.

_____, "Miletos (*IG* 1^2.22 [1^3.21]) and the Structures of Alliances," 11-30. Edited by Wolfgang Schuller. *Studien zum Attischen Seebund (Xenia: Konstanzer althistorische Vorträge und Forschungen*; Heft 8). Konstanz 1984.

Baldwin, Agnes, *The Electrum Coinage of Lampsakos*. New York 1914.

_____, "The Electrum and Silver Coins of Chios, Issued during the Sixth, Fifth and Fourth Centuries B.C." *American Journal of Numismatics* 48 (1914). 1-60.

Baldwin, Barry, *Studies in Aulus Gellius.* Lawrence 1975.

Balkan, Kemal, "Inscribed Bullae from Daskyleion-Ergili." *Anatolia* 4 (1959). 123-8.

Balmuth, Miriam S., "Remarks on the Appearance of the Earliest Coins," 1-7. Edited by D. G. Mitten, J. Pedley, and J. A. Scott, *Studies Presented to George M. A. Hanfmann.* Cambridge, Mass. 1971.

Balogh, Elmer, *Political Refugees in Ancient Greece.* Witwatersrand 1943.

Bammer, Anton, *Die Architektur des jüngeren Artemision von Ephesos.* Wiesbaden 1972.

_____, "Recent Excavations at the Altar of Artemis in Ephesos." *Archaeology* 27 (1974). 202-5.

Bammer, Anton, Brein, Friedrich, and Wolff, Petra, "Das Tieropfer am Artemisaltar von Ephesos." Edited by Sencer Şahin, Elmar Schwertheim, and Jörg Wagner. *Studien zur Religion und Kultur Kleinasiens: Festschrift für Friedrich Karl Dörner zum 65. Geburtstag am 28. Februar 1976.* Vol. 1. Leiden 1978.

Barnett, R. D., "ᶜAnath, Baᶜal and Pasargadae." *Mélanges de l'Université Saint-Joseph, Beirut* 45 (1969). 407-22.

_____, "Ancient Oriental Influences on Archaic Greece," 212-38. Edited by S. S. Weinberg, *The Aegean and the Near East: Studies Presented to Hetty Goldman.* Locust Valley 1956.

_____, "Early Greek and Oriental Ivories." *JHS* 68 (1948). 1-25.

_____, "The Epic of Kumarbi and the Theogony of Hesiod." *JHS* 65 (1945). 100-1.

_____, "Persepolis." *Iraq* 19 (1957). 55-77.

_____, "Some Contacts between Greek and Oriental Religions," 143-53. Edited by Otto Eissfeldt, *Éléments orientaux dans la religion Grecque ancienne.* Paris 1960.

Barns, John, "Cimon and the First Athenian Expedition to Cyprus." *Historia* 2 (1953). 163-76.

Barron, John P., "Milesian Politics and Athenian Propaganda, c. 460-440 B.C." *JHS* 82 (1962). 1-6.

_____, "Religious Propaganda of the Delian League." *JHS* 84 (1964). 35-48.

_____, *The Silver Coins of Samos.* London 1966.

_____, "The Sixth-Century Tyranny at Samos." *CQ* 14 (1964). 210-29.

_____, "The Fifth-Century Diskoboloi of Kos," 75-89. Edited by C. M. Kraay and G. K. Jenkins, *Essays in Greek Coinage Presented to Stanley Robinson.* Oxford 1968.

Barth, Fredrik, "Ecologic Relationships of Ethnic Groups in Swat, North Pakistan." *American Anthropologist* 58 (1956). 1079-89.

_____, ed., *Ethnic Groups and Boundaries.* Bergen 1969.

Bauer, Adolf, *Die Kyros-Sage und Verwandtes.* Vienna 1882.

Bean, George E., *Aegean Turkey: An Archaeological Guide.* New York 1967.

_____, *Journeys in Northern Lycia 1965-1967. Ergänzungsbände zu den Tituli Asiae Minoris* 4. Vienna 1971.

_____, *Lycian Turkey: An Archaeological Guide*. London 1978.

_____, "Notes and Inscriptions from Caunus." *JHS* 73 (1953). 10-35.

_____, "Notes and Inscriptions from Caunus." *JHS* 74 (1954). 85-110.

_____, *Turkey Beyond the Maeander*. London 1971.

_____, *Turkey's Southern Shore*. New York 1968.

Bean, George E. and Cook, J. M., "The Carian Coast III." *BSA* 52 (1957). 58-146.

_____, "The Cnidia." *BSA* 47 (1952). 171-212.

_____, "The Halicarnassus Peninsula." *BSA* 50 (1955). 85-171.

Bean, George E. and Mitford, Terence B., *Journeys in Rough Cilicia in 1962 and 1963*. Vienna 1965.

_____, *Journeys in Rough Cilicia 1964 - 1968. Ergänzungsbände zu den Tituli Asiae Minoris* 3. Vienna 1970.

Bekker, Immanuel, *Anecdota Graeca*. Berlin 1814.

Bell, Harold Idris, *Egypt: From Alexander the Great to the Arab Conquest*. Oxford 1948.

Bellen, Heinz, "Der Rachegedanke in der griechisch-persischen Auseinandersetzung." *Chiron* 4 (1974). 43-67.

Beloch, Julius, *Griechische Geschichte*. Vol. 2.1. Strassburg 1914.

Benedict, Warren C. and von Voigtlander, Elizabeth, "Darius' Bisitun Inscription, Babylonian Version, Lines 1-29." *JCS* 10 (1956). 1-10.

Bengtson, Hermann, "Die 'Ionier' in der Überlieferung des Alten Orients." *Philologus* 92 (1937). 148-55.

_____, *Die Staatsverträge des Altertums: Die Verträge der griechisch-römischen Welt von 700 bis 338 v. Chr.* Munich 1962.

_____, "Syria under the Persians," 402-8. *The Greeks and the Persians*. London 1969.

_____, "Zur Vorgeschichte der Schlact bei Salamis." *Chiron* 1 (1971). 89-94.

Ben-Gurion, David, "Cyrus, King of Persia." *Acta Iranica Hommage Universel* 1 (Leiden 1974). 127-34.

Benson, J. L., *Ancient Leros*. Durham 1963.

Bent, Theodore J., "On the Gold and Silver Mines of Siphnos." *JHS* 6 (1885). 195-8.

Benveniste, Emile, "Les classes sociales dans la tradition avestique." *Journal asiatique* 221 (1932). 117-34.

_____, *Indo-European Language and Society*. Coral Gables 1973.

_____, *Les Mages dans l'Ancien Iran*. Paris 1938.

Bequignon, Y., "Les 'Pyrgoi' de Teos." *Revue archeologique* 28 (1928). 185-208.

Bernard, Paul, "Les mortiers et pilons inscrits de Persépolis." *Studia Iranica* 1 (1972). 165-76.

Berve, Helmut, *Miltiades: Studien zur Geschichte des Mannes und seiner Zeit. Hermes Einzelschriften* 2. Berlin 1937.

_____, *Die Tyrannis bei den Griechen*, 2 Vol. Munich 1967.

Bickerman, Elias J., "Autonomia: Sur un passage de Thucydide (I.114.2)." *Revue internationale des droits de l'antiquité*, 3 s. 5 (1958). 313-43.

_____, *Chronology of the Ancient World*. London 1968.

_____, "The Edict of Cyrus in Ezra 1." *JBL* 65 (1946). 249-75.

_____, "Remarques sur le droit des gens dans la Grèce classique." *Revue internationale des droits de l'antiquité: Mélanges Ferdinand De Vissher* 4 (1950). 99-116.

_____, "A propos d'un passage de Charès de Mytilène." *La Parola del Passato* 91 (1963). 241-55.

_____, Review of M. A. Dandamaev, *Persien unter den Ersten Achämeniden (6. Jahrhundert v. Chr.)*. Wiesbaden 1976, in *Athenaeum* 56 (1978). 413-5.

_____, "The 'Zoroastrian' Calendar." *Archiv Orientální* 35 (1967). 197-207.

Bickerman, E. J. and Tadmor, H., "Darius I, Pseudo-Smerdis and the Magi." *Athenaeum* 56 (1978). 239-61.

Bicknell, P. J., "Again the Comet of 480 and the Owls of Athens." *The New Zealand Numismatic Journal* 15.2 (June 1980). 62-3.

_____, "The Comet of 480 B.C. and the Owls of Athens." *The New Zealand Numismatic Journal* 14.3 (Oct.1977). 18-21.

_____, "The Command Structure and Generals of the Marathon Campaign." *AC* 39 (1970). 427-42.

Bigwood, Joan M., "Ctesias' Account of the Revolt of Inarus." *Phoenix* 30 (1976). 1-25.

_____, "Ctesias as Historian of the *Persian Wars*." *Phoenix* 32 (1978). 19-41.

_____, "Ctesias' Description of Babylon." *AJAH* 3 (1978). 32-51.

_____, "Ctesias of Cnidus." Ph.D. dissertation, Harvard University 1964.

_____, Review of Robert Drews, *The Greek Accounts of Eastern History*. Washington D. C. 1973, in *Phoenix* 29 (1975). 199-200.

Billingmeier, J. -Chr. "Troy, Taruiša, and the Etruscans." *Talanta* 8-9 (1977). 5-10.

Bing, John Daniel, "A History of Cilicia during the Assyrian Period." Ph.D. dissertation, Indiana University 1969.

Bintliff, J. L., "New Approaches to Human Geography. Prehistoric Greece: A Case Study," 59-114. Edited by Francis W. Carter, *An Historical Geography of the Balkans*. London 1977.

Birmingham, J. M., "The Overland Route Across Anatolia in the Eighth and Seventh Centuries B.C." *Anatolian Studies* 11 (1961). 185-95.

Bittel, Kurt, *Grundzüge der Vor- und Frühgeschichte Kleinasiens*. Tübingen 1950.

Bivar, A. D. H., "Document and Symbol in the Art of the Achaemenids." *Acta Iranica Monumentum H. S. Nyberg* 1 (Leiden 1975). 49-67.

_____, "A Hoard of Ingot-Currency of the Median Period from Nūsh-i Jān, near Malayir." *Iran* 9 (1971). 97-112.

_____, "A Persian Monument at Athens, and its Connections with the Achaemenid State Seals," 43-61. Edited by Mary Boyce and Ilya Gershevitch, *W. B. Henning Memorial Volume*. London 1970.

_____, "A 'Satrap' of Cyrus the Younger." *NC* 7s.1 (1961). 119-27.

_____, "Religious Subjects on Achaemenid Seals," 90-105. Edited by J. R. Hinnell's, *Mithraic Studies* 1. Manchester 1975.

Blackman, David, "The Athenian Navy and Allied Naval Contribution in the Pentecontaetia." *GRBS* 10 (1969). 180-216.

Blamire, Alec, "Herodotus and Histiaeus." *CQ* 9 (1959). 142-54.

_____, "Pausanias and Persia." *GRBS* 11 (1970). 295-305.

Bleeker, C. J., "Wer war Zarathustra?" *Persica* 7 (1975-1978). 25-41.

Blegen, Carl W., Boulter, Cedric G., Caskey, John L., and Rawson, Marion, *Troy: Settlements VIIa, VIIB and VIII*, Vol. IV, pt.1. Princeton 1958.

Bleicken, Jochen, "Zur Entstehung der Verfassungstypologie im 5. Jahrhundert v. Chr." *Historia* 28 (1979). 148-72.

Blinkenberg, Chr., *Die lindische Tempelchronik*. Bonn 1915.

Bloch, Marc, *Feudal Society*. Chicago 1961.

Bloedow, Edmund F., "Corn Supply and Athenian Imperialism." *AC* 44 (1975). 20-9.

Boardman, John, *Athenian Black Figure Vases*. New York 1974.

_____, "Chian and Early Ionic Architecture." *Antiquaries Journal* 39 (1959). 170-218.

_____, "Excavations at Pindakas in Chios." *BSA* 53/4 (1958/59). 295-309.

_____, *Greek Sculpture: The Archaic Period*. New York 1978.

_____, *The Greeks Overseas*. Harmondsworth 1964.

_____, *Pre-Classical: From Crete to Archaic Greece*. Harmondsworth 1967.

_____, "Pyramidal Stamp Seals in the Persian Empire." *Iran* 8 (1970). 19-45.

Bockisch, Gabriele, "Die Karer und ihre Dynasten." *Klio* 51 (1969). 117-75.

Bodenstedt, Friedrich, *Phokäisches Elektron-Geld von 600-326 v. Chr*. Mainz 1976.

_____, "Studien zur Elektronprägung von Phokaia und Mytilene." *RSN* 52 (1973). 17-51.

Bodéüs, Richard, "Le premier cours occidental sur la royauté Achéménide." *AC* 42 (1973). 458-72.

Boehlau, Johannes and Schefold, Karl, eds., *Larisa am Hermos*. Vol. 1, *Die Bauten*. Berlin 1940.

Boersma, Joh. S., *Athenian Building Policy from 561/0 to 405/4 B.C.* Groningen 1970.

Bogoliubov, M. N., "Titre honorifique d'un chef militaire achéménide en Haute-Égypte." *Acta Iranica Hommage Universel* 2 (Leiden 1974). 109-14.

Bon, A., "Les ruines antiques dans l'île de Thasos et en particular les tours héllenique," *BCH* 54 (1930). 147-94.

Bonner, Robert J., *Evidence in Athenian Courts*. Chicago 1905.

_____, "The Use and Effect of Attic Seals." *CP* 3 (1908). 399-407.

Bonner, Robert J. and Smith, Gertrude, *The Administration of Justice from Homer to Aristotle* Vol. 2. Chicago 1938.

Bonsor, G., *Tartesse*. New York 1922.

Borchhardt, Jürgen, "Eine Doppelaxtstele aus Limyra," 183-91. Edited by Sencer Şahin, Elmar Schwertheim, and Jörg Wagner, *Studien zur Religion und Kultur Kleinasiens: Festschrift für Friedrich Karl Dorner zum 65. Geburtstag am 28. Februar 1976* Vol. 1. Leiden 1978.

Borsay, Laszlo A., "Lydia: Its Land and History." Ph.D. dissertation, University of Pittsburgh 1965.

Bossert, Helmuth T., *Altanatolien*. Berlin 1942.

_____, *Asia*. Istanbul 1946.

Bosworth, A. B., "The Congress Decree: Another Hypothesis." *Historia* 20 (1971). 600-16.

Bousquet, Jean, "Arabinas, fils de Gergis, dynastie de Xanthos." *CRAI* (1975). 138-50.

Bovon, Anne, "La Représentation des guerriers perses et la notion de Barbare dans la 1re moitié du Ve siècle." *BCH* 87 (1963). 579-602.

Bowman, Johnston Alexander, "Studies in Ctesias." Ph.D. dissertation, Northwestern University 1938.

Bowman, Raymond A., *Aramaic Ritual Texts from Persepolis*. Chicago 1970.

Bowra, C. M., *Greek Lyric Poetry*, 2nd ed. Oxford 1961.

_____, "Polycrates of Rhodes." *CJ* 29 (1934). 375-80.

_____, "Xenophanes, Fragment 3." *CQ* 35 (1941). 119-26.

Boyce, Mary, *A History of Zoroastrianism*, Vol. 1. Leiden 1975.

_____, *A History of Zoroastrianism*, Vol. 2. Leiden 1982.

_____, "On Mithra, Lord of Fire." *Acta Iranica Monumentum H. S. Nyberg* 1 (Leiden 1975). 69-76.

_____, *A Persian Stronghold of Zoroastrianism*. Oxford 1977.

_____, "Iconoclasm among the Zoroastrians," 93-111. Edited by J. Neusner, *Greco-Roman Cults: Christianity, Judaism and Other Studies for Morton Smith at Sixty*, Vol. 4. Leiden 1975.

Bradeen, Donald W., "The Popularity of the Athenian Empire." *Historia* 9 (1960). 257-69.

Bradeen, Donald W. and McGregor, Malcolm F., *Studies in Fifth-Century Attic Epigraphy*. Norman 1973.

Brandenstein, Wilhelm, "Der persische Satz bei Aristophanes, ᾿Αχαρνῆς, Vers. 100." *Wiener Zeitschrift für die Kunde Süd- und Ostasiens* 8 (1964). 43-58.

Brandenstein, Wilhelm and Mayrhofer, Manfred, *Handbuch des Altpersischen*. Wiesbaden 1964.

Brannan, Patrick T., "Herodotus and History: The Constitutional Debate Preceding Darius' Accession." *Traditio* 19 (1963). 427-38.

Braun, Martin, *History and Romance in Graeco-Oriental Literature*. Oxford 1938.

Bravo, Benedetto, "Une lettre sur plomb de Berezan: Colonisation et modes de contact dans le Pont." *Dialogues d'histoire ancienne* 1 (1974). 111-87.

Brehm, Jack W. and Cohen, Arthur R., *Explorations in Cognative Dissonance*. New York 1962.

Bresciani, Edda, "Egypt and the Persian Empire," 333-53. In Hermann Bengtson, *The Greeks and the Persians*. London 1969.

_____, "La satrapia d'Egitto." *Studi classici e orientali* 7 (1958). 132-88.

Briant, Pierre, "Des Achéménides aux rois hellenistiques: Continuités et ruptures." *Annali della Scuola Normale Superiore di Pisa* 9 (1979). 1375-1414.

_____, "Appareils d'Etat et developpement des Forces productives au Moyen-Orient ancien: le cas de l'Empire achéménide." *La Pensée* 217/8 (1981). 9-23.

_____, " 'Brigandage', Dissidence et Conquête en Asie Achéménide et Hellenistique." *Dialogues d'histoire ancienne* 2 (1976). 165-279.

_____, "Communautes rurales, forces productives et mode de production tributaire en Asie Achéménide." *Zaman* 2-3 (1980). 75-100.

_____, "Conquête territoriale et stratégie idéologique: Alexandre le Grand et l'idéologie monarchique Achéménide." *Prace Historyczne* 63 (1980). 37-83.

_____, "Contrainte militaire, dépendance rurale et exploitation des territoires en Asie achéménide." *Index: Quaderni camerti di studi romanistici* 8 (1978-79). 48-98.

_____, "Dörfer und Dorfgemeinschaften im achämenidischen und hellenistischen Asien." *Jahrbuch für Wirtschaftsgeschichte* 4 (1975). 115-33.

_____, *Etat et pasteurs au Moyen-Orient ancien*. Cambridge 1982.

_____, "Produktivkräfte, Staat und tributäre Produktionswise im Achämenidenreich," 351-72. Edited by Joachim Herrmann and Irmgard Sellnow, *Produktivkräfte und Gesellschaftsformationen in vorkapitalistischer Zeit*. Berlin 1982.

Bright, John, *A History of Israel*. Philadelphia 1959.

Bringmann, Klaus, "Die Verfassungsdebatte bei Herodot 3, 80-82 und Dareios' Aufstieg zur Königsherrschaft." *Hermes* 104 (1976). 266-79.

British Naval Intelligence Division, Geographic Handbook Series, Greece: Regional Geography 3. London 1945.

Broadhead, H. D., *The Persae of Aeschylus*. Cambridge 1960.

Brown, Truesdall S., "Aeneas Tacitus, Herodotus and the Ionian Revolt." *Historia* 30 (1981). 385-93.

_____, "Aristodicus of Cyme and the Branchidae." *AJP* 99 (1978). 64-78.

Brundage, Burr C., "Feudalism in Ancient Mesopotamia and Iran," 108-10. Edited by Rushton Coulbourn, *Feudalism in History*. Princeton 1956.

Brunnsåker, S., *The Tyrant-Slayers of Kritios and Nesiotes*. Lund 1955.

Brunt, P. A., "The Hellenic League against Persia." *Historia* 2 (1953/4). 135-62.

Bryce, T. R., "The Other Pericles." *Historia* 29 (1980). 377-81.

Buck, Carl Darling, *The Greek Dialects*. Chicago 1955.

Buckler, W. H., *Sardis, Publication of the American Society for the Excavation of Sardis*, Vol. VI, pt. II: *Lydian Inscriptions*. Leiden 1924.

Buckler, W. H. and Robinson, David M., *Sardis: Greek and Latin Inscriptions* Vol. 7.1. Leiden 1932.

Burford, Allison, *Craftsmen in Greek and Roman Society*. London 1972

Burkert, Walter, "Iranisches bei Anaximandros." *Rheinisches Museum* 106 (1963). 97-134.

_____, *Structure and History in Greek Mythology and Ritual*. Berkeley 1979.

Burn, Andrew Robert, *The Lyric Age of Greece*. New York 1960.

_____, *Persia and the Greeks: The Defense of the West, c. 546-478 B.C.* New York 1962.

Burney, Charles, *From Village to Empire: Introduction to Near Eastern Archaeology*. Oxford 1977.

Burney, Charles and Lang, David Marshall, *The Peoples of the Hills*. London 1971.

Burstein, Stanley Mayer, *The Babyloniaca of Berossus*. Malibu 1978.

_____, "Herodotus and the Emergence of Meroe." *Journal of the Society for the Study of Egyptian Antiquities* 11 (1981). 1-5.

_____, *Outpost of Hellenism: The Emergence of Heraclea on the Black Sea*. Berkeley 1974.

Bury, J. B., "The European Expedition of Darius." *CR* 11 (1897). 277-82.

Buschor, Ernst, *Altsamische Standbilder*. Berlin 1934.

Busink, T. A., *Der Tempel von Jerusalem von Salomo bis Herodes*, Vol. 2 *von Ezechiel bis Middot*. Leiden 1980.

Busolt, Georg, *Griechische Staatskunde*, Vol. 1. Munich 1920.

Cadoux, C. J., *Ancient Smyrna*. Oxford 1938.

Cadoux, T. J., "The Duration of the Samian Tyranny." *JHS* 76 (1956). 105-6.

Cahn, Herbert A., "Asiut: Kritische Bemerkungen zu einer Schatzfundpublikation." *RSN* 56 (1977). 279-87.

_____, Knidos: *Die Münzen des sechsten und des fünften Jahrhunderts v. Chr.* Berlin 1970.

Calder, W. M., "The Royal Road in Herodotus." *CR* 39 (1925). 7-11.

Calder, W. M. and Bean, George E., *A Classical Map of Asia Minor.* London 1958.

Caldwell, Wallace E., *Hellenic Conceptions of Peace. Studies in History, Economics and Public Law*, Vol. 84. New York 1919.

Calhoun, G., "Ancient Athenian Mining." *Journal of Economic and Business History* 3 (1931). 333-61.

_____, "Athenian Magistrates and Special Pleas." *CQ* 14 (1919). 338-50.

Calmeyer, Peter, *Datierbare Bronzen aus Luristan und Kirmanshan.* Berlin 1969.

_____, "Zur Genese altiranischer Motive." *AMI* 8 (1975). 99-113.

_____, "Zur Genese altiranischer Motive: III. Felsgräber. IV. 'Persönliche Krone' und Diadem. V. Synarchie." *AMI* 9 (1976). 45-96.

_____, "Zur Genese altiranischer Motive. V. Synarchie." *AMI* 10 (1977). 191-95.

_____, "Stand der archäologische Forschung den Iranischen Kronen." *AMI* 10 (1977). 168-90.

_____, "The Subject of the Achaemenid Tomb Reliefs." *Proceedings of the IIIrd. Annual Symposium on Archaeological Research in Iran, Nov. 1974.* Teheran 1975, 233-42.

Calmeyer, P. and Eilers, W., "Vom Reisehut zur Kaiserkrone." *AMI* 10 (1977). 153-90.

Cameron, George G., "Cyrus the 'Father' and Babylonia." *Acta Iranica, 1er S.: Hommage Universel* 1 (Leiden 1974). 45-8.

_____, "Darius and Xerxes in Babylonia." *AJSL* 58 (1941). 314-25.

_____, "Darius Carved History on Ageless Rock." *National Geographic Magazine* 98.6 (Dec. 1950). 825-44.

_____, "Darius' Daughter and the Persepolis Inscriptions." *JNES* 1 (1942). 214-8.

_____, "Darius, Egypt, and the 'Lands beyond the Sea'." *JNES* 2 (1943). 307-13.

_____, "Darius the Great and his Scythian (Saka) Campaign, Bisitun and Herodotus." *Acta Iranica, Vol. 4, Monumentum H. S. Nyberg* (Leiden 1975). 76-88.

_____, "The Elamite Version of the Bisitun Inscriptions." *JCS* 14 (1960). 59-68.

_____, "An Inscription of Darius from Pasargadae." *Iran* 5 (1967). 7-10.

_____, "The Monument of King Darius at Bisitun." *Archaeology* 13 (1960). 162-71.

_____, "New Tablets from the Persepolis Treasury." *JNES* 24 (1965). 167-92.

_____, "The Old Persian Text of the Bisitun Inscription." *JCS* 5 (1951). 47-54.

_____, "The Oriental Institute Archaeological Report on the Near East."
AJSL 50 (1933-34). 272.

_____, *Persepolis Treasury Tablets.* Chicago 1948.

_____, "Persepolis Treasury Tablets Old and New." *JNES* 17 (1958). 161-76.

_____, "The Persian Satrapies and Related Matters." *JNES* 32 (1973). 47-56.

_____, "A Photograph of Darius' Sculptures at Behistan." *JNES* 2 (1943). 115-
6.

_____, "Zoroaster the Herdsman." *Indo-Iranian Journal* 10 (1968). 261-81.

_____, "Ancient Persia," 79-97. Edited by R. C. Dentan, *The Idea of History
in the Ancient Near East.* New Haven 1955.

Campanile, Enrico, "Ant. Pers. xšāyaθiya xšāyaθiyānām." In *Studi Linguistici in onore di
Tristano Bolelli.* Pisa 1974, 110-8.

Cannizzaro, F. A., *Il capitolo georgico dell'Avesta.* Messina 1913.

Cardascia, Guillaume, *Les Archives des Muraŝū.* Paris 1951.

_____, "Armée et fiscalité dans la Babylonie Achéménide." In *Armées et
fiscalité dans le Monde Antique.* Paris 1977, 3-10.

_____, "Le fief dans la Babylonie achéménide." *Recueil de la Société Jean
Bodin* 2nd ed. Brussels 1958, 55-88.

_____, *Le ḫaṭru et les collectivités en Babylonie, d' après les archives de la
maison Muraŝū. Mémoire présenté à l'École des Hautes Etudes.* Paris 1946.

Cargill, Jack, "The Nabonidus Chronicle and the Fall of Lydia." *AJAH* 2 (1977). 97-116.

_____, *The Second Athenian League.* Berkeley 1981.

Carney, T. F., *The Shape of the Past: Models and Antiquity.* Lawrence 1975.

Carpenter, Rhys, *The Architects of the Parthenon.* Baltimore 1970.

_____, *Folk Tale, Fiction and Saga in the Homeric Epic.* Berkeley 1946.

Carratelli, G. Pugliese, "Greci d'Asia in Occidente tra il secolo VII e il VI." *La Parola del
Passato* 21 (1966). 155-63.

_____, "Greek Inscriptions of the Middle East." *East and West* 16 (1966). 31-
6.

Cary, Max, "The Ionian Revolt." *CAH* Vol. 4, 1st ed. Cambridge 1939, 214-28.

_____, "Sources of Silver for the Greek World." In *Mélanges Gustave Glotz*
Vol. 1. Paris 1932, 133-42.

Caskel, Werner, "Arabia," 409-20. In Hermann Bengtson, *The Greeks and the Persians.*
London 1969.

Caspari, M. O. B., "The Ionian Confederacy." *JHS* 35 (1915). 173-88.

_____, "A Survey of Greek Federal Coinage." *JHS* 37 (1917). 168-83.

Cassola, Filippo, "Sull'alienabilità del suolo nel mondo Greco." *Labeo* 11 (1965). 206-19.

_____, *La Ionia nel mondo Miceneo*. Naples 1957.

_____, "La struttura della lega ionica." *Labeo* 4 (1958). 153-71.

Casson, Stanley, "A Greek Settlement in Thrace." *Antiquity* 7 (1933). 324-8.

Castritius, Helmut, "Die Okkupation Thrakiens durch die Perser und der Sturz des athenischen Tyrannen Hippias." *Chiron* 2 (1972). 1-15.

Cavaignac, E., *Études sur l'histoire financière d'Athenes au Ve siècle*. Paris 1908.

Cawkwell, G. L., "The Power of Persia." *Arepo* 1 (1968). 1-5.

Chadwick, John, "The Berezan Lead Letter." *Proceedings of the Cambridge Philological Society* 199 (1973). 35-7.

_____, "The Ionian Name," 106-9. Edited by K. Kinzl, *Greece and the Eastern Mediterranean in Ancient History and Prehistory, Studies Presented to F. Schachermeyr*. Berlin 1977.

Chambers, James T., "The Fourth-Century Athenians' View of their Fifth-Century Empire." *La Parola del Passato* 30 (1975). 177-91.

Chambers, Mortimer, "The Significance of the Themistokles' Decree." *Philologus* 3 (1967). 157-69.

Chapman, G. A. H., "Herodotus and Histiaeus' Role in the Ionian Revolt." *Historia* 21 (1972). 546-68.

Childe, V. Gordon, "India and the West before Darius." *Antiquity* 13 (1939). 5-15.

Childs, William A. P., "The Authorship of the Inscribed Pillar of Xanthos." *Anatolian Studies* 29 (1979). 97-102.

_____, *The City-Reliefs of Lycia*. Princeton 1978.

Chiller, P., Ἐπιγραφαὶ, Ῥόδου, Θήρας, Νάξου, Ἀρκαδίας. Ἀρχαιολογικὴ Ἐφημερίς (1914). 130-5.

Christensen, Arthur E., *Les gestes des rois dans les traditions de l'Iran antique*. Paris 1936.

_____, "Die Iranier." In *Kulturgeschichte des alten Orients*. Munich 1933, 203-309.

Christensen, Richard, "De jure et condicione sociorum Atheniensium quaesto historica." In *Opuscula philologica ad Ioannem Nicolaum Madvigium*. Copenhagen 1876, 1-20.

Cizek, Alexandru, "From the Historical Truth to the Literary Convention: The Life of Cyrus the Great viewed by Herodotus, Ctesias and Xenophon." *AC* 44 (1975). 531-52.

Clader, Linda Lee, *Helen: The Evolution from Divine to Heroic in Greek Epic Tradition*. Leiden 1976.

Clarke, David L., "A Provisional Model of an Iron Age Society and its Settlement System," 801-69. Edited by David L. Clarke, *Models in Archaeology*. London 1972.

_____, "Towns in the Development of Early Civilization," 435-43. Edited by David L. Clarke, *Analytical Archaeologist*. London 1979.

Clay, Albert T., "Aramaic Indorsements on the Documents of the Murašū Sons," 287-321. In *Old Testament and Semitic Studies in Memory of William Rainey Harper*, Vol. 1. Chicago 1908.

Clemen, C. D., *Fontes Historiae religionis persicae*. Bonn 1920.

Clermont-Ganneau, "Le Paradeisos royal Achéménide de Sidon." *Revue biblique* 30 (1921). 106-9.

Closs, Alois, "Vorzarathustrische Religionen in Iran und in den Randgebieten als Hintergrund des Zarathustrischen und des spätern Mazdaismus." *Acta Iranica Hommage Universel* 3. (Leiden 1974). 111-21.

Cobet, C., "Miscellanea Philologica et Critica." *Mnemosyne* n.s. 1 (1873). 1-58.

Cogan, Mordechai and Tadmor, Hayim, "Gyges and Assurbanipal." *Orientalia* 46 (1977). 65-85.

Cohen, Gerald, "Origin of Persian Cuneiform." *Comments on Etymology* 6 (1976). 1-11.

Cohen, Getzel M., *The Seleucid Colonies: Studies in Founding, Administration and Organization*. Wiesbaden 1978.

Coldstream, J. N., *Geometric Greece*. London 1977.

Colinvaux, Paul, "An Ecologist's View of History." *The Yale Review* 64 (1975). 357-69.

_____, *The Fates of Nations: A Biological Theory of History*. New York 1980.

_____, "In the Grand Scheme of Things Every Species has its 'Niche'." *Science Digest* 87 (1980). 72-7.

_____, "The Human Breeding Strategy." *Nature* 261 (June 1976). 356-7.

Collitz, H. and Bechtel, F., *Sammlung der griechischen Dialekt-Inschriften*. Göttingen 1884-1915.

Condurachi, Emil, "Problemi della πόλις e della χώρα nelle città greche del Ponto Sinistro." *La Città e il suo Territorio: Atti del settimo convegno di Studi sulla Magna Grecia, Taranto 8-12 Ottobre 1967*. Naples 1968, 143-63.

Connor, W. Robert, "Theseus in Classical Athens," 143-74. Edited by A. G. Ward, *The Quest for Theseus*. New York 1970.

_____, "Tyrannis Polis," 95-109. Edited by John H. D'Arms and John W. Eadie, *Ancient and Modern: Essays in Honor of Gerald F. Else*. Ann Arbor 1977.

Coogan, Michael D., "Life in the Diaspora: Jews at Nippur in the Fifth Century B.C." *BA* 37 (1974). 6-12.

_____, "Patterns in Jewish Personal Names in the Diaspora." *Journal for the Study of Judaism* 4 (1973). 184-91.

Cook, J. M., "Archaeology in Greece, 1948-1949." *JHS* 70 (1950). 1-15.

_____, "Archaeology in Greece, 1949-1950." *JHS* 71 (1951). 233-53.

_____, "Greek Archaeology in Western Asia Minor." *Archaeological Reports for 1959-1960*. (1960). 27-57.

_____, "Greek Settlement in the Eastern Aegean and Asia Minor." *CAH* 3rd ed., Vol. 2. pt. 2. Cambridge 1975, 773-804.

_____, *The Greeks in Ionia and the East*. New York 1963.

_____, "Old Smyrna, 1948-1951." *BSA* 53-4 (1958-9). 1-34.

_____, "The Problem of Classical Ionia." *Proceedings of the Cambridge Philological Society* 7 (1961). 9-18.

_____, *The Troad: An Archaeological and Topographical Study*. Oxford 1973.

Cook, J. M. and Bean, G. E., "The Carian Coast III." *BSA* 52 (1957). 106-16.

Cook, Robert M., "Amasis and the Greeks in Egypt." *JHS* 57 (1937). 227-37.

_____, "Ionia and Greece in the 8th and 7th Centuries B.C." *JHS* 66 (1946). 67-98.

_____, "A Terracotta Sarcophagus in the Fitzwilliam Museum." *JHS* 56 (1936). 58-63.

Cooks, S. A., "The Age of Zerubbabel," 19-36. Edited by H. H. Rowley, *Studies in Old Testament Prophecy Presented to Theodore H. Robinson*. Edinburgh 1950.

Cornford, F. M., *Before and After Socrates*. Cambridge 1962.

Coupel, Pierre and Demargne, Pierre, *Fouilles de Xanthos*, Vol. 3: *Le Monument des Néréides*. Paris 1969.

Cousin, G. and Deschamps, G., "Lettre de Darius, fils d'Hystaspes." *BCH* 13 (1889). 529-42.

Cowley, A. E., *Aramaic Papyri of the Fifth Century B.C.* Oxford 1923.

Cramer, John A., *A Geographical and Historical Description of Asia Minor*. Amsterdam 1971, reprint.

Cross, Frank M. Jr., "An Aramaic Inscription from Daskyleion." *BASOR* 184 (1966). 8-9.

Culham, Phyllis, "The Delian League: Bicameral or Unicameral?" *AJAH* 3 (1978). 27-31.

Culican, William, *The Medes and Persians*. New York 1965.

Dalton, George, "Karl Polanyi's Analysis of Long-Distance Trade and His Wider Paradigm," 63-132. Edited by J. A. Sabloff and C. C. Lamberg-Karlovsky, *Ancient Civilization and Trade*. Albuquerque 1975.

Dandamayev, Muhammad A., "Achaemenid Babylonia." In *Ancient Mesopotamia*. Moscow 1969, 296-311.

_____, "The Dynasty of the Achaemenids in the Early Period." *AAH* 25 (1977). 39-42.

_____, "Die Lehnsbeziehungen in Babylonien unter den ersten Achämeniden." In *Festschrift für Wilhelm Eilers*. Wiesbaden 1967, 37-42.

_____, "New Data on Religion in Persia at the turn of the VI-V Centuries B.C." *VDI* 128 (1974). 18-33 [in Russian].

_____, *Persien unter den Ersten Achämeniden (6. Jahrhundert v. Chr.)*. Wiesbaden 1976.

_____, "La politique religiouse des Achéménides." *Acta Iranica Monumentum H. S. Nyberg* 1 (Leiden 1975). 193-200.

_____, "Politische und Wirstschaftliche Geschichte," 15-58. Edited by Gerald Walser, *Beiträge zur Achämenidengeschichte.* Wiesbaden 1972.

_____, "Social Stratification in Babylonia (7th-4th Centuries B.C.)." *AAH* 22 (1974). 433-44.

Dandamayev, M. A. and Lukonin, V. G., *The Culture and Economic-System of Ancient Iran.* Moscow 1980 [in Russian].

Danov, Christo M., "Social and Economic Development of the Ancient Thracians in Homeric, Archaic, and Classical Times." *Études historiques* 2 (1960). 3-29.

_____, *Altthrakien.* Berlin 1976.

d'Aspremont, Lynden G., "L'Empire d'Athenes et la democratie sociale de Pericles." *Lettres d'humanité* 5 (1946). 74-131.

Daube, David, *Civil Disobedience in Antiquity.* Edinburgh 1972.

Daux, G., "Serments amphictyioniques et serment de Platées," 775-82. Edited by George Mylonas, *Studies Presented to David Moore Robinson,* Vol. 2. St. Louis 1953.

_____, "Le Serment de Platées." *RA* 17 (1941). 176-83.

Daverio Rocchi, Giovanna, "Aristocrazia genetica ed organizzazione politica arcaica." *La Parola del Passato* 28 (1973). 92-116.

Davidson, J. A., "The First Greek Triremes." *CQ* 41 (1947). 18-24.

_____, "Notes on the Panathenaia." *JHS* 78 (1958). 23-41.

Davies, J. K., *Athenian Propertied Families: 600-300 B.C.* Oxford 1971.

Davis, J. K., *People of the Mediterranean: An Essay in Comparative Social Anthropology.* London 1977.

Deane, Philip, *Thucydides' Dates 465-431 B.C.* Don Mills 1972.

Debevoise, Neilson C., "The Rock Reliefs of Ancient Iran." *JNES* 1 (1942). 78-80.

Delaunay, J. A., "A propos des Aramaic 'Ritual texts from Persepolis' de R. A. Bowman." *Acta Iranica Hommage Universel* 2 (Leiden 1974). 193-217.

_____, "L'Arameen d'Empire et les debuts de l'ecriture en Asie centrale." *Acta Iranica Hommage Universel* 2 (Leiden 1974). 219-46.

_____, "Remarques sur quelques noms de personne des archives élamites de Persepolis." *Studia Iranica* 5 (1976). 9-31.

de Liagre Böhl, F. M. T., "Die babylonischen Prätendenten zur Zeit Xerxes." *Bibliotheca Orientalis* 19 (1962). 110-4.

Demandt, Alexander, "Die Ohren des falschen Smerdis." *Iranica Antiqua* 9 (1972). 94-101.

de Mecquenem, Jean, "La Ziq-kurat." *Gazette des Beaux Arts* 18 (1937). 201-14.

Dengate, James A., "A Mint for the Coinage of the Ionian Revolt." *AJA* 72 (1968). 164.

_____, "The Coinage of Klazomenai." Ph.D. dissertation, University of Pennsylvania 1967.

de Romilly, Jacqueline, "Le classement de constitutions d'Hérodote à Aristote." *REG* 72 (1959). 81-99.

_____, "La crainte dans l'oeuvre de Thucydide." *Classica et Mediaevalia* 17 (1956). 119-27.

_____, *The Rise and Fall of States According to Greek Authors.* Ann Arbor 1977.

_____, *Thucydide et l'impérialisme athénien.* Paris 1947.

_____, "Guerre et paix entre cities," 207-20. Edited by J. P. Vernant, *Problèmes de la guerre en Grèce ancienne.* Paris 1968.

De Sanctis, Gaetano, "Aristagora di Mileto." *Rivista di filologia* 59 (1931). 48-72.

_____, "I Molpi di Mileto." In *Studi in onore di Pietro Bonfante* Vol. 2. Milan 1930, 669-80.

Desborough, V. R. d'A., *The Greek Dark Ages.* London 1972.

de Ste Croix, G. E. M., "The Character of the Athenian Empire." *Historia* 3 (1954/55). 1-41.

_____, *The Class Struggle in the Ancient Greek World.* London 1981.

_____, *The Origins of the Peloponnesian War.* London 1972.

de Vaux, Roland, "Les décrets de Cyrus et de Darius sur la reconstruction du Temple." *Revue biblique* 46 (1937). 29-57.

Diakonoff, I. M., "On Cybele and Attis in Phrygia and Lydia." *AAH* 25 (1977). 333-40.

_____, "On the Interpretation of § 70 of the Bisutūn Inscription (Elamite Version)." *AAH* 17 (1969). 105-7.

_____, "The Origin of the 'Old Persian' Writing System and the Ancient Oriental Epigraphic and Annalistic Traditions," 98-124. Edited by Mary Boyce and Ilya Gershevitch, *W. B. Henning Memorial Volume.* London 1970.

Dicks, Brian, *The Ancient Persians: How they Lived and Worked.* Newton Abbot 1979.

Diehl, Ernest, *Anthologia Lyrica Graeca* (Teubner Text) 3 Vols. Leipzig 1949-1952.

Diels, Hermann, *Die Fragmente der Vorsokratiker*, 3 Vols. Berlin 1934.

Dienelt, K., *Die Friedenspolitik des Perikles.* Vienna 1958.

Diesner, H.-J., "Die Gestalt des Tyrannen Polykrates bei Herodot." *AAH* 7 (1959). 211-9.

_____, *Griechische Tyrannis und griechische Tyrannen.* Berlin 1960.

Diller, Aubrey, *Race Mixture among the Greeks before Alexander.* Urbana 1937.

Diller, Hans, "Die Hellenen-Barbaren-Antithese im Zeitalter der Perserkriege." In *Greces et Barbares. Fondation Hardt pour l'Étude de l'antiquité classique.* Entretiens 8. Geneva 1962, 39-68.

_____, "Zwei Erzählungen des Lyders Xanthos." In *Navicula Chiloniensis: Festschrift für F. Jacoby.* Leiden 1956, 66-78.

Dinsmoor, William Bell, *The Architecture of Ancient Greece.* New York 1975 edition.

Dittenberger, Wilhelm, *Orientis Graeci inscriptiones selectae.* Leipzig 1905.

_____, *Sylloge Inscriptionum Graecum.* 3rd ed. Leipzig 1915-1924.

Dodd, C. H., "The Samians at Zankle-Messana." *JHS* 28 (1908). 56-76.

Donlan, Walter, *The Aristocratic Ideal in Ancient Greece.* Lawrence 1980.

_____, "The Tradition of Anti-Aristocratic Thought in Early Greek Poetry." *Historia* 22 (1973). 145-54.

Donner, H. and Röllig, W., *Kanaanäische und aramäische Inschriften.* Vol. 1. Wiesbaden 1962. Vol. 2. Wiesbaden 1964.

Dorjahn, A., "On the Athenian Anakrisis." *CP* 36 (1941). 182-5.

Dougherty, Raymond Philip, *Nabonidus and Belshazzar: A Study of the Closing Events of the Neo-Babylonian Empire.* New Haven 1929.

_____, "Writing upon Parchment and Papyrus among the Babylonians and Assyrians." *JAOS* 48 (1928). 109-35.

Dover, Kenneth J., *Greek Homosexuality.* London 1978.

Dow, Sterling, "The Purported Decree of Themistokles: Stele and Inscription." *AJA* 66 (1962). 352-68.

Doxiadis, C. A., "Ancient Greek Settlements." *Ekistics* 182 (1971). 4-21.

_____, *Ekistics: An Introduction to the Science of Human Settlements.* London 1969.

Drews, Robert, *Basileus: The Evidence for Kingship in Geometric Greece.* New Haven 1983.

_____, "The Fall of Astyages and Herodotus' Chronology of the Eastern Kingdoms." *Historia* 18 (1969). 1-11.

_____, "The First Tyrants in Greece." *Historia* 21 (1972). 129-44.

_____, *The Greek Accounts of Eastern History.* Washington D.C. 1973.

_____, "Herodotus' Other Logoi." *AJP* 91 (1970). 181-91.

_____, "Sargon, Cyrus and Mesopotamian Folk History." *JNES* 33 (1974). 387-93.

Drioton, Étienne and Vandier, Jacques, *L'Égypte.* Paris 1952.

Driver, G. R., *Aramaic Documents of the Fifth Century B.C.* 2nd ed. Oxford 1957.

Dubberstein, Waldo, "The Chronology of Cyrus and Cambyses." *AJSL* 55 (1938). 417-9.

Duchesne-Guillemin, Jacques, "Le Dieu de Cyrus." *Acta Iranica Hommage Universel* 3 (Leiden 1974). 11-21.

_____, "Fire in Iran and in Greece." *East and West* 13 (1962). 198-206.

_____, *Ormazd et Ahriman.* Paris 1953.

_____, "Die Religion der Achämeniden." *AAH* 19 (1971). 25-35.

_____, "Religion et politique, de Cyrus à Xerxès." *Persica* 3 (1967/1968). 1-9.

_____, *The Western Response to Zoroaster.* Oxford 1958.

_____, *Zoroastre: Étude critique avec une traduction commentée des Gāthā.* Paris 1948.

_____, *Zoroastrianism: Symbols and Values.* New York 1970.

_____, "La Religion des Achéménides," 59-82. Edited by Gerald Walser, *Beiträge zur Achämenidengeschichte.* Wiesbaden 1972.

Dufková, Marie and Pečírka, Jan, "Excavations of Farms and Farmhouses in the Chora of Chersonesos in the Crimea." *Eirene* 8 (1970). 123-74.

Duleba, Wladyslaw, "Was Darius a Zoroastrian?" *Folia Orientalia* 18 (1977). 205-9.

Dumézil, Georges, *L'idéologie tripartie des Indo-Européens.* Brussels 1958.

_____, *Mitra-Varuṇa: Essai sur deux représentations indo-européennes de la Souveraineté.* Paris 1940.

_____, "Note sur un Roman Scythique d'Hérodote: Skylès." *Acta Iranica Monumentum H. S. Nyberg* 1 (Leiden 1975). 215-22.

Dunbabin, T. J., *The Greeks and their Eastern Neighbors.* London 1957.

Dunham, Adelaide Glynn, *A History of Miletos.* London 1915.

Dupont-Sommer, A., *Les Araméens.* Paris 1949.

_____, "L'ostracon araméen d'Assour." *Syria* 24 (1944-5). 24-61.

_____, "Un ostracon araméen inedit de Larsa." *Revue d'Assyriologie* 40 (1945-1946). 143-7.

_____, "Un papyrus araméen d'époque saïte decouvert à Saqqara." *Semitica* 1 (1948). 43-68.

Dyer, Robert, "Asia/*Aswia and Archilochus Fr. 23." *La Parola del Passato* 101 (1965). 115-32.

Dyson, Robert H., Jr., "Problems of Protohistoric Iran as seen from Hasanlu." *JNES* 24 (1965). 193-217.

Earp, A. J., "Athens and Miletos ca 450 B.C." *Phoenix* 8 (1954). 142-7.

East, W. Gordon, *The Geography Behind History.* New York 1967.

Ebeling, E., "Die Rüstung eines babylonischen Panzerreiters nach einem Vertrage aus der Zeit Darius II." *Zeitschrift für Assyriologie* 16 (1952). 203-13.

Ebner, Pietro, "Il mercato dei metalli preziosi nel secolo d'oro dei Focei (640-545 a. C.)." *La Parola del Passato* 21 (1966). 111-27.

Eddy, Samuel K., "The Cold War Between Athens and Persia, ca 448-412 B.C.," *CP* 68 (1973). 241-53.

_____, "ΕΠΙΦΟΡΑ in the Tribute Quota Lists." *AJP* 89 (1968). 129-43.

_____, "Four Hundred Sixty Talents Once More." *CP* 63 (1968). 184-95.

_____, "The Gold in the Athena Parthenos." *AJA* 81 (1977). 107-11.

_____, *The King is Dead*. Lincoln 1961.

_____, "On the Peace of Callias." *CP* 65 (1970). 8-14.

_____, Review of Chester G. Starr, *Athenian Coinage*. Oxford 1970, in *AJP* 94 (1973). 308-10.

Edinger, H. D., "Vocabulary and Imagery in Aeschylus' Persians." Ph.D. dissertation, Princeton University 1961.

Edmonds, John Maxwell, *Elegy and Iambus* 1. Loeb Edition. Cambridge, Mass. 1931.

_____, *The Fragments of Attic Comedy* Vol. 1. Leiden 1957.

_____, *Lyra Graeca*. Loeb Edition. Vol. 1. Cambridge, Mass. 1963. Vol. 2. Cambridge, Mass. 1964.

Ehrenberg, Victor, "The Foundation of Thurii." *AJP* 69 (1948). 149-70.

_____, "Freedom-Ideal and Reality." In *The Living Heritage of Greek Antiquity*. The Hague 1967, 132-46.

_____, "Das Harmodioslied." *Wiener Studien* 69 (1956). 57-69.

_____, "The Origins of Democracy." *Historia* 1 (1950). 515-48.

_____, When did the *Polis* Rise?" *JHS* 57 (1937). 147-59.

Ehtécham, Mortéza, *L'Iran sous les achéménides*. Fribourg 1946.

Eilers, Wilhelm, "The End of the Behistan Inscription." *JNES* 8 (1948). 106-10.

_____, "Iranische Beamtennamen in der keilschriftlichen Überlieferung." *Abhandlungen für die Kunde des Morgenlandes, Deutschen morgenländische Gesellschaft* 25 (1940). 22-37.

_____, "Iranisches Lehngut im arabischen Lexicon: über einige Berufsnamen und Titel." *Indo-Iranian Journal* 5 (1961-62). 203-32.

_____, "Kleinasiatisches." *ZDMG* 94 (1940). 189-233.

_____, "The Name of Cyrus." *Acta Iranica Hommage Universel* 3 (Leiden 1974). 3-9.

_____, "Vom Reisehut zur Kaiserkrone: A. Das Wortfeld." *AMI* 10 (1977). 153-68.

_____, "Le texte cuneiforme du Cylindre de Cyrus." *Acta Iranica Hommage Universels* 2 (Leiden 1974). 25-34.

Ekholm, K. and Friedman, J., " 'Capital' Imperialism and Exploitation in Ancient World Systems," 41-58. Edited by Mogens Trolle Larsen, *Power and Propaganda: A Symposium on Ancient Empires*. Copenhagen 1979.

Eliot, C. William J., *Coastal Demes of Attika*. Toronto 1962.

_____, "Where did the Alkmaionidai Live?" *Historia* 16 (1967). 279-86.

Emlyn-Jones, C. J., *The Ionians and Hellenism: A Study of the Cultural Achievement of Early Greek Inhabitants of Asia Minor*. London 1980.

Engelmann, H. and Merkelbach, Reinhold, *Die Inschriften von Erythrai und Klazomenai.* Vol. 1. Bonn 1972.

Erbse, Hartmut, "Über Herodots Kroisoslogos." In *Ausgewählte Schriften zur klassischen Philologie.* Berlin 1979, 180-202.

Erxleben, Erhard, "Das Münzgesetz des delisch-attischen Seebundes I." *Archiv für Papyrusforschung* 19 (1969). 91-139.

_____, "Das Münzgesetz II." *Archiv für Papyrusforschung* 20 (1970). 66-132.

_____, "Das Münzgesetz III." *Archiv für Papyrusforschung* 21 (1971). 145-62.

Erzen, Afif, *Kilikien bis zum Ende Perserherrschaft.* Leipzig 1940.

Etienne, H. J., *The Chisel in Greek Sculpture.* Leiden 1968.

Evans, J. A. S., "Herodotus and the Gyges Drama." *Athenaeum* 43 (1955). 333-6.

_____, "Herodotus and the Ionian Revolt." *Historia* 25 (1976). 31-7.

_____, "Histiaeus and Aristagoras: Notes on the Ionian Revolt." *AJP* 84 (1963). 113-28.

_____, "What Happened to Croesus?" *CJ* 74 (1978). 34-40.

Farkas, Ann, *Achaemenid Sculpture.* Leiden 1974.

_____, "The Horse and Rider in Achaemenid Art." *Persica* 4 (1969). 57-76.

_____, "Is there Anything Persian in Persian Art?," 15-21. Edited by D. Schmandt-Besserat, *Ancient Persia: The Art of an Empire.* Malibu 1980.

Farnell, Lewis Richard, *The Cults of the Greek States.* 5 Vols. Oxford 1896-1909.

Farrington, B., *Greek Science.* Harmondsworth 1961 edition.

Farron, S. G., "The Odyssey as an Anti-Aristocratic Statement." *Studies in Antiquity* 1 (1979-80). 59-101.

Fauth, Wolfgang, "Der königliche Gärtner und Jäger im Paradeisos." *Persica* 8 (1979). 1-53.

Feodora Prinzessin von Sachsen-Meiningen. "Proskynesis in Iran," 125-66. Edited by F. Altheim, *Geschichte der Hunnen.* Vol. 2. Berlin 1960.

Ferrill, Arther, "Herodotus and the Strategy and Tactics of the Invasion of Xerxes." *American Historical Review* 72 (1966). 102-15.

_____, "Herodotus on Tyranny." *Historia* 27 (1978). 385-98.

Fertonani, Roberto, "Ecateo di Mileto e il suo razionalismo." *La Parola del Passato* 7 (1952). 18-29.

Festinger, Leon, *A Theory of Cognitive Dissonance.* Stanford 1957.

_____, *When Prophecy Fails.* New York 1964 edition.

Figueira, Thomas J., "Aeginetan Membership in the Peloponnesian League." *CP* 76 (1981). 1-24.

Filippani-Ronconi, Pio, "La conception sacrée de la royauté iranienne." *Acta Iranica Hommage Universel* 1 (Leiden 1974). 90-101.

Finley, M. I., "The Alienability of Land in Ancient Greece: A Point of View." *Eirene* 7 (1968). 25-32.

——————————, *The Ancient Economy*. London 1973.

——————————, *Ancient Slavery and Modern Ideology*. New York 1980.

——————————, "Empire in the Greco-Roman World." *Greece & Rome*. 2nd. s. 25 (1978). 1-15.

——————————, "The Freedom of the Citizen in the Greek World." *Talanta* 7 (1976). 1-23.

——————————, *The World of Odysseus*. 2nd ed. London 1977.

——————————, "The Fifth-Century Athenian Empire: A Balance Sheet," 103-26. Edited by P. D. A. Garnsey and C. R. Whittaker, *Imperialism in the Ancient World*. Cambridge 1978.

——————————, "Sparta," 143-60. Edited by J. P. Vernant, *Problèmes de la guerre en Grèce ancienne*. Paris 1968.

Fisher, W. B., ed., *The Cambridge History of Iran*. Vol. 1. *The Land of Iran*. Cambridge 1968.

Fitzmyer, Joseph A., "Some Notes on Aramaic Epistolography." *JBL* 93 (1974). 20 1-25.

Fleischer, Robert, "Artemis von Ephesos und Verwandte Kultstatuen aus Anatolien und Syrien Supplement," 324-58. Edited by Sencer Şahin, Elmar Schwertheim, and Jörg Wagner, *Studien zur Religion und Kultur Kleinasiens: Festschrift für Friedrich Karl Dorner zum 65. Geburtstag am 28. Februar 1976*. Vol. 1. Leiden 1978.

Fogazza, Giovanni, "Per una storia della lega ionica." *La Parola del Passato* 28 (1973). 157-69.

Fol, Alexander and Marazov, Ivan, *Thrace and the Thracians*. London 1977.

Fornara, Charles W., *Archaic Times to the End of the Peloponnesian War*. Baltimore 1977.

——————————, "On the Chronology of the Samian War." *JHS* 99 (1979). 7-18.

——————————, "The Cult of Harmodius and Aristogeiton." *Philologus* 114 (1970). 155-80.

——————————, "The Date of the 'Regulations for Miletos'." *AJP* 92 (1971). 473-5.

——————————, *Herodotus*. Oxford 1971.

——————————, "Some Aspects of the Career of Pausanias of Sparta." *Historia* 15 (1966). 257-71.

Fränkel, Hermann, *Early Greek Poetry and Philosophy*. New York 1975.

Francis, E. D., "Greeks and Persians: The Art of Hazard and Triumph," 53-86. Edited by D. Schmandt-Besserat, *Ancient Persia: The Art of an Empire*. Malibu 1980.

Franke, Peter R., "Geschichte, Politik und Münzprägung in frühen Makedonien." *Jahrbuch für Numismatik und Geltgeschichte* 3-4 (1952-3). 99-112.

Frankel, David, *The Ancient Kingdom of Urartu*. London 1979.

Frankenstein, Susa, "The Phoenicians in the Far West: A Function of Neo-Assyrian Imperialism," 263-94. Edited by Mogens Trolle Larsen, *Power and Propaganda: A Symposium on Ancient Empires*. Copenhagen 1979.

Frankfort, Henri, "Achaemenian Sculpture." *AJA* 50 (1946). 6-14.

_____, *The Art and Architecture of the Ancient Orient*. Baltimore 1970.

_____, *Kingship and the Gods*. Chicago 1948.

Frankfort, Henri, *et al.*, *Before Philosophy*. Harmondsworth 1949.

Fraser, P. M. and Bean, G. E., *The Rhodian Peraea and Islands*. Oxford 1954.

Freeman, Kathleen, *Companion to the Pre-Socratic Philosophers*. Cambridge, Mass. 1966.

French, A., "Athenian Ambitions and the Delian Alliance." *Phoenix* 33 (1979). 134-41.

_____, *The Athenian Half-Century*. Sidney 1971.

_____, *The Growth of the Athenian Economy*. London 1964.

_____, "The Tribute of the Allies." *Historia* 21 (1972). 1-20.

French, D. H., "Archaeology, Prehistory and Religion," 375-83. Edited by Sencer Şahin, Elmar Schwertheim, and Jörg Wagner, *Studien zur Religion und Kultur Kleinasiens: Festschrift für Friedrich Karl Dorner zum 65. Geburtstag am 28. Februar 1976*. Vol. 1. Leiden 1978.

Fried, Morton H., "On the Evolution of Social Stratification and the State," 713-31. Edited by S. Diamond, *Culture in History*. New York 1960.

Friedel, Hans, "Der Tyrannenmord in Gesetzgebung und Volksmeinung der Griechen." *Würzburger Studien zur Altertumswissenschaft*. Stuttgart 1937.

Friedl, Ernestine, *Vasilika: A Village in Modern Greece*. New York 1962.

Friedrich, Johannes, *Kleinasiatische Sprachdenkmäler*. Berlin 1932.

_____, "Ein phrygisches Siegel und ein phrygisches Tontäfelchen." *Kadmos* 4 (1965). 154-6.

Frisch, Peter, *Die Träume bei Herodot*. Meisenheim am Glan 1968.

Frost, Frank J., "A Note on Xerxes at Salamis." *Historia* 22 (1973). 118-9.

_____, "Pericles, Thucydides, Son of Melesias, and Athenian Politics before the War." *Historia* 13 (1964). 385-99.

_____, *Plutarch's Themistocles*. Princeton 1980.

Frye, Richard N., "The Charisma of Kingship in Ancient Iran." *Iranica Antiqua* 4 (1964). 36-54.

_____, "Gestures of Deference to Royalty in Ancient Iran." *Iranica Antiqua* 9 (1972). 102-7.

_____, *The Heritage of Persia*. Cleveland 1963.

_____, "Persepolis Again." *JNES* 33 (1974). 383-6.

_____, Review of David Stronach, *Pasargadae*. Oxford 1978, in *AJA* 83 (1979). 234-6.

_____, "The Institutions," 83-93. Edited by Gerald Walser, *Beiträge zur Achämenidengeschichte*. Wiesbaden 1972.

_____, "Mithra in Iranian History," 62-7. Edited by J. R. Hinnells, *Mithraic Studies*. Vol. 1. Manchester 1975.

Gadd, C. J., *Ideas of Divine Rule in the Ancient East*. London 1948.

Gaebler, Hugo, "Die Silberprägung von Lampsakos." *Nomisma* 12 (1933). 1-33.

Gallet de la Santerre, Hubert, "Chronique des Fouilles en 1950: Asie Mineure." *BCH* 75 (1951). 128-9.

Galling, Kurt, "Von Naboned zu Darius: Studien zur chaldäischen und persischen Geschichte." *Zeitschrift des deutschen Palästina-Vereins* 69 (1953). 42-64.

_____, "Von Naboned zu Darius." *Zeitschrift des deutschen Palästina-Vereins* 70 (1954). 4-32.

_____, *Studien zur Geschichte Israels im persischen Zeitalter*. Tübingen 1964.

_____, "Syrien in der Politik der Achämeniden bis zum Aufstand des Megabyzos 448 v. Chr." *Der Alte Orient* 36. Heft 3/4 (1937). 5-49.

Galtung, Johan., "A Structural Theory of Imperialism." *Journal of Peace Research* 8 (1971). 81-117.

Ganshof, F. L., *Feudalism*. New York 1961.

Gardner, P., "Coinage of the Athenian Empire." *JHS* 33 (1913). 147-88.

_____, "The Coinage of the Ionian Revolt." *JHS* 31 (1911). 151-60.

_____, *A History of Ancient Coinage 700-300 B.C.* Oxford 1918.

_____, "Note on the Coinage of the Ionian Revolt." *JHS* 33 (1913). 105.

Gauthier, Phillipe, "Les tyrans dans le monde Grec antique." *REG* 81 (1968). 555-61.

Gehrke, Hans-Joachim, "Zur Geschichte Milets in der Mitte des 5. Jahrhunderts v. Chr." *Historia* 29 (1980). 17-31.

Gentili, Bruno, ed., *Anacreon*. Rome 1958.

Georgiades, A. and Pritchett, W. Mc., "The Koan Fragment of the Athenian Monetary Decree." *BCH* 89 (1965). 400-40.

Gernet, Louis, *The Anthropology of Ancient Greece*. Baltimore 1981.

Gershevitch, Ilya, "Amber at Persepolis." In *Studia classica et orientalia Antonino Pagliaro Oblata*. Vol. 2. Rome 1969, 167-251.

_____, *The Avestan Hymn to Mithra*. Cambridge 1959.

_____, "An Iranist's View of the Soma Controversy," 52-75. Edited by P. Gignoux and A. Tafazzoli, *Mémorial Jean de Menasce*. Louvain 1974.

_____, "Zoroaster's Own Contribution." *JNES* 23 (1964). 12-38.

Ghirshman, Roman, "L'Apadana de Suse." *Iranica Antiqua* 3 (1963). 148-54.

_____, "Les Daivadāna." *AAH 24 (1976).* 3-14.

_____, *"La frontalité dans l'art iranien et ses origines."* CRAI (1975). 51-60.

_____, *Iran.* Harmondsworth 1954.

_____, *Iran, Parthians, and Sassanans.* London 1962.

_____, "Masjid-i-Solaiman, Résidence des premiers Achéménides." *Syria* 27 (1950). 205-20.

_____, "Notes iraniennes VII, à propos de Persépolis." *Artibus Asiae* 20 (1957). 265-78.

_____, Review of I. M. Diakonov, *Istoria Midii-Histoire de la Medie* [in Russian]. Moscow 1956, in *Bibliotheca Orientalis* 15.6 (Nov. 1958). 257-61.

_____, "Les tribus perses el leur formation tripartite." *CRAI* (1973). 210-21.

_____, *Village Perse-Achéménide. Memoires de la Mission Archéologique en Iran.* Vol. 36 Paris 1954.

Gielow, Hertha E., "Die Silberprägung von Dankle-Messana (ca. 515-396 v. Chr.)." *Mitteilungen der Bayerischen Numismatischen Gesellschaft* 48 (1930). 1-68.

Gigon, Olof, "Die Theologie der Vorsokratiker." *La Notion du Divin depuis Homère jusqu'à Platon. Fondation Hardt, Entretiens sur l'Antiquité Classique.* Vol. 1. Geneva 1954, 127-55.

Gignoux, P., "Le dieu Baga en Iran." *AAH* 25 (1977). 119-27.

Gillis, Daniel, *Collaboration with the Persians.* Wiesbaden 1979.

Ginsberg, H. L., " 'King of Kings' and 'Lord of Kingdoms'." *AJSL* 57 (1940). 71-4.

Giovannini, Adalberto and Gottlieb, Gunther, "Thukydides und die Anfänge der athenischen Arche." *Sitzungsberichte der Heidelberger Akademie der Wissenschaften. Philosophisch-historische Klasse* (1980). 7-45.

Glotz, Gustave, "Une inscription de Milet." *CRAI* (1906). 511-29.

Gnoli, Gherardo, "Politique religieuse et conception de la royauté sous les Achéménides." *Acta Iranica Hommage Universel* 2 (Leiden 1974). 117-90.

Goblot, Henri, *Les qanats. Une technique d'acquisition de l'eau.* Paris 1979.

Goff, Clare, "Bābā Jān." In "Survey of Excavations in Iran During 1968-69." *Iran* 8 (1970). 175-6.

_____, "Excavation at Bābā Jān, 1968." *Iran* 8 (1970). 141-56.

_____, "Excavations at Baba Jan: The Architecture of the East Mound, Levels II and III." *Iran* 15 (1977). 103-40.

_____, "Excavations at Baba Jan: The Pottery and Metal from Levels III and II." *Iran* 16 (1978). 29-68.

_____, "Luristan Before the Iran Age." *Iran* 9 (1971). 131-51.

Goldman, Bernard, "Politicking in Ancient Persia." *Natural History* 85 (April 1976). 36-45.

Gomme, Arnold Wycombe, "The Citizenship Law of 451-0." *Essays in Greek History and Literature.* Oxford 1937, 86-8.

_____, *A Historical Commentary on Thucydides.* Vol. 1. Oxford 1959.

_____, "Herodotos and Marathon." *More Essays in Greek History and Literature.* Oxford 1952, 29-37.

_____, *The Population of Ancient Athens.* Oxford 1933.

_____, "Thucydides ii. 13.3: An Answer to Professor Meritt." *Historia* 3 (1954/55). 333-8.

Gow, A. S. F., "Notes on the *Persae* of Aeschylus." *JHS* 48 (1928). 133-59.

Graf, David Frank, "Medism: Greek Collaboration with Achaemenid Persia." Ph.D. dissertation, University of Michigan 1979.

Graham, A. J., *Colony and Mother City in Ancient Greece.* Manchester 1964.

Gray, D. H. F., Review of C. W. Blegen *et al.*, *Troy* 4. Princeton 1958, in *JHS* 82 (1962). 195-7.

Gray, John, *The Krt Text in the Literature of Ras Shamra: A Social Myth of Ancient Canaan.* 2nd ed. Leiden 1964.

Green, Peter, *Xerxes at Salamis.* New York 1970.

Greenberg, Moshe, "Ezekial 17 and the Policy of Psammetichus II." *JBL* 76 (1957). 304-9.

Greenewalt, Crawford H., Jr., "An Exhibitionist from Sardis," 29-46. Edited by D. G. Mitten, J. G. Pedley, and J. A. Scott, *Studies Presented to George M. A. Hanfmann.* Cambridge, Mass. 1971.

_____, *Ritual Dinners in Early Historic Sardis.* Berkeley 1976.

Greenfield, J. C., "On Some Iranian Terms in the Elephantine Papyri." *AAH* 25 (1977). 113-8.

Greenhalgh, P. A. L., *Early Greek Warfare.* Cambridge 1973.

Grelot, Pierre, *Documents araméens d'Égypte.* Paris 1972.

Griffiths, J. Gwyn, Βασιλεὺς Βασιλέων: Remarks on the History of a Title." *CP* 48 (1953). 145-54.

Grosso, F., "Gli Eretriese deportati in Persia." *Rivista di filologia e di istruzione classica* 86 (1958). 350-75.

Groten, F. J., Jr., "Herodotus' Use of Variant Versions." *Phoenix* 17 (1963). 79-87.

Gruben, G., "Das archaische Didymaeion." *Jahrbuch des deutschen archäologischen Instituts* 78 (1963). 78-182.

Grundy, G. B., *The Great Persian War and its Preliminaries.* London 1901.

Gschnitzer, Fritz, *Die sieben Perser und das Königtum des Dareios.* Heidelberg 1977.

_____, "Stadt und Stamm bei Homer." *Chiron* 1 (1971). 1-17.

Guépin, J. P., "Le Cours du Cyzicène." *AC* 34 (1965). 199-203.

_____, "Greek Artists under Achaemenid Rule." *Persica* 1 (1963-64). 34-52.

Güterbock, Hans G., "The Hittite Version of the Hurrian Kumarbi Myths: Oriental Forerunners of Hesiod." *AJA* 52 (1948). 123-34.

_____, "Narration in Anatolian, Syrian and Assyrian Art." *AJA* 61 (1957). 62-71.

Gurney, O. R., *The Hittites*. Harmondsworth 1952.

Gusmani, M. Roberto, "Der lydische Name der Kybele." *Kadmos* 8 (1969). 158-61.

_____, *Lydisches Wörterbuch mit grammatischer Skizze und Inschriftensammlung*. Heidelberg 1964.

_____, *Neue epichorische Schriftzeugnisse aus Sardis* (1958-1971). Cambridge, Mass. 1975.

_____, "Onomastica iranica nei testi epicorici lidi." In *Umanita e Storia: Scritti in onore de Adelchi Attisani*. Vol. 2. Naples 1971, 3-10.

Gutherie, W. K. C., *A History of Greek Philosophy*. Vol. 1. Cambridge 1962.

_____, *The Greek Philosophers from Thales to Aristotle*. London 1967.

_____, "The Presocratic World-Picture." *The Harvard Theological Review* 45 (1952). 87-104.

Gyles, Mary Francis, *Pharaonic Policies and Administration, 663 to 323 B.C.* Chapel Hill 1959.

Habicht, Christian, "Falsche Urkunden zur Geschichte Athens im Zeitalter der Perserkriege." *Hermes* 89 (1961). 1-35.

Hagg, T., "Photius at Work." *GRBS* 14 (1973). 213-22.

Hahn, I., "Aspekte der spartanischen Aussenpolitik im V. Jh." *AAH* 17 (1969). 285-96.

Hainsworth, J. B., *The Flexibility of the Homeric Formula*. Oxford 1968.

_____, *Homer. Greece & Rome. New Surveys in the Classics*. Vol. 3. Oxford 1969.

Hallock, Richard T., "Darius I, the King of the Persepolis Tablets." *JNES* 1 (1942). 230-2.

_____, "The Elamite Texts from Persepolis," 177-9. Edited by Herbert Franke, *Akten des vierundzwanzigsten internationalen Orientalisten-Kongresses, München*. Wiesbaden 1959.

_____, "The Evidence of the Persepolis Tablets." *Cambridge History of Iran*. Vol. 2. Cambridge forthcoming.

_____, "New Light from Persepolis." *JNES* 9 (1950). 237-52.

_____, "A New Look at the Persepolis Treasury Tablets." *JNES* 19 (1960). 90-100.

_____, "On the Old Persian Signs." *JNES* 29 (1970). 52-5.

_____, "The 'One Year' of Darius I." *JNES* 19 (1960). 36-9.

_____, "The Persepolis Fortification Archive." *Orientalia* 42 (1973). 320-3.

_____, *Persepolis Fortification Tablets.* Chicago 1969.

_____, "The Use of Seals on the Persepolis Fortification Tablets." *Bibliotheca Mesopotamica* 6 (1977). 127-33.

Hammond, N. G. L., "The Battle of Salamis." *JHS* 76 (1956). 32-54.

_____, "The Campaign and the Battle of Marathon." *JHS* 88 (1968). 13-57.

_____, "The Extent of Persian Occupation in Thrace." *Chiron* 10 (1980). 53-61.

_____, *A History of Greece to 322 B.C.* 2nd ed. Oxford 1967.

_____, "The Origins and the Nature of the Athenian Alliance of 478/7 B.C." *JHS* 87 (1967). 41-61.

_____, "Studies in Greek Chronology of the Sixth and the Fifth Centuries B.C." *Historia* 4 (1955). 371-411.

Hampl, Fritz, "Poleis ohne Territorium." *Klio* 32 (1939). 1-60.

Hands, A. R., "In Favour of a Peace of Kallias." *Mnemosyne* s.4. 28 (1975). 193-5.

Hanfmann, G. M. A., "Archaeology in Homeric Asia Minor." *AJA* 52 (1948). 135-55.

_____, "Excavations at Sardis—1959." *AJA* 64 (1960). 185.

_____, "The Fourth Campaign at Sardis (1961)." *BASOR* 166 (1962). 1-57.

_____, *From Croesus to Constantine.* Ann Arbor 1975.

_____, "Greece and Lydia: The Impact of Hellenic Culture." In *Le Rayonnement des Civilisations grecque et romaine sur les cultures périphériques.* Paris 1965, 491-500.

_____, "Ionia, Leader or Follower?" *HSCP* 61 (1953). 1-37.

_____, *Letters from Sardis.* Cambridge, Mass. 1972.

_____, "Lydiaka." *HSCP* 63 (1958). 65-88.

_____, "On the Palace of Croesus," 145-54. Edited by U. Höckmann and A. Krug, *Festschrift für Frank Brommer.* Mainz 1977.

_____, "Pediment of the Persian Era from Sardis." In *Mélanges Arif Müfid Mansel.* Ankara 1974, 289-301.

_____, "Prehistoric Sardis," 160-83. Edited by George Mylonas, *Studies Presented to David M. Robinson.* Vol. 1. St. Louis 1951.

_____, "Sardis und Lydien." *Akademie der Wissenschaften und Literatur. Abhandlungen der geistes und sozialwissenschaftlichen Klasse* 6 (1960). 499-536.

_____, "The Tenth Campaign at Sardis." *BASOR* 191 (1968). 2-41.

_____, "The Third Campaign at Sardis (1960)." *BASOR* 162 (1961). 8-49.

Hanfmann, G. M. A. and Balmuth, M. S., "The Image of an Anatolian Goddess at Sardis." *Jahrbuch für Kleinasiatische Forschung* 2 (1965). 261-9.

Hanfmann, G. M. A. and Detweiler, A. H., "From the Heights of Sardis." *Archaeology* 14 (1961). 3-12.

_____, "New Exploration of Sardis." *Archaeology* 12 (1959). 53-61.

_____, "Sardis through the Ages." *Archaeology* 19 (1966). 90-7.

Hanfmann, G. M. A. and Ramage, Nancy H., *Sculpture from Sardis: The Finds through 1975.* Cambridge, Mass. 1978.

Hanfmann, G. M. A. and Waldbaum, Jane C., "The Eleventh and Twelfth Campaigns at Sardis (1968, 1969)." *BASOR* 199 (1970). 7-58.

_____, "Kybele and Artemis: Two Anatolian Goddesses at Sardis." *Archaeology* 22 (1969). 264-9.

_____, *A Survey of Sardis and the Major Monuments outside the City Walls.* Cambridge, Mass. 1975.

Hansman, John, "An Achaemenian Stronghold," *Acta Iranica* 2nd s. 6 (Leiden 1975). 289-309.

_____, "Elamites, Achaemenians and Anshan." *Iran* 10 (1972). 101-25.

Hansen, Mogens Herman, "Seven Hundred *Archai* in Classical Athens." *GRBS* 21 (1980). 151-73.

Hanson, Richard S., "Aramaic Funerary and Boundary Inscriptions from Asia Minor." *BASOR* 192 (1968). 3-11.

Harden, Donald, *The Phoenicians.* New York 1963.

Harmatta, János, "The Bisitun inscription and the introduction of the Old Persian Cuneiform script." *AAH* 14 (1966). 255-83.

_____, "Darius' Expedition against the Sakā Tigraxaudā." *AAH* 24 (1976). 15-24.

_____, "Irano-Aramaica." *AAH* 7 (1959). 337-409.

_____, "The Literary Patterns of the Babylonian Edict of Cyrus." *AAH* 19 (1971). 217-31.

_____, "Migrations of the Indo-Iranian Tribes." *AAH* 26 (1978). 185-94.

_____, "Les modèles littéraires d l'édit babylonian de Cyrus." *Acta Iranica Hommage Universel* 1 (Leiden 1974). 29-44.

_____, "A Recently Discovered Old Persian Inscription." *AAH* 2 (1953). 1-16.

_____, "The Rise of the Old Persian Empire." *AAH* 19 (1971). 3-15.

Harper, Richard P., "Two Carian Notes: II. What does Gerga Mean?," 384-8. Edited by Sencer Şahin, Elmar Schwertheim and Jörg Wagner, *Studien zur Religion und Kultur Kleinasiens: Festschrift für Friedrich Karl Korner zum 65. Geburtstag am 28. Februar 1976.* Vol. 1. Leiden 1978.

Harris, George, "Ionia under Persia: 547-477 B.C. — A Political History." Ph.D. dissertation, Northwestern University 1971.

Harrison, Evelyn B., "Athena and Athens in the East Pediment of the Parthenon." *AJA* 71 (1967). 27-58.

Hartner, Willy, "The Earliest History of the Constellations in the Near East, and the Motif of the Lion-Bull Combat." *JNES* 24 (1965). 1-16.

Hartner, W. and Ettinghausen, R., "The Conquering Lion, The Life Cycle of a Symbol." *Oriens* 17 (1964). 161-71.

Harvey, David, "Leonidas the Regicide?"   253-60.   Edited by G. W. Bowersock, W. Burkert and M. C. J. Putnam Jr., *Arktouros: Hellenic Studies Presented to Bernard M. W. Knox on the Occasion of his 65th Birthday.* Berlin 1979.

Harvey, F. D., "The Political Sympathies of Herodotus." *Historia* 15 (1966). 254-5.

Hasebroek, Johannes, *Trade and Politics in Ancient Greece.* New York 1965, reprint.

Hasluck, Frederick Wm., *Cyzicus.* Cambridge 1910.

Hauben, Hans, "The Chief Commanders of the Persian Fleet in 480 B.C." *Ancient Society* 4 (1973). 23-37.

_____, "The King of the Sidonians and the Persian Imperial Fleet." *Ancient Society* 1 (1970). 1-8.

Hauri, Christoph., *Das pentathematische Schema der Altpersischen Inschriften.* Wiesbaden 1973.

Hausoullier, B., "Offrande à Apollo Didymeen." *Mémoires, Délégation française en Perse* 7 (1905). 155-65.

Havelock, Eric A., "Prologue to Greek Literacy." In *Lectures in Memory of Louise Taft Semple.* 2nd. 5. Cincinnati 1971, 1-61.

Haynes, Sybille, *Land of the Chimaera: An Archaeological Excursion in the South-West of Turkey.* London 1974.

Head, Barclay V., *Catalogue of the Greek Coins of Ionia in the British Museum.* Bologna 1964 edition.

_____, "On the Chronological Sequence of the Coins of Ephesus." *NC* n.s. 20 (1880). 85-173.

_____, "Coinage of Ephesus." *NC* 3.1 (1881). 13-23.

_____, *Historia Numorum.* Oxford 1911.

Hegyi, D., "Athens and Aigina on the Eve of the Battle of Marathon." *AAH* 13 (1965). 171-81.

_____, "The Historical Background of the Ionian Revolt." *AAH* 14 (1966). 285-302.

_____, "Notes on the Origins of Greek Tyrannis." *AAH* 13 (1965). 303-18.

Heichelheim, Fritz M., "Ezra's Palestine and Periclean Athens." *Zeitschrift für Religions und Geistesgeschichte* 3 (1951). 251-3.

Heidegger, Martin and Fink, Eugen, *Heraclitus Seminar 1966/67.* University 1970.

Heidel, A., *The Babylonian Genesis.* Chicago 1951.

Heilbroner, Robert L., *An Inquiry into the Human Aspect.* New York 1974.

Heinhold-Krahmer, Susanne, *Arzawa: Untersuchungen zu seiner Geschichte nach den hethitischen Quellen.* Heidelberg 1977.

Helm, Payton R., "Herodotus' *Mēdikos Logos* and Median History." *Iran* 19 (1981). 85-90.

Hemmy, A. S., "The Weight-Standards of Ancient Greece and Persia." *Iraq* 5 (1938). 65-80.

Henning, W. B., "The Murder of the Magi." *Journal of the Royal Asiatic Society* (1944). 135-44.

_____, *Zoroaster: Politician or Witch-Doctor?* London 1951.

Henrichs, Albert, "Despoina Kybele: Ein Beitrag zur religiösen Namenkunde." *HSCP* 80 (1976). 253-86.

Hereward, D., "Miltiades' Speech at the Bridge." *Kodaigaku: Palaeologia* 6 (1957/8). 113-23.

_____, "Miltiades' Speech at the Bridge." *Proceedings of the Classical Association* 52 (1955). 24-5.

Herington, C. J., "Athena in Athenian Literature and Cult." *Greece & Rome. Suppl.* to 10 (1963). 61-73.

_____, *Athena Parthenos and Athena Polias, A Study in the Religion of Periclean Athens.* Manchester 1955.

Herrenschmidt, C., "Les créations d'Ahuramazda. Essai sur la royauté perse impériale." *Studia Iranica* 6 (1977). 17-58.

_____, "Désignation de l'Empire et Concepts Politiques de Darius 1 er d'après ses inscriptions en vieux-Perse." *Studia Iranica* 5 (1976). 33-65.

_____, "La religion des Achéménides: État de la question." *Studia Iranica* 9 (1980). 325-39.

Herrmann, Fritz, "Die Silbermünzen von Larissa in Thessalien." *Zeitschrift für Numismatik* 35 (1924). 1-69.

Herrmann, Georgina, *The Iranian Revival.* Oxford 1977.

Herrmann, Peter, "Zu den Beziehungen zwischen Athen und Milet im 5. Jahrhundert." *Klio* 52 (1970). 163-73.

_____, "Men, Herr von Axiotta," 415-23. Edited by Sencer Şahin, Schwertheim, Elmar and Jörg Wagner. *Studien zur Religion und Kultur Kleinasiens: Festschrift für Friedrich Karl Dorner zum 65. Geburtstag am 28. Februar 1976.* Vol. 1. Leiden 1978.

_____, *Der römische Kaisereid.* Göttingen 1968.

_____, "Teos und Abdera im 5. Jahrhundert v. Chr. Ein neues Fragment der Teiorum Dirae." *Chiron* 11 (1981). 1-30.

Herzfeld, Ernst E., *Archaeological History of Iran.* London 1935.

_____, "Pasargadae." *Klio* 8 (1908). 1-68.

_____, *The Persian Empire: Studies in Geography and Ethnology of the Ancient Near East.* Wiesbaden 1968.

_____, "Der Tod des Kambyses." *BSOAS* 8 (1935-7). 589-97.

_____, *Am Tor von Asien: Felsdenkmale aus Irans Heldenzeit.* Berlin 1920.

_____, *Zoroaster and His World.* 2 Vols. Princeton 1947.

Heubeck, Alfred, *Lydiaka.* *Erlanger Forschungen. Reihe A: Geisteswissenschaften Band*
9. Erlangen 1959.

_____, *Praegraeca. Erlanger Forschungen. Reihe A. Geisteswissenschaften*
Band 12. Erlangen 1961.

Heydemann, H., "Ellas ed Asia sul vaso dei Persiani nel Museo di Napoli." *Annali
dell'Istituto di Correspondenza Archeologica* 45 (1837). 20-52.

Highby, Leo I., "The Erythrae Decree." *Klio Beiheft* 36 (1936).

Hignett, Charles, *Xerxes' Invasion of Greece.* Oxford 1963.

Hill, B. H. and Meritt, B. D., "An Early Athenian Decree Concerning Tribute." *Hesperia*
13 (1944). 1-15.

Hill, G. F., *Sources for Greek History between the Persian and Peloponnesian Wars.*
Oxford 1951 edition.

Hill, George, *A Handbook of Greek and Roman Coins.* London 1899.

Hill, Ida Thallon, *The Ancient City of Athens.* Chicago 1969 reprint.

Hiller von Gaertringen, Friedrich, "Das Köngitum bei den Thessalern im sechsten und
fünften Jahrhundert." *Aus der Anomia.* Berlin 1890. 1-16.

Hinz, Walther, "Achämenidische Hofverwaltung." *Zeitschrift für Assyriologie* 61 (1971).
260-311.

_____, *Altiranische Sprachgut der Nebenüberlieferungen.* Wiesbaden 1975.

_____, "Zur Behistun-Inschrift des Dareios." *ZDMG* 96 (1942). 326-49.

_____, *Darius und der Perser: Eine Kulturgeschichte der Achämeniden.* Vol.
2 Baden-Baden 1979.

_____, "Die Einführung der altpersischen Schrift." *ZDMG* 102 (1952). 28-38.

_____, "Zu den elamischen Burgbau-Inschriften Darius I. aus Susa." *AAH* 19
(1971). 17-24.

_____, "The Elamite Version of the Record of Darius's Palace at Susa." *JNES*
9 (1950). 1-7.

_____, "Die Entstehung der altpersischen Keilschrift." *AMI* n.f. 1 (1968). 95-
8.

_____, "Das erste Jahr des Grosskönigs Dareios." *ZDMG* 92 (1938). 136-73.

_____, "'Glückwunsch' aus Persepolis." In *Mémorial Jean de Menasce.*
Louvain 1974, 125-9.

_____, *The Lost World of Elam.* London 1972.

_____, *Neue Wege im Altpersischen.* Wiesbaden 1973.

_____, "Zu den Mörsern und Stösseln aus Persepolis." *Acta Iranica
Monumentum H. S. Nyberg* 1 (Leiden 1975). 371-85.

_____, "Die Quellen," 5-14. Edited by Gerald Walser, *Beiträge zur
Achämenidengeschichte.* Wiesbaden 1972.

Hirsch, Marga, "Die athenischen Tyrannenmörder in Geschichtsschreibung und Volkslegende." *Klio* 20 (1926). 129-67.

Hodder, Ian, ed., *The Spatial Organisation of Culture*. London 1978.

_____, "Spatial Studies in Archaeology," 33-64. Edited by C. Board, *Progress in Human Geography*. Vol. 1. London 1977.

Hodge, A. Trevor, "Marathon: The Persians' Voyage." *TAPA* 105 (1975). 155-73.

Höck, Adelbert, "Das Odrysenreich in Thrakien." *Hermes* 26 (1891). 76-117.

Hörhager, Herbert, "Zu den Flottenoperation am Kap Artemision." *Chiron* 3 (1973). 43-59.

Hofstetter, Josef, *Die Griechen in Persien*. Berlin 1978.

_____, "Zu den griechischen Gesandtschaften nach Persien," 94-107. Edited by Gerald Walser, *Beiträge zur Achämenidengeschichte*. Wiesbaden 1972.

Hogarth, David G., *Ionia and the East*. Oxford 1909.

_____, "Lydia and Ionia." *CAH* Vol. 3, 1st ed. Cambridge 1929, 501-26.

Holloway, R. Ross, "The Crown of Naxos." *The American Numismatic Society Museum Notes* 10 (1962). 1-8.

Hooker, J. T., *Mycenaean Greece*. London 1976.

Hopper, R., "The Mines and Miners of Ancient Athens." *Greece & Rome* 8 (1961). 138-51.

_____, *Trade and Industry in Classical Greece*. London 1979.

Houwink ten Cate, P. H. J., "Anatolian Evidence for Relations with the West in the Late Bronze Age," 141-61. Edited by R. A. Crossland and Ann Birchall, *Bronze Age Migrations in the Aegean*. London 1973.

_____, *The Luwian Population Groups of Lycia and Cilicia Aspera during the Hellenistic Period*. Leiden 1965.

How, W. W. and Wells, J., *A Commentary on Herodotus*. 2 Vols. Oxford 1928.

Huart, Clément, *Ancient Persia and Iranian Civilization*. New York 1927.

Hübner, Alfred, "Zum Tod des Kambyses." *Zeitschrift für vergleichende Sprachforschung* 68 (1944). 57.

Hüsing, Georg, *Porušātiš und das achamanidische Lehenswesen*. Vienna 1933.

Hughes, J. Donald, *Ecology in Ancient Civilizations*. Albuquerque 1975.

Humphreys, S. C., *Anthropology and the Greeks*. Boston 1978.

_____, "Archaeology and the Economic and Social History of Classical Greece." *La Parola del Passato* 22 (1967). 374-400.

_____, "Economy and Society in Classical Athens." *Annali della Scuola normale superiore di Pisa* 39 (1970). 1-26.

Hunt, D. W. S., "Feudal Survivals in Ionia." *JHS* 67 (1947). 68-76.

Hunter, Virginia, *Past and Process in Herodotus and Thucydides*. Princeton 1982.

Hussey, Edward, *The Presocratics*. London 1972.

Hutchinson, G. Evelyn, *An Introduction to Population Ecology*. New Haven 1978.

Huxley, George, *The Early Ionians*. London 1966.

_____, "Mimnermus and Pylos." *GRBS* 2 (1959). 103–7.

_____, "Titles of Midas." *GRBS* 2 (1959). 85–99.

Imbert, J., "L'épigramme grecque du Stèle de Xanthe." *REG* 7 (1894). 267–75.

Immerwahr, Henry I., *Form and Thought in Herodotus*. Cleveland 1966.

_____, "The Samian Stories of Herodotus." *CJ* 52 (1957). 312–22.

in der Smitten, Wilhelm T., "Xerxes und die Daeva." *Bibliotheca Orientalis* 30 (1973). 368a–369b.

Ingalls, Daniel H. H., "Remarks on Mr. Wasson's Soma." *JAOS* 91 (1971). 188–91.

Insler, S., *The Gāthās of Zarathustra*. *Acta Iranica* 3rd. s. 1. Leiden 1975.

Jackson, A. H., "The Original Purpose of the Delian League." *Historia* 18 (1969). 12–6.

Jacoby, Felix, "Zu den älteren griechischen Elegikern: II. Zu Mimnermos." *Hermes* 53 (1918). 262–307.

_____, *Atthis: The Local Chronicles of Ancient Athens*. Oxford 1949.

_____, *Die Fragmente der griechischen Historiker*. Berlin and Leipzig 1923–58.

_____, "Some Athenian Epigrams from the Persian Wars." *Hesperia* 14 (1945). 156–211.

Jaeger, Werner, *Paideia: The Ideals of Greek Culture*. Vol. 1. Bk. 1. New York 1965 edition.

_____, *The Theology of the Early Greek Philosophers*. Oxford 1947.

Jameson, Michael H., "Agriculture and Slavery in Classical Athens." *CJ* 73 (1977–78). 122–45.

_____, "A Revised Text of the Decree of Themistokles from Troizen." *Hesperia* 31 (1962). 301–5.

_____, "The Provisions for Mobilization in the Decree of Themistokles." *Historia* 12 (1963). 385–404.

Jankowska, N. B., "Some Problems of the Economy in the Assyrian Empire," 253–76. Edited by I. M. Diakoff, *Ancient Mesopotamia*. Moscow 1969.

Jarvie, I. C., *The Revolution in Anthropology*. Chicago 1969.

Jeffery, L. H., *Archaic Greece*. London 1976.

_____, "The Courts of Justice in Archaic Chios." *BSA* 51 (1956). 157–67.

_____, *The Local Scripts of Archaic Greece*. Oxford 1961.

Jenkins, G. K., *Ancient Greek Coins*. London 1972.

_____, "Coin Hoards from Pasargadae." *Iran* 3 (1965). 41-52.

Johansen, K. Friis, "Clazomenian Sarcophagus Studies." *Acta Archaeologica* 13 (1942). 1-64.

Johnston, A. E. M., "The Earliest Preserved Greek Map: A New Ionian Coin Type." *JHS* 87 (1967). 86-94.

Johnston, J., "An International Managed Currency in the Fifth Century." *Hermathena* 47 (1932). 132-57.

Jones, John Ellis, "Town and Country Houses in Attica in Classical Times," 63-140. Edited by H. Mussche, P. Spitaels and F. Goemaere-De Poerck, *Miscellanea Graeca* I, *Thorikos and Laurion in Archaic and Classical Times.* Ghent 1975.

Jones, W., *The Law and Legal Theory of the Greeks.* Oxford 1956.

Judeich, W., "Griechische Politik und persische Politik im V. Jahrhundert v. Chr." *Hermes* 58 (1923). 1-19.

_____, "Zur ionischen Wanderung." *Rheinisches Museum* 82 (1933). 305-14.

Junge, Peter Julius, *Dareios I. König der Perser.* Leipzig 1944.

_____, "Satrapie und Natio, Reichsverwaltung und Reichpolitik im Staate Dareios' I." *Klio* 34 (1941). 1-55.

_____, "Hazaraptiš.' *Klio* 33 (1940). 13-38.

Justi, Ferdinand, "Der Chiliarch des Dareios." *ZDMG* 50 (1896). 659-66.

Kagan, Donald, "The Dates of the Earliest Coins." *AJA* 86 (1982). 1-18.

_____, *The Outbreak of the Peloponnesian War.* Ithaca 1969.

Kahn, Charles H., *Anaximander and the Origins of Greek Cosmology.* New York 1960.

_____, *The Art and Thought of Heraclitus.* Cambridge 1979.

Kahrstedt, Ulrich, "Sparta und Persien." *Hermes* 56 (1921). 320-5.

_____, *Staatsgebiet und Staatsangehörige in Athen.* Stuttgart 1934.

Kantor, Helene J., "Achaemenid Jewelry in the Oriental Institute." *JNES* 16 (1957). 1-23.

_____, "Narration in Egyptian Art." *AJA* 61 (1957). 44-54.

Karavites, Peter, "Realities and Appearances, 490-480. B.C." *Historia* 26 (1977). 129-47.

Kardara, Chrysoula P., "On Theseus and the Tyrannicides." *AJA* 55 (1951). 293-300.

_____, "The Tyrannicides Once More." *AJA* 64 (1960). 281.

Kawerau, Georg and Rehm, A., *Das Delphinion in Milet.* Berlin 1914.

Keil, J., "Die Kulte Lydiens." In *Anatolian Studies presented to Sir William Mitchell Ramsay.* Manchester 1923, 239-66.

Kent, Roland G., "VIII. Addenda on Naqš-i-Rustam B." *JNES* 4 (1945). 232-3.

_____, "VIII. Artaxerxes I, Persepolis A." *JNES* 4 (1945). 228-32.

_____, "Cameron's Old Persian Readings at Bisitun: Restorations and Notes." *JCS* 5 (1951). 55-7.

_____, "More Old Persian Inscriptions." *JAOS* 54 (1934). 34-52.

_____, "IX. Naqš-i-Rustam D." *JNES* 4 (1945). 233.

_____, *Old Persian: Grammar, Texts, Lexicon.* 2nd ed. New Haven 1953.

_____, "Old Persian Texts." *JNES* 1 (1942). 415-23.

_____, "Old Persian Texts: III.   Darius' Behistan Inscription, Column V." *JNES* 2 (1943). 105-14.

_____, "Old Persian Texts: IV. The Lists of Provinces." *JNES* 2 (1943). 302-6.

_____, "Old Persian Texts: V. Darius' Behistan Inscription, Column V: A Correction." *JNES* 3 (1944). 232-3.

_____, "Old Persian Texts: VI. Darius' Naqš-i-Rustam B. Inscription." *JNES* 4 (1945). 39-51.

_____, "The Restoration of Order by Darius." *JAOS* 58 (1938). 112-21.

Keramopoullos, Ant. D., Ὁ Κῦρος καὶ τὸ Ὑρκανιον Πεδίον Ἀθηνᾶ, 16 (1904). 161-88.

Kervan, M., Stronach, D., Vallat, F., and Yoyotte, J., "Une statue de Darius découverte à Suse." *Journal asiatique* 260 (1972). 235-66.

Kiechle, Franz, "Athens Politik nach der Abwehr der Perser." *Historische Zeitschrift* 204 (1967). 265-304.

Kienitz, Friedrich Karl, *Die politische Geschichte Ägyptens vom 7. bis zum 4. Jahrhundert vor der Zeitwende.* Berlin 1953.

Kierdorf, Wilhelm, *Erlebnis und Darstellung der Perserkriege.* Göttingen 1966.

King, Leonard W. and Thompson, R. C., *The Sculptures and Inscription of Darius the Great on the Rock of Behistun in Persia.* London 1907.

Kinzl, Konrad H., ed., *Die ältere Tyrannis bis zu den Perserkriegen.* Darmstadt 1979.

_____, *Miltiades-Forschungen.* Vienna 1968.

Kirk, G. S., *Heraclitus: The Cosmic Fragments.* Cambridge 1970.

_____, *Homer and the Epic.* Cambridge 1965.

_____, "Homer and Modern Oral Poetry: Some Confusions." *CQ* 10 (1960). 271-81.

_____, *Homer and the Oral Tradition.* Cambridge 1976.

_____, *The Nature of Greek Myths.* Harmondsworth 1974.

_____, *The Songs of Homer.* Cambridge 1962.

Kirk, G. S. and Raven, J. E., *The Presocratic Philosophers.* Cambridge 1966 edition.

Kirsten, Ernst, *Die griechische Polis als historisch-geographisches Problem des Mittelmeerraumes.* Bonn 1956.

Kiyonaga, S., "The Date of the Beginnings of Coinage in Asia Minor." *RSN* 52 (1973). 5-16.

Klasens, A., "Egypte onder Perzen en Grieken-Romeinen—Cambyses en Egypte." *Vooraziatisch-Egyptisch Gezelschap, "Ex Oriente Lux" Jaarbericht* 65 (1946). 339-49.

Kleiner, Gerhard, *Alt-Milet.* Wiesbaden 1966.

_____, *Die Ruinen von Milet.* Berlin 1968.

Kleiss, Wolfram, "Ein Abschnitt der achämenidischen Königsstrasse von Pasargadae und Persepolis nach Susa, bei Naqshi-i Rustam." *AMI* 14 (1981). 45-53.

_____, "Der Takht-i Rustam bei Persepolis und das Kyrosgrab in Pasargadae." *Archäologischer Anzeiger* 86 (1971). 157-62.

Kleiss, Wolfram and Calmeyer, Peter, "Das unvollendete Achämenidische Felsgrab bei Persepolis." *AMI* 8 (1975). 81-98.

Klima, Otakar, "Gaumāta der Magier." *Archiv Orientální* 31 (1963). 119-21.

Kluge, Theodor, "Die Lykier: Ihre Geschichte und ihre Inschriften." *Der Alte Orient.* Vol. 11. Leipzig 1910.

Knox, A. D., *Herodes, Cercidas and the Greek Choliamibic Poets.* (Loeb Edition). London 1953.

Knox, Bernard M. W., *Oedipus at Thebes.* New Haven 1957.

Koch, Heidemarie, *Die religiösen Verhältnisse der Dareioszeit.* Göttingen 1977.

König, Friedrich Wilhelm, *Der falsche Bardija: Dareios der Grosse und die Lügenkönige.* Vienna 1938.

_____, *Die Persika des Ktesias von Knidos.* Graz 1972.

_____, *Die Stele von Xanthos.* Vienna 1936.

Kolars, John F., *Tradition, Season, and Change in a Turkish Village.* Chicago 1963.

Kolbe, Walther, "Die Anfänge der attischen Arché." *Hermes* 73 (1938). 249-68.

Koldewey, Robert, *Neandria.* Berlin 1891.

Konishi, Haruo, "Thucydides' Method in the Episodes of Pausanias and Themistocles." *AJP* 91 (1970). 52-69.

Korošec, Viktor, *Hethitische Staatsverträge: Ein Beitrag zu ihrer juristischen Wertung.* Leipzig 1931.

Kothe, Heinz, "Der Skythenbegriff bei Herodot." *Klio* 51 (1969). 15-88.

Kraay, Colin M., *Archaic and Classical Greek Coins.* London 1976.

_____, "Gold and Copper Traces in Early Greek Silver," *Archaeometry* 1 (1958). 1-5.

_____, "Monnaies provenant du site de Colophon." *RSN* 42 (1962/63). 5-13.

_____, "Review-Article: The Asyut Hoard: Some Comments on Chronology." *NC* s.7.17 (1977). 189-98.

Kraay, Colin M. and Emeleus, Vera M., *The Composition of Greek Silver Coins.* Oxford 1962.

Kraeling, C. H. and Adams, R. M., eds., *The City Invincible.* Chicago 1960.

Kraft, Konrad, "Bemerkungen zu dem Perserkriegen." *Hermes* 92 (1964). 144-71.

Krappe, Alexander H., "Solomon and Ashmodai." *AJP* 54 (1933). 260-8.

Krefter, Friedrich, *Persepolis Rekonstruktionen.* Berlin 1971.

Kreissig, Heinz, *Die sozialökonomische Situation in Juda zur Achämenidenzeit.* Berlin 1973.

Kroll, John H., "Wappenmünzen, Gorgoneia, Owls." *American Numismatic Society Museum Notes* 26 (1981). 1-32.

Krumbholz, Paul, *De Asiae Minoris Satrapis Persicis.* Leipzig 1883.

Kübler, Paul, "Die persische Politik gegenüber dem Griechentum in der Pente-kontaetia." Unpublished inaugural dissertation, Ruprecht-Karl-Universität, Heidelberg 1950.

Kuhn, Thomas S., *The Structure of Scientific Revolutions.* Chicago 1970.

Kurtz, Donna C. and Boardman, John, *Greek Burial Customs.* Ithaca 1971.

Kutsher, J. and Polotsky, J., "An Aramaic Scroll from the Fifth Century B.C.E." *Kedem* 2 (1945). 66-74 [in Hebrew].

Labarbe, J., "Un décalage de 40 ans dans la chronologie de Polycrate." *AC* 31 (1962). 153-88.

_____, "Un Putsch dans la Grèce antique: Polycrate et ses frères à la conquête de pouvoir." *Ancient Society* 5 (1974). 21-42.

Lacey, W. K., *The Family in Classical Greece.* Ithaca 1968.

Lacroux, Leon, "A propos des monnaies de Cyzique et de la legende d'Oreste." *AC* 15 (1946). 209-24.

Laidlow, William A., *A History of Delos.* Oxford 1933.

Laloux, Monique, "La circulation des monnaies d'électrum de Cyzique." *Revue Belge de Numismatique* 117 (1971). 31-69.

Lamberg-Karlovsky, C. C., "Tepe Yahya." *Iran* 12 (1974). 228-31.

Lambert, G., "La Restauration juive sous les rois Achéménides." *Cahiers Sioniens* 1 (1947). 314-37.

Lang, Mabel L., "Again the 'Marathon' Epigram," 80. Edited by D. W. Bradeen and M. F. McGregor, ΦOPOΣ: *Tribute to Benjamin Dean Meritt.* Locust Valley 1974.

_____, "Herodotus and the Ionian Revolt." *Historia* 17 (1968). 24-36.

_____, "Scapegoat Pausanias." *CJ* 63 (1967). 79-85.

Langlotz, Ernst, *Die kulturelle und künstlerische Hellenisierung der Küsten des Mittelmeers durch die Stadt Phokaia.* Cologne 1966.

Lanzani, Carolina, "Ricerche su Pausania, regente di Sparta." *Rivista di Storica Antica* 7 (1903). 105-14.

Laroche, Emmanuel, "Koubaba, déesse anatolienne, et le problème des origines de Cybèle," 113-28. Edited by Otto Eissfeldt, *Éléments orientaux dans la religion Grecque ancienne.* Paris 1960.

Larsen, J. A. O., "The Constitution and Original Purpose of the Delian League." *HSCP* 51 (1940). 175-213.

_____, "The Constitution of the Peloponnesian League." *CP* 28 (1933). 257-76.

_____, "Federation for Peace in Ancient Greece." *CP* 39 (1944). 145-62.

_____, *Representative Government in Greek and Roman History.* Berkeley 1955.

_____, "Sparta and the Ionian Revolt." *CP* 37 (1932). 136-50.

Larsen, Mogens Trolle, ed., *Power and Propaganda: A Symposium on Ancient Empires.* Copenhagen 1979.

Lateiner, Donald, "The Failure of the Ionian Revolt." *Historia* 31 (1982). 129-60.

_____, "No Laughing Matter: A Literary Tactic in Herodotus." *TAPA* 107 (1977). 175-82.

_____, "A Note on ΔΙΚΑΣ ΔΙΔΟΝΑΙ in Herodotus." *CQ* 30 (1980). 30-2.

Lattimore, Richmond, "Aeschylus on the Defeat of Xerxes." In *Classical Studies in Honor of William Abbott Oldfather.* Urbana 1943, 82-93.

_____, "The Wise Advisor in Herodotus." *CP* 34 (1939). 24-35.

Lawrence, A. W., "The Acropolis and Persepolis." *JHS* 71 (1951). 111-9.

_____, *Greek Architecture.* Harmondsworth 1957.

Lazenby, J. F., "Pausanias, Son of Kleombrotos." *Hermes* 103 (1975). 235-51.

_____, "The Strategy of the Greeks in the Opening Campaign of the Persian War." *Hermes* 92 (1964). 264-84.

Leach, Edmund, *Custom, Law, and Terrorist Violence.* Edinburgh 1977.

Leahy, D. M., "The Spartan Embassy to Lygdamis." *JHS* 77 (1957). 272-5.

Lecoq, Pierre, "La Langue des inscriptions Achéménides." *Acta Iranica Hommage Universel* 2 (Leiden 1974). 55-62.

_____, "Le problème de l'écriture cunéiforme vieux-perse." *Acta Iranica Hommage Universel* 3 (Leiden 1974). 25-107.

Legon, Ronald P., "Samos in the Delian League." *Historia* 21 (1972). 145-58.

Lehmann-Haupt, C. F., "Dareios und sein Ross." *Klio* 18 (1923). 59-64.

Lemerle, P., *Le Premier humanisme Byzantin.* Paris 1971.

Lenardon, Robert J., "Charon, Thucydides, and Themistokles." *Phoenix* 15 (1961). 28-40.

_____, "The Chronology of Themistokles' Ostracism." *Historia* 8 (1959). 23-48.

_____, *The Saga of Themistocles.* London 1978.

Lenschau, Thomas, "Zur Geschichte Ioniens." *Klio* 13 (1913). 175-83.

_____, "Die Gründung Ioniens und der Bund am Panionion." *Klio* 36 (1944). 201-37.

Lentz, W., "Has the Function of Persepolis been Fully Recognized so Far?" *The Memorial Volume: Vth International Congress of Iranian Art and Archaeology* 1 (Teheran 1972). 289-90.

Lentz, W., Schlosser, Worfhard, and Gropp, Gerd, "Persepolis—Weitere Beiträge zur Funktionsbestimmung." *ZDMG* 121 (1971). 254-68.

Leuze, Oscar, *Die Satrapieneinteilung in Syrien und im Zweistromlande von 520-320.* Halle 1935.

Levi, Mario A., "La Spedizione scitica di Dario." *Rivista di Filologia* 61 (1933). 58-70.

Levine, Baruch A., "Aramaic Texts from Persepolis." *JAOS* 92 (1972). 70-9.

Levine, Louis D. and Young, T. Cuyler, Jr., eds., *Mountains and Lowlands: Essays in the Archaeology of Greater Mesopotamia.* Malibu 1977.

Levy, Reuben, trans., *The Epic of Kings: Shah-Nama, the National Epic of Persia by Ferdowsi.* London 1967.

Lewis, David M., "Additional Notes." *JHS* 99 (1979). 18-9.

_____, "The Public Seal of Athens." *Phoenix* 9 (1955). 32-4.

_____, *Sparta and Persia.* Leiden 1977.

Lewy, Hildegard, "The Babylonian Background of the Kay Kāūs Legend." *Archiv Orientální* 17 (1949). 28-109.

Lewy, Julius, "The Problems Inherent in Section 70 of the Bisitun Inscription." *HUCA* 25 (1954). 169-208.

Libourel, Jan M., "The Athenian Disaster in Egypt." *AJP* 92 (1971). 605-15.

Lidzbarski, Mark, "Aramäische Inschriften aus Kappadocien." *Ephemeris für semitische Epigraphik* 1 (1900-2). 67-9.

Lincoln, Bruce, *Priests, Warriors, and Cattle: A Study in the Ecology of Religions.* Berkeley 1980.

Lintott, Andrew, *Violence, Civil Strife and Revolution in the Classical City.* London 1982.

Lipínski, E., "Western Semites in Persepolis." *AAH* 25 (1977). 101-12.

Lippold, Adolf, "Pausanias von Sparta und die Perser." *Rheinisches Museum* 108 (1965). 320-41.

Littleton, C. Scott, *The New Comparative Mythology.* Berkeley 1966.

Littman, Enno, *Sardis.* Vol. 6.1. *Lydian Inscriptions.* Leiden 1916.

Littman, Robert J., "Kinship in Athens." *Ancient Society* 10 (1979). 5-31.

_____, "The Religious Policy of Xerxes and the *Book of Esther*." *The Jewish Quarterly Review* 65 (1975). 145-55.

Lloyd, G. E. R., *Early Greek Science: Thales to Aristotle.* London 1970.

Lloyd, Seton, *The Art of the Ancient Near East*. New York 1961.

———————, *Early Anatolia*. Harmondsworth 1956.

Lobel, Edgar and Page, Denys, eds., *Poetarum Lesbiorum Fragmenta*. Oxford 1955.

Lochner-Hüttenbach, F., "Brief des Königs Darius an den Satrapen Gadatas," 91-8. Edited by W. Brandenstein and M. Mayrhofer, *Handbuch des Altpersischen*. Wiesbaden 1964.

Loenen, Dirk, *Polemos: een Studie over oorlog in de griekse oudheid*. Amsterdam 1953.

———————, *Stasis: Enige Aspecten von de Begrippen Partÿ-en Klassenstrÿd in Ord-Griekenland*. Amsterdam 1953.

Lombardo, Giuseppina, *Cimone: ricostruzione della biografia e discussioni storiografiche*. Rome 1934.

Lommel, H., "Die Späher des Varuna und Mitra und das Auge des Königs." *Oriens* 6 (1953). 323-33.

L'Orange, H. P., *Studies on the Iconography of Cosmic Kingship in the Ancient World*. Oslo 1953.

Lorenz, Manfred, "Zarathustras Friedenbotschaft." *Acta Iranica Hommage Universel* 3 (Leiden 1974). 123-32.

Losada, Luis A., *The Fifth Column in the Peloponnesian War*. Leiden 1972.

Lotze, Detlef, Μεταξὺ 'Ελευθέρων καὶ Δούλων. Berlin 1959.

Loughran, C. P. and Raubitschek, A. E., "Three Attic Proxeny Decrees." *Hesperia* 16 (1947). 78-81.

Luria, S., "Kureten, Molpen, Aisymneten." *AAH* 11 (1963). 31-6.

———————, "Ein milesischer Männerbund im Lichte ethnologischer Parallelen." *Philologus* 83 (1928). 113-36.

Lukács, Georg, *History and Class Consciousness*. Cambridge, Mass. 1971.

Luschey, Heinz, "Zum Problem der Stilentwicklung in der Achämenidischen und Sasanidischen Reliefkunst." *Iranica Antiqua* 11 (1975). 113-33.

———————, "Studien zu dem Darius-Relief in Bisutun." *AMI* n.f. 1 (1968). 63-94.

Lutz, H. F., "An Agreement between a Babylonian Feudal Lord and his Retainer in the Reign of Darius II." *The University of California Publications in Semitic Philology* 9 (1928). 269-77.

McCarthy, Dennis J., *Treaty and Covenant: A Study in Form in the Ancient Oriental Documents and in the Old Testament*. Rome 1963.

McCown, Donald E., "The Material Culture of Early Iran." *JNES* 1 (1942). 424-49.

McCredie, James R., "Hippodamos of Miletos," 95-100. Edited by D. G. Mitten, J. G. Pedley, and J. A. Scott, *Studies Presented to George M. A. Hanfmann*. Cambridge, Mass. 1971.

McEwan, C. W., *The Oriental Origin of Hellenistic Kingship*. Chicago 1934.

MacDonald, Brian R., "The Authenticity of the Congress Decree." *Historia* 31 (1982). 120-3.

MacDowell, D., "Aigina and the Delian League." *JHS* 80 (1960). 118-21.

———————, *Athenian Homicide Law in the Age of the Orators.* Manchester 1963.

———————, *The Law in Classical Athens.* London 1978.

McGregor, Malcolm F., "Athenian Policy, at Home and Abroad." In *Lectures in Memory of Louise Taft Semple.* Cincinnati 1967, 1-32.

———————, "The Pro-Persian Party at Athens." *HSCP Suppl.* 1 (1940). 71-95.

McKenzie, John L., ed., *The Anchor Bible: Second Isaiah.* Garden City 1968.

MacQueen, J. G., "The First Arrival of Indo-European Elements in Greece. Some Observations from Anatolia." *Acta of the 2nd International Colloquium on Aegean Prehistory.* Athens 1972, 142-5.

———————, "Geography and History in Western Asia Minor in the Second Millennium B.C." *Anatolian Studies* 18 (1968). 168-86.

———————, *The Hittites.* London 1975.

Maddoli, Gianfranco, "Erodoto e i Ioni: per l'interpretazione di I.143." *La Parola del Passato* 34 (1979). 256-66.

Mallowan, Max, "Cyrus the Great (558-529 B.C.)." *Iran* 10 (1972). 1-18.

Manville, P. B., "Aristagoras and Histiaios: The Leadership Struggle in the Ionian Revolt." *CQ* 27 (1977). 80-91.

Marg, W., "Zur Stategie der Schlact bei Salamis." *Hermes* 90 (1962). 116-9.

Marinos, G. and Petraschek, W., *Laurium.* Athens 1956 [in Greek].

Marschall, M. B. H., "Urban Settlement in the Second Chapter of Thucydides." *CQ* 25 (1975). 26-40.

Martin, Hubert, *Alcaeus.* New York 1972.

Martin, Roland, *L'Urbanisme dans la Grèce antique.* Paris 1956.

Martin, Victor, "La politique des Achéménides. L'exploration prélude de la conquête." *Museum Helveticum* 22 (1965). 38-48.

Martin, William J., "Tribut und Tributleistungen bei den Assyrern." *Studia Orientalia* 8 (1936). 3-50.

Mas^{c}ūdī, *Les Prairies d'Or.* Barbier de Meynard and Pavet de courteille. Pellat, Charles, trans. Vol. 1. Paris 1962. Vol. 2. Paris 1965.

Masson, Olivier, *Les fragments du poète Hipponax: Édition critique et commentée.* Paris 1962.

Mather, Maurice W. and Hewitt, Joseph W., eds., *Xenophon's Anabasis.* Books 1-IV. Norman 1962.

Matthews, Victor J., *Panyassis of Halikarnassos: Text and Commentary.* Leiden 1974.

Mattingly, Harold B., "The Athenian Decree for Miletos (IG 1^2.22+ = ATL II, D II): A Postscript." *Historia* 30 (1981). 113-7.

———————, "Athenian Imperialism and the Foundation of Brea." *CQ* 16 (1966). 172-92.

_____, "The Athenian Proxeny Decree, IG 1².30+23 (SEG.10.20)." *Phoenix* 29 (1975): 284-6.

_____, "Periclean Imperialism." In *Ancient Societies and Institutions*. New York 1967. 193-224.

Matzat, Heinrich, "Über die Glaubwürdigkeit der geographischen Angaben Herodots über Asien." *Hermes* 6 (1872). 393-486.

Maurice, F., "The Size of the Army of Xerxes in the Invasion of Greece 480 B.C." *JHS* 50 (1930). 210-35.

Mavrogordato, J., "A Chronological Arrangement of the Coins of Chios." *NC* 4.15 (1915), I. 1-52; II. 361-429.

Mayrhofer, Manfred, *Die Arier im Vordern Orient—Ein Mythos?* Vienna 1974.

_____, "Altpersische Späne." *Orientalia* 33 (1964). 72-87.

_____, "Alttagsleben und Verwaltung in Persepolis." *Anzeiger der phil.-hist. Klasse der Österreichischen Akademie der Wissenschaften* 109 (1972). 192-202.

_____, "Kleinasien zwischen Agonie des Persereiches und Hellenistischem Frühling." *Anzeiger der phil.-hist. Klasse der Österreichischen Akademie der Wissenschaften* 112 (1975). 274-82.

_____, *Onomastica Persepolitana*. Vienna 1973.

_____, "Aus dem perserzeitlichen Ägypten." *Anzeiger der phil.-hist. Klasse der Österreichischen Akademie der Wissenschaften* 109 (1972). 317-20.

_____, "Der Rekonstruktion des Medischen." *Anzeiger der phil.-hist. Klasse der Österreichischen Akademie der Wissenschaften* 105 (1968). 1-22.

_____, "Überlegungen zur Entstehung der altpersischen Keilschrift." *BSOAS* 42 (1979). 290-6.

_____, "Ein unpubliziertes Beschriftetes eichgewicht der Dareios-Zeit." *Anzeiger der phil.-hist. Klasse der Österreichischen Akademie der Wissenschaften* 116 (1979). 25-7.

_____, "Xerxès-le-Grand." *Acta Iranica Hommage Universel* 1 (Leiden 1974). 108-116.

Mazzarino, Santo, *Fra Oriente e Occidente*. Florence 1947.

Meade, Clare Goff, "Excavations at Bābā Jān 1967: Second Preliminary Report." *Iran* 7 (1969). 115-30.

_____, "Luristan in the First Half of the First Millennium B.C." *Iran* 6 (1968). 105-34.

_____, "Bābā Jān." In "Survey of Excavations in Iran During 1966-67." *Iran* 6 (1968). 157-8.

Meiggs, Russell, *The Athenian Empire*. Oxford 1972.

_____, "The Crisis of Athenian Imperialism." *HSCP* 67 (1963). 1-36.

_____, "The Growth of Athenian Imperialism." *JHS* 63 (1943). 21-34.

_____, "The Political Implication of the Parthenon." *Greece & Rome. Suppl.* to Vol. 10 (1963). 36-45.

Meiggs, Russell and Lewis, David, *A Selection of Greek Historical Inscriptions.* Oxford 1969.

Meissner, Bruno, "Die Achämenidenkönige und das Judentum." *Sitzungsberichte der preussischen Akademie der Wissenschaften (Phil.-hist. Klasse).* (1938). 6-26.

Mellaart, James, *The Archaeology of Ancient Turkey.* London 1978.

Mellink, Machteld J., "Archaeology in Asia Minor." *AJA* 59 (1955). 235-6.

_____, "Archaeology in Asia Minor." *AJA* 78 (1974). 105-30.

_____, "Archaeology in Asia Minor." *AJA* 80 (1976). 261-90.

_____, "Archaeology in Asia Minor." *AJA* 82 (1978). 315-38.

_____, "Archaeology in Asia Minor." *AJA* 83 (1979). 331-44.

_____, "Archaeology in Asia Minor." *AJA* 85 (1981). 463-79.

_____, ed., *Dark Ages and Nomads c. 1000 B.C.: Studies in Iranian and Anatolian Archaeology.* Istanbul 1964.

Mendenhall, George E., *Law and Covenant in Israel and the Ancient Near East.* Pittsburgh 1955.

Mercer, Samuel A. B., "The Oath in Cuneiform Inscriptions." *AJSL* 29 (1913). 65-94.

Meritt, Benjamin Dean, "An Athenian Casualty List." *Hesperia* 25 (1956). 375-7.

_____, "Athens and the Amphiktyonic League." *AJP* 69 (1948). 312-4.

_____, "Athens and the Amphiktyonic League." *AJP* 75 (1954). 369-73.

_____, "Attic Inscriptions of the Fifth Century (Athens and Erythrai)." *Hesperia* 14 (1945). 82-3.

_____, "The Early Years of the Delian League." *Proceedings of the Classical Association* 43 (1946). 10-1.

_____, "Epigrams from the Battle of Marathon," 268-80. Edited by S. S. Weinberg, *The Aegean and the Near East: Studies Presented to Hetty Goldman.* Locust Valley 1956.

_____, "Greek Inscriptions." *Hesperia* 5 (1936). 355-8.

_____, "Greek Inscriptions: An Early Archon List." *Hesperia* 8 (1939). 59-65.

_____, "Greek Inscriptions." *Hesperia* 13 (1944). 210-68.

_____, "Greek Inscriptions (77. Erythrai and Athens)." *Hesperia* 15 (1946). 246-9.

_____, "Inscriptions of Colophon." *AJP* 56 (1935). 358-97.

_____, "The Marathon Epigrams Again." *AJP* 83 (1962). 294-8.

_____, "Perikles, the Athenian Mint, and the Hephaisteion." *Proceedings of the American Philosophical Society* 119 (1975). 267-74.

_____, "The Tribute Quota-List of 454/3 B.C." *Hesperia* 41 (1972). 403-17.

Meritt, B. D. and Wade-Gery, H. T., "The Dating of Documents to the Mid-Fifth Century—I." *JHS* 82 (1962). 67-74.

Meritt, B. D., Wade-Gery, H. T., and McGregor, Malcolm, *The Athenian Tribute Lists.* Vol.1. Cambridge, Mass. 1939. Vol. 2. Princeton 1949. Vol. 3. Princeton 1950.

Métraux, G. P. R., "Western Greek Land Use and City Planning in the Archaic Period." Ph.D. dissertation, Harvard University 1972.

Metzger, Henri *et al.*, *Fouilles de Xanthos. Vol.* 6: *La Stèle trilinque de Létöon.* Paris 1979.

_____, "La Stéle trilinque recémment découverte au Létoon de Xanthos." *CRAI* (1974). 82-93, 115-25, 132-49.

Meuleau, Maurice, "Mesopotamia under Persian Rule," 354-85. In H. Bengtson, *The Greeks and the Persians.* London 1969.

Meyer, Eduard, *Geschichte des Altertums.* Vol. 4.1. Stuttgart 1944.

Meyer, Hans D., "Vorgeschichte und Gründung des delisch-attischen Seebundes." *Historia* 12 (1963). 405-46.

Miller, Molly, "The Early Persian Dates in Herodotus." *Klio* 37 (1959). 29-52.

_____, "The Herodotean Croesus." *Klio* 41 (1963). 58-94.

_____, *The Thalassocracies: Studies in Chronography.* Vol. 2. Albany 1971.

Miller, Naomi Frances, "Economy and Environment of Malyan, A Third Millennium B. C. Urban Center in Southern Iran." Ph.D. dissertation, University of Michigan 1982.

Milne, J. G., *Kolophon and its Coinage: A Study. Numismatic Notes & Monographs.* 96. New York 1941.

Milton, Marcus P., "The Date of Thucydides' Synchronism of the Siege of Naxos with Themistokles' Flight." *Historia* 28 (1979). 257-75.

Misch, Georg, *The Dawn of Philosophy.* Cambridge, Mass. 1951.

Mitchell, B. M., "Herodotus and Samos." *JHS* 95 (1975). 75-91.

_____, "Notes on the Chronology of the Reign of Arkesilas III." *JHS* 94 (1974). 174-7.

Mitten, David Gordon, "A New Look at Ancient Sardis." *BA* 29 (1966). 38-68.

Mitten, D. G. and Yüğrüm, G., "The Gygean Lake, 1969: Eski Balikhane, Preliminary Report." *HSCP* 75 (1971). 191-5.

Moggi, Mauro, "Autori Greci di Persika I: Dionysio di Mileto." *Annali della Scuola Normale Superiore di Pisa* 2 (1972). 433-68.

_____, "I furti di Statue attribuiti a Serse e le relative restituzioni." *Annali della Scuola Normale Superiore di Pisa* 3 (1973). 1-42.

_____, *I sinecismi interstatali Greci.* Vol. 1. Pisa 1976.

_____, "La tradizione delle guerre persiane in Platone," *Studi Classici e Orientali* 17 (1968). 213-26.

Momigliano, Arnaldo, *Alien Wisdom: The Limits of Hellenization.* Cambridge 1975.

_____, "The Place of Herodotus in the History of Historiography." In *Studies in Historiography.* New York 1966, 127–41.

_____, "La spedizione ateniese in Egitto." *Aegyptus* 10 (1929). 190–206.

_____, "Dalla spedizione scitica di Filippo, alla spedizione scitica di Dario." *Athenaeum* 11 (1933). 336–59.

_____, "Sull'amministrazione del Minere del Laurio." *Athenaeum* 10 (1932). 247–58.

_____, "Tradizione e invenzione in Ctesia." *Atene e Roma* 12 (1931). 15–44.

Momigliano, Arnaldo and Humphreys, Sally C., "The Social Structure of the Ancient City." *Annali della Scuola Normale Superiore de Pisa* s. 3.4 (1974). 331–67.

Moorey, P. R. S., "Some Elaborately Decorated Bronze Quiver Plaques made in Luristan, c. 750–650 B.C." *Iran* 13 (1975). 19–30.

_____, "Towards a Chronology for the 'Luristan Bronzes'." *Iran* 9 (1971). 113–30.

Morgenstern, J., "Further Light from the Book of Isaiah upon the Catastrophe of 485 B.C." *HUCA* 37 (1966). 1–28.

_____, "Jerusalem—485 B.C." *HUCA* 27 (1956). 101–79.

_____, "Jerusalem—485 B.C. (Concluded)." *HUCA* 31 (1960). 1–29.

_____, "Jerusalem—485 B.C. (Continued)." *HUCA* 28 (1957). 15–47.

_____, "Two Prophecies from 520–516 B.C." *HUCA* 22 (1949). 365–431.

Mosley, Derek J., "Diplomacy and Disunion in Ancient Greece." *Phoenix* 25 (1971). 319–30.

_____, "The Size of Embassies in Ancient Greek Diplomacy." *TAPA* 96 (1965). 255–66.

Mossé, Claude, *La Tyrannie dans la Grèce antique.* Paris 1969.

Mosshammer, Alden A., *The Chronicle of Eusebius and Greek Chronographic Tradition.* Lewisburg 1979.

Mourelatos, Alexander P. D., ed., *The Pre-Socratics.* Garden City 1974.

Müller, C. and Müller, T., eds., *Fragmenta Historicum Graecorum.* Paris 1841–1872.

Müller, Dietram, "Von Doriskos nach Therme. Der Weg des Xerxes-Heeres durch Thrakien und Ostmakedonien." *Chiron* 5 (1975). 1–11.

Müller, Karl, *Geographi Graeci Minores.* 2 Vols. Paris 1882.

Muffs, Yochanan, *Studies in the Aramaic Legal Documents from Elephantine.* Leiden 1969.

Muhly, James D., "Hittites and Achaeans: Ahhijawā Redomitus." *Historia* 23 (1974). 129–45.

Munro, J. A. R., "Dascylium." *JHS* 32 (1912). 57–67.

_____, "Pelasgians and Ionians." *JHS* 54 (1934). 109–28.

Murison, C. L., "The Peace of Callias: Its Historical Context." *Phoenix* 25 (1971). 12-31.

Murray, Oswyn, Ο ΑΡΧΑΙΟΣ ΔΑΣΜΟΣ. *Historia* 15 (1966). 142-56.

_____, *Early Greece.* Atlantic Highlands 1980.

_____, *Early Greece and Her Eastern Neighbours.* Harvester Press 1979.

Muscarella, Oscar W., "The Archaeological Evidence for Relations between Greece and Iran in the First Millennium B.C." *The Journal of the Ancient Near Eastern Society of Columbia University* 9 (1977). 31-57.

_____, "Excavated and Unexcavated Achaemenian Art," 23-42. Edited by D. Schmandt-Besserat, *Ancient Persia: The Art of an Empire.* Malibu 1980.

Musiolek, P., "Themistokles und Athen." *AAH* 6 (1958). 301-19.

Mustili, D., "L'occupazione ateniese di Lemnos e gli scavi di Hephaistia." In *Studi offerte a E. Ciaceri.* Genoa 1940, 149-58.

Myers, J. M., ed., *The Anchor Bible: Ezra. Nehemiah.* Garden City 1965.

Myres, John L., *Herodotus.* Chicago 1971 edition.

_____, "Persia, Greece and Israel." *Palestine Exploration Quarterly.* 85 (1953). 8-22.

Naster, Paul, "De laatste Lydische Herakliden." *Philologische Studien* 7 (1935-36). 3-16.

Naveh, Joseph and Shaked, Shane, "Ritual Texts or Treasury Documents?" *Orientalia* 42 (1973). 445-57.

Nease, A. S., "Garrisons in the Athenian Empire." *Phoenix* 3 (1949). 102-11.

Nenci, Giusseppe, *Hecataei Milesii Fragmenta.* Florence 1954.

_____, "La monetazione della revolta ionica nei suoi aspetti economici e politici." In *Studi in onore di Amintore Fanfani.* Vol. 1. Milan 1962, 71-83.

Nesselhauf, Herbert, "Untersuchungen zur Geschichte der delisch-attischen Symmachie." *Klio* 30 (1933). 1-141.

Netzer, Amnon, "Some Notes on the Characterization of Cyrus the Great in Jewish and Judeo-Persian Writings." *Acta Iranica Hommage Universel* 2 (Leiden 1974). 35-52.

Neufeld, E., *The Hittite Laws.* London 1951.

Neumann, Günther, *Untersuchungen zum Weiterleben hethitischen und luwischen Sprachgutes in hellenistischer und römischer Zeit.* Wiesbaden 1961.

_____, "Ein weiteres Fragment der Synagogen-Inschrift aus Sardeis." *Kadmos* 7 (1968). 94-5.

Nicholls, R. V., "Old Smyrna: The Iron Age Fortifications and Associated Remains on the City Perimeter." *BSA* 53-4 (1958-59). 35-137.

Nicol, M. B., "Dorudzan." *Iran* 5 (1967). 137-8.

Nilsson, Martin P., *Cults, Myths, Oracles, and Politics in Ancient Greece.* New York 1972 edition.

_____, *The Mycenaean Origin of Greek Mythology.* Berkeley 1932.

Noonan, Thomas S., "The Grain Trade of the Northern Black Sea in Antiquity." *AJP* 94 (1973). 231-42.

_____, "The Origins of the Greek Colony at Panticopaeum." *AJA* 77 (1973). 77-81.

Nordin, Richard, "Aisymnetie und Tyrannis." *Klio* 5 (1905). 392-409.

Noth, Martin, *The History of Israel.* New York 1958.

Notopoulos, James A., "Homer, Hesiod and the Achaean Heritage of Oral Poetry." *Hesperia* 29 (1960). 177-97.

Nyberg, Henrik Samuel, "Das Reich der Achämeniden." *Historia Mundi* 3 (1954). 56-115.

_____, *Die Religionen des alten Iran.* Leipzig 1938.

Nylander, Carl, "Al-Bērūnī and Persepolis." *Acta Iranica Hommage Universel* 1 (Leiden 1974). 137-50.

_____, "Anatolians in Susa — and Persepolis (?)." *Acta Iranica* 2nd. s. 6 (Leiden 1975). 317-23.

_____, "ΑΣΣΥΡΙΑ ΠΡΑΜΜΑΤΑ: Remarks on the 21st Letter of Themistokles." *Opuscula Atheniensia* 8 (1968). 122-36.

_____, *The Deep Well.* London 1969.

_____, *Ionians in Pasargadae.* Uppsala 1971.

_____, "Mason's Marks in Persepolis: A Progress Report." *Proceedings of the IInd Annual Symposium on Archaeological Research in Iran, Nov. 1973.* Teheran 1974, 216-22.

_____, "Old Persian and Greek Stonecutting and the Chronology of Achaemenian Monuments: Achaemenian Problems I." *AJA* 69 (1965). 49-55.

_____, "The Toothed Chisel in Pasargadae: Further Notes on Old Persian Stone Cutting." *AJA* 70 (1966). 373-77.

_____, "Who Wrote The Inscriptions at Pasargadae?" *Orientalia Suecana* 16 (1967). 135-80.

_____, "Achaemenid Imperial Art," 345-59. Edited by Mogens Trolle Larsen, *Power and Propaganda: A Symposium on Ancient Empires.* Copenhagen 1979.

Obed, Bustenay, *Mass Deportations and Deportees in the Neo-Assyrian Empire.* Wiesbaden 1979.

Oettinger, Norbert, *Die militärischen Eide der Hethiter.* Wiesbaden 1976.

Oliva, Pavel, "Die Bedeutung der frühgriechischen Tryannis." *Klio* 38 (1960). 81-6.

_____, ΠΑΤΡΙΚΗ ΒΑΣΙΛΕΙΑ. In ΓΕΡΑΣ: *Studies Presented to George Thomson on the Occasion of his 60th Birthday.* Prague 1963. 171-81.

_____, "La Tyrannie, première forme de l'état en Grèce, et son role historique." *La Pensée* 66 (1956). 102-13.

Oliver, James H., "The Athenian Decree Concerning Miletos in 450/49 B.C." *TAPA* 66 (1935). 177-98.

_____, *Demokratia, the Gods and the Free World.* Baltimore 1960.

_____, "The Peace of Callias and the Pontic Expedition of Pericles." *Historia* 6 (1957). 254-5.

_____, "The Text of the So-Called Constitution of Chios from the First Half of the Sixth Century B.C." *AJP* 80 (1959). 296-301.

Olmstead, Albert T., "The Assyrians in Asia Minor." In *Anatolian Studies Presented to Sir William Mitchell Ramsay*. Manchester 1923, 282-96.

_____, "Critical Note: Darius as Lawgiver." *AJSL* 51 (1935). 247-9.

_____, "Darius and his Behistun Inscription." *AJSL* 55 (1938). 392-416.

_____, *History of Assyria*. New York 1923.

_____, *History of the Persian Empire*. Chicago 1948.

_____, "Oriental Imperialism." *American Historical Review* 23 (1918). 755-62.

_____, "Persia and the Greek Frontier Problem." *CP* 34 (1939). 305-22.

_____, "A Persian Letter in Thucydides." *AJSL* 49 (1933). 154-61.

_____, "Tattenai, Governor of Across the River." *JNES* 3 (1944). 46.

_____, "Wearing the Hat." *American Journal of Theology* 24 (1920). 94-111.

Olmstead, Cleta Margaret, "A Greek Lady from Persepolis." *AJA* 54 (1950). 10-8.

Oppenheim, A. L., "Akkadian pul(u)ḫ(t)u and Melammu." *JAOS* 63 (1943). 31-4.

_____, *Ancient Mesopotamia: Portrait of a Dead Civilization*. Chicago, 1964.

_____, "The Eyes of the Lord." *JAOS* 88 (1968). 173-80

_____, "The Interpretation of Dreams in the Ancient Near East." *Transactions of the American Philosophical Society*. n.s. Vol. 46 (1956). 179-371.

Orlin, Louis L., "Athens and Persia ca 507 B.C.: A Neglected Perspective." In *Michigan Oriental Studies in Honor of George G. Cameron*. Ann Arbor 1976. 255-66.

Ostwald, Martin, *Autonomia: Its Genesis and Early History*. *American Classical Studies* 11 (1982).

_____, *Nomos and the Beginnings of Athenian Democracy*. Oxford 1969.

Oxtoby, Willard Gurdon, "Interpretations of Iranian Dualism." In *Iranian Civilization and Culture*. Montreal 1972. 59-70.

Özgüç, Tahsin, "Excavations at the Hittite Site, Maşat Höyük: Palace, Archives, Mycenaean Pottery." *AJA* 84 (1980). 304-9.

Page, Denys, *Poetae Melici Graeci*. Oxford 1962.

_____, *Sappho and Alcaeus*. Oxford 1955.

Pagliaro, Antonio, "Cyrus et l'Empire Perse." *Acta Iranica Hommage Universel* 2 (Leiden 1974). 3-23.

_____, "Riflessi de etimologie iraniche nella tradizione storiografica greca." *Rendiconti della sedute dell'Accademia Nazionale dei Lincei* 9 (1954). 133-53.

Pallis, Svend Aage, *The Babylonian Akītu Festival.* Copenhagen 1926.

Paoli, Ugo Enrico, *Studi di diritto Attico.* Florence 1930.

_____, *Studi sul processo attico.* Padua 1933.

Papantionios, G. A., Ὁ Μηδισμὸς τῶν Θεσσαλῶν, των Βοιωτῶν καὶ τῶν Φωκέων. *Platon* 15 (1956). 18-30.

Papp, Harald, "Zum Verhältnis Athens zu seinen Bündern im attisch-delischen Seebund." *Historia* 17 (1969). 425-43.

Parain, Charles, "Les caractères spécifiques de la lutte des classes dans l'Antiquité classique." *La Pensée* 108 (1963). 3-25.

Parker, R. A., "Darius and his Egyptian Campaign." *AJSL* 58 (1941). 373-7.

_____, "Persian and Egyptian Chronology." *AJSL* 58 (1941). 285-301.

Parker, Richard A. and Dubberstein, Waldo, *Babylonian Chronology 626 B.C.-A.D. 75.* Providence 1956.

Parker, S. Thomas, "The Objectives and Strategy of Cimon's Expedition to Cyprus." *AJP* 97 (1976). 30-8.

Parlato, Sandra, "La cosiddetta campagna scitica di Dario." *Annali, Istituto Orientale di Napoli* 41 (1981). 213-50.

Parshikov, A. Y., "Pausanias and the Political Struggle in Sparta." *VDI* (1968). 126-38 [in Russian].

Paton, W. R. and Hicks, E. L., *The Inscriptions of Cos.* Oxford 1891.

Pearson, Lionel, "Credulity and Scepticism in Herodotus." *TAPA* 72 (1941). 335-55.

_____, *Early Ionian Historians.* Oxford 1939.

Pease, Samuel James, "Xenophon's *Cyropaedia*, 'The Compleat General'." *Classical Journal* 29 (1934). 436-40.

Pečírka, Jan, "Homestead Farms in Classical and Hellenistic Greece," 113-47. Edited by M. I. Finley, *Problèmes de la terre en Grèce ancienne.* Paris 1973.

_____, "Land Tenure and the Development of the Athenian Polis." In ΓΕΡΑΣ: *Studies Presented to G. Thomson.* Prague 1963, 183-201.

Pedley, John G., *Ancient Literary Sources on Sardis.* Cambridge, Mass. 1972.

_____, "Carians in Sardis." *JHS* 94 (1974). 96-9.

_____, *Sardis in the Age of Croesus.* Norman 1968.

Peek, Werner, "Die Kämpfe am Eurymedon." *HSCP Suppl.* 1 (1940). 97-120.

_____, "Zu den Perser-Epigrammen." *Hermes* 88 (1960). 494-8.

_____, "Ein Seegefecht aus den Perserkriegen." *Klio* 32 (1939). 289-306.

_____, "Aus der Werkstatt," 304-33. Edited by George Mylonas, *Studies Presented to David Moore Robinson.* Vol. 2. St. Louis 1953.

Penella, Robert J., "Scopelianus and the Eretrians in Cissia." *Athenaeum* n.s. 52 (1974). 295-300.

Périphanakis, Constantin E., *La Théorie grecque du Droit et le Classicisme actuel.* Athens 1946.

Perkins, Ann, "Narration in Babylonian Art." *AJA* 61 (1957). 54-62.

Perlman, S., "Panhellenism, the Polis and Imperialism." *Historia* 25 (1976). 1-30.

Perrot, Jean, "Le Palais de Darius le Grand à Šuš." *Proceedings of the IInd Annual Symposium on Archaeological Research in Iran, Nov. 1973.* Teheran 1974, 91-101.

Philarétos, Georges W., "Un congrès à Athènes sous Périclès pour la liberté des mers et la paix." *L'Acropole Revue Mensuelle* 1 (1920). 104-11.

Phillips, E. D., "Saneunos the Scythian." *GRBS* 9 (1968). 385-8.

Piotrovskii, B. B., *Urartu: The Kingdom of Van and its Art.* New York 1967.

Pizzagalli, A. M., "L'epica iranica e gli scrittori greci." *Atene e Roma* s. 3.10 (1942). 33-43.

Plescia, Joseph, "Herodotus and the Case for Eris (Strife)." *La Parola del Passato* 27 (1972). 301-11.

Podlecki, Anthony J., trans. and comm., *Aeschylus: The Persians.* Englewood Cliffs 1970.

——————, "Cimon, Skyros and 'Theseus' Bones'." *JHS* 91 (1971). 141-3.

——————, *The Life of Themistocles.* Montreal 1975.

——————, "The Political Significance of the Athenian 'Tyrannicide'-Cult." *Historia* 15 (1966). 129-41.

Poebel, Arno, "Chronology of Darius' First Year of Reign." *AJSL* 55 (1938). 142-65, 285-314.

——————, "The Duration of the Reign of Smerdis, the Magian, and the Reigns of Nebuchadnezzar III and Nebuchadnezzar IV." *AJSL* 56 (1939). 121-45.

——————, "The King of the Persepolis Tablets: The Nineteenth Year of Artaxerxes I." *AJSL* 56 (1939). 301-4.

——————, "The Names and the Order of the Old Persian and Elamite Months during the Achaemenian Period." *AJSL* 55 (1938). 130-41.

Pope, Arthur U., "Persepolis as a Ritual City." *Archaeology* 10 (1957). 123-30.

Porada, Edith, *The Art of Ancient Iran.* Baden-Baden 1964.

——————, *Corpus of Ancient Near Eastern Seals in North American Collections. The Collection of the Pierpont Morgan Library.* Vol. 1. Washington D. C. 1948.

——————, Review of Ann Farkas, *Achaemenid Sculptures* Leiden 1974, in *The Art Bulletin* 58 (1976). 612-3.

Porten, Bezalel, *Archives from Elephantine.* Berkeley 1968.

Posener, Georges, *La premiére domination Perse en Égypte.* Cairo 1936.

Pounds, N. J. G., *An Historical Geography of Europe, 450 B.C. - A.D. 1330.* Cambridge 1973.

_____, "The Urbanization of the Classical World." *Annals of the Association of American Geographers* 59 (1969). 135-57.

Prakken, D., "Note on the Apocryphal Oath of the Athenians at Plataia." *AJP* 61 (1940). 62-5.

Prášek, Justin, *Dareios I. Der Alte Orient.* Vol. 14. Leipzig 1914.

_____, *Geschichte der Meder und Perser bis zur makedonischen Eroberung.* Gotha Vol. 1 1906, Vol. 2 1910.

_____, "Hekataios als Herodots Quelle zur Geschichte Vorderasiens." *Klio* 4 (1904). 193-208.

_____, *Kambyses. Der Alte Orient.* Vol. 14. Leipzig 1913.

_____, *Kyros der Grosse. Der Alte Orient.* Vol. 13. Leipzig 1912.

Price, Martin J., Review of Liselotte Weidauer, *Probleme der frühen Elektronprägung* in *NC* s. 7.16 (1976). 273-5.

Price, Martin J. and Waggoner, Nancy, *Archaic Greek Coinage: The 'Asyut' Hoard.* London 1975.

Pritchard, James B., ed., *Ancient Near Eastern Texts Relating to the Old Testament.* Princeton 1955.

Pritchett, W. Kendrick, "The Attic Stelai, Part I." *Hesperia* 22 (1953). 225-99.

_____, "The Attic Stelai, Part II." *Hesperia* 22 (1956). 178-317.

_____, *The Greek State at War.* Vol. 1. Berkeley 1974.

_____, *Marathon: University of California Publications in Classical Archaeology.* Berkeley 1960.

_____, "The Transfer of the Delian Treasury." *Historia* 18 (1969). 17-21.

Puhvel, Jaan, "The Death of Cambyses and Hittite Parallels." In *Studia Classica et Orientalia Antonio Pagliaro Oblata.* Vol. 3. Rome 1969. 169-75.

Quinn, Trevor J., *Athens and Samos, Lesbos and Chios: 478-404 B.C.* Manchester 1981.

_____, "Political Groups at Chios: 412 B.C." *Historia* 18 (1969). 22-30.

_____, "Political Groups in Lesbos during the Peloponnesian War." *Historia* 20 (1971). 405-16.

_____, "Thucydides and the Unpopularity of the Athenian Empire." *Historia* 13 (1964). 257-66.

Raaflaub, Kurt, "Athens 'Ideologie der Macht' und die Freiheit des Tyrannen," 45-86. Edited by Wolfgang Schuller. *Studien zum Attischen Seebund (Xenia: Konstanzer althistorische Vorträge und Forschungen; Heft 8).* Konstanz 1984.

_____, "Beute, Vergeltung, Freiheit?" *Chiron* 9 (1979). 1-22.

_____, "Polis Tyrannos: Zur Entstehung einer politischen Metapher," 237-52. Edited by G. W. Bowersock, W. Burkert, and M. C. J. Putnam, *Arktouros: Hellenic Studies presented to Bernard M. W. Knox on the Occasion of his 65th Birthday.* Berlin 1979.

Radermacher, Ludwig, *Mythos und Sage bei den Griechen.* Baden 1938.

Radet, G., *La Lydie et le monde grec au temps des Mermnades.* Paris 1893.

Radt, W., *Siedlungen und Bauten auf der Halbinsel von Halikarnassos.* *Beiheft* 3. *Istanbuler Mitterlungen.* Tübingen 1970.

Ramage, Andrew, "City Area: Pactolus North." In G. M. A. Hanfmann, "The Tenth Campaign at Sardis." *BASOR* 191 (1968). 11-3.

_____, *Lydian Houses and Architectural Terracottas.* Cambridge, Mass. 1978.

Ramage, Andrew and Ramage, Nancy Hirschland, "The Siting of Lydian Burial Mounds." 143-60. Edited by D. G. Mitten, J. G. Pedley, and J. A. Scott, *Studies Presented to George M. A. Hanfmann.* Cambridge, Mass. 1971.

Ramage, Nancy H., "A Lydian Funerary Banquet." *Anatolian Studies* 29 (1979). 91-5.

Ramsay, William M., *The Historical Geography of Asia Minor.* London 1890.

_____, "Military Operations on the North Front of Mount Taurus." *JHS* 40 (1920). 89-112.

Raubitschek, A. E., "The Covenant of Plataea." *TAPA* 91 (1960). 178-83.

_____, "Das Datislied," 234-42. Edited by K. Schauenburg, *Charites, Studien zur Altertumswissenschaft.* Bonn 1957.

_____, *Dedications from the Athenian Acropolis.* Princeton 1949.

_____, "Gyges in Herodotus." *Classical World* 48 (1955). 48-50.

_____, "The Peace Policy of Pericles." *AJA* 70 (1966). 37-42.

_____, Theopompos on Thucydides the Son of Melesias." *Phoenix* 14 (1960). 81-95.

_____, "Treaties between Persia and Athens." *GRBS* 5 (1964). 151-9.

_____, "Two Monuments Erected after the Victory of Marathon." *AJA* 44 (1940). 53-9.

Rawlings, Hunter R., III, "Thucydides on the Purpose of the Delian League." *Phoenix* 31 (1977). 1-8.

Reade, Julian, "Elam and the Elamites in Assyrian Sculpture." *AMI* 9 (1976). 97-105.

Redfield, Robert, *Peasant Society and Culture.* Chicago 1956.

_____, *The Primitive World and its Transformations.* Ithaca 1953.

Redfield, Robert, *et al.*, "Memorandum for the Study of Acculturation." *American Anthropologist* 38 (1936). 149.

Reich, N. J., "The Codification of the Egyptian Laws by Darius and the Origin of the 'Demotic Chronicle'." *Mizraim* 1 (1933). 178-85.

Reiner, E., "The Location of Anshan." *Revue d'Assyriologie* 67 (1973). 57-62.

Renfrew, Colin, "Trade as Action at a Distance," 3-54. Edited by Jeremy A. Sabloff and C. C. Lamberg-Karlovsky, *Ancient Civilization and Trade.* Albuquerque 1975.

Reverdin, Olivier, "Crise spirituelle et évasion." In *Grecs et Barbares. Fondation Hardt, pour l'Étude de l'antiquité classique. Entretiens* 8. Geneva 1962. 85-107.

Rhodes, P. J., "Thucydides on Pausanias and Themistocles." *Historia* 19 (1970). 387-400.

Richardson, Emeline, *The Etruscans.* Chicago 1964.

Richter, Gisela M. A., *Archaic Greek Art: Against its Historical Background.* New York 1949.

_____, "Greeks in Persia." *AJA* 50 (1946). 15-30.

_____, *Korai: Archaic Greek Maidens.* London 1968.

Ries, Gerhard, *Die neubabylonischen Bodenpachtformulare.* Berlin 1976.

Rig Veda. trans. Doniger O'Flaherty. Harmondsworth 1981.

Ringgren, H., *Religions of the Ancient Near East.* Philadelphia 1973.

Roaf, Michael and Stronach, David, "Tepe Nūsh-i Jan, 1970: Second Interim Report." *Iran* 11 (1973). 129-40.

Robert, Louis, "Décrits de Kolophon." *Revue philologique* s.3. Vol. 10 (1936). 158-70.

_____, "Hyrcania." *Hellenica* 6 (1948). 16-26.

_____, "Inscription of the Sepulchral Stele from Sardis." *AJA* 64 (1960). 53-6.

_____, *Noms indigènes dans l'Asie-Mineure gréco-romaine.* Pt. 1. Paris 1963.

_____, "Une nouvelle Inscription grecque de Sardis: Règlement de L'autorité perse relatif à un culte de Zeus." *CRAI* (1975). 306-30.

_____, "Philologie et Geographie." *Anatolia* 4 (1959). 1-12.

_____, "Sur Quelques Ethniques." *Hellenica* 2 (1946). 65-93.

_____, "Types Monétaires à Hypaipa." *Revue Numismatique* 6th s.18 (1976). 25-48.

_____, *Villes d'Asie Mineure: Études de Geographie antique.* Paris 1935.

Robinson, C. A., Jr., "Athenian Politics 510-486 B.C." *AJP* 66 (1945). 243-54.

Robinson, E. S. G., "The Athenian Currency Decree and the Coinage of the Allies." *Hesperia, Suppl.* 8 (1949). 324-40.

_____, "Coins from the Ephesian Artemision Reconsidered." *JHS* 71 (1951). 156-67.

_____, "Greek Coins Acquired by the British Museum 1938-1948. I." *NC* 6th s. 8 (1948). 43-65.

_____, Review-notice of J. G. Milne, *Kolophon and its Coinage: A Study: Numismatic Notes & Monographs* 96 (1941), in *Numismatic Literature* 5 (Oct. 1948). 133-4.

_____, "Rhegion, Zankle-Messana, and the Samians." *JHS* 66 (1946). 13-20.

_____, "Some Electrum and Gold Greek Coins." In *Centennial Publication of the American Numismatic Society.* New York 1958. 585-94.

Robinson, John M., *An Introduction to Early Greek Philosophy.* Boston 1968.

Robertson, H. Grant, *The Administration of Justice in the Athenian Empire.* Toronto 1924.

Robertson, Noel D., "The True Nature of the 'Delian League'." *AJAH* 5 (1980). 64-96.

_____, "The True Nature of the 'Delian League' II." *AJAH* 5 (1980). 110-33.

Roebuck, Carl, "The Early Ionian League." *CP* 50 (1955). 26-40.

_____, "The Economic Development of Ionia." *CP* 48 (1953). 9-16.

_____, *Ionian Trade and Colonization.* New York 1959.

_____, "Tribal Organization in Ionia." *TAPA* 92 (1961). 495-507.

Röllig, Wolfgang, "Politische Heiraten im Alten Orient." *Saeculum* 25 (1974). 11-23.

Roes, Anne, "The Achaemenid Robe." *Bibliotheca Orientalis* 8 (1951). 137-41.

Rogers, Robert William, *A History of Ancient Persia.* New York 1929.

Roos, Paavo, *The Rock-Tombs of Caunus I: The Architecture.* Göteborg 1972.

Root, Margaret Cool, *The King and Kingship in Achaemenid Art. Acta Iranica* 3s. Vol. 9. Leiden 1979.

_____, "The Persepolis Perplex: Some Prospects Borne of Retrospect," 5-13. Edited by D. Schmandt-Besserat, *Ancient Persia: The Art of an Empire.* Malibu 1980.

Roscher, Wilhelm H., "Das Alter der Weltkarte in 'Hippokrates' περὶ ἐβδομάδον und die Reichskarte des Darius Hystaspis." *Philologus* 70 (1911). 529-38.

Rosen, Stanley H., "Herodotus Reconsidered." *Giornale di metafisica* 18 (1963). 194-218.

Rowton, M. B., "The Woodlands of Ancient Western Asia." *JNES* 26 (1967). 261-77.

Roy, J., "The Mercenaries of Cyrus." *Historia* 16 (1967). 287-323.

Rtskhiladze, R., "La specificite d l'Orient dans les 'Histoires' d'Hérodote." *AAH* 22 (1974). 487-94.

Rubincam, Catherine Reid, "A Note on Oxyrhynchus Papyrus 1610." *Phoenix* 30 (1976). 357-66.

Rumpf, Andreas, "Zu den klazomenischen Denkmälern." *Jahrbuch des deutschen archäologischen Instituts* 48 (1933). 55-83.

Säflund, Gösta, "Karische Inschriften aus Labranda." *Opuscula Atheniensa* 1 (1953). 199-205.

Saggs, H. W. F., *The Greatness that was Babylon.* New York 1962.

Şahin, Sencer; Schwertheim, Elmar; and Wagner, Jörg, *Studien zur Religion und Kultur Kleinasiens: Festschrift für Friedrich Karl Dorner zum 65. Geburtstag am 28. Februar 1976.* Vols. 1-2. Leiden 1978.

Sahlins, Marshall D., *Tribesmen.* Englewood Cliffs 1968.

Sakellariou, Michel B., *La migration grecque en Ionie.* Athens 1958.

Sallis, John and Maly, Kenneth, eds., *Heraclitean Fragments: A Companion Volume to the Heidegger/Fink Seminar on Heraclitus.* University 1980.

Salmon, Pierre, *La Politique Égyptienne d'Athènes (VIe et Ve siècles avant J.-C.).* Brussels 1965.

Sanders, Irwin Taylor, *Rainbow in the Rock: The People of Rural Greece.* Cambridge, Mass. 1962.

Sarfaraz, A. A., "Borazjān," in "Survey of Excavations in Iran 1971-1972." *Iran* 11 (1973). 188-9.

Sarre, Friedrich and Herzfeld, Ernst, *Iranische Felsreliefs.* Berlin 1910.

Sauer, Georg, "Serubbabel in der Sicht Haggais und Sacharjas." In *Das Ferne und Nahe Wort, Festschrift Leonhard Rost.* Berlin 1967, 199-207.

Sayce, A. H., *Aramaic Papyri Discovered at Assuan.* London 1906.

Schachermeyr, Fritz, "Athen als Stadt der Grosskönig." *Grazer Beiträge* 1 (1973). 211-20.

_____, *Geistesgeschichte der Perikleischen Zeit.* Stuttgart 1971.

_____, "Marathon und die persische Politik." *Historische Zeitschrift* 172 (1951). 1-35.

_____, *Perikles.* Stuttgart 1969.

Schaeder, H. H., "Das Auge des Königs." *Abhandlungen der Gesellschaft der Wissenschaften zu Göttingen (Phil.-hist. Klasse)* 3 s. 10 (1934). 3-24.

_____, *Iranische Beitrage* I. Halle 1930.

_____, "Das persische Weltreich." In *Die Weltreiche der Geschichte und die Grossraumidee der Gegenwart.* Breslau 1942.

Schäfer, Hans, "Die Autonomie-Klausel des Kalliasfriedens." In *Probleme der alten Geschichte.* Göttingen 1963, 253-68.

Scharf, Joachim, "Die erste ägyptische Expedition der Athener." *Historia* 3 (1954/5). 308-25.

Schefold, Karl, *Die Griechen und ihre Nachbarn: Propyläen Kunstgeschichte* Vol. 1. Berlin 1967.

_____, "Die Tyrannenmörder." *Museum Helveticum* 1 (1944). 189-202.

Schehl, Francis W., "Darius' Letter to Gadatas." *AJA* 54 (1950). 265.

Scheil, P., "Esagil ou le temple de Bēl-Marduk." *CRAI* (1914). 293-308.

Schmidt, Bernhard, *Griechische Märchen, Sagen, und Volkslieder.* Leipzig 1877.

Schmidt, Erich F., *Flights over Ancient Cities of Iran.* Chicago 1940.

_____, *Persepolis.* 3 Vols. Chicago 1953-1970.

_____, *The Treasury of Persepolis and Other Discoveries in the Homeland of the Achaemenids.* Chicago 1939.

Schmidt, Rüdiger, "Die achaimenidische Satrapie TAYAIY DRAYAHYĀ." *Historia* 21 (1972). 522-7.

_____, *Altpersische Siegel-Inschriften.* Vienna 1981.

_____, *Die Iranier-Namen bei Aischylos.* Vienna 1978.

_____, "Medisches und persisches Sprachgut bei Herodot." *ZDMG* 117 (1967). 119-45.

_____, "The Medo-Persian Names of Herodotus in the Light of the New Evidence from Persepolis." *AAH* 24 (1976). 25-35.

_____, "Der Numerusgebrauch bei Länder -und Völkernamen im Alt-persischen." *AAH* 25 (1977). 91-9.

_____, "Die Verfassungsdebatte bei Herodot 3, 80-82 und die Etymologie des Dareios-Namens." *Historia* 26 (1977). 243-4.

Schnitzler, Hans-Jürgen, "Der Sakenfeldzug Dareios' des Grossen." In *Antike und Universalgeschichte: Festschrift für Hans Erich Stier.* Münster 1972, 52-71.

Schrader, Carlos, *La Paz de Calias: Testimonios e Interpretacion.* Barcelona 1976.

Schreiner, Johan Henrik, "Thucydides 1.93 and Themistokles during the 490's." *Symbolae Osloensis* 44 (1969). 23-41.

Schubert, R., *Geschichte der Könige von Lydien.* Breslau 1884.

Schuller, Wolfgang, "Die Einführung der Demokratie auf Samos im 5. Jahrhundert v. Chr." *Klio* 63 (1981). 281-8.

_____, "Zur Entstehung der griechischen Demokratie ausserhalb Athens," 432-47. Edited by Horst Sund and Manfred Timmermann, *Auf den Weg Gebracht.* Konstanz 1979.

_____, *Die Herrschaft der Athener im Ersten Attischen Seebund.* Berlin 1974.

_____, *Die Stadt als Tyrann: Athens Herrschaft über seine Bundesgenossen.* Konstanz 1978.

Schulten, A., ed., *Avieno Ora Maritima.* Barcelona 1955.

_____, *Tartessos.* Hamburg 1950.

Schulze, Wilhelm, "Der Tod des Kambyses." *Sitzungsberichte der königlich preussischen Akademie der Wissenschaft, Berlin (Phil.-hist. Klasse).* (1912). 685-703.

Schwabacher W., "Lycian Coin-Portraits," 111-24. Edited by C. M. Kraay and G. Jenkins, *Essays in Greek Coinage Presented to Stanley Robinson.* Oxford 1968.

Schwabl, Hans, "Das Bild der Fremden Welt bei den Frühen Griechen." In *Grecs et Barbares. Fondation Hardt pour l'Étude de l'Antiquité classique. Entretiens 8.* Geneva 1962. 3-23.

Schwenzner, Walther, "Gobryas." *Klio* 18 (1923). 41-58. 226-52.

Schwyzer, Eduard, *Dialectorum Graecarum exempla epigraphica potiora.* Leipzig 1923.

Seager, R., "The Congress Decree: Some Doubts and Hypotheses." *Historia* 18 (1969). 129-41.

Seager, R. J. and Tuplin, C. J., "The Freedom of the Greeks of Asia: On the Origins of a Concept and the Creation of a Slogan." *JHS* 100 (1980). 141-54.

Sealey, Raphael, "On the Athenian Concept of Law." *Classical Journal* 77 (1982). 289-302.

_____, "Ephialtes." *CP* 59 (1964). 11-22.

_____, "Notes on Tribute-Quota Lists 5, 6, and 7 of the Athenian Empire." *Phoenix* 24 (1970). 13-28.

_____, "The Origin of the Delian League." In *Ancient Society and Institutions.* New York 1967, 233-55.

_____, "The Pit and the Well: The Persian Heralds of 491 B.C." *Classical Journal* 72 (1976). 13-20.

_____, "Thucydides, Herodotus, and the Causes of War." *CQ* 51 (1957). 1-12.

Seel, Otto, "Herakliden und Mermnaden," In *Navicula Chiloniensis: Festschrift für Felix Jacoby.* Leiden 1956, 37-65.

_____, "Lydiaka." *Wiener Studien* 69 (1956). 212-36.

Segal, Charles, "Croesus on the Pyre: Herodotus and Bacchylides." *Wiener Studien* 84 (1971). 39-51.

Segall, Berta, "Notes on the Iconography of Cosmic Kingship." *The Art Bulletin* 38 (1956). 75-80.

Segré, Mario, "La legge ateniese sull'unificazione della moneta." *Clara Rhodos* 9 (1938). 151-78.

Seibt, Gunter, *Griechische Söldner im Achaimenidenreich.* Bonn 1977.

Seidl, Erwin, *Ägyptische Rechtsgeschichte der Saïten- und Perserzeit.* Glückstadt 1956.

Seidl, Ursula, "Ein Relief Dareios' I. in Babylon." *AMI* 9 (1976). 125-30.

Seligman, Paul, *The 'Apeiron' of Anaximander.* London 1962.

Seltman, Charles, *Greek Coins.* London 1955.

Semple, E. C., *The Geography of the Ancient Mediterranean.* New York 1931.

Ševoroškin, Vitali, "Karisch, Lydisch, Lykisch." *Klio* 50 (1968). 53-69.

Shafer, Robert, "A Break in the Carian Dam." *AC* 34 (1965). 398-424.

Shahbazi, A. Shapur, "An Achaemenid Symbol." *AMI* n.f. 7 (1974). 135-44.

_____, "An Achaemenid Symbol: II. Farnah '(God given) Fortune'." *AMI* 13 (1980). 119-47.

_____, "The 'One Year' of Darius Re-examined." *BSOAS* 35 (1972). 609-14.

_____, *The Irano-Lycian Monuments.* Teheran 1975.

_____, "From Pārsa to Taxt-e Jamšīd." *AMI* 10 (1977). 197-208.

_____, "The Persepolis 'Treasury Reliefs' Once More." *AMI* 9 (1976). 151-6.

_____, "The 'Traditional Date of Zoroaster' Explained." *BSOAS* 40 (1977). 25-35.

Shear, T. L., Jr., "The Early Projects of the Periklean Building Program." Ph.D. dissertation, Princeton University 1967.

Shefton, B. B., "Some Iconographic Remarks on the Tyrannicides." *AJA* 64 (1960). 173-9.

Sidersky, D., "L'onomastique hébraïque des Tablettes de Nippur." *Revue des Études juives* 87 (1929). 178-99.

Siegel, Bernard J., *et al.*, "Acculturation: An Exploratory Formulation." *American Anthropologist* 56 (1954). 973-1002.

Siewert, Peter, *Der Eid von Plataiai.* Munich 1972.

Six, Jan Pieter, "Die Münzen von Abydos." *Zeitschrift für Numismatik* 3 (1876). 237-9.

Sjöquist, F., *Sicily and the Greeks.* Ann Arbor 1973.

SkJadanek, Bogdan, "The Structure of the Persian State." *Acta Iranica Hommage Universel* 1 (Leiden 1974). 117-9.

Smart, J. D., "Kimon's Capture of Eion." *JHS* 87 (1967). 136-8.

_____, "Review Article: The Athenian Empire." *Phoenix* 31 (1977). 245-57.

Smith, Carol A., ed., *Regional Analysis: Vol. 1. Economic Systems.* New York 1976.

Smith, Gertrude, "Athenian Casualty Lists." *CP* 14 (1919). 351-64.

Smith, Morton, "II Isaiah and the Persians." *JAOS* 83 (1963). 415-21.

_____, *Jesus the Magician.* New York 1978.

_____, "Palestinian Judaism in the Persian Period," 386-401. In H. Bengtson, *The Greeks and the Persians.* London 1969.

_____, *Palestinian Parties and Politics that Shaped the Old Testament.* New York 1971.

Smith, Sidney, *Isaiah Chapters XL-LV.* London 1944.

Snell, Bruno, *The Discovery of the Mind: The Greek Origins of European Thought.* Oxford 1953.

Snodgrass, A. M., *Archaeology and the Rise of the Greek State.* Cambridge 1977.

_____, *Archaic Greece: The Age of Experiment.* London 1980.

_____, *Arms and Armour of the Greeks.* London 1967.

_____, *The Dark Age of Greece.* Edinburgh 1971.

_____, "An Historical Homeric Society." *JHS* 94 (1974). 114-25.

Sokolowski, F., *Lois Sacrées de l'Asie Mineure.* Paris 1955.

Solmsen, Lieselotte, "Speeches in Herodotus' Account of the Ionian Revolt." *AJP* 64 (1943). 194-207.

Sordi, M., "La posizione di Delfi a dell'Anfizionia nel decennio tra Tanagra e Coronea." *Rivista di Filologia* 86 (1958). 48-65.

Soyez, Brigitte, "Le Phénicien Thalès et le synoecisme de l'Ionie." *AC* 43 (1974). 74-82.

Spalinger, Anthony J., "The Date of Gyges and its Historical Implications." *JAOS* 98 (1978). 400-9.

Speiser, E. A., *Anchor Bible: Genesis.* Garden City 1964.

——————————, "Cultural Factors in Social Dynamics in the Near East." *Middle East Journal* 7 (1953). 133-52.

Spiegelberg, Wilhelm, *The Credibility of Herodotus' Account of Egypt in Light of the Egyptian Monuments.* Oxford 1927.

——————————, *Die sogenannte demotische Chronik des Papyrus 215 der Bibliotheque Nationale zu Paris.* Leipzig 1914.

Spooner, Brian, "Iranian Kinship and Marriage." *Iran* 4 (1966). 51-60.

Stahl, Johannes Matthias, *De Sociorum atheniensium judiciis commentatio.* Münster 1881.

Starcky, J., "Une tablette araméenne de l'an 34 de Nebuchadonosor." *Syria* 37 (1960). 99-115.

Starr, Chester G., *Athenian Coinage: 480-449 B.C.* Oxford 1970.

——————————, "The Decline of the Early Greek Kings." *Historia* 10 (1961). 129-38.

——————————, "The Early Greek State." *La Parola del Passato* 12 (1957). 97-108.

——————————, *The Economic and Social Growth of Early Greece, 800-500 B.C.* New York 1977.

——————————, "Greeks and Persians in the Fourth Century B.C." *Iranica Antiqua* 11 (1975). 44-99.

——————————, *Political Intelligence in Classical Greece.* Leiden 1974.

——————————, "A Sixth-Century Athenian Tetradrachm used to Seal a Clay Tablet from Persepolis." *NC* 7th s. 26 (1976). 219-22.

——————————, "Why did the Greeks Defeat the Persians?" *La Parola del Passato* 17 (1962). 321-32.

Stein, Aurel, "An Archaeological Journey in Western Iran." *Geographical Journal* 92 (1938). 313-42.

——————————, "An Archaeological Tour in the Ancient Persis." *Iraq* 3 (1936). 1-225.

——————————, *Old Routes of Western Iran.* London 1940.

Stève, M.-J., "Inscriptions de Achéménides à Suse." *Studia Iranica* 3 (1974). 7-28, 135-69.

——————————, "Inscriptions de Achéménides à Suse." *Studia Iranica* 4 (1975). 7-26.

Stewart, Douglas J., "Thucydides, Pausanias, and Alcibiades." *Classical Journal* 61 (1966). 145-52.

Stolper, Matthew W., "The Genealogy of the Murašū Family." *JCS* 28 (1976). 189-200.

——————————, "Management and Politics in Later Achaemenid Babylonia: New Texts from the Murašū Archive." 2 Vols. Ph.D. dissertation, University of Michigan 1974.

——————————, "A Note on Yahwistic Personal Names in the Murašū Texts." *BASOR* 222 (1976). 25-8.

——————————, Review of G. Ries, *Die neubabylonische Bodenpachtformulare.* Berlin 1976, in *Bibliotheca Orientalis* 35 (1978). 230-33.

Strasburger, Hermann, "Herodot und das perikleische Athen." *Historia* 4 (1955). 1-25.

Stronach, David, "Achaemenid Village I at Susa and the Persian Migration to Fars." *Iraq* 36 (1974). 239-48.

_____, "A Circular Symbol on the Tomb of Cyrus." *Iran* 9 (1971). 155-8.

_____, "Excavations at Pasargadae, First Preliminary Report." *Iran* 1 (1963). 19-42.

_____, "Excavations at Pasargadae, Second Preliminary Report." *Iran* 2 (1964). 21-40.

_____, "Excavations at Pasargadae, Third Preliminary Report." *Iran* 3 (1965). 9-40.

_____, "Excavations at Tepe Nūsh-i Jān, 1967." *Iran* 7 (1969). 1-20.

_____, "A Fourth Season of Excavations at Teppeh Nuši Jān." In *Proceedings of the IIIrd Annual Symposium on Archaeological Research in Iran, Nov. 1974.* Teheran 1975. 203-12.

_____, *Pasargadae.* Oxford 1978.

_____, "Tappeh Nuši-Jān: A Case for Building Rites in 7th/6th Century B.C. Media?" In *Proceedings of the IInd Annual Symposium on Archaeological Research in Iran, Nov. 1973.* Teheran 1974, 223-38.

_____, "Tepe Nūsh-i Jān" in "Survey of Excavations in Iran, 1969-70." *Iran* 9 (1971). 175.

_____, "Tepe Nush-i Jan," in "Survey of Excavations in Iran—1973-4." *Iran* 13 (1975). 187-8.

_____, "Tepe Nush-i Jan," in Survey of Excavations in Iran—1977." *Iran* 16 (1978). 195.

_____, "Tepe Nush-i Jan: A Mound in Media." *The Metropolitan Museum of Art Bulletin* 27 (Nov. 1968). 177-86.

_____, "Urartian and Achaemenian Tower Temples." *JNES* 26 (1967). 278-88.

Stronach, D. and Roaf, M., "Excavations at Tepe Nush-i Jan." *Iran* 16 (1978). 1-28.

Struve, V. V., "Chronology of the Sixth Century B.C. and the Work of Herodotus." *VDI* (1952). 60-78 [in Russian].

_____, "The Dating of the Behistun Inscription." *VDI* (1952). 26-48 [in Russian].

_____, "The Reform of the Written Language under Darius I." *VDI* (1951). 186-91 [in Russian].

_____, "The Religion of the Achaemenides and Zoroastrianism." *Cahiers d'Histoire Mondiale* 5 (1959-60). 529-45.

Stubbs, H. W., "Thucydides 1.2.6." *CQ* 22 (1972). 74-7.

Sumner, G. V., "A Note on Thucydides 1.2.6." *CP* 54 (1959). 116-8.

Sumner, William Marvin, "Cultural Development in the Kur River Basin, Iran: An Archaeological Analysis of Settlement Patterns." Ph.D. dissertation, University of Pennsylvania 1972.

Sundwall, Johannes, *Die einheimischen Namen der Lykier, nebst einem Verzeichnisse kleinasiatischer Namenstämme. Klio Beiheft* 11. Leipzig 1913.

_____, "Zu den karischen Inschriften und den darin vorkommenden Namen." *Klio* 11 (1911). 464-80.

Sventsitskaya, I. S., "The Status of the Dependent Population in Asia Minor in the Fifth and Fourth Centuries B.C." *VDI* (1967). 80-6 [in Russian].

Svoronos, J. N., "L'Hellénisme primitif de la Macédoine prouvé par la numismatique et l'or du Pangée." *Journal international d'Archeologie numismatique* 19 (1918-19). 1-261.

Szemerenyi, Oswald, *Four Old Iranian Ethnic Names: Scythian - Skudra - Sogdian - Saka.* Vienna 1980.

Tadmore, Hayim, "The Inscriptions of Nabunaid: Historical Arrangement." *Assyriological Studies* 16 (1965). 351-63.

Talamo, Clara, "Per la storia de Colofone in età arcaica." *La Parola del Passato* 28 (1973). 343-75.

Teixidor, Javier, "The Aramaic Text in the Trilingual Stele from Xanthus." *JNES* 37 (1978). 181-5.

Ténékidès, Georges, *La notion juridique d'indépendance et la traditon hellénique.* Athens 1954.

Thieme, P., "The Concept of Mitra in Aryan Belief," 21-39. Edited by J. R. Hinnells, *Mithraic Studies.* Vol. 1. Manchester 1975.

Thomas, Carol G., "Homer and the Polis." *La Parola del Passato* 21 (1966). 5-14.

_____, "On the Origin of the Institution of Slavery." *The Ancient World* 1 (1978). 109-10.

_____, ΠΑΤΡΙΚΗ ΒΑΣΙΛΕΙΑ: Η ΥΠΟΛΗΨΙΣ. *Historia* 15 (1966). 368-9.

_____, "The Roots of Homeric Kingship." *Historia* 15 (1966). 387-407.

_____, "The Territorial Imperative of the Polis." *The Ancient World* 2 (1979). 35-9.

Thomas, D. Winton, "The Sixth Century B.C.: A Creative Epoch in the History of Israel." *Journal of Semitic Studies* 6 (1961). 33-46.

Thompson, David, "The Possible Hittite Sources for Hesiod's 'Theogony'." *La Parola del Passato* 22 (1967). 241-51.

Thompson, Dorothy Burr, "The Persian Spoils in Athens," 281-91. Edited by S. S. Weinberg, *The Aegean and the Near East: Studies Presented to Heddy Goldman.* Locust Valley 1956.

Thompson, Georgina, "Iranian Dress in the Achaemenian Period." *Iran* 3 (1965). 121-6.

Thompson, Paul, *The Voice of the Past: Oral History.* New York 1978.

Thompson, Stith, *Motif-Index of Folk Literature.* 2nd ed. 6 Vols. Bloomington 1955-8.

Thompson, Stith and Balys, Jonas, *The Oral Tales of India.* Bloomington 1958.

Thompson, Wesley E., "The Chian Coinage in Thucydides and Xenophon." *NC* 7s. 11 (1971). 323-4.

_____, "The Peace of Callias in the Fourth Century." *Historia* 30 (1981). 164-77.

Tilia, Ann Britt, "Discovery of an Achaemenian Palace near Takht-i Rustam to the North of the Terrace of Persepolis." *Iran* 12 (1974). 200-4.

_____, *Studies and Restorations at Persepolis and Other Sites of Fārs.* Vol. 1. Rome 1972.

_____, *Studies and Restorations at Persepolis and Other Sites of Fārs.* Vol. 2. Rome 1978.

Tobler, W. and Wineberg, S., "A Cappadocian Speculation." *Nature* 231 (May 1971). 39-41.

Tölle, Renate, *Die antike Stadt Samos.* Mainz 1969.

Töttössy, C., "Graeco—Indo-Iranian." *AAH* 25 (1977). 129-35.

Tomlinson, Richard A., *Greek Sanctuaries.* London 1976.

Torrey, Charles C., "An Aramaic Inscription from Cilicia, in the Museum of Yale University." *JAOS* 35 (1915-17). 370-4.

_____, "The Bilingual Inscription from Sardis." *AJSL* 34 (1917-1918). 185-98.

_____, "The Chronicler's History of the Return under Cyrus." *AJSL* 37 (1920-21). 81-100.

_____, *Ezra Studies.* New York 1970.

_____, "The Two Persian Officers Named Bagoas." *AJSL* 56 (1939). 300-1.

Tozzi, Pierluigi, *La rivolta Ionica.* Pisa 1978.

_____, "Per la storia della politica religiosa degli Achemenidi: distruzioni persiane di templi greci agli inizi del V Secolo." *Rivista Storica Italiana* 89 (1977). 18-32.

Travlos, John, *Pictorial Dictionary of Ancient Athens.* New York 1971.

Treuber, Oskar, *Geschichte der Lykier.* Stuttgart 1887.

Tritsch, F. J., "The Harpy Tomb at Xanthus." *JHS* 62 (1942). 39-50.

Trümpelmann, Leo, "Zur Entstehungsgeschichte des Monumentes Dareios' I. von Bisutun und zur Datierung der Einführung der altpersischen Schrift." *Archäologischer Anzeiger* 82 (1967). 281-98.

_____, "Das Heiligtum von Pasargadae." *Studia Iranica* 6 (1977). 7-16.

Tsereteli, G. V., "The Achaemenid State and the World Civilization." *Acta Iranica Hommage Universel* 1 (Leiden 1974). 102-7.

Unger, Eckhard, "Die Dariusstele am Tearos." *Archäologischer Anzeiger* 30 (1915). 3-18.

Vallat, François, "Corpus des Inscriptions Royales en Élamite Achemenide." Thèse présentée pour l'obtention du Doctorat de IIIe Cycle, Paris 1977.

_____, "Deux Inscriptions Élamites de Darius 1er (DSf et DSz)." *Studia Iranica* 1 (1972). 3-13.

_____, "Deux Nouvelles 'Chartes de Fondation' d'un Palais de Darius Ier à Suse." *Syria* 48 (1971). 53-9.

_____, "L'inscription trilingue de Xerxes à la porte de Darius." *Cahiers de la Délégation Archéologique Française en Iran* 4 (1974). 171-80.

_____, "Table Élamite de Darius Ier." *Revue d'Assyriologie* 64 (1970). 149-60.

Vallet, Georges, "La cité et son territoire dans les colonies grecques d'occident." In *La Città e il suo Territorio. Atti del settimo convegno di Studi sulla Magna Grecia, Taranto 8-12 Ottobre 1967.* Naples 1968. 67-142.

Vallet, Georges and Villard, François, "Les Phocéens en Mediterranée occidentale a l'époque archaïque et la fondation de Hyélè." *La Parola del Passato* 21 (1966). 166-90.

Van Compernolle, René, "La date de la bataille navale de Lade." *AC* 27 (1958). 383-9.

Van de Maele, S., "Le Livre VIII de Thucydide et la Politique de Sparte en Asie Mineure (412-411 av. J. C.)." *Phoenix* 25 (1971). 32-50.

Vanden Berghe, Louis, "Cyrus le Grand et le Rayonnement de la civilisation iranienne." *Acta Iranica Hommage Universel* 1 (Leiden 1974). 60-7.

van den Hout, Michiel, "Studies in Early Greek Letter-Writing II." *Mnemosyne* 2 (1949). 141-52.

Vanderpool, Eugene, "A Monument to the Battle of Marathon." *Hesperia* 35 (1966). 93-106.

_____, "Some Ostraka from the Athenian Agora." *Hesperia Suppl.* 8 (1949). 400-1.

Vernant, Jean-Pierre, "Remarques sur la lutte de classe dans la Grèce ancienne." *Eirene* 4 (1965). 5-19.

Vinogradoff, Paul, *Outlines of Historical Jurisprudence: Vol. 2. The Jurisprudence of the Greek City.* Oxford 1922.

Vlastos, Gregory, "Equality and Justice in the Early Greek Cosmogonies." *CP* 48 (1947). 156-78.

Vogt, Joseph, "Die Hellenisierung der Perser in der Tragödie des Aischylos: Religiöse Dichtung und historisches Zeugnis." In *Antike und Universalgeschichte: Festschrift für Hans Erich Stier.* Münster 1972. 131-45.

Voigtländer, Walter, "Quellhaus und Naiskos im Didymaion nach den Perserkriegen." *Istanbuler Mitteilungen* 22 (1972). 93-112.

von der Osten, Hans Henning, *Die Welt der Perser.* Stuttgart 1956.

von Gall, Hubertus, "Die Grosskönigliche Kopfbedeckung bei den Achämeniden." *Proceedings of the IIIrd Annual Symposium on Archaeological Research in Iran, Nov. 1974.* Teheran 1975. 219-32.

_____, "Die Kopfbedeckung des persischen Ornats bei den Achämeniden." *AMI* 7 (1974). 145-61.

_____, "Das persische Königszeit und die Hallenarchitektur in Iran und Griechenland," 119-32. Edited by U. Höckmann and A. Krug, *Festschrift für Frank Brommer.* Mainz 1977.

_____, "Persische und Medische Stämme." *AMI* 5 (1972). 261-83.

von Hagen, Victor W., "Along the First Road," *Geographical Magazine* 46.9 (June 1974). 456-61.

_____, "Clue to a Tigris Source," *Geographical Magazine* 48.6 (March 1976). 365-8.

_____, "Horror of the Tomissa Crossing," *Geographical Magazine* 48.5 (February 1976). 278-81.

von Voigtlander, Elizabeth N., *The Bisitun Inscription of Darius the Great: Babylonian Version.* London 1978.

von Wilamowitz-Moellendorff, Ulrich, "Über die ionische Wanderung." *Sitzungsberichte der königlich preussischen Akademie der Wissenschaften,* Berlin 4 (1906). 59-79.

_____, "Panionion." *Sitzungsberichte der königlich preussischen Akademie der Wissenschaften,* Berlin 4 (1906). 38-57.

Wade-Gery, H. T., "Hesiod." *Phoenix* 3 (1949). 81-93.

_____, "The Peace of Kallias." *HSCP. Suppl.* 1 (1940). 121-56.

_____, "The Question of Tribute in 449/8 B.C." *Hesperia* 14 (1945). 212-29.

_____, "Thucydides the Son of Melesias." *JHS* 52 (1932). 205-27.

Wade-Gery, H. T. and Meritt, B. D., "Athenian Resources in 449 and 431 B.C." *Hesperia* 26 (1957). 163-97.

Wagner, M., *Zur Geschichte der attischen Kleruchien.* Tübingen 1914.

Wagstaff, J. M., "A Note on Settlement Numbers in Ancient Greece." *JHS* 95 (1975). 163-8.

Walbank, Michael B., "Honors for Parianos of Issa and his Sons Athenodoros and Ikesios." *Hesperia* 42 (1973). 334-9.

Walcot, P., *Greek Peasants, Ancient and Modern.* Manchester 1970.

_____, *Hesiod and the Near East.* Cardiff 1966.

_____, "The Text of Hesiod's Theogony and the Hittite Epic of Kumarbi." *CQ* 50 (1956). 198-206.

Wallace, Anthony F. C., "Revitalization Movements." *American Anthropologist* 58 (1956). 264-80.

Wallace, W., "The Public Seal of Athens." *Phoenix* 3 (1949). 70-3.

Wallis, Gerard, "Jüdische Bürger in Babylonien während der Achämeniden-Zeit." *Persica* 9 (1980). 129-88.

Walser, Gerold, *Audienz beim persischen Grosskönig.* Zurich 1965.

_____, ed. *Beiträge zur Achämenidengeschichte.* Wiesbaden 1972.

_____, "Griechen am Hofe des Grosskönigs." In *Festgabe Hans von Greyerz.* Bern 1976, 189-202.

_____, "La notion de l'Etat chez les Grecs et les Achemenides." In *Assimilation et Résistance à la Culture Gréco-Romaine dans le Monde Ancient Travaux du VIe Congrès International d'Etudes Classiques (Madrid 1974)*. Bucharest 1976, 227-31.

_____, *Die Völkerschaften auf den Reliefs von Persepolis*. Berlin 1966.

Walsh, John, "The Authenticity and the Dates of the Peace of Callias and the Congress Decree." *Chiron* 11 (1981). 31-63.

Wardman, A. E., "Herodotus on the Cause of the Greco-Persian Wars." *AJP* 82 (1961). 133-50.

Wason, Margaret O., *Class Struggles in Ancient Greece*. London 1947.

Wasson, R. Gordon, "The Soma of the Rig Veda: What was it?" *JAOS* 91 (1971). 169-86.

Waszýnski, S., "De l'authenticité de la correspondance de Pausanias avec Xerxes." *Eos* 6 (1900). 113-7.

Waters, Kenneth H., "Herodotus and the Ionian Revolt." *Historia* 19 (1970). 504-8.

_____, *Herodotus: On Tyrants and Despots*. Wiesbaden 1971.

_____, "The Purpose of Dramatisation in Herodotus." *Historia* 15 (1966). 157-71.

Weber, Max, *The Agrarian Sociology of Ancient Civilizations*. London 1976.

Webster, T. B. L., *Potter and Patron in Classical Athens*. London 1972.

Weidauer, Liselotte, *Probleme der frühen Elektronprägung*. Fribourg 1975.

Weiler, Ingomar, "Greek and Non-Greek World in the Archaic Period." *GRBS* 9 (1968). 21-9.

Weinberg, Joël P., "Bemerkungen zum Problem 'Der Vorhellenismus im Vorderen Orient'." *Klio* 58 (1976). 5-20.

Weisberg, David B., *Guild Structure and Political Allegiance in Early Achaemenid Mesopotamia*. New Haven 1967.

Weissbach, F. H., *Babylonische Miszellen*. Leipzig 1903.

_____, "Die fünfte Kolumne der Grossen Bisutun-Inschrift." *Zeitschrift für Assyriologie* 46 (1940). 53-82.

_____, *Die Keilinschriften der Achämeniden*. Leipzig 1911.

Wells, C. Bradford, *Royal Correspondence in the Hellenistic Period*. London 1934.

Wells, J., "The Persian Friends of Herodotus." *JHS* 27 (1907). 37-47.

Welwei, Karl-Wilhelm, "Die 'Marathon'-Epigramme von der athenischen Agora." *Historia* 19 (1970). 295-305.

Werner, Rudolf, *Hethitische Gerichtsprotokolle*." Wiesbaden 1967.

West, Martin L., *Early Greek Philosophy and the Orient*. Oxford 1971.

West, William C., III, "Saviours of Greece." *GRBS* 11 (1970). 271-82.

_____, "The Trophies of the Persian Wars." *CP* 64 (1969). 7-19.

Westermann, William Linn, "Between Slavery and Freedom." *American Historical Review* 50 (1945). 213-27.

Westlake, H. D., "The Medism of Thessaly." *JHS* 56 (1936). 12-24.

_____, "Thucydides on Pausanias and Themistocles—A Written Source." *CQ* 27 (1977). 95-110.

Wheeler, Mortimer, *Flames over Persepolis*. New York 1968.

Wheelright, Philip, *Heraclitus*. Princeton 1959.

White, Mary, "The Duration of the Samian Tyranny." *JHS* 74 (1954). 36-43.

_____, "Greek Tyranny." *Phoenix* 9 (1955). 1-18.

_____, "Herodotus' Starting Point." *Phoenix* 23 (1969). 39-48.

_____, "Some Agiad Dates: Pausanias and His Sons." *JHS* 84 (1964). 140-52.

Whitehead, John David, "Early Aramaic Epistolography: The Arsames Correspondence." Ph.D. dissertation, University of Chicago 1974.

Whittaker, Robert H. and Levin, Simon A., *Niche Theory and Application*. Stroudsburg 1975.

Whittick, G. Clement, "Σαγηνεύουσι δε τόνδε τον τρόπον: Herodotus VI. 31." *AC* 22 (1953). 27-31.

Wick, T. E., "A Note on Thucydides I, 23.6." *AC* 44 (1975). 176-83.

Widengren, G., *Der Feudalismus im alten Iran*. Cologne 1969.

_____, "Recherches sur le feodalisme l'Iran antique." *Orientalia Suecana* 5 (1956). 79-182.

_____, "La royaute de l'Iran antique." *Acta Iranica Hommage Universel* 1 (Leiden 1974). 84-9.

_____, "The Sacral Kingship of Iran." *Numen Suppl.* 4 (1959). 242-57.

Wiegand, Theodor, *Achter vorläufiger Bericht über die von den Staatlichen Museen in Milet und Didyma*. Berlin 1924.

Wiesehöfer, Josef, *Der Aufstand Gaumātas und die Anfänge Dareios' I.* Bonn 1978.

_____, "Die 'Freunde' and 'Wohltäter' des Grosskönigs." *Studia Iranica* 9 (1980). 7-21.

Wiesen, David S., "Herodotus and the Modern Debate over Race and Slavery." *The Ancient World* 3 (1980). 3-16.

Wilber, Donald W., *Persepolis*. London 1969.

Wilcken, Ulrich, "Der Anonymus Argentinensis." *Hermes* 42 (1907). 374-418.

Wilhelm, A., "IG 1² 26." *Mnemosyne* 4s. 2 (1949). 286-93.

Wilkinson, Charles K., "Assyrian and Persian Art." *The Metropolitan Museum of Art Bulletin* 13 (1955). 213-24.

Will, Édouard, *Korinthiaka*. Paris 1955.

_____, *Le Monde grec et l'Orient I. Le Ve siècle* (510-403). Paris 1972.

_____, "Les tyrannies dans la Grece antique." *REG* 69 (1956). 439-44.

Williams, G. M. E., "The Image of the Alkmeonidai between 490 B.C. and 487/6 B.C." *Historia* 29 (1980). 106-10.

Wilson, John A., *Herodotus in Egypt*. Leiden 1970.

Wilson, N. G., "The Composition of Photius' *Bibliotheca*." *GRBS* 9 (1968). 451-5.

_____, "Two Notes on Byzantine Scholarship: II. Photius' *Bibliotheca:* A Supplementary Note." *GRBS* 12 (1971). 559-60.

Windfuhr, Gernot, "Notes on the Old Persian Signs." *Indo-Iranian Journal* 12 (1970). 121-5.

Winton, Richard I., "Φιλοδικεῖν δοκοῦμεν: Law and Paradox in the Athenian Empire." *Museum Helveticum* 37 (1980). 89-97.

Wiseman, D. J., *Chronicles of Chaldean Kings (626-556 B.C.) in the British Museum.* London 1956.

_____, *Cylinder Seals of Western Asia*. London 1958.

Wittfogel, Karl A., *Oriental Despotism: A Comparative Study of Total Power.* New Haven 1957.

Wolff, Hans Julius, "The Origin of Judicial Litigation among the Greeks." *Traditio* 4 (1946). 31-87.

Wolski, Josef, "La constitution de l'empire d'Iran et son rôle dans l'histoire de l'Antiquité." *Acta Iranica Hommage Universel* 1 (Leiden 1974). 71-83.

_____, "Les Grecs et les Ioniens au temps des Guerres médiques." *Eos* 58 (1969). 33-49.

_____, "Μηδισμός et son importance en Grèce à l'époque des Guerres Médiques." *Historia* 22 (1973). 3-15.

_____, "Pausanias et le problème de la politique spartiate (480-470)." *Eos* 47 (1956). 75-7.

Woodcock, George, *The Greeks in India*. London 1966.

_____, "Persia and Persepolis, Part I." *History Today* 17 (1967). 236-41.

_____, "Persia and Persepolis, Part II." *History Today* 17 (1967). 301-7.

Woodhead, A. G., "The Institution of the Hellenotamiae." *JHS* 79 (1959). 149-52.

_____, "The Second Capture of Sestos." *Proceedings of the Cambridge Philological Society.* 181 (1950-51). 9-12.

_____, *Thucydides on the Nature of Power*. Cambridge, Mass. 1970.

_____, "West's Panel of Ship-Payers," 170-8. Edited by D. Bradeen and M. McGregor, ΦΟΡΟΣ: *Tribute to Benjamin Dean Meritt*. Locust Valley 1974.

Wormell, D. E. W., "Studies in Greek Tyranny: I—The Cypselids." *Hermathena* 66 (1945). 1-24.

Wüst, Fritz R., "Amphiktyonie, Eidgenossenschaft, Symmachie." *Historia* 3 (1954/5). 129-53.

Wüst, Walther, "Bestand die Zoroastrische Urgemeinde aus Ekstatikern und Rinderhirten der Steppe?" *Archiv für Religionswissenschaft* 36 (1939). 234-49.

Wycherly, R. E., *The Stones of Athens*. Princeton 1978.

Yavis, Constantine G., *Greek Altars: Origins and Typology*. St. Louis 1949.

Young, John H., "Ancient Towers on the Island of Siphnos." *AJA* 60 (1956). 51-5.

_____, "Studies in South Attica: Country Estates at Sounion." *Hesperia* 25 (1956). 122-46.

Young, Rodney, "The Campaign of 1955 at Gordion: Preliminary Report." *AJA* 60 (1956). 249-66.

_____, "Progress at Gordion, 1951-1952." *University Museum Bulletin* 17.4 (Dec. 1953). 2-39.

_____, "Gordion: Problems of Western Phrygia." In *Le Rayonnement des Civilisations grecque et romaine sur les cultures périphérique*. Paris 1965. 481-98.

Young, T. Cuyler, Jr., "An Archaeological Survey of the Kangāvar Valley." *Proceedings of the IIIrd Annual Symposium on Archaeological Research in Iran, Teheran 1974*. Teheran 1975. 23-30.

_____, "A Comparative Ceramic Chronology of Western Iran, 1500-500 B.C." *Iran* 3 (1965). 53-86.

_____, *Excavation at Godin Tepe: First Progress Report*. Toronto 1969.

_____, "Excavations at Godin Tappeh 1973." *Proceedings of the IInd Annual Symposium on Archaeological Research in Iran, Nov. 1973*. Teheran 1974. 80-90.

_____, "The Iranian Migration into the Zagros." *Iran* 5 (1967). 11-34.

_____, "Godin Tepe," in "Survey of Excavations in Iran During 1968-69." *Iran* 8 (1970). 175-6.

_____, "Godin Tepe," in "Survey of Excavations in Iran During 1970-71." *Iran* 10 (1972). 184-6.

Young, T. Cuyler, Jr. and Levine, Louis D., *Excavations of the Godin Project: Second Progress Report*. Toronto 1974.

Zadok, Ron, "On the Connections between Iran and Babylonia in the Sixth Century B.C." *Iran* 14 (1976). 61-78.

_____, "Nippur in the Achaemenid Period: Geographical and Ethnical Aspects." Ph.D. dissertation, Hebrew University 1974.

Zaehner, R. C., *The Dawn and Twilight of Zoroastrianism*. London 1961.

_____, "Zoroastrian Survivals in Iranian Folklore." *Iran* 3 (1965). 87-96.

Zeilhofer, Gerhard, *Sparta, Delphoi und die Amphikytonen im 5. Jahrhundert vor Christus*. Erlangen 1961.

Ziatkovskaia, T. D., "South Thracian Tribal Alliances in the 6th-5th Centuries B.C." *VDI* (1967). 147-58 [in Russian].

Zimmern, Alfred, *The Greek Commonwealth*. New York 1931.

Zoumpos, A. N., *Herakleitos von Ephesos als Staatsmann und Gesetzgeber*. Athens 1956.

Zschietzschmann, W., "Branchidae," 1039–43. Edited by G. Mylonas, *Studies Presented to David Moore Robinson*. Vol. 2. St. Louis 1953.

INDEX

Lightning Source UK Ltd.
Milton Keynes UK
UKOW04f1937060915

258160UK00001B/253/P